# The Wiley Blackwell Handbook of the Psychology of Coaching and Mentoring

GW00672430

## Wiley Blackwell Handbooks in Organizational Psychology

Series Editor: Jonathan Passmore

The aim of the Wiley Blackwell Handbooks in Organizational Psychology is to create a set of uniquely in-depth reviews of contemporary research, theory and practice across critical sub-domains of organizational psychology. Series titles will individually deliver the state-of-the-art in their discipline by putting the most important contemporary work at the fingertips of academics, researchers, students and practitioners. Over time, the series will grow in into a complete reference for those seeking to develop a comprehensive understanding of the field.

**The Wiley Blackwell Handbook of the Psychology of Coaching and Mentoring**
*Edited by Jonathan Passmore, David B. Peterson, and Teresa Freire*

**The Wiley Blackwell Handbook of the Psychology of Leadership, Change and Organizational Development**
*Edited by H. Skipton Leonard, Rachel Lewis, Arthur M. Freedman, and Jonathan Passmore*

**The Wiley Blackwell Handbook of the Psychology of Training, Personal Development and E-Learning**
*Edited by Kurt Kraiger, Jonathan Passmore, Nuno Rebelo dos Santos, and Sigmar Malvezzi*

**The Wiley Blackwell Handbook of the Psychology of Occupational Safety and Workplace Health**
*Edited by Sharon Clarke, Tahira M. Probst, Frank Guldenmund, and Jonathan Passmore*

**The Wiley Blackwell Handbook of the Psychology of Team Working and Collaborative Processes**
*Edited by Eduardo Salas, Ramon Rico, and Jonathan Passmore*

**The Wiley Blackwell Handbook of the Psychology of Recruitment, Selection and Employee Retention**
*Edited by Harold Goldstein, Elaine D. Pulakos, Jonathan Passmore, and Carla Semedo*

**The Wiley Blackwell Handbook of the Psychology of Positivity and Strengths-Based Approaches at Work**
*Edited by Lindsay G. Oades, Michael F. Steger, Antonelle Delle Fave, and Jonathan Passmore*

**The Wiley Blackwell Handbook of the Psychology of the Internet at Work**
*Edited by Guido Hertel, Dianna L. Stone, Richard Johnson, and Jonathan Passmore*

# The Wiley Blackwell Handbook of the Psychology of Coaching and Mentoring

Edited by Jonathan Passmore,
David B. Peterson, and Teresa Freire

**WILEY** Blackwell

*Library of Congress Cataloging-in-Publication Data*

The Wiley Blackwell handbook of the psychology of coaching and mentoring / edited by Jonathan Passmore, David B. Peterson, and Teresa Freire.
     p.   cm.
   Includes index.
   ISBN 978-1-119-99315-5 (cloth) – ISBN 978-1-119-23790-7 (paperback)
   1. Personal coaching.   2. Employees–Coaching of.   3. Mentoring in business.
I. Passmore, Jonathan.   II. Peterson, David B.   III. Freire, Tereza.
   BF637.P36W535 2013
   158.3–dc23
                                        2012029596

A catalogue record for this book is available from the British Library.

Cover image: © Steve Goodwin / iStockphoto

Set in 9.5/12pt Galliard by SPi Global, Pondicherry, India

1   2016

# Contents

# About the Editors

**Jonathan Passmore, D.Occ.Psych,** is professor of psychology at Evora and managing director of Embrion, a psychology consulting company. He is a chartered psychologist, holds five degrees and has an international reputation for his work in coaching and leadership. He has published 14 books on the themes of leadership, personal development, and change, including editing the Association for Coaching series of coaching titles. He speaks widely at conferences across the world from the USA to Europe and Asia and has published over 100 journal papers and book chapters and has won several awards for his writing, research and practice.

**David B. Peterson, PhD** David is Director, Executive Coaching and Leadership at Google, Inc. Prior to that, he served as SVP and leader of PDI Ninth House's coaching services. A pioneer in the field of executive coaching, he has written best-selling books and dozens of popular articles on coaching and leadership development, as well as conducting ground-breaking research. A Fellow of the American Psychological Association, the Society of Consulting Psychology, and Society for Industrial and Organizational Psychology, he received his PhD in I/O and counseling psychology from the University of Minnesota. David lives in San Francisco, with wife Alexis and an adorable Tibetan terrier named Pinot.

**Teresa Freire, PhD** Teresa is assistant professor in the School of Psychology, at the University of Minho (Braga, Portugal), where she teaches graduate and postgraduate students. She coordinates the research line on positive psychology for master and doctoral students and leads the research group for the study of optimal functioning. She develops group and community interventions, being the coordinator of the Peer Tutoring and Coaching Project, and the Director of the Service of Psychology in the School of Psychology, University of Minho, Portugal. She belongs to the European Network for Positive Psychology (ENPP), and is a member of the Management Board Committee. She has a number of national and international publications in books and peer review journals.

# About the Contributors

**Geoffrey Abbott**  Geoffrey is Corporate Educator at the Queensland University of Technology Business School in Brisbane, Australia. Geoff is an experienced international coach and is co-editor of the *Routledge Companion to International Business Coaching*. Geoff's doctoral thesis explored how executive coaching might assist expatriate managers in cultural adjustment. He can be contacted at: geoffa@internationalbusinesscoaching.com

**Julie Allan**  Julie coaches and consults to organizations and is an educator, supervisor, and speaker. She serves on the British Psychological Society Committees for Ethics and Coaching Psychology, is involved in developing coaching psychology standards and has chapters in *The Handbook of Coaching Psychology* (Gestalt) and *Supervision in Coaching* (Ethics). Her practitioner research concerns developing corporate wisdom. She can be contacted at: julie@irvingallan.com.

**Tim Anstiss**  Tim is a medical doctor with a Master's degree in sports medicine and a diploma in occupational medicine. A member of the British Psychological Society, Tim spends a lot of his time working with clinicians and managers, helping them have more person-centered, guiding, and empowering conversations with patients and employees respectively. He can be contacted at shl@btinternet.com.

**Kathleen M. Ayers**  Kathleen has worked in the mental health field since 1991, providing assessment and psychotherapy for all age groups. She has also worked in research and currently teaches psychology graduate students, medical students, and physician assistant students. Kathleen has also had extensive experience in civil forensic neuropsychology. She can be contacted at: dr_kathleen_ayers@hotmail.com.

**Tatiana Bachkirova**  Tatiana is an academic, coach, and coaching supervisor with a particular expertise in coaching psychology and coaching supervision. She is based at Oxford Brookes University and leads the MA in Coaching and Mentoring Supervision, as well as supervising doctoral students. Tatiana is an active researcher and author.

**Miles Bowman**  Miles received his doctorate from Queen's University in Kingston, Ontario, Canada. After completing his degree, he joined the coaching profession and obtained his certification through CTI shortly thereafter. He presently lives in Port Hope, Ontario where he runs his coaching business and does sessional work with universities in the surrounding area. He can be contacted at: kilometers@gmail.com.

**Camala Boyce** Camala is a consulting psychologist working globally to bring greater trust and cohesion to virtual, geographically distributed teams and coaching high performing leaders for increased success. She leads workshops on emotional intelligence and is on faculty at the California School of Professional Psychology, Alliant International University.

**Mary Wayne Bush** Mary Wayne holds a Master 's degree from Yale University and a doctorate in Organizational Change from Pepperdine University. In addition to writing and speaking on the subject of coaching, she teaches in a doctoral program at Colorado Technical University. Mary Wayne is a member of several international editorial and advisory boards that contribute to the field of coaching, and she was the Director of Research for the Foundation of Coaching, (now known as the Harvard Institute of Coaching).

**Alison Carter** Alison is an independent researcher and evaluator in HR, leadership and coaching, and a Principal Associate with the Institute for Employment Studies (IES) in the UK. She has an MBA from Henley Business School and a professional doctorate. Alison was a founding Director of the European Mentoring and Coaching Council (2003–5), Co-chair of the 2nd International Coaching Research Forum (2009) and is on the editorial board of Coaching at Work magazine.

**Michael J. Cavanagh** Michael is both a Coaching and Clinical Psychologist. He holds a BA (Hons, first class) in Psychology from the University of Sydney, and a PhD and Masters of Clinical Psychology from Macquarie University. Michael is Deputy Director of the Coaching Psychology Unit at the University of Sydney and was the key instigator of the Global Convention on Coaching. He has published widely and is the editor of the *International Coaching Psychology Review*.

**Sabine Dembkowski** Sabine is founder and director of the Coaching Centre in London and Cologne. With her team she supports senior executives and high-potentials in Fortune 500, DAX 30, and other leading firms across Europe. Previously she was a strategic management consultant with A.T. Kearney and Monitor Company in London.

**Michael A. Diamond** Michael A. Diamond is Professor and Director of the Center for the Study of Organizational Change at the University of Missouri. His latest (2009) book *Private Selves in Public Organizations* is published by Palgrave Macmillan. He is past president of the International Society for the Psychoanalytic Study of Organizations. He can be contacted at: http://csoc.missouri.edu.

**Fiona Eldridge** Fiona is director of The Coaching and Communication Centre and also Senior Leadership Advisor at the National College of Police Leadership. She is an experienced non-executive Director and Chairman, taking one organization from start up to a mature top three business in its field via three MBOs and CEOs.

**Robert Garvey** Bob is Professor of Business Education at York St John Business School, York. He is one of Europe's leading academic practitioners in coaching and mentoring. He is in demand internationally as a keynote conference speaker and has presented papers and made keynote conference presentations around the world. Bob is widely published in a range of journals and books.

**Niloofar Ghods**  Niloofar is a consultant with Cisco's Center for Collaborative Leadership's Executive Development Practice, where she assesses and coaches Cisco's SVP and VP talent pipeline. Prior to Cisco, Niloofar consulted for YSC, assessing and coaching senior executives of Fortune 100 multinational organizations and Dell's Global Talent Management Team.

**Kate Gilbert**  Kate is Senior Lecturer in Coaching and Mentoring at Oxford Brookes University. She has been fascinated by the potential of cultural experiences for personal growth ever since her first trip to the United States as a young student. Her doctoral research was on the cultural aspects of management development programs for Russian leaders in the 1990's transition period, and it was during this period that she was converted to coaching. Kate is currently researching attitudes to cultural awareness in UK businesses, and enjoys teaching research methods.

**Lucy L. Gilson**  Lucy is an Associate Professor at the University of Connecticut (PhD and MBA Georgia Institute of Technology, BSc from Georgetown School of Foreign Service). She serves as the Management's PhD Coordinator and Women's MBA Association faculty advisor. Lucy's research primarily focuses on teams and creativity. She is also interested in mentoring, employee empowerment, diversity, fairness issues, and virtual communication.

**Anthony M. Grant**  Tony is Director of the world's first Coaching Psychology Unit at Sydney University and Visiting Professor at Oxford Brookes University. In 2007 he was awarded a British Psychological Society Award for outstanding scientific contribution to Coaching Psychology. In 2009 he was awarded the "Vision of Excellence Award" from Harvard University for his pioneering work in developing a scientific foundation to coaching. He also plays loud (but not very good) blues guitar.

**Jane Brodie Gregory**  Brodie is currently a Visiting Assistant Professor of Social and Organizational Psychology at Washington & Lee University. Most recently she worked in Global Leadership Development with the Procter & Gamble Company, where she led the coaching program and performance management process. Dr Gregory completed her PhD in Industrial/Organizational Psychology at The University of Akron.

**Siegfried Greif**  Siegfried is managing director of a consulting institute (www.ifp.de). He was professor at the Free University of Berlin and had the chair of Work and Organizational Psychology at the University of Osnabrueck (Germany). He is editor of a book series on *Innovative Management* and the editor/author of 14 titles, including a German book series on coaching.

**Peter Hawkins**  Peter is Emeritus Chairman of Bath Consultancy Group, Professor of Leadership at Henley Business School, and is a leading coach, consultant, writer, and researcher in organizational strategy, leadership, team, and board development. He is the author of many books, including Leadership Team Coaching, Creating a Coaching

Culture, and Coaching, Mentoring and Organizational Consultancy: Supervision and Development with Nick Smith.

**Kate Hefferon**  Kate graduated from the University of Ottawa with a BA in English Literature and Psychology, followed by a BA in Psychology from Carleton University. This led to the completion of an MSc in Performance Psychology at Edinburgh University. Kate's PhD thesis was on the experience of post-traumatic growth among female breast cancer survivors and the role of the body in the recovery and growth process. She now teaches positive psychology at the University of East London.

**Joan C. King**  Joan received her PhD in neuroscience from Tulane (1972). Currently a Professor Emeritus Tufts University School of Medicine, Master Certified Coach and Board Certified Coach, Joan directed research and taught neuroscience prior to founding Beyond Success LLC (1998). Joan trains coaches in the Success Unlimited Network™ Program and mentors coaches in several coaching programs. Her concept of Cellular Wisdom™ is explored in a series of books. She can be contacted at: joanking@cellular-wisdom.com.

**Kathy E. Kram**  Kathy is the Shipley Professor in Management at the Boston University School of Management. Her primary interests are in the areas of adult development, mentoring, relational learning, and diversity issues in executive development. She is currently exploring the nature of peer coaching dyads, group peer coaching, and developmental networks. She can be contacted at: kekram@bu.edu.

**Robert J. Lee**  Robert is Managing Director of iCoachNewYork, a coach training group. He is affiliated with The New School University and Baruch College. Previously he was the CEO of the Center for Creative Leadership and of Lee Hecht Harrison. He is co-author of *Becoming an Exceptional Executive Coach.*

**Robin Leichtman**  Robin is finishing her PhD in Counseling Psychology at Cleveland State University and engaged in Gestalt Training (GTP XIV) at the Gestalt Institute in Cleveland, Ohio. With two Master's degrees, she is a licensed teacher and a licensed professional counselor in the State of Ohio.

**Paul E. Levy**  Paul is a Professor and Chair of the Department of Psychology at The University of Akron. Dr Levy received his PhD in I/O psychology from Virginia Tech in 1989. He is a fellow of the Society for Industrial and Organizational Psychology and the American Psychological Association. His research interests include performance appraisal, feedback, coaching, and motivation.

**Rodney L. Lowman**  Rodney is Distinguished Professor at Alliant International University, San Diego and President, Lowman & Richardson Consulting Psychologists. He has written or edited nine books (including *The Ethical Practice of Psychology in Organizations*), over one hundred articles, and made hundreds of conference presentation. He is a Fellow in three of the American Psychological Association divisions 12, 13, and 14 and past president of two psychology associations, the Society of Consulting Psychology and the Society of Psychologists in Management. He received his PhD in psychology (specializing in I-O and clinical psychology) at Michigan State University, USA.

**Lis Merrick** Lis is Managing Director of Coach Mentoring Ltd, a consultancy, which specializes in mentoring and coaching solutions to clients on a global basis. She is also a Module Leader and Senior Lecturer within the Coaching and Mentoring Research Unit (C&MRU) at Sheffield Business School and a Senior Consultant at Clutterbuck Associates.

**Rowena Ortiz-Walters** Rowena is an Associate Professor of Management at Quinnipiac University. Her research interests include mentoring relationships as a career developmental tool for women and racial minorities, and issues of diversity in the workplace. She received her PhD from the University of Connecticut. Her research has appeared in the *Journal of Organizational Behavior* and *Journal of Vocational Behavior*.

**Esra Ozkan** Esra is a cultural anthropologist and holds a doctorate in Science, Technology, and Society from MIT. She wrote her dissertation on the emergence and development of coaching as a professional field of expertise in the United States. Currently, Esra is a visiting scholar at Parsons, the New School for Design, where she teaches and conducts research on the field of information visualization.

**Linda J. Page** Linda is President and Founder of Adler Graduate Professional School located in Toronto, Canada. A graduate of Princeton University and Adler's Professional Coaching Program, Linda is Co-Chair of the Academic Standards Committee of the Graduate School Alliance for Executive Coaching (GSAEC). She is co-author with David Rock of *Coaching with the Brain in Mind* (2009). She can be contacted at: ljpage@adler.ca.

**Stephen Palmer** Stephen is the Founder Director of the Centre for Coaching, International Academy for Professional Development. He is an Honorary Professor of Psychology at City University London and Director of their Coaching Psychology Unit. He is president of the International Society for Coaching Psychology. He has authored numerous articles on coaching, stress management, and counseling, and has authored or edited over 40 books.

**Philippe Rosinski** Philippe is the author of several books, including *Coaching Across Cultures* and *Global Coaching*. He was the first European ICF Master Certified Coach and is a visiting professor at universities in Tokyo and Prague. He is the principal of Rosinski & Company.

**Gordon B. Spence** Gordon is a lecturer and researcher at Sydney Business School, University of Wollongong. He is a qualified psychologist with particular interests in leadership, mindfulness, peak performance, employee engagement, and workplace well-being. Gordon has over 20 refereed articles and book chapters, regularly speaks at national and international conferences and is Co-chair of the Scientific Advisory Council, Institute of Coaching at McLean Hospital/Harvard University.

**Juliann Spoth** Juliann is an executive coach, consultant, educator, author, and speaker with over 30 years of experience in individual, team, and organizational development and coaching practice that has spanned 14 countries. Juliann is the principal of Spoth & Associates, the principal of Spoth & Associates, the Chair and faculty for the Gestalt Institute of Cleveland (GIC) Coach Certification Program coaching faculty for the National Training Institute

(NTL) and a Master Coach for Case Western Reserve University. She has published in the organizational behavior field. She can be contacted at: jspoth@ameritech.net.

**Reinhard Stelter** Reinhard, PhD in psychology, is an accredited member and honorary vice-president of the International Society of Coaching Psychology, is professor of Coaching and Sport Psychology and head of the Coaching Psychology Unit, Department of Nutrition, Exercise and Sport Sciences, University of Copenhagen, visiting professor at Copenhagen Business School, and fellow at the Institute of Coaching at Harvard. He can be contacted at: www.rstelter.dk.

**Paul Stokes** Paul is a senior lecturer at Sheffield Hallam University where he teaches on the coaching and mentoring program. He is a member of the European Mentoring and Coaching Council, external examiner at the universities of Hertfordshire and Teeside, and has published widely in the field.

**Sunny Stout-Rostron** Sunny is Executive Director of Sunny Stout-Rostron Associates (Cape Town), and Research Mentor at the Institute of Coaching at Harvard/McLean Medical School. With a wide range of experience in leadership development and business strategy, and over 20 years as an executive coach, Sunny works with international leaders to help them achieve individual, team, and organizational goals. Sunny recently published *Business Coaching International.*

**Sarah Toman** Sarah is an associate professor at Cleveland State University and faculty at the Gestalt Institute of Cleveland. Sarah has published in both the career development and Gestalt therapy fields. She and Ansel Woldt co-edited, *Gestalt Therapy: History, Theory and Practice.* Sarah maintains a psychotherapy practice in Medina, Ohio.

**Chloé Tong** Chloé is a Business Psychologist. She has particular knowledge and expertise in designing and delivering high quality assessment and development programs. She has previously published in the field of emotional intelligence development through coaching.

**Gunnela Westlander** Gunnela is Professor Emeritus in Social and Organizational Psychology and has held since 1995 expert appointments with the University of Linköping, the Royal Institute of Technology, and Stockholm University. Research areas include: quality of work life; human-computer interaction; technological change; human aspects of intervention strategies; organizational change; and development.

**Helen Williams** Helen is an occupational and coaching psychologist specializing in solution-focused and cognitive behavioral coaching. An associate consultant at the Centre for Coaching, she is an HPC registered member and a member of the BPS SGCP, ISCP, and AC. Helen has co-authored several publications on assessment, coaching in organizations, cognitive behavioral and solution-focused coaching.

# Foreword

This book is an important addition to the library of books on the psychology of coaching and mentoring. It bridges the gap that exists between scholars and practitioners, helping establish the science behind the practice. I understand this conflict well since I studied psychology as a practice and felt that that was much more valuable than any academic theory. In fact I believe that many academics lack real hands-on experience and therefore fall short of good therapeutic or applied process.

I would argue that the same is true of coaching and I have little time for theoretical coaches who talk up an essay but don't deliver well. Jonathan, David, and Teresa have proven track records in both academic research and in workplace practice in the United Kingdom, United States, and Portugal. I think this book bridges the gap well. It illustrates practice well with a wide number of models that are wisely used by coaches and mentors, and offers insights into the growing research literature across coaching and mentoring, with contributions from the leading names in this emerging field of psychology.

I have personally worked with Jonathan on a number of projects, including improving police car driving, and Jonathan has published a number of research studies which provide evidence that coaching is a highly effective method for learning. In this book Jonathan, David, and Teresa offer value material for Master's students and academics to build a scientific basis for their studies and future research. They also aims to win over the skeptics who still tend to hold onto the long redundant autocracy and hierarchy still found in the workplace, by providing clear evidence of coaching's impact and potential.

The authors refer to a large number of examples provided by coaches from across the globe showing the importance of subtle language and cultural differences and the role coaching can play in helping build effective leaders and better organizations.

I believe it is worth adding here that coaching and its derivatives are not simply a useful tool, but a more advanced way of leading and managing others than instruction. Since a primary goal of coaching is to build self-responsibility in others, it is, in fact, an evolutionary need for humankind, for we have to move on beyond parental autocracy and hierarchy which are in general rather primitive states for adults. Humanity needs to continue to grow up and coaching and this book will contribute to our evolutionary process for many years to come. Defining it well and clearly, as this book does, will contribute to this process.

Sir John Whitmore, PhD
Coach and author

# Series' Preface

Welcome to this second book in the Wiley Blackwell Industrial and Organizational Psychology series. This title in the series focus is on coaching and mentoring, which are two fairly recent developments in I/O psychology. In terms of research, coaching and mentoring have only really come to the fore since 2000.

Over this period in the United States, Australia, and the United Kingdom we have seen a growing number of university programs offer coaching or coaching and mentoring Master's programs, including a small number of coaching psychology programs. In addition we have seen a significant growth in the number of coaching and mentoring PhDs and published research papers, which have made a book such as this possible.

We believe this series differs in three significant ways from other titles in the field.

First, the focus for the title is towards the researcher and student, as opposed to the practitioner, although scholar practitioners may also find this an interesting read. The aim of this book is to offer a comprehensive coverage of the main topics of inquiry within the domain and in each of these to offer a comprehensive critical literature review. Each chapter is thus an attempt to gather together the key papers, book chapters, and ideas and to present these for the serious researcher, student, and academic as a starting point for research in the key topics of I/O psychology.

Second, while many books take a UK/European or a US/North American approach with contributors drawn predominately from one continent or the other, in this series we have made strenuous efforts to create an international feel. For each title in the series we have drawn contributors from across the globe, and encouraged them to take an international as opposed to national or regional focus. Such an approach creates challenges. Challenges in terms of language and spelling, but also in the way ideas and concepts are applied in each region. We have encouraged our contributors to highlight such differences. We encourage you as the reader to reflect on these to better understand how and why these differences have emerged and what implications these have for your research and practice.

Third, the chapters avoid offering a single perspective, based on the ideas of the contributor. Instead we have invited leading writers in the field to critically review the literature in their areas of expertise. The chapters thus offer a unique insight into the literature in each of these areas, with leading scholars sharing their interpretation of the literature in their area.

Finally, as series editor I have invited contributors and editors to contribute their royalties to a charity. Given the international feel for the title we selected an international charity – Railway Children. This means approximately 10 percent of the cover price has been donated to charity.

With any publication of this kind there are errors; as editors we apologies in advance for these.

Jonathan Passmore
Series Editor, I/O Psychology

# Railway Children

Railway Children supports children alone and at risk on the streets of India, East Africa, and the United Kingdom. Children migrate to the streets for many reasons, but once there they experience physical and sexual abuse, exploitation, drugs, and even death. We focus on early intervention, getting to the street kids before the street gets to them, and where possible we reunite them with their families and communities.

In addressing the issue we work through our three-step change agenda to:

- Meet the immediate needs of children on the streets – we work with local organizations to provide shelter, education or vocational training, counseling, and, if possible, reintegration to family life.
- Shift perception in the local context – we work with local stakeholders to ensure that street children are not viewed as commodities to be abused and exploited – but as children in need of care and protection.
- Hold governments to account – if we are to see a long-term, sustainable change for the children with whom we work, we must influence key decision makers, ensuring that provisions for safeguarding children are made within their policies and budgets.

Last year we reached over 60,000 children across India, East Africa and the UK. In 2010 we launched an extensive qualitative piece of research 'Off The Radar' which highlighted the reasons behind children leaving or being forced from their homes and the services they needed to be safe. The recommendations from this report informed our model of practice here in the UK we call 'Reach', that offers services to children both before, during and after they runaway from home. Last year we reached over 37,000 children here in the UK through preventative work in schools, emergency refuge, detached street work and therapeutic family intervention.

To find out more about our work, or to help us support more vulnerable children, please go to: www.railwaychildren.org.uk or call 01270 757596

# 1

# The Psychology of Coaching and Mentoring

## Jonathan Passmore, David B. Peterson, and Teresa Freire

## Introduction

In this short introduction we aim to explore the nature of coaching and mentoring as tools for individual and organizational change. We will also consider the developing notion of coaching psychology and what this means for mentoring. Finally, we will briefly set out for the reader what follows in this edited title.

## What is Coaching?

The issue of a definition in coaching is one which has been actively explored in the literature, in a way which is not found in mentoring. A host of papers have considered the question, some focusing on reviewing previous definitions, others offering new definitions. This activity reflects the immature nature of the domain and the desire to delineate boundaries and mark out territory for coaching being a different and distinctive intervention to other organizational interventions such as mentoring, careers counseling, appraisals, and feedback. The reality, in our view, is that coaching has many similarities and overlaps with many of these interventions.

Tobias (1996) suggested a more extreme position, arguing that executive coaching was really a repackaging of activities and techniques borrowed from other disciplines such as counseling, psychology, learning, and consulting. This position, however, is not typical, and most writers have suggested that coaching is different and distinctive, while having areas of overlap with many other interventions.

Several papers have reviewed and debated the nature of coaching and its boundaries with counselling (Bachkirova and Cox, 2004; Passmore, 2007), as well as the emerging domain of coaching psychology (Sperry, 2008; Stewart et al., 2008). However, after a decade of debate, there is as yet no agreed standard definition of coaching. This diversity

*The Wiley Blackwell Handbook of the Psychology of Coaching and Mentoring*, First Edition.
Edited by Jonathan Passmore, David B. Peterson, and Teresa Freire.
© 2013 John Wiley & Sons, Ltd. Published 2016 by John Wiley & Sons, Ltd.

may reflect both the multiple applications of the approach, with multiple clients and multiple environments, and more importantly a lack of a single body to pull together diverse strands and establish a single overarching definition.

Key early writers such as Whitmore (1992) and Whitworth *et al.* (1998) provide definitions that have informed the course of the debate. One of the most frequently quoted definitions is Whitmore's. He suggests that: "Coaching is unlocking people's potential to maximise their own performance. It is helping them to learn rather than teaching them" (Whitmore, 1992, p. 10). Here Whitmore draws on the work of Gallwey's *Inner Game* (1986). Gallwey notes in his own writing the critical nature of the self in enhancing personal performance; the "opponent within one's own head is more formidable that the one on the other side of the net." Whitmore's response to overcome the self, is to use the self as a tool for reflection, raising self-awareness and through this personal responsibility for success or failure.

Whitworth places a stronger focus on the relational aspects of coaching, which are fostered by the coach. She notes coaching is, "a form of conversation with unspoken ground rules of certain qualities that must be present: respect, openness, compassion, and rigour, our committment to speaking the truth" (Whitworth *et al.*, 1998).

Both definitions are simple and widely drawn. In this sense it may be argued that they fail to delineate coaching from many of the other interventions identified above, although their wide embracing nature makes them attractive. In short these may be considered "big tent" definitions of coaching.

Other writers have attempted to be more specific in defining the nature of coaching, with the objective of more clearly establishing boundaries with other interventions. Grant and Stober (2001) in their largely Australian edited textbook of evidenced based coaching offer a definition: "A collaborative and egalitarian relationship between a coach, who is not necessarily a domain-specific specialist, and Client, which involves a systematic process that focuses on collaborative goal setting to construct solutions and employ goal attainment process with the aim of fostering the on-going self-directed learning and personal growth of the Client" (Grant and Stober, 2006, p. 2). This view of coaching can be contrasted with other definitions in edited texts.

Peltier (2001) in his US edited textbook of executive coaching psychology suggested that those trying to define coaching often start by stating what coaching is not: "Coaching is specifically not therapy." After a review of systems and consulting psychology, Peltier offers his own definition of coaching: "Someone from outside an organisation uses psychological skills to help a person develop into a more effective leader. These skills are applied to specific present moment work problems in a way that enables this person to incorporate them into his or her permanent management or leadership repertoire" (Peltier, 2001, p. xx). Peltier's definition reflects his background in psychology, combined with a desire to encourage the development of a stronger evidenced-base approach. This contrasts with earlier writers, such as Whitworth, who highlighted the strong intuitive nature of coaching.

As a comparison with another popular UK edited title Cox and her colleagues (Cox *et al.*, 2010) offer a "workman-like" definition: "Coaching can be seen as a human development process that involves structured, focused interaction and the use of appropriate strategies, tools, and techniques to promote desirable and sustained change for the benefit of the coachee and potentially other stakeholder" (Cox *et al.*, 2010). However, in the following debate they acknowledge that coaching is difficult to define. They note that definitions often seek to define coaching through reference to its ultimate purpose (what's it for), the type of clients (who uses the service), or the process (how is it done). They note that many definitions offer little fresh insight, as their broad and all encompassing natures fail to distinguish them from other human development interventions.

For a more organizational perspective, Kilburg suggested that coaching needed to offer  both individual and organizational benefits. He suggested the following definition of coaching:

> Helping a relationship formed between a client who has managerial authority and responsibility in an organization and a consultant who uses a wide variety of behavioural techniques and methods to help the client achieve a mutually identified set of goals to improve his or her professional performance and personal satisfaction and, consequently, to improve the effectiveness of the client's organization within a formally defined coaching agreement. (Kilburg, 2000, p. 142)

Kilburg's definition mixes psychological practice with organizational consulting and has become a standard defintion, frequently quoted alongside Whitmore's catchy definition, offering a contrast for readers in peer reviewed papers between the simple and more complex.

In reflecting on the research and publications over the past decade, Passmore and Fillery-Travis (2011) have attempted to offer a broad definition of coaching, which captures the three elements, "how, what and who for" highlighted by Cox and colleagues in their discussion about definitions. Passmore and Fillery-Travis suggest coaching is: "A Socratic based future focused dialogue between a facilitator (coach) and a participant (coachee/ client), where the facilitator uses open questions, summaries and reflections which are aimed at stimulating the self-awareness and personal responsibility of the participant."

Passmore and Fillery-Travis suggested that the "who for" can be vaguely defined as a "participant", that is someone actively and voluntarily participanting in the activity. The "how" of the process are the common techniques which underpin all coaching interventions, from cognitive behavioral to solution focus, and motivational interviewing to GROW. The outcome in this definition, too, is vaguely stated and is not goal focused, although this is included, but is instead rooted in Whitmore's view that in essence coaching is about self-awareness and personal responsibility.

In this definition the writters suggest, in using the term "Socratic dialogue", that the coachee already has within them the answer to the question, and thus the role of the coach is not socio-educational as it might be within approaches such as CBT, but is primarily faciliative.

## What is Coaching Psychology?

Alongside the debate about the nature of coaching, a new debate has emerged with the growing popularization in the United Kingdom, Australia, and Europe of coaching psychology. Writers have suggested that coaching psychology is different from coaching, and by implication psychologically trained practitioners operate in a different way to coaching. Some of the coaching writers have alluded to psychological principles, while not making an explicit coaching psychology definition, for example Peltier (2001).

The coaching psychology movement has emerged from two corners – in Australia from the work of Anthony Grant, who's doctoral thesis examined the emerging phenomena of coaching in 2001 and led to the creation of the Coaching Psychology Unit at Sydney University, with Michael Cavanagh in 2001. This unit was later supported by the emergence of an Australian Psychology Society's Interest Group in Coaching Psychology. Second, the work of a small group of coaching psychology practitioners in the UK, led by Stephen Palmer, but including Alison Whybrow, Pauline Willis, and Jonathan Passmore, who in 2002 formed the Coaching Psychology Forum. The forum led to the development of the British Psychology Society's Special Interest Group in coaching psychology. Over the following years, coaching psychology groups have emerged across the world.

In parallel with its growth in popularity, there is discussion as to whether coaching psychology or coaching psychologists are distinctive and if so in what way are they distinctive to others who practice coaching. At the heart of this is the question: "What is coaching psychology?" Grant and Palmer (2002) defined coaching psychology as: "Coaching psychology is for enhancing performance in work and personal life domains with normal, non-clinical populations, underpinned by models of coaching grounded in established therapeutic approaches."

This definition implies that coaching psychology is distinctive from coaching. Further, this definition of coaching psychology makes clear that the intervention is one targeted at "normal" and "non-clinical" populations. While this may have been true in 2002, the spread of coaching has taken coaching into new areas, including health (Anstiss and Passmore, in press) and education (Van Nieuwerburgh, in press). Coaching psychologists now work with non-adult populations in schools, with clinical populations in hospitals and with a wide range of individuals in care settings. Second, Grant and Palmer's original definition suggests that coaching psychology must draw on models grounded in therapeutic approaches. This definition thus limited coaching pscyhology and restricted the development of this emerging approach. In response to these, and other points, Palmer and Grant updated their definition. A revised version of the definition for coaching psychology offered by the writers is: "Coaching Psychology is for enhancing well-being and performance in personal life and work domains, underpinned by models of coaching grounded in established adult learning or psychological approaches" (adapted from Grant and Palmer, 2002).

While this deals with many of the concerns expressed about the original definition, some writers (including ourselves) have been concerned about creating an artifical distinction between coaching practice and coaching psychology practice, without evidence to support such a distinction. In fact research by Passmore *et al.* (2010) has suggested that there is little evidence to support differences in practice, at least within the UK coaching population – when comparing chartered pscyhologsits with the practices of coaches from other professional coaching bodies. A US survey, on which the UK survey was based, did find some small differences in practice, but these were tiny in comparison to the areas of commonality between coaching practitioners and coaching psychologists (Bono *et al.*, 2009). In short, coaching practitioners and coaching psychology practitioners appear to use similar behaviors within their coaching practice.

This is not to say that there is not a distinction between evidenced-based coaching practice and some of the practices adopted by coaches who Sherman and Freas (2004) might have included within their "wild west" of coaching when they highlighted concerns about a lack of training, regulation, and maturity in organizations in appointing professional practitioners. In fact many of these concerns still exist today. Coaching still has zero barriers to entry, there is no regulation of coaches and there are frequent examples of poor quality coach commisioning by organizations, reflecting the immature nature of the market.

Given this evidence, an alternative approach to coaching psychology is to consider it as the study of coaching practice as opposed to a distinctive aspect of coaching practice itself. Passmore (2010) has offered the following definition: "Coaching psychology is the scientific study of behaviour, cognitive and emotion within coaching practice to deepen our understanding and enhance our practice within coaching."

This approach to coaching psychology mirrors the definitions used for health, occupational, and other psychology disciplines and reflects a view that psychology is the scientific study of practice as opposed to the practice itself – which maybe evidenced based or not. Coaching psychology can study both and identify areas of excellence and areas of concern. We would argue that all coaching practice should be evidenced based and that while this is not the case at present, coaches should be asserting their voice to protect their domain from spurious practices, which in the long term will have a detrimental impact on the reputation of coaching.

This book has adopted this defintion of coaching psychology. Coaching psychology is concerned with the study, critical review, and sharing of evidenced-based coaching practice, as opposed to a distinct or seperate way of undertaking coaching with clients.

One issue not explored in this discussion is the lack of recognition around group and team coaching, as well as virtual coaching. The research on team coaching is at a lower level of maturity than one-to-one coaching, but there is a developing literature within the realm of team effectiveness (Mathieu *et al.*, 2008). Specifically, Wageman (1997, 2001) has made a substantial contribution, culminating in the publication of a theory of team coaching with Hackman (Hackman and Wageman, 2005). In addition, there is a small literature on virtual coaching. We have included both issues within this publication.

## What is Mentoring?

The complexity of the debate on definition within coaching has been matched in mentoring. Jacobi (1991) identified 15 different definitions of mentoring across the education, psychological, and management literature. Other researchers have made similar observations, noting the diversity in defining this organizational intervention (Burke, 1984; Merriam, 1983). As with coaching, the debate on definitions has created a challenge in trying to clarify the issue of impact and also the distinctive practices within mentoring that contribute to successful outcomes.

Given mentoring researchers longer history, over the past three decades, the topic has broadened and developed, allowing the emergence of both greater clarity on definitions and acceptance of diversity of practice depending on the mentoring goal and the client.

Within organizational mentoring, there is broad agreement about the nature of the topic. As Ragins and Kram (2007) note, the term "mentoring" is popularly used to denote a relationship between an older, more experienced mentor and a younger, less experienced protégé for the purposes of supporting the career development of the protégé. The mentor may not work in the same organization as the protégé, but is likely to work in the same sector or bring a deep understanding of the issues and challenges faced by the protégé.

Eby *et al.* (2007) offer the following definition, which we have used for this publication: "Workplace mentoring involves a relationship between a less experienced individual (protégé) and a more experienced person (the mentor), where the purpose is the personal and professional growth of the protégé … and where the mentor may be a peer at work, a supervisor someone else within the organization, but outside the protégé's chain of command" (Eby *et al.*, p. 16). What is of interest, since the seminal work by Kram (1985) and the emergence of a mentoring research agenda, is that there has been no discussion about "mentoring psychology" as a distinct or separate area of practice or research. We would hold the view that coaching and mentoring share many qualities and as coaching has looked to counseling, coaching should over the coming decade also look to mentoring research for insights into the design of mentoring/coaching programs and how coaching can contribute to individual development. Given this belief we have asked leading mentoring researchers to share their insights from three decades of work.

## The Developing Research Agenda for Coaching and Mentoring

Our hope is that this title will be a useful resource for postgraduate researchers, students, and academics alike, looking for a comprehensive review of the literature as a starting point for their own research and for scholar-practitioners to gain a full understanding of the depth and scope of the literature in their area of interest, with the objective of enhancing evidence-based practice and stimulating further research.

The book is structured using four sections focused on coaching, mentoring, theories and models, and a final section on issues in coaching and mentoring. We recognize this is only one of a number of ways we could have clustered these chapters. Together these sections combine what are the most important questions, conceptual frameworks, and practices related to the coaching and mentoring fields.

The first section comprises nine chapters devoted to coaching in general. The aim of this section is to present the state of the art about coaching issues that have been studied from a psychological perspective. A set of scholars, researchers, and professionals in the area of coaching discuss different concepts considered relevant for a better understanding of coaching science and practice.

Chapter 2 of this volume explores the efficacy of coaching. In this chapter Anthony Grant discusses two main questions, about organizational coaching efficacy and cost effectiveness. The author offers processes for answering these questions, which includes the discussion and definition of other main aspects, such as, the meaning of coaching, the nature of coaching-related evidence, the measurement of coaching effectiveness, and effective methodologies for assessing coaching outcomes. Grant also presents some broad delineations of coaching and the possible future directions for the measurement of coaching efficacy.

In Chapter 3 Robert Lee discusses the role of contracting in coaching, balancing individual and organizational issues. Lee reviews the literature regarding contracting as used in the field of executive coaching to provide insight into methods for establishing productive expectations among the multiple parties involved in an executive coaching engagement. Along the chapter all aspects related to contracting are discussed, underlying the notion that good contracts among all parties are a requirement for good coaching.

The development of meaning and identity within coaching is the focus of Chapter 4. This chapter explores how issues of meaning and identity relate to coaching individuals and groups. The authors argue that meaning and identity are foundational to all coaching practice and that these topics become involved at some point in all coaching. Such issues arise for both individuals and groups at key times of change and transition: when there are endings and/or new beginnings; when a person or team seems "stuck", or unable to move forward.

The importance of ethics is highlighted in Chapter 5, where Rodney Lowman discusses whether coaching is (or has the potential) to become a separate and distinct profession. The chapter moves on to consider the nature of ethics and its application by three bodies: the American Psychological Association (APA), the Canadian Psychological Association (ACA), and the British Psychology Society (BPS). Finally, the chapter offers a review of the small but growing list of papers which have explored coaching ethics.

In a more internal perspective, Bowman and colleagues present the neuroscience of coaching in Chapter 6. They provide an overview of some of the emerging science from neuro-psychology and raise questions about the implications for coaching practice. They argue that while neuroscience may be a new field, it has potential to be a useful ally for those engaged in personal development.

Mindfulness in coaching is the focus of Chapter 7. In this chapter Michael Cavanagh and Gordon Spence seek to answer several main questions about mindfulness as a construct or as an intervention. The authors examine the conceptual and definitional issues related to mindfulness, and present a model to assist in clarifying these. They also consider the potential mechanisms by which mindfulness may have its beneficial effects in coaching, presenting a theoretical model of these mechanisms. Cavanagh and Spence show the important contributions that mindfulness makes to coaching efficacy at the level of the coach, the coachee and the coaching relationship itself.

Coaching is also discussed from a developmental perspective. In line with this, Tatiana Bachkirova discusses developmental coaching in Chapter 8, presenting a new theory and framework for practice. She discusses two potential perspectives on developmental coaching, namely developmental coaching and practical approaches based on adult development theories. Bachkirova offers a new approach to developmental coaching based on re-conceptualization of the self that leads to facilitating change in coaching.

Gender issues in business coaching, is considered by Sunny Stout-Rostron in Chapter 9. This chapter reviews the contemporary literature relevant to gender as it affects organizational and institutional coaching. The author explores gender diversity and gender coaching, discussing the definition of gender; the challenges which gender presents; the wider research on the gender debate and coaching as a solution to build organizations.

Finally, and as the last chapter of this first section, Alison Carter and Peter Hawkins focus on team coaching. The two authors critically review the team literature and explore its relevance for coaching in group and team settings.

Section II of the book focuses on mentoring, with four chapters from leading authors around the world. The first chapter of this section – Chapter 11 – relates to designing mentoring schemes. Lis Merrick and Paul Stokes critically examine the design of mentoring schemes and programs, drawing out the lessons for future practice in relation to issues concerning the different modes of mentoring, in particular electronic and mutual mentoring.

Kath Kram and Chloe Tong provide a comprehensive review of the literature relating to the efficacy of mentoring in Chapter 12. The chapter introduces the reader to the various benefits of mentoring, exploring the benefits of traditional mentoring relationships for the individual partners, the protégé, and the mentor, and the benefits to the organization. The difficulties with the mentoring literature to date are discussed, followed by the variations on traditional mentoring relationships and their unique benefits. The authors highlight the need to consider the changes in contemporary organizational contexts.

In Chapter 13, Robert Garvey and Gunnela Westlander explore the issue of training mentors. The chapter considers the behaviors in mentoring that bring positive outcomes. The authors discuss the main issues related to mentoring, with a particular emphasis on mentor education and curriculum for mentors. They highlight the need for training, recognizing the underlying complexity of these processes and the dynamic nature of organizational environments, where successful behaviors in the previous year can spell disaster in the following year.

Finally in this section, in Chapter 14, Rowena Ortiz-Walters and Lucy Gilson discuss mentoring programs for under-represented groups. They highlight the fact that although companies around the world and across industries are implementing mentoring programs to provide career, leadership, and personal development for employees, the employees have limited access to mentoring. For this, the authors argue that research and broader understanding is greatly needed.

Section III of this title focuses on theories and models with implications for coaching. Leading authors present different psychological theories and models, drawing on their expertise and previous publications. They offer insights into the origins of each model, its research and theoretical framework, and finally its application within coaching. In total, eight chapters on models are presented.

In the first chapter of this section – Chapter 15 of the book – entitled "Humanistic and Person-centered Approaches," Jane Brodie Gregory and Paul Levy discuss how to provide structure and clarity to the notion of humanistic coaching, including techniques that can be incorporated into its practice. Some contributions from other psychological areas are discussed, namely the contribution from positive psychology, showing how coaches can maximize human potential of their clients throughout the practice of humanistic coaching.

Next, in Chapter 16, Sabine Dembkowski and Fiona Eldridge consider behavioral coaching. In this chapter the authors explore the influence and impact of behaviorism on developing effective executive coaching practice. For the authors, behavioral-based coaching is one of the most popular coaching models, although coaches and aspiring coaches are unaware of the theoretical basis of the models they learn about and apply, and of the consequences for their practice. This chapter aims to redress this balance.

Cognitive behavioral approaches are the focus of Chapter 17 authored by Stephen Palmer and Helen Williams. The authors review the historical development of the cognitive behavioral approach, detailing its philosophical routes and theoretical foundations, summarize the research evidence for the approach, detail the development of CBC in coaching and offer some examples of how the concept has been applied by coaching practitioners through new models and tools.

Tim Anstiss and Jonathan Passmore discuss, in Chapter 18, the motivational interviewing approach. After reviewing the origins, theory, and practice of motivational interviewing with clinical populations, the authors suggest that the approach has equal value with non-clinical clients where readiness to change is a challenge. They suggest that while the research with non-clinical populations is less extensive the approach will offer significant benefits in helping individuals prepare for change.

Michael Diamond in Chapter 19 presents psychodynamic executive coaching, aiming to explain the three major perspectives that underline this kind of coaching. Each of these theories illuminates different dimensions that executive coaches encounter relative to leadership, groups, and organizational dynamics. Along the chapter, the author shows how psychodynamic approaches to executive coaching offer consultants a better understanding and consideration of the impact of psychological reality on organizational roles and working relationships; and how it is intended to help leaders and executives by engaging them in authentic and reflective dialogue.

From another point of view, Juliann Spoth, Sarah Toman, Robin Leichtman, and Julie Allen, in Chapter 20, present how gestalt approach can create a unique approach to coaching. Along their chapter on gestalt coaching the authors explore gestalt theoretical approaches and their applications to coaching, with an emphasis also on gestalt coaching methods, that enables gestalt coaches to work at a deeper level and bring about powerful shifts.

In Chapter 21, Reinhard Stellar discusses the characteristics and potentialities of narrative approaches for coaching, showing how narrative coaching is representative of the new wave – or third generation – of coaching practice. The chapter is aimed to present coaching as a narrative-collaborative practice, an approach that is based on phenomenology, social constructionism, and narrative theory. Seeing narrative coaching as a collaborative practice, the author highlights how it leads to reflecting on the relationship between coach and coachee(s) in a new way. Stellar underlines the contribution of using coaching as a narrative-collaborative practice to the development of social capital.

Finally in Chapter 22, the last in the Third section, Teresa Freire discusses how coaching can benefit from the science of positive psychology, specifically in relation to questions regarding work, life, and organizations. The author presents the main concepts and approaches that justify the intersection of positive psychology and coaching in terms of research, methodologies, and practices, contributing to the definition of the positive coaching psychology field.

In the final section in this book, related to issues in coaching and mentoring, four chapters are presented. These explore issues of equal consideration for both coaching and mentoring such as evaluation, emotions, relationship, cross-cultural perspectives, and virtual working.

Chapter 23, by Siegfried Greif, deals with conducting organizational based evaluations of coaching and mentoring programs. This chapter highlights the main issue related to the evaluation of the effects of coaching and mentoring programs in organizations. Therefore, the primary aim of this chapter is to inform the reader about evaluation models and methods that meet high standards of quality and can be recommended for use in program evaluation studies.

In Chapter 24 Kate Hefferon focuses on the area of emotion research and its role in coaching and mentoring, from both the coach/mentor and client perspective, with special emphasis on the importance of happiness in the development of fulfilled individuals.

In Chapter 25, Geoffrey Abbott, Kate Gilbert, and Philippe Rosinski explore the role of cross-cultural themes in coaching and mentoring. They consider the differences of each and their cultural fit, as well as reviewing different models which may be helpful in deepening our understanding of culture within coaching and mentoring within organizations.

In the final chapter of the book *Niloofar Ghods* and *Camala Boyce* explore virtual coaching and mentoring. Virtual work involves working with those who are not co-located in the same space or are working with technology (i.e. telephone, email, text) as a replacement for face-to-face interactions. The authors note the particular challenges such media bring, and share the growing research in this area of practice.

## Conclusion

In this title we have taken a strongly academic approach to coaching, which contrast with other popular texts such as Peltier (2001, 2010), Passmore (2006, 2010), Palmer and Whybrow (2007), Cox *et al.* (2010), and Wildflower and Brennan (2011), which each offer a stronger practitioner focus. Our aim has been to offer an edited title, with leading international writers and critical literature reviews across a wide area of both coaching and mentoring, and through this to encourage stronger cross-fertilization between these areas of research, as well as to encouraging researchers to draw on the wider psychological (research-based) literature to inform further research and practice. We believe the development of evidenced based practice through high quality research is vital if coaching and mentoring are to achieve their full potential as tools to support individuals at work reaching their full potential.

## References

Anstiss, T. and Passmore, J. (in press) *Health Coaching*. London: Karnac Press.

Bachkirova, T. and Cox, E. (2004) A bridge over troubled water: Bring together coaching and counselling. *International Journal of Mentoring and Coaching*, 11(1).

Bono, J., Purvanova, R.,Towler, A.J., and Peterson, D.B. (2009) A survey of executive coaching practices. *Personnel Psychology*, 62, 361–404.

Burke, R. (1984) Mentoring in organizations. *Group and Organizational Studies*, 9, 355–72.

Cox, E., Bachkirova, T., and Clutterbuck, D. (2010) *The Complete Handbook of Coaching*. London: Sage.

Eby, L.T., Rhodes, J., and Allen, T.D. (2007) Definition and evolution of mentoring. In: T.D. Allen and T.D. Eby (eds) *Blackwell Handbook of Mentoring: A Multiple Perspectives Approach*. Oxford: Blackwell. pp. 7–20.

Gallwey, W.T. (1986) *The Inner Game of Tennis*. London: Pan Books.

Grant, A.M. and Palmer, S. (2002) Coaching psychology workshop. Annual conference of the Division of Counselling Psychology, BPS, Torquay, May 18.

Grant, A.M. and Stober, D. (2001) Introduction. In: D. Stober and A. Grant (eds) *Evidence Based Coaching: Putting Best Practices to Work for your Clients*. New Jersey: Wiley and Sons. pp. 1–14.

Grant, A.M. and Stober, D. (2006) Introduction. In: D. Stober and A. Grant (eds) *Evidence Based Coaching: Putting Best Practices to Work for your Clients*. New Jersey: Wiley and Sons. pp. 1–14.

Hackman, J.G. and Wageman, R. (2005) A theory of team coaching. *Academy of Management Review*, 30(2), 269–87.

Jacobi, M. (1991) Mentoring and under graduate academic success. A literature review. *Review of Educational Research*, 61, 505–32.

Kilburg, R.R. (2000) *Executive Coaching: Developing Managerial Wisdom in a World of Chaos*. Washington, DC. American Psychological Association.

Kram, K. (1985) *Mentoring at Work: Developmental Relationships at Work*. Glenview, II: Scott, Foreman and Co.

Mathieu, J., Maynard, M.T., Rapp, T., and Gilson, L. (2008) Team Effectiveness 1997–2007: A review of recent advancements and a glimpse into the future. *Journal of Management*, 34(3), 410–76.

Merriam, S. (1983) Mentors and protégés: A critical review of the literature. *Adult Education Quarterly*, 33, 161–73.

Passmore, J. (2007) Coaching and mentoring: The role of experience and sector knowledge *International Journal of Evidence based Coaching and Mentoring*, Summer, 10–16.

Passmore, J (2010) *Excellence in Coaching: The Industry Guide* (2nd edn). London: Kogan Page.

Passmore, J. and Fillery-Travis, A. (2011) A critical review of executive coaching research: A decade of progress and what's to come. *Coaching: An International Journal of Theory, Practice and Research*, 4(2), 70–88.

Passmore, J. Palmer, S., and Short, E. (2010) Results of an online UK survey of coaching and coaching psychology practitioners. Unpublished survey.

Peltier, B. (2001) *The Psychology of Executive Coaching. Theory and Application.* New York: Brunner-Routledge.

Peltier, B. (2010) *The Psychology of Executive Coaching: Theory and Application* (2nd edn). New York: Brunner-Routledge.

Ragins, B.R. and Kram, K. (2007) *The Handbook of Mentoring at Work: Theory, Reseach and Practice.* Thousand Oaks, CA: Sage.

Sherman, S. and Freas, A. (2004) *The Wild West of Coaching.* Harvard Business Review. November. Retrieved on December 7, 2011 from http://www.rocroseconsulting.com.au/Pdf%20Files/ The%20Wild%20West%20of%20Executive%20Coaching%20(2).pdf.

Sperry, L. (2008) Executive coaching: An intervention, role function or profession? *Consulting Psychology Journal: Practice and Research,* 60(1), 33.

Stewart, L.J., O'Riordan, S., and Palmer, S. (2008) Before we know how we've done, we need to know what we're doing: Operationalising coaching to provide a foundation for coaching evaluation. *The Coaching Psychologist,* 4(3), 127–33.

Tobias, L.L. (1996) Coaching executives. *Consulting Psychology Journal: Practice and Research,* 48(2), 87–95.

Van Nieuwerburgh, C. (in press) *Coaching in Education.* London: Karnac Press.

Wageman, R. (1997) Critical success factors for creating superb self-managing teams. *Organisational Dynamics,* 26(1), 49–61.

Wageman, R. (2001) How leaders foster self-managing team effectiveness: Design choices versus hands-on coaching. *Organisation Science,* 12(5), 559–77.

Wildflower, L. and Brennan, D. (2011) *The Handbook of Knowledge Based Coaching.* San Francisco: Jossey Bass.

Whitmore, J. (1992) *Coaching for Performance.* London: Nicholas Bearley.

Whitworth, L., Kimsey-House, H., Kimsey-House, K., and Sandahl, P. (1998) *Co-active Coaching: New Skills for Coaching People Toward Success in Work and Life.* London: Nicholas Brealey.

# Section I
# Coaching

# 2

# The Efficacy of Coaching

## Anthony M. Grant

## Introduction

Is coaching effective? Is it cost-effective? The answers to these questions depend heavily on the contextual and situational factors at play and who is asking the question – and why. A professional coach or purveyor of coaching services asking the above questions may well take the growth of the coaching industry worldwide as one indicator of whether coaching is effective and "works", and it is clear that in the last 10 or 15 years workplace and executive coaching has grown from a relatively novel and little used intervention to a mainstream activity in organizations worldwide.

The annual revenue expended on corporate coaching has been estimated to be in the region of US$1.5 billion, and in 2009 it was estimated that there were approximately 40,000 professional coaches globally (Frank Bresser Consulting, 2009) up from approximately 30,000 in 2006 (International Coach Federation, 2006), and the figures are probably even higher today despite the Global Financial Crisis (GFC). Indeed for some organizations the pressures and tensions inherent in the GFC served only to highlight the need to provide good coaching to key staff (Farndale *et al.*, 2010). In the United States, 93 percent of US-based Global 100 companies use executive coaches (Bono *et al.*, 2009). In the United Kingdom, 88 percent of organizations use coaching (Jarvis *et al.*, 2005). In 2006 in Australia, 64 percent of business leaders and 72 percent of senior managers reported using coaches (Leadership Management Australia, 2006), and following the GFC, Australian businesses perceived a need for coaching in terms of the increased importance of developing new perspectives in tough economic times, renewed emphasis on communicating effectively with employees, and building trust and resilience with staff increased dramatically (Leadership Management Australia, 2009).

But the growth of the coaching industry and industry's recognition of the important role of coaching in both good and tough economic times is not a reliable indicator of coaching's efficacy or validity. Indeed, given that coaching is playing an increasing role in

*The Wiley Blackwell Handbook of the Psychology of Coaching and Mentoring*, First Edition.
Edited by Jonathan Passmore, David B. Peterson, and Teresa Freire.
© 2013 John Wiley & Sons, Ltd. Published 2016 by John Wiley & Sons, Ltd.

organizations worldwide, it is important that we are able to reliably access the effectiveness of coaching interventions and develop an evidence base for professional coaching. Is coaching effective and do we yet have an evidence base for coaching?

To begin the process of answering these questions, we need to determine what we mean by coaching, delineate the nature of coaching-related evidence, work out how to measure coaching effectiveness, and determine effective methodologies for assessing coaching outcomes, and do so in relation to the extant coaching literature. Drawing on past work in this area (Grant, 2011; Grant *et al.*, 2010), and beginning with some broad delineations of coaching, I review the recent extant research into the efficacy of coaching and highlight possible future directions for the measurement of coaching efficacy.

## Seek First to Understand

Before we can meaningfully discuss the efficacy of coaching we need to understand the nature of coaching itself. Although the widespread use of the term "coaching" suggests that it is a monolithic activity, in fact coaching methodologies are highly diverse and heterogeneous approaches to creating and facilitating purposeful positive individual and organizational change.

Despite such diversity, most understandings of coaching are underpinned by the view of coaching as a collaborative relationship formed between a coach and the coachee for the purpose of attaining professional or personal development outcomes which are valued by the coachee (Spence and Grant, 2007). Thus, typically, coaching is a goal-focused activity; clients come to coaching because there is a problem they need or want to solve or a goal they want to attain, and they a looking for help in constructing and enacting solutions to that problem.

At its core the coaching process is a relatively straightforward one in which the coach helps stretch and develop the coachee's current capacities or performance, by helping individuals to: (1) identify desired outcomes, (2) establish specific goals, (3) enhance motivation by identifying strengths and building self-efficacy, (4) identify resources and formulate specific action plans, (5) monitor and evaluate progress towards goals, and (6) modify action plans based on such feedback. The monitor-evaluate-modification steps of this process constitute a simple cycle of self-regulated behavior, and this is a key process in creating intentional behavior change (Carver and Scheier, 1998). The role of the coach is to facilitate the coachee's movement through this self-regulatory cycle by helping the coachee to develop specific action plans and then to monitor and evaluate progression towards those goals (Grant *et al.*, 2010).

## Sounds Simple: So Coaching Should be Easy to Evaluate?

Thus, in theory at least, the essence of coaching is a relatively straightforward process of setting goals, developing action plans, and managing progress towards those goals. Therefore, it might be entirely reasonable to assume that assessing the efficacy of coaching should be a comparatively easy process.

However, coaching as a broadly-applied human change methodology has been used with a vast range of issues, including: reducing workplace stress (Wright, 2007); creating organizational cultural change (Anderson *et al.*, 2008); business coaching (Clegg *et al.*, 2005); facilitating work performance in cross cultural contexts (Peterson, 2007); dealing with resistance to change in low-performing managers (Passmore, 2007); enhancing sales force performance (Agarwal *et al.*, 2009); helping learner drivers develop driving skills (Passmore and Mortimer, 2011); improving communication and leadership skills (Wilson, 2004); helping with career development (Scandura, 1992); team building and group development (Cunha and Louro, 2000); and coaching to improve performance in job interviews (Maurer *et al.*, 1998) – an almost endless list of applications.

In addition to these rich and diverse applications, coaching in the workplace is conducted at all levels of the organization. Executive coaching for executive level employees is typically conducted within a formal coaching agreement with external coaches, using sit-down coaching sessions and encompasses a vast range of services and specialties: coaching for enhanced strategic planning; presentation skills; anger and stress management; executive management team building; and leadership development – all outcomes that are difficult to quantify. In contrast, workplace coaching in organizations can be understood as coaching that takes place in workplace settings with non-executive employees aimed at enhancing workplace performance and work-related skills. As such, it is often an internal coaching intervention delivered on the job by line managers and supervisors, or by employees specially designated as being in the coaching role. This kind of coaching often involves impromptu or "corridor coaching", rather than formal sessions (Grant *et al.*, 2010). Thus, the aims and processes of workplace coaching interventions are often somewhat different to those in executive coaching. Furthermore, and adding to the complexity of evaluating coaching in the workplace, is the fact that organizations tend to use a combination of both external and internal coaching approaches, for example one UK survey found that 51 percent of UK organizations used external coaches, 41 percent trained their own internal coaches, and 79 percent used managers as coaches (Kubicek, 2002).

## Reviewing the Efficacy of Coaching is Complex, and the Literature is Disjointed

Because coaching interventions cover such a broad range of applications, and are conducted with such a wide and diverse range of participants, it is perhaps not surprising that the academic outcome literature on coaching is disjointed and somewhat fragmented. There is an increasing amount of coaching-specific, practitioner-generated research. Practitioner research in general tends to be conducted by independent practitioners on client outcomes associated with their own personal business. Practitioner research, especially as part of one's reflective practice, has the potential to be extremely valuable and has made a significant contribution to the emergence and development of an evidence base for coaching. However, a key limitation of practitioner research is that many practitioners are not trained in research methods or in the dissemination of findings. Further, most practitioner research tends not to use standardized or validated outcome measures, typically constructing pre-post surveys or questionnaires that target the specific behaviors that are the focus of the coaching intervention, or presenting estimates of financial return on investment (ROI: McGovern *et al.*, 2001).

Whilst such idiosyncratic outcome measures may be very useful to the client and often form valuable material in terms of marketing for coaching service providers, their relevance to the broader coaching-specific knowledge base is often limited. It should be noted, however, that the quality of coaching practitioner research is improving. Where some past coaching research seemed to be primarily aimed at marketing coaching services

(Corbett, 2006), recently there are many more well-grounded examples of contemporary thought in this area, particulary in relation to the evaluation of executive coaching (for some useful examples see Coutu and Kauffman, 2009; Hernez-Broome and Boyce, 2011).

As regards the peer-reviewed academic literature on the efficacy of coaching: as of January 2011 there were a total of 634 published scholarly papers or dissertations on coaching listed in the databases PsycINFO and Business Source Premier, beginning with Gorby's (1937) report of senior staff coaching junior employees on how to save waste. This figure of 634 includes life (or personal coaching) and executive and workplace coaching, but excludes papers on other applications of coaching such as sports or athletic coaching, forensic, clinical or psychotherapeutic populations, educational coaching or coaching for faking on psychometric or educational tests, which are not relevant to this chapter.

It is clear that the coaching literature has grown significantly in recent years. Between 1937 and January 1, 2011 there were a total of 634 published papers. In terms of assessing the efficacy of coaching there have been 234 outcome studies published since 2000 (to January 2011); 131 case studies, 77 within-subject studies, and 25 between-subject studies. Of the 25 between-subject studies, 14 were randomized studies (see Table 2.1 for a summary of the 25 between-subject studies).

Many of the published empirical papers are surveys about different organizations' use of coaching (e.g., Douglas and McCauley, 1999; Vloeberghs *et al.*, 2005), or studies examining the characteristics of coach training schools (e.g., Grant and O'Hara, 2006). That is, most of the empirical literature to date is contextual or survey-based research about the characteristics of coaches and coachees or the delivery of coaching services. Whilst this is useful information for both the coaching industry and the purchasers of coaching services, it does not tell us a great deal about the efficacy of coaching *per se*.

## Outcome Studies

The first published empirical outcome study exploring the efficacy of coaching in the academic literature was Gershman's (1967) dissertation on the effects of specific factors of the supervisor-subordinate coaching climate upon improvement of attitude and performance of the subordinate, showed initial support of the efficacy of coaching approaches in the workplace. No other coaching outcome studies were published until Duffy's (1984) dissertation on the effectiveness of a feedback-coaching intervention in executive outplacement. Peterson's (1993) thesis on behavior change in an individually tailored management coaching program marked the dawning of a contemporary phase of coaching outcome research (prior to 1990 there had been only six published coaching outcome studies examining the efficacy of coaching).

Most of the 131 case studies in the coaching literature are purely descriptive, tending to emphasize practice-related issues rather than presenting rigorous evaluations of the coaching intervention. Very few of these case studies used established and validated quantitative measures, and few used case study methodology beyond a purely descriptive fashion.

## Two Key Case Studies

From this author's perspective two case studies stand out in the coaching literature as exemplifying good practice in using case study methodologies to explore the efficacy of coaching. The first is Libri and Kemp's (2006) A-B-A-B single case design with a sales

**Table 2.1** Summary of 25 between-subjects studies to January 1, 2011.

| Study | Intervention overview | Type of study | Key findings |
|---|---|---|---|
| Miller (1990) | 33 employees. Some received coaching by their managers over 4 weeks. | Quasi-experimental field study<br>(a) Coaching group; (b) Control group. | No sig. differences pre-post for interpersonal communication skills. |
| Deviney (1994)* | 45 line supervisors at a nuclear power plant. Some received feedback and coaching from their managers over 9 weeks. | Randomized controlled study<br>(a) Feedback plus coaching;<br>(b) Feedback with no coaching;<br>(c) Control group. | No sig. differences in pre-post feedback behavior. |
| Taylor (1997)* | Participants undergoing a medical college admission test preparation course. | Randomized controlled study<br>(a) Training only; (b) Coaching only;<br>(c) Training plus coaching;<br>(d) Control group. | Coaching reduced stress more than training. |
| Grant (2002)* | 62 trainee accountants received group coaching over one semester. | Randomized controlled study<br>(a) Cognitive coaching only;<br>(b) Behavioral coaching only;<br>(c) Combined cognitive and behavioral coaching; (d) Control groups for each condition. | Combined cognitive and behavioral coaching most effective in increasing grade point average, study skills, self-regulation, and mental health. GPA gains maintained in 12 month follow-up. |
| Miller *et al.* (2004)* | 140 licensed substance abuse professionals learnt motivational interviewing via a range of methods. | Randomized controlled study<br>(a) Workshop only; (b) Workshop plus feedback; (c) Workshop plus coaching; (d) Workshop, feedback, and coaching; or (e) Waitlist control group. | Relative to controls, the 4 trained groups had gains in proficiency. Coaching and/or feedback increased post-training proficiency. |
| Sue-Chan and Latham (2004) | 53 MBA students in two studies in Canada and Australia. | Random assignment<br>(a) External coach; (b) Peer coach or<br>(c) Self-coached. | Study 1: External coaching associated with higher team playing behavior than peer coaching; Study 2: External and self coaching associated with higher grades than peer coaching. |

*(continued)*

**Table 2.1**  (continued)

| Study | Intervention overview | Type of study | Key findings |
|---|---|---|---|
| Bennett and Perrin (2005)* | 111 individuals randomized to nurse coaching group or usual-care control group with coaching conducted by nurses on phone and email. | Randomized controlled study (a) Health coaching; (b) Control group. | Intervention group had significantly less illness intrusiveness and health distress than controls at 6 months. Nurse-delivered MI, primarily using the telephone and email, is a feasible method to facilitate well-being with older adults. |
| Gattellari et al. (2005)* | 277 GPs in total. Some received 2 phone-based peer coaching sessions integrated with educational resources. | Randomized controlled study (a) Peer coaching and educational resources; (b) Control group. | Compared to controls, peer coaching increased GPs' ability to make informed decisions about prostate-specific antigen screening. |
| Gyllensten and Palmer (2005) | 31 participants from UK finance organization. | Quasi-experimental field study (a) Coaching group; (b) Control group. | Anxiety and stress decreased more in the coaching group compared to control group. |
| Evers et al. (2006) | 60 managers of the federal government. | Quasi-experimental field study (a) Coaching group; (b) Control group. | Coaching increased outcome expectancies and self-efficacy. |
| Green et al. (2006)* | 56 adults (community sample) took part in SF-CB life coaching program | Randomized controlled study (a) Group-based life coaching; (b) Waitlist control. | Coaching increased goal attainment, well-being, and hope. 30-week follow-up found gains were maintained. |
| Green et al. (2007)* | 56 female high school students took part in SF-CB life coaching program for 10 individual coaching sessions over 2 school terms. | Randomized controlled study (a) Coaching group; (b) Waitlist control group. | Coaching increased cognitive hardiness, mental health and hope. |
| Spence and Grant (2007)* | 63 adults (community sample) took part in SF-CB life coaching program. | Randomized controlled study (a) Professional coaching group; (b) Peer coaching group; (c) Waitlist control group. | Professional coaching more effective in increasing goal commitment, goal attainment and environmental mastery. |
| Duijts et al. (2007) * | Dutch employees assessed for the effectiveness of a preventive coaching program on sickness absence due to psychosocial health complaints and on well-being outcomes | Randomized controlled study: (a) 6 month course of preventive coaching; (b) control group. | Significant improvements in health, life satisfaction, burnout, psychological well-being but no improvement in self-reported sickness absence. |

| Study | Sample / Design | Method | Findings |
|---|---|---|---|
| Spence et al. (2008)* | 45 adults (community sample) took part in mindfulness-based health coaching over 8 weeks. | (a) Randomized controlled study: SF-CB coaching followed by mindfulness training (MT); (b) Mindfulness training followed by SF-CB coaching; (c) Health education only control group. | Goal attainment greater in coaching than in the educative/directive format. No significant differences were found for goal attainment between the two MT/CB-SF conditions. |
| Fielden et al. (2009) | Nurses from 6 UK health care trusts were allocated to a coaching group (N=15) or a mentoring group (N=15). | Quasi-experimental field study (a) Coaching group; (b) Mentoring group in six-month coaching/mentoring program. Qualitative and quantitative data at (T1=baseline, T2=4 months and T3=9 months). | Mentoring was perceived to be "support" and coaching was "action". Both reported significant development in career development, leadership skills, and capabilities; mentees reported the highest level of development, with significantly higher scores in 8 areas of leadership and management and in 3 areas of career impact. |
| Franklin and Doran (2009)* | First-year students: co-coaching with preparation, action, adaptive learning coaching, or self-regulation coaching PAAL (N=27) or self-regulation (N=25) | A double-blind random control trial in which participants were randomly allocated to either a preparation, action, adaptive learning (PAAL), or a self-regulation co-coaching. | Both co-coaching conditions produced significant increases in self-efficacy and resilience; however, only those in the PAAL condition performed significantly better on decisional balance, hope, self-compassion, the incremental theory of change, and independently assessed academic performance. |
| (Grant et al., 2009)* | 41 executives in a public health agency received 360-degree feedback and four SF-CB coaching sessions over 10-week period. | Randomized controlled study (a) Coaching group; (b) Waitlist control group. | Coaching enhanced goal attainment, resilience and workplace well-being and reduced depression and stress and helped participants deal with organizational change. |

(continued)

**Table 2.1** (*continued*)

| Study | Intervention overview | Type of study | Key findings |
|---|---|---|---|
| Aust *et al.* (2010) | Seven intervention units (N=128) and seven non-randomized reference units (N=103) of a large hospital in Denmark participated in an intervention project with the goal of improving the psychosocial working conditions. | Quasi-experimental field study (a) Coaching group; (b) Control group. | In the intervention units there was a statistically significant worsening in 6 out of 13 work environment scales. The decrease was most pronounced for aspects of interpersonal relations and leadership. In comparison, the reference group showed statistically significant changes in only 2 scales. Process evaluation revealed that a large part of the implementation failed and that different implicit theories were at play. |
| Cerni *et al.* (2010) | 14 secondary school principals: all school staff in the 14 schools were invited to rate their school principal using the MLQ (5X) questionnaire. | Pre-test, post-test control-group research design (a) Coaching group; (b) Control group. | This study provides initial evidence that by creating changes to rational and constructive thinking, it is possible to increase coachee's use of transformational leadership techniques. |
| Grant *et al.* (2010)* | 44 high school teachers were randomly assigned to either SF-CB coaching or a waitlist control group. | This study was both an experimental (randomly assigned) and a WS (pre-post) study. | Participation in coaching was associated with increased goal attainment, reduced stress and enhanced workplace well-being and resilience. Pre-post analyses for the coaching group indicated that coaching enhanced self-reported achievement and humanistic-encouraging components of constructive leadership styles. |
| Kauffeld and Lehmann-Willenbrock (2010) | Spaced and massed training are compared using behavioral and outcome criteria; 64 bank employees (N=32 in each training group). | Quasi-experimental follow-up research design with a sample of 64 bank employees (N=32 in each training group) is used. | Spaced rather than massed training practice resulted in greater transfer quality, higher self-reports of sales competence and improved key figures. Spaced training did not surpass massed training in terms of transfer quantity. |

| Study | Intervention | Design | Findings |
|---|---|---|---|
| Kines *et al.* (2010) | Foremen in 2 intervention groups are coached and given bi-weekly feedback about their daily verbal safety communications with their workers. | A pre-post intervention-control design with 5 construction work gangs: foremen-worker verbal safety exchanges (experience sampling method, N=1693 interviews), construction site safety level (correct vs. incorrect, N=22,077 single observations), and safety climate (7 dimensions, N=105 questionnaires), measured over 42 weeks. | Coaching construction site foremen to include safety in their daily verbal exchanges with workers has a significantly positive and lasting effect on the level of safety, which is a proximal estimate for work-related accidents. |
| Kochanowski *et al.* (2010) | Experimental group of managers received individual coaching several weeks after attending a feedback workshop. The control group of managers also attended a feedback workshop but did not receive the follow-up coaching. | Quasi-experimental field study (a) Feedback plus coaching group; (b) Feedback only control group. | Coaching significantly increased the use of collaboration with subordinates, but results for the other three "core" tactics were mixed. |
| Leonard-Cross (2010) | Investigated the impact and process of developmental coaching evaluating coaching which took place over a two-year period. | The study used action research (Lewin, 1946) and a quasi-experimental method. Coachees and the comparative group of non-coached staff completed questionnaires. | Participants that had received developmental coaching (N=61) had higher levels of self-efficacy than the control group of participants (N=57) who had not received coaching. |

Notes: SF-CB=solution-focused cognitive behavioral; * = randomized controlled study.

executive that used established and validated self-report quantitative measures of anxiety (Beck and Steer, 1993), depression (Beck *et al.*, 1996), and core self-evaluations (Judge *et al.*, 2003), in addition to objective measures of sales performance, including the number of client leads, client loan interviews, loan applications, and number of loans approved each week. This case study of the efficacy of coaching serves as a useful case study exemplar of the blending of the psychological with the pragmatic in that the case reports both on quantitative psychological facets and workplace performance.

The second case study, that in many ways is the antitheses of the Libri and Kemp (2006) paper, is Freedman and Perry's (2010) qualitative report. This detailed and highly descriptive paper describes the development and trajectory of an initially non-voluntary shadow coaching and consulting engagement with a somewhat reluctant client in the nuclear industry. The case study explores the efficacy of coaching from both the coach's and the client's perspective, and the paper is somewhat unusual in that both coach and client jointly contributed to its writing. This paper gives the reader detailed insight into the actual process of shadow coaching and consulting, including access to the cognitive and emotional responses of both the coach and client, and in this way sheds light on inner workings of the executive coaching relationship. From the perspective of Freedman and Perry's (2010) paper, investigation of the efficacy of coaching is more than just reports of coaching outcomes or goal attainment.

Such narrative accounts of the coach's and client's internal process provide valuable information about the efficacy of coaching from a completely different perspective to that offered by numerical data, and are of great value to those seeking such insights. However, they do not allow us to make more generalized evaluations of the efficacy of coaching or compare results between different coaching interventions. For that type of evaluation we need to turn our attention to group-based evaluations of the efficacy of coaching.

## Within-subject Outcome Research

Within-subject studies are those that compare the impact of coaching on a group of individuals. The group was assessed before and following the coaching interventions. The 74 within-subject studies published to January 2011 represent the largest single group-based methodological approach to quantitative empirical coaching research. This group of studies into the efficacy of coaching cover a wide range of issues including: workplace coaching to reduce waste (Sergio, 1987); improvement in managers' leadership skills as a result of feedback and coaching (Conway, 2000); the impact of life coaching on goal attainment, insight and mental health (Grant, 2003); the use of team coaching in supporting team reflection and learning in global research and development project teams (Mulec and Roth, 2005); the cognitive and behavioral flexibility in executives who received coaching (Jones *et al.*, 2006); the attainment of organizational quota and personal goals within an army recruiting organization (Bowles *et al.*, 2007); changes in leadership competencies and learning agility amongst senior executives in the IT industry (Trathen, 2008); increases in measures of operational and fiscal performance in medical settings (Bacigalupo *et al.*, 2009) and the impact of peer coaching on well-being amongst psychology undergraduate students (Short *et al.*, 2010).

Of particular interest in the group of within-subject studies is Solansky's (2010) evaluation of two key leadership development program components. This paper is of interest to those concerned with the development of the literature base on the efficacy of coaching as it is one of few coaching-related empirical papers published in a top-tier academic journal. To date, the vast majority of coaching research has been published in second- or third-level journals. Whilst the level of prestige accorded to a journal by an elitist section of the academic community may have little or no relevance for the vast majority of readers interested in coaching, the small but increasing number of coaching publications in top-tier journals indicates that coaching as a human change methodology is finding increasing acceptance within the academic community. To the extent that such publications are an indicator of the increasing recognition of coaching as a valid approach to facilitating human change, this trend is welcome and it is hoped it will continue.

Within-subject studies can provide useful quantitative data and allow for the use of inferential statistics, provided that the studies are well designed and use validated and reliable measures. However, by comparing the results of the intervention to a matched group that did not receive coaching, a between-subject design can give greater assurance that the results are due to the coaching intervention itself, and not to some broader influence such as the mere passage of time or changes in, for example, workplace culture or environment. The use of random assignment to a coaching or non-coaching control group means greater control over extraneous, individual differences, and gives some sections of the coaching community and interested onlookers greater comfort in the certainty of reported coaching efficacy.

## Between-subject and Randomized Controlled Studies

Conducting evaluations of real-life coaching intervention is a complex and time consuming process. Recruiting participants, managing the process of collecting data, organizing the coaches and coachees, and ensuring that there is a broad consistency in the way that the actual coaching is conducted presents unique and difficult challenges. These are made particularly complicated when the coaching is conducted in organizational settings where there are often competing political or operational agendas, and the structure and priorities of the organization may change substantially over the course of the coaching engagement.

It is thus not surprising that there are few between-subject studies in the coaching literature. As of January 2011 in the PsycINFO database there are only 25 published between-subject studies and only 14 of those used randomized controlled designs. The 14 randomized controlled studies of coaching that have been conducted to date indicate that coaching can indeed improve performance in various ways.

Four of these fourteen studies have been in the medical or health areas of work. Taylor (1997) found that solution-focused coaching fostered resilience in medical students. This study appears to be the first reporting on the impact of solution-focused coaching. Solution-focused approaches parallel the aims of appreciative inquiry (Cooperrider *et al.*, 2000), in that solution-focused coaching focuses specifically on the individual's strengths and goals, rather than taking a reductionist, diagnostic approach.

Gattellari *et al.* (2005) found that peer coaching by general practitioners improved the coachee's ability to make informed decisions about prostate-specific antigen screening. Miller *et al.* (2004) found that coaching with feedback was superior to training-only conditions, in a program designed to help clinicians learn motivational interviewing skills. Spence *et al.* (2008) found that goal attainment in a health coaching program was greater in the coaching condition when compared to an education-only intervention.

Four outcome studies have been in the life (or personal) coaching domain with community samples and with students. These have indicated that coaching can improve or indeed facilitate goal attainment and reduce anxiety and stress (Grant, 2003), enhance psychological and subjective well-being (Green *et al.*, 2006; Spence and Grant, 2007) and resilience, while reducing depression, stress, or anxiety (Green *et al.*, 2007).

There have been only two randomized controlled studies of workplace coaching. Deviney (1994) examined the efficacy of supervisors acting as internal workplace coaches, finding no changes in supervisors' feedback skills following a multiple-rater feedback intervention and coaching from their managers over nine weeks. The reason for this is not clear, but it may be because the training processes for giving the supervisors' workplace coaching skills was not effective. The difficulties of developing managers' coaching skills is well-recognized (Grant, 2010).

Duijts *et al.* (2008) examined the effectiveness of coaching as a means of reducing sickness absence due to psychosocial health complaints and on well-being outcomes and found that coaching led to significant improvements in health, life satisfaction, burnout, and psychological well-being, but found no improvement in self-reported sickness absence, concluding that coaching can enhance the general well-being of employees. There has been only one randomized controlled study of the effectiveness of executive coaching, with participants receiving 360-degree feedback followed by four sessions of executive coaching. The coaching was found to improve goal attainment, increase resilience, and reduce stress and depression (Grant *et al.*, 2009).

For some observers the small number of randomized controlled outcome studies may be considered to be the major shortcoming in the literature on coaching efficacy. Although the data obtained from quantitative, randomized, controlled outcome studies cannot provide the rich detailed insights afforded by well-written qualitative case studies (e.g., see Peterson and Millier, 2005), and many might contest their practical utility, they are currently held to be the "gold standard" in quantitative outcome research (for discussion on this issue in relation to coaching see Cavanagh and Grant, 2006). Certainly there is a considerable section of the coaching and general scientific community that sees randomized controlled studies as essential for establishing the credibility of coaching interventions, and in this author's view such research indeed provides one extremely important part of the foundation for an evidence-based approach to coaching.

However, in real-life coaching research, unlike laboratory-based studies or clinical drug trials, genuine randomized allocation to intervention or control is often extremely difficult, if not impossible. Because of these difficulties many coaching outcome studies have used single group, pre-post, within-subject designs (e.g., Grant 2003, Jones *et al.*, 2006; Olivero *et al*, 1997; Orenstein, 2006).

There have been a number of quasi-experimental studies that have used pre-test and post-test comparisons with non-randomized allocation to a coaching or control group. Miller (1990) examined the impact of coaching on transfer of training skills, but the drawing of conclusions was restricted by a high rate of participant drop out: 91 participants began the study but only 33 completed the final measures. Gyllensten and Palmer (2005) found that, compared with a no-coaching control group, coaching was associated with lower levels of anxiety and stress. Evers *et al.* (2006) found that executive coaching enhanced participants' self-efficacy and their beliefs in their ability to set personal goals, but they did not measure actual goal attainment. Barrett (2007) used a quasi-experimental, modified post-test only control group design, finding that group coaching reduced burnout but did not improve productivity.

In an interesting use of workplace coaching to improve safety in the building industry, Kines *et al.* (2010) found that coaching construction site foremen to include safety in their daily verbal exchanges with workers had a significant positive and lasting effect on the level of safety. Kochanowski *et al.* (2010) compared a feedback only group with a feedback plus coaching group of managers on a leadership development program, finding that coaching significantly increased the use of collaboration with subordinates. Recent research also includes quasi-investigations into the differential effects of spaced versus massed training and coaching strategies, finding that spaced rather than massed training practice resulted in greater transfer quality, higher self-reports of sales competence and improved key performance criteria (Kauffeld and Lehmann-Willenbrock, 2010).

## Longitudinal Studies: Is Coaching Effective Over Time?

In order to truly assess the efficacy of coaching interventions we need to know if any reported effects maintain over time. However, thus far there have been very few longitudinal studies. The few that have been conducted indicate that coaching can indeed produce sustained change.

In a 12-month follow-up, Miller *et al.* (2004) found coaching with feedback was superior to training-only conditions in maintaining clinicians' interviewing skills. Green *et al.* (2006) found that gains from participation in a ten-week solution-focused cognitive-behavioral life coaching were maintained at a 30-week follow-up. Using an A-B-A-B design in a signal subject case study with an 18-month follow-up, Libri and Kemp (2006) found that cognitive-behavioral coaching enhanced sales performance and core self-evaluations.

## Gauging Efficacy Through Measuring Outcomes of Coaching

It would appear from this review that coaching outcome research, as a relatively new area of empirical study, is progressing through the "natural" stages of research development, from descriptive or qualitative case studies, through to quantitative within-subject studies, and on to quasi-experimental and randomized, controlled between-subject designs. Indeed, the 234 outcome studies published between 2000 and January 2011 provide a useful foundation for future research and are indicative of the emergence of an evidence base for coaching, and the amount of research is increasing over time.

However, a major potential problem for the development of a coherent body of knowledge about the effectiveness of coaching, and further establishment of an evidence-based framework for coaching, is the fact that there is little consistency in the use of outcome measures in coaching research. Indeed, the lack of consistency could prove to be a significant barrier to the development of an evidence base for coaching, and could even possibly lead to the decline of a coherent coaching literature as onlookers struggle to make sense of a potentially amorphous mass of data.

For example, in relation to executive coaching, the topics addressed within the coaching interventions vary widely and include interpersonal skills, stress management, strategic thinking, time management, dealing with conflict, leadership and management styles, delegation, staffing issues, as well as sales or financial performance (Bono *et al.*, 2009). Not surprisingly the ways such goals are measured also vary considerably. However, there is considerable variation between studies in the use of outcome measures, which makes it

*Coaching*

very difficult to draw meaningful comparisons between studies, and this is an important issue that researchers into coaching will need to address if a coherent body of knowledge about coaching efficacy is to be developed over time.

An overview of the outcome literature in executive and workplace coaching illustrates the diversity of variables used to measure the outcome of executive coaching. The following are some representative examples of outcome measure from the literature.

## Executive Coaching Efficacy Measures

Peterson (1993) provides a valuable example of how to develop coaching assessments to suit the idiosyncratic goals of individual coaching clients. Peterson used multiple customized rating inventories and rating scales based on each coachee's individual training objectives, and drew data from a number of raters to assess the effectiveness of an individualized coaching program for managers and executives. Steinbrenner and Schlosser (2011) and Orenstein (2006) have reported on the use of similar techniques.

Not surprisingly in executive coaching, customized surveys targeting the specific goals of the coaching intervention, and reports completed by the coachee, their managers, or peers form the largest single group of outcome measures in executive coaching outcome research. For example, Jones *et al.* (2006) developed a customized self-report inventory based on aspects of transactional and transformational leadership (Bass and Avolio, 1994), and self-reported measures of managerial flexibility. Although in this case such measures were theoretically grounded, no reliability or validity data (beyond face validity) was reported – a common shortcoming in much of this literature. Olivero *et al.* (1997) used behavioral, task-specific outcome measures (the timely completion of patient evaluation forms), to assess the relative impact of training and coaching, reporting that coaching and training combined was more effective than training alone. Gravel (2007) investigated the efficacy of executive coaching workshops with high school principals using customized surveys assessing time spent on administrative tasks and overall job satisfaction.

Given that most executives and senior managers participate in 360-degree assessments, and that such assessments are frequently used at the beginning of a coaching assignment in order to define the coaching goals (Coutu and Kauffman, 2009), it is surprising that more outcome studies do not use 360-degree assessments or validated leadership style assessments as outcome measures. Of those that did, Kampa-Kokesch and Anderson (2002) used the Multi-factor Leadership Questionnaire (MLQ; Bass and Avolio, 1990), a well-validated and widely-used leadership assessment tool (Lowe *et al.*, 1996), to assess changes in leadership style. However, only coachees' self-ratings were taken following the coaching program – probably due to the complexity of conducting follow-up research with non-participants (Grant *et al.*, 2010).

Thach (2002) used a customized 360-degree feedback tool which drew on previously validated items to assess the impact of executive coaching, collecting ratings from the coachees themselves, their mangers, and their direct reports, finding that coaching increases leadership effectiveness. Moving beyond merely assessing outcomes, Thach (2002) also conducted a number of additional analysis including exploring and reporting positive correlational relationships between the number of coaching sessions attended and increases in self-reported leadership effectiveness, giving possibly useful insights into some of the mechanisms underpinning effective coaching.

Also exploring both outcomes and the mechanisms underpinning effective coaching, Trathen (2008) used Choices Architect®, a research-based 360-tool designed to measure learning agility (Lominger, 2009), collecting data from both participates and their managers before and after coaching, finding a meaningful and significant association between changes in leadership competences and learning agility among those participating in executive coaching.

In a randomized controlled study of executive coaching in the health industry Grant *et al.* (2009) reported on the use of the Human Synergistics Life Styles Inventory (LSI; Lafferty, 1989) for 360-degree feedback, and on the use of the Depression, Anxiety and Stress Scale (DASS; Lovibond and Lovibond, 1995), and the Workplace Well-being Index (WWBI; Page, 2005) for assessment of the impact of coaching on individual participants' mental health. For an assessment of the impact of coaching on goal attainment Grant *et al.* (2009) used goal attainment scaling (see Spence, 2007), a process in which participants set personal goals and rate their goal progression before and after the coaching intervention. Coaching was associated with improved outcomes on all these measures.

More recently Cerni *et al.* (2010) used a pre-test, post-test control-group research design to assess the impact of a ten-week coaching intervention program based on cognitive-experiential self theory on transformational leadership among 14 secondary school principals using the MLQ (Bass and Avolio, 1990), finding a significant difference between the pre-test and post-test scores for the intervention group, as rated by their school staff, whereas the control group remained unchanged. Cerni *et al.* (2010) reported qualitative findings indicating that school principals in the intervention group became more reflective about their thinking processes and leadership practices.

However, although the aforementioned studies that have employed 360-degree feedback assessments show that such assessment is indeed a viable outcome measure in coaching, it is nevertheless true that one key barrier to the common use of 360-degree assessments, as an assessment of the efficacy of coaching interventions, is that the collection of such data pre- and post-coaching intervention is often an extremely time consuming and challenging process, involving coordinating time-poor employees and senior executives at multiple time points. Nevertheless, when reliable and well-validated 360-degree tools are used appropriately, such research can provide important standardized data about the efficacy of coaching that is important for the advancement of coaching. It is recommended that far more research be conducted long these lines.

## Workplace and Personal Coaching Measures

A similarly diverse pattern is evident in the outcome literature on workplace coaching with non-executive employees. It is also notable that a number of these studies have employed objective outcome measures, important indices in assessing the efficacy of coaching interventions. For example, Sergio (1987) reported on a workplace coaching intervention aimed at modifying six specific behaviors of 24 male forming-machine operators in a mid-sized fastener manufacturing organization with the outcome measures being actual observed behaviors, and most importantly, a reduction in actual wasted material.

Another interesting study that used actual observable behaviors as a measure of the efficacy of workplace coaching was Kines *et al.* (2010) who explored the use of coaching to improve safety behaviors on construction sites. Foremen were coached to increase the number of times that they included safety-related comments in their day-to-day dealings with construction site workers. The foremen set specific personal goals about the number of times they wished to refer to safety behaviors in their interactions with workers, and the foremen then received bi-weekly feedback and coaching on their actual performance. Compared to control groups the coaching condition increased safety on a number of observable measures, including the number of times workers reported having had a safety-related conversation with their foreman, observed safety performance, and the authors concluded that feedback-based coaching to construction site foremen regarding the content of their daily verbal exchanges resulted in significant increases in workers' safety performance and the physical safety level of the work site.

Also exploring the effect of coaching on objective measures of performance in university students, Franklin and Doran (2009) conducted a well-designed, double-blind, random, control trial in which participants were randomly allocated to either a preparation, action, adaptive learning (PAAL) coaching condition, or to a self-regulation co-coaching program with blind assessment of subsequent academic performance – an objective behavioral measure of the efficacy of the coaching intervention. A third no-treatment condition was used for additional comparison and control of expectancy effects. Participants in both coaching conditions reported significant improvements in self-efficacy and resilience, but only those in the PAAL condition experienced significant increases in decisional balance, hope, self-compassion, and belief in the incremental theory of change. Moreover, participants in the PAAL condition experienced significantly greater increases in six of the seven dependent variables than participants in the self-regulation condition. Relative to the no treatment control group, PAAL participants performed 10 percent better in independently assessed academic performance, whereas those in the self-regulation coaching condition only performed 2 percent better.

Other workplace coaching studies have used self-reported measures of workplace performance and mental health to good effect. Duijts *et al.* (2008) conducted a randomized controlled study into the impact of coaching on employees' sickness absence due to psychosocial health complaints and on the general well-being of employees using self-reported measures including the Short Form Health Survey (Ware and Sherbourne, 1992), the General Health Questionnaire (Koeter and Ormel, 1991), the Dutch Questionnaire on Perception and Judgment of Work (Veldhoven and Meijmen, 1994), and the Dutch version of the Maslach Burnout Inventory (Schaufeli and Dierendonck, 2000), which are all well-validated measures.

In a quasi-experimental study examining the impact of workplace coaching on mental health with finance industry employees, Gyllensten and Palmer (2005) used the DASS (Lovibond and Lovibond, 1995) as an outcome measure and found that levels of anxiety and stress had decreased more in the coaching group compared to the control group, and were lower in the coaching group compared to the control group at the end of the study.

Evers *et al.* (2006) report on an executive coaching intervention with managers of the US federal government using self-report measures of self-efficacy beliefs and outcome expectancies that were linked to three central domains of functioning: setting one's own goals, acting in a balanced way, and mindful living and working.

Comparing the relative impact of a feedback workshop with attendance at the workshop followed by coaching sessions, Kochanowski *et al.* (2010) found that coaching significantly increased manager's use of collaboration with subordinates, which was assessed using the Influence Behaviour Questionnaire (IBQ; Yukl *et al.*, 2008) which measures 11 proactive influence tactics.

In relation to coaching in non-workplace settings, the outcome measures used to assess the efficacy of coaching interventions have been similarly varied and have included personality inventories (Norlander, 2002), students' well-being (Short *et al.*, 2010), improvement of techniques in Aikido (Negi and Shimamline, 2010), goal self-concordance (Burke and Linley, 2007), and body mass index (Zandvoort *et al.*, 2009), as well as measures of mental health (Spence and Grant, 2007), well-being (Green *et al.*, 2007), and self-refection and insight (e.g., Grant, 2008).

The observed extensive variations in outcome measures is to be expected given that coaching is a highly individualized human change methodology and is used in a wide range of contexts. Coaching outcome measures are purposefully aligned with individual client's goals; thus, it is inevitable that outcome measures will vary considerably between studies. However, as previously mentioned, the idiosyncratic use of measures means that it is difficult for a coherent body of knowledge to develop over time. For such a body of knowledge to develop we need to augment the idiosyncratic measures necessary to assess the efficacy of specific coaching engagement with common standardized, validated, and psychometrically reliable measures (Passmore, 2008).

## Using Validated Measures to Assess Efficacy: Mental Health and Goal Attainment

It is surprising that few studies have used commonly-available, well-validated measures of mental health and well-being given that coaching is frequently promoted as being effective as a means of enhancing both goal attainment and well-being (e.g., Levine *et al.*, 2006; Passmore and Gibbes, 2007). This is despite the fact that there are many such measures designed for use in non-clinical populations. Such measures include the Depression, Anxiety and Stress Scale (Lovibond and Lovibond, 1995), the Psychological Well-being Scale (Ryff and Keyes, 1996), the Satisfaction With Life Scale (Diener *et al.*, 1985), and the Cognitive Hardiness Scale (Nowack, 1990).

Coaching is a goal-orientated change methodology. Thus, goal attainment is an important outcome measure in coaching. However, few outcome studies have used goal attainment scaling as a measure of coaching efficacy. Goal Attainment Scaling (GAS) techniques offer a useful methodology for measuring goal progression towards predetermined objective success benchmarks. For a comprehensive discussion of the use of GAS in coaching see Spence (2007). The broader use of GAS could provide a means of making comparisons between studies and its use in coaching efficacy research would significantly help to further build a coherent body of knowledge about the efficacy of coaching. GAS would also help address the serious limitations of the few studies that have examined return on investment (ROI) in coaching using subjective post-coaching ratings of success (e.g., McGovern *et al.*, 2001).

## Is Return on Investment a Reliable Measure of Coaching Efficacy?

Return on investment is often presented as being the most important indicator of coaching efficacy in organizational coaching contexts. Return on investment data is calculated using metrics such as growth in sales, market share, or organizational profitability, and is frequently used by coaching and consulting organizations as a marketing tool in order to promote and sell their coaching and consulting services. Return on investment figures of 788 percent (Kampa-Kokesch and Anderson, 2001) and 545 percent (McGovern *et al.*, 2001) are commonly reported as being *the* ROI for executive coaching and are frequently touted as being a key rationale of the use of coaching in organizational settings (Grant *et al.*, 2010).

But is ROI a reliable measure of coaching efficacy? On the surface the idea that spending money on coaching services will make the organization more money in return, seems like a persuasive argument for the use of ROI as both a measure of coaching efficacy and as a means of promoting coaching as a viable and reliable change methodology. However, I believe that there are some significant problems in using ROI as a measure of coaching efficacy.

To understand these problems we need to examine how ROI is typically calculated. In essence, ROI is calculated by subtracting the value of the outcomes of coaching from the costs of coaching and then expressing this as a percentage (((coaching benefits – costs of coaching)/costs of coaching)) x 100 percent). There are a number of different variations on this formula, for example, including factoring into the calculation a rating of the coachee's level of confidence that all or some of the perceived benefits are in fact due to coaching, or deliberately underestimating the financial return (Grant *et al.*, 2010).

However, whilst ROI can provide some indications about the impact of a specific coaching intervention in a specific context, I argue that ROI has serious limitations as a benchmark outcome measure for coaching effectiveness. The use of ROI may well give purchasers of coaching services and those who seek to market their coaching and consultancy services a sense of comfort and some reassurance that their coaching is effective and valuable, but does ROI really measure the true impact of coaching? Most definitely not.

It is important to note that the ROI metric depends on two key things: (1) the costs of the coaching intervention, including the amount that the coaches charge and associated costs of implantation, and (2) the financial benefit obtained by the organization. These are highly idiosyncratic factors. Thus at best ROI can only be indicative of a single specific coaching engagement, and is a somewhat spurious measure of coaching outcome.

## Do We Yet Have an Evidence Base for the Efficacy of Coaching?

It is clear from this review of the literature on the efficacy of coaching that the amount and quality of coaching outcome research is increasing and, importantly, applications are becoming more diverse over time. The quality and sophistication of the research is increasing, but it is also clear that there are no standardized or even particularly commonly used measures of coaching efficacy. The indicators of efficacy reviewed here include leadership style, reductions in wastage in manufacturing settings, psychological well-being, employees' absence due to sickness, personal resilience, workplace well-being, sales performance, safety behaviors on construction sites, ROI, and goal attainment, to name just a few. It is indeed heartening to see coaching methodologies being used so broadly. But the wide success of coaching also brings its own problems. The questions remain: Do we yet have an evidence-base for the efficacy of coaching? Can we now say that coaching is an effective human change methodology?

I suggest that the above review indicates that we do indeed have an emergent evidence base for the efficacy of coaching, and that we can certainly say that coaching can be a very effective human change methodology.

But we must also recognize that the evidence base at present is somewhat unsophistic-ated in comparison to areas such as medicine and health – domains typically taken to rep-resent aspirational benchmarks as other disciplines move towards their own evidence base (for discussion on this point in relation to the debate on an evidence base for industrial and organizational psychology see Potworowski and Green, 2011). Indeed, alternative per-spectives could suggest that we do not have sufficient well-conducted between-subject studies to constitute a true evidence base for coaching and, furthermore, the notion of evidence-based coaching is highly unrealistic because coaching does not have and is unlikely to ever develop a sophisticated knowledge base such as that found in the domains of medicine and health. In short, they might argue, the notion of an evidence-base for coaching is simply not achievable.

However, such an argument is based on the assumption that a discipline of professional coaching should aspire to development along the lines of evidence-based practice (EBP) as delineated by the medical model. I am not at all convinced that this should be the case. Where much of the medical, health, and clinical psychological literature appears to hold tightly to the medical model of EBP, prizing randomized controlled trials above other forms of empirical enquiry, there has been considerable debate about the applicability of evidence based approaches to "real world" organizational contexts in the industrial and organizational (I/O) psychology literature (e.g., Briner and Rousseau, 2011) – contexts highly familiar to much coaching research and practice. It is important to note that an evidence base *per se* does not purport to prove that any specific intervention is guaranteed to be effective, nor does it require that a double-blind, randomized, controlled trial is held as being inevitably and objectively better than a qualitative case study approach.

## Inclusivity in Establishing Efficacy

An evidence-base for coaching should recognize that, as in the case of I/O psychology, real-world research is not easy. In the real world, allocation to intervention or control is not always possible, and moreover, as this chapter's earlier discussion of the Freedman and Perry (2010) case study clearly shows, well-conducted qualitative research into coaching can provide important insights that are simply not possible with quantitative approaches – and a true evidence base for any discipline should recognize and respond to diversity of practice by providing reliable information for a wide range of applications, contexts, and methodologies. This view of evidence-based approaches is deliberately broad, and this broad perspective represents current thinking in this area (Cronin and Klimoski, 2011) – and I posit that it is this view that should inform the development of an evidence base for coaching.

Within this view many forms of enquiry are welcome and valued. The key criteria for evaluation and tests of efficacy should thus be the rigor and coherence of the enquiry, the insights it generates, and its contribution to the broader knowledge research and practice of coaching, rather than whether it is a qualitative, single case study or a large-scale randomized controlled study. Each has its place and each can contribute to the continued development of our understanding of the efficacy of this exciting human change methodology that we call coaching.

# Conclusion

There can be little doubt that the academic and research base for coaching has grown substantially, and all signs indicate that this growth will continue into the near to mid future at the very least. Coaching has definitely moved from fad to fixture in organizational contexts, and in the areas of personal and developmental coaching, too. Applications of coaching are highly diverse and measures of coaching efficacy are similarly varied. The lack of consistency associated with such diversity could prove to be a significant obstacle in the development of an evidence base for coaching as onlookers struggle to make sense of a potentially amorphous mass of data.

In order to move the evidence base for coaching further forward we need to increase the use of standardized outcome measures and this will give greater consistency to the research literature. This is not to decry the use of idiosyncratic measures that reflect the individualistic goals that often lie at the heart of the coaching endeavor. Rather, it is a call to augment those so that a common language of coaching efficacy can develop. Goal attainment scaling may be one measure of efficacy that can provide the syntax necessary to enable this language, and could well provide the framework to facilitate communication across the broad range of contexts in which contemporary coaching is practiced and researched. In this way we have the opportunity to demonstrate that the diversity of coaching is indeed its key strength.

# References

Agarwal, R., Angst, C.M., and Magni, M. (2009) The performance effects of coaching: A multilevel analysis using hierarchical linear modeling. *International Journal of Human Resource Management*, 20(10), 2110–34.

Anderson, M.C., Anderson, D.L., and Mayo, W.D. (2008) Team coaching helps a leadership team drive cultural change at Caterpillar. *Global Business and Organizational Excellence*, 27(4), 40–50.

Bacigalupo, A., Hess, J., and Fernandes, J. (2009) Meeting the challenges of culture and agency change in an academic health center. *Leadership and Organization Development Journal*, 30(5), 408–20.

Barrett, P.T. (2007) The effects of group coaching on executive health and team effectiveness: A quasi-experimental field study. *Dissertation Abstracts International Section A*, 67, 26–40.

Bass, B.M. and Avolio, B.J. (1990) *Transformational Leadership Development: Manual for the Multifactor Leadership Questionnaire*. Palo Alto, CA: Consulting Psychologists Press.

Bass, B.M. and Avolio, B.J. (1994) *Improving Organisational Effectiveness through Transformational Leadership*. London: Sage.

Beck, A.T. and Steer, R.A. (1993) *Beck Anxiety Inventory Manual*. San Antonio: The Psychological Corporation.

Beck, A.T. Steer, R.A., and Brown, B.S. (1996) *Beck Depression Inventory Manual* (2nd edn). San Antonio: The Psychological Corporation.

Bennett, J.A. and Perrin, N.A. (2005) Healthy aging demonstration project: Nurse coaching for behavior change in older adults. *Research in Nursing and Health*, 28(3) June.

Bono, J.E., Purvanova, R.K., Towler, A.J., and Peterson, D.B. (2009) A survey of executive coaching practices. *Personnel Psychology*, 62(2), 361–404.

Bowles, S., Cunningham, C.J., De La Rosa, G.M., and Picano, J. (2007) Coaching leaders in middle and executive management: Goals, performance, buy-in. *Leadership and Organization Development Journal*, 28, 388–408.

Briner, R.B. and Rousseau, D.M. (2011) Evidence-based I–O psychology: Not there yet. *Industrial and Organizational Psychology*, 4(1), 3–22.

Burke, D. and Linley, P. (2007) Enhancing goal self-concordance through coaching. *International Coaching Psychology Review*, 2(1), 62–9.

Carver, C.S. and Scheier, M.F. (1998) *On the Self-regulation of Behavior*. Cambridge, UK: Cambridge University Press.

Cavanagh, M. and Grant, A.M. (2006) Coaching psychology and the scientist-practioner model. In: S. Corrie and D. Lane (eds) *The Modern Scientist Practitioner*. New York: Routledge. pp. 146–57.

Cerni, T., Curtis, G.J., and Colmar, S.H. (2010) Executive coaching can enhance transformational leadership. *International Coaching Psychology Review*, 5(1), 81–5.

Clegg, S., Rhodes, C., Kornberger, M., and Stilin, R. (2005) Business coaching: Challenges for an emerging industry. *Industrial and Commercial Training*, 37(5), 218–23.

Conway, R.L. (2000) The impact of coaching mid-level managers utilizing multi-rater feedback. *Dissertation Abstracts International*, 60(7-A), 2672.

Cooperrider, D.L., Sorensen, P.F., Whitney, D., and Yaeger, T.F. (2000) *Appreciative Inquiry: Rethinking Human Organization Toward a Positive Theory of Change*. Champaign, IL: Stipes Publishing.

Corbett, K. (2006) *The Sherpa Report (2006)*. Ohio: Sasha Corp.

Coutu, D. and Kauffman, C. (2009) *The Realities of Executive Coaching*. Cambridge, MA: Harvard Business Review Research Report.

Cronin, M.A. and Klimoski, R. (2011) Broadening the view of what constitutes "evidence". *Industrial and Organizational Psychology*, 4(1), 57–61.

Cunha, P.V. and Louro, M.J. (2000) Building teams that learn. *Academy of Management Executive*, 14(1), 152.

Deviney, D.E. (1994) The effects of coaching using mulitple rater feedback to change supervisor behavior. *Dissertation Abstracts International Section A*, 55, 114.

Diener, E., Emmons, R.A., Larsen, R.J., and Griffin, S. (1985) The satisfaction with life scale. *Journal of Personality Assessment*, 49(1), 71–5.

Douglas, C.A. and McCauley, C.D. (1999) Formal developmental relationships: A survey of organizational practices. *Human Development Quarterly*, 10(3), 203–20.

Duffy, E.M. (1984) A feedback-coaching intervention and selected predictors in outplacement. *Dissertation Abstracts International Section B*, 45(1611).

Duijts, S.F.A.P., Kant, I.P., van den Brandt, P.A.P., and Swaen, G.M.H.P. (2008) Effectiveness of a preventive coaching intervention for employees at risk for sickness absence due to psychosocial health complaints: Results of a randomized controlled trial. *Journal of Occupational and Environmental Medicine*, 50(7), 765–76.

Evers, W.J., Brouwers, A., and Tomic, W. (2006) A quasi-experimental study on management coaching effectiveness. *Consulting Psychology Journal: Practice and Research*, 58(3), 174–82.

Farndale, E., Scullion, H., and Sparrow, P. (2010) The role of the corporate HR function in global talent management. *Journal of World Business*, 45(2), 161–8.

Fielden, S.L., Davidson, M.J., and Sutherland, V.J. (2009) Innovations in coaching and mentoring: Implications for nurse leadership development. *Health Services Management Research*, 22(2), 92–9.

Frank Bresser Consulting (2009) The state of coaching across the globe: The results of the Global Coaching Survey 2008/2009 retreived March 29, 2011 from http://www.frank-bresser-consulting.com/globalcoachingsurvey.html.

Franklin, J. and Doran, J. (2009) Does all coaching enhance objective performance independently evaluated by blind assessors? The importance of the coaching model and content. *International Coaching Psychology Review*, 4(2), 128–44.

Freedman, A.M. and Perry, J.A. (2010) Executive consulting under pressure: A case study. *Consulting Psychology Journal: Practice and Research*, 62(3), 189–202.

Gattellari, M., Donnelly, N., Taylor, N., Meerkin, M., Hirst, G., and Ward, J. (2005) Does peer coaching increase GP capacity to promote informed decision making about FSA screening? A cluster randomised trial. *Family Practice*, 22, 253–65.

Gershman, L. (1967) The effects of specific factors of the supervisor-subordinate coaching climate upon improvement of attitude and performance of the subordinate. *Dissertation Abstracts International Section B*, 28, 2122.

Gorby, C.B. (1937) Everyone gets a share of the profits. *Factory Management and Maintenance*, 95, 82–3.

Grant, A.M. (2002) Towards a psychology of coaching: The impact of coaching on metacognition, mental health and goal attainment. *Dissertation Abstracts International Section A: Humanities and Social Sciences*, 63/12, (June), 6094.

Grant, A.M. (2003) The impact of life coaching on goal attainment, metacognition and mental health. *Social Behavior and Personality*, 31(3), 253–64.

Grant, A.M. (2008) Personal life coaching for coaches-in-training enhances goal attainment, insight and learning. *Coaching: An International Journal of Theory, Research and Practice*, 1(1), 54–70.

Grant, A.M. (2010) It takes time: A stages of change perspective on the adoption of workplace coaching skills. *Journal of Change Management*, 10(1), 61–77.

Grant, A.M. (2011) Workplace, executive and life coaching: An annotated bibliography from the behavioural science and business literature (January 1). Unpublished paper: Coaching Psychology Unit, University of Sydney, Australia.

Grant, A.M. and O'Hara, B. (2006) The self-presentation of commercial Australian life coaching schools: Cause for concern? *International Coaching Psychology Review*, 1(2), 20–32.

Grant, A.M., Curtayne, L., and Burton, G. (2009) Executive coaching enhances goal attainment, resilience and workplace well-being: A randomised controlled study. *Journal of Positive Psychology*, 4(5), 396–407.

Grant, A.M., Passmore, J., Cavanagh, M.J., and Parker, H. (2010) The state of play in coaching today: A comprehensive review of the field. *International Review of Industrial and Organisational Psychology*, 25, 125–68.

Gravel, T. M. (2007) Principal time commitment and job satisfaction before and after an executive coaching workshop. *Dissertation Abstracts International Section A: Humanities and Social Sciences*, 68(4-A), 1247.

Green, L., Oades, L., and Grant, A. (2006) Cognitive-behavioral, solution-focused life coaching: Enhancing goal striving, well-being, and hope. *The Journal of Positive Psychology*, 1(3), 142–9.

Green, L.S., Grant, A.M., and Rynsaardt, J. (2007) Evidence-based life coaching for senior high school students: Building hardiness and hope. *International Coaching Psychology Review*, 2(1), 24–32.

Gyllensten, K. and Palmer, S. (2005) Can coaching reduce workplace stress: A quasi-experimental study. *International Journal of Evidence Based Coaching and Mentoring*, 3(2), 75–85.

Hernez-Broome, G. and Boyce, L.A. (eds) (2011) *Advancing Executive Coaching*. San Francisco CA: Josey-Bass.

International Coach Federation (2006) *Global Coaching Study*. International Coach Federation, TX: International Coach Federation.

Jarvis, J., Lane, D., and Fillery-Travis, A. (2005) *Making the Case for Coaching: Does it Work*. London: Chartered Institute of Personnel and Development.

Jones, R.A., Rafferty, A.E., and Griffin, M.A. (2006) The executive coaching trend: Towards more flexible executives. *Leadership and Organization Development Journal*, 27, 584–96.

Judge, T.A., Erez, A., Bono, J.E., and Thoresen, C.J. (2003) The core self-evaluation scale: Development of a measure. *Personnel Psychology*, 56, 303–31.

Kampa-Kokesch, S. (2002) Executive coaching as an individually tailored consultation intervention: Does it increase leadership? *Dissertation Abstracts International: Section B: the Sciences and Engineering*, 62(7-B), 3408.

Kampa-Kokesch, S. and Anderson, M.Z. (2001) Executive coaching: A comprehensive review of the literature. *Consulting Psychology Journal: Practice and Research*, 53(4), 205–28.

Kauffeld, S. and Lehmann-Willenbrock, N. (2010) Sales training: Effects of spaced practice on training transfer. *Journal of European Industrial Training*, 34(1), 23–37.

Kines, P., Andersen, L.P., Spangenberg, S., Mikkelsen, K.L., Dyreborg, J., and Zohar, D. (2010) Improving construction site safety through leader-based verbal safety communication. *Journal of Safety Research*, 41(5), 399–406.

Kochanowski, S., Seifert, C.F., and Yukl, G. (2010) Using coaching to enhance the effects of behavioral feedback to managers. *Journal of Leadership and Organizational Studies*, 17(4), 363–9.

Koeter, M.W.J. and Ormel, J. (1991) *General Health Questionnaire Manual, Dutch Version*. Lisse: Swete and Zeitlinger.

Kubicek, M. (2002) Is coaching being abused? *Training*, 12–14.

Lafferty, J.C. (1989) *Life Style Inventory LSI 1: Self-development Guide*. Plymouth, MI: Human Synergistics.

Leadership Management Australia (2006) *The LEAD Survey 2005/6*. Melbourne: Leadership Management Australia.

Leadership Management Australia (2009) *Learnings for the New World of 2009*. Melbourne: Leadership Management Australia.

Levine, T., Kase, L., and Vitale, J. (2006) *The Successful Coach: Insider Secrets to Becoming a Top Coach*. New York: John Wiley and Sons Ltd.

Libri, V. and Kemp, T. (2006) Assessing the efficacy of a cognitive behavioural executive coaching programme. *International Coaching Psychology Review*, 1(2), 9–18.

Lominger (2009) *Choices Architect®*. Minneapolis, MN: Lominger International.

Lovibond, S.H. and Lovibond, P.F. (1995) *Manual for the Depression Anxiety Stress Scales*. Sydney: Psychology Foundation of Australia.

Lowe, K.B., Kroeck, K.G., and Sivasubramaniam, N. (1996) Effectiveness correlates of transformation and transactional leadership: A meta-analytic review of the MLQ literature. *Leadership Quarterly*, 7(3), 385–425.

McGovern, J., Lindermann, M., Vergara, M.A., Murphy, S., Barker, L., and Warrenfelz, R. (2001) Maximizing the impact of executive coaching: Behavioral change, organizational outcomes and return on investment. *The Manchester Review*, 6(1), 1–9.

Maurer, T., Solamon, J., and Troxtel, D. (1998) Relationship of coaching performance with performance in situational employment interviews. *Journal of Applied Psychology*, 83(1), 128–36.

Miller, D.J. (1990) The effect of managerial coaching on transfer of training. *Dissertation Abstracts International Section B*, 50(2435).

Miller, W.R., Yahne, C.E., Moyers, T.B., Martinez, J., and Pirritano, M. (2004) A randomized trial of methods to help clinicians learn motivational interviewing. *Journal of Consulting and Clinical Psychology*, 72(6), 1050–62.

Mulec, K. and Roth, J. (2005) Action, reflection, and learning and coaching in order to enhance the performance of drug development project management teams. *R&D Management*, 35, 483–91.

Negi, S. and Shimamline, S. (2010) Behavioral coaching and skill improvement in Aikido. *The Japanese Journal of Behavior Analysis*, 24(1), 59–65.

Norlander, T., Bergman, H., and Archers, T. (2002) Relative constancy of personality characteristics and efficacy of a 12-month training program in facilitating coping strategies. *Social Behavior and Personality*, 30(8), 773–83.

Nowack, K.M. (1990) Initial development of an inventory to assess stress and health. *American Journal of Health Promotion*, 4, 173–180.

Olivero, G., Bane, K., and Kopelman, R.E. (1997) Executive coaching as a transfer of training tool: Effects on productivity in a public agency. *Public Personnel Management*, 26(4), 461–9.

Orenstein, R.L. (2006) Measuring executive coaching efficacy? The answer was right here all the time. *Consulting Psychology Journal: Practice and Research*, 58, 106–16.

Page, K. (2005) Subjective wellbeing in the workplace. Unpublished thesis, Deakin University, Melbourne, Australia.

Passmore, J. (2007) Addressing deficit performance through coaching – using motivational interviewing for performance improvement at work. *International Coaching Psychology Review*, 2(3), 265–75.

Passmore, J. (ed.) (2008) *Psychometrics in Coaching*. London: Kogan Page.

Passmore, J. and Gibbes, C. (2007) The state of executive coaching research: What does the current literature tell us and what's next for coaching research? *International Coaching Psychological Review*, 2(2), 116–28.

Passmore, J. and Mortimer, L. (2011) The experience of using coaching as a learning technique in learner driver development: An IPA study of adult learning. *International Coaching Psychology Review*, 6(1), 33–45.

Peterson, D.B. (1993) *Skill learning and behavior change in an individually tailored management coaching program.* Unpublished doctoral dissertation. University of Minnesota, Minneapolis, MN.

Peterson, D.B. (2007) Executive coaching in a cross-cultural context. *Consulting Psychology Journal: Practice and Research*, 59(4), 261–71.

Peterson, D.B. and Millier, J. (2005) The alchemy of coaching: "You're good, Jennifer, but you could be really good." *Consulting Psychology Journal: Practice and Research*, 57(1), 14–40.

Potworowski, G. and Green, L.A. (2011) Assessing the uptake of evidence-based management: A systems approach. *Industrial and Organizational Psychology*, 4(1), 54–6.

Ryff, C.D. and Keyes, C.L.M. (1996) The structure of psychological wellbeing revisited. *Journal of Personality and Social Psychology*, 96, 719–27.

Scandura, T. (1992) Mentoring and career mobility: An empirical investigation. *Journal of Organizational Behavior*, 13(2), 169–74.

Schaufeli, W.B. and Dierendonck, D. (2000) *UBOS, Utrechtse Bournout Schaal, Handeiding*. Lisse: Swets Test Publishers.

Sergio, J.P. (1987) Behavioral coaching as an intervention to reduce production costs through a decrease in output defects. *Dissertation Abstracts International*, 47(8-B), 3566–7.

Short, E., Kinman, G., and Baker, S. (2010) Evaluating the impact of a peer coaching intervention on well-being amongst psychology undergraduate students. *International Coaching Psychology Review*, 5(1), 27–35.

Solansky, S.T. (2010) The evaluation of two key leadership development program components: Leadership skills assessment and leadership mentoring. *Leadership Quarterly*, 21(4), 675–81.

Spence, G.B. (2007) GAS powered coaching: Goal Attainment Scaling and its use in coaching research and practice. *International Coaching Psychology Review*, 2(2), 155–67.

Spence, G.B. and Grant, A. (2007) Professional and peer life coaching and the enhancement of goal striving and well-being: An exploratory study. *The Journal of Positive Psychology*, 2, 185–94.

Spence, G.B., Cavanagh, M.J., and Grant, A.M. (2008) The integration of mindfulness training and health coaching: an exploratory study. *Coaching: An International Journal of Theory, Research and Practice*, 1(2), 145–63.

Steinbrenner, D. and Schlosser, B. (2011) The coaching impact study (TM). In: G. Hernez-Broome and L.A. Boyce (eds) *Advancing Executive Coaching*. San Francisco CA: Jossey-Bass. pp. 369–400.

Sue-Chan, C. and Latham, G.P. (2004) The relative effectiveness of expert, peer and self coaches. *Applied Psychology*, 53(2), 260–78.

Taylor, L.M. (1997) The relation between resilience, coaching, coping skills training, and perceived stress during a career-threatening milestone. *Dissertation Abstracts International*, 58(5), 2738.

Thach, L.C. (2002) The impact of executive coaching and 360 feedback on leadership effectiveness. *Leadership and Organization Development Journal*, 23(4), 205–14.

Trathen, S.A. (2008) Executive coaching, changes in leadership competencies and learning agility amongst Microsoft senior executives. *Dissertation Abstracts International: Section B: The Sciences and Engineering*, 69(1-B), 2008, 727.

Veldhoven, M. and Meijmen, T. (1994) *Questionnaire on Perception and Judgment of Work*. Amsterdam: NIA.

Vloeberghs, D., Pepermans, R., and Thielemans, K. (2005) High-potential development policies: An empirical study among Belgian companies. *Journal of Management Development*, 24(6), 546–58.

Ware, J.E. and Sherbourne, C.D. (1992) The MOS 36-item short-form health survey (SF-36): Concpetual framework and item selection. *Med Care*, 30, 473–83.

Wilson, C. (2004) Coaching and coach training in the workplace. *Industrial and Commercial Training*, 36(3), 96–8.

Wright, J. (2007) Stress in the workplace: A coaching approach. *Work: Journal of Prevention, Assessment and Rehabilitation*, 28, 279–84.

Yukl, G., Seifert, C.F. and Chavez, C. (2008) Validation of the extended Influence Behavior Questionnaire. *Leadership Quarterly*, 19, 609–21.

Zandvoort, M. v., Irwin, J. D., and Morrow, D. (2009) The impact of co-active life coaching on female university students with obesity. *International Journal of Evidence Based Coaching and Mentoring*, 7(1), 104–8.

# 3

# The Role of Contracting in Coaching: Balancing Individual Client and Organizational Issues

## Robert J. Lee

## Introduction

This chapter reviews the ideas of coaching writers to provide insight into methods for establishing productive expectations among the multiple parties involved in an executive coaching engagement. Contracting includes the agreements and commitments made among the principals during an executive coaching engagement. As used in this chapter, contracting refers broadly to official and casual documents as well as to verbal statements describing intended outcomes, the business arrangements, or the methods the coach will be using. The principal agents in the contract are the client, the coach, and the sponsor's representatives.

Contracting is most visible at the outset of an engagement, although important agreements and commitments are formed or changed along the way as well. Contracting is a universally acknowledged step early in coaching; good contracting is viewed as important or even central to coaching success.

Yet only a few texts on coaching have a chapter or a section on the topic of contracting. Sadly, the indexes of many coaching texts do not even mention the word. Further, there is almost no research specifically on contracting in coaching. Given the importance of the topic and the scarcity of the research, it thus seems appropriate to cast a very wide net, including a survey of the larger field, and provide typologies and distinctions useful for discussing this topic.

This chapter looks at contracting from multiple perspectives:

1 Pre-contracting, the decisions that precede the formal contracting efforts.
2 Change contracts, describing the ways the client hopes to develop as an executive with the support of the coach and sponsoring organization.
3 Process contracts, which contain the methods and responsibilities of the coach, the client, and others that combine to make coaching happen.

*The Wiley Blackwell Handbook of the Psychology of Coaching and Mentoring*, First Edition.
Edited by Jonathan Passmore, David B. Peterson, and Teresa Freire.
© 2013 John Wiley & Sons, Ltd. Published 2016 by John Wiley & Sons, Ltd.

4   Business contracts specifying the commercial and legal arrangements between the coach and the sponsor.
5   Psychological contracts, the tacit but potentially powerful expectations among the parties.

# Underlying Issues

Contracting in executive coaching rests on a foundation of assumptions that give purpose and shape to the contracts. These include: a defining characteristic of executive coaching (formality), a core tension between individual client's and the organizational sponsor's interests (balance), and two important assumptions (clarity and trust).

## Formality

Formality in executive coaching is important because it sets this professional service apart from the myriad of casual conversations people have with each other in the organizational and social worlds, as well as from other forms of assistance with which clients may be more familiar. Executive coaching cannot occur through well-intended lunchtime conversations, nor is it mentoring, supervisory in-the-moment coaching, consulting, personal counseling or other kinds of helping. Clients should be educated about what executive coaching will look like as practiced by a particular coach in a particular setting. An important mechanism for creating this formality, and for providing this education, is the process of contracting.

Kilburg (2007) strongly underlines the point about formality: "First, executive coaching is a formal consulting relationship between an individual executive client and a professional coach." Stern's (2004) description also emphasizes the formal character of coaching: "A professional executive coach formally contracts with an executive and his or her organization to work in a collaborative partnership with the executive and others in the organization to achieve identified business results and the executive's learning objectives. Such a formal contract needs to incorporate agreed-upon ground rules, time frames, goals, and specific measures of success."

The definitions just quoted both refer to a "professional" coach, someone who provides this service on a regular basis to internal or external clients.

## Balance

Executive coaching necessarily involves at least three parties (coach, client, sponsor) and may involve several additional sponsors and a variety of stakeholders. The interests and perspectives of these parties are likely to partially but not entirely overlap. It is the coach's responsibility to be aware of all these viewpoints, to work toward reasonable alignment of them, or to identify important differences. This can be a continuous balancing act.

The term "client" can be used to refer to any one or several of the persons involved in the coaching arrangement, or even to the larger organization. Kramer *et al.* (1994) surveyed 576 consultants regarding: "Who is the client?" and found that consultants have difficulty agreeing on this matter. An important symbolic step is taken when the coach designates one or two of these parties as "the client".

In many coaching engagements the client's manager and the HR director are central figures. If the individual is the client, then it is useful to refer to these people as "sponsors" since they made it possible for it to happen. Other individuals, such as the client's direct reports and peers, can be described as "stakeholders".

A strong argument can be made for using the word "client" to mean the individual person receiving the coaching. This choice has the advantage of clarifying where the coach's primary responsibility lies, and how the coach needs to resolve questions of ethics and confidentiality. This is the view of APECS in their ethical guidelines (2007), and of the Executive Coaching Forum (2008). This usage is followed in this chapter.

There are those who take an alternate position. Stern (2009) and Dotlich and Cairo (1999) see the organization as the primary client. Stern's perspective is outlined very succinctly: "There are multiple clients in most executive coaching projects. The first and primary client is usually the organization ... The second client is the individuals or groups being coached. The third is the individuals' or groups' managers/boards and their human resources professionals."

This is not just a semantic distinction. Dotlich and Cairo place first priority on the organization's goals. If there is a gap between the client's objectives and those of the sponsor, they see it as the coach's role to motivate the client to move in the direction of the organization's interests.

Desrosiers and Oliver (2011) and Stomski *et al.* (2011) offer descriptions of how programmatic coaching works in two different large organizations. The need for aligning the individual efforts with organizational goals is an explicit, on-going discussion. The concern isn't that coaching won't be valued, or will be valuable only to the client, although these could be valid concerns in some situations. The concern expressed by these authors is that the coaching of many individuals has to aggregate in a way that helps the organization achieve much larger objectives such as shifting its operating culture.

## Clarity

Contracting is a way of putting executive coaching into operational form so that ambiguity is replaced with predictability. All the writers on coaching seem to make the assumption that by formally specifying the roles, rules, and expectations there will be increased clarity, a greater sense of partnership and trust, and therefore greater likelihood of a successful outcome.

The challenge of reducing uncertainty and creating clarity has attracted the attention of many writers. Bluckert (2006) states: "The purpose of contracting is twofold: firstly, to facilitate more productive outcomes and, secondly, to reduce the likelihood of misunderstandings and failed expectations in the future. You do this by establishing both the personal and organizational objectives for the coaching and by clarifying everyone's roles and responsibilities in the process." Kilburg (2001) offers a list of features of a good contract, the first two items being clarity of agreement and goal clarity.

Lusch and Brown (1996), referring to contracts in the business world, note that "contracts are mechanisms that are used in exchange relationships to reduce risk and uncertainty." How well contracts do that can depend on many things, of course. These authors point out that people cannot predict all future outcomes, so there is a "tacit assumption" involved in all contracts that other cues – such as those coming from their relationships with each other – may guide behavior outside the contractual terms. However imperfect, good initial contracts are assumed to be essential to building solid relationships by reducing feelings that the other party may be unfair or opportunistic.

Bacon and Spear (2003) emphasize the multi-party nature of the clarification process: "Negotiating expectations means bringing the coach's expectations and the client's into alignment within the organizational context in which the coaching is occurring." They emphasize that contracting is largely meant to achieve unity of process and purpose, rather than be just a binding legal document.

> The word "contracting" makes this part of the process seem very formal, but it doesn't need to be. Contracting can be as simple as saying, "What kind of help would you like?" The purpose is to reach a mutual understanding of what will most benefit the client and to ensure that you understand the client's needs and expectations from the coaching process. If you clarify the client's expectations about the kind of coaching you are going to provide, then you can be reasonably certain that you are being most helpful to him or her. If you aren't explicit about the agreement, then you run the very real risk of doing the wrong kind of coaching, which will frustrate both of you. (pp. 22–3)

The Executive Coaching Forum (2008) prepared an *Executive Coaching Handbook* that covers this territory in detail. They note (p. 50) that the purposes of contracting are to, "ensure productive outcomes, clarify roles, prevent misunderstandings, establish learning goals, and define business and interpersonal practices."

No one seriously argues against having reasonable clarity at the beginning of this kind of relationship. Achieving that clarity is not as easy as saying it is needed, even if we agree that more clarity is always better – which it isn't. Some practitioners consider it important to leave a lot of room for issues that emerge along the way, or otherwise don't feel they should tie themselves down too early.

There is no gold standard for determining how much clarity is "reasonable". It is difficult to know when one has achieved the optimum degree of clarity. There are, however, some outcomes from a good contracting process that can serve as guidelines.

One of these outcomes is informed consent, particularly around the topic of confidentiality. Does the client know what information can be shared with whom? A second outcome is responsible participation: Does the client know enough about how the coaching will proceed so that he or she can be an active partner in the process?

Third, there are boundaries about "content". The client and coach should agree on what is not to be part of the coaching discussion as well as what will be discussed. As Frederic Hudson (1999) wrote: "The focus is to establish what is inside and outside the agreement … The overt goal is to establish mutual expectations for the coaching relationship. The covert goal is to keep the relationship within the agreed-upon boundaries which can be renegotiated by either party" (p. 27).

## Trust

Writers on coaching agree that safety and trust should be maintained in coaching relationships, and this starts with the contracting process. The literature from the clinical and counseling professions is very clear about the need to create a safe psychological environment so that trust can be built. These authors assume that clear contracting reduces anxiety, thus promoting greater disclosure. Gyllenstein and Palmer (2007) and Luebbe (2005) both emphasize that trust is the most important factor in coaching, and that a safe relationship is necessary for risk taking. Other authors use such terms as "the relationship" (Davis and McKenna, 2011), the "coaching alliance" (Passmore, 2007a) or "the coach-client alliance" (Kemp, 2011) but seem to be referring to much the same element.

How are safety and trust created during contracting? There are various opinions on this matter, and not a great deal of consensus. This seems to be an area where a coach's style and experience are the major factors. Hare-Mustin *et al.* (1979) suggested that a coach or other professionals can appear as a threat to clients, and such threats can be dealt with during the contracting process. Alvey and Barclay (2007) focus on the idea that promises of confidentiality are important for trust building.

Some coaches focus a good deal of attention on the formal aspects of contracting in the first couple of sessions with a client. Other coaches deal with the contracting topics more briefly so that "arrangements" don't get in the way of building a productive relationship. Kilburg's (2000) list of the components of executive coaching interventions begins with, "Developing an intervention agreement," and then Step 2 is, "Building a coaching relationship," Hudson's (1999) list of stages has, "Formulate a coaching agreement" in second place after, "Building a relationship."

In practice, both clarity and trust have to be accomplished as the coaching engagement starts. Experienced coaches have found ways to integrate these two objectives so the contracting process becomes a way of building a trusting relationship.

# Five Kinds of Contracting

## Pre-contracting

What comes before contracting? Three parties don't just jump into a contracting process without each first agreeing to do so. Before there can be written or explicit contracts there must be agreement among the principals to work together to negotiate them. In some business environments this phase might be called "qualifying" the client or customer. Another name for this might be "reaching an agreement in principle."

Bluckert (2006) refers to these activities as a, "detailed preliminary exercise undertaken before" the contracting phase is reached. He refers to checking out the credibility of the coach, and assessing the fit among the coach, client, and sponsor.

These early information gathering activities serve some important contracting purposes:

- Determining appropriateness of this client for a coaching engagement.
- Assessing the client's readiness and capability to engage in coaching.
- Checking out the chemistry among client, coach, and sponsors.

The outcome of these activities will be a preliminary decision, which is seldom written, but is often accompanied by a handshake or a phone call to say, "Yes, let's get started."

*Appropriateness*　Appropriateness refers to having reasonable assurance that we are dealing with a realistic coaching opportunity – that we're not dealing with a selection problem, a team building challenge, or a highly personal matter that calls for another kind of helping professional.

- Are we dealing with a person who is in the wrong job? If so, the changes the organization expects may be beyond the client's reach, with or without a good coach. If the root issue is a selection one, a coach is the wrong person to bring in.
- Team and system problems can be "blamed" on a single person. This person might be the leader of a low-performing unit, or one of its members. If the system is badly

designed, or under-resourced or highly dysfunctional for other reasons, the resolution will likely be beyond the ability of one person to make things right. Although the coach might be able to do some organizational development (OD) work, such efforts are likely to be limited in their impact unless the coach renegotiates the contract and creates a very different client relationship.

- Coaches are sometimes brought in when an individual is underperforming for reasons of a very personal nature. This could be a temporary matter (e.g., illness, financial pressure) or a chronic condition (serious physical or mental health concerns). In either case, an appropriate next step is to defer the start of the assignment or to bring in another type of professional.

Appropriateness includes some very basic issues. Ting and Hart (2004) identify time and schedule compatibility as one such issue. Making sure there is an appropriate room available is another. Fielder and Starr (2008) comment on discovering what goals the client already seems to have settled on. Frisch (2001) reviews many of the issues having to do with appropriateness.

Additionally, there has to be an adequate amount of support for the coaching from the client's immediate management. There should not be job jeopardy, that is, "This is your last chance ... if this doesn't get fixed soon, you're out of here!" The manager and the HR representative should show good understanding of what coaching is; this may require a bit of education by the coach. An important element of that understanding has to do with the trade-offs between confidentiality and reporting.

Hodgetts (2002) is very clear about the importance of appropriateness:

> Be sure that executive coaching, and not some other approach to executive development, is the correct intervention. Proceed with coaching only if you are reasonably certain that the issues involved are primarily individual, not organizational, and only if the desired behavioral changes can be linked to business goals and strategy and will improve business effectiveness. Even if these initial conditions are met, proceed with coaching only if the individual to be coached seems relatively open to feedback and change and if others in the organization are likely to support these changes. (p. 221)

*Readiness and capability*   Does the executive really want to be a coaching client? This cannot be assumed, since organizational sponsors may have arm-twisted the person into a coaching relationship. To be successful, coaching must begin with a client who is voluntarily entering the relationship (Valerio and Lee, 2005; Winum, 1995).

Kretzschmar (2010) developed a model for assessing readiness, which she finds helpful for discussing this issue with clients and sponsors. Readiness probably is not something that can be assessed at only one point in time. It makes sense that a client's readiness for coaching or change can vacillate. Passmore and Whybrow (2007) emphasize this point: "First, then, is the need for the coach to continually assess the coachee's state of readiness to change towards the targeted behaviour."

Prior to negotiating a firm contract, some coaches will initiate a few coaching interactions to see how the client responds. O'Neill (2007) says the client must be receptive to early feedback, or the coaching may not work – and of course this isn't easy to determine until some coaching has taken place.

It is important to see if the client understands that a coaching need exists. If there's a "problem", Dotlich and Cairo (1999) want the coach to make sure the client acknowledges it. If the coaching is being initiated for more positive reasons, such as preparation for a promotion or a recent transition into the present role, does the client agree that coaching is desirable?

Is this a good time for the client to engage in coaching? The client may want the coaching, but need to start at a later date. Are there too many other claims on the individual's time and energy? If too many important or demanding pressures are on the client, it's better to reconsider when to start the coaching.

An additional aspect of pre-contracting is capability, which refers to an assessment of whether the proposed client is within reach of the objectives expected. Are the basic skills in place? Is the client's behavior close enough to the desired performance that it can be improved sufficiently within the timeframe?

A related issue has to do with the coach's own capabilities. There probably are several hundred thousand people who do some kind of coaching work with managers and executives. Clearly we are not all similarly skilled. It is the coach's responsibility to know his or her strengths and limitations as they apply to a client's needs.

*Chemistry*   And finally there is the chemistry factor. Both the coach and the proposed client should have a positive sense of chemistry, and the same is true for the coach/sponsor relationship. If the chemistry isn't right, there may be good reason to request that another coach steps in.

## Change contracts

*Changing behavior*   At a fundamental level, every coach, regardless of theoretical background, is a behaviorist. We all are trying to help a client make changes in behavior and performance. How complex is that process? It is, of course, extremely complex – well beyond what any explicit contract could describe at the beginning of the relationship. Learning, changing and goal setting processes have been addressed in thousands of articles and books, and need not be summarized here (see the chapter on behavioral coaching).

Despite this enormous body of knowledge, a measure of humility is appropriate in this domain, especially as it applies to organizational leaders. We know a lot, but there's a lot we don't know. Avolio and Hannah (2008) remind us, "that there has been relatively little discussion on how to best set the conditions to successfully accelerate development before placing leaders through leader development programs." This is equally true for the version of leadership development we call coaching.

*Goal setting*   How does the literature address contracting for the purpose of changing behavior? The typical vehicle is through goal setting, a topic dealt with at great length in every book on coaching (see, for example, Passmore, 2007b). Some general themes from that literature are that goals should be challenging, attainable, specific, participatory, and incremental.

Whitmore (2002) says the goals should be as challenging as possible, while still being realistic. Locke and Latham (1990), in their text on goal setting and task performance, ask that we set goals as highly specific as possible, thus allowing the client to measure success.

Hodgetts (2002) adds another reason to have clear goals: eventual assessment of success. "In coaching, as in many other organizational activities, it is vital to establish clear contractual agreement on objectives among all interested parties. Otherwise, it will be nearly impossible later to measure progress, gauge effectiveness, or know when the need for coaching has ended."

Goal evolution seems to be one of the less understood yet very important elements of goal setting (Lee and Frisch, 2011). Coaching engagements begin with needs felt by the client and the stakeholders, but these may not be aligned with each other nor stated in ways that facilitate good coaching. The initial felt needs are negotiated into more usable goals, and then eventually "nailed down" in the form of specific, actionable, measurable objectives. As expressed by Bacon and Spear (2003): "The presenting problem is rarely the real one ... Sometimes the goals may not be clear until the coaching process has begun and the client has discovered enough to know what the desired outcome should be."

A development plan (or action plan, or action learning plan) becomes a very real kind of contract. Frisch (2001) states that: "One document that is key to the success of coaching and represents the most specific contract is the development plan." At a minimum it is a contract between coach and client and will guide their discussions. In a great many instances this plan is shared with and approved by the client's manager, thus becoming even more of a contract.

*Relationship*   Throughout the contracting process there is a theme that plays constantly in the minds of both the coach and client. That theme is: "Do we have a workable relationship?" All the rest of the contracting work will be largely useless without a strong, productive relationship between coach and individual client.

Davis and McKenna (2011) report that four factors account for almost all the systematic variance in psychotherapy outcomes (citing Asay and Lambert, 1999). The two large components of the variance are factors in the client (40 percent), and the therapeutic relationship (30 percent). They see these results equally applicable to coaching as well as to therapy. The remaining variance is divided equally (15 percent each) between therapists' theories and techniques, and a factor having to do with hope and expectancy.

This perspective is echoed by Kemp (2011), who examines the formation of a "developmental alliance built phenomenologically between coach and client." O'Broin and Palmer (2007) also explore this issue (in Palmer and Whybrow, 2007). There is a solid stream of concurring views on this matter (see Bluckert, 2005; Davis and Barnett, 2010; Lambert and Barley, 2001; Martin *et al.*, 2000; Wasylyshyn, 2003) which have been summarized elsewhere (Passmore (2007b)).

Stober and Grant (2006) state the case directly: "Regardless of preferred theoretical perspective, the foundation of effective coaching is the successful formation of a collaborative relationship." For these authors this means there will be a meaningful relationship, the client believes the coach will be working in the client's best interest, and that the coach will guide the development process to achieve good results.

Whether the phrase being used is relationship or any of its cousins, such as alliance or bonding, the intent is the same. As Peterson (1996) put it, if there is no partnership, the coach's entire effort to guide the client is at risk.

*Commitment*   "Until now, the coach has been doing most of the work solo. In the next stage, enrollment, the coach/client partnership becomes explicit and the work shared. In enrollment, both the client and the coach make explicit what they are committed to accomplishing in the coaching program." This quote from Flaherty (2010, p. 117) introduces a core issue in any coaching engagement: commitment to changing behavior. Flaherty uses the term "enrollment" rather than contract to emphasize the psychological nature of the commitment.

Coaching requires the commitment of an active, eager, and responsible client as a partner. Good contracts can increase a client's sense of control and responsibility, which will facilitate making the desired changes. The client participates in the decisions, and then knows what he or she has to do.

Kilburg (1996) mentions how the client needs to commit time and resources to the coaching effort, taking an active role. O'Neill (2007) comments on how the client must own his or her part of the issue. Witherspoon (2000) says that nothing important will be done until all parties are committed to achieving the goals. Hargrove (2008) takes the issue of commitment even further. He emphasizes that: "The commitment to create an extraordinary coaching relationship is a transformational act, not just a matter of working out the details."

Flaherty (2010) describes a standard for knowing when the contracting is adequately completed: "As a coach, you'll know this processes is complete when both you and the client know exactly what the outcomes are and what the commitment of each is to the program, and when both have a general idea about what it will take to achieve the outcome."

However, commitment goes two ways. Bush (2005) describes how the coach's degree of commitment impacts coaching outcomes in important ways.

*Learning*  Although behavior changes are important, some coaches reach for what they consider to be a higher level of result: that the client should learn *how* to change and develop. A real success would be that the client finishes the coaching engagement with strong self-awareness into his or her best ways of growing as an executive. The next time the client confronts a transition or challenge there will be greater ability to manage it smoothly either with or without a coach. This notion can be traced to the writings of Argyris and Schön (1978) and Argyris (1991).

Hawkins and Smith (2010) employ this learning approach when they describe how coaching can move from a focus on skills or performance to development and even transformation. Stokes and Jolly (2010) make a similar point by outlining three levels of learning: behavior change, self-image, and eventually purpose and meaning.

For this to happen, the coach has to be aware of how adults learn. Peterson (2002, 2011) has been a strong advocate for the position that coaches should have a solid understanding of how each of their clients learn and develop. No one disputes this point, but it typically isn't the first thing that comes into people's minds when they think of what goes into successful coaching.

## Process contracts

Coaching happens through a structured process, one that has steps, activities, rules, outcomes, and so forth. Let's briefly look at the components of a typical contract that structures the relationship between coach and client. There are many lists of what should go into a coaching contract. The Executive Coaching Forum (2008) and Silsbee (2010, Chapter 5) have useful discussions.

For purposes of this review we consider these components:

- Confidentiality
- Responsibilities
- Rhythm

- Boundaries and ethics
- Data gathering

*Confidentiality* Confidentiality is always mentioned in discussions of coaching agreements. It is easy to say: "Everything is confidential," but that isn't really true in most coaching engagements. The counterpoint to confidentiality is reporting – there are sponsors and other stakeholders, often the client's manager and the HR representative, who need to be informed about some of what's going on in the privacy of the coach/client relationship. A typical way of expressing this balance is that "conversations" are confidential, and "progress" will be reported. In the strictest sense, then, the word "confidentiality" is probably too strong for the reality of executive coaching engagements, but it's the word that is generally used.

Complications can set in. Fisher (2008) states that clients have a right to know if there is a potential for confidentiality to be breached under certain conditions. What are those conditions? For Fisher the conditions have to do with such things as serious mental health problems, criminal activity, sexual abuse or harassment, and subpoenas issued by courts. This tends to be more important for coaches who have connections with psychology, counseling, psychiatry, or social work professions. Similar points are made by others who write from a clinical psychology perspective (e.g. Hare-Mustin *et al.*, 1979; Beahrs and Gutheil, 2001; Martindale *et al.*, 2009). In practice, some coaches never mention that these limits to confidentiality might arise, and other coaches routinely go into some detail about them.

There has been much informal talk about whether external, professional coaches are bound by the same rules as are internal staff who do coaching or HR work. Do organizations expect coaches to act as their agents, as if they were employees? Are external coaches buffered by their independent status from the norms of their sponsors? There doesn't appear to be a resolution of this matter.

*Responsibilities* One would think that in a coaching engagement it would be obvious who does which activities, but such is not necessarily the case. Although perhaps not spelled out in a written document, there should be agreement about:

- Who takes notes.
- Who prepares the development plan.
- Who keeps the client's manager and HR staff up to date.
- What "homework", journaling, and reading expectations are applicable.
- The rules about cancellations, rescheduling, and missed appointments.
- Where the coaching discussions will happen – whose office? (In this age of virtual employees and cubicles, a responsibility may be to arrange a private space.)

It is probably wiser to discuss and agree on these roles earlier rather than "when they come up."

*Rhythm* Contracting always includes some discussion of the time period for the coaching, which for executive-level clients is often in the 3–12-month range. Within that time period there will be expectations for "how often and for how long" coaching conversations may be held. Some organizations have contracts with coaches that specify the number of sessions as well as the overall engagement length.

Time pressure is almost always a factor in executive coaching. One benefit of a contract with a clearly stated series of coaching appointments is that it provides discipline, making the coaching a priority among all the other urgent matters. "For harried and time-challenged managers today, this behavioral accountability makes all the difference in the world" (Dotlich and Cairo, 1999). Underhill *et al.* (2007), who are involved with a large consulting organization, report that: "Coaches state that their engagements are lasting longer than what organizations report. One possible reason for this discrepancy is that organizations are referring to the actual contract time, whereas coaches reference the relationship time, which includes follow-up conversations after the contract ends."

*Boundaries and ethics*   Clients are embedded in their teams and organizations, and in their personal lives and communities. Coaching conversations often wander off into any of these spaces. Coaches differ in their views as to what should be included or even known about – in our terms, where are the boundaries and what are the ethical considerations? De Haan and Burger (2005) provide a helpful discussion of this topic. They point to conflicts of interest that can arise if boundaries aren't discussed and maintained by mutual agreement.

Most texts on coaching have guidelines regarding a boundary between coaching and other forms of helping, especially therapy. The boundary in this case has to do with what's really "personal" and what should be included in a work-related conversation. Relevant considerations are the coach's skills, the client's privacy, and the sponsor's mandate, which is predictably to keep the discussions on the organization's business and the client's performance.

Pomerantz and Eiting (2004) have written an article specifically on ethics in coaching. They discuss the coaching/therapy boundary and offer guidance on how to clarify expectations about what is shared by the coach. As a general rule the topic is not confidential while the content of the discussions remains private.

*Data gathering*   A very popular type of data gathering is "360 interviewing". The coach, client, and sponsor need to agree on who will be included in such interviews. It is good practice for the coach and client to agree on the key questions and topics to be covered. This data may be obtained through electronic surveys, by in-person meetings or by telephone calls.

Another kind of data gathering is through psychometric instruments. Some organizations have preferences for certain measurement methods, and the coach may be expected to use them or interpret the ones that have already been administered. Both Herd and Russell (2011) and Passmore (2008) have provided reviews of the measures used by coaches. Clients should be advised in advance regarding the use of these instruments, and what will be done with the resulting information.

Other kinds of data gathering might include "shadowing" the client as he/she goes about daily activities, reviewing performance documents for previous time periods, or observing the client in role plays.

All of these methods can be used only with the agreement of the client, and sometimes with approval of sponsors. These agreements may be in written documents, emails or perhaps only verbal, but there must be agreement before the coach implements the data gathering.

## Business contracts

The first association most people have with the notion of contracting in coaching is with the business arrangement between the coach and the sponsoring organization. These contracts can be limited or extensive, depending on many factors. Importantly, they affect the coach/client relationship in a number of ways. Unfortunately, information about business contracts is not generally found in the behavioral science literature.

The traditional paradigm for establishing a business contract for coaching engagements has been between the coach and a human resources representative. This relationship continues to be very important, and in smaller organizations it is still probably the norm. Either the coach or the HR person may offer a document spelling out the primary dimensions of the relationship: fees, timeframes, terms such as confidentiality, possibly something about the purpose of the coaching and whatever else seems important.

In larger, more complex, worldwide organizations, however, negotiating a contract has become more complicated. More interested parties are involved. There may be an overall coordinator of coaching within the company, or lead on coaching. This lead may be based in another country, so cultural factors will also influence how the organization does its contracting. Patel (2008) discusses how multiple contracts, going beyond the client and coach, are involved in a global coaching program. Contracts will be given to the coach to sign, with some slight amount of negotiation flexibility available. These organizations are likely to have a list of sanctioned coaches, known as a "pool", which may number from less than ten to well over a hundred.

There may be an important role played by a purchasing department. These departments treat providers of coaching as "vendors", along with the firms that supply the organization with every other kind of product or service. The business contracts from purchasing departments may say very little about coaching since they are designed to cover so many other purposes. The description of the coaching services and relevant terms are included in a statement of work (SOW) that accompanies the master contract.

One aspect of any business contract will be fees. Coaching can be provided on a per hour basis or on a flat-fee basis (sometimes called a project fee). Business contracts also usually specify payment terms, for example half at initiation and the balance at the conclusion, or monthly, based on invoices indicating the hours spent, or some other arrangement. Along with fees there will be language regarding reimbursement of expenses such as travel or video conferencing.

Several clauses in corporate contracts are designed to protect the interests of the corporation. Often there will be a non-disclosure agreement (NDA) which requires that the coach does not disclose anything that is "owned" by the sponsor, such as its business strategies or dealings. Another clause may require the coach to show evidence of liability insurance. Of particular interest to coaches will be the absence in these large corporate contracts of a clause regarding confidentiality. If this isn't in the corporate version of the contract or SOW it should be added by the coach. There may be a clause addressing satisfactory performance. Sponsors sometimes place greater priority on change in performance than they do on other aspects of the coaching engagement, which is quite understandable. Whether they (or the coach) make this matter part of the business contract is an open question. How the results are to be measured is a very complex subject (see DeMeuse *et al.*, 2009).

Another recent trend in the coaching profession is affecting the way business is contracted by independent coaches. Consulting firms of all varieties have established executive coaching as one of their lines of service, but often have only a few full-time employees doing this work. They, too, have been forming "pools" of affiliated coaches who sub-contract to do the actual work. The consulting firm has a contract with the sponsoring organization, and the coach has a contract with the consulting firm.

The contract between the coach and consulting firm will specify the fees, services to be delivered, and other terms. It is also likely to contain a non-compete clause blocking the coach from doing business directly with the sponsoring organization for some period of time. The coach may also be asked to carry the consulting firm's business card, and the coach may be "requested" not to join the affiliate pools of other consulting firms.

## Psychological contracts

At least passing reference should be made to the notion of psychological contracts. They aren't much discussed in the coaching literature but perhaps they play an important role in the coaching process.

Rousseau (1995, 2004) makes the point that any specific contract resides within a larger context of social and psychological contracts. This unwritten, unspoken psychological contract fills in the gaps left by a formal contracting process. Kilburg and Levinson (2008) make a similar point, with the addition of an unconscious component: "Psychological contracts have many elements, from those that are conscious and thus easily observable ... to those that are completely unconscious."

Because they aren't articulated, a psychological contract becomes evident primarily when it is violated. There hasn't been much investigation into the nature of psychological contracts in coaching, but causes for breach might include overpromising by the coach or wishful interpretations and unrealistic expectations by a client.

## Two additional thoughts on contracting

*Contracts are dynamic*   It is helpful for all parties to understand that circumstances change and therefore so must the agreements. Kilburg (2002) is clear that contracts "must be reworked as reality forces new considerations on the people involved." Hudson (1999) says the initial coaching agreement is the first edition of a living document. Frisch (2001), who connects the revising of development plans to maintaining client commitment, notes that the plan needs to be a "joint effort and a living document."

Whitworth *et al.* (1998) refer to their coaching approach as co-active, with responsibility and power shared by coach and client. An implication of this approach is that a contract set several months earlier may be revised as coaching progresses so it makes sense to the client.

*Contracting is personal*   "No two coaches work in quite the same way. Nor should they" (Frisch *et al.*, 2012). Just as there can be no one right way to coach, nor is there only one right way to do the contracting that is central to it. Contracting is ultimately a reflection of the coach and his or her way of doing coaching. Lee and Frisch (2011) make this point clearly: "Ideally, contracting reflects a melding of case-specific requirements and a coach's individual approach to coaching ... Contracting empowers coaches to bring their practice judgment to the foreground."

Hargrove's (2008) personal model of coaching is based on being clear about his commitments: "The stand that I take is to be a Masterful Coach and have my way of being come from my commitments versus my reactions." From this foundation he designs and re-designs his contracts with clients and sponsors. Kilburg (2002) reminds coaches that an important element in contracting is: "Understanding your own needs, strengths and weaknesses … A successful agreement begins with the parties recognizing that they both have needs and they both bring value to the bargaining table."

Perhaps the ultimate contract for coaches is with themselves, and everything else flows from it.

## Future Research

Coaching is an emerging professional field and is led much more by its practitioners than by researchers. Much of the "evidence" we have for our work is borrowed from neighboring disciplines. The good news here is this is a wide-open field for researchers. Some of the research questions in regard to contracting are:

1 The underlying issues – formality, balance, clarity, trust – should be examined. How much formality is useful? How should a coach integrate formality and relationship building? What describes a good balance between client interests and sponsor expectations? Does clarity serve the purpose of channeling productive effort, or of prematurely solidifying an adaptive process? How is a trusting relationship to be formed between employees in a highly structured organization where confidentiality is never absolute?

2 The typology of five kinds of contracts hasn't been subjected to thorough discussion or research. Are there other kinds of contracts too? Are there important sub-categories? What other agreements can be found in coaching engagements, either explicit or implicit?

3 The evolution from felt needs to negotiated coaching goals to designed outcome objectives is fascinating, uncharted territory. We know that goals in coaching engagements shift over time, but the process remains unclear. What are the contributions of values, long-term life goals, acknowledgment of short-term realities, increasing trust levels, or compromises between individual and sponsor interests?

4 Executive coaching necessarily involves multiple parties. This chapter has used the term *client* to refer to the individual coaching recipient, but alternative views also are supportable. This tension is reflected in the various contracts used concurrently by coaches. How should they overlap? Should they be separate documents? Who should have access to them? How should changes be negotiated?

5 Almost nothing is known about the psychological contracts that are certain to exist among the parties to executive coaching.

There is real need to make progress in these and other areas of research on contracting. As a professional service, coaching is moving rapidly toward standardization, certification of practitioners, centralized organizational control, electronic delivery, and implementation worldwide at many organizational levels. These evolutions of the coaching art should all be premised on a solid understanding of the contractual bases for successfully helping the clients.

## Conclusion

This chapter surveyed the literature regarding contracting as used in the field of executive coaching. A wide net was cast because the concept of contracting in coaching hasn't been a focus for contributors to the field. Although every coach and writer about coaching talks about contracting, and they acknowledge its centrality to what they're doing, the term remains poorly defined. In the hope of improving that situation this chapter offered a broad definition of coaching contracts and identified four underlying issues and five kinds of coaching contracts. The four underlying issues are formality, balance among competing interests, clarity, and trust. These may be seen as values or assumptions or as foundations for theorizing about the nature of contracting in coaching. The five kinds of coaching contracts represent a rough but hopefully useful typology. As with the four underlying issues, this typology is meant to be heuristic rather than definitive.

It is commonly heard that good coaching is based on a good relationship between client and coach, and that is certainly true. Equally valid is the notion that good contracts among all parties are a requirement for good coaching. These statements appear to be mutually supportive.

# References

Alvey, S. and Barclay, K. (2007) The characteristics of dyadic trust in executive coaching. *Journal of Leadership Studies*, 1(1), 18–27.

Argyris, C. (1991) Teaching smart people how to learn. *Harvard Business Review*, 69(3), 99–109.

Argyris, C. and Schön, D. (1978) *Organizational Learning*. Reading, MA: Addison-Wesley.

Asay, T.P. and Lambert, M.J. (1999) The empirical case for the common factors in therapy: Quantitative findings. In: M.A. Hubble, B.J. Duncan and S. Miller (eds) *The Heart and Soul of Change: What Works in Therapy*. Washington, DC: American Psychological Association.

Association for Professional Executive Coaching and Supervision (APECS) (2007) Ethical Guidelines. Retrieved from http://www.apecs.org/coachingEthicalGuidelines.asp.

Avolio, B.J. and Hannah, S.T. (2008) Developmental readiness: Accelerating leader development. *Consulting Psychology Journal: Practice and Research*, 60(4), 331–47.

Bacon, T.R. and Spear, K.I. (2003) *Adaptive Coaching*. San Francisco, CA: Davies-Black.

Beahrs, J.O. and Gutheil, T.G. (2001) Informed consent in psychotherapy. *American Journal of Psychiatry*, 158(1), 4–10.

Bluckert, P. (2005) Critical factors in executive coaching – the coaching relationship. *Industrial and Commercial Training*, 37(7), 336–40.

Bluckert, P. (2006) *Psychological Dimensions of Executive Coaching*. Buckingham, UK: Open University Press.

Bush, M. (2005) Client perceptions of effectiveness in executive coaching. Unpublished doctoral dissertation, Pepperdine University, Malibu, CA.

Davis, S.L. and Barnett, R.C. (2010) Changing behavior one leader at a time. In: R.F. Silzer and B.E. Dowell (eds) *Strategy-driven Talent Management: A Leadership Imperative*. San Francisco, CA: Jossey-Bass.

Davis, S.L. and McKenna, D.D. (2011) Activating the active ingredients of leadership coaching. In: G. Hernez-Broome and L.A. Boyce (eds) *Advancing Executive Coaching: Setting the Course for Successful Leadership Consulting*. San Francisco, CA: Jossey-Bass.

DeMeuse, K.P., Dai, G., and Lee, R.J. (2009) Evaluating the effectiveness of executive coaching: Beyond ROI? *Coaching: An International Journal of Theory, Research and Practice*, 2(2), 118–35.

Desrosiers, E. and Oliver, D.H. (2011) Maximizing impact: Creating successful partnerships between coaches and organizations. In: G. Hernez-Broome and L.A. Boyce (eds) *Advancing Executive Coaching: Setting the Course for Successful Leadership Consulting*. San Francisco, CA: Jossey-Bass.

Dotlich, D. and Cairo, P. (1999) *Action Coaching: How to Leverage Individual Performance for Company Success*. San Francisco, CA: Jossey-Bass.

Executive Coaching Forum (2008) *The Executive Coaching Handbook: Principles and Guidelines for a Successful Coaching Partnership* (4th edn). Boston: The Executive Coaching Forum. Retrieved on August 3, 2011from http://www.theexecutivecoachingforum.com/manuals/ECHandbook 4thEdition032009.pdf.

Fielder, J.H. and Starr, L.M. (2008) What's the big deal about coaching contracts? *International Journal of Coaching in Organizations*, 15(4), 15–27.

Fisher, M.A. (2008) Protecting confidentiality rights: The need for an ethical practice model. *American Psychologist*, 63(1), 1–13.

Flaherty, J. (2010) *Coaching: Evoking Excellence in Others* (3rd edn). Burlington, MA: Elsevier.

Frisch, M.H. (2001) The emerging role of the internal coach. *Consulting Psychology Journal: Practice and Research*, 53(4), 240–50.

Frisch, M.H., Lee, R.J., Metzger, K.L., Robinson, J. and Rosemarin, J. (2012) *Becoming an Exceptional Executive Coach*. New York: AMACOM.

Gyllenstein, K. and Palmer, S. (2007) The coaching relationship: An interpretative phenomenological analysis. *International Coaching Psychology Review*, 2(2), 168–77.

de Haan, E. and Burger, Y. (2005) *Coaching with Colleagues: An Action Guide for One-to-one Learning*. Basingstoke, UK: Palgrave Macmillan.

Hare-Mustin, R.T., Marecek, J., Kaplan, A.G., and Liss-Levinson, N. (1979) Rights of clients, responsibilities of therapists. *American Psychologist*, 34(1), 3–16.

Hargrove, R. (2008) *Masterful Coaching*. San Francisco, CA: Jossey-Bass.

Hawkins, P. and Smith, N. (2010) Transformational coaching. In: E. Cox, T Bachkirova, and D. Clutterbuck (eds) *The Complete Handbook of Coaching*. London: Sage Publications.

Herd, A.M. and Russell, J.E.A. (2011) Tools and techniques: What's in your toolbox? In: G. Hernez-Broome and L.A. Boyce (eds) *Advancing Executive Coaching: Setting the Course for Successful Leadership Consulting*. San Francisco, CA: Jossey-Bass.

Hodgetts, W.H. (2002) Using executive coaching in organizations: What can go wrong (and how to prevent it). In: C. Fitzgerald and J. Garvey Berger (eds) *Executive Coaching: Practices and Perspectives*. Palo Alto, CA: Davies-Black.

Hudson, F.M. (1999) *The Handbook of Coaching*. San Francisco, CA: Jossey-Bass.

Kemp, T. (2011) Building the coaching alliance: Illuminating the phenomenon of relationship in coaching. In: G. Hernez-Broome and L.A. Boyce (eds) *Advancing Executive Coaching: Setting the Course for Successful Leadership Consulting*. San Francisco, CA: Jossey-Bass.

Kilburg, R.R. (1996) Toward a conceptual understanding and definition of executive coaching. *Consulting Psychology Journal: Practice and Research*, 48(2), 134–44.

Kilburg, R.R. (2000) *Executive Coaching: Developing Managerial Wisdom in a World of Chaos*. Washington, DC: American Psychological Association Press.

Kilburg, R.R. (2001) Facilitating intervention adherence in executive coaching: A model and methods. *Consulting Psychology Journal: Practice and Research*, 51, 251–67.

Kilburg, R.R. (2002) Individual interventions in consulting psychology. In: R.L. Lowman (ed.) *Handbook of Organizational Consulting Psychology*. San Francisco, CA: Jossey-Bass.

Kilburg, R.R. (2007) Introduction: The historical and conceptual roots of executive coaching. In: R.R. Kilburg and R.C. Diedrich (eds) *The Wisdom of Coaching*. Washington, DC: American Psychological Association.

Kilburg, R.R. and Levinson, H. (2008) Executive dilemmas: Coaching and the professional perspectives of Harry Levinson. *Consulting Psychology Journal: Practice and Research*, 60(1), 7–32.

Kramer, T.J., Kleindorfer, K.L., and Colarelli-Beatty, K.M. (1994) Who is the client: A replication and extension. *Consulting Psychology Journal: Practice and Research*, 46(3), 11–18.

Kretzschmar, I. (2010) Exploring clients' readiness for coaching. *International Journal of Evidence Based Coaching and Mentoring*, 4, 1–20.

Lambert, M.J. and Barley, D.E. (2001) Research summary on the therapeutic relationship and psychotherapy outcome. *Psychotherapy: Theory, Research, Practice, Training*, 38, 357–61.

Lee, R.J. and Frisch, M.H. (2011) Learning to coach leaders. In: G. Hernez-Broome and L.A. Boyce (eds) *Advancing Executive Coaching: Setting the Course for Successful Leadership Consulting*. San Francisco, CA: Jossey-Bass.

Locke, E. and Latham, G. (1990) *A Theory of Goal Setting and Task Performance*. Englewood Cliffs, NJ: Prentice-Hall.

Luebbe, D.M. (2005) The three-way mirror of executive coaching. *Dissertation Abstracts International: Section B: The Sciences and Engineering*, 66(3-B) 1771. Ann Arbor, MI: Proquest, International Microfilms International.

Lusch, R.F. and Brown, J.R. (1996) Interdependency, contracting, and relational behavior in marketing channels. *Journal of Marketing*, 60, 19–38.

Martin, D.J., Garske, J.P., and Davis, M.K. (2000) Relation of the therapeutic alliance with outcome and other variables: A meta-analytic review. *Journal of Consulting and Clinical Psychology*, 68, 438–50.

Martindale, S.J., Chambers, E., and Thomson, A.R. (2009) Clinical psychology service users' experiences of confidentiality and informed consent: A qualitative analysis. *Psychology and Psychotherapy: Theory, Research and Practice*, 82, 355–68.

O'Broin, A. and Palmer, S. (2007) Reappraising the coach-client relationship: The unassuming change agent in coaching. In: S. Palmer and A. Whybrow (eds) *Handbook of Coaching Psychology: A Guide for Practitioners*. London: Brunner-Routledge.

O'Neill, M.B. (2007) *Executive Coaching with Backbone and Heart: A Systems Approach to Engaging Leaders with Their Challenges*. San Francisco, CA: Jossey-Bass.

Passmore, J. (2007a) Integrative coaching: a model for executive coaching. *Consulting Psychology Journal: Practice and Research, America Psychology Association*, 59(1), 68–78.

Passmore, J. (2007b) Behavioural coaching. In: S. Palmer and A. Whybrow (eds) *Handbook of Coaching Psychology: A Guide for Practitioners*. London: Brunner-Routledge.

Passmore, J. (ed.) (2008) *Psychometrics in Coaching: Using Psychological and Psychometrics Tools for Development*. London: Kogan Page.

Passmore, J. and Whybrow, A. (2007) Motivational interviewing: A specific approach for coaching psychologists. In: S. Palmer and A. Whybrow (eds) *Handbook of Coaching Psychology: A Guide for Practitioners*. London: Brunner-Routledge.

Patel, J. (2008) Six degrees of contracting: Approaches and lessons from a global coaching program. *International Journal of Coaching in Organizations*, 6(4), 28–45.

Peterson, D.B. (1996) Executive coaching at work: The art of one-on-one change. *Consulting Psychology Journal: Practice and Research*, 48(2), 78–86.

Peterson, D.B. (2002) Management development: Coaching and mentoring programs. In: K. Kraiger (ed.) *Creating, Implementing, and Managing Effective Training and Development: State-of-the-art Lessons for Practice*. San Francisco, CA: Jossey-Bass.

Peterson, D.B. (2011) Good to great coaching: accelerating the journey. In: G. Hernez-Broome and L.A. Boyce (eds) *Advancing Executive Coaching: Setting the Course for Successful Leadership Consulting*. San Francisco, CA: Jossey-Bass.

Pomerantz, S. and Eiting, J. (2004) Drawing lines in the sand: Ethics in coaching, contracting, and confidentiality. *International Journal of Coaching in Organizations*, 2(3), 38–44.

Rousseau, D.M. (1995) *Psychological Contracts in Organizations: Understanding Written and Non-written Agreements*. Thousand Oaks, CA: Sage Publications.

Rousseau, D.M. (2004) Psychological contracts in the workplace: Understanding the ties that motivate. *Academy of Management Executive*, 18, 120–27.

Silsbee, D. (2010) *The Mindful Coach: Seven Roles For Facilitating Leader Development*. San Francisco, CA: Jossey-Bass.

Stern, L.R. (2004) Executive coaching: A working definition. *Consulting Psychology Journal: Practice and Research*, 56, 154–62.

Stern, L. (2009) Challenging some basic assumptions about psychology and executive coaching: Who knows best, who is the client, and what are the goals of executive coaching? *Industrial and Organizational Psychology*, 2(3), 268–71.

Stober, D.R. and Grant, A.M. (2006) Towards a conceptual approach to coaching models. In: D.R. Stober and A.M. Grant (eds) *Evidence Based Coaching Handbook: Putting Best Practices to Work for your Clients*. Hoboken, NJ: Wiley.

Stokes, J. and Jolly, R. (2010) Executive and leadership coaching. In: E. Cox, T. Bachkirova and D. Clutterbuck (eds) *The Complete Handbook of Coaching*. London: Sage Publications.

Stomski, L., Ward, J., and Battista, M. (2011) Coaching programs: Moving beyond the one-on-one. In: G. Hernez-Broome and L.A. Boyce (eds) *Advancing Executive Coaching: Setting the Course for Successful Leadership Consulting*. San Francisco, CA: Jossey-Bass.

Ting, S. and Hart, E. (2004) Formal coaching. In: C.D. McCauley and E.V. Velsor (eds) *The Center for Creative Leadership Handbook of Leadership Development*. San Francisco, CA: Jossey-Bass.

Underhill, B.O., McAnally, K.L., and Koriath, J.J. (2007) *Executive Coaching for Results: The Definitive Guide to Developing Organizational Leaders*. San Francisco, CA: Berrett-Koehler Publishers, Inc.

Valerio, A.M. and Lee, R.J. (2005) *Executive Coaching: A Guide for the HR Professional*. San Francisco, CA: John Wiley & Sons.

Wasylyshyn, K.M. (2003) Executive coaching: An outcome study. *Consulting Psychology Journal: Practice and Research*, 55(2), 94–106.

Whitmore, J. (2002) *Coaching for Performance*. London: Nicholas Brealey.

Whitworth, L., Kimsey-House, H. and Sandahl, P. (1998) *Co-active Coaching*. Palo Alto, CA: Davies-Black.

Winum, P.C. (1995) Anatomy of an executive consultation: Three perspectives. *Consulting Psychology Journal: Practice and Research*, 47(2), 114–21.

Witherspoon, R. (2000) Starting smart: Clarifying coaching goals and roles. In: M. Goldsmith, L. Lyons, and A. Freas (eds) *Coaching for Leadership: How the World's Greatest Coaches Help Leaders Learn*. San Francisco, CA: Jossey-Bass.

# 4

# The Development of Meaning and Identity Within Coaching

## Mary Wayne Bush, Esra Ozkan, and Jonathan Passmore

## Introduction

This chapter identifies how issues of meaning and identity relate to coaching individuals and groups. We believe issues of meaning and identity are important, even foundational, to all coaching, and that these topics become involved at some point in all coaching. Issues of meaning and identity arise for both individuals and groups at key times of change and transition: when there are endings and/or new beginnings; when a person or team seems "stuck", or unable to move forward, reach a goal, or be productive; and when new resources, people, opportunities, or directions are presented. There are four existential "inflection points" that can trigger questions or issues about meaning and identity in clients, whether groups or individuals. The following sections present a brief review of the literature, discussions of both individual and team coaching for meaning and identity (using the four inflection points noted above) and resources, tools, and coaching considerations for working with issues of meaning and identity.

## Theories of Identity

The study of self has a long tradition in sociology, including Mead (1934) who explored the self as a social construct developed in the context of social activity and experience where we come to know ourselves only through imaging what others think of us (Cooley, 1902; Mead, 1934). One of the earliest theories of identity was developed by Erickson who made a distinction between ego identity (self-personal differences that separate one person from the next) and social identity (Erickson, 1959). Based on these early theories, sociologists developed symbolic interaction perspective that saw the self as constructed by others through communication and interaction (Blumer, 1969; Denzin, 1992; Garfinkel, 1967; Glaser and Strauss, 1967; Goffman, 1959; Rosenberg, 1981). Goffman (1959)

*The Wiley Blackwell Handbook of the Psychology of Coaching and Mentoring*, First Edition.
Edited by Jonathan Passmore, David B. Peterson, and Teresa Freire.
© 2013 John Wiley & Sons, Ltd. Published 2016 by John Wiley & Sons, Ltd.

used the symbolic interaction model to examine human interaction in social settings and developed an analysis of face-to-face interactions in everyday life and within organized structures such as the workplace and school. He employed the theater model as a means of analyzing how we maintain a certain self-image acceptable to others who have social and economic power. The symbolic interactionist model has been criticized for relying too heavily on everyday interactions and for not paying enough attention to the larger social context in which these interactions happen (Callero, 2003; Hewitt, 1989). Stryker argued that positions are defined as elements of social structure. When the meanings of social roles are internalized, they are said to have become a part of the self and identity (Stryker 1980). Family systems therapists and psychiatrists, drawing on Gregory Bateson's (1972) cybernetic theories as well as other traditions, have adapted similar ideas, viewing people not as isolates but as members of larger systems (Minuchin, 1974).

Social psychologists shifted the emphasis to the study of social roles and social identity (Gubrium and Holstein, 2000; Stryker, 1980; Stryker and Burke, 2000). Social identity theory was developed by Tajfel (1974) who insisted that the key to understanding inter-group conflict, prejudice, and discrimination is found in an individual's social identity as defined by group membership not in individual defects of personality or attitude.

Anthropological studies cross-culturally have studied quite different notions of self and identity and explored how they provide different ideals for the individual's self-fashioning and ability to deal with conflicts as embedded in various social systems and role structures (Geertz, 1973; Hallowell, 1955; Kondo, 1997; Levy, 1973; Lock ,1993; Malinowski, 1927; Mauss, 1985 (1938); Myers, 1979; Rosaldo, 1980; Rosenberger, 1989; see also survey of approaches in anthropology Marcus and Fischer 1986). Identity became important to anthropologists especially in the 1970s when ethnicity and social movements emerged.

In recent years, identity and image have become central subjects in organizational studies. Scholars have written about personal versus organizational identity, threats to identity, organizational image and identification, adaptation, and member commitment, and so forth. They have explored how a person's self-concept is shaped by membership in occupational and work groups and by the knowledge/awareness of their membership. And certain coaching approaches build heavily on identity and meaning, such as narrative coaching, ontological coaching, and gestalt coaching (Bluckett, 2011; Drake, 2011; Sieler and Drake, 2010).

When an organization's collective identity is challenged by major events such as regulatory changes, competitive moves, structural changes resulting from mergers or acquisition, or larger events such as an economic depression, organizational attributes become visible. As the number of organization-based roles, and the rate at which organizations change is increasing, role transitions become more important. Each role has a distinct identity, a set of values, beliefs, norms, interaction styles, and time horizons (Weick and Ashford, 2001).

Organizational identity has traditionally been defined as distinctive and enduring but evidence suggests that organizational identity is dynamic and fluid, and the durability of identity is somewhat illusionary (Gioia *et al.*, 2000). Continuity is essential to organizations, but they also have to adapt quickly to changing environments.

So far questions have revolved around: "Who are we as an organization?" "Who do we think we are?" "Who do they think we are?" or "Who do they think we should be?" But considering organizational identity is negotiated, interactive, and reflexive, the main question to ask should be:

"Is this who we really are as an organization?"
"Is this who we are becoming as an organization?" or even,
"Is this who we want to be?"

Identity-image discrepancy suggests two major options: change something about the way we see ourselves, or change the way others perceive us. Major transitions can be facilitated by reducing the value of the current organizational identity by helping members loosen or negate their ties to it and/or and facilitating a change in individuals' sense of their working selves within a new set of defining parameters that are limited, concrete, and role based (Gioia *et al.*, 2000).

## How Coaching Helps to Define Meaning and Identity

This section will trace the connection between coaching and issues of meaning and identity, offering case examples from practicing coaches, as well as drawing on the theoretical framework and a model of coaching. Best practices will be identified and the case will be made for coaching as the optimal intervention for working with clients on issues of meaning and identity.

Whereas efficiency was previously posed as an organizational problem, coaches demonstrate that today efficiency is a matter of individual psychology. Coaches and coaching clients continuously talk about a work ethic that emphasizes increased knowledge about the individual and the social world in which the individual operates. This is where multiple aspects of identity and meaning take on a central role.

Identity is a product of both of the social roles to which individuals are assigned (or to which they have been previously assigned themselves) and of the choices that individuals make within the constraints of the role they play within the larger society. One could explore identity at three related levels. Personal identity is the self-exploration of individual goals, values and meaning, strengths and weaknesses, personality, motivation, work ethic, and so forth. This is also referred to as "personal brand" by writers such as Clark (2011, p. 79).

Another level of identity in organizations is the group, including team membership and leadership, collaboration, and competition. Group identity is more than the combination of the individuals' identities in the group: each group takes on an identity derived from its function and performance in the organization. In addition, coaches must consider factors of cultural identity in both individuals and teams they work with. Gender, ethnicity, race, generation, class, and multicultural contexts play an important role in leadership and individual effectiveness in the workplace, more so in the complex environment of multinational or global companies.

Cultural identity is a product of the larger contextual forces, including ethnicity, social class, skin color, stereotypical perceptions, as well as the social context and realities of the communities in which people have been acculturated. Cultural identity can also be associated with "organizational culture", which is the set of expectations and (often) unwritten rules that govern behavior in organizations. Abrahams (2007) argues that: "Corporations as entities and people as individuals share certain characteristics. Over time, they develop personalities that shape their philosophies and motivate their actions" (p. 2). To be most successful, individuals and groups need to be aware of, and adapt to, the organizational culture in which they are working. The goal or challenge for coaches is three-fold: first, to have an understanding of the coachee's identity at all these three levels; second, to help coaches explore their personal, group, and cultural identity and align them with the organizational identity in order to improve personal and professional performance; and third, to help coaches adapt their identity to changes within the organization and business environment. Often, one of the biggest challenges for executives is to accept that they may have to change what they consider part of their identity.

There might also be discrepancies between the ways in which people experience their own identity, and the ways in which their identity is perceived from outside. It is essential for coaches to help clients recognize these discrepancies and explore the unspoken anxieties and concerns regarding these experiences and perceptions. Bluckert (2011) argues that a reflective coaching approach, such as existential coaching, can be particularly helpful with these issues. Psychometric assessments such as multi-rater feedback can also be important in helping a client understand whether a gap exists between his or her self-image and the perceptions of others.

## Issues of Meaning and Identity in Coaching Individuals

This section will focus on how the coach can identify and work with issues of meaning and identity with individuals. Identity work can surface as questions about an executive's "fit" in an organization, or in transitioning to a new role. Identity can also play a part in career development and executive presence work. This section will address coaching's contribution to how people see themselves and the development of their identity. In addition, this section will explore coaching for personal meaning: life purpose, values, and satisfaction.

Executive coaches may be invited into an organization where a manager is not performing to expectations. Here coaching becomes a "remedial" tool to enhance performance and effectiveness through eliminating unhelpful patterns of behaviors. The executive coaching process might also be a part of succession planning processes or executive development initiatives. In these "developmental" situations a coach is hired to help the executive to function more effectively on the present job or to be well positioned for future career responsibilities. In each of these assignments there are aspects which are related to identity and meaning for the coachees that the coach should explore.

Coaches enlist a set of techniques to increase their clients' efficiency in increasing self-awareness, as well as exploring models of individual development. Bachkirova (2012) has explored some of these development themes in her chapter within this book. However, it is also worth exploring some of the methods and tools used by coaches in their engagement with their executive clients. Many coaches also use structured tools such as the Myers-Briggs Type Indicator (MBTI) and the California Personality Inventory (CPI) to document their executive clients' beliefs, values, assumptions, character traits, strengths and weaknesses, mental and emotional intelligence, and assess their capacities, potential and vision (or lack thereof) through a variety of structured psychometric tools (see, for example, Passmore, 2008). Multi-rater or "360 feedback" assessments are also important tools used to provide clients with awareness about how they are perceived (Morgenson, 2005). Such tools also provide a useful insight for coaches, helping them to reflect on who they are and how they learn and engage with others.

## Psychodynamic approaches

Coaching delves into an executive's unknown psychic territory and poses questions such as: What does he think? How does he feel? Where do these thoughts and feelings come from? What do others feel and think about him? What does he think and feel others think and feel about him? How does this web of assumptions, feelings, thoughts, and affects influence his effectiveness? It is through the exploration of the world of identity and meaning that organizations can take further steps to improve the efficiency of their executives. These issues are explored in more detail in Chapter 19.

## Issues of meaning and identity in coaching teams and organizations

Typically, issues of meaning and identity that are presented in group, team, or organizational settings revolve around the entity's mission and membership roles and responsibilities, as individuals coordinate action toward the organization's goals. However, issues of organizational identity and the business can impact of a firm's reputation and market share. While coaching individuals on issues of meaning and identity often involves waiting until these issues arise naturally in the course of the coaching engagement, it is more common for coaches to take a proactive stance when working with groups or teams on this subject. An important aspect of the basic organizational development work to be done with any group or team involves clarifying its mission and vision, or – said another way – its "identity and meaning".

Coaching conversations about the organization's vision and mission not only help the group come to agreement on foundational issues of meaning and identity, but they create alignment and solidarity, which helps to develop trust and build the foundation for effective functioning. The work of defining a shared agreement around the organization's mission and vision is the work of developing and declaring the group's meaning and identity. Abrahams reminds us that: "The group's mission is a description of the group's purpose, answering the questions, 'Why do we exist?'" and 'What are we convened or mandated to do or provide?'" (p. 2).

A group's vision is a statement of a desired future state or contribution: it speaks to an ideal or possibility that is not yet realized, toward which the group will strive. Both mission and vision statements are designed to promote stability and focus for the group, and to aid in alignment and decision making. Both are also meant to stay the same, for years in most cases, and it is a good team exercise to re-validate the mission and vision annually. However, in times of change, for example mergers and acquisitions, new product launches or economic and environmental impacts on an organization, both the vision and mission need to be re-examined to ensure that they remain current and supportive of the group's effective functioning.

Identifying the group's mission and vision, and getting team agreement about them, is foundational to the team's effective functioning. These agreements inform the team's strategic direction and brand, whether the group is a production team on a factory floor, or thousands of employees in a large, multi national corporation. Agreements about the group's vision and mission help clarify the scope and strategy of the key initiatives, goals, and actions that the group will take to carry out its vision and mission.

Many groups carry this identity conversation further, defining specific values about how the work will be done and how they will conduct themselves with each other, key stakeholders, and the public. These groups not only declare what they will strive for, but they also identify characteristics of the process they will take.

Discussing and clarifying a group's values is a way to link to personal meaning for each of the members, giving individuals the opportunity to express what is important to them, and what is most meaningful about the work of the team, as well as the teamwork experience itself. Identifying and documenting group values can also set a tone for the way the group does its work: for instance, a group whose declared values are accuracy, productivity, and excellence will most likely have a different "spirit" than a group whose values are collaboration, customer service, and enjoyment – even though both teams are successful and productive. This "spirit" is a demonstration of its values in action, and contributes to its identity and meaning, both for members and for external stakeholders. It is also important that the group's values are congruent with the overall culture and values of the larger organizational context in which they function.

While this work to develop a shared understanding of mission and vision is recommended at the outset for any team or group that is being formed or chartered, it is also useful for a coach to introduce the subjects of mission and vision when the team adds new members, when there is some form of organizational change that impacts the unit, team or group, and when the group is experiencing some dysfunction or trouble. These conversations should be re-visited to validate the continued shared understanding and agreements about mission and vision on a regular basis.

Coaches working with groups or teams (or any organizations) should inquire about the existence of the vision or mission, how widely it is known, used, and how it is documented. In situations where there are neither (or only one) mission and vision, the coach can help the team draft and agree to a mission and/or vision statement for itself. The coach can help the group assess how well their mission and vision fit with the larger organizational context, and enhance or enlarge the group's "brand". A next step for coaching the group can be to get data from key internal and external stakeholders (by surveys or interview processes) to evaluate whether the behavior and results of the group are perceived by others to be congruent with its stated mission and vision. The coach can also help the group and its members notice how they are applying the mission and vision in their work, their behaviors toward each other, and with their key stakeholders.

It is also important for a coach to help each individual find a personal link to the team's mission and vision and values. The coach can work with the team to help foster pride in their identity.

## Issues of Meaning and Identity in Coaching in Changing Times

This section will examine issues of identity and meaning through times of transition and change. Such changes might be the result of organizational restructuring practices such as mergers and acquisitions or larger cultural and economic changes such as globalization and economic recession. The section will explore the ways in which coaches address issues of identity and meaning within teams and organizations going through change.

In today's business environment, change is accelerated and enabled by many factors: globalization, technology advances, complex multinational organizations, and more frequent partnering across national borders and company boundaries. A study by IBM Corporation (2008) claimed that "change is the new normal" (p. 1). Companies no longer have the luxury of expecting day-to-day operations to maintain static or predictable patterns that are occasionally interrupted by short bursts of change. "In reality, the new normal is continuous change – not the absence of change" (p. 6). According to research from the Corporate Leadership Council (2003), most organizations acknowledge change as a continuous process that impacts the way organizations change.

Issues of meaning and identity take center stage during organizational change. Whether change is the result of mergers or acquisitions, downsizing, introducing new products or venturing into new markets, issues of meaning and identity are among the first that need to be addressed. During mergers or acquisitions, an organization's identity needs to be clarified and re-articulated. Issues of meaning translate into organizational vision and mission, and both need to be understood and adopted by the new, larger group. In downsizing, the organization must grapple with the questions of, "Who are we now that we have lost a percent of our workforce?" and, "What will this mean to our brand, our reputation in the industry, and our ability to keep production up and ensure customer satisfaction?"

The latter issue is also important to address when organizations venture into new products or territories, but there are also issues of new stakeholders and new cultures to consider. Coaching can be an invaluable asset to help with these issues during organization change (Bennett and Bush, 2009).

Executive coaches often work with leaders whose organizations are undergoing change. One important way coaching supports meaning and identity is in helping the leader assess and communicate the changes to the organization's brand or mission. This fundamental work must be done when there is any type of organizational change, to determine whether or not the organization's prior identity and meaning (its mission and vision) is still appropriate and powerful. Coaches also help leaders define and implement a change management strategy, incorporating best practices for project success as well as addressing the psychological impacts of transition on employees and group members.

As mentioned above, there are four key focus areas related to meaning and identity coaching that directly support leaders in dealing with organizational change. The first of these is helping the leader assess and re-evaluate any changes in the organization's meaning and identity, as a result of the change. This involves supporting the leader to formulate and articulate the new meaning and identity (i.e. vision and mission), and helping members of the organization adopt it, both as it relates to their behaviors and their professional functions. Often, this means helping organization members disconnect from the prior vision and mission (and the behaviors associated with them), and reframing the new organizational identity in a meaningful way that directly connects with their professional role. An example of this is the outsourcing of work to other countries. This practice can change the organization's identity as part of a more global workplace, and alter the work patterns by necessitating more virtual interaction, an expanded workday, and new forms of communication and consideration.

The second area is ensuring that the leader establishes and communicates a new (or updated) structure and artifacts that support the new organizational vision and mission. While much of this is the basic work of organizational development in terms of defining vision, mission, strategy, values, goals, and roles, it also includes creating new logos and organization charts which reflect the changes. The coach's aim is to help the leader and other organization members clarify their role or job function, and align their "working selves" with the new organizational identity, which may involve adopting new behaviors, work patterns or learning new equipment or skills. The leader should also highlight achievements related to the change to reinforce the stability and permanence of the new way of being. In the outsourcing example above, organization members may need to adjust time schedules to be available for international meetings, and hold these meetings virtually using online video-conferencing or other media. The outsourced partners, now also organization members, also have to learn new systems, policies, procedures, and language. The coach can help the leader notice and celebrate evidence of the organization members adapting to new, positive, behaviors that will solidify the new organization identity and help sustain it.

The third area is reflecting with (and to) the leader about his or her own behaviors and ways of being that support the new organization identity (or do not). The coach can help the leader adopt and display behaviors that are congruent with the new vision and mission, and be aware of his or her function as a role model for other organization members. The coach can act as a professional "sounding board" to help the leader examine his or her own behavior apropos of the new organization vision and mission, to identify areas that are going well and those that are still challenging and need further attention.

The final area is confirming and sustaining the new organizational identity through communication, celebration of successes, and reinforcement of the soundness of the new identity and meaning and the reasons for the change.

The coach can help the leader develop a strategy to stay in front of the organization members and the public with communication about the new organization identity and meaning, and the ways it is unfolding and taking hold. The leader needs to be the principle advocate and champion of the change, and cannot rest until the new vision, mission, and brand are established – not only within the organization, but to external stakeholders as well. In the case of the corporation, the stakeholders will be financial and industry communities, while in the case of an internal organization that is changing, the stakeholders will be peers and internal customers. Regardless, the leader must be the champion for the change, and keep everyone informed of progress, achievements, and the impact of the changes. The coach can help the leader devise a strategy to reach out to, connect, and stay networked with the key stakeholders, to provide up-to-date communication about the change, and take opportunities to get important feedback from stakeholders as well.

The evolving global, technological, and economic trends that we see today impact organizations in many ways, not the least of which is that their missions, visions, and strategies also must keep pace. This means that leaders at all levels need to continually re-evaluate and re-interpret the organizational identity and meaning, and help organization members to reframe and adjust their own work selves in support of the organizational changes. We know that organizational coaching is an important strategy for organization change and leadership development. "As leaders at all levels and sectors face increasingly difficult challenges in complex business environments, the use of organizational coaching rises" (Bennett-Bush, 2009, p. 12). As change becomes the "new normal", leaders who partner with coaches to help clarify and express organization meaning and identity during times of change may find themselves more successful at transformation on both personal as well as professional levels.

# Conclusion

People and organizations seek coaching because they want something to happen – and most of the time, that "something" is change. Typical coaching engagements will, at some point, involve considerations of meaning and/or identity for the client or group. Coaches often work with clients who are unhappy in their work or lives, who haven't identified or examined their core values, and who may not be living life in a way that fulfills and satisfies them – either physically, spiritually, emotionally or intellectually. We also often work with teams and organizations that are fragmented, unclear on purpose and direction, lacking the integrative function of vision and mission, and may not be seen as useful or important to others in the company.

# References

Abrahams, J. (2007) *101 Mission Statements from Top Companies.* Berkeley, CA: Ten Speed Press.

Bachkirova, T. (2012) Developmental coaching. In: J. Passmore, D. Peterson, and T. Freire (eds) *The Wiley-Blackwell Handbook of the Psychology of Coaching and Mentoring.* Chichester: Wiley.

Bateson, G. (1972). *Steps to an Ecology of Mind: Collected Essays in Anthropology, Psychiatry, Evolution and Epistemology.* San Francisco: Chandler Publications Company.

Bennett, J.L. and Bush, M.W. (2009) Coaching in organizations: Current trends and future opportunities. *OD Practitioner,* 41(1), 2–7.

Bluckert, P. (2011) The gestalt approach to coaching. In: E. Cox, T. Bachkirova, and D. Clutterbuck (eds) *The Complete Handbook of Coaching.* London: Sage Publications. pp. 80–93.

Blumer, H. (1969) *Symbolic Interactionism: Perspectives and Method.* Englewood Cliffs, NJ: Princeton-Hall.

Callero, P.L. (2003) The sociology of self. *Annual Review of Sociology,* 23, 115–33.

Cooley, C. (1902) *Human Nature and the Social Order.* New York: Schribners.

Corporate Leadership Council Report. (2003) *Change Management Models* Washington, DC: (Catalog Number CLC1XOGAX).

Denzin, N.K. (1992) *Symbolic Interactionism and Cultural Studies: The Politics of Interpretation.* Cambridge, MA: Blackwell.

Drake, D. (2011) Narrative coaching. In: E. Cox, T. Bachkirova, and D. Clutterbuck (eds) *The Complete Handbook of Coaching.* London: Sage Publications. pp. 120–31.

Erickson, E.H. (1959) *Identity and the Life Cycle – Selected Papers.* Madison, CT: International University Press.

Garfinkel, H. (1967) *Studies in Ethnomethodology.* Englewood Cliffs, NJ: Prentice-Hall.

Geertz. C. (1973) *The Interpretation of Cultures: Selected Essays.* New York: Basic Books.

Gioia, D.A., Thomas, J.B., Clark, S.M., and Chittipeddi, K. (1994) Symbolism and strategic change in academia: The dynamics of sensemaking and influence. *Organization Science ,* 5(3), 363–83.

Glaser, B.G. and Strauss, A.L. (1967) *The Discovery of Grounded Theory: Strategies for Qualitative Research.* Chicago: Aldine Pub. Co.

Goffman, E. (1959) *The Presentation of Self in Everyday Life.* New York: Anchor.

Gubrium, J.F. and Holstein, J.A. (2000) *The Self We Live by: Narrative Identity in a Postmodern World.* New York: Oxford University Press.

Hallowell, A.I. (1955) *Culture and Experience.* Philadelphia: University of Pennsylvania Press.

Hewitt, J.P. (1989) *Dilemmas of the American Self.* Philadelphia: Temple University Place.

IBM (2008) *Making Change Work.* New York: IBM.

Kondo, D. (1997) *About Face: Performing Race in Fashion and Theatre.* New York and London: Routledge.

Levy, R. (1973) *Tahitians: Mind and Experience in the Society Islands.* Chicago: University of Chicago Press.

Lock. M. (1993) *Encounters with Aging: Mythologies of Menopause in Japan and North America.* Berkeley: University of California Press.

Malinowski, B. (1927) *Sex and Repression in Savage Society.* London: Routledge and Kegan Paul.

Marcus G.E. and Fischer M.J. (1986) *Anthropology as Cultural Critique: An Experimental Moment in the Human Sciences.* Chicago and London: The University of Chicago Press.

Mauss, M. (1985) (1938) Category of the person: The notion of person, The notion of self. In: M. Carrithers, S. Collins, and S. Lukes (eds) *The Category of the Person: Anthropology, Philosophy, History*. Cambridge and New York: Cambridge University Press.

Mead, G.H. (1934) *Mind, Self and Society*. Chicago: University Chicago Press.

Minuchin, S. (1974) *Families and Family Therapy*. Cambridge, MA.: Harvard University Press.

Morgeson, F.P. (2005) The external leadership of self-managing teams: Intervening in the context of novel and disruptive events. *Journal of Applied Psychology*, 90, 497–508.

Myers, F. (1979) Emotions and the self: A theory of personhood and political order among Pintupi Aborigines. *Ethos*. 7, 343–70.

Passmore, J. (ed.) (2008) *Psychometrics in Coaching: Using Psychological and Psychometrics Tools for Development*. London: Kogan Page.

Rosaldo, M. (1980) *Knowledge and Passion: Ilongot Notions of Self and Social Life*. Cambridge: Cambridge University Press.

Rosenberg, M. (1981) The self-concept: Social product and social force. In: M. Rosenberg and R. Turner (eds) *Social Psychology: Sociological Perspectives*. New York: Basic Books. pp. 593–624.

Rosenberger, N.R. (1989) Dialectic balance in the polar model of self: The Japanese case. *Ethos*. 17, 88–113.

Sieler, A. and Drake, D. (2011) Ontological Coaching. In: E. Cox, T. Bachkirova, and D. Clutterbuck (eds) *The Complete Handbook of Coaching*. London: Sage Publications. pp. 107–19.

Stryker, S. (1980) *Symbolic Interactionism: A Social Structural Version*. Menlo Park: CA: Benjamin/Cumings.

Stryker, S. and Burke, P.J. (2000) The past, present and future of an identity theory. *Social Psychology Quarterly*, 63, 284–97.

Tajfel, H. (1974) Social identity and intergroup behaviour. *Social Science Information*, 13, 65–93.

Weick, K. E. and Ashford, S.J. (2001) Learning in organizations. In: F.M. Jablin and L.L. Putnam (eds) *The New Handbook of Organizational Communication: Advances in Theory, Research, and Methods*. Thousand Oaks, CA: Sage. pp. 704–31.

# 5

# Coaching Ethics

## Rodney L. Lowman

## Introduction

By most standards, coaching practice has greatly exceeded empirical research addressing its effectiveness. From whatever professional discipline one comes to coaching its practice currently rests more on lore, prescription, and conventions than on any extensive body of solid scientific evidence (although that evidence is beginning to grow; see, for example, Peltier, 2010; Stober and Grant, 2006; various articles in *Consulting Psychology Journal: Practice and Research* and in some of the emerging journals that specialize in coaching, such as *International Coaching Psychology Review* and *Coaching: An International Journal*). This raises a fundamental question: what is the most ethical way to proceed when practice exceeds science? To what extent can the ethical procedures useful in other areas of professional practice or from disciplines that were not created with coaching in mind, serve as guides to ethical practice? And, what are the important ethical issues commonly encountered in the practice of coaching?

## Is Coaching a Profession?

Let's start with some basic questions. Is coaching a profession or is it more akin to a set of activities like counseling or psychotherapy that can be performed by persons who come to the activity from different professional backgrounds? I argue for the latter view, but first it is important to consider what constitutes a profession. By most standards, a profession would include among its defining characteristics: mastery of an extensive and usually complex knowledge base typically learned over many years and usually requiring undergraduate and postgraduate university education, professional autonomy with the assumption of self-policing by the profession, an enforced code of ethics, expectation of career-long learning, and a carefully developed supervised experience component of

*The Wiley Blackwell Handbook of the Psychology of Coaching and Mentoring*, First Edition.
Edited by Jonathan Passmore, David B. Peterson, and Teresa Freire.
© 2013 John Wiley & Sons, Ltd. Published 2016 by John Wiley & Sons, Ltd.

training (Elliott, 1972; see Lefkowitz, 2003, for a detailed discussion). Members of a profession are in turn granted respect by society, often allowed to create and to enforce their own rules of conduct, and are generally well compensated for their work.

The American Psychological Association's (APA) Joint Interim Committee for the Identification and Recognition of Specialties and Proficiencies (Joint Interim Committee, 2008) has differentiated between specialties and proficiencies. The Joint Committee defined a *proficiency* "as a circumscribed activity in the general practice of professional psychology or one or more of its specialties that is represented by a distinct procedure, technique, or applied skill set used in psychological assessment, treatment and/or intervention within which one develops competence" (Joint Interim Committee, 1995, unpaginated). A *specialty*, in contrast, was defined by the APA's Joint Interim Committee (2008) as being, "a defined area of psychological practice which requires advanced knowledge and skills acquired through an organized sequence of education and training" (unpaginated). The Joint Interim committee also noted:

> The advanced knowledge and skills specific to a specialty are obtained subsequent to the acquisition of core scientific and professional foundations in psychology ... every defined specialty in professional psychology will contain: (a) core scientific foundations in psychology; (b) a basic professional foundation; (c) advanced scientific and theoretical knowledge germane to the specialty; and (d) advanced professional applications of this knowledge to selected problems and populations in particular settings, through use of procedures and techniques validated on the same. (Joint Interim Committee, 2008, unpaginated)

Although we could debate whether coaching would fit better into the definition of a specialty or a proficiency, or perhaps neither one, it would appear that at present the practice of coaching is more akin to a proficiency than to a specialty, although some have argued that coaching should seek to establish itself as a profession. A proficiency as a stand-alone area of practice brings with it some challenges since, absent mastery of a profession to which the proficiency is additive, some of the assumptions that could otherwise be taken for granted (e.g., mastery of a scientific foundation for practice, science-based practice, socialization in the ethics of a profession) cannot be taken for granted.

I will therefore assert that all those practicing coaching, regardless of their level of prior training or experience in another specialization or profession, need to learn how to incorporate ethics into their coaching practices and that includes those who come to coaching without benefit of any prior professional training. In this chapter I will examine various approaches to the ethical practice of coaching and consider several broad issues that transcend specific areas of professional practice.

## Ethical by What Standard?

Before we begin considering specific practices of coaching and specific ethical standards to guide them, we need first to recognize that there are no ethics codes universally agreed to be applicable for those who practice coaching. There are, however, several codes of practice that can be looked to as guides to ethical professional practice in this area. These include, to name just four, the ethics codes of the American Psychological Association (APA, 2002), the British Psychological Society (BPS, 2009), the Canadian Psychological Association (CPA, 2000) and the International Coaching Federation (ICF, 2008). Of course any country that has a psychological association usually also has a code of ethics so this list is necessarily quite truncated. Fortunately most of the codes cover similar territory, so we can consider broad, overarching ethical issues that transcend specific ethical standards. Still, the approaches of each of these codes to what is ethical and not in coaching will be compared and contrasted.

## American Psychological Association Code of Ethics

The APA is the largest professional association of psychologists in the world. American psychologists who provide coaching services from their roles as psychologists have a very advanced ethics code (Ethical Principles, 2002) widely used as a model for other professional associations. However, the APA Ethics Code (APA Code) only applies to members of the APA and other organizations such as the Society of Industrial-Organizational Psychology (SIOP) that have formally adopted the Code, and to psychologists who are licensed in jurisdictions that incorporate the APA Code into their licensing laws. Nevertheless, the APA code is often seen as a model for identifying ethical standards.

## International Coaching Federation Code of Ethics

The ICF is a professional association dedicated specifically to coaching. It also has a code of ethics, which was developed with just coaching in mind. The ICF Code of Ethics (ICF Code) defines coaching as, "partnering with clients in a thought-provoking and creative process that inspires them to maximize their personal and professional potential" (ICF Code, ICF, 2008, p. 1) a definition that is problematic for a number of reasons, including that it might also define the effects of going to a powerful and impactful movie.

The ICF code identifies a number of ethical standards that specify what the coach can and cannot do. The code also states in its preamble that: "ICF Professional Coaches aspire to conduct themselves in a manner that reflects positively upon the coaching profession; are respectful of different approaches to coaching; and recognize that they are also bound by applicable laws and regulations" (ICF, 2008, p. 1).

## British Psychological Society Code of Ethics

The BPS Code of Ethics and Conduct (BPS, 2009) provides useful perspectives of how psychology ethics from a non-US country may help us think more broadly about ethics and coaching. The BPS code has been recently (2009) revised and covers many of the same areas as the APA code. It includes guidance about the process of ethical decision making, including an interesting discourse on the "British eclectic tradition" and moral reasoning.

> ...' British eclectic tradition'. Moral principles and the codes which spell out their applications can only be guidelines for thinking about the decisions individuals need to make in specific cases. Variable factors are involved such as the particular circumstances, the prevailing law, the cultural context, the likely consequences and the feelings colouring the judgement. However, if moral judgements are to retain some objectivity, that is if they can be judged to be right or wrong, they must be based on rational principles which serve as criteria. (BPS, 2009, p. 4)

Also of note, the BPS code provides some evidence of process guidance for psychologists trying to think through ethical issues. Many of these are found in a valuable section on ethical decision making (pp. 6–9). This includes practical things for psychologists to consider in deciding the appropriate steps to take, including identifying these important aspects of the situation at issue:

- What are the parameters of the situation?
- Is there research evidence that might be relevant?
- What legal guidance exists?
- What do peers advise?
- Is there guidance available from the Health Professions Council or other relevant bodies?

(BPS, 2009, p. 7)

Still, the BPS code does not have much to say directly about the practice of psychology in organizational or coaching contexts. It recognizes, as do most codes, basic principles such as issues involving multiple relationships, confidentiality, and the like, but there is little evidence that this code was written with organizational psychology practice in mind. The BPS code does protect specific "adjectival titles" including "Occupational Psychologist", under which the work of psychologist-coaches might be expected to fall. (Of note, however, all psychologists licensed in Britain are overseen by the Health Professions Council, even when non-health psychology is being practiced.)

## Canadian Psychological Association Code of Ethics

Another useful code is that of the Canadian Psychological Association's (CPA) Code of Ethics (CPA, 2000) Like the APA code, the Canadian code differentiates between broad, overarching principles and specific, enforceable standards. However, unlike the APA code, the CPA code also provides guidelines as to what psychologists should do when their ethical principles conflict in a particular application.

## Overarching Principles and Standards of Ethical Behavior in Coaching

From the time of Plato and Aristotle, ethical principles have dealt with morality, that is, the "right and wrong" thing to do in particular situations or in general. Although various efforts have been made to try to tie ethics to empirical approaches, almost always codes of ethics derive from philosophical underpinnings or pronouncements of the right (and wrong) thing to do. Professional ethics codes differ from generic ones that apply (or aim to apply) to all people and situations in that (1) they are limited to the behavior of professionals when practicing their profession and (2) they represent consensus among experts from that profession about appropriate behavior and about what constitutes misbehavior. There are various underlying philosophical approaches that codes may adopt but they are in each case essentially prescriptive standards or principles of behavior that are acceptable or not under a particular professional code of ethics.

Because most ethical codes in professions whose members practice coaching were not developed with coaching in mind (the exception is the ICF code) we cannot at this time point to one particular code of ethics that would universally be accepted as providing the ethical ground rules for the practice of coaching. Therefore, in this chapter, we will identify some generic principles that apply to coaching and consider the ways in which some representative codes address these issues.

## Scientific and Other Bases for Practice

The APA code requires that psychologists base their work on established scientific and professional knowledge. Its standard 2.04 Bases for Scientific and Professional Judgments states: "Psychologists' work is based upon established scientific and professional knowledge of the discipline" (APA, 2002, p. ).

The code also recognizes, however, that new areas of practice and knowledge emerge over time and, in effect, practice sometimes exceeds research. As the APA ethics code standard 2.01 (e) states: "In those emerging areas in which generally recognized standards for preparatory training do not yet exist, psychologists nevertheless take reasonable steps to ensure the competence of their work and to protect clients/patients, students, supervisees, research participants, organizational clients, and others from harm" (APA, 2002, p. 1064).

Other codes approach new areas of practice similarly to the APA code. The BPS code (BPS, 2009), for example, defines psychology as the "scientific study of behaviour" (p. 6). The Canadian Code (2000) does not address the scientific bases of practice in quite the same way as do the APA or BPS codes. However, it does specify that psychologists "conscientiously [apply] the ethical principles and values of the code to new and emerging areas of activity." Standard IV.3 requires that psychologists must: "Keep informed of progress in their area(s) of psychological activity, take this progress into account in their work, and try to make their own contributions to this progress" (CPA, 2000, p. 29). The ICF code (2008) does not explicitly address the issue of a scientific basis for coaching practice.

If, as I argue, there is not yet a sufficient scientific basis to define the practice of coaching (see also Gregory *et al.*, 2011), ethical issues still need to be confronted about what constitutes appropriate practice and appropriate preparation for coaching practice. Specific ethical issues include: is there enough current knowledge to justify practice?; is there an ethical obligation to base practice only on scientifically-validated findings?; what obligations does the professional coach have to keep up with the professional and scientific literature?; and happens when the literature does not support the practices that are assumed to be correct?

## Eight Generic Ethical Principles

It is not possible to identify all ethical issues that can arise in the practice of coaching. Prior efforts have helped to identify themes (see, for example, Lowman, 2006; Passmore, 2009) of ethical issues that arise in coaching, and casebooks have helped highlight some of the predictable areas that coaching ethics have to address. Here we examine eight such areas.

## Ethical Principle 1: Competence

Competence is an ethical requirement in most professional codes of ethics. The idea is that professionals need to practice their profession competently and well and usually on the basis of established knowledge – scientific and professional. This implies, of course, that there is consensus among competent professionals about the nature of competent professional behavior, that is, agreement on the desired competences of practicing professionals. The standard also suggests that competences are specific to a type of activity and to application of the competences to individuals or groups with whom they are trained and experienced.

The APA Ethical Principles (2002) specify in Standard 2.01a Boundaries of Competence: "Psychologists provide services, teach, and conduct research with populations and in areas only within the boundaries of their competence, based on their education, training, supervised experience, consultation, study, or professional experience" (p. 1063).

The BPS code charges psychologists to, "engage in additional areas of professional activity only after obtaining the knowledge, skill, training, education, and experience necessary for competent functioning" (Standard 2.3 (v), p. 16) and to: "Remain aware of and acknowledge the limits of their methods, as well as the limits of the conclusions that may be derived from such methods under different circumstances and for different purposes" (Standard 2.3 (vi), p. 17).

The Canadian Code (2000) in its "Responsible Caring" principle (II) includes the following statement: "Psychologists recognize the need for competence and self-knowledge. They consider incompetent action to be unethical per se, as it is unlikely to be of benefit and likely to be harmful. They engage only in those activities in which they have competence or for which they are receiving supervision, and they perform their activities as competently as possible" (p. 15). Those covered by the Canadian Code are also mandated in Standard 4 of Principle III (Integrity) to: "Maintain competence in their declared area(s) of psychological competence, as well as in their current area(s) of activity" (p. 23).

The ICF Code (2008) is a bit more elusive in its approach to competence but does note in its Standard 14 that the ICF coach, "will not give my prospective clients or sponsors information or advice ... know[n] or believe[d] to be misleading or false" (p. 3).

The following sample case is illustrative.

Case 1: Competence of coaches.

*Description of the case.* An executive coach came to coaching from another line of work. He had spent much of his career in commercial real estate. After two decades in that field he was bored and a bit depressed. He sought out the help of an executive coach who helped him better understand the sources of his unhappiness. Always good with people and always good in sales, he became inspired by his own coaching experience to start a coaching practice. At first he focused on helping other realtors be more effective in their sales, but in time he expanded his practice to others who were experiencing sales slumps and then to include a variety of other difficulties. He wrote a popular self-help book with a jazzy title and had no shortage of clients. He received no training in the field nor did he read the literature other than some popular self-help books on coaching.

*Interpretation.* To the extent that a real estate expert limited his consultation to helping other realtors become more effective in sales there might not be much of a concern about competence in this case. However, to pursue a new career in coaching, spanning a diversity of problems, and seeking no training in the new profession, suggests that competence was likely lacking in the new coaching roles. The failure to properly prepare for the new career, to be supervised in his new work or to read the literature suggests that the coach was not competent in the new profession even though his clients may have been satisfied with his work with them.

# Ethical Principle 2: Do No Harm

Most professional ethics codes, dating back to early versions of the physicians' Hippocratic Oath, state that the professional must do not harm to a client. The Hippocratic oath stated: "I will prescribe regimens for the good of my patients according to my ability and my judgment and never do harm to anyone" (Edelstein *et al.*, 1987, p. 6).

This issue is made explicit in the APA code, which states in its Standard 3.04 Avoiding Harm: "Psychologists take reasonable steps to avoid harming their clients/patients, students, supervisees, research participants, organizational clients, and others with whom they work, and to minimize harm where it is foreseeable and unavoidable" (Ethical Principles, APA, 2002, p. 1065).

The BPS code (2009) also articulates avoidance of harm to clients as both a value and expected behavior. Its Standard 3.1 mandates that psychologists: "Avoid harming clients, but take into account that the interests of different clients may conflict. The psychologist will need to weigh these interests and the potential harm caused by alternative courses of action or inaction" (p. 18). Here the focus is on harm avoidance but the standard introduces appropriate complexity as to what that entails.

The Canadian Code also mandates professionals do no harm. As it states: "A basic ethical expectation of any discipline is that its activities will benefit members of society or, at least, do no harm" (CPA, 2000, p. 15). The code explicitly mandates in its Ethical Standard II.2: "Avoid doing harm to clients, research participants, employees, supervisees, students, trainees, colleagues, and others" (p. 16). The Canadian Code goes on to elaborate a more nuanced model, balancing potential harm and potential gain. It states: "Responsible caring leads psychologists to take care to discern the potential harm and benefits involved, to predict the likelihood of their occurrence, to proceed only if the potential benefits outweigh the potential harms, to develop and use methods that will minimize harms and maximize benefits, and to take responsibility for correcting clearly harmful effects that have occurred as a direct result of their research, teaching, practice, or business activities" (CPA, 2000, p. 14).

Except for a statement on avoiding harm in research, the ICF Code does not directly specify the "do no harm" construct.

Here is a case that illustrates this concept.


Case 2: Avoiding harm.
*Description of the case.* A coach was working with a high level executive. The coach had been hired by the senior executive to whom the person being coached reported. The coach proceeded in good faith with the assignment, collecting 360-degree feedback and holding weekly sessions. The coaching had been presented to the coach as having been developmental ("to smooth out some rough edges"). The coaching seemed to be proceeding well and a plan had been developed to gather follow-up data to assess changes in the person being coached. After a few months of coaching, the coach received a call from a senior executive in the company's corporate offices who indicated the company had collected data (without knowledge of the coach or the coach's client) and "a decision had been made" to terminate the executive. The executive contacted the coach for information about what had happened. The coach had no idea.

*Interpretation.* In this case, it was not the coach who caused harm to the client but others in the institution. The coach had proceeded in good faith with a coaching assignment. However, others in the corporation made the decision to fire the executive despite the progress being made in coaching. At the point of learning of the termination the coach could attempt to minimize damage to the client from the termination, protect the good name of coaching by assuring the client that whoever made the decision did it without input from the coach, and help the client plan the next steps and to learn from the experience.

# Ethical Principle 3: Integrity

Integrity issues are almost always addressed in professional ethics codes. Integrity in professional ethics speaks to such factors as honesty and trustworthiness, a basic virtue found in most codes of ethics and in most professional codes of ethics. The virtue approach to ethics is based on the idea of character. For our purposes, Lefkowtiz's (2003) definition is helpful: character is "the relatively stable dispositional aspects of personality that account for relatively consistent attitudes and behavioral tendencies across a variety of circumstances" (p. 148). Although character may not be trainable (see, for example, Bersoff, 1996) professional ethics do not specify one's character outside the work environment, but they do require character ethics throughout one's professional activities. Integrity requires telling the truth, not misleading, and doing what one says one will do.

The APA Ethical Principles (2002, p. 1062) includes aspirational Principle C, Integrity, which states: "Psychologists seek to promote accuracy, honesty, and truthfulness in the science, teaching, and practice of psychology. In these activities psychologists do not steal, cheat, or engage in fraud, subterfuge, or intentional misrepresentation of fact. Psychologists strive to keep their promises and to avoid unwise or unclear commitments." These principles find their way into many aspects of the (enforceable) standards of the APA code.

The BPS Code (2008) includes a major section on integrity that articulates the following value: "Psychologists value honesty, accuracy, clarity, and fairness in their interactions with all persons, and seek to promote integrity in all facets of their scientific and professional endeavours" (p. 21). This Code goes on to define four very specific requirements organized around the following four themes: honesty and accuracy, avoiding of exploitation and conflicts of interest, maintaining professional boundaries, and addressing ethical misconduct.

The Canadian Code is similarly replete with integrity obligations. Although this Code has 40 specific standards in its Principle III, Integrity in Relationships, its general statement captures the essence of the ethical expectations. That Principle notes:

> The relationships formed by psychologists in the course of their work embody explicit and implicit mutual expectations of integrity that are vital to the advancement of scientific knowledge and to the maintenance of public confidence in the discipline of psychology. These expectations include: accuracy and honesty; straightforwardness and openness; the maximization of objectivity and minimization of bias; and, avoidance of conflicts of interest. Psychologists have a responsibility to meet these expectations and to encourage reciprocity. [These include] accuracy, honesty, [and] the obvious prohibitions of fraud or misrepresentation. (CPA, 2000, p. 22)

The ICF Code has a number of standards relating to integrity. These include: Section 1: Professional Conduct At Large "(1) I will not knowingly make any public statement that is untrue or misleading about what I offer as a coach, or make false claims in any written documents relating to the coaching profession or my credentials or the ICF. (2) I will accurately identify my coaching qualifications, expertise, experience, certifications and ICF Credentials" (ICF, 2008, p. 1). Section 3 in the ICF Code, Professional Conduct with Clients, includes the following standards: "(13) I will not knowingly mislead or make false claims about what my client or sponsor will receive from the coaching process or from me as the coach …(15) I will have clear agreements or contracts with my clients and sponsor(s). I will honor all agreements or contracts made in the context of professional coaching relationships" (ICF, 2008, p. 3).

The following case is illustrative of this principle.

Case 3: Integrity.

*Description of the case.* Marlon had a coaching practice. He was referred a case by a colleague with whom he frequently made referrals when either of them was too busy or did not want to work with a particular client. The referred individual was an articulate and somewhat aggressive manager who had been referred for coaching by her boss after several complaints about her managerial style. She asked the coach how many cases like hers he had coached and his success record in working with them. He said that he had seen "at least 100" such individuals and that all of them had turned out well. In fact, he exaggerated both the number of such clients he had seen and never bothered to follow up with his clients after they ended their coaching so he had no idea about his ultimate effectiveness with his clients.

*Interpretation.* In his efforts to get the referral, the coach lied about his experience and outcome results. By almost any ethical standard of integrity, including the four reviewed here, he behaved unethically and further materially influenced the client's decision making about working with him in a way that was problematic.

# Ethical Principle 4: Informed Consent

Informed consent refers to the process by which coaching clients have the right to agree to services that are provided to them and to know before agreeing what is expected, the known or anticipated risks and any limitations on possible implicit expectations, such as restrictions or possible compromises to confidentiality or a duty to report information (e.g., threat to harm oneself or others) that is mandated by law to be reported. Consent also applies to participation in research about coaching. Albala *et al.* (2010) described the evolution of consent forms for research over time and note some serious ethical breaches that have occurred in not disclosing known risks to participation in research.

The APA Ethical Principles (2002) Standard 3.10 is entitled "Informed Consent" but is only one of several sections in the code addressing relevant issues. Standard 3.10 (a) states: "When psychologists conduct research or provide assessment, therapy, counseling, or consulting services in person or via electronic transmission or other forms of communication, they obtain the informed consent of the individual or individuals using language that is reasonably understandable to that person or persons except when conducting such activities without consent is mandated by law or governmental regulation or as otherwise provided in this Ethics Code." Section (d) of this standard also notes: Psychologists appropriately document written or oral consent, permission, and assent" (APA, 2002, p. 1065).

The BPS Code (2008) includes a lengthy standard, 1.4, under the general heading of Respect that deals specifically with informed consent (BPS, 2008, pp. 12–14). The standard says, in particular, that psychologists are mandated to: "Ensure that clients, particularly children and vulnerable adults, are given ample opportunity to understand the nature, purpose, and anticipated consequences of any professional services or research participation, so that they may give informed consent to the extent that their capabilities allow" (p. 12). However, there is nothing in this part of the BPS code to suggest that the issues of coaching – or corporate consultations in general – have been thought through by the BPS code.

The Canadian Code (2000) addresses informed consent issues in its "Principle I: Respect for the Dignity of Person". There are 16 specific standards in this section of the Canadian code just on informed consent, 12 under the heading "Informed Consent" and the other 4 under a section labeled "Freedom of Consent". The former includes two important standards: " I.16 Seek as full and active participation as possible from others in decisions that affect them, respecting and integrating as much as possible their opinions and wishes." And, "I.17 Recognize that informed consent is the result of a process of reaching an agreement to work collaboratively, rather than of simply having a consent form signed" (p. 10).

"Freedom of Consent" addresses issues of whether the consent was truly voluntary rather than coerced. The Canadian Code in this section also specifies that, once given, consent may be withdrawn at any time, when it states that the psychologist must respect, "the right of persons to discontinue participation or service at any time, and be responsive to non-verbal indications of a desire to discontinue if a person has difficulty with verbally communicating such a desire (e.g., young children, verbally disabled persons) or, due to culture, is unlikely to communicate such a desire orally" (p. 15).

The ICF Code (2008) addresses informed consent in the standards in its Section 3, Professional Conduct with Clients, which state: "(15) I will have clear agreements or contracts with my clients and sponsor(s)" and "(16) I will carefully explain and strive to ensure that, prior to or at the initial meeting, my coaching client and sponsor(s) understand the nature of coaching, the nature and limits of confidentiality, financial arrangements, and any other terms of the coaching agreement or contract" (p. 3).

Each of these codes in this case is quite clear in its general intent. Voluntary consent with as complete information as possible is ethically mandated before undertaking coaching engagements. Such consent must clearly establish the rights, roles, and responsibilities for both the client and sponsor if they are not the same persons. At times this process is straightforward but at other times not. It is rarely possible in coaching contexts to anticipate all the things that could possibly happen during the course of an engagement.

Ethical issues abound in applying these standards and principles to coaching in organizational contexts. What constitutes informed consent when more than one party is involved (e.g., both a person being coached and the person's boss)? Is formal, written consent required? What issues need to be addressed in informed consent when every possibility can rarely be anticipated in advance? What happens to consent in a situation when coaching is, in effect, forced on a client? The following case is illustrative of the importance of some of these issues.

Case 4: Informed consent.

*Description of the case.* Hank was referred to a coach because of problems on the job. He had been put in an impossible managerial situation in which he was to lead a turnaround of a troubled division but his subordinates were given carte blanche access to his supervisors to complain about every initiative he had undertaken. His boss, tired of the complaints, insisted that Hank get some coaching help. He had little interest in receiving coaching and felt the problem was with his boss but, to minimize conflict, he agreed to go along with it. The coach obtained a signed consent form before beginning the coaching and proceeded, unaware that his "client" had little interest in being coached.

*Interpretation.* Voluntary consent, as the Canadian code notes, is not simply about signing a form to go into the record. In coaching with parties other than the coachee involved, coaching may not be truly voluntary. It is up to the coach to explore with the potential client whether coaching has, in effect, been forced and, if so, what the individual wants to do about it. Consent in coaching in organizational contexts is particularly rife with situations in which "voluntary" consent is compromised.

## Ethical Principle 5: Avoiding or Effectively Managing Multiple Relationships

Because multiple relationships are the rule rather than the exception in coaching in organizational contexts, those involved in coaching need to understand how having dual or multiple parties involved in coaching affects the nature of the intervention. The need to identify obligations and mutual expectations up front is an ethical one. At the least, explicit rules of engagement need to be articulated at the start of the coaching.

The APA Ethical Principles (2002) has a standard, 3.05, on multiple relationships. It states:

> (a) A multiple relationship occurs when a psychologist is in a professional role with a person and (1) at the same time is in another role with the same person, (2) at the same time is in a relationship with a person closely associated with or related to the person with whom the psychologist has the professional relationship, or (3) promises to enter into another relationship in the future with the person or a person closely associated with or related to the person. A psychologist refrains from entering into a multiple relationship if the multiple relationship could reasonably be expected to impair the psychologist's objectivity, competence, or effectiveness in performing his or her functions as a psychologist, or otherwise risks exploitation or harm to the person with whom the professional relationship exists. Multiple relationships that would not reasonably be expected to cause impairment or risk exploitation or harm are not unethical.
>
> Standard 3.05 (b) notes that if a "potentially harmful" relationship develops "due to unforeseen factors, the psychologist takes reasonable steps to resolve it with due regard for the best interests of the affected person and maximal compliance with the Ethics Code" (p. 1065).

The BPS code (2008) includes a separate standard on multiple relationships. 4.2 Standard of avoiding exploitation and conflicts of interest. Reasonably, psychologists are ethically mandated by this code to "(i) Remain aware of the problems that may result from dual or multiple relationships" (p. 22), but none of the examples noted by the Standard cover anything related to organizational consulting or coaching. Nonetheless, psychologists are mandated by the BPS Code to: "(iii) clarify for clients and other relevant parties the professional roles currently assumed and conflicts of interest that might potentially arise" (p. 22). In an interesting final point, the BPS code raises the requirement that psychologists must: "Recognise that conflicts of interests and inequity of power may still reside after professional relationships are formally terminated, such that professional responsibilities may still apply" (p. 22). This suggests that conflicts of interest may outlast a professional's relationship even when the engagement is apparently over. The Canadian Code (2000) explicitly addresses multiple relationships as a subset of conflicts of interests. Its Standard III.33 mandates psychologists to: "Avoid dual or multiple relationships (e.g., with clients, research participants, employees, supervisees, students, or trainees) and other situations that might present a conflict of interest or that might reduce their ability to be objective and unbiased in their determinations of what might be in the best interests of others. The code does not rule out dual/multiple relationships but does state in Standard III.34 that psychologists: "Manage dual or multiple relationships that are unavoidable due to cultural norms or other circumstances in such a manner that bias, lack of objectivity, and risk of exploitation are minimized. This might include obtaining ongoing supervision or consultation for the duration of the dual or multiple relationship, or involving a third party in obtaining consent (e.g., approaching a client or employee about becoming a research participant)" (p. 27).

The ICF Code (2008) provides some interesting definitions of client ("the person(s) being coached") and "sponsor", "the entity (including its representatives) paying for and/ or arranging for the coaching services to be provided" (p. 1). The code further elaborates that "the 'client' is the person(s) being coached" and that "The 'sponsor' is the entity (including its representatives) paying for and/or arranging for coaching services to be provided" (p. 1). This generally helpful distinction is a good start in recognizing that multiple parties are often involved in a coaching engagement. However, such definitions do not begin to describe all possible multiple relationships that may arise in the course of coaching. The ICF Code does address an issue also elaborated in the APA and Canadian codes by stating explicitly as an ethical standard "(18) I will not become sexually intimate with any of my current clients or sponsors" (ICF Code, 2008, p. 3).

Case 5: Multiple relationships.

*Description of the case.* A male coach was coaching a female executive on some issues related to her style and presentation. The client suggested that, since her schedule was very crowded, they meet over dinner. The coach explained that confidentiality might be violated if they were to meet in a public place. The executive suggested they meet at her home for dinner. Over the course of the dinner the executive suggested that she had begun to develop feelings for the coach and suggested they consider a romantic relationship.

*Interpretation.* A romantic relationship, sexual or otherwise, between a coach and a client would constitute an undesirable and entirely avoidable multiple relationship. Nor would it be sufficient to simply stop the coaching relationship and to begin a romantic one. In this case, the decision to go to a client's home for a business meeting was probably ill advised. When the client's intentions were noted, the coach would not only have to decline the romantic involvement but also to determine the impact of the suggestion of the coach's ability to be effective with this client.

# Ethical Principle 6: Confidentiality

Ethical obligations include the need to protect confidentiality of communication between the professional and the person being coached and to make clear at the beginning of the consultation (or as an issue arises during the coaching) what exceptions may exist to confidentiality. Unless one is practicing coaching as a licensed professional whose communications with clients are legally protected, confidentiality cannot be assured or promised. In coaching in job contexts, there may also be exceptions to confidentiality.

A coach who does not have a professional license that confers privilege (i.e., the right not to disclose information shared in confidence in a coaching engagement) cannot promise confidentiality.

The APA Code (2002) discusses confidentiality obligations in several standards. APA Ethical Standard 4.01 Maintaining Confidentiality states: "Psychologists have a primary obligation and take reasonable precautions to protect confidential information obtained through or stored in any medium, recognizing that the extent and limits of confidentiality may be regulated by law or established by institutional rules or professional or scientific relationship" (APA, 2002, p. 1066). The code also mandates (in its Standard 4.02) that " (a) Psychologists discuss with persons … and organizations with whom they establish a scientific or professional relationship (1) the relevant limits of confidentiality and (2) the fore-seeable uses of the information generated through their psychological activities" (p. 1066).

The BPS Code (2008) mandates that psychologists: "Normally obtain the consent of clients who are considered legally competent or their duly authorised representatives, for disclosure of confidential information (p. 10). Although the espoused standards are reasonable in the clinical context, there is no elaboration of how this ethical mandate is to be carried out in the coaching context.

The Canadian Code (2000) discusses confidentiality in several parts of the code, including those on informed consent. Three specific ethical standards are noted in the section that elaborates confidentiality, including 1.45 "Share confidential information with others only with the informed consent of those involved, or in a manner that the persons involved cannot be identified, except as required or justified by law, or in circumstances of actual or possible serious physical harm or death" (p. 13).

The ICF Code (2008) includes the following standards: "(7) I will maintain, store, and dispose of any records created during my coaching business in a manner that promotes confidentiality, security, and privacy, and complies with any applicable laws and agreements" (p. 2), and, "(22) I will maintain the strictest levels of confidentiality with all client and sponsor information. I will have a clear agreement or contract before releasing information to another person, unless required by law; (23) I will have a clear agreement upon how coaching information will be exchanged among coach, client, and sponsor; (24) When acting as a trainer of student coaches, I will clarify confidentiality policies with the students" (pp. 3–4).

Coaches should not promise confidentiality (or leave the client assuming that anything said will remain confidential) if that promise cannot be assured. Reports of coaching also raise issues about ethical treatment of their content. Who "owns" the notes and reports on a client's progress and what information can be shared in billing, are exemplary of the issues of confidentiality that need to be sorted out in advance of the coaching engagement. Also, if a coach is not licensed in a profession that includes privilege (essentially, the legal right of a client not to have information revealed in treatment released without consent) the coach should make this known at the outset of the coaching.

Case 6: Confidentiality.

*Description of the case.* A senior executive received feedback from an assessment program held prior to implementing a coaching program in a major corporation. The assessments were to be for purposes of development. One of the coaches working on the project with relevant training in assessment and a relevant license to practice in this area provided feedback to the executive who was highly upset with the results. He attacked the process and the conclusions. Consistent with the agreed upon plan, a copy of the assessment report went to the individual and a copy went to the Talent Management office in the company. The executive refused to participate in the coaching program. Somehow, the results of the assessment, and the executive's reaction to it, became widely known among the senior executives who worked with the individual as well as the executive's boss. Shortly thereafter, the executive was fired, largely for concerns similar to those raised in the assessment. The coach proceeded with the intervention program as planned.

*Interpretation.* Confidentiality in a coaching context is a critical component in establishing trust, a necessary ingredient for successful personal coaching. In psychotherapy the rules of engagement are well defined and confidentiality is expected and usually required. In coaching, there are many threats to confidentiality, particularly when coaching is done in the context of "live" organizations. In this case, it is difficult to know what actually happened such that presumably confidential information became publicly known. Perhaps it was the assessee himself who complained to others about the assessment process and his refusal to participate in the coaching. Perhaps providing a copy of the report to someone in the company compromised confidentiality.

The coach in this case faced a difficult situation. Because confidentiality had been compromised, it would be difficult to proceed with the coaching engagement without re-assessing the procedures that were being used in the coaching engagement. Frank conversations with those executives in positions of authority over this project would be needed to dissect what had happened and how the potential damage to the assumptions of confidentiality could be repaired before proceeding with the intervention. No coach can predict everything that might happen even when an intervention is carefully planned. As unforeseen compromises to basic ethical principles arise, the coach has an ethical responsibility to determine what happened and why, to take corrective action, and to minimize damage, including to the reputation of coaching.

## Ethical Principle 7: Conflicts of Interest

Conflicts of interest in coaching include situations in which the coach has a vested interest in the outcome of a particular coaching engagement that may be incompatible with the needs of the client or in which a conflict of interest clouds judgment. Conflicts of interest are not per se ethically forbidden in most codes of ethics but they must be identified and managed. In general, they are to be avoided altogether.

The APA Ethical Principles (2002) Principle B, Fidelity and Responsibility, includes the following statement: "Psychologists uphold professional standards of conduct, clarify their professional roles and obligations, accept appropriate responsibility for their behavior, and seek to manage conflicts of interest that could lead to exploitation or harm" (p. 1062). This principle is operationalized in Standard 3.06 Conflict of Interest: "Psychologists refrain from taking on a professional role when personal, scientific, professional, legal, financial, or other interests or relationships could reasonably be expected to (1) impair their objectivity, competence, or effectiveness in performing their functions as psychologists or (2) expose the person or organization with whom the professional relationship exists to harm or exploitation" (p. 1065).

The BPS Code (2008) Standard 4.2 identifies the need to avoid exploitation and conflicts of interest Beyond the issue of multiple relationships already discussed, the BPS Code addresses several aspects of conflicts of interest. A general guideline is well stated: Psychologists "avoid forming relationships that may impair professional objectivity or otherwise lead to exploitation of or conflicts of interest with a client." As with some of the other codes, the psychologist bound by the BPS Code has a pro-active responsibility to: "Clarify for clients and other relevant parties the professional roles currently assumed and conflicts of interest that might potentially arise," and must: "Refrain from abusing professional relationships in order to advance their sexual, personal, financial, or other interests" (p. 22).

The Canadian Code (2000) contextualizes conflicts of interest in its Principle III: Integrity in Relationships: "The relationships formed by psychologists in the course of their work embody explicit and implicit mutual expectations of integrity that are vital to the advancement of scientific knowledge and to the maintenance of public confidence in the discipline of psychology. These expectations include: accuracy and honesty; straightforwardness and openness; the maximization of objectivity and minimization of bias; and, avoidance of conflicts of interest" (p. 22). Five specific standards are elaborated concerning conflicts of interest in this code, which also include multiple and dual relationships. One of these, Standard III.3, mandates that psychologists must not:

> Exploit any relationship established as a psychologist to further personal, political, or business interests at the expense of the best interests of their clients, research participants, students, employers, or others. This includes, but is not limited to: soliciting clients of one's employing agency for private practice; taking advantage of trust or dependency to encourage or engage in sexual intimacies (e.g., with clients not included in Standard II.27, with clients' partners or relatives, with students or trainees not included in Standard II.28, or with research participants); taking advantage of trust or dependency to frighten clients into receiving services; …giving or receiving kickbacks or bonuses for referrals; seeking or accepting loans or investments from clients; and, prejudicing others against a colleague for reasons of personal gain. (p. 26)

The ICF Code (2008) states in its Section 1: "(4) I will, at all times, strive to recognize personal issues that may impair, conflict, or interfere with my coaching performance or my professional coaching relationships. Whenever the facts and circumstances necessitate, I will promptly seek professional assistance and determine the action to be taken, including whether it is appropriate to suspend or terminate my coaching relationship(s)." Section 2 of the code includes four standards related to conflicts of interest:

> (9) I will seek to avoid conflicts of interest and potential conflicts of interest and openly disclose any such conflicts. I will offer to remove myself when such a conflict arises; (10) I will disclose to my client and his or her sponsor all anticipated compensation from third parties that I may pay or receive for referrals of that client; (11) I will only barter for services, goods or other non-monetary remuneration when it will not impair the coaching relationship; (12) I will not knowingly take any personal, professional, or monetary advantage or benefit of the coach-client relationship, except by a form of compensation as agreed in the agreement or contract. (p. 2)

Conceptually, then, conflicts of interest are to be avoided because they can cloud professional judgment and they result in the needs of the coach taking precedence over the needs of the client. Anytime a coach finds her/himself in a situation where personal interests stand to cloud judgment it is time to step back and correct the situation. At the least, the conflict needs to be acknowledged and managed.

Case 7: Conflicts of interest.
*Description of the case.* A well-known coach appeared on a television talk show in which he made it clear that he had been called in to coach a major elected government figure during a difficult and highly publicized period in the individual's personal life. This occurred while the individual was still in office. The talk show host asked about the advice he had given to the individual and the coach responded that his advice was confidential.
*Interpretation.* Bragging about providing coaching services to a nationally prominent figure in a highly visible context undermines the integrity of all coaching. It can be argued that the coach behaved unethically by indicating the identity of his client, even if that information was first revealed by the television host. The appropriate response when asked to confirm whether

indeed he had provided coaching services to the famous figure should have been: "I do not discuss the identity of my coaching clients." By acknowledging that he had provided such services, the coach indulged in a conflict of interest between his own desire for publicity or recognition and the needs of his client. Even if the client had given permission for the client–coach relationship to be revealed, it would have been ethically inappropriate to have discussed even the existence of the relationship in so public a context because it was likely to have been based more on the needs of the coach than then needs of his client (see, for example, Law, 2010).

## Ethical Principle 8: Being Multiculturally and Internationally Competent

Coaching skills cannot be expected to generalize to all types of clients. The extent to which the coaching professional is competent in working with clients of different ethnicities, sexual orientation, gender, or nationality require careful consideration in order to ensure that the practice is competent and ethical.

The APA Ethical Principles (2002) Principle E, Respect for People's Rights and Dignity, states that:

> Psychologists are aware of and respect cultural, individual, and role differences, including those based on age, gender, gender identity, race, ethnicity, culture, national origin, religion, sexual orientation, disability, language, and socioeconomic status and consider these factors when working with members of such groups. Psychologists try to eliminate the effect on their work of biases based on those factors, and they do not knowingly participate in or condone activities of others based upon such prejudices. (p. 1063).

The APA has also promulgated multicultural guidelines for use in education, training, research, practice, and organizational change (APA, 2003; see also Lowman, 2013).

The BPS Code's (2008) Standard of General Respect provides a proactive admonition for respecting cultural differences, not just a admonition not to disparage or discriminate. It states: "Psychologists should: (i) Respect individual, cultural and role differences, including (but not exclusively) those involving age, disability, education, ethnicity, gender, language, national origin, race, religion, sexual orientation, marital or family status and socio-economic status" (p. 10).

The Canadian Code (2000) specifies:

> Psychologists accept as fundamental the principle of respect for the dignity of persons; that is, the belief that each person should be treated primarily as a person or an end in him/herself, not as an object or a means to an end. In so doing, psychologists acknowledge that all persons have a right to have their innate worth as human beings appreciated and that this worth is not dependent upon their culture, nationality, ethnicity, colour, race, religion, sex, gender, marital status, sexual orientation, physical or mental abilities, age, socio-economic status, or any other preference or personal characteristic, condition, or status. (p. 8)

The Canadian Code's Principle I, Respect for the Dignity of Persons, includes ethical Standard, which states: "1.2 Not engage publicly (e.g., in public statements, presentations, research reports, or with clients) in degrading comments about others, including demeaning jokes based on such characteristics as culture, nationality, ethnicity, colour, race, religion, sex, gender, or sexual orientation" (p. 9).

The ICF Code (2008) does not address these issues except for the following standard in its Section 3: Professional Conduct with Clients: "(17) I will be responsible for setting clear, appropriate, and culturally sensitive boundaries that govern any physical contact I may have with my clients or sponsors" (ICF Code, 2008, p. 3).

Case 8: Multicultural competence.

*Description of the case.* An executive coach was hired to work with the senior management team of a medium-sized corporation. Those to be coached included two women and an African American male. The coach, a solo practitioner, was asked by these individuals if they could work with, respectively, a female or African American male. The coach, a white male, indicated that he had been working in this area for 30 years and he felt confident he could help them.

*Interpretation.* The coach erred in not further exploring the issues raised by the women and African American male. Bringing in other relevant coaches to assist with the project would probably have been a desirable course of action in this case, even if the coach's profits were lessened. Multicultural competence does not mean that every client must be matched with a comparable service provider. However, access to a competent and diverse staff is highly desired when working with a diverse population. At the least, the multiculturally/internationally competent coach will recognize the issues and explore them as appropriate with clients before making a decision on how best to proceed.

## Consequences of Unethical Behavior

What happens when a professional coach behaves unethically? The ICF requires members to take a pledge to honor ethical and legal obligations to coaching clients and sponsors. "If I breach this Pledge of Ethics or any part of the ICF Code of Ethics," the ICF Code (2008) states, "I agree that the ICF in its sole discretion may hold me accountable for so doing. I further agree that my accountability to the ICF for any breach may include sanctions, such as loss of my ICF membership and/or my ICF Credentials" (p. 4). For psychologists or other professionals required to be licensed, ethical violations can result in expulsion from their professional associations or, in the case of serious violations, they may lose their license and their economic livelihood. It is also worth noting that both the APA (2002) and the Canadian (2000) codes require psychologists encountering unethical behavior by other psychologists to take appropriate action to confront the apparent violation or, in certain circumstances, to report the problematic behavior. Professions take ethics seriously and set up a mechanism by which charges of ethical violations can be addressed.

## Emerging Literature on Coaching Ethics

As the field of coaching has expanded and developed new journals, a literature on the ethics of coaching has slowly begun to emerge (see, for example, Allan *et al.*, 2011; Brenan and Wildflower, 2010; Passmore, 2011; Williams and Anderson, 2006). Some of these studies are empirically based, attempting to understand how samples of coaches view various ethical issues. Others, more typically, are more theoretical. Ethics, of course, has both theoretical and empirical aspects (see Lefkowtiz, 2003; Lefkowitz and Lowman, 2010).

To date, most of the empirical research on ethics has been done on business ethics and ethical issues in organizational contexts. Business ethics, in particular, has become an important topic in empirical research. This literature has explored such topics as the role of individual, group, and organizational levels in influencing ethical behavior by managers and employees (see, for example, Dalal, 2005; Elango *et al.*, 2010; Kaptein, 2010; and Kish-Gephart *et al.*, 2010). Studies (e.g., Wimbush *et al.*, 1997) have also examined the relationship or organizational climate to ethical behavior of employees. Bear *et al.* (2010), for example, found that more ethnically and gender diverse boards of directors had better ethical climates and reputations. The value of ethics codes for assuring ethical behavior has been studied by other researchers (e.g., McKinney *et al.*, 2010). What can be suggested at this point is that a multimodal approach is needed to maximize ethical behavior and minimize unethical behavior. Such an approach would include a clearly defined and enforced code of ethics, a whistle blowing program (e.g., Vandekerckhove and Tsahuridu, 2010), ethical leaders at the top, modeling of ethical behavior, low to no tolerance for ethical breaches and the creation of an environment in which ethical behavior becomes automaticized (Reynolds *et al.*, 2010).

There are a few empirical studies that have been specific to coaching. Duffy and Passmore (2010) conducted a small sample (N =11) qualitative study using interviews and a focus group on the topic of ethical decision making (see also Passmore and Mortimer, 2011). Based on their data they advocated a six-step process for addressing ethical dilemmas in coaching: (N =11). These included: (1) awareness of applicable ethical stanadards; (2) identifying the relevant issues in the case at hand; (3) personal refection on the issues; (4) identifying options on handling the problems; (5) choosing from among these options; and (6) initiating a course of action. The literature of ethics does not need to be only empirical. As Lefkowitz (2003) has demonstrated, ethics has a philosophical underpinning. Lowman (2006) has also shown that ethics in professional practice largely stem from consensus judgment and reflect judgments about the right thing to do at a particular point in time (see also, Eliott, 1972). Since coaching is an emerging area of practice, it will be many years before there is consensus on the ethically appropriate thing to do in diverse situations.

## Managing Ethical Conflicts

In this chapter we have identified eight ethical principles that need to be taken into account in coaching, as well as reviewing the published literature on coaching ethics. Since all ethical issues can never be anticipated, coaches need methods to think through ethical issues. Here are some basic suggestions.

First, the professional coach needs to be aware of the ethical standards that need to guide practice. There is not one code of ethics that adequately covers all issues that are likely to come up in coaching practice. Having thought through these issues in advance the coach is likely to be sensitive to behaving in a professionally appropriate way.

Second, the professional coach needs to monitor practice situations continuously for possible ethical concerns. Those ethical issues that are anticipated in advance of a coaching engagement are less likely to happen.

Third, a professional coach cannot practice in isolation. Reading articles, chapters, and books on ethics are ways to stay professionally connected. Having colleagues with whom one can discuss ethical issues as they arise is also recommended.

There are many guidelines that are useful for thinking through ethical problems and issues. Ethical casebooks (e.g., Lowman, 2006; see also, Allan, 2010; Bersoff, 2008;

Lefkowitz and Lowman, 2010; Nagy, 2005; Passmore and Mortimer, 2011) provide examples that are useful in thinking through how the various codes apply to typical and sometimes complex ethical situations. Of particular interest is an unusual feature of the Canadian code (2000). This code provides useful practical guidance about what to do when ethical principles conflict and a helpful set of guidelines for ethical decision making (pp. 2–3). Other practical books and articles are also relevant (see, for example, Fisher, 2008; Nagy, 2005).

# Conclusion

Professional coaching raises a number of important ethical issues but there is not one way to address these issues. This chapter identifies a number of commonly encountered ethical concerns and ways effectively to address these. It makes clear that certain ethical principles and standards are common no matter what the specific ethics code is used. The wise and prudent coach will take ethical issues seriously in their professional practice.

# References

Albala, I., Doyle, M., & Appelbaum, P.S. (2010). The evolution of consent forms for research: A quarter century of changes. *IRB: Ethics and Human Research*, 32(3), 7–11.

Allan, J. (2010) The ethics column. *The Coaching Psychologist*, 6(1), 52.

Allan, J., Passmore, J., & Mortimer, L. (2011). Coaching ethics. The ACTION model. In J. Passmore (ed.), *Supervision in coaching: Understanding coaching supervision, ethics, CPD and the law*. London: Kogan Page.

American Psychological Association (APA) (2002). Ethical principles of psychologists and code of conduct. *American Psychologist*, 57, 1060–1073.

American Psychological Association (2003). Guidelines on multicultural, education, training, research, practice, and organizational change for psychologists. *American Psychologist*, 58, 377–402.

Bear, S., Rahman, N., & Post, C. (2010). The impact of board diversity and gender composition on corporate social responsibility and firm reputation. *Journal of Business Ethics*, 97, 207–21.

Bersoff, D.N. (1996). The virtue of principle ethics. *The Counseling Psychologist*, 24, 86–91.

Bersoff, D.N. (2008). *Ethical conflicts in psychology* (4th ed.). Washington, DC: American Psychological Association.

Brenan, D., & Wildflower, L. (2010). Ethics in coaching. In E. Cox, T. Bachkirova and D. Clutterbuck (Eds.), *The complete handbook of coaching* pp. 369–80. London: Sage.

British Psychological Society (BPS) (2009). *Code of ethics and conduct. Guidance published by the Ethics Committee of the British Psychological Society*. Leicester, UK: Author. Retrieved July 29, 2011 from http://www.bps.org.uk/sites/default/files/documents/code_of_ethics_and_conduct.pdf.

Canadian Psychological Association (CPA) (2000). *Canadian code of ethics for psychologists*. Ottawa, Canada: Canadian Psychological Association.

Dalal, R.S. (2005). A meta-analysis of the relationship between organizational citizenship behavior and counterproductive work behavior. *Journal of Applied Psychology*, 90, 1241–1255.

Duffy, M. & Passmore, J. (2010). Ethics in coaching: An ethical decision making framework for coaching psychologists. *International Coaching Psychology Review*, 5, 140–51.

Edelstein, L., Temkin, O.C., & Temkin, L. (Eds.) (1987) *Ancient medicine*. Baltimore, MA: Johns Hopkins University Press.

Elango, B.B., Paul, K., Kundu, S.K., & Paudel, S.K. (2010). Organizational ethics, individual ethics, and ethical intentions in international decision-making. *Journal of Business Ethics*, 97, 543–61.

Elliot, P. (1972). *The sociology of the professions*. New York: Herder and Herder.

Ethical principles of psychologists and code of conduct. (2002). *American Psychologist, 57*, 1060–73.

Fisher, C. (2008). *Decoding the ethics code: A practical guide for psychologists* (2nd ed.). Thousand Oaks, CA: Sage Publications.

Gregory, J. Beck, J.W., & Carr, A.E. (2011). Goals, feedback, and self-regulation: Control theory as a natural framework for executive coaching. *Consulting Psychology Journal: Practice and Research, 63*, 26–38.

International Coaching Federation (ICF) (2008). *International Coaching Federation code of ethics*. Retrieved from: http://www.coachfederation.org/ethics/.

Joint Interim Committee for the Identification and Recognition of Specialties and Proficiencies (1995). *Principles for the recognition of proficiences in professional psychology*. Washington, DC: Joint Interim Committee for the Identification and Recognition of Specialties and Proficiencies. Retrieved from: http://www.apa.org/ed/graduate/specialize/proficiency-principles.aspx

Joint Interim Committee for the Identification and Recognition of Specialties and Proficiencies (2008). *Principles for the recognition of specialties in professional psychology*. Washington DC: Joint Interim Committee for the Identification and Recognition of Specialties and Proficiencies. Retrieved from: http://www.apa.org/about/governance/council/policy/principles-recognition.pdf.

Kaptein, M. (2010). The ethics of organizations: A longitudinal study of the U.S. working population. *Journal of Business Ethics, 92*, 601–18.

Kish-Gephart, J. J., Harrison, D.A., & Treviño, L. (2010). Bad apples, bad cases, and bad barrels: Meta-analytic evidence about sources of unethical decisions at work. *Journal of Applied Psychology, 95*, 1–31.

Law, H. (2010). Coaching relationships and ethical practice. In, S. Palmer, A. McDowall, S. Palmer, & A. McDowall (Eds.), pp. 182–202. *The coaching relationship: Putting people first*. New York: Routledge/Taylor and Francis Group.

Lefkowitz, J. (2003). *Ethics and values in industrial and organizational psychology*. New York: Erlbaum (Francis and Taylor).

Lefkowitz, J., & Lowman, R.L. (2010) Ethics of employee selection. In J.L. Farr and N. Tippins (Eds) (pp. 571–590). *Handbook of employee selection* (pp. 571–590). New York: Psychology Press (Taylor and Francis).

Lowman, R.L. (2006). *The ethical practice of psychology in organizations* (2nd ed.). Washington, DC: American Psychological Association.

Lowman, R.L. (Ed.) (in press, 2013). *Internationalizing multiculturalism: Expanding professional competencies in a globalized world*. Washington, DC: American Psychological Association.

McKinney, J.A., Emerson, T.L., & Neubert, M.J. (2010). The effects of ethical codes on ethical perceptions of actions toward stakeholders. *Journal of Business Ethics, 97*, 505–16.

Nagy, T.F. (2005). *Ethics in plain English: An illustrative case book for psychologists* (2nd ed.). Washington, DC: APA Books.

Passmore, J. (2009). Coaching ethics: Making ethical decisions – novices and experts. *The Coaching Psychologist, 5* (1), 6–10.

Passmore, J. (Ed.) (2011) *Supervision in coaching: Understanding coaching supervision, ethics, CPD and the law*. London: Kogan Page.

Passmore, J. & Mortimer, L. (2011). Ethics in coaching. In: L. Boyce and G. Hernez-Broome (eds) *Advancing Executive Coaching: Setting the Course for Successful Leadership Coaching*. San Francisco, CA: Jossey-Bass. pp. 205–28.

Peltier, B. (2010). *The psychology of executive coaching: Theory and application* (2nd ed.). New York: Routledge/Taylor and Francis Group.

Reynolds, S.J., Leavitt, K., & DeCelles, K.A. (2010). Automatic ethics: The effects of implicit assumptions and contextual cues on moral behavior. *Journal of Applied Psychology, 95*, 752–60.

Smith, D. (2003). Ten ways practitioners can avoid frequent ethical pitfalls. *APA Monitor, 34* (1), 50.

Stober, D.R. and Grant, A.M. (eds) (2006). *Evidence based coaching handbook: Putting best practices to work for your clients*. Hoboken, NJ: Wiley.

Vandekerckhove, W. & Tsahuridu, E.E. (2010). Risky rescues and the duty to blow the whistle. *Journal of Business Ethics, 97*, 365–80.

Williams, P. and Anderson, S. (2006). *Law and ethics in coaching*. Hoboken, NJ: Wiley.

Wimbush, J.C., Shepard, J.M., & Markham, S.E. (1997). An empirical examination of the relationship between ethical climate and ethical behavior from multiple levels of analysis. *Journal of Business Ethics, 16*, 1705–1716.

# 6

# The Neuroscience of Coaching

## Miles Bowman, Kathleen M. Ayers, Joan C. King, and Linda J. Page

## Introduction

Our conscious experience is so dense and multi-faceted that we puzzle how such complexity arises from a single source: the brain. This is not to say that the brain acts in isolation – as we shall see, brain function is influenced by its connection with the central nervous system (CNS), by multiple systems throughout the body, and by social and developmental factors. Recent developments in understanding the brain and nervous system's function and influence – in essence the expanding field of neuroscience – have promulgated a myriad of applications for behavioral-based professions, including coaching. Neuroscience is one of the fastest growing areas of research in science; its popularity is not dissimilar to the surge of interest in coaching. Thus, as neuroscience research continues to propagate alongside coaching, an obvious question emerges: "Can a synergism be forged between these fields in the future?"

It may not readily be apparent why neuroscience is relevant to coaching. Yet, like coaching, neuroscience is multi-leveled and multi-disciplinary. Investigations range from the specific, as when examining the signals that start and stop motor activities starting in a circuit of neurons (Jin and Costa, 2010), to systemic, as when recording activity in pain pathways arising from social rejection (Eisenberger *et al.*, 2003; Eisenberger and Lieberman, 2004). Such research has the potential to ratify (i.e., validate) widely-employed coaching practices and to inform empirically-supported future approaches. Because coaches are concerned with engaging clients to produce results, it behooves the coaching community to examine how neuroscience might impact current and future strategies within the coaching profession.

This chapter is intended to be a primer for coaches who wish to integrate fundamental aspects of neuroscience research and its applications into their practice. We provide examples that link neuroscience research to coaching processes. Section one introduces neuroscience research, describes the ways in which it is performed, and elaborates upon

*The Wiley Blackwell Handbook of the Psychology of Coaching and Mentoring*, First Edition.
Edited by Jonathan Passmore, David B. Peterson, and Teresa Freire.
© 2013 John Wiley & Sons, Ltd. Published 2016 by John Wiley & Sons, Ltd.

potential mechanisms involved in coaching processes. Section two details the contributions of neuroscience in understanding human behavior and highlights those contributions that impact coaching. Section three suggests potential future collaborations between coaching and neuroscience.

## Section One: Neuroscience and Understanding the Nervous System

As part of a general orientation, coaches claim to work with individuals as a whole, including their physical beings (Olalla, 2004; Whitworth *et al.*, 1998). Asking whether mind and body affect each other presupposes that they are separable. They are not (McEwen, 1998; Sapolsky, 2004; Segerstrom and Miller, 2004), although full understanding of the interaction between the brain and the body has yet to be elucidated. The brain is a major component of a system of nerves that extends throughout the entire body and is involved in our conscious experience and sense of self. Coaches who ignore the interrelatedness of brain–body–mind relationships are ignoring substantial research.

The brain governs behavior with both incredible complexity and elegant simplicity. There is a common fallacy that we use only 10 percent of our brains; however, even simple problem solving draws upon an array of interconnected systems throughout the cortex. The brain is functionally organized such that discrete areas are devoted to performing particular skill-types; broad examples of such organization include vision, touch, speaking, and movement. In addition, areas of greater refinement have been identified, for example cerebral specialization for error identification in planned goal-directed movements (Holroyd and Coles, 2002), or recognizing that your arm is your own (van den Bos and Jeannerod, 2002).

Anatomically, the various regions of the brain are intricately interconnected. One such example is the insular cortex, an area located deep within each hemisphere between the temporal and frontal lobes that plays a role in autonomic regulation, emotion, and cognition. The insular cortex connects with the amygdala, medial prefrontal cortex, anterior cingulate gyrus, frontal, parietal, and temporal cortical areas (Berntson *et al.*, 2011). Simply mapping these connections is an enormous task, let alone understanding how they relate to behavior. These types of cerebral organization are roughly consistent for all humans and analogous to other primates; this has important implications. For example, despite the varying contexts in which they might occur, fear responses result from activity in the same brain areas across species. That is, the ubiquity in the design of the brain and its relation to the body indicates that some level of standardization may be possible when designing behavioral treatments.

Exploring the links between wellness and performance – common background considerations in coaching – has revealed noteworthy relationships between physical and mental health (Walsh, 2011). For example, physical exercise relates robustly to physical health (Richardson *et al.*, 2004; Smart and Marwick, 2003), mental health, and cognitive ability (Pereira *et al.*, 2007; van Praag, 2009; Voss *et al.*, 2011) even when practiced later in life (Gates *et al.*, 2011; Kramer *et al.*, 2006). Physical self-care is the domain of many specialized coaches; its influence on mental processes is only beginning be understood. Several branches of behavioral sciences are exploring these findings using combinations of neuroimaging, studies of brain lesions, clinical observations, and laboratory experiments. The findings are still preliminary, therefore coaches should not be compelled, as a result of these findings, to prescribe exercise as part of their practice; however, the potential application to coaching practice is profound.

Exercise-induced effects are but one of many possible underlying mechanisms relevant to coaches who want to gain a basic knowledge of how our central nervous system (CNS) processes information. Consider that neuroscience has aided understanding in coaching-relevant processes, including: the basis for motivation to reach a goal (Mizuno *et al.*, 2008); what mitigates stress responses when a threat is perceived (Arnsten, 2009; van den Bos *et al.*, 2009); and how change can be effectively adopted into long-term behavior (Bandura, 2004). These examples point to just three important elements that relate to successful coaching. Here, we suggest three levels of analysis at which the fundamentals of neuroscience may be understood:

1  Molecular and/or subcellular influences on behavior (e.g., hormones, neurotransmitters).
2  Intrapersonal – influences on the individual arising from the functional organization of the brain (e.g., emotion, motivation).
3  Interpersonal – behaviors that emerge as a result of interactions with the environment and, indeed, all complex human behavior (e.g., empathy, social interactions, culture).

Because of the wide variety of questions that neuroscientists attempt to answer, there are many different methods by which data can be gathered. We turn next to a brief summary of methodology, before returning to how neuroscience can facilitate coaching.

## Section Two: Studying Neuroscience and Observing Behavior

A large part of what we know about human behavior stems from observational studies of individuals with known brain injuries. Individuals who have suffered a damaging cerebellar incident (e.g., ischemia, thrombosis, lesion, ablation) can provide examples of impairment resulting from the loss of a specific functional area. However, bleeding, swelling, and infection produce non-discrete damage and sometimes tissue damage opposite a site of injury (Courville, 1942). Therefore an ability to generalize from a single case study is often limited. To protect against a limited ability to generalize from case studies, meta-analyses are often conducted that examine large sets of data to allow researchers to extrapolate the requirements for normal functioning in healthy brains (Berntson *et al.*, 2011).

Neuroscientists are also able to infer the underlying drivers of human behavior by observing changes in non-human organisms that result from experimental manipulation. Animal models range from simple organisms like fruit flies and yeast to more complex organisms such as rats and monkeys. In all cases animal models allow investigations and discoveries that would otherwise not be feasible on human participants, while still allowing generalization and comparison to human behavior.

Before the advent of imaging technology, efforts to determine the link between brain damage and behavioral changes were limited to postmortem confirmation. However, it is now possible to image the brain *in vivo* using technologies to record and reconstruct neural activity patterns *post hoc*. These reconstructions are therefore not indications of brain activity per se, but rather indirect measures or approximations constrained by the specifications of the equipment. Such limitations may, at first pass, hamper the ability to generalize these findings to behavior writ large. However, scientific design and the ability to replicate testing can somewhat alleviate concerns over technical limitations by requiring specific questions that address finite problems. Admittedly, the design of the equipment described below may prevent participants from moving or talking freely; nonetheless, experiments may be conducted that allow participants to respond to pertinent questions. To fully understand measures of *in vivo* activity and how they can apply to coaching processes, we briefly review these technologies.

When neurons communicate they produce an electrical signal that moves along the membrane of an initiating neuron and is converted to a chemical signal that spans the space between two neurons to a receiving neuron. The junction between the initiating and receiving neurons is referred to as a synapse. These signals from neurons can be measured in volume from the surface of the skull. Using sensors placed upon the scalp, an electroencephalogram (EEG) can measure electrical activity in the brain. The EEG measurements typically represent a signal generated by larger sets of neurons related to a particular stimulus in the environment (known as an event related potential, or ERP). Since individual neurons fire regularly, it is difficult to isolate one neuron's response relative to the stimulus; however, the response of a population of neurons will produce an ERP that allows precise temporal measures related to cerebral activity. The electrical current flow within the brain that results from neural activity is similarly used in magneto-encephalography (MEG) scanners to provide precise estimates of when certain brain areas respond to a variety of stimuli. Thus, EEG and MEG studies are often used in investigating the timing of cerebral activation.

Greater spatial specificity related to cerebral activation is better obtained through positron emission tomography (PET). This method provides clear anatomical images with more detailed spatial precision but less temporally precise measures. This type of imaging does not provide direct measures of synaptic activity; instead researchers infer activity based on changes in metabolism in active areas. Positron emission tomography combines magnetic resonance imaging (MRI) and computed tomography (CT) scanning technology to measure blood flow via metabolic rates that are measured using radioactive deoxyglucose (or sugar) that is injected into the bloodstream shortly before performing the to-be-measured task. This radioactive material quickly decays and poses no serious risk while allowing researchers to measure which cells are active during the task by recording those that metabolize the deoxyglucose. When neural activity in a given cortical area demands an increase in metabolism, oxygen-rich blood, the source of energy, is supplied to that area and so, too, is the radioactive marker. Researchers can indirectly measure neural processing by recording the radioactivity in given brain regions.

In the example in Figure 6.1, researchers treated depressed patients with transcranial magnetic stimulation (TMS) to induce a weak electrical current in participants' mid-dorsal lateral frontal cortex. Paus *et al.* (2001) suggest that rehabilitating activity levels in the frontal cortex may be a means of treating depression. Positron emission tomography images taken following treatment show areas of decreased metabolism and other areas of increased metabolism in the patients' brains. Such a procedure enables researchers to directly engage with one area of cortex and then measure the subsequent changes in connected areas that result from the manipulations at a single treatment site.

Transcranial magnetic stimulation affects the natural changes in magnetic field properties in the brain that result from metabolism and is a non-invasive procedure that produces minimal discomfort. Transcranial magnetic stimulation equipment can be used to administer directed magnetic field disruptions to a selected brain region and may result in elevation or depression of neural activity, as illustrated in Figure 6.1. By rehabilitating activity levels in the frontal cortex using TMS, disorders such as depression can be treated (Paus *et al.*, 2001; but see also Paus and Barrett, 2004). Transcranial magnetic stimulation can also be used

(a)
TMS1–BASE1

(b)
TMS1–BASE1

(c)
TMS4–TMS1

(d)
Regression with MDLFC

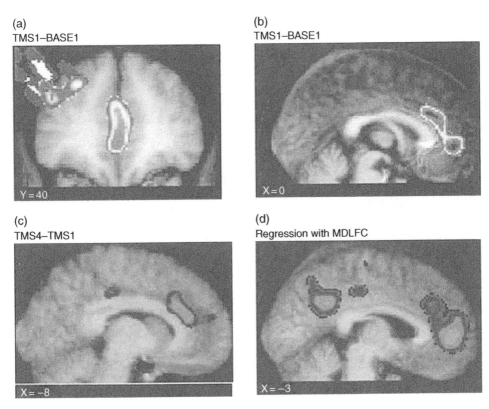

**Figure 6.1** Examples of PET measured changes in metabolism following clinical TMS treatment. Participants with depression were treated with TMS stimulation to the mid-dorsal lateral frontal cortex (placement of TMS coil shown in top left of (a); target of stimulation in crosshairs). Following treatment with TMS, metabolic rates in the brain were measured using PET imaging. Areas of decreased metabolism (i.e. inhibited activity) were seen at the stimulation site and several distal sites (a–b). Areas of increased metabolism (c) and correlated increases in blood flow also resulted (d) (adapted from Paus *et al.*, 2001).

to temporarily disrupt behavior in a focused brain area by inhibiting neural activity without causing permanent damage. This ability has led many to describe its effects as a virtual lesion, which, as discussed above, can reveal contributions of specific brain areas to behavior.

Studies using functional magnetic resonance imaging (fMRI) also record the flow rates of oxygenated blood (i.e., hemoglobin). When hemoglobin is deoxygenated, the magnetic property of the hemoglobin changes and produces a signal that can be detected by the MRI scanner. Thus, greater neural activity in the brain during a cognitive task produces a change in the magnetic field in that brain region. Figure 6.2 compares examples of fMRI recordings during creative and uncreative thinking (Howard-Jones *et al.*, 2005). In both cases, activity shared in both creative and uncreative thinking is not shown. Images such as these enable researchers to "see" inside a functioning brain and to determine which cortical areas are necessary for a variety of cognitive tasks.

While each current technique has its limitations, these approaches are not easily dismissed. Both PET and fMRI measurement have become increasingly useful in recent years, as their ability to record more rapid time-sensitive readings with greater accuracy has progressed. Bennett and Miller (2010) report that while the "reliability of fMRI may not be high relative

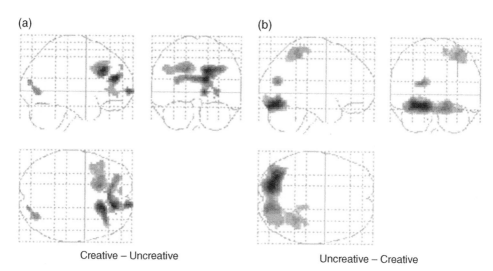

Creative – Uncreative        Uncreative – Creative

**Figure 6.2**  Examples of fMRI recordings during creative and uncreative thinking. (a) Activation patterns recorded during creative thought which are achieved by "subtracting out" activity that also occurs during uncreative thinking; areas of shared activity are not represented. (b) Activity patterns during uncreative thought which are achieved by subtracting out activity that also occurs during creative thought; areas of shared activity are not displayed (adapted from Howard-Jones *et al.*, 2005). Note that creative thinking uses frontal areas (used in problem solving) while uncreative thinking uses areas that process visual information.

to other scientific measures … it is presently the best tool available for *in vivo* investigation of brain function" (p. 150). To account for these challenges, Logothetis (2008) suggests a "multimodal approach is more necessary than ever for the study of brain's function and dysfunction … [including] further improvements to MRI technology and its combination with other non-invasive techniques that directly assess the brain's electrical activity" (p. 877).

Indeed, several researchers have begun employing more than one approach in their studies to minimize equipment-specific limitations and to bolster the robustness of their findings (see Figure 6.1). For example, certain researchers are using multiple tools to capture brain activity with the temporal specificity of MEG and the spatial specificity of fMRI (Sawyer, 2011). Taken together these approaches reveal that there are multiple avenues of exploration available to neuroscientists to study behavior as it occurs. Unsurprisingly, with so many tools at its disposal neuroscience research has grown rapidly in recent years.

We turn now to the application of neuroscience findings to coaching processes by reviewing findings at the three levels and how each can impact coaching. A quick caveat: coaching discussions include abstract concepts such as social awareness, empathy, and creativity. These abstract concepts are difficult, though not impossible, to examine in a laboratory setting. And while exactly how the brain gives rise to these more complex faculties is not yet fully understood (Brothers, 2001; Siegel, 2010), significant progress has been made. The lack of clarity stems in part from the fact that abstract concepts such as empathy and fear emerge from interactions between multiple brain areas (Preston *et al.*, 2007; Zahn *et al.*, 2009). Still another factor that will be familiar to coaches is that many abstract concepts are difficult to define operationally. Ask yourself what consciousness entails and you'll soon find yourself in good company, as this is a current dilemma for many neuroscientists. Thus, although still preliminary, evidence is mounting to suggest that even the more complex mental processes can be investigated using modern equipment.

## Molecular and subcellular influences

Although studying behavior at a microscopic level may initially seem to simplify experimentation, these pursuits require extraordinary precision and highly-detailed paradigms. For example, studying how neurons communicate takes great care. Synaptic transmission – the result of chemical reactions within the cell and between neurons – can be influenced in their development and function from the release of neurotransmitters (Greengard, 2001), can be influenced by other chemical influences such as endocannabinoids (Alger, 2002), as well as the components of the neuronal membrane (Zamponi *et al.*, 2010), past connections between cells and more. Each of these components can influence the activity of single cells and circuits of many neurons related to the behavior we see in an individual. As just one example, a defect in the way a protein is synthesized in the structure involved in generating the synapse in neurons has recently been found to contribute to epilepsy (Zamponi *et al.*, 2010).

At the molecular level, investigators employ a number of state-of-the-art technologies and methodologies. These may include the analysis of a cell's DNA and the localization of specific molecules within cells using specific antibodies, cell-body staining, using radioactive markers to monitor deoxyglucose uptake in neurons during metabolism, or using genetic color markers that dye certain proteins in order to trace neuronal connections throughout the brain. While these methods are beyond the scope of this chapter, they contribute to understanding of the connectivity and function and are often the first step neuroscientists employ in understanding behavior at the next level of analysis.

An awareness of the interrelatedness of neural connections and their influences could benefit coaches who desire to understand the mechanisms that underlie behavioral strategies they may wish to employ with clients. As an example, gonadotropin releasing hormone (GnRH) stimulates the pituitary to secrete luteinizing hormone, which in turn induces ovulation in females and spermatogenesis in males. Neurons that stimulate GnRH production are heavily represented in the hypothalamus (a gateway to the limbic system), the autonomic nervous system (responsible for, among other things, both stress and relaxation responses), and the endocrine system. Thus, the production and availability of just one hormone can have far-reaching implications for a number of behaviors.

The majority of applications to coaching at the molecular level are, for now, beyond our reach, though they may still provide the foundation to the intrapersonal and interpersonal level of analysis relevant to coaches. A few examples provide some points of reference. Van den Bos and colleagues (2009) have noted differences between men and women in how cortisol reactivity relates to performance. Many coaches are also familiar with the behavioral indicators of attention deficit hyperactivity disorder (ADHD), an area of concerted investigatory focus in neuroscience. Although there remains a great deal to be learned about this disorder, having an awareness of the underlying mechanisms may provide coaches with a better understanding of approaches they can use to mediate a client's emotional response or to help them battle feelings of being overwhelmed.

## Intrapersonal influences: Mediating individual behaviors

Research in psychology in the mid-twentieth century explored myriad behavioral topics related to individual behavior, including perception, memory, reasoning, language, problem-solving, and decision making; as technology improved, neuroscience-influenced questions began to follow. The rapid expansion rate of investigation has engendered considerable understanding of behavior, both developmentally (Hua and Smith, 2004) and with regard to adults (Johnson and Taylor, 2006). Among the array of coaching-related topics invest-igated by neuroscience researchers are creativity (Limb and Braun, 2008), problem solving (Kounios, *et al.*, 2006), and the effects of optimism (Schacter and Addis, 2007). In all cases these findings have led to a greater understanding of how the environment and behavior reciprocally influence the individual – the topic of our next section.

At first pass, coaching might be described as a process to facilitate the learning (and remembering) of new behaviors. In the brain, memory is in part influenced by activity in the hippocampus (Davachi and Wagner, 2002). Recalling memories is subject to a variety of influences and can be improved by allowing elaboration in relation to closely-valued concepts and autobiographical details (Tambini *et al.*, 2010). Learning is also benefited by aerobic exercise (Ratey and Hagerman, 2008), sleep patterns (Tambini *et al.*, 2010), distributed practice (Litman and Davachi, 2008), and even taking tests (Roediger and Karpicke, 2006), and is conversely inhibited by distraction (Arnsten, 1998, 2009). Learning is too broad to be included in the scope of this chapter, and is instead presented in more detail in Chapter 11. Coaches can benefit greatly from researching and applying empirically substantiated learning methods in their practice.

Coaching requires more than providing an environment in which the client remembers and develops action goals, it also requires acknowledging feelings as a crucial component in facilitating change behaviors. Indeed, recent trends in neuroscience place emotion at the center of coaching issues (Camille *et al.*, 2004; Davidson *et al.*, 2000; Izard, 2010; Jaremka *et al.*, 2010). Emotional self-regulation – considered central to maturational development (Posner and Rothbart, 2009) – positively relates to effective socialization (Rand *et al.*, 2009), achievement (Blair and Diamond, 2008; Pekrun *et al.*, 2002), productivity in adults (O'Connor *et al.*, 2010), and avoidance of psychopathology (Schore, 2006). Evidence is amassing to suggest that emotion reciprocally influences cognition; emotions do not corrupt rational decision making – they are necessary to it (Bechara, 2004; Bliss-Moreau and Barrett, 2009). Part of the coach's job, then, is to create an environment in which clients integrate their emotional experience to generate cogent decision making.

Emotional and cognitive processes, while interdependent, are at least partially segregated in the brain (Critchley, 2005). Self-reflections relative to emotional states have been shown to occur separately in the brain from reflections on self-conceptualization (Lieberman, 2007). Conscious cognitive strategies may thus be used to regulate emotional responses that would otherwise reduce cognitive capacity and make falling into implicit patterns more likely (Mak *et al.*, 2009; Ochsner and Gross, 2005, 2008). Strategies to determinatively select emotional states that are conducive to decision making can arise from helping an individual name an experienced emotion (Lieberman *et al.*, 2007) and from reappraising emotion – in other words, to reassess assumptions that associate tears with sadness rather than joy (McRae *et al.*, 2010).

Becoming aware of automatic patterns and deciding to regulate our emotions requires metacognition, or the ability to observe our own thoughts, feelings, and behaviors. A popular technique for this is mindfulness training. Using an approach that taught part-icipants mindfulness meditation, Farb and colleagues (2007) found participants were able to dissociate between self-evaluative measures that are momentary (present) and those that are persistent (ongoing). In doing so participants differentially engaged frontal cor-tical resources and effectively changed the way they thought about an issue (Farb *et al.*, 2007). Similar training also influenced how participants' experience of sadness is expressed in the brain (Farb *et al.*, 2010). Such changes may occur in response to physical changes in brain structures associated with attention and emotional integration that have been recorded following mindfulness training (Hölzel *et al.*, 2011).

Present-based focus (through mindfulness) may be a critical component of changing how clients process an event and find viable alternatives by suggesting that clients reframe how they think about an issue. Directed attentional control is required to guide our thinking patterns when we are tempted to focus only on an emotion-arousing event (Hedden and Gabrieli, 2006). Though evidence is just emerging, mindfulness training appears to be a solid candidate for an empirically validated coaching skill that benefits attention (Lutz *et al.*, 2008; Tang *et al.*, 2007), measures of general well-being (Brown and Ryan, 2003), and memory and emotional experience (Jha *et al.*, 2010).

Clients often seek coaching to create change in their lives. However, there is a gap between recognizing the need for change and choosing what must be done. In such cases, coaches would benefit from understanding how to inspire creative thinking in order to provide unusual or unexpected solutions. Recent work on creativity has revealed that the frontal cortex plays a pivotal role in creative thinking (Heilman *et al.*, 2003). Heightened frontal cortical activity has been recorded in activities such as divergent creativity tasks in music (Gibson *et al.*, 2009) improvisation for jazz musicians (Limb and Braun, 2008) and storytelling (Howard-Jones *et al.*, 2005). These are just a few examples of important skills used in solution finding.

Electroencephalogram (EEG) measures reveal a distinct pattern of electrical activity in the brain known as alpha wave activity during the creative process (Fink *et al.*, 2008). That is, creative thinking is activity-level dependent (Heilman *et al.*, 2003) and requires investment from a great many cortical structures. Indeed, one of the hallmarks of creative thinking is a vastly distributed activation pattern (i.e., creativity is not a strictly right hemisphere task – Sawyer, 2011). Importantly, training can help participants produce creative thinking (Fink *et al.*, 2008), suggesting that creative thinking can be instigated under certain circumstances. While the components necessary for creative thought are only just being identified, coaches may already be able to draw from these discoveries. Creative thinking occurs when the perception of threats are mitigated (Berns, 2010); it often does not result from "thinking about a problem" but instead stems from insights that occur when distracted (Kounios *et al.*, 2008).

Maintaining a positive mindset – at least while solution finding – may be what keeps individuals open to possibility. When positive and negative experiences occur at a ratio of three to one, problem-solving abilities improve (Frederickson, 2009). Similar findings have surfaced in work with couples and relationship enhancement (Gottman, 1994), business team dynamics (Losada and Heaphy, 2004), and psychotherapy success (Schwartz *et al.*, 2002). The possibility that positive behavior influences the brain is suggested by research showing resilient individuals (those who resist succumbing to setbacks or challenges) show distinct physiological and psychological profiles (Frederickson, 2001, 2009). Waugh and colleagues (2008) show corresponding evidence in brain-scanning work, concluding that neural activation patterns correlated with resilience (i.e., ability to recover following setback).

Mindset and expectation can affect the body in many ways, including our next topic – the negative. Negative behavioral strategies such as emotional suppression have been linked with the physical side effects of increased blood pressure and heart rate. However, there are mental artifacts as well. There are important reasons why a coach should identify instances when a client attends to the negative. For example, focusing on the negative increases the salience of negative stimuli (Barrett *et al.*, 2007) that are then remembered more often than positive stimuli (Ray *et al.*, 2005). Fixating on the negative may also limit social and self-awareness, relationship management, and self-regulation (Beauregard, 2007). Thus, a negative mindset can lead to a familiar downward spiral that actively inhibits a client's capacity to help themselves and, over protracted periods of time, may contribute to depression.

When circumstances are perceived as sufficiently negative, a threat response may be triggered in the amygdala (a component of the limbic system and important for emotional regulation). The strength of amygdala activation depends, in part, on the level of threat appraisal and results in activation of the sympathetic nervous system's fight or flight response. Amygdala activation produces the subjective experience of a strong emotional surge that inhibits frontal cortical areas while increasing self-protecting behaviors (Arnsten, 1998, 2009). The inhibition of frontal cortical areas limits creativity and meta-thinking, and encourages fixating upon more proximal and immediate details of the task at hand (Phelps, 2006) that can significantly hamper decision making (Feinstein *et al.*, 2011; Mui *et al.*, 2008), emotional memory encoding (Murty *et al.*, 2010), and social status evaluation (Borsook and McDonald, 2010; Zink *et al.*, 2008). Accordingly, old habits that may exacerbate the situation are more likely acted upon while analytical capabilities are sacrificed – a familiar profile to many coaches.

As we have said, amygdala activation arises in response to perceived threats. Coaches may deal predominantly with those stemming from social threats. Researchers have identified what may be considered to be five key areas in which social threats are perceived: social status related to dominance hierarchies (Chiao *et al.*, 2004; Zink *et al.*, 2008); autonomy, or self-governance of the individual (Leotti *et al.*, 2010; Rodin, 1986); belonging or alienation from social groups (Baumeister and Leary, 1995; Baumeister *et al.*, 2002); fairness estimates (Tabibnia *et al.*, 2008); and uncertainty related to decision making and producing errors in judgment (Heilman *et al.*, 2010). Thus, an important consideration for clients emerges: situational evaluations may promote threat assessments and shut down cognitive ability related to solution finding. Indeed, the type of thinking that coaches encourage for their clients might require regulating fear responses – especially fear of public ridicule, failure, and uncertainty (Berns, 2010). In some cases, coaches must keep clients from "thinking too much" in order to continue to promote productive creativity.

Taken together, the above-detailed neural activation patterns provide coaches with good reason to remain aware of – and in some cases increase – the client's awareness of his or her emotional state while offering strategies for self-management. Mediating emotional extremes is necessary to maintaining the cognitive capacity to identify options in coaching. For example, the client's naming of an emotion (affective labeling) interrupts activity in the amygdala and promotes right ventrolateral prefrontal cortical activity and results in a calming effect (Lieberman *et al.*, 2007). Thus, talking about feelings in the present may implicitly calm a client, while talking about narrative details may freeze them (recall the similar effects of mindfulness training).

Coaches are familiar with the common route of solution finding to decision making that leads to action. But is one path better than another? And, should coaches be at liberty to prescribe it? Consider that the positive outlooks discussed earlier can be learned and therefore do not need to be imposed upon a client. One strategy for improving outlook is keeping a daily gratitude journal, which has been shown to protect against depression and to help individuals identify components of their lives that they enjoy (Emmons and McCullogh, 2003). Accordingly, coaches may encourage clients to be self-directed while also indicating options that incorporate the coach's input into decision making.

However, coaches must be aware that providing too many options may also be problematic as the client pursues his or her goals. Making choices involves conscious processes influenced by the pre-frontal cortex (PFC; Gold and Shadien, 2007). When tired or otherwise depleted, we literally may not have the energy to interrupt an established pattern (Gailliot *et al.*, 2007). Even when well rested, too many choices will negatively affect decision making (Halford *et al.*, 2005; Shiffrin and Nosofsky, 1994) by, for example, dividing attentional resources (Einstein *et al.*, 2003; Kensinger *et al.*, 2003). As a result of overwhelming choice, implicit habitual responses are more likely to be selected rather than potentially adaptive behaviors. Some researchers have suggested that considering only two options is the ideal circumstance for making a decision (Schwartz, 2004). Others suggest that having and following explicit procedures in making decisions can help regulate the emotional arousal that interferes with decision making (Seo *et al.*, 2010). Here, the coach's influence in helping the client design such systems becomes apparent.

Not only can emotional state influence a client's view of himself or herself, it also colors their perception of others. Moreover, creativity, optimism, and confidence, may well impact interpersonal relationships and the workplace (Peterson *et al.*, 2008). Helping clients understand their peers can produce several benefits within organizations.

We turn next to social relationships because while it is clear that there are many internal influences on an individual, recent findings in social neuroscience have revealed important interactions between the social environment and the individual as well.

## Interpersonal influences: Complex social interactions and dynamics

Cozolino (2006) argues: "The individual neuron or a single human brain does not exist in nature," referring instead to social interactions as "our natural habitat" (p. 11). Indeed, many professionals, including coaches, are interested in behaviors that arise from social interactions and their potential to influence brain structure (Siegel, 1999). Neuroscience research has begun to elucidate the underpinnings of relationship management, social awareness and how we view others (Amodio and Frith, 2006; Lieberman, 2007; Mitchell *et al.*, 2006).

An undeniably large part of our social skill set is learned during maturation. Child-caregiver attachment styles shape how an individual will later relate to their social sphere (Ainsworth *et al.*, 1978; Bowlby, 1951, 1969, 1973, 1980). Siegel (1999) suggests that adult relationships both reflect and heal childhood attachment deficits. Using imaging studies, Schore (2001) has reviewed the caregiver's influence on infant limbic system development (the amygdala and more), suggesting that parenting styles influence how a child self-regulates, copes with stress, and relates to others, and whether they are susceptible to mental disorder. Life experiences will influence how a client sees their social world, but is this immutable?

Despite such established patterns, coaches may explore using brain-based approaches with clients to influence how they perceive others. Coaches may have heard of one of the more vaunted discoveries from neuroscience: mirror neurons (Gallese *et al.*, 1996). This discovery is both new and far-reaching so it calls for careful consideration. Mirror neuron studies cite activation patterns in specialized subsets of neurons involved in both the generation and observation of action (Gallese *et al.*, 1996; Iacoboni *et al.*, 2005). Rather than being a specialized type of neuron, mirror neuron activity is linked to populations of neurons that respond to actions of another (Dinstein *et al.*, 2008). Mirror neurons point to a common specialized circuitry that is tuned to respond to activities that are self-generated as well as those generated by others. This has been substantiated with common activity patterns found in the frontal cortex during self-evaluative judgments and evaluations of others (Mitchell *et al.*, 2005). The idea of shared neural circuits suggests to some that it may be possible to influence how a person sees others by coaching the individual on how they see themselves.

Indeed, some researchers have even gone so far as to claim mirror neurons may be a source for empathy (Carr *et al.*, 2003; Iacoboni, 2009). Mirror neuron activity associated with empathic response is sensitive to perceived similarities to others and previous observation of fairness (Singer and Lamm, 2009). Further, engaging in positive social interactions reciprocally promote pro-social behaviors (Rand *et al.*, 2009). How social interactions are influenced by mirror neurons is only beginning to be investigated (Montgomery and Haxby, 2008), but the mere presence of socially-based behavioral primers underscores the importance of the social environment and its link to understanding ourselves.

Our capacity for theory of mind, or the ability to surmise what others are thinking, may also be influenced by mirror neurons (Gallese and Goldman, 1998; Lombardo *et al.* 2009; Vogeley *et al.*, 2001). Pro-social behaviors such as altruism and empathy are contingent upon the capacity for theory of mind (Batson, 1987) and can trigger the release of oxytocin, a hormone associated with bonding (Mitchell *et al.*, 2006). Bonding can in turn positively influence self-evaluations of well-being and measures of trust (Kosfeld *et al.*, 2005). When we perceive ourselves as similar to others, we are more likely to feel good about their good fortune (Mobbs *et al.*, 2009) and to act with compassion toward them (Decety and Batson, 2007; Decety and Ickes, 2009). Interestingly, displays of compassion from leaders in the workplace have been shown to promote healthy workplace environments (Boyatzis *et al.*, 2006).

On the other hand, fear responses can promote projectionist and antagonistic behaviors; that is, a me-against-them perspective. Amygdala activation is negatively associated with altruistic behavior (Marsh *et al.*, 2007; Marsh and Blair, 2008) as well as the ability to accurately interpret the fear response of others (Marsh *et al.*, 2007; Marsh and Blair, 2008). Managing negative response toward others is particularly important in organizations (Gibson and Callister, 2010). A lack of structure for resolving issues can contribute to an emotional contagion, whereas explicit problem-solving strategies can reduce this (Johnson, 2008). This supports the legitimacy and efficacy of a coach's role in devising and using conscious procedures for decision making.

Because not every social interaction ends well, coaches must be prepared to deal with the after effects in coaching sessions. Consider our earlier cited source of amygdala activation: social rejection. There is good reason to regard rejection as threat – the social pain of rejection registers in the same brain areas as physical pain (Eisenberger and Lieberman, 2004; Eisenberger *et al.*, 2003). Acetaminophen can even relieve social pain (DeWall *et al.*, 2010). Paradoxically, mildly negative social interactions reduce pain sensitivity (Borsook and MacDonald, 2010). Such findings challenge the assumption that social pain is imagined and add significant weight to the importance of giving clients the appropriate space and resources they need to deal with these types of pain.

Social behaviors are complex, and their interpretation can vary due to individual differences (Grabner *et al.*, 2006) and emotional states (Arnsten, 1998); however, it is also important to recognize culture's influence on social behavior (Kitayama *et al.*, 2003). Cultural differences may have profound effects in our personal expression, as when interpreting emotional display on the face (Masuda *et al.*, 2004). Culture's influence may also be imperceptible, as when recent eye-gaze studies found basic differences in how Chinese and American participants focused on a complex image (Chua *et al.*, 2005). These kinds of findings have led to the inception of a new field of cultural neuroscience that suggests culturally mediated brain activity (Chiao *et al.*, 2010; Kitayama and Thompson, 2010). As we know, culture is variable and because the environment can have such a profound effect on the brain, coaches must add this to the list of influencing factors.

In our final section we discuss three main questions that coaches are presented with and how neuroscience is being applied in each case: how to manage approach-avoidance; mitigating factors in adopting change behavior; and how to inspire and maintain motivation when dealing with clients. These three issues are raised in an effort to point to possible synergisms between coaches and neuroscientists. We point to an overarching theme of coaches understanding what is required to help individuals move from relationships of projection, or distance, to relationships of engagement – from egocentric to collaborative and cooperative.

## Section Three: Applications and Future Directions

Rock and Page (2009) have argued that coaching emerged from the type of crossover that occurs when disciplines meet. A similar emergence occurred when neuroscience arose from its cross-disciplinary beginnings. As in neuroscience, coaches must resist confusing common concepts or shared terminology. Coaching is additionally faced with the challenge of building an evidence base to validate it as a field. These needs are occurring at the very moment that neuroscience is developing new techniques for studying coaching-related issues. The coincident timing points toward a potential synergism that may help establish coaching as a neuroscience-backed discipline. However, in order for that to happen, the direction and goals of coaching as a discipline must be clarified.

Neuroscience findings are only beginning to be integrated into coaching applications (Rock and Page, 2009; Street, 2010). As yet, there is little research that directly addresses the neural underpinnings of coaching per se, perhaps because the questions have remained too broad to be scientifically investigated. Questions such as: "Does coaching affect a client's brain?" are often where conversations begin, but such a question is unanswerable because of its lack of scientific focus – it cannot properly be tested. Answering more testable questions like: "Does approach X diminish amygdala-based fear-response more than approach Z?" remains a long way off because we do not have competing theories to pit against each other. This lack of generative models is perhaps the biggest limit to scientific progress in the coaching industry. While there are several frameworks available for how to coach from a given perspective, we do not know of any models that currently generate research-related questions as a result of their explanatory power or theoretical stance. Until coaching can establish a base of questions that can be empirically tested, the gap between coaching and neuroscience will persist. The onus of responsibility rests with coaches to operationalize and parameterize key concepts for the field such that they can be subjected to scientific inquiry.

Yet, despite these shortfalls, there are still coaching issues that can be addressed here. The three levels of analysis in neuroscience described above might be a suitable framework for asking coaching questions. First, and largely undiscovered, are those questions that arise around the unseen factors (chemical, hormonal, perhaps unconscious) that produce changes in behavior. Second, questions related to a client-focused approach might ask how environmental control, subjective reappraisal and emotional triggers can promote or discourage positive thinking, resilience, and creative solution finding. Third, questions can be asked pertaining to how to assist clients to be more receptive to social cues or to promote collaborative and engaging social environments and what effects such training might have (Logan *et al.*, 2008).

*Approach-avoidance*: As discussed earlier, mindset can greatly influence an individual's perceptions. Individuals assigned to coaching, especially following poor performance review may be tuned to a negative assessment of the experience (Baumeister *et al.*, 2001); for some, just the word "feedback" may set off neural alarms (Kluger and DeNisi, 1996). Establishing a meaningful relationship might therefore be predicated on first working on the client–coach relationship and the prescribed issue later. This example, while facile, serves to illustrate that coaches must be aware while they are coaching of how the client views others, themselves, *and* the coach.

There is good reason for coaches to be attending to the literature in this area. For example, using TMS to selectively inhibit regions of the brain, van Rijn and colleagues (2005) have revealed dissociation between detecting approach emotions (happiness, anger) and avoidance emotions (sadness, fear). While still preliminary, the advent of differential emotional detection systems may have a significant impact on how coaches develop a relationship with their clients. The importance of this distinction is highlighted by Boyatzis and colleagues' (2010) recent finding that positive and encouraging remarks from coaches prepared clients to be more open and ready for change compared with negative or neutral comments.

Rock's (2008) SCARF model, based upon assessing amygdala response to threats of Status, Certainty, Autonomy, Relatedness, and Fairness, is an example of an attempt to develop a framework to help coaches promote healthy relationships. Recent studies suggest that using this framework facilitates organizational cohesion (e.g., Martin-Kniep, 2010; Street, 2010). Similar models are sorely needed that apply to coach/client dynamics and to client-centered assessment.

*Change*: Change is not a simple, one-step process. To change, clients must become aware of what needs to be changed; however, change-related issues are often indicated by discontent, hope, worry, expectation or fear; that is, by emotions. While we have highlighted above a number of findings that indicate the importance of emotional valance in change management, a cohesive theory is yet to be developed. There may be types of change programs that are more responsive to positive emotional valence than to negative. For example, smokers show greater success when quitting is framed in terms of gains rather than losses (Toll *et al.*, 2007). Similar queries around other change behaviors remain to be investigated; yet there are clues that such investigations would be worthwhile.

Programs to encourage lasting change can be drawn from neuroscience research. For example, because the resources required for working memory are limited and easily disrupted (Halford *et al.*, 2005), being able to automate behaviors, or make them habitual, bestows advantages – at least when we want that behavior to propagate or to be selected in high-stress situations. However, the lack of competing theories limits coaches in developing an actual template for such programs.

*Motivation and reward*: Motivation is influenced by and dependent upon emotion (Yerkes and Dodson, 1908). With too little emotion clients are uninterested, unengaged, and unmotivated. Similarly, too much investment makes us so "frazzled" that our capacity to solve problems is greatly reduced (Arnsten, 1998; Mather *et al.*, 2006). Coaches may need to help clients engage, but not be overwhelmed in solution finding and decision making.

Gollwitzer and Bargh (1996) suggest making desired goals more salient, and their achievement more likely, by implementing "if-then" planning. Describing specific actions, taking contingencies into account, and asking for accountability are common practices in encouraging goal achievement (Gollwitzer and Bargh, 1996), though such approaches are limited by marginal success, qualifiers (Gollwitzer *et al.*, 2009) and frequent outliers (Powers *et al.*, 2005, 2011).

Because selected change behaviors can be related to a number of motivational factors, coaches might benefit from learning to identify the basis of reward for a desired change (e.g., social, physiological), and from looking at the timing of when reward is given. Although there are a number of reward circuits in the brain, each relies on its ability to associate reward with behavior. One future avenue for coaches may lie in increasing the salience not only of rewards but also the consequence of refusing to change, depending on the nature of the to-be changed behavior (see Toll *et al.*, 2007).

## Conclusion

Research in coaching of any kind is still in its early stages, so the small number of applications of neuroscience to coaching is hardly surprising. Neuroscience may come to provide an empirical foundation for coaching and mentoring but the matter is complicated because coaching tends to be framed in high-level abstractions and cognitive processes that are difficult to operationalize. Yet techniques from neuroscience research are already becoming an integral part of inquiry in all the disciplines from which coaching draws its theoretical and empirical nurturance. For these reasons, coaching-specific questions will help to provide much needed direction to the profession as a whole. As coaching is operationalized and data are gathered, meta-analyses will soon follow, leading to a better understanding of the questions that specifically relate to or can be elucidated by, neuroscience.

Knowledge about brain function will have considerable value for coaches. We have reviewed several behaviors that can be influenced by coaches. Yet the potential power of brain-based explanations comes with a caveat. Neuroscience findings are commonly portrayed in print, broadcast, and electronic media as definitive explanations for why we behave as we do, and often with conflated elaborations. For example, recent reports in the media cited that watching the television show Spongebob Squarepants caused braindamage (Liete, 2011; Spongebob Study, 2011). However, the Lillard and Peterson cited report (2011) in fact claimed only a short-term decrease in executive function (e.g., working memory, self control) after watching a segment of the show. Many of the attention-grabbing sound bites about the brain may in fact be inaccurate or downright wrong. As professionals, it is our responsibility to seek out the source before determining if current findings apply to coaching. Such a responsibility only further highlights the need for the coaching profession to be asking its own questions ensuring the validity and applicability of results.

It is our hope that readers are not discouraged at this point. After reading this litany of factors that often complicate issues rather than resolving them this would not be surprising. However, this complexity is precisely what we, the authors, would choose to celebrate about neuroscience, or indeed science in general. Neuroscience cannot and will not provide all the answers about human behavior. In many cases it may just provide us with more questions. As with all scientific and intellectual pursuits, the preponderance and patterns of questions will indicate not only what is understood, but also how much more is left to discover. Neuroscience is an approach for exploring the neural basis of thinking. It can help coaches and clients think about thinking. Its pursuit will generate more questions each time one is answered, but this is, as coaches know, the real value. The real power after all, lies in the questions.

# References

Ainsworth, M.D.S., Blehar, M.C., Waters, E., and Wall, R. (1978) *Patterns of Attachment: A Psychological Study of the Strange Situation*. Hillsdale, NJ: Erlbaum.

Alger, B.E. (2002) Retrograde signaling in the regulation of synaptic transmission: Focus on endocannibanoids. *Progress in Neurobiology*, 68, 247–86.

Amodio, D.M. and Frith, C.D. (2006) Meeting of minds: The medial frontal cortex and social cognition. *Nature Reviews Neuroscience*, 7, 268–77.

Arnsten, A.F.T. (1998) The biology of being frazzled. *Science*, 280, 1711–12.

Arnsten, A.F.T. (2009) Stress signaling pathways that impair prefrontal cortex structure and function. *Nature Reviews Neuroscience*, 10, 410–22.

Bandura, A. (2004) Health promotion by social cognitive means. *Health Education and Behaviour*, 31(2), 143–64.

Barrett, L.F., Bliss-Moreau, E., Duncan, S.L., Rauch, S.L., and Wright, C.I. (2007) The amygdala and the experience of affect. *Social Cognitive Affective Neuroscience*, 2, 73–83.

Batson, C.D. (1987) Prosocial motivation: Is it ever truly altruistic? In: L. Berkowitz (ed.) *Advances in Experimental Social Psychology*, 20, 65–122.

Baumeister, R.F. and Leary, M.R. (1995) The need to belong: Desire for interpersonal attachments as a fundamental human motivation. *Psychological Bulletin*, 117, 497–529.

Baumeister, R.F., Bratslavsky, E., Finkenauer, C., and Vohs, K.D. (2001) Bad is stronger than good. *Review of General Psychology*, 5, 323–70.

Baumeister, R.F., Twenge, J.M., and Nuss, C.K. (2002) Effects of social exclusion on cognitive processes: Anticipated aloneness reduces intelligent thought. *Journal of Personality and Social Psychology*, 83(4), 817–27.

Beauregard, M. (2007) Mind does really matter: Evidence from neuroimaging studies of emotional self-regulation, psychotherapy, and placebo effect. *Progress in Neurobiology*, 81, 218–36.

Bechara, A. (2004) The role of emotion in decision-making: Evidence from neurological patients with orbitofrontal damage. *Brain and Cognition*, 55, 30–40.

Bennett, C.M. and Miller, M.B. (2010) How reliable are the results from functional magnetic resonance imaging? *Annals of the New York Academy of Sciences*, 1191, 133–55.

Berns, G. (2010) *Iconoclast: A Neuroscientist Reveals How to Think Differently*. Boston: Harvard Business Press.

Berntson, G.G., Norman, G.J., Bechara, A., Bruss, J., Tranel, D., and Cacioppo, J.T. (2011) The insula and evaluative processes. *Psychological Science*, 22(1), 80–6.

Blair, C. and Diamond, A. (2008) Biological processes in prevention and intervention: The promotion of self-regulation as a means of preventing school failure. *Development and Psychopathology*, 20(3), 899–11.

Bliss-Moreau, E. and Barrett, L.F. (2009) What's reason got to do with it? Affect as the foundation of learning. *Behavioural and Brain Sciences*, 3, 201–2.

Borsook, T.K. and MacDonald, G. (2010) Mildly negative social encounters reduce physical pain sensitivity. *Pain*, 151(2), 372–7.

Bowlby, J. (1951) *Maternal Care and Mental Health*. Geneva: World Health Organization.

Bowlby, J. (1969) *Attachment, Attachment and Loss*. Vol. I. London: Hogarth.

Bowlby, J. (1973) *Separations: Anger and Anxiety, Attachment and Loss*. Vol. II. London: Hogarth.

Bowlby, J. (1980) *Loss: Sadness and Depression, Attachment and Loss*. Vol. III. London: Hogarth Press.

Boyatzis, R.E., Jack, A., Cesaro, R., Khawaja, M., and Passarelli, A. (2010) Coaching with Compassion: An fMRI Study of Coaching to the Positive or Negative Emotional Attractor. Paper presented at Academy of Management Annual Conference, Montreal, August.

Boyatzis, R.E., Smith, M., and Blaize, N. (2006). Developing sustainable leaders through coaching and compassion. *Academy of Management Journal on Learning and Education*, 5(1), 8–24.

Brothers, L. (2001) *Mistaken Identity: The Mind-brain Problem Reconsidered*. Albany: State University of New York Press.

Brown, K.W. and Ryan, R.M. (2003) The benefits of being present: Mindfulness and its role in psychological well-being. *Journal of Personality and Social Psychology*, 84, 822–48.

Camille, N., Corecelli, G., Sallet, J., Pradat-Diehl, P., Duhamel, J.R., and Sirigu, A. (2004) The involvement of the orbitofrontal cortex in the experience of regret. *Science*, 304, 1167–70.

Carr, L., Iacoboni, M., Dubeau, M.C., Mazziota, J.C., and Lenzi, G.L. (2003) Neural mechanisms of empathy in humans: A relay from neural systems for imitation to limbic areas. *Proceedings of the National Academy of Science, USA*, 100, 5497–502.

Chiao, J.Y., Bordeaux, A.R., and Ambady, N. (2004) Mental representations of social status. *Cognition*, 93(2), 49–57.

Chiao, J.Y., Hariri, A.R., Harada, T., Mano, Y., Sadato, N., Parrish, T.B. *et al.* (2010) Theory and methods in cultural neuroscience. *Social Cognitive and Affective Neuroscience*, 20, 2167–74.

Chua, H.F., Boland, J.E., and Nisbett, R.E. (2005) Cultural variation in eye movements during scene perception. *Proceedings of the National Academy of Sciences of the USA*, 102, 12629–33.

Courville, C.B. (1942) Coup-contrecoup mechanisms of cranio-cerebral injuries: Some observations. *Archives of Surgery*, 45, 19–43.

Cozolino, L. (2006) *The Neuroscience of Human Relationships: Attachment and the Developing Social Brain*. New York: WW Norton and Co.

Critchley H.D. (2005) Neural mechanisms of autonomic, affective and cognitive integration. *The Journal of Comparative Neurology*, 493, 154–66.

Davachi, L. and Wagner, A.D. (2002) Hippocampal contributions to episodic encoding: Insights from relational and item-based learning. *American Physiological Society*, 88, 982–90.

Davidson, R.J., Jackson, D.C., and Kalin, N.H. (2000) Emotion, plasticity, context and regulation: Perspectives from affective neuroscience. *Psychological Bulletin*, 126(6), 890–909.

Decety, J. and Batson, C.D. (2007) Social neuroscience approaches to interpersonal sensitivity. *Social Neuroscience*, 2(3–4), 151–7.

Decety, J. and Ickes, W. (eds) (2009) *The Social Neuroscience of Empathy*. Cambridge: MIT Press, Cambridge.

DeWall, C.N., MacDonald, G., Webster, G.D., Masten, C.L., Baumeister, R.F., Powell, C. *et al.* (2010) Acetaminophen reduces social pain: Behavioral and neural evidence. *Psychological Science*, 21(7), 931–7.

Dinstein, I., Thomas, C., Behrmann, M., and Heeger, D.J. (2008) A mirror up to nature. *Current Biology*, 18(1), R13–18.

Einstein, G.O., McDaniel, M.A., Williford, C.L., Pagag, J.L., and Dismukes, R.K. (2003) Forgetting of intentions in demanding situations is rapid. *Journal of Experimental Psychology: Applied*, 9(3), 147–62.

Eisenberger, N.I. and Lieberman, M.D. (2004) Why it hurts to be left out: The neurocognitive overlap between physical and cognitive pain. *Trends in Cognitive Sciences*, 8, 294–330.

Eisenberger, N.I., Lieberman, M.D., and Williams, K.D. (2003) Does rejection hurt? An fMRI study of social exclusion. *Science*, 302(5643), 290–2.

Emmons R.A. and McCullough M.E. (2003) Counting blessings versus burdens: An experimental investigation of gratitude and subjective well-being in daily life. *Journal of Personality and Social Psychology*, 84(2), 377–89.

Farb, N.A.S., Anderson, A.K., Mayberg, H., Bean, J., McKeon, D., and Segal, Z. (2010) Minding one's emotions: Mindfulness training alters the neural expression of sadness. *Emotion*, 10(1), 25–33.

Farb, N.A.S., Segal, Z.V., Mayberg, H., Bean, J., McKeon, D., Fatima, Z., and Anderson, A.K. (2007) Attending to the present: Mindfulness meditation reveals distinct neural modes of self-reference. *Social Cognitive and Affective Neuroscience*, 2(4), 313–22.

Feinstein, J.S., Adolphs, R., Damasio, A., and Tranel, D. (2011) The human amygdala and the induction and experience of fear. *Current Biology*, 21, 1–5.

Fink, A., Grabner, R.H., Benedek, M., Reishofer, G., Hauswirth, V., Fally, M. *et al.* (2009) The creative brain: Investigation of brain activity during creative problem solving by means of EEG and fMRI. *Human Brain Mapping*, 30, 734–48.

Frederickson, B.L. (2001) The role of positive emotions in positive psychology: The broaden-and-build theory of positive emotions. *American Psychologist*, 56, 218–26.

Frederickson, B.L. (2009) *Positivity: Top-notch Research Reveals the 3-to-1 Ratio that will Change your Life*. New York: Three Rivers Press.

Gailliot, M.T., Baumeister, R.R., DeWall, C.N., Maner, J.K., Plant, E.A., Tice, D.M. *et al.* (2007) Self-control relies on glucose as a limited energy source: Willpower is more than a metaphor. *Journal of Personality and Social Psychology*, 92, 325–36.

Gallese, V. and Goldman, A (1998) Mirror neurons and the simulation theory of mind-reading. *Trends in Cognitive Sciences*, 2(12), 493–501.

Gallese, V., Fadiga, L., Fogassi, L., and Rizzolatti, G. (1996) Action recognition in the premoter cortex. *Brain*, 119(2), 593–609.

Gates, N.J., Valenzuela, M., Sachdev, P.S., Singh, N.A., Baune, B.T., Brodaty, H. *et al.* (2011) Study of mental activity and regular training (SMART) in at risk individuals: A randomized double blind, sham controlled, longitudinal trial. *BMC Geriatrics*, 11(19). (Epub ahead of print).

Gibson, D.E. and Callister, R.R. (2010) Anger in organizations: Review and integration. *Journal of Management*, 36(1), 66–93.

Gibson, C., Folley, B.S., and Park, S. (2009) Enhanced divergent thinking and creativity in musicians: A behavioural and near-infrared spectroscopy study. *Brain and Cognition*, 69, 162–9.

Gold, J.I. and Shadien, M.N. (2007) The neural basis of decision-making. *Annual Review of Neuroscience*, 30, 535–74.

Gollwitzer, P.M., and Bargh, J.H. (eds) (1996) *The Psychology of Action: Linking Cognition and Motivation to Behavior*. New York: Guilford Press.

Gollwitzer, P.M., Sheeran, P., Michalski, V., and Seifert, A.E. (2009) When intentions go public: Does social reality widen the intention-behaviour gap? *Psychological Science*, 20(5), 612–18.

Gottman, J.M. (1994) *What Predicts Divorce? The Relationship Between Marital Process and Marital Outcomes*. Hillsdale, NJ: Erlbaum.

Grabner, R.H., Neubauer, A.C., and Stern, E. (2006) Superior performance and neural efficiency: The impact of intelligence and expertise. *Brain Research Bulletin*, 69, 422–39.

Greengard, P. (2001) The neurobiology of slow synaptic transmission. *Science*, 294, 1024–30.

Halford, G.S., Baker, R., McCredden, J.E., and Bain, J.D. (2005) How many variables can humans process? *Psychological Science*, 16(1), 70–6.

Hedden, T. and Gabrieli, J.D.E. (2006) The ebb and flow of attention in the human brain. *Nature Neuroscience*, 9(3), 145–62.

Heilman, K.M., Nadeau, S.E., and Beversdorf, D.O. (2003) Creative innovation: Possible brain mechanisms. *Neurocase*, 9(5), 369–79.

Heilman, R.M., Liviu, G., Crişan, L.G., Houser, D., Miclea, M., and Miu, A.C. (2010) Emotion regulation and decision making under risk and uncertainty. *Emotion*, 10(2), 257–65.

Holroyd, C.B. and Coles, G.H. (2002) Dorsal anterior cingulate cortex integrates reinforcement history to guide voluntary behaviour. *Cortex*, 44, 548–59.

Hölzel, B.K., Carmody, J., Vangel, M., Congleton, C., Yerramsetti, S.M., Gard, T. *et al.* (2011) Mindfulness practice leads to increases in regional brain gray matter density. *Psychiatry Research: Neuroimaging*, 191(1), 36.

Howard-Jones, P.A., Blakemore, S., Samuel, E.A., Summers, I.R., and Claxton, G. (2005) Semantic divergence and creative story generation: An fMRI investigation. *Cognitive Brain Research*, 25, 240–50.

Hua, J.Y. and Smith, S.J. (2004) Neural activity and the dynamics of central nervous system development. *Nature Neuroscience*, 7, 327–32.

Iacoboni, M. (2009) Imitation, empathy, and mirror neurons. *Annual Review of Psychology*, 60, 653–70.

Iacoboni, M., Molnar-Szakacs, I., Gallese, V., Buccino, G., Mazziotta, J.C., and Rizzolatti, G. (2005) Grasping the intentions of others with one's own mirror neuron system. *PLoS Biology*, 3(3), 79.

Izard C.E. (2009).The many meanings/aspects of emotion: Definitions, functions, activation, and regulation. *Emotion Review*, 2, 363–70.

Jaremka, L., Gabrial, S., and Carvallo, M. (2010) What makes us feel the best also makes us feel the worst: The emotional impact of independent and interdependent experiences. *Self and Identity*, 10, 44–63.

Jha, A.P., Stanley, E.A., Kiyonaga, A., Wond, L., and Gelfand, L. (2010) Examining the protective effects of mindfulness training on working memory capacity and affective experience. *Emotion*, 10(1), 54–64.

Jin, X. and Costa, R.M. (2010) Start/stop signals emerge in nigrostriatal circuits during sequence learning. *Nature*, 466, 457–62.

Johnson, S. and Taylor, K. (eds) (2006) The neuroscience of adult learning. *New Directions for Adult and Continuing Education*, 10 (special issue).

Johnson, S.K. (2008) I second that emotion: Effects of emotional contagion and affect at work on leader and follower outcomes. *The Leadership Quarterly*, 19, 1–19.

Kensinger, E.A., Clarke, R.J., and Corkin, S. (2003) What neural correlates underlie successful encoding and retrieval? A functional magnetic resonance imaging study using a divided attention paradigm. *Journal of Neuroscience*, 23, 2407–15.

Kitayama, S. and Thompson, S. (2010) Envisioning the future of cultural neuroscience. *Asian Journal of Social Psychology*, 13(2), 92–101.

Kitayama, S., Dufy, S., Dawamura, T., and Larsen, J.T. (2003) Perceiving an object and its context in different cultures: A cultural look at new look. *Psychological Science*, 13, 201–6.

Kluger, A.N. and DeNisi, A. (1996) The effects of feedback interventions on performance: A historical review, a meta-analysis, and a preliminary feedback intervention theory. *Psychological Bulletin*, 119(2), 254–84.

Kosfeld, M., Heinrichs, M., Zak, P.J., Fischbacher, U., and Fehr, E. (2005) Oxytocin increases trust in humans. *Nature*, 435, 673–6.

Kounios, J., Fleck, J.L., Green, D.L., Payne, L., Stevenson, J. L., Bowden, M. *et al.* (2008) The origins of insight in resting-state brain activity. *Neuropsychologica*, 46, 281–91.

Kounios, J., Frymiare, J., Bowden, E., Fleck, J., Subramaniam, K. Parrish, T. *et al.* (2006). The prepared mind: Neural activity prior to problem presentations predicts subsequent solution by sudden insight. *Psychological Science*, 17, 882–90.

Kramer, A.F., Erickson, K.I., and Colcombe, S.J. (2006) Exercise, cognition, and the aging brain. *Journal of Applied Physiology*, 101(4), 1237–42.

Leotti, L.A., Iyengar, S.S., and Ochsner, K.N. (2010) Born to choose: The origins and value of the need for control. *Trends in Cognitive Sciences*, 24, 457–63.

Lieberman, M.D. (2007) Social cognitive neuroscience: A review of core processes. *Annual Review of Psychology*, 58, 259–89.

Lieberman, M.D., Eisenberger, N.I., Crockett, M.J., Tom, S.M., Pfeifer, J.H., and Way, B.M. (2007) Putting feelings into words: Affect labeling disrupts amygdala activity in response to affective stimuli. *Psychological Science*, 18(6), 421–8.

Liete, P. (2011) Watching Spongebob Causes Brain Damage (Web post). Retrieved from http://www.luuux.com/entertainment/watching-spongebob-causes-brain-damage (September 16).

Lillard, A.S. and Peterson, J. (2011) The immediate impact of different types of television on young children's executive function. *Pediatrics*, 128(4), e1–e6.

Limb, C.J. and Braun, A.R. (2008) Neural substrates of spontaneous musical performance: An fMRI study of jazz improvisation. *PLoS ONE*, 3, 1–9.

Litman, L. and Davachi, L. (2008) Distributed learning enhances relational memory consolidation. *Learning and Memory*, 8, 711–16.

Logan, D., King, J., and Fisher-Wright H. (2008) *Tribal Leadership: Leveraging Natural Groups to Build a Thriving Organization*. New York: Harper Business.

Logothetis, N.K. (2008). What we can do and what we cannot do with fMRI. *Nature*, 453, 869–78.

Lombardo, M.V., Chakrabarti, B., Bullmore, E.T., Wheelwright, S.J., Sadek, S.A., Suckling, J. *et al.* (2009) Shared neural circuits for mentalizing about the self and others. *Journal of Cognitive Neuroscience*, 22, 1623–35.

Losada, M. and Heaphy, E. (2004) The role of positivity and connectivity in the performance of business teams: A nonlinear dynamics model. *American Behavioral Scientist*, 47, 740–65.

Lutz, A., Slagter, H.A., Dunne, J.D., and Davidson, R.J. (2008) Attention regulation and monitoring in meditation. *Trends in Cognitive Science*, 12(4), 163–9.

McEwen, B.S. (1998) Protective and damaging effects of stress mediators. *New England Journal of Medicine*, 338, 171–9.

McRae, K., Hughes, B., Chopra, S., Gabrieli, J.J.D., Gross, J.J., and Ochsner, K.N. (2010) The neural correlates of cognitive reappraisal and distraction: An fMRI study of emotion regulation. *Journal of Cognitive Neuroscience*, 22, 248–62.

Mak, A.K.Y., Hu, Z., Zhang, J., Xiao, Z., and Lee, T.M.C. (2009) Neural correlates of regulation of positive and negative emotions: An fMRI study. *Neuroscience Letters*, 457(2), 101–6.

Marsh A.A. and Blair, R.J. (2008) Deficits in facial affect recognition among antisocial populations: A meta-analysis. *Neuroscience of Biobehaviour Review*, 32, 454–65.

Marsh, A.A., Kozak, M.N., and Ambady N. (2007) Accurate identification of fear facial expressions predicts prosocial behavior. *Emotion*, 7, 239–51.

Martin-Kniep, G.O. (2010) Neuroscience of engagement and SCARF: Why they matter in schools. *NeuroLeadership Journal*, 3, 87–96.

Masuda, T., Ellsworth, P.C., Mesquita, B., Leu, J., Tanida, S., and Van de Veerdonk, E. (2004) Placing the face in context: Cultural differences in the perception of facial emotion. *Journal of Personality and Social Psychology*, 94(3), 365–81.

Mather, M., Mitchell, K.J., Raye, C.L., Novak, D.L., Greene, E.J., and Johnson, M.K. (2006) Emotional arousal can impair feature binding in working memory. *Journal of Cognitive Neuroscience*, 18, 614–25.

Mitchell, J.P., Banaji, M.R., and Marae, C.N. (2005) The link between social cognition and self-referential thought in the medial prefrontal cortex. *Journal of Cognitive Neuroscience*, 17(8), 1306–15.

Mitchell, J.P., Macrae, C.N., and Banaji, M.R. (2006) Dissociable medial prefrontal contributions to judgments of similar and dissimilar others. *Neuron*, 50, 655–63.

Mizuno, K., Tanaka, M., Ishii, A., Tanabe, H.C., Onoe, H., Sadato, N., and Watanabe, Y. (2008) The neural basis of academic achievement motivation. *NeuroImage*, 42(1), 369–78.

Mobbs, D., Yu, R., Meyer, M., Passamonti, L., Seymour, B., Calder, A.J. *et al.* (2009) A key role for similarity in vicarious reward. *Science*, 324, 900.

Montgomery, K.J. and Haxby, J.V. (2008) Mirror neuron system differentially activated by facial expressions and social hand gestures: A functional magnetic resonance imaging study. *Journal of Cognitive Neuroscience*, 20(10), 1866–77.

Mui, A.C., Heilman, R.M., and House, D. (2008) Anxiety impairs decision-making: Psychophysiological evidence from the Iowa gambling task. *Biological Physiology*, 77, 353–8.

Murty, V.P., Ritchey, M., Adcock, R.A., and LaBar, K.S. (2010) fMRI studies of successful memory encoding: A quantitative meta-analysis. *Neuropsychologia*, 48, 3459–69.

Ochsner, K.N. and Gross J.J. (2005) The cognitive control of emotion. *Trends in Cognitive Science*, 9, 242–9.

Ochsner, K.N. and Gross, J.J. (2008) Cognitive emotion regulation: Insights from social cognitive and affective neuroscience. *Currents Directions in Psychological Science*, 17, 153–8.

O'Connor, M., Cooper, N. J., Williams, L.M., DeVarney, S., and Gordon, E. (2010) Neuroleadership and the productive brain. *Neuro leadership Journal*, 3, 37–42.

Olalla, J. (2004) *From Knowledge to Wisdom: Essays on the Crisis in Contemporary Learning*. Boulder, CO: Newfield Network.

Paus, T. and Barrett, J. (2004) Transcranial magnetic stimulation (TMS) of the human frontal cortex: Implications for repetitive TMS treatment of depression. *The Journal of Psychiatry and Neuroscience*, 29(4), 268–79.

Paus, T., Castro-Alamancos, M.A., and Petrides, M. (2001) Cortico-cortical connectivity of the human mid-dorsolateral frontal cortex and its modulation by repetitive transcranial magnetic stimulation. *European Journal of Neuroscience*, 14, 1405–11.

Pekrun, R., Goetz, T., Titz, W., and Perry, R.P. (2002) Academic emotions in students' self-regulated learning and achievement: A program of qualitative and quantitative research. *Educational Psychologist*, 37(2), 91–105.

Pereira, A.C., Huddleston, D.E., Brickman, A.M., Sosunov, A.A., Hen, R., McKhann, G.M. *et al.* (2007). An in vivo correlate of exercise-induced neurogenesis in the adult dentate gyrus. *PNAS*, 104(13), 5638–48.

Peterson, S.J., Waldman, D.A., Balthazard, P.A., and Thatcher, R.W. (2008) Neuroscientific implications of psychological capital: Are the brains of optimistic, hopeful, confident, and resilient leaders different? *Organizational Dynamics*, 37(4), 342–53.

Phelps, E.A. (2006) Emotion and cognition: Insights from studies of the human amygdala. *Annual Review of Psychology*, 57, 27–53.

Posner, M.I. and Rothbart, M.K. (2009) Toward a physical basis of attention and self-regulation. *Physical Life Review*, 6, 103–20.

Powers, T.A., Koestner, R., and Topciu, R.A. (2005) Implementation intentions, perfectionism, and goal progress: Perhaps the road to hell is paved with good intentions. *Personality and Social Psychology Bulletin*, 31(7), 902–12.

Powers, T.A., Koestner, R., Zuroff, D.C., Milyavskaya, M., and Corin, A.A. (2011) The effects of self-criticism and self-oriented perfectionism on goal pursuit. *Personality and Social Psychology Bulletin*, 37(7), 964–75.

Preston, S.D., Bechara, A., Damasio, H., Grabowski, T.J., Stansfield, R.B., Mehta, S., and Damasio, A.R. (2007) The neural substrates of cognitive empathy. *Social Neuroscience*, 2(3–4), 254–75.

Rand, D.G., Dreber, A., Ellingsen T., Fudenberg, D., and Maritn, A.N. (2009) Positive interactions promote public cooperation. *Science*, 325, 1272–5.

Ratey, J.J. and Hagerman, E. (2008) *Spark: The Revolutionary New Science of Exercise and the Brain*. New York: Little, Brown.

Ray, R.D., Ochsner, K.N., Cooper, J.C., Roberston, E.R., Gabrieli, J.D.E., and Gross, J.J. (2005) Individual differences in trait rumination and the neural systems supporting cognitive reappraisal. *Cognitive, Affective, and Behavioral Neuroscience*, 5(2), 156–68.

Richardson, C.R., Kriska, A.M., Lantz, P.M., and Hayward, R.A. (2004) Physical activity and mortality across cardiovascular disease risk groups. *Medical Science of Sports and Exercise*, 36(11), 1923–29.

Rock, D. (2008) SCARF: A brain-based model for collaborating with and influencing others. *NeuroLeadership Journal*, 1, 44–52.

Rock, D. and Page, L. (2009) *Coaching with the Brain in Mind: Foundations for Practice*. Hoboken, NJ: John Wiley and Sons.

Rodin, J. (1986) Aging and health: Effects of the sense of control. *Science*, 233, 1271–6.

Roediger, H.L. and Karpicke, J.D. (2006) Test-enhanced learning: Taking memory tests improves long-term retention. *Psychological Science*, 17, 249–55.

Sapolsky, R.M. (2004) *Why Zebras Don't Get Ulcers* (3rd edn). New York: Harper Collins.

Sawyer, K. (2011) The cognitive neuroscience of creativity: A critical review. *Creativity Research Journal*, 23(2), 137–54.

Schacter, D.L. and Addis D.R. (2007) The optimistic brain. *Nature Neuroscience*, 10, 1345–47.

Schore, A.N. (2001) Effects of a secure attachment relationship on right brain development, affect regulation, and infant mental health. *Infant Mental Health Journal*, 22(1–2), 7–66.

Schore, A.N. (2006) Attachment, affect regulation, and the developing right brain: linking developmental neuroscience to pediatrics. *Pediatrics in Review*, 26(6), 204–17.

Schwartz, B. (2004) *The Paradox of Choice: Why Less is More*. New York: Harper Perennial.

Schwartz, R.M., Reynolds, C.F., Thase, M.E., Frank, E., Fasiczka, A.L., and Haaga, D.A.F. (2002) Optimal and normal affect balance in psychotherapy of major depression: Evaluation of the balanced states of mind model. *Behavioural and Cognitive Psychotherapy*, 30, 439–50.

Segerstrom, S.C. and Miller, G.E. (2004) Psychological stress and the human immune system: A meta-analytic study of 30 years of inquiry. *Psychological Bulletin*, 130(4), 601–30.

Seo, M.G., Bartunek, J.M., and Barrett, L.F. (2010).The role of affective experience in work motivation: Test of a conceptual model. *Journal of Organizational Behavior*, 31, 951–68.

Shiffrin, R.M. and Nosofsky, R.M. (1994) Seven plus or minus 2: A commentary on capacity limitations. *Psychological Review*, 101(2), 357–61.

Siegel, D.J. (1999) *The Developing Mind: Toward a Neurobiology of Interpersonal Experience*. New York: Guilford Press.

Siegel, D.J. (2010) *Mindsight: The New Science of Personal Transformation*. New York: Bantam Books.

Singer, T. and Lamm, C. (2009).The social neuroscience of empathy. *The Year in Cognitive Neuroscience 2009: Ann. N.Y. Acad. Sci*, 1156, 81–96.

Smart, N. and Marwick, T.H. (2003) Exercise training for patients with heart failure: A systematic review of factors that improve mortality and morbidity. *American Journal of Medicine*, 116(10), 693–706.

Spongebob Study: "Spongebob" can cause brain damage (nd). Retrieved September 27, 2011, from Little Green Footballs website: http://littlegreenfootballs.com/page/257478_SpongeBob_study-_SpongeBob_Can

Street, C. (2010) Application of neuroscience in executive team coaching: The WSR case. *Neuroleadership Journal*, 3, 64–77.

Tabibnia, G., Satpute, A.B., and Lieberman, M.D. (2008) The sunny side of fairness: Preference for fairness activates reward circuitry (and disregarding unfairness activates self-control circuitry). *Psychological Science*, 19(4), 339–47.

Tambini, A., Ketz, N., and Davachi, L. (2010) Enhanced brain correlations during rest are related to memory for recent experiences. *Neuron*, 65, 280–90.

Tang, Y.Y., Ma, Y., Wang, J., Fan, Y., Feng, S., Lu, Q. *et al.* (2007) Short-term meditation training improves attention and self-regulation. *Proceedings of the National Academy of Sciences of the United States of America*, 104, 17152–6.

Toll, B.A., O'Malley, S.S., Katuluk, N.A., Wu, R., Dubin, J.A., Latimer, A. *et al.* (2007) Comparing gain- and loss-framed messages for smoking cessation with sustained-release bupropion: A randomized controlled trial. *Psychology of Addictive Behaviors*, 21(4), 534–544.

van den Bos, R., Harteveld, M., and Stoop, H. (2009) Stress and decision-making in humans: Performance is related to cortisol reactivity, albeit differently in men and women. *Psychoneuroendocrinology*, 34, 1149–58.

van den Bos, E. and Jeannerod, M. (2002) Sense of body and sense of action both contribute to self-recognition. *Cognition*, 85, 177–87.

van Praag, H. (2009) Exercise and the brain: something to chew on. *Trends in Neuroscience*, 32(5), 283–90.

van Rijn, S., Aleman, A., van Diessen, E., Berckmoes, C., Vingerhoets, G., and Kahn, R.S. (2005) What is said or how it is said makes a difference: Role of the right parietal operculum in emotional prosody as revealed by repetitive TMS. *European Journal of Neuroscience*, 21, 3195–200.

Vogeley, K., Bussfelds, P., Newen, A., Herrmann, S., Happé, F., Falkai, P. *et al.* (2001) Mind reading: Neural mechanisms of theory of mind and self-perspective. *NeuroImage*, 14, 170–81.

Voss, M.W., Nagamatsu, L.S., Liu-Ambrose, T., and Kramer, A.F. (2011) Exercise, brain, and cognition across the lifespan. *Journal of Applied Physiology* (Epub ahead of print).

Walsh, R. (2011) Lifestyle and mental health. *American Psychologist*, 66, 579–92.

Waugh, C.E., Wager, T.D., Fredrickson, B.L., Noll, D.N., and Taylor, S.F. (2008) The neural correlates of trait resilience when anticipating and recovering from threat. *Social Cognitive and Affective Neuroscience*, 3, 322–32.

Whitworth, L., Kimsey-House, H., and Sandahl, P. (1998) *Co-active Coaching: New Skills for Coaching People Toward Success in Work and Life*. Palo Alto, CA: Davies-Black Publishing.

Yerkes, R.M. and Dodson, J.D. (1908) The relation of strength of stimulus to rapidity of habit-formation. *Journal of Comparative Neurology and Psychology*, 18, 459–82.

Zahn, R., Moll, J., Paiva, M., Garrido, G., Krueger, F., Huey, E.D., and Grafman J. (2009) The neural basis of human social values: Evidence from functional MRI. *Cerebral Cortex*, 19, 276–83.

Zamponi, G.W., Lory, P., and Perez-Reyes, E. (2010) Role of voltage-gated calcium channels in epilepsy. *Pflugers Archives – European Journal of Physiology*, 460, 395–403.

Zink, C.R., Tong, Y., Chen, Y.O., Bassett, D.S., Stein, J.L., and Meyer-Lindenberg, A. (2008) Know your place: Neural processing of social hierarchy in humans. *Neuron*, 58, 273–83.

# 7

# Mindfulness in Coaching: Philosophy, psychology or just a useful skill?

## Michael J. Cavanagh and Gordon B. Spence

### Introduction

For over 30 years mindfulness meditation has been used within medical and therapeutic settings to assist people to deal with physical and mental illness and to enhance well-being (Marianetti and Passmore, 2010). In these settings it has been shown to be highly effective. However, it has not been without controversy. As a construct it is beset with conceptual and definitional confusion. As an intervention, its mechanisms of action are unclear. Mindfulness has more recently begun making its way into coaching practice and the coaching literature, carrying with it the unanswered definitional, theoretical, and practical questions: What is mindfulness? What is it good for? Does it work? If so, how does it work? How can it be used in coaching? What is its place in evidence-based coaching practice?

This chapter seeks to answer the above questions. We begin by examining the conceptual and definitional issues surrounding mindfulness, and present a model to assist in clarifying these. After a brief review of the literature we also consider the potential mechanisms by which mindfulness may have its beneficial effects in coaching, and present a theoretical model of these mechanisms. We suggest that mindfulness has important contributions to make to coaching efficacy at the level of the coach, the coachee, and the coaching relationship itself.

### The Changing World

William James once wrote, "compared to what we ought to be, we are only half awake" (James, 1911/1924). It seems we live in a world deliberately designed to keep us half awake; a state where we respond automatically – mindlessly. This is true of Western society and increasingly of modern cities in societies all around the globe. Passive and solitary forms of entertainment and information delivery are ubiquitous in the virtually connected

*The Wiley Blackwell Handbook of the Psychology of Coaching and Mentoring*, First Edition.
Edited by Jonathan Passmore, David B. Peterson, and Teresa Freire.
© 2013 John Wiley & Sons, Ltd. Published 2016 by John Wiley & Sons, Ltd.

world. Organizations pay billions of dollars each year to shape the way people think and act, while ensuring that this shaping of our choices remains below the level of consciousness. Shopping malls, product placement, lighting, media messages, advertising, television shows are all scientifically designed to maximize the automatic responding desired by the purveyors of these services. Our needs and wants are given to us, and even our very sense of self becomes disconnected from our actual experience and is invested in things outside ourselves. The result is a growing sense of disconnection, both between people and within the person.

It is no accident, then, that mindfulness has arisen as a major theme in the psychological literature, and that it continues to attract great attention among researchers, clinicians and coaches alike. Articles, books, and reviews are constantly appearing, covering all aspects of mindfulness, from definition and theory (Bishop *et al.*, 2004; Brown *et al.*, 2003; Shapiro *et al.*, 2006) to its cultivation (e.g., Baer, 2003; Hayes *et al.*, 2003; Linehan *et al.*, 2001; Teasdale, 2004), measurement (Baer *et al.*, 2006; Brown *et al.*, 2003; Cardaciotto *et al.*, 2008), and outcomes in therapeutic and counseling practice (e.g., Brown *et al.*, 2007; Shapiro *et al.*, 2006). Discussions examining the role of mindfulness in supporting therapeutic and non-therapeutic relationships are also emerging (e.g., Barnes *et al.*, 2007; Bruce *et al.*, 2010; Martin, 1997).

Mindfulness as a coaching intervention has received some recent attention in the scholarly coaching literature (e.g., Marianetti and Passmore, 2010; Spence, 2008; Spence *et al.*, 2008). However, this literature is somewhat narrowly focused on exploring the effects of formal and informal mindfulness practice on the coachee. In this chapter we seek to present a more thorough exploration of mindfulness in the coaching engagement by viewing it through the prism of the five reflective spaces created by the coaching engagement (Cavanagh, 2006). These spaces are centred on the coachee, the coach, and the shared space of the coaching relationship itself. They represent distinct loci of experience and reflection. It is our contention that the practice of mindfulness in these five reflective spaces produces linked but different consequences for the coach, the coachee, and the coaching process.

We believe that a nuanced understanding of mindfulness is critical for effective coaching practice. Coaching is fundamentally concerned with the enhancement of human self-regulation. As research is increasingly showing, mindfulness is a multifaceted psychological phenomena (or, as we will argue, a state, trait, process, and philosophy) that appears to reduce emotional and behavioral reactivity and support adaptive, goal-directed self-regulation (Baer and Lykins, 2011; Barnes *et al.*, 2007; Brown *et al.*, 2007; Evans *et al.*, 2009; Spence *et al.*, 2008). The more detailed our understanding of mindfulness, the more effective we can be in using it to enhance our client's capacity to self-regulate.

## Mindfulness: A Confused Construct

What is meant by mindfulness? In both the coaching and wider psychological literatures mindfulness has proven to be difficult to define and a good deal of fuzziness currently surrounds the construct. Current usage of the term is quite elastic. Mindfulness appears to cover a wide range of practices and beliefs, depending on the authors' background and perspective. It has been variously defined in secular and religious terms, and has been used to connote everything from a simple attentional process, to a committed lifestyle choice (Brown *et al.*, 2007; Friedman, 2010). Practices as diverse as focusing on the breath and loving kindness meditation fall under the banner of mindfulness, although this is not without some controversy among mindfulness scholars (Dhimam, 2009).

This lack of definitional clarity and consistency of practice across research studies, has led some commentators to seriously question the overall validity of claims made about mindfulness and its utility in practice (for discussions see Mikulas, 2011; Rapgay and Bystrisky, 2009) . The definitional debate also engenders a surprising amount of emotion among adherents of different perspectives – a somewhat ironic outcome for a construct that is ostensibly about non-clinging and acceptance. Notwithstanding this debate, the scientific study of mindfulness has progressed at a rapid rate and a substantial body of empirical work has accumulated over the past decade (Sauer and Baer, 2011).

The definitional debate has also yielded several different approaches to measuring mindfulness. As Sauer and Baer (2011) note, at least six independent research teams have published self-report measures of mindfulness and led to the accumulation of a sizable body of knowledge about its nature, relationship to other variables and beneficial effects. It can, however, be difficult to summarize findings across this literature as some measures are based on conceptualizations that vary from one factor (e.g., the Mindful Attention Awareness Scale; Brown and Ryan, 2003) to many (e.g., the Five Facet Mindfulness Questionnaire; Baer *et al.*, 2006). Nonetheless, given all these measures are moderately correlated with each other and strongly correlated with other related constructs, such as self-compassion (+ve) and neuroticism(-ve) (see Baer *et al.*, 2006), it would seem that the pessimism about whether conclusions can be drawn from this literature may be overstated.

## If it is so fuzzy, why bother with mindfulness?

Despite the definitional and measurement challenges in mindfulness research, research does suggest a range of benefits may accrue to individuals who display a mindful disposition or engage in practices designed to enhance mindfulness. Several reviews and meta-analyses suggest mindfulness is associated with a wide variety of beneficial effects. These include: enhanced mental and physical health, psychological well-being, behavioral regulation, and interpersonal dynamics (e.g., Baer and Lykins, 2011; Brown *et al.*, 2007; Grossman *et al.*, 2004).

Well-conducted studies have shown that high levels of trait mindfulness are associated with less emotional disturbance and psychological distress (Baer *et al.*, 2006; Brown and Ryan, 2003; Thompson and Waltz, 2007), more benign stress appraisals and less avoidant coping (Weinstein *et al.*, 2009), greater vitality (Brown and Ryan, 2003), and numerous other markers of subjective and psychological well-being (see Baer and Lykins, 2011). Barnes *et al.* (2007) found higher levels of mindfulness predicted greater relationship satisfaction, lower emotional reactivity, and more constructive responses to relationship stress.

The main body of mindfulness research is to be found in clinical settings, both medical and psychological. This growing body of mindfulness-based intervention research consistently reports that mindfulness training (usually involving some form of meditative practice) is effective for treating a wide variety of psychological disorders, stress-related conditions, and behavioral difficulties. Kabat-Zinn's (1990) well-documented Mindfulness-Based Stress Reduction (MBSR) program is an example of a program designed to bring mindfulness into medical settings.

According to Brown *et al.* (2007), by promoting sustained, non-discriminatory observation of momentary experience, all the prominent intervention modalities appear to help individuals develop "insight into psychological and behavioral sources of suffering and thereby leverage well-being enhancement or actions taken to facilitate it" (p. 219).

Studies on the impact of mindfulness on leaders, workers, and organizational functioning are also beginning to emerge. To date, however, this branch of the literature is restricted to studies focused on discreet behaviors associated with workplace performance. For example, Langer (1997) found mindfulness to be associated with improved memory, motivation, and creativity, whilst others have found it to improve other work-related metrics, such as job satisfaction (Kriger and Hanson, 1999), emotional awareness (Shefy and Sadler-Smith, 2006) and social capital and workplace learning (Adams, 2007). Recent studies have also reported links between mindfulness and improved workplace problem identification and coping skills (Walach *et al.*, 2007), depression prevention and improved personal effectiveness (Williams *et al.*, 2010), and mental resilience and psychosocial functioning in the workplace (Burton *et al.*, 2010). Finally, Marrs (2007) examined the impact of a program designed to address fear in the workplace and found mindfulness to be associated with the capacity to make new meanings of familiar situations, think more clearly, and feel calmer, more empowered, and empathetic.

It should be noted that much of the literature involving workplace mindfulness uses small sample sizes and uncontrolled interventions, which requires a cautious interpretation of these findings. For a more comprehensive review of the literature on mindfulness in the workplace see Marianetti and Passmore (2010).

In sum, despite differences in the measurement of mindfulness, enough empirical evidence exists to suggest that the cultivation of mindfulness is a good thing. That is, people who report high levels of mindfulness seem to have a better quality of life experience. Fortunately, for those who report lower levels of mindfulness, a variety of programs appear to reliably enhance mindful qualities and with it one's cognitive, affective, behavioral, and social functioning.

## So, What is Mindfulness?

Although numerous definitions of mindfulness have been proposed in the literature, most see mindfulness as a psychological process that involves both cognitive and emotional elements. Several common elements have been noted across conceptualizations. According to Dane (2010) most definitions refer to mindfulness as (1) a mental *state* that is, (2) focused on *present moment* realities, and that (3) encompasses both internal and external phenomena. Unsurprisingly, these commonalities led to a definition of mindfulness as, "a state of consciousness in which attention is focused on present-moment phenomena occurring both externally and internally" (Dane, 2010, p. 4).

Whilst doubt has recently been cast on the adequacy of several, widely cited definitions of mindfulness (refer to critiques in Brown *et al.*, 2007; Mikulas, 2011), we believe that a relatively minimalist definition of mindfulness (similar to that proposed by Dane (2010)) has some merit and avoids ascribing more to the construct than is warranted.

### Is mindfulness more than bare awareness?

One of the most contentious issues in the study of mindfulness concerns whether the definition should include facets of experience and practice related to the construct. For some the answer is no. For example, Niemiec *et al.* (2010) see mindfulness as a quality of consciousness typified by a "receptive state of mind wherein attention, informed by awareness of present experience, simply observes what is taking place" (p. 345). According to this view, mindfulness is little more than bare awareness; a state in which the person's own mental processes and overt behaviors are merely the object of awareness and not subject to cognitive operations such as judging, categorizing, or appraising (Mikulas, 2011).

Other theorists argue that the experience of mindfulness is much more than bare awareness. For example, Shapiro *et al.* (2006) hold that mindfulness requires attitudinal qualities, such as openness and acceptance, and motivational qualities, such as intentionality. Relatedly, Rapgay and Bystrisky (2009) argue that goal directedness is an essential feature of mindfulness. Drawing on a detailed understanding of Buddhist tradition, they state that mindfulness is fundamentally concerned with the reduction of maladaptive thoughts and the increase of adaptive thinking. Other authors (e.g., Davidson, 2010) are happy to include practices such as loving kindness meditation under the banner of mindfulness. Loving kindness meditation involves the deliberate holding of loving and compassionate feelings toward to the object of the meditation.

Brown *et al.* (2007) point out the prevailing clinical context that surrounds the application of mindfulness in Western psychology has heavily influenced the way it has been defined. They argue that definitions advocated by several structured mindfulness training programs have tended to emphasize important antecedents of mindfulness. For example, Kabat-Zinn's (1990) reference to "purposeful use of attention" makes an act of will (via intention) a part of the conceptualization, whilst other definitions and models include a variety of cognitive operations such as the describing or labeling of thoughts with words (Baer *et al.*, 2004).

It should be noted that not all definitions of mindfulness have been developed alongside clinical treatment packages focused on the development of mindfulness skills. A notable example is Langer's (1989) multi-component socio-cognitive model. Langer's model emerged from research conducted in a variety of settings, both clinical and non-clinical (e.g., education, aged care). She contrasts mindfulness with mindlessness – a type of automatic responding to stimuli unmediated by deliberate conscious processing of data. According to Langer's model, mindfulness encompasses five factors: (1) an orientation in the present, (2) sensitivity to context, (3) openness to experience, (4) adoption of multiple perspectives, and (5) the drawing of novel distinctions (Langer, 1989).

Whilst Langer's focus on the present moment, sensitivity to context and openness to experience is consistent with definitions of mindfulness as bare awareness, the final two factors represent cognitive operations that move well beyond this understanding of mindfulness. The adoption of multiple perspectives requires a deliberate attempt to construct experience in multiple ways. The drawing of novel distinctions requires that imagination, creativity, and evaluation are actively engaged and applied to the object of awareness. This moves mindfulness from an awareness of one's perception to an active construction of one's reality – a move that is out of step with more minimalistic definitions.

## Mindfulness as state, trait, process and philosophy

We believe that a significant portion (but not all) of the definitional debate over mindfulness is due to an unwitting conflation of different categories of phenomena. In other words, the mindfulness literature does not adequately distinguish between mindfulness as (1) a present moment state, (2) a trait or characteristic predisposition toward experience, (3) a deliberate attentional practice, and (4) a commitment toward a set of beliefs about the nature of the self, the world, and experience (i.e., a philosophy). The conflation of

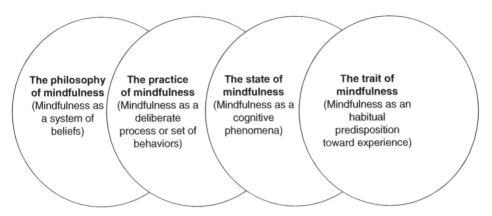

**Figure 7.1** Defining mindfulness – four definitional categories.

these four areas means that definitional disagreements (e.g., Mikulas, 2011) arise because they are actually focused on different types of phenomena.

One way to resolve this issue is to propose that a full understanding of mindfulness needs to encompass all four of these categories (as shown in Figure 7.1), and to recognize that some definitions are focused toward one or more of these perspectives. The minimalist approach tends to focus on mindfulness as a state (the bare awareness approach). For others mindfulness is an attentional process (the act of deliberately focusing attention in a particular way), or alternatively, attitudinal predispositions and habitual intentions toward experience that incline one towards mindful states (the trait approach). Finally, some authors are particularly concerned with articulating the conceptual and philosophical foundations that give meaning to the practice of mindfulness (e.g., Wallace and Shapiro, 2006); an approach that has recently been the subject of some critique (see Friedman, 2010).

## A proposed definition

Based on the preceding discussion we propose that mindfulness is: "A motivated state of decentered awareness brought about by receptive attending to present moment experience." Whilst this definition is reflective of many definitions that currently exist in the literature, we prefer it because it clearly differentiates the state of mindfulness (i.e., decentered awareness) from the process by which the state of mindfulness is attained and maintained (i.e., receptive attending to current experience).

Notably, this definition does not speak to the notion of mindfulness as a trait or as a system of philosophical or religious beliefs. Rather, we have chosen to focus the definition on those aspects of mindfulness most likely to be responsible for the purported beneficial effects of mindfulness: decentered awareness and intentional attending. Whilst the impact of mindfulness has been studied using meditational models (e.g., Barnes *et al.*, 2007), it remains an open empirical question whether these features of mindfulness mediate the positive effects of trait mindfulness, or whether trait mindfulness carries benefits above and beyond those found in the state and practice of mindfulness.

Several aspects of our definition require further elaboration. First, in keeping with other authors, we see mindfulness as a decentered state of awareness. This refers to the position from which experience is observed. In mindfulness, awareness is shifted from a position in which the viewer is central referent, to a position in which the phenomena being observed is central. Our viewpoint on the solar system is a useful analogy for this notion of decentered awareness (Breuer and Roth, 2003). When observed from the perspective of the earth, the sun and planets appears to move in a circular path with the earth at the centre. However, when the viewer moves away from an "earthcentric" perspective, a very different observation can be made. Now the earth and planets are seen to move around the sun. Galileo's great contribution of the heliocentric solar system was enabled by taking a decentered perspective on the movement of the sun.

To continue the analogy, Einstein's theory of relativity tells us that both the earth-centric and heliocentric views are equally valid and equally illusory. The movement of the earth, planets, and sun appears to change again when viewed from the perspective of the galaxy, and will change again if perspectives outside the galaxy are taken. Again, when the timeframe of the perspective is changed, so is the pattern of their movement.

In mindfulness one attempts to observe one's experience from a decentered or non-egocentric position, thereby decoupling the phenomena under observation from the obvious (and apparently immutable) interpretations suggested when the perspective of the viewer is taken as stable and given. The question of which perspective of the solar system is true is really a nonsense question when viewed in a decentered way. So, too, with mindfulness. Mindfulness does not seek to define any particular view of reality as correct or true. Rather, mindfulness practices are intended to assist the practitioner in gaining access to different aspects of the phenomena under observation – aspects hidden when one's habitual interpretations and meanings are taken as stable.

Second, the term "receptive attending" is preferred because it gives primacy to that which is the object of attention. It is the ability of the person to approach the object of attention from a decentered perspective – with the beginner's mind as it were – and so be receptive to it as it emerges in the here and now. In so doing, a person becomes more able to remain non-defensively engaged with present realities. It is this receptivity that often used descriptors of mindfulness such as curiosity, openness, and acceptance, seek to capture. We believe these qualities of attention are best seen as process elements because they can be enhanced via training and purposefully generated at any time (assuming one possesses the requisite skill).

Finally, our definition does not address the notion of mindfulness as a philosophy, or coherent system of beliefs about the nature of oneself, events, and the world. The purpose of our definition is to provide a conceptual starting point to direct research and practice toward those elements of mindfulness thought to be psychologically "active" and hence most likely to be responsible for the beneficial effects that mindfulness practice hopes to achieve. That is not to suggest that a philosophical or religious commitment underpinning mindfulness is therefore psychologically irrelevant. In our definition, mindfulness is con-ceived of as an intentional or motivated state and practice. People may have quite different reasons for engaging in mindfulness practice. It seems to us that the worldviews that support or give rise to these intentions and motivations are one step further removed from its effects. Nevertheless, like trait mindfulness, the contribution of such belief systems to the outcomes of mindfulness practice remain an open question empirically.

## Mindfulness Practice and Purposeful, Positive Change

As outlined above, the research literature reports studies attesting to the positive impact that mindfulness training has on psychological flexibility and purposeful, positive change. Indeed, the reported benefits of mindfulness training seem so vast and wide ranging that a reader could be excused for seeing it as a panacea or "silver bullet" for the optimization of human behavior and general functioning. However, more recent reviews would suggest such an interpretation may be misplaced (Mikulas, 2011; Rapgay and Bystrisky, 2009). We would strongly argue that mindfulness has an important role to play in successful coaching outcomes, and thus would recommend it as a useful addition to coaching practice. However, we also believe that mindfulness represents only one aspect of the coaching engagement.

In order to better articulate the role that mindfulness plays in coaching, we begin by examining a hypothesized effect pathway (see Figure 7.2). This effect pathway has been designed to highlight some potential mechanisms of change, with the hope that it might stimulate further research and better inform practice.

Consistent with our definition, Figure 7.2 suggests that the state of mindfulness results from deliberate attention, supported by a set of attitudinal inputs or postures such as receptivity and openness. It is this attentional focus and attitudinal posture that engagement in structured mindfulness practice is designed to produce. The degree to which a practitioner achieves a state of mindfulness will depend on a range of variables (which are not included in the model for reasons of graphical clarity). These include their history of mindfulness practice, trait mindfulness and personality, and contextual variables. The state of mindfulness then enables a range of potential changes and leads to the practitioner outcomes regularly reported in the research literature. We hypothesize that this effect pathway can be divided into first, second, and third order psychological effects that cumulatively lead to the personal outcomes shown (and potentially many others). In the context of the current discussion, the mindfulness practitioner may be either the coachee or the coach.

As mentioned, for mindfulness practice to be beneficial it must be grounded in some basic attitudinal and behavioral inputs provided by the practitioner. These include the *intention* to only engage in mindful acts and to do so with *acceptance* of what emerges. This basic stance of openness or receptivity to the objects of attention, involves a certain curiosity about the phenomena being observed, and a non-clinging to previous and current interpretations, concerns and thoughts. These preconditions correspond to those proposed by Bishop *et al.* (2004) and Shapiro *et al.* (2006).

If a practitioner can bring these qualities to their practice, then over time, they are likely to develop an enhanced capacity to experience a state of decentered awareness. The object of practice is to develop the ability to greet one's unfolding experience (either during practice or in life) in a more dispassionate way – a more objective observer of one's own subjective experience. A range of outcomes or effects are thought to flow from this decentered stated of awareness (i.e., state mindfulness).

## First order effects

The first order effects include an increased control over one's attention, decreased emotional reactivity, intrapersonal attunement, and access to new sources of information.

*Attentional control*: Increased control over attention is an important outcome of mindfulness. In practicing deliberate focused attention, the practitioner is able to experience him/herself as actively in control of their attention. For many, consciousness is experienced as something that happens to us. That is, our thoughts come and go unbidden, our attention is "captured" by stimuli external to us, and seemingly this occurs

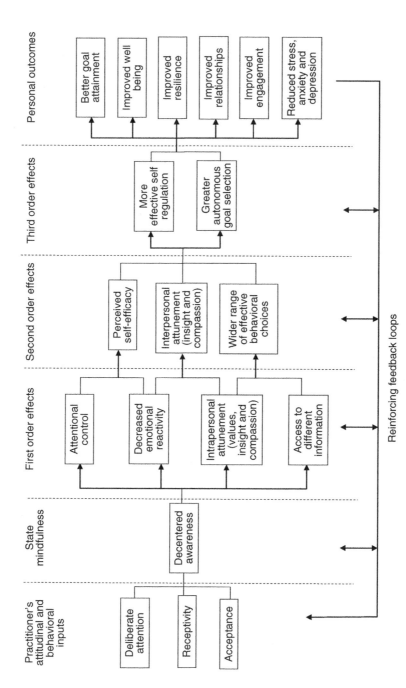

**Figure 7.2** Hypothesized effect pathway showing how the practice of mindfulness influences processes associated with purposeful, positive change.

independent of our choice. Indeed, much of modern life seeks to distract us and hold us in a state of passive receptivity. Watching television, for example, produces brain wave activity more akin to a comatose state (Krugman, 1971) and is characterized by its passivity. This is very different to the deliberate, engaged focus of attention that is characteristic of mindfulness. As Langer (1989) noted, mindfulness is a "limber state of mind" (p. 70). It is an attentionally active state. We hypothesize that this increased capacity to control attention is a key component to an enhanced sense of self-efficacy and greater self-regulation.

*Decreased emotional reactivity.* Emotional reactivity is also associated with a passive stance toward consciousness, wherein the person experiences him/herself as *subject* to their perceptions and the emotions that arise from them are experienced as automatic and immutable. The decentered awareness of experience associated with mindfulness enables the person to make their perceptions an *object* of attention, rather than being subject to them. In breaking this nexus, the person creates a moment of choice or "a small interval of time" (Martin, 1997) in which they can see their experience differently and chose an appropriate response. Without this decentered position, the person's response is effectively choosing them.

*Intrapersonal attunement.* Bruce and colleagues (2010) describe intrapersonal (or self) attunement as the type of relationship that a person has with him/herself. They argue it is a relationship characterized by curiosity, openness, acceptance, and love (COAL; Siegel, 2007). According to Bruce *et al.* (2010) mindfulness is critical to intrapersonal attunement because it promotes a more "secure attachment to oneself" (p. 86), one that promotes experiential engagement rather than avoidance (Hayes, 2003). In other words, the security afforded by an affirming and curious relationship with oneself enables the individual to engage with their ongoing experience and derive important insights from it. This leads to better self-understanding and, ultimately, better understanding of others.

For example, if Sarah normally relates to herself with criticism and derision and finds herself performing poorly on a task, it is unlikely she will wish to dwell on that experience and may instead display defensive response patterns (e.g., blaming self or others). If so, she loses an opportunity to know and accept herself more. She is also less likely to gain insight into other's failures to perform.

*Access to "new" information:* It is generally accepted that the human attentional system has limited capacity (Ward, 2004). A multitude of stimuli bombard the senses in any moment and people can only direct attention towards a small fraction of the available stimuli. Numerous clinical studies have shown that some affective states, such as anxiety, exert a powerful influence on the attentional system (Wells and Matthews, 1994) and tend to bias the selection and recall of information (often towards self-relevant information, e.g., the possibility of a feared event occurring) and impair judgment and evaluation. We believe that mindfulness practice helps to counteract this tendency toward egocentric processing by helping people to either notice information that was previously missed (e.g., another person's delight, rather than one's own fear) or by allowing an opportunity to select (choose) a new interpretation for familiar stimuli (e.g., understanding job performance feedback as constructive, not personal criticism).

## Second order effects

The key second order effects include perceived self-efficacy, interpersonal attunement, and a wider range of effective behavioral choices.

*Perceived self-efficacy.* Alexander *et al.* (1998) note that one advantage of practicing a self-directed mental technique is that individuals gain a sense of empowerment from within. This observation suggests that mindfulness training may positively impact goal-directed behavior via improvements in self-efficacy. That is, when the experience of attentional control is coupled with reduced emotional reactivity, a person is likely to feel that they can better manage their emotional responses and utilize their cognitive resources more fully in the service of self-regulation.

*Interpersonal attunement.* In addition to greater attentional control and emotional regulation, the intrapersonal attunement of mindfulness is likely to enhance the practitioner's capacity for effective empathy or interpersonal attunement. Intrapersonal attunement plays an important role in the development of interpersonal attunement (Bruce *et al.*, 2010). Familiarity with one's own psychological process is an essential starting point for the understanding of others. Through mindfulness practitioners become aware of the interplay between emotions, desires, motivations, and behavior (Rapgay and Bystrisky, 2009), and come to an experience of our common humanity. Importantly for this discussion, research has gone some way to confirming the existence of this relationship in the psychotherapeutic context (e.g., Henry *et al.*, 1990) and there is good reason to suspect this relationship would also extend to the coaching context.

*Behavioral flexibility.* Finally, mindfulness also helps to prevent the enactment of automatic, habitual patterns of behavior and widen the range of one's behavioral choices. This is a consequence following on from the first order effect of decreased emotional reactivity. The process of stepping back and observing momentary experience (cognitive, affective, behavioral, physiological, environmental), encourages conscious rather than reactive responding (Martin, 1997). This corresponds to Watson and Tharp's (1997) observation that "attention breaks up automatic behaviors" (p. 115) and provides a moment of choice in which unsatisfactory, mindless thought-action sequences can be brought under the control of the self and permit the selection of alternative responses. This increase in thought action repertoires contributes to a sense of self-efficacy and control, and enables more effective and adaptive responding.

## Third order effects (with links to personal outcomes)

We hypothesize that the above effects, though useful and welcome in themselves, are most effective because they facilitate greater autonomous goal selection and more effective self-regulation. Furthermore, these third order effects moderate many of the personal outcomes relevant to goal attainment and well-being associated with mindfulness.

*Autonomous goal selection:* One way to understand the effect of interpersonal attunement is via the satisfaction of psychological needs, most especially the needs for relatedness and autonomy. Whilst the experience of being heard, understood and securely connected to others is undoubtedly a satisfying experience, self-determination theory (Deci and

Ryan, 1985) argues that feelings of relatedness have important implications beyond simple satisfaction. That is, when a person feels someone is attuned to them, it can be a clarifying experience, insofar as the process of being understood by another can help a person better understand themselves. This clarity makes the selection of autonomous goals more likely. There is a vast literature attesting to the importance of autonomous goal setting to effective goal-directed self-regulation (see Deci and Ryan, 2000). Research strongly indicates that when people become clearer about their values and interests, they tend to select more self-concordant (autonomous) goals and direct more effort towards the attainment of those goals (Sheldon *et al.*, 2002). Not surprisingly, they also report higher levels of goal attainment and greater levels of subjective and psychological well-being (Sheldon, 2009).

*Effective self-regulation*: The capacity to effectively self-regulate has a direct impact on goal attainment (Carver and Scheier, 1998) and its importance for coaching should require no elaboration here. However, it is useful to note that self-regulation can also provide a person with a sense of mastery that further enhances self-efficacy and motivation. As proposed by expectancy theory (Vroom, 1964), motivational force is a function of three cognitive states: valence (importance placed on the outcomes of goal attainment), instrumentality (the belief goal attainment with yield the desired outcome) and, most importantly for this discussion, expectancy (the belief one's effort will result in goal attainment).

As one might expect, across time feedback loops develop between each of the levels of effect in the model. Later effects reinforce earlier effects in the next iteration. Feedback loops also exist within effect levels (e.g., decreased emotional reactivity enhances access to new information).

## The Coaching Engagement – Five Reflective Spaces

To better understand the multifaceted role that mindfulness plays in coaching, it is useful to consider its influence from several different perspectives. To assist our exploration, we will regard the coaching engagement as consisting of five reflective spaces, or "five conversations that interact together to create the coaching conversation" (Cavanagh, 2006, p. 338). A graphical representation of these five reflective spaces is provided in Figure 7.3.

According to Cavanagh (2006), the five conversations (spaces) of interest are:

1  The internal conversation of the coachee.
2  The conversation between the coachee and coachee's world.
3  The internal conversation of the coach.
4  The conversation between the coach and the coach's world.
5  The shared space created between the coach and the coachee – the external coaching conversation.

In each of these reflective spaces information or data is processed, for the purpose of deciding on action. Those actions can be as simple as deciding what to say or when to intervene, or as complex as creating a case conceptualization collaboratively with a coachee and agreeing an action plan for goal attainment. Mindfulness is considered to be important for enhancing the quality of the conversations that occur in each of the reflective spaces.

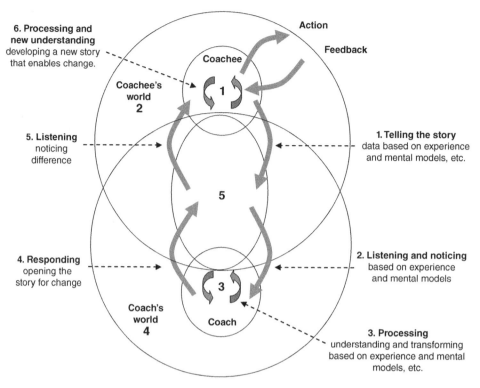

**6. Processing and new understanding**
developing a new story that enables change.

**Action**

**Feedback**

Coachee

Coachee's world
2

**5. Listening**
noticing difference

**1. Telling the story**
data based on experience and mental models, etc.

5

**4. Responding**
opening the story for change

**2. Listening and noticing**
based on experience and mental models

Coach's world
4

Coach

**3. Processing**
understanding and transforming based on experience and mental models, etc.

**Figure 7.3**   The five reflective spaces – a dynamic model of the coaching conversation.

## First reflective space: The internal conversation of the coachee

The stories a coachee shares throughout any coaching engagement are shaped by the way s/he understand themselves, others, and the world. Oftentimes these understandings are challenged during coaching. When this happens coachees are faced with the (usually) uncomfortable task of integrating alternative perspectives with their prevailing mental models, before trying to open up pathways for purposeful, positive action. How coachees "talk" to themselves about their change experience has important implications for coaching success. For example, a coachee may be assisted by internal conversations that involve recalling how their change is personally meaningful, or the generation of self-compassion when faced with unmet performance expectations. With another coachee, however, continued engagement in change efforts might be hampered by an internal dialogue that does not tolerate uncomfortable feelings (e.g., confusion, anxiety) or eschews personal responsibility for change and seeks to locate it in others (e.g., "It's the coach's role to fix the problem").

As we have seen from the foregoing discussion, mindfulness practice can make an important contribution to the coachee's capacity to be dispassionately aware of their internal dialogue, thoughts, and assumptions (e.g., see Jain *et al.*, 2007; Marrs, 2007). The decentered awareness characteristic of mindfulness can help coachees break ruminative cycles or other unhelpful thought-action sequences and, by liberating attention and processing capacity, greater access can be gained to the information needed for adaptive responding. As mentioned earlier, mindfulness also plays a role in enhancing emotional control, goal-setting, and self-regulation (for an example see Davidson *et al.*, 2003).

## Second reflective space: The conversation between the coachee and their world

The impact of mindfulness on the relationship the coachee has to their world is of critical importance for the coaching engagement. Indeed, change in the way the coachee sees, experiences, and operates in the world is the point of coaching. For our purposes in this chapter, the major impacts of mindfulness in this sphere correspond to the second and third order effects outlined in Figure 7.2, and discussed in more detail above.

As Marrs (2007) has reported, mindfulness positively impacts the way in which a person makes meaning in the world, and flowing on from this, enhances the person's behavioral, emotional, and social flexibility. This suggests that mindfulness may help a coachee to act upon the behavioral and cognitive changes that are stimulated during coaching sessions, enhance their ability to notice relevant feedback that is present in their world, and to use that feedback to regulate their behavior. Any improvement in the coachee's capacity to act, monitor feedback, and adapt will substantially increases the likelihood of success for the coaching engagement.

## Third reflective space: The internal conversation of the coach

Simply put, we see a coach's engagement in mindfulness practice as being not unlike the experience of any practitioner. As described earlier (and illustrated in Figure 7.2), the practitioner brings both an attitude and an intention to their practice, and then seeks to become better by paying close attention to the effects of that practice (via a series of feedback loops). We believe that a mindful coach would do much the same thing (see Figure 7.4). That is, they would prepare for each coaching session (their practice) by cultivating mindful qualities like openness and acceptance, along with an overarching intention that provides a reason for such a stance (e.g., "to create a safe, productive space for the coachee," or "be an effective coach"). Having cultivated these qualities, the coach is likely to be less emotionally reactive and more self-attuned (both first order effects), which is likely to enhance coaching confidence levels (self-efficacy) and lead to better attunement with the coachee (interpersonal attunement) – both of which are second order effects.

*Coach mindfulness – session level effects.* Having explored the salutary effects that mindfulness may have for the coach, we now turn our attention to the benefits that coach mindfulness may have for the coachee and the coaching session. It should be noted that the model presented in Figure 7.4 does not imply that the coach is responsible for the outcomes of coaching sessions, nor the coachee's outcomes overall. Rather, it merely proposes that these outcomes will be influenced by the degree to which a coach is mindful during coaching conversations.

Consistent with our earlier discussion, state mindfulness is considered to have much the same antecedents, and the same first and second order effects as indicated in Figure 7.2. However, the effect pathway depicted in Figure 7.4 diverges beyond the second order effects, where the new model focuses on the effects that greater perceived self-efficacy, interpersonal attunement, and behavioral flexibility have on the coach's ability to conduct

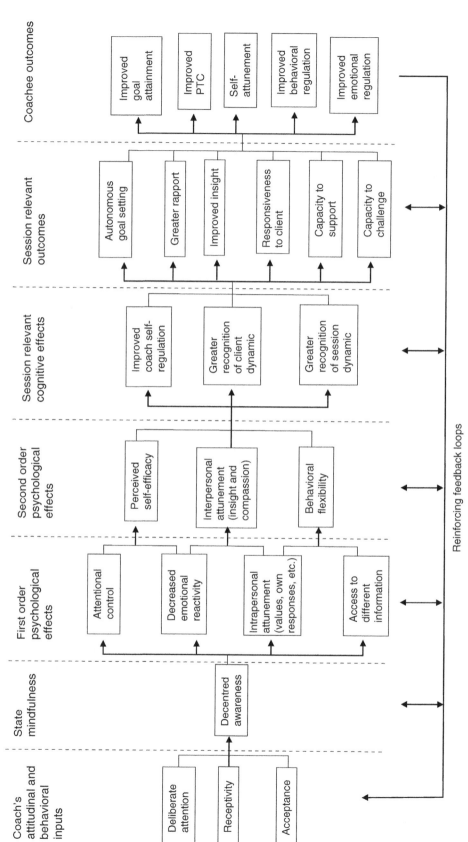

**Figure 7.4** Hypothesized effect pathway linking coach mindfulness to coaching outcomes.

an effective session (i.e., improved coach self-regulation). Here we are specifically referring to the use of core micro-skills (i.e., ask good questions, listen reflectively, manage time, etc.) that constitute good coaching (Zeus and Skiffington, 2002).

The model also focuses on the coach's capacity to notice and understand the verbal or non-verbal data being generated by the coachee (i.e., the client dynamic) and the relationship patterns that emerge throughout the coach–coachee interaction (i.e., the session dynamic). As these dynamics are often only discernible through the recognition of subtle cues (e.g., changes in voice tone, body language), it is vital that a coach be present and attentive to all that the coachee is communicating, and all that is occurring in the session. Yet sustaining mindfulness can be particularly challenging during coaching conversations. In our experience supervising professional coaches and students, we have noticed that there are almost an infinite number of ways that coaches can become distracted or inattentive to the messages a coachee might send.

For example, coaches will often bring a wealth of experience and domain-specific expertise to their practice. Whilst this is often an advantage, coaches often report to us that their expertise can impede coaching outcomes, particularly if a coach begins to "trade" too heavily on their knowledge and use it to direct the coachee's efforts (more in keeping with the style of a mentor or teacher). Although this is a perfectly valid approach to take in many situations (see Cavanagh, 2006), engagement in reflective coaching practice often leads coaches (the authors included) to the uncomfortable realization that the use of expert knowledge in coaching is often triggered by the needs of the coach (e.g., to regain control of a session, to "add value" and/or avoid the discomfort of witnessing a coachee's confusion), rather than the needs of the coachee.

For student or trainee coaches inattentiveness is often related to the use of simple process models, such as the Goal-Reality-Options-Wrap-up model (GROW; Whitmore, 1996). With GROW the challenge is often that the trainee coach becomes consumed by a need to apply the model in a linear G-R-O-W sequence. The unfortunate effect of this is that they often fail to attend to what the coachee is saying (often losing track of the conversation or missing important details) and/or attempt to force the coachee to fit their story into the coach's mental model. More often than not these effects will have a detrimental impact on important aspects of the working alliance (e.g., rapport, trust, and confidence).

Given these potential pitfalls, a coach who is able to bring a high level of mindfulness to their coaching conversations is more likely work effectively with a coachee because they will be less prone to succumbing to such acts of mindlessness and, should that happen, they would be more likely to recognize its occurrence and resume a mindful mode of processing.

*Coach mindfulness–session effects and coachee benefits.* Figure 7.4 also lists some of the key benefits that are likely to flow from a coaching session(s) characterized by a high degree of mindfulness. These include outcomes related to the coachee being better able to reflect on their values and then use them as the basis for setting goals (i.e., autonomous goal setting), more trusting, open dialogue (i.e., greater rapport), greater appreciation of what leads the coachee to act habitually (i.e., improved insight) and more immediate recognition of the coachee's needs (i.e., responsiveness to coachee). It should also be expected that the creation of a space that allows a coachee to safely notice and explore intra- and interpersonal processes would also lead to a greater preparedness to receive and provide help (i.e., capacity to support), as well as a greater preparedness to be stretched and to be stretching (i.e., capacity to challenge). These effects are consistent with those noted by other authors (Passmore and Marianetti, 2007; Siegel, 2007).

Should these session-relevant effects occur, a wide variety of outcomes might be expected to accrue for the coachee. These include improved behavioral regulation and goal attainment, greater self-attunement, better emotional regulation, and an enhanced capacity to take and hold a perspective on oneself, others and/or the external world or system that one operates within.

## Fourth reflective space: The coach's conversation with their world

How the coach interacts with their world outside the coaching engagement also has consequences for the quality of that engagement. The most obvious way that coach mindfulness might impact coaching is through their capacity to notice their own patterns of meaning making and behavior (e.g., stress reactivity) that might have consequences for their coaching practice. For a mindful coach, such observations are likely to become the basis for ongoing growth and development and be introduced into professional development activities (e.g., supervision) in an attempt to develop cognitive, behavioral, and emotional flexibility.

## Fifth reflective space: The shared conversation of coach and coach

Finally, we would like to discuss the role of mindfulness as a characteristic of the shared conversation between coach and coachee. As we have seen, the personal mindfulness of the coach and coachee can make an important contribution to the coaching endeavor. Yet, the coaching relationship is not simply the sum of what the coach and coachee bring to it. Coaching is a complex adaptive system, and as such, the conversation between the coach and coachee is a unique place of reflection and action in its own right (Cavanagh, 2006). This raises questions about how we might consider this shared conversation as the site of mindfulness. What does a mindful coaching space look like? How might it be fostered?

We propose that a mindful shared space is one within which there is a shared expectation and process for collaborative and non-defensive noticing of the changing flow of data that constitutes the coaching relationship. Put more simply, the coach and coachee work together in a way that creates receptive awareness of the present moment, and then seek to use the data that emerges from this awareness in the service of the coaching goals. Several pathways are apparent for creating such a coaching space and these will now be very briefly outlined.

*Modeling mindfulness.* The coach can seek to model mindfulness in the way they deal with the shared content of the session. This would include, where appropriate, using immediacy to make his/her thinking explicit (as it unfolds) and/or sharing with the coachee instances where the coach has noticed they have become captured by their own thinking and feelings. The coach might then model how to let go of such "clinging" behaviors.

*Cultivating mindfulness.* The coach and coachee could set up explicit processes that assist them to cultivate and maintain mindfulness. These processes might include:

1   Commencing each session with a short period of mindfulness practice. This could be as simple as bringing one's intentions for the session to mind or a short breathing-space exercise (see Williams *et al.*, 2007, pp. 183–4).

2   Modifying the physical space (e.g., no telephones, computers or other sources of potential distraction).
3   Setting up cues to remind the coach and coachee to be mindful throughout the session (e.g., a visual symbol or setting a mobile device to softly chime at regular intervals).
4   Creating the expectation that one's present moment internal states are valued in coaching and useful to share because they provide an important source of data that assist understanding and decision making processes. Useful questions can include: What are you feeling now? What tensions or feeling of discomfort might be arising as we discuss this?

*Mindful noticing*: Making shared emotions and fears explicit in the session can be helpful for maintaining a non-reactive and mindful reflective space. This is important at times when the coaching space is suffused with confusion and ambiguity, such as when high stakes issues are being considered. In moments like these it is often the case that neither the coach nor the coachee know what to make of what is emerging, goals can seem illusive and pathways of action invisible. Such moments can be quite aversive for both parties and can easily lead to reactive responses (such as rushing to closure on the goal, blaming other people, or blaming the process). Being able to mindfully notice and articulate such confusion (and its associated emotions) can help both coach and coachee to better manage the tension that accompanies ambiguity and lead to more adaptive responding (e.g., persevering with the conversations despite the discomfort).

*Turning towards tensions*: Mindfulness is difficult to maintain in the face of anxiety and distrust. If the shared coaching space is to be a place of mindfulness, it must also be a place of safety. This means that issues arising in the coaching relationship need to be attended to early, and in a non-judgmental, mindful fashion. One of the most potent ways that a coach can model mindfulness is to turn toward tensions in the coaching relationship, particularly situations that are potentially threatening for the coach (e.g., non-defensively approaching a coachee's criticism). By doing this a coach can help the coachee to see what it is like to remain mindful in the face of tension and anxiety. Structures and practices like those mentioned above can help scaffold both the coach and coachee into more mindful behaviors. This can occur not only during coaching sessions but also beyond those sessions. They represent potent ways of helping both the coach and coachee to learn to trust in the coaching process, and build flexibility into the coaching process. In essence, these practices help us turn toward tensions that occur in the here and now – tensions that we might otherwise seek to avoid or ignore. They may be as simple as a coach thinking "umm, I'm not sure I would do it that way," or "I'm not sure I understand," to the more confronting tensions that emerge during conflict between people ("I am right and you are wrong").

In complex systems, such tensions are best thought of as simply the consequence of different information flowing through a system at any particular point in time. The tensions that arise as a result of these differences are pointers to this new information, and new sites for creativity and innovation. As such, tensions are sought and welcomed. They are potentially a valuable source of new solutions. Indeed they are the very stuff of which coaching is made (Cavanagh, 2006; Cavanagh and Lane, 2012).

# Future Directions for Research

This chapter has explored issues related to the definition of mindfulness, proposed two new models (hypothesized effect pathways) that seek to clarify the role that mindfulness plays in coaching engagements, and situated these models within a multidimensional understanding of the coaching process (i.e. the Five Reflective Spaces model). We hope these contributions will help to stimulate research and can offer four recommendations for further work in this area.

First, the definitional challenges associated with mindfulness will continue to be of critical importance. Delineating the state, trait, process, and philosophical aspects of the construct hold promise in meeting some of these definitional issues. Like Brown and Ryan (2004), we believe that simply defining mindfulness in terms of traditional forms of meditation is likely to prove unhelpful. Distinguishing between the process, attitudinal, and qualitative, and predispositional components of mindfulness may help us to better understand how and why mindfulness creates its beneficial effects.

Second, the hypothesized pathway models presented here (Figure 7.2 and Figure 7.4) require empirical testing and validation. To what degree are the effect pathways postulated here accurate and what other mechanisms of action might be at play? While work has begun in clinical and counseling research literatures on identifying mechanisms of action and pathway models in mindfulness (e.g., Barnes *et al.*, 2007) much more empirical work is needed to assess the sort of detailed effect pathways here.

Third, the collaborative development of mindfulness practices for coaching is an area ripe for exploration. By this we are suggesting that coaches work creatively with coachees to develop practices that may make coaching conversations more mindful. Qualitative studies may be particularly useful in understanding the experiences of coachees applying mindfulness in the workplace, in session, and elsewhere in their lives. The development of such practices should also be subjected to scrutiny via scientific methods and become the focus of outcome studies in their own right.

Finally, to our knowledge only one study has explicitly situated mindfulness training into coaching practice (Spence *et al.*, 2008). More work is clearly needed. Mindfulness based coaching outcome studies should be characterized by clearly articulated definition mindfulness, and detailed description of the mindfulness practices undertaken. In addition, there is need for comparative outcome studies (e.g., comparing mindfulness based coaching with cognitive-behavioral, solution-focused coaching (CB-SF; see Green *et al.*, 2006; Spence and Grant, 2007)). Alternatively, the efficacy of simple mindfulness-practice could be compared with mindfulness based treatment models that have relevance to coaching, such as Acceptance and Commitment Therapy (Hayes *et al.*, 2003; Hayes and Smith, 2005).

# Conclusion

Given that mindfulness seems to play a critical role in human functioning (particularly the process of purposeful positive change), its relative absence from the scholarly coaching literature is somewhat strange. In writing this chapter it has been our hope that the ideas contained herein will give readers a different way to think about mindfulness and help to stimulate scientific investigation of the construct and, most importantly, lead to enhancements in evidence-based coaching practice.

While we might live in a world that encourages mindlessness, we also live in a time that, like no other time before, needs mindful leaders. The complex challenges that face our organizations, societies, and planet require us to be alive to the ever changing dynamic at play within us and between us – and within and between the systems in which we live. The question facing us as coaches is: "How well are we preparing ourselves and our clients to face those challenges and respond in intentional, thoughtful and creative ways?"

## Acknowledgement

This work was in part made possible through funding by the Australian Research Council (Linkage Grant No. LP0776814).

## References

Adams, H.L. (2007) Mindful use as a link between social capital and organizational learning: An empirical test of the antecedents and consequences of two new constructs. Dissertation Abstracts International Section A: *Humanities and Social Sciences*, 67(11-A), 4243.

Baer, R.A. (2003) Mindfulness training as a clinical intervention: A conceptual and empirical review. *Clinical Psychology: Science and Practice*, 10(2), 125–43.

Baer, R.A. and Lykins, E.L.B. (2011) Mindfulness and positive psychological functioning. In: K.M. Sheldon, T.B. Kashdan, and M.F. Steger (eds) *Designing Positive Psychology: Taking Stock and Moving Forward*. New York: Oxford University Press. pp. 335–48.

Baer, R.A., Smith, G.T., and Allen, K.B. (2004) Assessment of mindfulness by self-report: The Kentucky Inventory of Mindfulness Skills. *Assessment*, 11, 191–206.

Baer, R.A., Smith, G.T., Hopkins, J., Krietemeyer, J., and Toney, L. (2006) Using self-report assessment methods to explore facets of mindfulness. *Assessment*, 13(1), 27–45.

Barnes, S., Brown, K.W., Campbell, W.K., and Rogge, R.D. (2007) The role of mindfulness in romantic relationship satisfaction and responses to relationship stress. *Journal of Marital and Family Therapy*, 33(4), 482–500.

Bishop, S.R., Lau, M., Shapiro, S., Carlson, L., Anderson, N.D., Carmody, J. *et al.* (2004) Mindfulness: A proposed operational definition. *Clinical Psychology: Science and Practice*, 11(3), 230–41.

Breuer, F. and Roth, W. (2003) Subjectivity and reflexivity in the social sciences: Epistemic windows and methodical consequences. *Forum: Qualitative Social Research*, 4(2), Art. 25.

Brown, K.W. and Ryan, R.M. (2003) The benefits of being present: Mindfulness and its role in psychological well-being. *Journal of Personality and Social Psychology*, 84(4), 822–48.

Brown, K.W. and Ryan, R.M. (2004) Perils and promise in defining and measuring mindfulness: Observations from experience. *Clinical Psychology: Science and Practice*, 11(3), 242–8.

Brown, K.W., Ryan, R.M., and Cresswell, J.D. (2007) Mindfulness: Theoretical foundations and evidence for its salutary effects. *Psychological Inquiry*, 18(4), 211–37.

Bruce, N.G., Manber, R., Shapiro, S.L., and Constantino, M.J. (2010) Psychotherapist mindfulness and the psychotherapy process. *Psychotherapy Theory, Research, Practice, Training*, 47(1), 83–97.

Burton, N.W., Pakenham, K.I., and Brown, W.J. (2010) Feasibility and effectiveness of psychosocial resilience training: A pilot study of the READY program. *Psychology, Health and Medicine*, 15(3), 266–77.

Cardaciotto, L., Herbert, J.D., Forman, E.M., Moitra, E., and Farrow, V. (2008) The assessment of present-moment awareness and acceptance: The Philadelphia mindfulness scale. *Assessment*, 15(2), 204–23.

Carver, C.S. and Scheier, M.F. (1998) *On the Self-regulation of Behavior*. Cambridge: Cambridge University Press.

Cavanagh, M. (2006) Coaching from a systemic perspective: A complex adaptive conversation. In: D.R. Stober and A.M. Grant (eds) *Evidence Based Coaching Handbook: Putting Best Practices to Work for your Clients*. Hoboken, NJ: Wiley & Sons. pp. 313–54.

Cavanagh, M.J. and Lane, D. (2012) Coaching psychology coming of age: The challenges we face in the messy world of complexity? *International Coaching Psychology Review*, 7(1), 75–90.

Dane, E. (2010) Paying attention to mindfulness and its effects on task performance in the workplace. *Journal of Management*, 37(4), 997–1018.

Davidson, R.J. (2010) Empirical explorations of mindfulness: Conceptual and methological conundrums. *Emotion*, 10(1), 8–11.

Davidson, R.J., Kabat-Zinn, J., Schumacher, J., Rosenkranz, M., Muller, D., Santorelli, S.F. *et al.* (2003) Alterations in brain and immune function produced by mindfulness meditation. *Psychosomatic Medicine*, 65, 564–70.

Deci, E.L. and Ryan, R.M. (1985) *Intrinsic Motivation and Self-Determination in Human Behaviour*. New York: Plenum Press.

Deci, E.L. and Ryan, R.M. (2000) The "what" and "why" of goal pursuits: Human needs and the self-determination of behavior. *Psychological Inquiry*, 11(4), 227–68.

Dhimam, S. (2009) Mindfulness in life and leadership: An exploratory survey. *Interbeing*, 3(1), 55–80.

Evans, D.R., Baer, R.A., and Segerstrom, S.C. (2009) The effects of mindfulness and self-consciousness on persistence. *Personality and Individual Differences*, 47, 379–82.

Friedman, H. (2010) Is buddhism a psychology: Commentary on romanticism in "mindfulness in psychology". *The Humanistic Psychologist*, 38, 184–9.

Green, L.S., Oades, L.G., and Grant, A.M. (2006) Cognitive-behavioural, solution-focused life coaching: Enhancing goal striving, well-being, and hope. *Journal of Positive Psychology*, 1(3), 142–9.

Grossman, P., Niemann, L.G., and Walach, H. (2004) Mindfulness-based stress reduction and health benefits: A meta-analysis. *Journal of Psychosomatic Research*, 57(1), 35–43.

Hayes, S.C. and Smith, S. (2005) *Get Out of Your Mind and Into Your Life: The New Acceptance and Commitment Therapy*. Oakland, CA: New Harbinger Publications.

Hayes, S.C., Strosahl, K.D., and Wilson, K.G. (2003) *Acceptance and Commitment Therapy: An Experiential Approach to Behavior Change*. New York: Guilford Press.

Henry, W.P., Schacht, T.E., and Strupp, H.H. (1990) Patient and psychotherapist introject, interpersonal process, and differential psychotherapy outcome. *Journal of Consulting and Clinical Psychology*, 58, 768–74.

Jain, S., Shapiro, S.L., Swanick, S., Roesch, S.C., Mills, P.J., Bell, I. *et al.* (2007) A randomized controlled trial of mindfulness meditation versus relaxation training: Effects on distress, positive states of mind, rumination, and distraction. *Annals of Behavioral Medicine*, 33, 11–21.

James, W. (1911/1924) *Memories and Studies*. New York: Longmans, Green & Co.

Kabat-Zinn, J. (1990) *Full Catastrophe Living: Using the Wisdom of Your Body and Mind to Face Stress, Pain, and Illness*. New York: Delacorte.

Kriger, M.P. and Hanson, B.J. (1999) A value-based paradigm for creating truly healthy organizations. *Journal of Organizational Change Management*, 12(4), 302–17.

Krugman, H.E. (1971) Brain wave measures of media involvement. *Journal of Advertising Research*, 11(1), 3–9.

Langer, E.J. (1989) *Mindfulness*. Reading, MA: Addison-Wesley.

Langer, E.J. (1997) *The Power of Mindful Learning*. Reading, MA: Addison-Wesley.

Linehan, M.M., Cochran, B.N., and Kehrer, C.A. (2001) Dialectical behavior therapy for borderline personality disorder. In: D.H. Barlow (ed.) *Clinical Handbook of Psychological Disorders: A Step-by-step Treatment Manual*. New York: Guilford Press. pp. 470–522.

Marianetti, O. and Passmore, J. (2010) Mindfulness at work: Paying attention to enhance well-being and performance. In: P.A. Linley, S. Harrington, and N. Garcea (eds) *Oxford Handbook of Positive Psychology and Work*. Oxford, Oxford University Press. pp. 189–200.

Marrs, P.C. (2007) The enactment of fear in conversations-gone-bad at work. *Dissertation Abstracts International Section A: Humanities and Social Sciences*, 68(6-A), 2545.

Martin, J.R. (1997) Mindfulness: A proposed common factor. *Journal of Psychotherapy Integration*, 7(4), 291–12.

Mikulas, W.L. (2011) Mindfulness: Significant common confusions. *Mindfulness*, 2, 1–7.

Niemiec, C.P., Brown, K.W., Kashdan, T.B., Cozzolino, P.J., Breen, W.E., Levesque, C.S., *et al.* (2010) Being present in the face of existential threat: The role of trait mindfulness in reducing defensive responses to mortailty salience. *Journal of Personality and Social Psychology*, 99(2), 344–65.

Passmore, J. and Marianetti, O. (2007) The role of mindfulness in coaching. *The Coaching Psychologist*, 3(3), 131–8.

Rapgay, L. and Bystrisky, A. (2009) Classical mindfulness: An introduction to its theory and practice for clinical application. *Annals of the New York Academy of Science*, 1172(148–62).

Sauer, S. and Baer, R.A. (2011) Mindfulness and decentering as mechanisms of change in mindfulness and acceptance-based interventions. In: R.A. Baer (ed.) *Assessing Mindfulness and Acceptance Processes*. Oakland, CA: Context Press. pp. 25–50.

Shapiro, S.L., Carlson, L., Astini J.A., and Freedman, B. (2006) Mechanisms of mindfulness. *Journal of Clinical Psychology*, 62(3), 373–86.

Shefy, E. and Sadler-Smith, E. (2006) Applying holistic principles in management development. *Journal of Management Development*, 25(4), 368–85.

Sheldon, K.M. (2009). Changes in goal-striving across the life span: Do people learn to select more self-concordant goals as they age? *Handbook of Research on Adult Learning and Development*. New York, NY: Routledge/Taylor & Francis Group; US. pp. 553–69.

Sheldon, K.M., Kasser, T., Smith, K., and Share, T. (2002) Personal goals and psychological growth: Testing an intervention to enhance goal attainment and personality integration. *Journal of Personality*, 70(1), 5–31.

Siegel, D.J. (2007) *The Mindful Brain: Reflection and Attunement in the Cultivation Of Well-being*. New York: W.W. Norton & Co.

Spence, G.B. (2008) *New Directions in Evidence-based Coaching: Investigations into the Impact of Mindfuness Training on Goal Attainment and Well-being*. Saarbrucken: VDM Verlag Dr Muller.

Spence, G.B. and Grant, A.M. (2007) Professional and peer life coaching and the enhancement of goal striving and well-being: An exploratory study. *Journal of Positive Psychology*, 2(3), 185–94.

Spence, G.B., Cavanagh, M.J., and Grant, A.M. (2008)The integration of mindfulness training and health coaching: An exploratory study. *Coaching: The International Journal of Theory, Research and Practice*, 1(2), 145–63.

Teasdale, J.D. (2004) Mindfulness-based cognitive therapy. In: J. Yiend (ed.) *Cognition, Emotion and Psychopathology: Theoretical, Empirical and Clinical Directions*. New York: Cambridge University Press. pp. 270–89.

Thompson, B.L. and Waltz, J. (2007) Everyday mindfulness and mindfulness meditation: Overlapping constructs or not? *Personality and Individual Differences*, 43, 1875–85.

Vroom, V.H. (1964) *Work and Motivation*. New York: Wiley & Sons.

Walach, H., Nord, E., and Zier, C. (2007) Mindfulness-based stress reduction as a method for personnel development: A pilot evaluation. *International Journal of Stress Management*, 14(2), 188–98.

Wallace, B.A., Shapiro, S.L., Dietz-Waschkowski, B., Kersig, S., and Schüpbach, H. (2006) Mental balance and well-being: Building bridges between Buddhism and western psychology. *American Psychologist*, 61(7), 690–701.

Ward, A. (2004) *Attention: A Neuropsychological Approach*. Hove, UK: Psychology Press.

Watson, D.L. and Tharp, R.G. (1997) *Self-directed Behavior: Self-modification for Personal Adjustment*. Pacific Grove, CA: Brooks/Cole.

Weinstein, N., Brown, K.W., and Ryan, R.M. (2009) A multi-method examination of the effcts of mindfulness on stress atribution, coping, and emotional well-being. *Journal of Research in Personality*, 43, 374–85.

Wells, A. and Matthews, G. (1994) *Attention and Emotion: A Clinical Perspective*. Hove: Psychology Press.

Whitmore, J. (1996) *Coaching for Performance*. London: Nicholas Brealey.

Williams, M., Teasdale, J., Segal, Z., and Kabat-Zinn, J. (2007) *The Mindful Way Through Depression: Freeing Yourself From Chronic Unhappiness*. New York: Guilford Press.

Williams, V., Ciarrochi, J., and Deane, F.P. (2010) On being mindful, emotionally aware, and more resilient: Longitudinal pilot study of police recruits. *Australian Psychologist*, 45(4), 274–82.

Zeus, P. and Skiffington, S. (2002) *The Coaching at Work Toolkit: A Complete Guide to Techniques and Practices*. Sydney: McGraw Hill.

# 8

# Developmental Coaching – Developing the Self

## Tatiana Bachkirova

## Introduction

Although coaching is often portrayed in the literature and amongst coaches as a developmental enterprise, the concept of developmental coaching is less than clear and open to misinterpretations. This term is often used to emphasize that coaching of a developmental nature is different from remedial (e.g., Bennett, 2003) or from merely skills and performance coaching (e.g., Hawkins and Smith, 2006). However, what is specific to coaching when it is defined as such is rarely discussed, and no references to theoretical underpinning are usually offered. Interestingly, there are other types of coaching which are significantly informed by theories (e.g., Kegan, 1982; Torbert, 2004), but their authors do not usually use the term "developmental coaching" when describing their practical application.

In this chapter two potential perspectives on developmental coaching will be discussed: first, developmental coaching as a genre and second, practical approaches based on adult development theories. This will help to elicit different advantages and issues associated with each perspective. As one possible solution for addressing most significant issues a new approach to developmental coaching will be suggested (Bachkirova, 2011). This includes a theory specifically developed for coaching practice that is drawing at the same time from the existing perspectives on development of individuals. The theory is based on a new conceptualization of the self, which leads to a range of specific mechanisms for facilitating change in coaching. The new theory and developmental framework will be evaluated and discussed in the light of existing literature and current research, concluding with a range of questions for further research.

*The Wiley Blackwell Handbook of the Psychology of Coaching and Mentoring*, First Edition.
Edited by Jonathan Passmore, David B. Peterson, and Teresa Freire.
© 2013 John Wiley & Sons, Ltd. Published 2016 by John Wiley & Sons, Ltd.

## Literature on Developmental Coaching as a Genre

Although the term "developmental coaching" is not new it is only recently that some serious attempts have been made to discuss what this type of coaching would entail and how it differs from other genres such as performance coaching, leadership coaching, and peer-coaching (Berman and Bradt, 2006; Hawkins and Smith, 2006, 2010; Cox and Jackson, 2010). In the past, the term "developmental coaching" has been used, for example, in contrast to "remedial coaching" (Bennett, 2003; Grant and Cavanagh, 2004). One of the most recent uses of the term developmental coaching is an umbrella term for coaching that aims to help individuals at different periods during their lifespan (Palmer and McDowall, 2010). Although this is a good use of coaching for particular issues during the life transitions, it seems that the term "developmental" in this case does not refer to a purpose of coaching or a corresponding process, method or techniques of it. Perhaps "developmental" here mainly indicates an association with the subject knowledge of human development during the lifespan.

In a wider arena of training courses and Internet-based business offers of coaching, the term "developmental coaching" has been increasingly used synonymously with "coaching". Titles of courses and business offers such as "Executive Developmental Coaching", "Strategy Based Developmental Coaching", or "Developmental Sales Coaching" suggest that the use of "developmental" as a term in these cases is superfluous. Unfortunately, a similar trend is also apparent in research-based papers (e.g., Hunt and Weintraub, 2004; Leonard-Cross, 2010), when it is assumed that newly trained managers or students in the process of learning to coach can deliver developmental coaching.

Only three attempts to conceptualize developmental coaching as a genre have been identifiable so far. These are Berman and Bradt's (2006) description of developmental coaching as one of the types in their typology of coaching, Hawkins and Smith's (2006, 2010) continuum of types of coaching that includes developmental coaching and Cox and Jackson's (2010) position.

Berman and Bradt (2006) describe developmental coaching as one type in their model of executive coaching comprising of four categories: facilitative, executive, restorative, and developmental coaching. Their model defines the differences between these types in terms of the goals of the coaching assignment, the scope of work, and the kind of business scenarios involved. For example, facilitative coaching has a business focus, is short term and targeted towards specific goals. Restorative coaching is also short term but has a personal focus. Executive consulting (rather than coaching) is business focused but long term and exploratory. It is interesting that Berman and Bradt have chosen the term "developmental" to describe a type of coaching that addresses longstanding behavior problems of executives in both personal and work settings (p. 245). They describe potential clients for developmental coaching as those "who have substantial difficulties in some aspect of their management style, but for a variety of reasons are able to retain their jobs" (p. 250). They may be highly successful but with serious flaws of character, for example poorly controlled anger. These authors suggest that many theories and techniques developed in clinical psychology and psychodynamic therapy may be needed in this work. Therefore, a significant overlap between this conceptualization of developmental coaching and psychotherapy is apparent.

Although Berman and Bradt provide some evidence for their typology they also admit a current lack of research and only claim that their model may be of heuristic value for practitioners. However, the use of the term "developmental" is difficult to justify even under this condition. There seems to be very little in the description of this coaching that is coherent with the idea of development. In contrast to already mentioned uses of this term it seems unusual to name a form of coaching "developmental" when it is clearly remedial. As for the specific methods suggested, it is not clear why other clients, without longstanding psychological problems, would not benefit from them.

The next authors to offer a distinct conceptualization of developmental coaching are Hawkins and Smith (2006, 2010). Building on earlier work by Whitherspoon, (2000) they propose a continuum of different types of coaching according to their focus:

- Skills coaching
- Performance coaching
- Developmental coaching
- Transformational coaching

According to Hawkins and Smith, skills coaching is aimed at development of competences, while performance coaching involves more general applied capabilities in a particular professional role. These types of coaching could be offered by the manager as coach or by an internal coach. Developmental coaching, in contrast, is focused on the long-term development of the client as a whole, by helping to increase "their broader human capacities" (2010, p. 242). To introduce the difference between developmental and transformational coaching Hawkins and Smith (2010, p. 242) refer to the stage theory developed by Torbert (2004). They argue that developmental coaching "will tend to focus on increasing capacity within one life stage," while transformational coaching "will be more involved with enabling the coachee to shift levels or 'action logics' and thereby make a transition from one level of functioning to a higher one." They also claim that in transformational coaching this shift happens right there in the coaching room. Consequently, both "developmental coaching" and "transformational coaching" require a more substantial training than the first two.

The logic of this model reflects the different levels of complexity of clients' goals that coaches might face and aim to facilitate. The distinction between the first two levels is clearly explained. However, I have argued elsewhere that there is no sufficient justification for the proposed distinction between transformational and developmental coaching (Bachkirova, 2011). They both focus on development of broader human capacities. It seems that transformational coaching particularly relies on producing insight in clients that allows them to see their situation from a different-and it is hoped-a wider perspective. However, in both types of coaching the insights or shifts may or may not happen and may or may not lead to a change in the client's action logic in the long run. It is more reasonable to hope that developmental coaching might lead to transformation rather than to promise the transformation upfront.

Cox and Jackson (2010) also explore a natural progression from skills and performance coaching to a process that aspires to facilitate some progressive and permanent change. However, they only tentatively suggest that such change may lead to the growth of the whole person. These authors justify the value of this type of coaching in organizations by arguing that "the capacity of the system in which the client sits (organization, family, society) is itself enhanced by the individual's capacity" (Cox and Jackson, 2010, p. 221). In terms of the process of coaching as a genre, the main task of the coach is to ensure "ongoing improvement in the coachee's ability to respond to future events." Another important feature of developmental coaching, they claim, is the self-determination of the client: "It is not for the coach to decide that something will be good for the client 'in the end' just as it is not for the coach to decide where 'the end' is, or if there is such a thing at all" (p. 221).

Cox and Jackson describe developmental coaching as a genre; however, it is apparent that it is strongly informed by the philosophy and theory of the person-centered tradition. Although on some level it is a strength of the approach, it could be argued that this allegiance potentially limits the scope of developmental coaching. As a genre developmental coaching can accommodate a number of theoretical perspectives rather than a particular one. At the same time the account of developmental coaching by Cox and Jackson (2010) presents a most coherent and consistent argument on this topic. They also gave a fair overview of the state of knowledge in relation to developmental coaching, identifying in particular the lack of an overarching theory to guide its practice.

The review of literature on developmental coaching as a genre suggests that descriptive characteristics of it can overlap but also can contradict each other as the following list shows:

- It is holistic – addresses the whole person rather than only work-related goals.
- It addresses longstanding behavior problems.
- It is for working through transitions during the lifespan.
- It aims to increase the broader human capacities of clients.
- A coach is a "thought partner" who assumes a non-directive approach.
- It is a more suitable approach for a better trained external coach rather than for a manager as coach or an internal coach.

As has been said before, the fact contradictions exist is not surprising considering the differing conceptualizations of developmental coaching and the lack of a unifying theory behind the approach. However, in spite of conceptual and theoretical weaknesses, the actual practice of developmental coaching as a genre is apparently vast and growing.

## Developmental Coaching as an Application of Adult Development Theories

In relation to these types of developmental coaching the situation is quite the reverse. There is a multitude of well-known and respected theories in the field of adult development (e.g., Cook-Greuter, 1999; Graves, 1970; Kegan, 1982, 1994; Torbert, 2004; Wilber, 1979, 2000) that have prompted development of various applications to coaching. However, in spite of the quality and obvious value of these theories there seem to be many issues related to their application. Interestingly, none of these authors refer to the practical approaches that follow from their theoretical contribution as a form of developmental coaching. Similarly, other authors, who have published on the application of these theories (e.g., Berger, 2006; Berger and Fitzgerald, 2002, Laske, 2006), rarely described their coaching as developmental, with the exception of Laske.

The work of these authors follows in the footsteps of Freud, Piaget (1976), Kohlberg (1969), Perry (1970), Graves (1970), Loevinger (1976), and many others who studied changing patterns in the development of individuals in relation to the cognitive ability, moral reasoning, emotional maturity, ego strength, and other aspects of human nature.

These theories suggest that people undergo significant changes in terms of the above aspects during their lifetime. These changes occur in a logical sequence of stages throughout the life of each individual and influence the way people feel, make meaning, and engage with their environment. They argued that development can be influenced by other people who can provide appropriate support and challenge in a timely way if they are able to identify the developmental trajectories of those they aim to help.

A comprehensive overview of adult development theories can be found in Wilber (1979, 2000, 2006). He suggests an overarching and a multidimensional model of development emphasizing specific principles of development. One of the most important principles is "holarchy", which means that stages take considerable time to develop and cannot be "skipped", because each is built upon the previous one. Another principle is of independent development of various developmental aspects (cognitive, emotional, moral, etc.). This means that for each individual, development of a number of aspects could be far from synchronic. This relates to a disagreement between some authors, for example Loevinger, who believed that:, "If the stages really reflect a common 'deep structure', the stages of those variables should all proceed in tandem" (1987, p. 242). Similarly, other authors (Beck and Cowan, 1996; Laske, 2006; Wade, 1996) argued that it is their theories that describe such a structure. However, Wilber (2000) disputes such claims and the whole idea of overall development: "Although substantial empirical evidence demonstrates that each line develops through these holarchical stages in an invariant sequence, nonetheless, because all two dozen of them develop relatively independently, overall growth and development is a massively complex, overlapping, nonlinear affair, following no set sequence whatsoever" (Wilber, 1999, pp. 291–2).

As an overview of these theories, Table 8.1 presents only three stages under the names that will be explained in the next section of this chapter. The choice to reduce the number of stages, that usually is higher, is made for simplicity and because various statistical data suggest that these are the most characteristic for the majority of adults (Beck and Cowan, 1996; Torbet, 1991; Wilber, 2000). It is more likely that they will represent a clientele of coaches. The stages are described in four major aspects of the individual: cognitive style, interpersonal style, conscious preoccupations, and character development as most descriptive according to Loevinger (1976). The main input for each of these aspects is drawn from the theories of Kegan (1982), Graves (1970), Wade (1996), Torbert (1991) Cook-Greuter (1999), and Wilber (2000), with the use of another simplifying meta-perspective on these theories offered by McCauley *et al.* (2006).

The theories featured in this description of adult development have strong support from research including long-term longitudinal studies (e.g., Kolhberg, 1969). However, as with any theory some aspects will always remain questionable. The first potential issue is most crucial. It relates to the fact that both the developmental theories and the measurements of development in each of them are intertwined. This means that the theory provides a convincing framework, but the means for examining it are part of the theory, obviously restricting independence of judgment. There is also a good critique of some particular aspects of research supporting these theories (McCauley *et al.*, 2006; Manners and Durkin, 2001) such as small samples, mostly from cohorts of college students in the same cultural setting and lack of longitudinal studies of the whole spectrum of stages. Several more specific aspects can potentially interfere with the quality of measurement, such as verbal fluency and educational and social background (McCauley *et al.*, 2006; Manners and Durkin, 2001). There are also concerns about the prediction of progressive sequence in development. Although several longitudinal studies provide

**Table 8.1** A cumulative description of the three stages in adult development (Bachkirova, 2011, p. 49).

| Stages | Unformed ego | Formed ego | Reformed ego |
|---|---|---|---|
| **Cognitive style** (based mostly on Kegan) | Socialized mind; Ability for abstract thinking and self-reflection | Self-authoring mind; Can see multiplicity and patterns; critical and analytical | Self-transforming mind; Systems view; tolerance of ambiguity; change from linear logic to holistic understanding |
| **Interpersonal style** (Loevinger and Cook-Greuter) | Dependent; Conformist/self-conscious; Need for belonging; socially expected behavior in relationships; peacemakers/keepers | Independent; Conscientious/individualist; Separate but responsible for their own choices; communication and individual differences are valued | Inter-independent; Autonomous/integrated; Take responsibility for relationship; respect autonomy of others; tolerance of conflicts; non-hostile humor |
| **Conscious preoccupations** (Graves) | Multiplistic | Relativistic/individualistic | Systemic/integrated |
| **Character development** (Loevinger, Cook-Greuter and Kohlberg) | Social acceptance, reputation, moral "shoulds and oughts"; Rule-bound; "Inappropriate" feelings are denied or repressed. Rules of important others are internalized and obeyed. | Achievement of personal goals according to inner standards. Conscientious; Self-reliant, conscientious; follow self-evaluated rules; judge themselves and critical of others | Individuality; self-fulfilment; immediate present; understanding conflicting needs; Self-regulated; Behavior is an expression of own moral principles. Concerned with conflicting roles, duties, value systems |

support for sequentuality of stages, they also challenge the theorized irreversibility, for example, of ego development (Adams and Fitch; 1982; Bursik, 1990; Kohlberg, 1969; Manners and Durkin, 2001; Redmore, 1983; Westenberg and Gjerde, 1999).

At the same time the values of these theories to coaching is obvious. They elicit individual differences of the nature not accountable by personality theories and thus allow better understanding of clients in the light of their developmental process. They clearly explain why some coaching approaches might be better suited than others when working with people at different developmental stages. They also emphasize the importance of the personal growth of practitioners themselves (Bachkirova and Cox, 2007). We argued that coaches who are aware of their own stages of development might be in a better position to understand their own role in the coaching process and the dynamics of the coaching relationship and thus able to articulate, influence, and change more critical situations in the coaching process. Practical applications of some theories described, for example, by Berger and Fitzgerald (2002), Kegan and Lahey (2009), and Berger and Atkins (2009) show how useful these theories can be for coaching practice.

However, in relation to coaching practice there are a number of issues that impede a wide use of these theories. I argued before (Bachkirova, 2010, 2011) that this is related to the fact that these theories were not conceived to serve coaching practice. They were developed in order to gain a better understanding of individual differences, for example how different people make meaning of their life tasks and how the way they think and make meaning changes over time. The purpose of this work was scientific: to observe, describe, and explain the differences between people in relation to the developmental aspects they chose to focus on. To make fine and important differentiations the measurement instruments had to be very sensitive and consequently labor-intensive. For example, the subject-object interview (SOI) developed by Lahey and associates (1988) is used for the assessment of 21 gradations within Kegan's orders of mind. It requires 60–90 minutes of recorded interview and a highly skilled scoring of the transcript. Though justified, a quality use of this instrument is restricted by the need for a serious, maybe even lifelong training in the diagnostics of the stages. There is also the Washington University Sentence Completion Test used to measure Loevinger's (1976) stages, which has been updated by Cook-Greuter (2004) and Torbert *et al.* (2004) as the Leadership Development Profile (LDP). Individual assessment with these tools can only by done through relevant organizations. Although their commitment to improving the quality of these instruments and inter-rater reliability amongst their trained scorers is reassuring, the actual fact that the assessment is done through the third party can deter coaches from using them.

There are two more concerns in applying cognitive developmental theories in coaching practice (Bachkirova, 2010, 2011). The first suggests that developmental stages, instead of being a source of deeper understanding of the client, may become a main focus of attention in coaching, creating an illusion that development can happen as the result of high motivation and efforts by the client or the magical skills of the coach. Second, even if the above is avoided, there is a limitation of each individual theory being focused on one particular developmental line. However, the actual coaching assignments are more complex and multifaceted. When coaches encounter an individual client, they may need to work with a variety of themes such as interpersonal, cognitive, emotional. This should involve addressing each area of development with an open mind in spite of the indication of a particular stage in some of the others (Bachkirova, 2011).

To summarize, this two-part literature review illustrates that developmental coaching as a genre is becoming widespread amongst practitioners. However, it suffers from the incompatibility of various conceptualizations of developmental coaching and the lack of a unifying theory behind the approach. On the other hand, there is a solid body of research behind adult development theories, but considerable restrictions to the competent use of the diagnostic instruments which they entail and a narrow focus on particular developmental aspects prevents wider applications of these theories in coaching practice.

## A New Theory and Practical Approach to Developmental Coaching

The rest of this chapter will describe and evaluate an approach to developmental coaching that is aimed to address the above limitations of developmental coaching. To create a theoretical foundation to the practice of developmental coaching this approach had to start from the very beginning: who we are, how we engage with the world and change, and how the change can be influenced in coaching. Therefore a new theory has been developed (Bachkirova, 2011), providing theoretical consistency to a set of ideas about the self, leading to the mechanisms of change and concluding with a step-by-step logical process of coaching that takes into consideration the significant diversity of coaching clients. The theory does not claim a discovery of new laws of human nature, rather a new synthesis of ideas that allows integration of many other approaches to facilitating individual development. It draws from the wider fields of knowledge such as psychology, philosophy, and neuroscience, as well as existing practical approaches to coaching.

The description of the theory will have to be reasonably concise given the space restrictions of this chapter; however, it should start with making explicit main assumptions and concepts involved. For example, development is conceived as a combination of changes in the organism manifested in a sustained increased capacity to engage with and influence the environment and to look after internal needs and aspirations. It happens as the result of the complex interaction between the individual organism and the world and so could be intensified under certain circumstances. The pace of development is different for different individuals; it may become static and even reverse in some circumstances. Coaching is seen as an individualized process of facilitating change in people with the focus on specific targets and/or enriching their lives. Developmental coaching is explicit in the intention to coach the whole individual even when the goals of coaching are specific. It is important that the developmental coach understands how in principle the mind/brain system of the client operates in the functioning of the whole organism and is committed to work in partnership with the client.

As this theory involves concepts that are still debated not only in science but also in philosophy a consistent attempt is made to clarify whether they are considered from the "first-person" (phenomenological) or the "third person" perspective (metaphysical), which assumes that reality of phenomena is established by observation. This is considered important in lieu of many misconceptions about the self when these perspectives are not clarified. For example, Harter (1999, p. 7) describes components of the I-self (James, 1999) as: "(1) *self-awareness*, an appreciation for one's internal states, needs, thoughts, and emotions; (2) *self-agency*, the sense of the authorship over one's thoughts and actions; (3) *self-continuity*, the sense that one remains the same person over time; and (4) *self-coherence*, a stable sense of the self as a single, coherent, bounded entity" (p. 6).

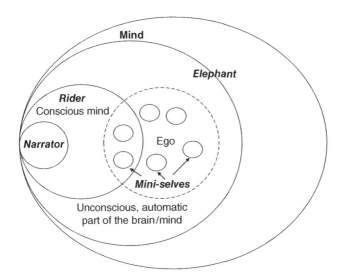

**Figure 8.1** Relationship between ego, narrator, and mini-selves (Bachkirova, 2011).

However correct this description could be phenomenologically, she proceeds to name them as "I-self capabilities, namely, those cognitive processes that define the knower" (1999, p. 7), which is obviously a too far-reaching assertion.

## The nature of the self

*We do not deal much in facts when we are contemplating ourselves.*
Mark Twain

It is important that in developmental coaching the coach understands how elements of the client's self operate in the functioning of their whole organism. However, the conception of self, consciousness, and agency are still subjects of huge disagreements and fierce debates in many fields of knowledge associated with these phenomena (Baumeister, 1999; Blackmore, 2003; Claxton, 1994, 2004; Damasio, 2000; Dennett, 1991; Gallagher and Zahavi, 2008; Hamachek, 1978; James, 1890; Strawson, 1999; 2009). The main split is usually between the first person and the third person perspectives on the self, with the latter defending a most radical view that there is no self. In the proposed theory I argue that both perspectives, however radical, have to be taken into account if we are interested in such a practice-oriented field as coaching. As a result this chapter will address at least three notions of self and the relationship they have with the common sense understanding of the self that we normally rely on in coaching. The proposed concepts will include a division between the conscious mind and the rest of the organism, including unconscious, automatic operations, and the body (Figure 8.1). I will use an analogy of the *rider* and the *elephant* in a slight variation from Haidt (2006), who first introduced it in his book, to illustrate that the role of the conscious mind, as a rider is significantly exaggerated in the functioning of the whole organism.

From the phenomenological perspective the self will be seen as an experiential dimension postulating a simple "I" as the most basic pre-reflective sense of self. From the third person perspective the properties and areas of the brain that are associated with the actions of the organism have to be considered. It is postulated that there is a neurological network, an executive center (ego), responsible for the coherent behavior and normal functioning of the individual in the world. Finally, the self is also seen as a narrative construction, an aspect of human nature (narrator) that explains the view of the self as we consciously and linguistically conceive. This should be consistent with phenomenology of our experience, but also make sense from the third person perspective. Overall, on the basis of current findings in various studies, a case is made that the three main elements for understanding the self are:

- Sense of *I* as a pre-reflective self-consciousness – center of awareness
- *Ego* as an executive center
- *Self-models* constructed by a *narrator* (conscious and reflective linguistic function of the mind/brain) – identity center

It is argued that the executive center or ego, as a network of mini-selves, is the most important notion for applied purposes. Each mini-self is a combination of brain/mind states and processes that are involved in the organism's engagement with a certain task or more precisely, it is a particular pattern of links between different areas of the brain that become activated or inhibited when the organism is involved in an act. These patterns may involve not only sensory stimuli, but memory, cognition, interpretation of meaning, and so on. Many mini-selves work simultaneously in different circumstances: "Every new situation gives a shake to the kaleidoscope of my personality" (Claxton, 1994, p. 124). Therefore, the ego, functioning mainly subconsciously, is responsible for satisfying the organism's needs. Consciousness may not be involved when these needs are unambiguous. However, when there is greater ambiguity, complexity, or greater leisure the mini-selves may involve conscious layers of information from memory, perception, or beliefs. When more conscious elements become involved in various mini-selves we may develop a habit of delaying a final evaluation and spend more time exploring nuances and subtle layers of significance and so become more conscious (Claxton, 2002; Gazzaniga, 1985). We may become aware of drives and instincts represented in some mini-selves being involved in conflicts between themselves or with the conscious rider.

The difference between the pre-reflective sense of I and self-models or various versions of "me", created by the narrator, is that the first is immediate and dynamic. It is so basic that even animals possess it. The second are conscious stories or theories of the self that we are able to put together because of our ability to use language. "Just as I can spin a hypothetical story to account for your funny little ways, so am I able to theorize about myself" (Claxton, 1994). These self-models may correspond to actual mini-selves or may not.

It is important to clarify that although these notions of self are called "centers" for uniformity, neither of them implies a reality of a specific place in the mind/brain, which could justify a vision of the self as a little operator in charge of the organism: another version of a homunculus. Only the first of these centers may feel like a center from the phenomenological perspective, but two other notions both imply multiplicity of mini-selves or self-models. Unfortunately, a more detailed description of these aspects of the self is beyond the limits of science at this stage, hence an extensive use of metaphors. My intention was at least not to contradict the current findings of science and the most plausible, in my view, theories of philosophers. On the other hand it is apparent that some of these metaphors are not in agreement with common sense, but I hope that the mechanism of change and coaching interventions that follows from these notions of self resonate with coaches in spite of this fact.

## Three mechanisms of developmental coaching

In identifying developmental coaching as a process that involves working with a whole organism it is important to introduce the idea of *organic* change. The organic change is one that is fully grounded in the whole organism of the client and is not just "a head" change – a rider's change. In some way it is a change that is already under way subconsciously and may not always be registered by the rider. This change is associated with the natural needs of the organism and requirements of the situation. Non-organic change, on the other hand, is generated by the rider and based on conscious desires rather than the needs of the whole organism in the current situation. When the change is not organic, the coach may face resistance, regular setbacks or breaks in the coaching relationship, which could be avoided if the change is organic.

The core of the organic change is in the executive center, implying that a new mini-self is getting ready to be formed to satisfy a need that is important to the whole organism. That is why there is a natural energy behind it. In order for a new mini-self to emerge most elements of it should be in place: channels to receive information from inside and outside the organism, necessary functional skills and motor-schemas to be activated, including links in the brain that can contribute to preparing this mini-self to go live. Good examples of such change are when people start new jobs or roles and adapt to changing demands seamlessly, as we say: "It comes naturally to him/her."

However, the organic change can be blocked and coaching may become a viable option. These blockages suggest that something is missing in the working cycle of the mini-self. It could be at any section of this cycle: input section, action sections, or communication between them. Therefore there could be at least three[1] types of blockages or obstacles to organic change which could be addressed by means of developmental coaching:

- Low quality of information at the input point
- Interruption from the narrator at the process of communication
- No obvious behavior routes exist at the action point

It is postulated that attention to these potential obstacles in developmental coaching will enhance a client's engagement with the change they are aiming at. Consequently it is proposed that the main mechanisms that allow an organic change to take place are:

- Improving the quality of perception
- Working with the multiplicity of self-models
- Working with the elephant (unconscious, automatic parts of mind/brain and body)

In order to improve the *quality of perception* both internally and externally coaches traditionally aim at development of active listening skills, observation skills, attention to body language, and so forth. However, if we agree with Koffka, that we see things not as they are but as we are, we also need a much better understanding of the nature of perception. It is important to know what we are up against when we try to improve it – what prevents us from seeing things as they are. According to Krishnamurti (1996, p. 54) it is only through

---

[1] Immunity to change, a concept developed by Kegan and Lahey (2009), is another potential blockage at the communication point that is useful to consider. It is discussed in the full description of the theory and approach to coaching (Bachkirova, 2011).

understanding the nature of the trap that one can be free of it. Therefore, in coaching two main issues which interfere with a quality of perception: *conditioning* and *self-deception* should be addressed.

Conditioning comes with getting "second-hand knowledge" and is useful to some extent. However, we are often conditioned by the culture of organizations, by circles of friends, by society as a whole in ways that prevent change and development. Various theoretical perspectives describe what happens when we "swallow the messages from other human beings without chewing." For example, transactional analysis discusses this as injunctions and counter-injunctions. The REBT approach explores how this adds to our innate tendency to irrationality, forming various "oughts" and "should". The person-centered approach describes how our organismic self gradually changes into self-concept through denial and distortion of our experiences. All the means for counteracting these influences advocated within these traditions are useful in developmental coaching.

The second obstacle to perception is self-deception. Whilst during conditioning the filters to perception of reality are polished by influential others, in self-deception this job is done internally. There is a significant body of literature (Ames and Dissanayake, 1996; Fingarette, 2000; Goleman, 1997; Gur and Sackheim, 1979; Lewis, 1996) that offers useful insights into the psychology of self-deception in individuals, explaining cases based on cognitive incompetence, faulty thinking, irrational beliefs and unconscious psychological mechanisms. Working with the holes in clients' perception created by self-deception is another task of developmental coaches.

The next mechanism of developmental coaching is *working with a multiplicity of self-models*. It appears that the narrator, being a linguistic function in the rider, has developed in evolution together with our ability to use language. The narrator puts together conscious stories or theories of self that we think we are. Some of these stories may be less then helpful in the process of change. Coaches can assist clients in *accepting the fact of multiplicity, matching a self-story with a real mini-self and working on the synthesis of self-models*. Seeing the multitude of self-stories is helpful for many reasons (Carter, 2008; Rowan, 2009). One of them is conscious openness to experimenting with new roles and not "holding a meeting every time we want to do something only slightly difficult, in order to find the self who is capable of undertaking it" (Midgley, 1984, p. 123). A research by Linville (1987), for example, found that the more distinct self-descriptions of themselves that participants were able to produce, the less they were likely to become depressed and even suffer somatically when under stress. Of course it would help if these conscious representations of our engagements with the world corresponded to how we actually act. Forming a meaningful and powerful story or self-model that is anticipating a new but not completed mini-self may serve as a missing link in the mind/brain. If a mini-self is being "ignored" it may be denied access to relevant memories that could be activated for its benefit. It is worth remembering, though, that the narrator, unfortunately, is not particularly trustworthy, because it has an agenda: to present us "in a favorable, or at least a sympathetic, light" (Claxton, 1994, p. 118) or to make a good synthesis of different self-models.

The third mechanism of change *working with the elephant* (the emotional unconscious mind and the body) is about better interaction between the rider and the elephant in the process of organic change. This is particularly important in circumstances where there seems to be no obvious route to achieving a change that is needed, or that something is missing in order for a new mini-self to emerge. Two forms of working with the elephant are proposed to facilitate better collaboration between the rider and the elephant. One is promotion of *soft thinking* (Claxton, 1999, p. 146) in addition to traditional hard reasoning, which implies the inhibition of other parts of the mind. Soft thinking instead implies a soft focus, "looking at" rather than "looking for" (Claxton, 1999; Claxton and Lucas, 2007) without forcing out new, unstable and fragile ideas that come from the unconscious. Gentle, rather than incisive questioning and simply slowing down also promote soft thinking.

Another way of working with the elephant is better *communication with the emotional body*, improving two-way traffic between the rider and elephant. The language of the elephant is non-verbal, so the developmental coach promotes attention to emotions and other signs that may not be easy to articulate: physical feelings, images and dreams, guesses, fleeting thoughts, and hunches. Gendlin (1962, 2003) suggests a step even further with his method "focusing": inviting the messages from the elephant, looking not only for unarticulated, but pre-logical, pre-conceptual, just felt dimensions of experiencing. In communicating messages to the elephant the use of imagery and metaphors is recommended and awareness of a particular sensitivity of the elephant to both the relationship with the coach and the coach's attitude towards the client. Each of these mechanisms, although seemingly rooted in different sides of the rider-elephant divide, are explicit in their intention to meet in the middle and thereby increase the harmony of working together rather than promoting the rider's control of the elephant (Bachkirova, 2011).

## Coaching according to developmental themes

Although it was proposed that the above mechanisms are fundamental for developmental coaching they must be applied in a different way for different people at different stages of life and for different problems that need to be tackled. That is why coaching is a creative process – it is impossible to give an exact recipe for each particular case. It does help, at the same time, if some patterns in individual differences are identified and some recommendations are given according to them. As I have been arguing before, the ego (executive center) should be determining the main configuration of these patterns, because it is the executive center that executes new behaviors. The ego could be developed to various degrees, from unformed to fully formed. When the ego is fully developed the mind/brain can act or refrain from action if necessary in a way that reasonably satisfies the organism as a whole with all the multiplicity of its needs and tasks. With the *unformed ego* there are needs that remain unsatisfied and tasks unfulfilled. For example, the person may have an ability to perform a task but would instead of carrying it out, freeze because of a fear of failure. They actually need more help or guidance from others.

The sign of a fully *formed ego* is the capacity of the whole organism to take ownership of the past, withstand anxiety about what the future holds, and build relationships with others without losing the sense of who they are. Their choices may be constructive or destructive, but they are made according to their own criteria that can be rationally explained. At the same time this stage of the ego is associated with other developmental challenges. The sense of control and self-ownership may lead to an overestimation of what is possible and realistic for the organism, which may result in a lack of attention to and even abuse of the body when working to achieve some specific targets.

The third category, a *reformed ego*, represents capacities of the ego that go beyond those of the formed ego. There is a much more harmonious relationship between the elephant and the rider, manifested in the ability of the organism to tolerate the ambiguity of some

**Table 8.2** Potential core assumptions and challenges with two columns* (adapted from the description of selected stages by Wade, 1996, p. 263).

| Stage | Core assumption* | Transitional dilemmas* | Corresponding challenge | Type of coaching |
|---|---|---|---|---|
| Unformed ego | The universe is fair, so I can ensure my security by being good. | Life is not fair. | Learning to stand on ones own feet. | Coaching towards a healthy ego. |
| Formed ego | I can be the master of my fate through my own initiative. | Some forces cannot be controlled. | Learning to see things from many perspectives. | Coaching the ego. |
| Reformed ego | I need to be all that I can be to fulfil my purpose in life. | I can only realize my potential by giving up myself. | Learning to live with paradoxes and see through constraints of language. | Coaching beyond the ego. |
| Ego with a soul | I seek to be one with the Ground of All Being. | Seeking or not seeking the Ground keeps me from it. | Learning a new way of being. | Coaching the soul. |

needs and tasks, thus minimizing energy wasted on conflicts between the various mini-selves. And finally *ego with a soul* is more complex because it involves at least three potentially overlapping groups of individuals:

1  Those who demonstrate unusual capacities (these capacities may indicate a stage reached by a few).
2  Those who have had special (spiritual) experiences (these experiences could indicate a state which may happen to a lot of people).
3  Those who have deep interest in the spiritual (an inclination that could be shared by anyone).

In Table 8.2 the stages indicating the maturity of the ego are suggested, together with indication of core assumptions, transitional dilemmas (Wade, 1996), and also corresponding challenge and the type of coaching required.

To illustrate the need for considering the stages of ego development here is an example of coaching involving a 360-degree feedback exercise with an aim to gain an insight into how the client is perceived by others. In the case of an unformed ego the clients are already highly influenced by others. Their view of themselves is practically an internalized view of how others see them. Therefore, if this view is fully confirmed in this exercise it would not make any difference to their development and so does not offer much for a coach to work with. If they receive feedback that they perceive as worse than they had expected it may be too overwhelming for them. The task of the coach in this case would be to help them cope with the psychological trauma rather than to focus

**Table 8.3**   Four groups of developmental themes.

| Unformed ego | Formed ego | Reformed ego | Ego with a soul |
|---|---|---|---|
| • Decision-making in difficult situations with a number of stake-holders<br>• Taking higher level of responsibility than they feel they can cope with<br>• Work–life balance connected to inability to say "no"<br>• Performance anxiety<br>• Issues of self-esteem | • Coping with high amount of self-created work<br>• Achievement of recognition, promotion, etc.<br>• Interpersonal conflicts<br>• Drive for success and underlying fear of failure<br>• Problem solving<br>• Learning to delegate<br>• Stress management | • Dissatisfaction with life in spite of achievements<br>• Internal conflict<br>• Not "fitting in"<br>• Search for meaning<br>• Overcoming life crisis<br>• Initiating a significant change<br>• Dealing with personal illusions<br>• Staying true to themselves in a complex situation | • Intention for spiritual development<br>• Lack of progress in a chosen path<br>• Making sense of a mystical experience<br>• Coming to terms with mortality of the organism<br>• Realization of incompleteness of work for a mission<br>• Overcoming spiritual illusions |

on development. Quite differently, the 360-degree feedback could be most useful for those with a formed ego. As they are confident in their own view of themselves their attitude to feedback will depend on how rigid this view is and if they are interested in development. If development is important for them the feedback would give very rich information to work with. If their view is rigid they may simply dismiss feedback that is incongruent to their view. In this case it is an indication that there is a need for much deeper work. Those with a reformed ego may be curious about 360-degree feedback, but the importance of this exercise will depend on what role it plays in other strategic areas of their life (Bachkirova, 2011).

It may be argued at the same time that this developmental framework is in principle no different to other cognitive developmental approaches and can suffer from the same criticism described earlier. For example, how can ego-development be assessed? How can we account for fluctuation between the stages? What if some clients occupy different stages in different areas of their life? These are the issues associated with attempts to make a judgment about a stage of the individual. These issues could be avoided, however, if we concentrate instead on what clients are concerned with in different periods of their life. Their concerns and their goals themselves show a pattern that is developmental. Therefore, it is proposed that for the purpose of coaching there is no need to assess where each client is according to any scale – instead coaches can and should work with *developmental themes* that are brought by clients themselves. The pattern in the themes (Table 8.3) would indicate the stage of the ego in each client and will help to shape an individual approach to coaching.

These themes are not only about goals – they are about the challenges that people face in life, what they find difficult, what their life circumstances demand from them (Tables 8.2 and 8.3). For example, the issues of confidence and self-esteem are typical for the first stage of ego development. It often becomes an overarching topic for coaching individuals with an unformed ego, because their well-being depends on how they are seen and valued by others. At the next stage the topic of self-esteem is not as prominent and unlikely to re-appear for the reformed ego.

## The task of the coach

The developmental coach would approach a new assignment initially in the same way as any other coach: identifying the clients' needs, exploring their situation fully, and clarifying the goals. This task should not be minimized by the focus on the clients' stage of development. However, the developmental coach would gradually uncover a sense of the state of the client's ego from taking into account the issues they both identified, the challenges the client faces and the difficulties he/she experiences. The task of the coach is to engage with whatever issue/goal is presented, but noticing at the same time a pattern in these: a developmental theme. The job to do between the sessions is to explore these patterns and consider relevant coaching strategies through reflection on the previous sessions, preparation for the coming sessions and discussion of these cases in supervision.

For example, the pattern of an unformed ego, which requires coaching towards a healthy ego, may be identified if the client expresses insufficient belief in his ability not only in relation to a particular task at work but also in other areas of life. He may find it quite challenging to disagree with significant people in his life. He may wish to develop a sense of control in himself and his environment and to have tangible results. The coach may feel that this client gives her too much power in their relationship and an unlimited opportunity to influence him.

In terms of selecting specific interventions, coaches may choose to use any appropriate tools and methods that they are familiar with. There are traditional coaching approaches particularly useful for some specific developmental themes. For example, cognitive behavioral coaching and transactional analysis have good methods suitable for coaching towards a healthy ego. The existential approach, on the other hand, fits well with coaching beyond the ego. In addition to these approaches, the developmental coach would also be considering the three main mechanisms that were discussed earlier: working with perception, the elephant and the multiplicity of self-models. Each of these would have significant variations when applied to different stages of ego-development. For example, in terms of improving the quality of perception, working with unformed ego needs more attention to conditioning: giving priority to experience and own voice, while the formed ego is more susceptible to self-deception, so the priority should be given to external input, feedback, and discrepancies.

It is important to note that this approach is flexible, appreciating that clients can bring in themes that belong to more than one group. It is possible that circumstances offer the challenges that may shift the focus from the themes of one stage to another. For example, illness may affect the theme of achievement that began unfolding but had to be put on hold and the client now may require coaching towards a healthy ego. The same illness may accelerate the developmental process and the client may begin to question the theme of achievement indicating the need for coaching beyond the ego. A new job and the expanded range of responsibilities may temporarily awake doubts about the capacity to manage them, so the issue of confidence may become prominent again even though it had been resolved in the past. Coaching the soul could be a part of any one of the other three types of coaching if clients' interests in spirituality are explicit.

# Future Research

This chapter introduced an approach to developmental coaching that starts with an assumption that the client acts as a whole organism which has a capacity to create multiple stories of the self. Developmental coaching, while keeping in mind the developmental significance of coaching themes, engages fully with them by improving the client's perception, mind-body communication, and sense of identity. The coach who works developmentally acts as a companion to the client in bringing about organic changes that stem from the whole organism. On the whole this approach to developmental coaching aims to offer a consistent theory developed specifically for coaching which at the same time makes use of other theories and traditions.

In comparison to other practical applications of adult development theories some features of this approach can present certain advantages:

- It does not require a diagnosis of the clients' state of development.
- It does not create a temptation to impose a developmental agenda by the coach.
- It shifts the weight of judgment from the person to the developmental theme and leaves more space for maneuver when themes from different stages are presented.
- It implies working with the whole individual rather than a particular developmental line.
- It appreciates the complexity of the human psyche and the organism as a whole in constant interaction with the external world.

At the same time there are, of course, certain limitations of it and room for further improvement. First of all it must be said that the exposition of the theory described in this chapter can only give a limited overview of the approach. However, even the full version may not be the easiest to learn and to apply in comparison to some others. Some coaches may need to suspend their assumptions about the value of particular practices and interventions, because the approach may sometimes clash with established tenets of coaching. This approach is quite demanding in relation to coaches themselves as individuals. There is an expectation that developmental coaches would be involved in their own development and mindful of the state of their own ego. And the most important one: although I tried as much as possible to illustrate all propositions of this theory with data from respected sources and research in many different fields, as a theory it needs targeted research from the field of coaching to support or question it and to explore it further in coaching practice.

Here are potential research questions that I would like to be investigated by interested researchers:

- What could be considered as indicators of the capacity of individuals to engage with their environment?
- What characteristics of organic change as opposed to non-organic can be identified and assessed?
- What other themes of coaching fall into the patterns suggested in the proposed theory?
- What are the typical dynamics of themes in the longer-term developmental coaching engagements? Would they support the developmental direction suggested?
- Which methods of coaching in terms of improving perception, working with the elephant and the multiplicity of self-models, are effective for intended change?

- What other methods are suitable for specific developmental themes?
- How can compatibility between the traditional coaching approaches and developmental coaching be evaluated?

# Conclusion

This theory and approach are one possible way of seeing the role of coaching on a wider scale of the psychological evolution and at the same time as an intimate one-to-one interaction with a focus on a concrete theme important for a client. As any theory, this is only one particular map to a vast territory of individual change and ways of facilitating it, which I hope could be useful for coaches and could contribute to the body of knowledge about influencing individual development.

# References

Adams, G. and Fitch, S. (1982) Ego stage and identity status development: A cross sequential analysis. *Journal of Personality and Social Psychology*, 43, 574–83.

Ames, A. and Dissanayake, W. (eds) (1996) *Self and Deception: A Cross-Cultural Philosophical Enquiry*. Albany: State University of New York Press.

Bachkirova, T. (2010) The cognitive-developmental approach to coaching. In: E. Cox, T. Bachkirova and D. Clutterbuck (eds) *The Complete Handbook of Coaching*, London: Sage. pp. 132–45.

Bachkirova, T. (2011) *Developmental Coaching: Working with the Self*. Maidenhead: Open University Press.

Bachkirova, T. and Cox, E. (2007) A cognitive developmental approach for coach development. In: S. Palmer and A. Whybrow (eds) *Handbook of Coaching Psychology: A Guide for Practitioners*. London: Routledge. pp. 325–50.

Baumeister, R.F. (ed.) (1999) *The Self in Social Psychology*. Philadelphia, PA: Psychology Press.

Beck, D. and Cowan, C. (1996) *Spiral Dynamics*. Oxford: Blackwell.

Bennett, B. (2003) Developmental coaching: Rejecting the remedial approach. *Development and Learning in Organizations*, 17(4), 16–19.

Berger, J. (2006) Adult development theory and executive coaching practice. In: D. Stober and A. Grant (eds) *Evidence Based Coaching Handbook: Putting Best Practices to Work for your Clients*. Chichester: John Wiley.

Berger, J. and Atkins, P. (2009) Mapping complexity of mind: using the subject-object interview in coaching. *Coaching: An International Journal of Theory, Research and Practice*, 2(1), 23–36.

Berger, J. and Fitzgerald, C. (2002) Leadership and complexity of mind: The role of executive coaching. In: C. Fitzgerald and J. Berger (eds) *Executive Coaching: Practices and Perspectives*. Palo Alto: Davies-Black Publishing. pp. 27–58.

Berman, W. and Bradt, G. (2006) Executive coaching and consulting: "Different strokes for different folks". *Professional Psychology: Research and Practice*, 37(3), 244–53.

Blackmore, S. (2003) *Consciousness: An Introduction*. Abingdon: Hodder and Stoughton.

Bursik, K. (1990) Adaptation to divorce and ego development in adult women. *Journal of Personality and Social Psychology*, 60, 300–6.

Carter, R. (2008) *Multiplicity: The New Science of Personality*. London: Little, Brown.

Claxton, G. (1994) *Noises from the Darkroom*. London: Aquarian.

Claxton, G. (1999) *Wise-Up: The Challenge of Lifelong Learning*. London: Bloomsbury.

Claxton, G. (2002) Moving the cursor of consciousness: Cognitive science and human welfare. In: F. Varela and J. Shear (eds) *The View From Within: First Person Approaches to the Study of Consciousness*. Thorverton: Imprint Academic, pp. 219–22.

Claxton, G. (2004) Proximal spirituality: Why the brains of angels are different from ours. In: D. Lorimer (ed.) *Science, Consciousness and Ultimate Reality*. Exeter: Imprint Academic. pp. 129–44.

Claxton, G. and Lucas, B. (2007) *The Creative Thinking Plan: How to Generate Ideas and Solve Problems in your Work and Life*. London: BBC Books.

Cook-Greuter, S. (1999) *Postautonomous Ego Development: Its Nature and Measurement*. Doctoral dissertation. Cambridge, MA: Harvard Graduate School of Education.

Cook-Greuter, S. (2004) Making the case for developmental perspective. *Industrial and Commercial Training*, 36(7), 275–81.

Cox, E. and Jackson, P. (2010) Developmental coaching. In: E. Cox, T. Bachkirova, and D. Clutterbuck (eds) *The Complete Handbook of Coaching*. London: Sage. pp. 217–30.

Damasio, A. (2000) *The Feelings of What Happens: Body, Emotion and the Making of Consciousness*. London: Vintage.

Dennet, D. (1991) *Consciousness Explained*. Boston and London: Little, Brown and Co.

Fingarette, H. (2000) *Self-Deception*. London: University of California Press.

Gallagher, S. and Zahavi, D. (2008) *The Phenomenological Mind: An Introduction to Philosophy of Mind and Cognitive Science*. London: Routledge.

Gazzaniga, M. (1985) *The Social Brain*. New York: Basic Books.

Gendlin, E. (1962) *Experiencing and the Creation of Meaning: A Philosophical and Psychological Approach to the Subjective*. Evanston, Il: Nothwestern University Press.

Gendlin, E. (2003) *Focusing*. London: Rider.

Goleman, D. (1997) *Vital Lies, Simple Truths: The Psychology of Self-Deception*. London: Bloomsbury.

Grant, A. and Cavanagh, M. (2004) Towards a profession of coaching: Sixty-five years of progress and challenges for the future. *International Journal of Evidence Based Coaching and Mentoring*, 2(1), 1–16.

Graves, C. (1970) Levels of existence: An open system theory of values. *Journal of Humanistic Psychology*, November.

Gur, R. and Sackheim, H. (1979) Self-deception: A concept in search of a phenomenon. *Journal of Personality and Social Psychology*, 37, 147–69.

Haidt, J. (2006) *The Happiness Hypothesis*. London: Arrow Books.

Hamachek, D.E. (1987) *Encounters with the Self* (3rd edn). New York: Holt, Rinehart and Winston, Inc.

Harter, S. (1999) *The Construction of the Self*. London: Guilford Press.

Hawkins, P. and Smith, N. (2006) *Coaching, Mentoring and Organizational Consultancy: Supervision and Development*. Maidenhead: Open University Press.

Hawkins, P. and Smith, N. (2010) Transformational coaching. In: E. Cox, T. Bachkirova, and D. Clutterbuck (eds) *The Complete Handbook of Coaching*. London: Sage. pp. 231–44.

Hunt, J. and Weintraub, J. (2004) Learning developmental coaching. *Journal of Management Education*, 28(Feb, 1), 39–61.

James, W. (1890) *The Principles of Psychology* (2 volumes). London: Macmillan.

James, W. (1999) The self. In: R. Baumeister (ed.) *The Self in Social Psychology*, Philadelphia: Psychology Press. pp. 69–77.

Kegan, R. (1982) *The Evolving Self: Problem and Process in Human Development*. London: Harvard University Press.

Kegan, R. (1994) *In Over Our Heads*. London: Harvard University Press.

Kegan, R. and Lahey, L. (2009) *Immunity to Change: How to Overcome it and Unlock the Potential in Yourself and Your Organisation*. Boston: Harvard Business Press.

Kohlberg, L. (1969) *Stages in the Development of Moral Thought and Action*. New York: Holt, Reinhart, and Winston.

Krishnamurti, J. (1996) *Questioning Krishnamurti*. London: Thorsons.

Lahey, L., Souvaine, E., Kegan, R., Goodman, R., and Felix, S. (1988) *A Guide to the Subject-Object Interview: Its Administration and Interpretation*. Cambridge, MA: Harvard University, Graduate School of Education, Laboratory of Human Development.

Laske, O. (2006) From coach training to coach education. *International Journal of Evidence Based Coaching and Mentoring*, 4(1, Spring), 45–57.

Leonard-Cross, E. (2010) Developmental coaching: Business benefit – fact or fad? An evaluative study to explore the impact of coaching in the workplace. *International Coaching Psychology Review*, 5(1), pp. 36–47.

Lewis, B. (1996) Self-deception: A post modern reflection. *Journal of Theoretical and Philosophical Psychology*, 16(1), 49–66.

Linville, P. (1987) Self complexity as a cognitive buffer against stress-related illness and depression. *Journal of Personality and Social Psychology*, 52, 663–76.

Loevinger, J. (1976) *Ego Development: Conceptions and Theories*. San Francisco: Jossey-Bass.

Loevinger, J. (1987) *Paradigms of Personality*. New York: M.H.Freeman and Company.

McCauley, C., Drath, W., Palus, P., and Baker, B. (2006) The use of constractive-developmental theory to advance the understanding of leadership. *The Leadership Quarterly*, 17, 634–53.

Manners, J. and Durkin, K. (2001) A critical review of the validity of ego development theory and its measurement. *Journal of Personality Assessment*, 77(3), 541–67.

Midgley, M. (1984) *Wickedness: A Philosophical Essay*. London: Ark.

Palmer, S. and McDowall, A. (eds) (2010) *The Coaching Relationship: Putting People First*. London: Routledge

Perry, W.G. (1970) *Forms of Intellectual and Ethical Development in the College Years*. New York: Holt, Rinehart and Winston, Inc.

Piaget, J. (1976) *The Psychology of Intelligence*. Totowa, NJ: Littlefield, Adams and Co.

Redmore, C. (1983) Ego development in the college years: Two longitudinal studies, *Journal of Youth and Adolescence*, 12, 301–6.

Rowan, J. (2009) *Subpersonalities – The People Inside Us*. London: Brunner-Routledge.

Strawson, G. (1999) The self and the SESMET. In: S. Gallagher and J. Shear (eds) *Models of the Self*. Thorverton: Imprint Academic. pp. 483–519.

Strawson, G. (2009) *Selves*. Oxford: Clarendon Press.

Torbert, W. (1991) *The Power of Balance*. Newbury Park, CA: Sage.

Torbert, W. and Associates (2004) *Action Inquiry: The Secret of Timely and Transforming Leadership*. San Francisco, CA: Berret-Koehler Publishers, Inc.

Wade, J. (1996) *Changes of Mind: A Holonomic Theory of the Evolution of Consciousness*. Albany: State University of New York Press.

Westenberg, P. and Gjede, P. (1999) Ego development during the transition form adolescence to young adulthood: A 9-year longitudinal study. *Journal of Research in Personality*, 33, 233–52.

Whitherspoon, R. (2000) Starting smart: Clarifying goals and roles. In: M. Goldsmith, L. Lyons, and A. Freas (eds) *Coaching for Leadership*. San Francisco, CA: Jossey-Bass, pp. 165–85.

Wilber, K. (1979) *No Boundary*. Boston: Shambhala.

Wilber, K. (2000) *Integral Psychology*. London: Shambhala.

Wilber, K. (2006) *Integral Spirituality*. Boston and London: Integral Books.

# 9

# Gender Issues in Business Coaching

## Sunny Stout-Rostron

## Introduction

The purpose of this chapter is to review the contemporary literature relevant to gender as it affects coaching within organizational and institutional environments. While gender already encompasses a wide range of theory and research, as a coaching issue it is relatively new (Stout-Rostron and Wilkins, 2011) and yet executives lead and manage in environments with considerable gender complexities.

I approach this chapter from a variety of perspectives in terms of the contemporary literature available to us. Contemporary research shows us that working with gender in organizations is often about who has power and who doesn't (Stout-Rostron, 2009, pp. 172–3). Gender, of course, refers to both men and women, and we will examine the current thinking on how men and women are socialized, the impact of organizational culture – and in what ways the dominant male organizational culture has affected the development of women in the workplace (Peltier, 2010, p. 192). Culture is our shared way of making sense of the world, informing our personal views, choices, and actions – and it is at this level of assumption that coaches need to work with their clients in order to understand how to manage gender diversity in the workplace (Marques Sampaio, 2009, p. 198).

This chapter focuses on academic and organizational research, peer reviewed journal articles, and bespoke models to explore gender diversity and gender coaching across five areas: defining gender; challenges which gender presents; wider research on the gender debate; coaching as a solution; and future research.

## Defining Gender

The distinction between sex and gender was recognized in the 1960s in feminist and other critical accounts of women's and men's positions in society (Broadbridge and Hearn, 2008,

*The Wiley Blackwell Handbook of the Psychology of Coaching and Mentoring*, First Edition.
Edited by Jonathan Passmore, David B. Peterson, and Teresa Freire.
© 2013 John Wiley & Sons, Ltd. Published 2016 by John Wiley & Sons, Ltd.

p. S39). Oakley (1972/1985) was one of the first to distinguish biological "sex" differences from "gender" as a set of socio-cultural constructions, identifying how what was often thought of as natural and biological was also social, cultural, historical, and political. However, some of the problems with the approaches in the 1960s and 1970s was with their cultural specificity, and relative lack of attention to power, change, and social structures (Broadbridge and Hearn, 2008, p. S40; Eichler, 1980).

Gatrell and Swan (2008) explore the background to the women's rights movement and the influence of liberal feminism on the equal opportunities agenda. The history of women's employment is positioned as a social issue within specific social contexts. Although formal workplace activism started in the 1960s and 1970s, the authors acknowledge that "women have always found ways to fight and resist discriminatory practices, individually and collectively" (Gatrell and Swan, 2008, p. 21). The theories of Marxist feminism, radical feminism, and patriarchy are considered as influences on our understanding of discrimination against women. Greer (1970/2006) and Friedan (1963) gave voice to feminist thinking on gender, work, and inequality. Radical feminism gave "a positive value to womanhood rather than supporting a notion of assimilating women into areas of activity with men" (Beasley, 1999, p. 54). Social and cultural perspectives are examined on how traditional stereotypes of masculinity and femininity have created the gendered division of labor at work, with particular emphasis on the discrimination of women with and without children (Gatrell and Swan, 2008, pp. 36–7).

During the 1970s and 1980s, the two dominant sets of literature on gender and management came from studies of gendered labor markets, "influenced by studies of political economy and by Marxist and socialist feminist work", and writings on "women and management" (Broadbridge and Hearn, 2008, p. S41). Rosabeth Moss Kanter's (1977) "extended case study of a large US corporation in *Men and Women of the Corporation*, significantly opened up the field, although Kanter stopped short of presenting a fully gendered account of power" (Broadbridge and Hearn, 2008, p. S41; Kanter, 1977).

By the late 1970s and 1980s, most relevant work was on gender divisions of labor, authority and hierarchy, and sexuality in management and organizations (Hearn and Parkin, 1983). With the move away from "women in management", to "gender in management", in 1986 *Women in Management Review* was renamed *Gender in Management: An International Journal*. In 1992, organizational theorist, Joan Acker set out to analyze gendered processes in organizations, describing how they intertwine with organizational culture, sexuality, and violations. A second journal, *Gender, Work and Organization*, was founded in 1994 due to the expansion of research in this area.

Butler (1990) argued that the sex-gender distinction is a socio-cultural construction. Although "the area of gender, organizations and management is now a recognized legitimate and important area," and it is recognized that there are "key issues of gender power relations in academic organizations and academic management which need urgent attention," gender "should not be isolated from other social divisions and oppressions, such as class or race" (Broadbridge and Hearn, 2008, pp. S38–40).

"The idea of 'gender and gendering', as opposed to 'women' in management as an analytic lens, means that the relationality between men and women, masculinity and femininity – the way they cannot be thought apart from each other – draws attention to the social construction of masculinity and femininity" (Gatrell and Swan, 2008, pp. 4–5). Gender, although a term widely used, finds "no common understanding of its meaning, even amongst feminist scholars" (Acker, 1992, p. 565). For most social theorists, gender is a social construction which means that "as for other social categories such as race, sexuality and disability – gender is the result of human social processes, actions, language, thought and practices" (Gatrell and Swan, 2008, pp. 4). Gender is seen as a process, rather than as given traits or essences, with "gender actively produced in and through the workplace" (Gatrell and Swan, 2008, p. 4).

Further trends since the 1990s have been the recognition of the specific gendering of men in organizations and management. Collinson and Hearn (1994) sought to contribute to the growing interest in naming men as part of a critical analysis of gendered power relations in organizations, arguing for an approach which addresses the issue of "multiple masculinities". Deborah Kolb (2009) highlights how the social construction of gender has generally changed the discourse from the concept of difference between men and women, to viewing gender as shifting complexities of identity shaped by the contexts in which "negotiation occurs". She considers how shifting feminist perspectives on gender can be incorporated into our understanding of gender relations in negotiation theory, practice, and research (Kolb, 2009, p. 515).

## Binary opposites which define gender

In Western cultures one of the key ways of making sense of the world is through binary oppositions. People construct meaning through the recognition of "opposites", defining what something is by knowing what it isn't: "Binary oppositions put the world into clearly defined categories ... between white and black ... masculine and feminine" (Marques Sampaio, 2009, pp. 189, 195–6). However, these "opposites" usually turn out to be based on unexamined assumptions about socially constructed categories, and human reality is much more complex than this kind of expedient simplification (Marques Sampaio, 2009, p. 195). A dualist view of gender (female/male, woman/man, feminine/masculine, femininity/masculinity, girls/boys) presents difficulties (Broadbridge and Hearn, 2008, p. S40; Richardson, 2007). This is because the division of experience into binary oppositions reflects a particular structure of power.

One side of this divide has traditionally been privileged (and often exercised that privilege) over the other: "Men (and masculinity) have traditionally been privileged over women (and femininity); whites over blacks; rich over poor" (Marques Sampaio, 2009, p. 196). In this sense, categories such as "masculine" and "feminine" are socially constructed; they depend on perceptions of gender which are contingent on the social or cultural beliefs of a particular society (see Abizadeh, 2001). In many societies, "characteristics such as assertiveness, initiative and leadership are seen as masculine, whereas obedience and a concern for the domestic sphere are seen as feminine qualities" (Marques Sampaio, 2009, p. 155). Gatrell and Swan (2008) examine the gendered binary of organizing the world, identifying how traditional stereotypes of masculinity and femininity have created the gendered division of labor at work, with particular emphasis on the discrimination of women with and without children (Gatrell and Swan, 2008, pp. 36–7).

To operate within an organizational context, human resources (HR), organizational development (OD) and coach practitioners must first work on themselves – learning from their own experience, developing self-awareness, and understanding the impact of their own limiting assumptions (Marques Sampaio, 2009, p. 198). This means being able to "see" through a multiplicity of lenses; in other words, not just our own individual perspective, but including the worldviews of our clients whose experience, education, background, hopes, and fears may be very different from our own (Stout-Rostron, 2009, p. 180).

## Organizational culture and gender

All organizations create their own values, language, rituals, and ways of seeing the world (Peters and Waterman, 1982). Corporate culture can be defined as "a set of understandings or meaning shared by a group of people", or "the rules for behavior in the organization" (Leimon *et al.*, 2011 p. 53). Part of understanding organizational culture is to clarify the cultural knowledge and social processes that operate within an organization on a daily basis. With organizations operating almost as if they are mini-societies, culture emerges through the social interactions and negotiations of the members of that organization (Czarniawska-Joerges, 1992; Legge, 1987/1995).

There are belief systems in operation about the rights and wrongs of how to do things, and it is through these belief systems that power operates within a company (Janse van Rensburg, 2009, p. 214). These power structures create worldviews about hierarchy, identity, performance, relationships, diversity, gender, and ethnicity. Also, the position that an individual holds within an organization shapes their attitudes, their values, and their behavior (Halford and Leonard, 2001, p. 65).

Organizational culture is articulated through some of the less tangible aspects of organizational life, such as the attitudes, beliefs, and values – as well as the symbols, languages, and practices of an organization. Organizational culture includes a way of "creating meaning" within the organizational system, but also helps to give employees a sense of identity and direction. Research shows that companies who have strong cultures tend to be highly performance-oriented, with hierarchies that create both a structure of power and a way for management to achieve consensus and performance delivery (Leimon *et al.*, 2011).

If women are to progress in their careers, it is essential that they understand corporate culture. Yet, "in many organizations, the culture is still based on a set of values and norms around the 'white male heritage' and women do not yet represent a critical mass … at the relevant level of management" (Leimon *et al.*, 2011, p. 53). This is where coaching and well-trained practitioners have a key role to play.

## Challenges Which Gender Presents

This section is an overview of the influence of cultural contexts on how gender issues in business are manifested and responded to by men and women, including historical and present challenges, and how these contexts need to be taken into account in coaching. In reviewing the available literature it is apparent that there are very few studies on gender coaching or gender diversity coaching. There are more studies on mentoring with an emphasis on gender.

Most contemporary coaching studies explore how and whether the coaching intervention works (Passmore and Fillery-Travis, 2011). The literature has explored the behaviors used by coaches (Passmore, 2011); what types of individuals make better coaches (Passmore and Fillery-Travis, 2010); issues including experience, gender, and personality (Passmore *et al.*, 2010); the coaching relationship, and the interplay between coach and coachee (see, for example, De Haan, 2008).

The gender diversity literature over the decades has primarily covered the areas of:

- Gender diversity and diversity constructs in organizations
- Gender diversity issues in hiring

- The dynamics of diversity within business teams
- The effects of gender diversity on business performance
- Gender-based communication styles
- Gender differences in management and leadership styles
- Women shattering the "glass ceiling" to become corporate directors
- Corporate board gender diversity and stock performance
- Women directors and corporate social responsibility
- Gender equity in the upper levels of the sciences, health professions, the judiciary, and government
- Mentoring for gender equality and organizational change

## The glass ceiling and gender disparity

The published literature suggests that coaching is one of the key strategies to help women break through the glass ceiling, a term coined in the 1960s to describe the "barrier which is transparent but impassable, so that women can see the top of the management hierarchy, but may not reach it" (Gatrell and Swan, 2008, p. 12). The glass ceiling is also described as the "unseen, yet unbreachable barrier that keeps minorities and women from rising to the upper rungs of the corporate ladder" (Federal Glass Ceiling Commission, 1995). This barrier grows ever stronger with higher positions, higher income, and prestige; and the result is that women are often denied access to – or a voice in most boardrooms (Sparrow, 2008, pp. 18–19). "A major obstacle to establishing managing diversity and glass ceiling initiatives as top priorities for industry and government is the failure to recognize the major implications for the economic performance of organizations" (Cox and Smolinsky, 1994, p. i).

Meyerson and Fletcher (1999) believed that the glass ceiling would be shattered in the new millennium, but only through a strategy that uses small wins – incremental changes aimed at biases so entrenched in the system that they're not noticed until they're gone. Although seemingly a common-sense argument, it may be too slow in addressing the continuing imbalance of gender diversity on corporate boards (Meyerson and Fletcher, 1999, p. 128). The authors' research shows that "the small-wins strategy is a powerful way of chipping away the barriers that hold women back without sparking the kind of sound and fury that scares people into resistance" (Meyerson and Fletcher, 1999, p. 128).

Statistics suggest that as women approach the top of the corporate ladder, many jump off, frustrated or disillusioned with the business world (Meyerson and Fletcher, 1999, p. 127). A growth in self-employment among women has also been observed in recent years; this is explained in two arguably interrelated ways. One explanation may be that women have been attracted to self-employment by a desire for autonomy and flexibility; another may be a wish to escape the "glass ceiling" constraints encountered in large organizations (Wirth, 2004, pp. 33–6). Gender discrimination is so deeply embedded in organizational life as to be virtually indiscernible, and although it is generally agreed that women add enormous value, organizational definitions of competence and leadership are still predicated on traits stereotypically associated with men: tough and aggressive (Meyerson and Fletcher, 1999, pp. 129–31).

The International Labor Organization (ILO) conducted research in 63 countries, and despite the fact that women represent over 40 percent of the global labor force, gender segregation in the workplace tends to manifest itself in two main ways: (1) on the concentration of women in traditionally "feminized" jobs such as nursing, teaching, and administration; and (2) on the difficulties in rising to senior positions or higher paid job categories in comparison with men (Wirth, 2004, pp. 1–3). Despite such segregation, Wirth's (2004) report provides evidence that women are breaking into fields which have been traditionally male dominated, such as law, science, engineering, and information and communication technology. That progress is, however, balanced by constraints that mean women at the highest levels of corporate life are still rare.

In Britain, claims persist that boardrooms continue to be afflicted by the "pale male" syndrome, with little sign or promise of change (Gatrell and Swan, 2008, p. 11). Women have been segregated into the "velvet ghetto", and are still segregated vertically in terms of the career ladder, and horizontally into particular jobs that are seen as less valued (Gatrell and Swan, 2008, p. 12). The velvet ghetto refers to positions that are considered to be "gendered", such as human resources, public relations, and marketing.

In the United States, women comprise 10 percent of senior managers in Fortune 500 companies; less than 4 percent of the uppermost ranks of CEO, president, executive vice president, and COO; and less than 3 percent of top corporate earners (Meyerson and Fletcher, 1999, p. 127). Women of color represent 23 percent of the US women's workforce, yet only account for 14 percent of women in managerial roles (Meyerson and Fletcher, 1999, p. 136).

Based on an extensive review of the literature, their own wide consulting experience and input from five leading companies on organization change to manage diversity, Cox and Smolinsky (1994) conclude that: (1) managing diversity can improve cost structures of organizations and increase the quality of human resources; and (2) organizations which excel at leveraging diversity, (including the hiring and advancement of women and non-white men into senior management jobs, providing a climate conducive to contributions from people of diverse backgrounds) will experience better financial performance in the long run than organizations which are not effective in managing diversity (Cox and Smolinsky, 1994, pp. 1–2).

Despite these recommendations, the main gender disadvantage for women remains the issue of maternity; maternity impacts on opportunities within the workplace and hinders upward movement with women's career development. Wirth observes that, as employers start to recognize that family-friendly policies have benefits not only to male and female employees but also in helping to increase overall business productivity, "personal characteristics of integrity, diligence and sincerity, traditionally attributed to women, are increasingly viewed as qualities that can enhance a company's image in a world riddled with corporate misconduct" (Wirth, 2004, p. 18).

In 2005, the Parliamentary Assembly of the Council of Europe published a paper listing the main reasons for discrimination against women as: lack of access to the labor market, the wage gap, and the "glass ceiling". The paper describes women as paying a "gender penalty as actual or potential mothers. Many employers wrongly fear the cost and hassle motherhood may entail. But women are not only discriminated against for economic reasons – they are mainly discriminated against because of stereotyping and misguided preconceptions of women's roles and abilities, commitment and leadership style" (Parliamentary Assembly, Council of Europe, 2005, p. 1).

The committee report explains that: "Women are routinely passed over when it comes to promotions. The higher the post, the less likely a woman – even one as qualified as her male colleague (or even more qualified) – is to get it." Women "who manage to break through this so-called 'glass-ceiling' into decision-making positions remain the exception to the rule, as even in female-dominated sectors where there are more women managers, a disproportionate number of men rise to the more senior positions" (Parliamentary Assembly, Council of Europe, 2005, p. 5). Their research shows a significant number of barriers to women's career development, including: lack of mentoring and role models for women at the highest levels; exclusion from informal networks and channels of communication; stereotyping of women's roles and abilities; sexual harassment; and unfriendly corporate culture (Parliamentary Assembly, Council of Europe, 2005, p. 5).

Peltier mentions the "glass ceiling" that still prevents women from progressing too high in the organization; and that "glass walls" keep women in the new "pink collar" jobs (Peltier, 2010, p. 193) such as HR, OD, and marketing. Although Peltier acknowledges that women are socialized differently today, his research was carried out prior to the so-called Generation Y, whose members have a very different outlook on work and career from the previous generation of "Baby Boomers". What Peltier calls "erroneous assumptions" about women in the workplace, for example that most leaders assume a woman's highest priority is the family, we can identify as "limiting assumptions" which deliberately exclude women from long-term career development. A major challenge facing women is their dislike of promoting themselves, combined with the "stereotyped perception of assertive women as pushy" (Peltier, 2010, p. 202).

Despite changes in UK legislation and policy focusing on equality of opportunity, "discrimination within the workplace remains widespread and persistent" (Gatrell and Swan, 2008, p. 1). The "glass ceiling" and the "glass wall" continue to frustrate black and minority ethnic women, so that "wherever they turn their career progress is limited, they are prevented by organizational practices and processes" from climbing to the "top of the career ladder" (Gatrell and Swan, 2008, p. 12). Similarly, women are often marginalized and excluded from the "family boardroom" (Mulholland, 1996, p. 78). Women play a "fundamental part in the establishment and running of family businesses", but are often "invisible" and "excluded from social and economic rewards" (Hamilton, 2006, p. 8).

More recently, the explosion of research on gender has been prompted by concerns about the gap in wages and achievement – the glass ceiling effects – in which women plateau before they reach top leadership positions (see Babcock and Laschever, 2003; Bowles *et al.*, 2005). Despite the fact that women make up close to 50 percent of the labor force, graduating from college in greater numbers than men, women are still not anywhere near parity in corporate senior positions (Catalyst, 2007).

## Broadening the gender discussion

It is important not to assume that women represent the only gender concerns, but to broaden the discussion to include men. Some research suggests that coaching men is different from coaching women, and Erlandson (2009) has argued that the coach should at least be aware of gender issues. One study suggests that gender issues are not at the forefront of a coach or coachee's mind, nor do they have any real effect on the coaching relationship or its aims (Bowers and Passmore, in press).

Ludeman and Erlandson, in a paper focusing on alpha males (2004, pp. 58, 62), depicted these individuals as "highly intelligent, confident and successful," and as "people who aren't happy unless they're the top dogs." Alpha males are described as natural leaders who get stressed only "when tough decisions don't rest in their capable hands" (Ludeman and Erlandson, 2004, p. 58).

In their research, they claim to have found few successful female leaders with equally strong personalities, or to find women who matched the "complete alpha profile". When asked why so many alpha executives need coaches, the authors explained that alpha "quintessential strengths are what make them so challenging, and often frustrating to work with; independent and action-oriented, alphas take extraordinarily high levels of performance for granted, in themselves and in others" (Ludeman and Erlandson, 2004, p. 58). The flip side is that alpha males have "little or no natural curiosity about people or feelings" (Ludeman and Erlandson, 2004, p. 58). Alphas "often make snap judgments about other people, which they hold on to tenaciously. They believe that paying attention to feelings, even their own, detracts from getting the job done; they're judgmental of colleagues who can't control emotions yet often fail to notice how they vent their own anger and frustration" (Ludeman and Erlandson, 2004, pp. 59–60).

Ludeman and Erlandson (2004) claim that although alphas make perfect mid-level managers, in the CEO role they don't necessarily become inspirational people managers. It is in the transition where the role of a competent coach is needed. Alphas aren't good at asking for help, and can be "typically stubborn and resistant to feedback." According to the authors, coaches shouldn't undermine the alpha's focus on results, but should improve the process for achieving them (Ludeman and Erlandson, 2004, p. 58).

Tannen (1999) picks up on the corporate appetite for conflict, debate, and argument – rather than dialogue. Corporations often operate on an adversarial approach to business, "settling disputes in litigation" (Tannen, 1999, p. 4). Tannen, whose earlier (1995) work explored the differences in communication styles between men and women, has helped practitioners to understand how the "argument culture" impacts the workplace. She draws attention to military and war metaphors which pervade managerial and board-room language, affecting behavior and thinking. Tannen's research has shown how deeply entrenched is the language divide between two polarized ways of thinking and speaking. Her work offers useful input for practitioners who are coaching men and women to resolve their differences.

Corporate conflict is where the role of the "alpha male", the dominant white male executive, plays a strong part. Peltier calls it the "testosterone culture" because business organizations are typically male-led, dominated by male culture and male assumptions (Peltier, 2010, p. 192). He also mentions that metaphors of sports and war are typical in the standard business environment – almost as if men are continuing to play children's fighting games, keeping score with "clear winners and losers" (Peltier, 2010, p. 192).

These analyses of "alpha" characteristics are interesting for both men and women executives, but is it crucial for business leaders to have such traits? Further research into coaching alpha executives would be useful to understand the frequency of these characteristics, as well as their importance for successful executive behavior.

## Wider Research on the Gender Debate

Catalyst was founded in 1962 in the United Kingdom by Felice Schwartz with the aim of introducing women to potential employers and educators. By the mid-1970s, women were being recruited in large numbers, but the workplace wasn't supportive for women as it was designed by and for men (Mattis, 2001, p. 371). By the mid-1980s, Catalyst began to work with business organizations "to enhance their ability to recruit, retain, develop, and advance women professionals and managers," and Catalyst is now best known for extensive research in eliminating barriers and leveraging opportunities to train, advance, and retain women professionals and managers (Mattis, 2001, p. 372).

## The gendered organization

Halford and Leonard define the "gendered organization" as one of male power in levels which gain "progressively more power" as they near the top (Halford and Leonard, 2001, p. 216). Although women managers have high levels of education and a desire to progress in their careers, few achieve the same status or salary as their male counterparts. Male managers are likely to be better paid; in more secure employment; on higher grades; less stressed; and to not have experienced prejudice and sexual discrimination (Calás and Smirnich, 2006; Chênevert and Tremblay, 2002; Davidson and Cooper, 1984; Fielden and Cooper, 2002; Gatrell and Cooper, 2007; Institute of Management, 1995; Institute of Management/Remuneration Economics, 1998).

Simpson and Lewis (2007) offer insight into how gender is linked to organizations and accounts for differences in the experiences of men and women in the world of work. Their study examines where some voices are privileged over others and how masculine voices silence and suppress other discourses such as femininity (Simpson and Lewis, 2007, p. 81). New to most practitioners will be men as the invisible gender(less) subject, with the invisible privileges and resources of masculinity.

Not all men identify with the oppressive, dominating, uncaring, socially and economically privileged representation of themselves. The differentiation between two types of men is based on their orientation to the principle of equality, with some supporting equality and others opposing it, believing instead in traditional roles for women (Simpson and Lewis, 2007, p. 57). However, this binary opposition allows for no middle ground. Simpson and Lewis have developed a practical framework integrating voice and visibility to develop female entrepreneurs, which needs to be researched for applicability in organizations.

The conclusion is that, despite legislation and campaign organizations such as the Equal Opportunities Commission and the lobbying group, Fawcett, there is a continuing debate on gender diversity in management. Not only are there differences between women, we also need to understand the complex ways in which gender operates and the ways that inequality is differentially formed and experienced (Gatrell and Swan, 2008, p. 88).

## Lack of academic gender parity

Barriers remain even though women "have risen to leadership positions in professional organizations, academic departments, and funding agencies" (Bell and Kastens, 2004, p. 292). A study by the Commission on the Status of Women at Columbia University, New York from 1990 to 2000 highlights that women are not progressing through the academic pipeline at the same rate as men; specifically, women are under-represented in the applicant pools for faculty positions, and few women are hired into the tenured faculty (Bell and Kastens, 2004, p. 292).

The percentage of women medical students in the United States has grown from 18 percent to 44 percent in the last 25 years (Bickel, 2001, p. 267). Gender stereotyping detracts from women's opportunities, and although having tripled in number, comparatively few women medical students enter surgery or specialized fields (Bickel, 2001, p. 267). Universities need to monitor gender-related barriers to education, and to create an environment of equal opportunity – "where assumptions and judgments about individuals' competencies and preferences are not coloured by their sex" (Bickel, 2001, p. 268).

## Gender diversity on corporate boards and financial performance

Gender diversity on corporate boards has become a core theme for governance reform efforts worldwide. A large literature documents that the gender composition of the board is positively related to measures of board effectiveness (Adams and Ferreira, 2008, p. 26).

Research in Europe and the United States suggests that "companies with higher numbers of women at senior levels are also companies with better organizational and financial performance" (Desvaux *et al.*, 2008, pp. 1–2). Researchers at the business schools of Columbia and Maryland Universities argue for greater gender diversity among corporate leaders. Using data from 1,500 US companies in 1992–2006, the authors found "evidence that greater female representation in senior-management positions leads to better firm quality and performance" (Desvaux *et al.*, 2008, p. 3).

Adams and Ferreira (2008) from the London School of Economics show that female directors have a significant and meaningful impact on board inputs and firm outcomes. Their sample consists of 86,714 directorships in 8,253 firm-years of data on 1,939 firms. Their results suggest that gender-diverse boards monitor more effectively, CEO turnover is more sensitive to stock performance, and directors receive more equity-based compensation (Adams and Ferreira, 2008, p. 1).

The benefits of having female directors translate into financial success (Bernardi and Threadgill, 2010, p. 16), and a relatively recent study shows that diversity on a board of directors is directly associated with shareholder value (Arfken *et al.*, 2004; Carter *et al.*, 2003; Daily and Dalton, 2003). As companies increase the number of women serving on their boards, they develop a more positive corporate environment with more satisfied customers; an increase in revenue and profit; and companies with diverse boards were significantly more profitable than those with homogeneous boards (Erhardt *et al.*, 2003).

According to Catalyst, companies with the highest percentage of female board members returned 34 percent more to shareholders than companies with the lowest percentage of women (Bernardi and Threadgill, 2010, p. 16; Speedy, 2004, p. 24). Additionally, boards with a higher percentage of women were significantly more likely to appear on Fortune's list of "Best companies to work for", and on Ethisphere's "Most Ethical Companies" list (Bernardi and Threadgill, 2010, pp. 19–20).

The conclusions of a McKinsey survey (Desvaux *et al.*, 2008, p. 6) studying over 230 organizations employing a total of 115,000 staff concluded that:

- Companies with three women or more in their top management teams scored systematically higher in nine organizational dimensions (leadership, direction, accountability, coordination and control, innovation, external orientation, capability, motivation and work environment, and values).
- Companies which did score higher in all nine dimensions had a systematically higher financial performance than their peers, an operational profitability that was 68 percent above the group average and a market value 62 percent above the group average.

This issue isn't without controversy. Farrell and Hersch (2005, p. 104) failed to find convincing evidence that gender diversity in the corporate boardroom is a value enhancing strategy. They found evidence that women serve on better performing firms, but document insignificant financial returns from a woman being added to the board. If gender diversity is not a value enhancing strategy, then why the demand? Organizations may be responding to outside pressure to create greater diversity, or there may be an internal demand so that corporates reflect the "tastes of society at large" (Farrell and Hersch, 2005, p. 104).

Researchers at the Utrecht School of Economics studied gender diversity and the overall performance of organizations, drawing evidence from Dutch and Danish Boardrooms. "Using empirical data on 186 listed firms observed in 2007 (102 Dutch and 84 Danish), almost 40 percent of these firms had at least one woman in the boardroom. Their findings indicate that there is no effect of board gender diversity on firm performance" (Marinova *et al.*, 2010, pp. 1–2, 16, 18). However, "an equal representation of women in top positions is not only a means to an end, but also a matter of social justice" (Marinova *et al.*, 2010, p. 18).

## Coaching as a Solution

How can coaching help women to better manage in the gendered organization? How is coaching helping to redress the gender imbalance on corporate boards worldwide? An evident gap in the literature is how coaching can, or is, being used to promote women into senior management roles, and ultimately to corporate board and chief executive positions. Another gap seems to be how those who are neither alpha male, nor alpha female, can be developed through executive coaching to step into senior executive and corporate board positions. In other words, how important is it for leaders to fulfil "alpha" executive characteristics, or are those characteristics no longer needed in today's world?

There are a range of studies on women and mentoring, and gender differences in mentoring – but very few studies on gender in coaching, except for one or two studies in athletic coaching (see, for example, Hawkes and Seggar, 2000). A variety of factors that affect mentoring have been investigated, but few have examined the influence of gender identity on the functioning of these relationships (Eddleston *et al.*, 2010, pp. 100–120). Woodd (1997) proposed that different gender cultures can create dilemmas for women in the workplace, and that mentoring can be one means of coping with this.

In the foreword to a seminal compilation of practitioner-researched papers on issues of diversity in psychotherapy (Chin *et al.*, 1993), Sue describes, "how ethnic and racial diversity issues, as well as other diversity issues such as gender and sexual orientation, are embedded in society in general and psychotherapy in particular" (Sue, 1993, p. ix). Brome (1993, p. 1) advocates that diversity and difference need to be respected and valued as assets instead of liabilities. Brome emphasizes the paradigmatic shift needed for practitioners to work effectively with gender diversity complexities in the workplace, advocating the need for cultural self-evaluation on the part of both practitioner and client (Brome, 1993, p. 2). The authors suggest for psychotherapists what is also critical for coach practitioners – that they begin to challenge "their own assumptions about diversity, in all its forms of race, gender, ethnicity, culture and empathy" (De La Cancela *et al.*, 1993, p. 9). The examples cited show how racial, ethnic and economic power differences have affected social esteem and gender role expectations within the groups they studied, and the depth at which historical and cultural experiences color our understanding of ourselves and of self-other relationships (Chin *et al.*, 1993).

Peltier (2010, p. 190) says that: "Women have arrived in all arenas of the workplace and they are not going back home." Peltier's view is that coaches need to understand how women function within an organization – the reverse of the standard approach to coaching women, which suggests that they need help in finding a way to fit into organizational culture (Peltier, 2010, pp. ix–xx). In grappling with the development of managerial leaders, it is critical that business/executive coaches understand the intrapersonal and interpersonal realms. Psychology and psychotherapy have well-established traditions in specialized fields of study such as ethics and supervision, including published research that is highly relevant to our fast-changing, complex organizational and societal systems. Business coaches need a practical grounding or "literacy" in psychological research and theory to understand an executive's behavior and performance (Stout-Rostron, 2009, p. 20). For our purpose, in terms of coaching women in organizations, practitioners also need an awareness of current studies on gender diversity.

## Organizational coaching

Leimon *et al.* (2011) interviewed 125 successful women leaders, of whom 107 were working in a corporate environment. The study identified the main barriers to women's advancement in organizations, and the following eight coping strategies thought to be commonly used to overcome these barriers: family and career balance; understanding corporate culture; systematic investment in career and development; confidence; knowledge of own strengths; networking; role models; and career planning (Leimon *et al.*, 2011, pp. 40–1).

A questionnaire survey was carried out to test the effectiveness of these coping strategies among women in corporate roles. It was found that the women were challenged in five of the eight coping strategies:

- Career progression emphasized the need for career planning.
- Confidence examined the major area for coaching, which is women's lack of self-belief.
- Organizational dynamics means developing a sufficient understanding of organizational culture, and more importantly, finding out the rules of the game.
- Relational support made it clear that women lack an understanding of the critical need for networking to progress their careers.
- Work–life balance is a factor that neither men nor women get right.

Out of this research women seemed to be seriously disadvantaged in "balancing personal life and career", and attempted to be all things to all people, personally and professionally (Leimon *et al.*, 2011, pp. 47–9).

Some of the other key aspects to emerge are important themes for coaching women in organizations. The interviews demonstrated the need to overcome personal insecurities and inadequacies and learning how to say no to other's expectations. Most women leaders have a deficit in understanding the culture of the organization in which they work – men consistently network to manage their careers, and women start to network at a later age than men to progress their careers. Due to the shortage of women in senior and executive management positions, women seriously lack female role models and can be excluded from a variety of informal "one-to-one relationship building sessions in male-dominated environments" such as the locker room and the golf course (Leimon *et al.*, 2011, p. 48).

Justifying why women professionals need coaching at various stages in their careers, Leimon *et al.* (2011) identify the most important factors needed to move out of middle management and to reach a board position. This is one of the few pieces of research looking at the need to differentiate coaching for men and women, developing a model for women's leadership development. According to the authors, each of the eight strategies is useful for coaching in organizations. However, to further the evidence base, it will be essential to conduct similar surveys in organizational cultures outside the United Kingdom.

One question is: "How is coaching impacting gender diversity on boards and the development of women for board positions?" Motsoaledi (2009) researched a doctoral study in South Africa on *Executive Coaching in Diversity From a Systems Psychodynamic Perspective*. In this empirical study, nine major themes and their related sub-themes were identified: gender, race, ethnicity, authority, disability, language, age, de-authorization of diversity work and the coaching process. The study found that "through the coaching, the executives gained insights into their intra-psychic environment and the complex, multi-faceted, and intersecting nature of diversity in their organizations. They were assisted to take up their leadership roles more effectively and to take action on behalf of their organizations" (Motsoaledi, 2009, p. xv).

## Role of gender within coaching practice

Although there is a variety of research exploring the different models of coaching practice, there has been a scarcity of research on the coaching relationship and almost no reference to the role of gender within the coach-coachee partnership. Using a Q-sort methodology, Passmore and Fillery-Travis (2011) explore the role of key factors which influence the coaching relationship – specifically the role of gender. According to Bowers and Passmore (in press), given the current imbalance at board level, the issue of gender is worth further exploring to better understand the gender dynamic within the coaching relationship.

There are very few studies in the selection process to match coach and coachee. Gray and Goregaokar's (2010) study describes the results from a coaching program in which coachees were asked to reflect on and justify their choice of coach. The initial qualitative results suggested that female coachees favored female coaches as a role model of business success; male coachees justified their selection of a female coach as more approachable, and able to discuss more sensitive, personal issues – a minority of male respondents displayed sexist attitudes. In a subsequent quantitative analysis of the data, there was no bias towards the choice of either female or male coach. The results apparently show no statistical significance in a coachee's gender choice, yet for a minority of coachees, gender is a factor (Gray and Goregaokar, 2010, pp. 525–6).

The results of a study at Villanova University in Pennsylvania, suggest that self-reported leadership styles of female accountants differ somewhat from the leadership styles reported by male accountants. Females are more likely than males to indicate that they use an interactive style of management called transformational leadership. Female accountants reported somewhat higher perceived effectiveness on two of these management skills: coaching and developing, and communicating. The findings also suggest that female accountants receive more developmental opportunities than do their male colleagues (Burke and Collins, 2001, pp. 244–57).

In her doctoral study into executive coaching in South Africa, Motsoaledi studied issues of male insubordination to female authority, finding that in several instances males refused to accept it, projecting inadequacies on to women leaders and using aggression as a tool to dominate them (Motsoaledi, 2009, p. 203). Although the women managers wielded power as individuals, they still had to deal with being a member of a subordinate group expected to comply with traditional patriarchal roles (Motsoaledi, 2009, p. 207). The unique position of the black female leader, who despite her formal authority still had to submit to male dominance within a patriarchal world, made it difficult for the black female to compete with her white female counterpart (Motsoaledi, 2009, p. 209).

The differences in these studies highlights the importance of research that takes not just gender, but culture into account.

## Retaining women to gain the competitive edge

Research shows a correlation between high numbers of female senior executives and stronger financial performance, which means that companies hiring and retaining more women gain a competitive edge – increasing retention rates by "offering flexible hours, maternity and child-care leave, and coaching to ease the return to the workforce" (Desvaux *et al.*, 2008, p. 5). Coaching is one of the key financial investments which may help to retain female talent and embed gender diversity positively. However, gender diversity coaching needs an integrated approach – and no change comes without cost, whether it be financial expenditure or time to implement and manage change.

Suitable policies to recruit and retain female talent will help organizations to create "a larger talent pool and stronger financial performance, which suggest that making gender diversity a significant goal is well worth the investment" (Desvaux *et al.*, 2008, p. 6). Organizations and educational institutions who are keen to promote gender diversity in the workplace need to understand existing government policies and practices that are in place, and to make aggressive efforts to recruit and retain female talent.

A universal finding from Catalyst's and other organizations' research on corporate diversity initiatives is that retaining and advancing women in corporate management requires a sustained and coordinated commitment from the top (Mattis, 2001, p. 372). For it to work, senior leaders need to create and link the business case for gender diversity to strategic business plans; all management and employees need to be convinced that eliminating barriers to success and recruiting the best female talent is in their personal best interests (Mattis, 2001, p. 373).

There is also a business case for maternity coaching to support new parents – men and women. Calling it the "new business environment", Liston-Smith (2010) advocates maternity coaching and HR/OD discussion forums in organizations to enable parents to continue to contribute and to develop leadership potential. Research that the Korea Labor Institute conducted in 2007 indicates that some "family-friendly policies are correlated with higher revenues per employee" (Desvaux *et al.*, 2008, p. 5).

A more even gender mix on the board of directors also helps a company better understand and attract the diverse population that has the potential to become its clients, allowing a company to better penetrate existing markets (Arfken *et al.*, 2004, pp. 177–86). Women are a huge market force, and understanding the female perspective is essential to generating goods and services that meet consumer wants and needs.

## Gender coaching strategies

Three years after the release of Workforce 2000, Roosevelt Thomas shifted the paradigm of diversity from compliance to a matter of business survival; he argued that recruitment was not the central problem; rather, the more serious problems began once someone was hired (Thomas, 1990, pp. 108–9). Thomas argued that something besides affirmative action was needed, that is, managing diversity which "consists of enabling people, in this case minorities and women, to perform to their potential" (Anand and Winters, 2008, p. 359; Thomas, 1990, p. 108).

Part of an enabling strategy is gender diversity coaching. Studies confirm that women tend to value relationships, teamwork and consensus-building, where men prefer analytical systems thinking and competitiveness (Ludeman, 2009, p. 238). Instead of trying to become like men, women are more successful being who they are, "strengthening under-developed skills to meet their goals" (Ludeman, 2009, p. 238). Ludeman and Erlandson (2006a, 2006b) assessed gender differences in leaders, identifying that beta characteristics are greater in women – and that women need to develop more alpha characteristics if they wish to be leaders. Ludeman advocates that coaches use different tools and techniques when coaching women leaders, and in particular acknowledging that the coachee's experience is real (Ludeman, 2009, p. 244).

Similarly, Erlandson advocates coaching for gender difference. Men are drawn to competition and attaining positions of dominance; women work more collaboratively, building relationships and networking (Erlandson, 2009, pp. 216–17). Although some women leaders do possess alpha traits, Erlandson focuses on the alpha male. Strengths become risks for alpha males, and they can fluctuate between healthy and unhealthy behaviors (Erlandson, 2009, p. 220).

Another reason often provided for the absence of women on boards is their lack of connections. Medland (2004) argues that the most important impediment to female directorships is that the informal social network linking directors consists primarily of men. "To win the game, you have to know the rules – the real rules. Women are often not included in the informal network in which information about promotion possibilities and job openings is exchanged; this isn't just the case in the business world; increasing the transparency of promotion and review procedures is also a challenge to universities and research centres" (Ragins and Sundstrom, 1989).

Internal research at Hewlett Packard showed that women apply for jobs only if they think they meet 100 percent of the criteria; whereas men apply if they feel they meet 60 percent of the requirements (Desvaux *et al.*, 2008, p. 4). Coaching, mentoring, and networking programs have proven quite successful in helping female executives to succeed, encouraging them to seek out new positions more aggressively.

## Future Research

The importance of gender diversity research cannot be underestimated. There is a huge need for research into the impact of coaching for both women and men on core diversity issues, particularly on how business and executive coaching can be tailored in a more gender-sensitive way to assist women to excel.

Mentoring and sponsorship programs within organizations have been shown to develop equity in the workplace (Ragins and Scandura, 1994). However, there is little research to show what the results would be for equity between men and women, if coaching was available to women on an equal basis to men at senior levels. There is coaching taking place worldwide, but we need evidence-based studies to see what the results are for women breaking through the glass ceiling.

In response to concerns about the imbalance between men and women in senior roles, and the lack of informal mentors and appropriate role models for women – the main body of gender-related research has taken place in the field of mentoring (see, for example, the chapters in this book on mentoring). It has been suggested that coaching could be the key to increase women's visibility and to challenge stereotypical perceptions, as long as the coach understands how women function within an organization and how organizations view them (Peltier and Irueste-Montes, 2010; Zeus and Skiffington, 2003). We therefore need to develop new theoretical approaches to gender coaching research, adopting a critical analysis of the gendered organization and the implications for coaching to influence gender equity in senior leadership positions.

In recent decades there has been considerable research into diversity, gender, and culture. However, in the current literature, there is little reference as to how coaching can influence gender balance within organizations, particularly at a senior level. We need more studies in organizations using coaching as a key driver for market differentiation and improved performance, and which are developing gender diversity as a business objective for organizational effectiveness.

# Conclusion

I have examined current thinking on how men and women are socialized, the impact of organizational culture – and in what ways the dominant male organizational culture has affected the development of women in the workplace. If we are to redress the imbalance of women in senior management and board positions, we need to develop coaching as a driver of business strategy. Coaching conversations can provide a real platform for creative thinking and strategic planning, using the real experiences of clients (Hernez-Broome and Boyce, 2011).

Although contemporary research has looked at whether coaching is different for men and for women (Erlandson, 2009), and whether there is a need for a more gender-specific style of coaching, the way forward is to ensure that coaching is available to help all executives develop self-awareness and an understanding of the "gendered organization", and how to negotiate the pitfalls of organizational culture, politics, and structure. Each coach practitioner has a responsibility to integrate knowledge and understanding of gender diversity issues into their own education and practice, evaluating themselves to understand their own worldview. It is only in this way that practitioners can increase their competence and empower their clients.

# References

Abizadeh, A. (2001) Ethnicity, race, and a possible humanity. *World Order*, 33(1), 22–34.

Acker, J. (1992) Gendering organizational theory. In: A.J. Mills and P. Tancred (eds) *Gendering Organizational Analysis*. Newbury Park, CA: Sage. pp. 248–60.

Adams, R.B. and Ferreira, D. (2008) Women in the boardroom and their impact on governance and performance. *Journal of Financial Economics*, 94(2), 291–309.

Anand, R. and Winters, M.-F. (2008) A retrospective view of corporate diversity training from 1964 to the present. *Academy of Management Learning and Education*, 7(3), 356–72.

Arfken, D.E., Bellar, S.L., and Helms, M.M. (2004) The ultimate glass ceiling revisited: The presence of women on corporate boards. *Journal of Business Ethics*, 50(2), 177–86.

Babcock, L. and Laschever, S. (2003) *Women Don't Ask: Negotiation and the Gender Divide*. Princeton, NJ: Princeton University Press.

Beasley, C. (1999) *What is Feminism? An Introduction to Feminist Theory*. London: Sage.

Bell, R.E. and Kastens, K.A. (2004) *Righting the Balance: Gender Diversity in the Geosciences*. Paper 47, ADVANCE Library Collection http://digitalcommons.usu.edu/advance/47 (accessed May 20, 2011).

Bernardi, R.A. and Threadgill, V.H. (2010) Women directors and corporate social responsibility. *Electronic Journal of Business Ethics and Organization Studies*, 15(2), 15–21.

Bickel, J. (2001) Gender equity in undergraduate medical education: A status report. *Journal of Women's Health and Gender-Based Medicine*, 10(3), 261–70.

Bowers, C. and Passmore, J. (in press). Exploring key factors in the coaching relationship: A Q-sort study. *Personnel Review*.

Bowles, H.R., Babcock, L., and McGinn, K.L. (2005) Constraints and triggers: Situational mechanics of gender in negotiation. *Journal of Personality and Social Psychology*, 89(6), 951–65.

Broadbridge, A. and Hearn, J. (2008) Gender and management: New directions in research and continuing patterns in practice. *British Journal of Management*, 19, S38–S49.

Brome, D.R. (1993) Part one. In: J.L. Chin, V. De La Cancela, and Y.M. Jenkins (eds) *Diversity in Psychotherapy: The Politics of Race, Ethnicity, and Gender*. Westport, CT and London: Praeger. pp. 1–4.

Burke, S. and Collins, K.M. (2001) Gender differences in leadership styles and management skills. *Women in Management Review*, 16(5), 244–57.

Butler, J. (1990) *Gender Trouble: Feminism and the Subversion of Identity*. New York and London: Routledge.

Calás, M.B. and Smircich, L. (2006) From 'the woman's point of view': Feminist approaches to organization studies. In: S.R. Clegg, C. Hardy, and W.R. Nord (eds) *Handbook of Organization Studies*. London: Sage. pp. 218–57.

Carter, D.A., Simkins, B.J., and Simpson, W.G. (2003) Corporate governance, board diversity, and firm value. *The Financial Review*, 38(1), 33–53.

Catalyst (2007) *The Double-Bind Dilemma for Women in Leadership: Damned if you Do, Doomed if you Don't*. www.catalyst.org/publication/83/the-double-bind dilemmafor-women-in-leadership-damned-if-you-do-doomed-if-you-dont (accessed May 20, 2011).

Chênevert, D. and Tremblay, M. (2002) Managerial career success in Canadian organizations: Is gender a determinant? *International Journal of Human Resource Management*, 13(6), 920–41.

Chin, J.L., De La Cancela, V., and Jenkins, Y.M. (eds) (1993) *Diversity in Psychotherapy: The Politics of Race, Ethnicity, and Gender*. Westport, CT: Praeger.

Collinson, D.L. and Hearn, J. (1994) Naming men as men: Implications for work, management and organizations. *Gender, Work and Organization*, 1(1), 2–22.

Cox, T. Jr., and Smolinski, C. (1994) *Managing Diversity and Glass Ceiling Initiatives as National Economic Imperatives*. Report to the US Department of Labor Glass Ceiling Commission. Federal Publications Paper 117, Cornell University ILR School Digital Commons. http://digitalcommons.ilr.cornell.edu/key_workplace/117 (accessed May 17, 2011).

Czarniawska-Joerges, B. (1992) *Exploring Complex Organizations: A Cultural Perspective*. Newbury Park, CA: Sage.

Daily, C.M. and Dalton, D.R. (2003) Are director equity policies exclusionary? *Business Ethics Quarterly*, 13(4), 415–32.

Davidson, M.J. and Cooper, C.L. (1984) Occupational stress in female managers: A comparative approach. *Journal of Management Studies*, 21, 185–205.

De Haan, E. (2008) *Relational Coaching: Journeys Towards Mastery, One To One Learning*. Chichester: Wiley.

De La Cancela, V., Jenkins, Y.M., and Chin, J.L. (1993) Chapter one: Diversity in psychotherapy: Examination of racial, ethnic, gender, and political issues. In: J.L. Chin, V. De La Cancela, and Y.M. Jenkins (eds), *Diversity in Psychotherapy: The Politics of Race, Ethnicity, and Gender*. Westport, CT and London: Praeger. pp. 5–16.

Desvaux, G., Devillard-Hoellinger, S., and Meaney, M.C. (2008) A business case for women. *McKinsey Quarterly*, September.

Eddleston, K.A., Simione, K., and Ortiz-Walters, R. (2010) Satisfaction with mentoring relationships: Does gender identity matter? *Career Development International*, 15, 100–20.

Eichler, M. (1980) *The Double Standard: A Feminist Critique of Feminist Social Science*. London: Croom Helm.

Erhardt, N.L., Werbel, J.D., and Shrader, C.B. (2003) Board of director diversity and firm financial performance. *Corporate Governance*, 11(2), 102–11.

Erlandson, E. (2009) Coaching with men: Alpha males. In: J. Passmore (ed.) *Diversity in Coaching: Working with Gender, Culture, Race and Age*. London and Philadelphia, PA: Association for Coaching and Kogan Page. pp. 216–36.

Farrell, K.A. and Hersch, P.L. (2005) Additions to corporate boards: The effect of gender. *Journal of Corporate Finance*, 11, 85–106.

Federal Glass Ceiling Commission (1995) *Solid Investment: Making Full Use of the Nation's Human Capital*. Washington, DC: US Department of Labor.

Fielden, S.L. and Cooper, C.L. (2002) Managerial stress: Are women more at risk? In: R.J. Burke and D. Nelson (eds) *Gender, Work and Stress*. Washington, DC: American Psychological Association.

Friedan, B. (1963) *The Feminine Mystique*. Harmondsworth: Penguin.

Gatrell, C. and Cooper, C.L (2007) (No) cracks in the glass ceiling: Women managers, stress and the barriers to success. In: D. Bilimoria and S.K. Piderit (eds) *Handbook on Women in Business and Management*. Cheltenham: Edward Elgar.

Gatrell, C. and Swan, E. (2008) *Gender and Diversity in Management: A Concise Introduction*. London: Sage.

Gray, D.E. and Goregaokar, H. (2010) Choosing an executive coach: The influence of gender on the coach-coachee matching process. *Management Learning*, 41(5), 525–44.

Greer, G. (1970/2006) *The Female Eunuch*. London: Harper Perennial.

Halford, S. and Leonard, P. (2001) New identities? Professionalism, managerialism and the construction of self. In: M. Exworthy and S. Halford (eds) *Professionals and the New Managerialism in the Public Sector*. Buckingham: Open University Press.

Hamilton, E. (2006) Whose story is it anyway? Narrative accounts of the roles of women in founding and establishing family businesses. *International Small Business Journal*, 23(3), 1–16.

Hawkes, N.R. and Seggar, J.F. (2000) *Celebrating Women Coaches: A Biographical Dictionary*. Westport, CT: Greenwood Press.

Hearn, J. and Parkin, W. (1983) Gender and organizations: A selective review, and a critique of a neglected area. *Organization Studies*, 4(3), 219–42.

Hernez-Broome, G. and Boyce, L.A. (eds) (2011) *Advancing Executive Coaching: Setting the Course for Successful Leadership Coaching*. San Francisco, CA: Wiley.

Institute of Management (1995) *National Management Salary Survey*. London: Institute of Management.

Institute of Management/Remuneration Economics (1998) *UK National Management Survey*. London: Institute of Management.

Janse van Rensburg, M. (2009) Marti Janse van Rensburg writes. In: S. Stout-Rostron. (ed.) *Business Coaching International: Transforming Individuals and Organizations*. London: Karnac. pp. 206–27.

Kanter, R.M. (1977) *Men and Women of the Corporation*. New York: Basic Books.

Kolb, D.M. (2009) Too bad for the women, or does it have to be? Gender and negotiation research over the past twenty-five years. *Negotiation Journal*, October, 515–31.

Legge, K. (1987) Women in personnel management: Uphill climb or downhill slide? In: A. Spencer and D. Podmore (eds) *In a Man's World*. London: Tavistock.

Leimon, A., Moscovici, F., and Goodier, H. (2011) *Coaching Women to Lead*. New York: Routledge.

Liston-Smith, J. (2010) Maternity coaching: The business case. *My Family Care*, www.myfamilycare.co.uk. UK ezine.

Ludeman, K. (2009) Coaching with women. In: J. Passmore (ed.) *Diversity in Coaching: Working with Gender, Culture, Race and Age*. London and Philadelphia, PA: Association for Coaching and Kogan Page. pp. 237–54.

Ludeman, K. and Erlandson, E. (2004) Coaching the alpha male. *Harvard Business Review*, May.

Ludeman, K. and Erlandson, E. (2006a) *Alpha Assessment.* www.alpha-assessment.com (accessed May 17, 2011).

Ludeman, K. and Erlandson, E. (2006b) *Alpha Male Syndrome.* Boston, MA: Harvard Business School Press.

Marinova, J., Plantenga, J., and Remery, C. (2010) *Gender Diversity and Firm Performance: Evidence from Dutch and Danish boardrooms.* Discussion Paper Series 10–03, Tjalling C. Koopmans Research Institute, Utrecht School of Economics. Utrecht: Utrecht University.

Marques Sampaio, D. (2009) Daniel Marques Sampaio writes. In: S. Stout-Rostron (ed.) *Business Coaching International: Transforming Individuals and Organizations.* London: Karnac. pp. 188–206.

Mattis, M.C. (2001) Advancing women in business organizations: Key leadership roles and behaviors of senior leaders and middle managers. *Journal of Management Development*, 20(4), 371–88.

Medland, D. (2004) Small steps for womankind. *Corporate Board Member Europe*, Winter.

Meyerson, D. and Fletcher, J.K. (1999) A modest manifesto for shattering the glass ceiling. *Harvard Business Review*, 78(1), 127–36.

Motsoaledi, L.S.P. (2009) Executive coaching in diversity from a systems psychodynamic perspective. Unpublished PhD (Consulting Psychology) dissertation. Pretoria: University of South Africa.

Mulholland, K. (1996) Gender, power and property relations within entrepreneurial wealthy families. *Gender, Work and Organisation*, 3(2), 78–102.

Oakley, A. (1972/1985) *Sex, Gender and Society* (revised edn). Aldershot: Gower.

Parliamentary Assembly, Council of Europe (2005) *Discrimination Against Women in the Workforce and the Workplace.* Report of the Committee on Equal Opportunities for Women and Men, Document 10484. http://assembly.coe.int/Documents/WorkingDocs/Doc05/EDOC10484. htm (accessed May 20, 2011).

Passmore, J. (2010) A grounded theory study of the coachee experience: The implications for training and practice in coaching psychology. *International Coaching Psychology Review*, 5(1), 48–62.

Passmore, J. and Fillery-Travis, A. (2011) A critical review of executive coaching research: A decade of progress and what's to come. *Coaching: An International Journal of Theory, Practice and Research*, 4(2) 70–88.

Passmore, J., Holloway, M., and Rawle-Cope, M. (2010). MBTI types and executive coaching: In search of a relationship. *Counselling Psychology Quarterly*, 23(1), 1–16.

Peltier, B. (2010) *The Psychology of Executive Coaching, Theory and application* (2nd edn). London/New York: Taylor and Francis Group.

Peltier, B. and Irueste-Montes, A.M. (2010) Coaching women in business. In: B. Peltier (ed.) *The Psychology of Executive Coaching: Theory and application* (2nd edn). London/New York: Taylor and Francis. pp. 259–83.

Peters, T. and Waterman, R. (1982) *In Search of Excellence.* London: Harper-Collins.

Ragins, B.R. and Scandura, T.A. (1994) Gender differences in expected outcomes of mentoring relationships. *Academy of Management Journal*, 37(4), 957.

Ragins, B.R. and Sundstrom, E. (1989) Gender and power in organizations: A longitudinal perspective. *Psychological Bulletin*, 105, 51–88.

Richardson, D. (2007) Patterned fluidities: Reimagining the relationship between gender and sexuality. *Sociology*, 41(3), 457–74.

Simpson, R. and Lewis, P. (2007) *Voice, Visibility and the Gendering of Organizations.* Basingstoke: Palgrave Macmillan.

Sparrow, S. (2008) Girls allowed. *Training and Coaching Today*, June, 18–19.

Speedy, B. (2004). Diverse view: Women directors are good for the bottom line. *The Australian*, October 5, 24.

Stout-Rostron, S. (2009) *Business Coaching International: Transforming Individuals and Organizations.* London: Karnac.

Stout-Rostron, S. and Wilkins, N. (2011) Gender issues in business coaching. *COMENSAnews*, April.

Sue, S. (1993) Foreword. In: J.L. Chin, V. De la Cancela, and Y.M. Jenkins (eds) *Diversity in Psychotherapy: The Politics Of Race, Ethnicity, and Gender*. Westport, CT and London: Praeger. pp. ix–x.

Tannen, D. (1995) The power of talk: Who gets heard and why. *Harvard Business Review*, September–October.

Tannen, D. (1999) *The Argument Culture: Stopping America's War of Words*. New York: Ballantine.

Thomas, R. R. Jr. (1990) From affirmative action to affirming diversity. *Harvard Business Review*, 90(2), 107–17.

Wirth, L. (2004) *Breaking Through the Glass Ceiling: Women in Management: Update 2004*. Geneva: International Labour Office.

Woodd, M. (1997) Gender differences in mentoring: A biographical reflection. *Educational Management and Administration*, 25, 25–34.

Zeus, P. and Skiffington, S. (2003) *Behavioural Coaching*. North Ryde, NSW: McGraw-Hill Australia.

# 10

# Team Coaching

## Alison Carter and Peter Hawkins

## Introduction

The primary aim of this chapter is to provide an overview of the current state of the theory, craft, and practice of team coaching in organizations, to review the limited amount of research that has been carried out in this field, with some guidance of where future research would be valuable.

Most coaching to date within organizations has been dyadic (one-to-one) and it is this form which has been the subject of most research to date. But more recently there has been a growing interest in team coaching by both organizational purchaser and providers. However, the field of team coaching is both complex and still very underdeveloped and can be likened to where individual coaching was in the 1980s. The practice is only beginning to be defined and theoretical models produced. Only when a field has defined itself, clarified the purpose and outcomes it endeavors to create, and developed clear frameworks, can meaningful research be carried out to test the hypotheses and evaluate the success of different approaches. So in this chapter we will first explore why there is a growing focus on teams, define what constitutes a team, explore the growing body of work to define team coaching and develop key models and approaches, show how this applies to different types of teams and then give an overview of what research has been done in the area and guidance for future research.

Throughout the chapter we view team coaching not just as the application of individual coaching to a larger collection of people belonging to the same part of the organization, but as a separate craft that draws not only on the field of coaching, but also the much older tradition of organization development, including the many approaches to team development, as well as combining learning from sports psychology's work with high performing teams.

The economic crisis of 2008–2011 and the harsh economic conditions in many Western countries has led to cuts in budgets as well as rapid organizational change. This has left organizations looking for new ways to engage their teams and maximize the efficiency

*The Wiley Blackwell Handbook of the Psychology of Coaching and Mentoring*, First Edition.
Edited by Jonathan Passmore, David B. Peterson, and Teresa Freire.
© 2013 John Wiley & Sons, Ltd. Published 2016 by John Wiley & Sons, Ltd.

of their employees in order to remain ahead of their competitors. Whilst many coaching providers are keen to offer their version of "team coaching", there is, as yet, only a small amount of specific literature that examines team coaching. This is not surprising in an immature profession such as coaching, which is still building the theoretical foundations for its dominant (dyadic) form. There is, however, a broader and long established litera- ture on teams within organizations which offers important contextual research for those studying the coaching of teams.

Since coaching teams is relatively under-researched, this chapter starts with a discussion of the broader literature encompassing development interventions as well as some parts of the management, leadership, and team effectiveness literature that address coaching. Then we address what the specific team coaching literature to date tells us about what it is, the forms in which it is found, and how its features compare to other team or group-based interventions, along with how outcomes are being measured and the benefits claimed. A consideration of the difficulties and limitations with the existing literature follows. Finally, future directions for research will be suggested.

## Why the Focus on Teams?

The use of teams has been prominent within modern organizational life for some years (Hackman, 2003; Thompson, 2004) and both public and private sector organizations are making increased use of team-orientated work. A study by Devine *et al.* (1999) estimated that half of all organizations in the United States made use of teams, while Guzzo and Shea (1992) and Offerman and Spiros (2001) both identified that over 80 percent of organizations with 100 employees or more reported using team structures (82 percent and 80 percent, respectively). A survey of high level managers in the United States found that 91 percent of them agreed with the statement: "Teams are central to organizational success" (Martin and Bal, 2006).

As Kozlowski and Ilgen state in their 2006 review of team effectiveness: "There is over fifty years of psychological research – literally thousands of studies – focused on understand- ing and influencing the processes that underlie team effectiveness" (p. 77). Management research also has a long tradition: over the last 20 years much attention has been given to studies on effective teams and how they can develop into high performance teams (e.g., Katzenbach and Smith, 1993a). The evidence from 'scientific' psychological research in the positivistic tradition  on the relationships between teams and absolute performance is by no means conclusive or consistent, but the prevailing view is that teamwork is a major contributor to improved performance, productivity, and quality of decision making. It has been argued that, in many circumstances, teams are more effective than individuals because team members can share workloads, monitor their colleagues' behaviours, and coordinate different areas of expertise (Mathieu *et al.*, 2000). Cases in support of this argument come from a variety of industries (Banker *et al.*, 1996; Wellins *et al.*, 1994). Ket- tley and Hirsh (2000) also highlighted the enormous potential of cross-functional teams for both individual and organizational learning.

More recently there has been an increased tendency to understand leadership in the twenty-first century as something that goes beyond the leader to a more collective and devolved leadership through the organization. Lynda Gratton writes: "In today's interconnected, dynamic, global and technically-enabled world, the creation of value and innovation rarely springs from isolated individual endeavours" (Gratton, 2007, p. 23). And Peter Hawkins has written elsewhere (2011a) how: "The current world challenges task us as a species to find a way of working together, across disciplines and borders, beyond local and self interest in a way that has never been attained before in history."

This is a reflection of the fundamental shifts in global interconnectedness, the speed of change and increasing political and economic volatility, technological innovation, and the nature of work, and therefore the nature of leadership required (Hawkins 2011a, 2011b; Ireland and Hitt, 1999; Pearce, 2004; Raelin, 2005). As a result of these arguments in-company development practice is focusing on two concepts: team effectiveness and empowerment. Development has moved beyond expecting major challenges to be met by the "great individual leader" to effective collective leadership and "high performing teams". The emphasis has moved to leadership development and away from leader development (Hawkins, 2010). Management research has been generally supportive of empowering and distributed leadership, with studies showing positive effects on creativity, performance, corporate culture, and team spirit (e.g., Kouzes and Posner, 2002; Manz and Sims, 1987; Srivastava *et al.*, 2006).

Hawkins (2011a, 2011b) argues that there is a significant increase in the need for strong leadership teams as the growing challenges for organizational leaders can no longer be met by single heroic leaders. However, many senior leaders have become successful through being strong, competitive, individualistic, and single minded, and consequently many leadership teams function at less than the sum of their parts. He cites the following growing challenges for collective leadership:

- Winning the hearts and minds of your people by engaging people with EQ not just IQ.
- Doing more with less – which means realizing the potential in others.
- Inspiring them to go beyond what they think they can achieve.
- Dealing with greater global interdependence and volatility.
- Embracing constant change.
- Orchestrating connections across boundaries.
- Relating transculturally.
- Creating shared value for all stakeholder groups.

Top leadership teams and boards play a crucial role in ensuring accountability as well as organization performance. Research at the top of organizations has risen in prominence in the wake of public concerns about governance and ethics (Bazerman and Tenbrunsel 2011). Evidence from 'ethnographic' research has been useful in exploring issues such as how skills, technical know-how, and experience are deployed to influence team processes (Samra-Fredericks, 2002), influence and decision-making within management team meetings (Clifton, 2009), and understanding collective 'blind spots' (Carter *et al.*, 2011).

So, if there is a need for more effective leadership teams, it is not surprising that team coaching is being thought of as a potential intervention to support the development of teams, team leaders, and team members.

## What Do We Mean by "A Team"?

### Team versus group

Within the literature there is much debate on the definition of a team and how it differs from a group of individuals (Fisher *et al.*, 1997; Robotham, 2009). Some scholars argue that the differences between groups and teams reflect only semantics and it is impossible, if not pointless, to separate the two (Guzzo and Dickson, 1996), whereas others have rejected this notion (Fisher *et al.*, 1997; Katzenbach and Smith, 1993b). Nevertheless, numerous definitions of teams have been developed. One that is commonly adopted is that of Kozlowski and Bell (2003) who stated that teams are: "Collectives who exist to perform organizationally relevant tasks, share one or more common goals, interact socially, exhibit task interdependencies, maintain, manage boundaries and are embedded in an organizational context that sets boundaries, constrains the team, and influences exchanges with other units in the broader entity." Katzenbach and Smith (1999) also described teams as: "A small number of people with complementary skills, who are committed to a common purpose, performance goals and approach, for which they hold themselves mutually accountable."

Both definitions explain why a team is different from a group or a collective and that this is to do with the team having a joint endeavor that they cannot achieve working either individually or in parallel. Teams have limitations in terms of size as the more people involved within them, the more complex the interactions and the less able the group is to function as a whole. The more people you have within a team, the more likely that subgroups will develop. Groups, on the other hand, do not have a limitation on their size. Second, team members need to identify with the team, interact with other team members, and have a clear sense of shared purpose and inter-dependence on other members (Kettley and Hirsh 2000, Hawkins 2011a). Katzenbach and Smith (1993b) believe that as teams rely on individual and collective accountability, team performance is higher as they produce outcomes based upon individual efforts and the joint contribution of their members: "A team is more than the sum of its parts."

As Brown and Grant (2010) observe, one of the problems in the coaching literature is that the terms "team" and "group" are frequently used interchangeably. Brown and Grant choose to use the broader category "group coaching" to cover any group of individuals including but not limited to teams, in their overview of non-dyadic group coaching and presentation of a model of group coaching. In this chapter we prefer to use the narrower category "team coaching" or "coaching teams" so that it relates only to individuals working together towards shared goals within or between their organizations.

We do not, however, discount the importance and tradition of group-based interventions within organizations, many of which are also used on teams. There is a substantial body of literature about organizational learning and organizational development interventions (Bate and Robert, 2007; Brown and Harvey, 2006; Pedler *et al.*, 1991; Schein, 1999; Senge, 1990). Specific OD methodologies are also documented, such as open space technology (Owen, 1997) and large-scale organizational change approaches (Bevan *et al.*, 2007; Garrow *et al.*, 2010; Gunnerson and Holling, 2002; Plsek, 2003). At the heart of all these group-based interventions is the need for development to be seen within an organization-wide scope and a systemic approach, which is also necessary for team coaching, as all teams operate within a wider systemic context.

## Team types

Teams can be complex to study and it is not always easy to identify the role of team leadership, let alone team coach (if we assume they might be different). Teamwork is characterized by recurring cycles of mutually dependent interaction (Kozlowski *et al.*, 1996a, 1996b). These cycles of goal-directed activity have been divided into the two distinct phases of transition (evaluation or planning activities) and action (performing work directly contributing to goal attainment) (Marks *et al.*, 2001). As teams work across the phases, they encounter numerous challenges that arise from within the team, organization, or environment within which the team operates (Morgeson *et al.*, 2009). In addition, interpersonal processes need to be managed, including fostering a climate for member motivation, promoting a sense of psychological safety (Edmondson, 1999), and dealing with conflict (Marks *et al.*, 2001). Internal or informal team leadership occurs when leadership responsibilities are shared among team members (Day *et al.*, 2004).

There are many types of teams within organizations and a number of ways of classifying them. Researchers have long sought to distinguish between different types of teams, based on the contexts in which they work, their type of task, and the length of time the team is together. Most studies have favored stable single-disciplinary teams engaged in routine tasks or interdisciplinary top management teams. One classification offered by Hawkins (2011b) is by team duration (e.g., project), function (e.g., marketing, production, etc.), geographical spread (e.g., regional, international, virtual), customer group focus (the X account team, the Y account team, etc.), position in the hierarchy (board, leadership, operational, etc.), mode of operating (e.g., decision-making, consultative, advisory), and by leadership style (self-managed, manager-led, etc.). Clutterbuck (2007) offers a classification based on dimensions: stable (members and tasks constant), cabin crew (tasks stay the same but membership changes constantly, standing project (relatively stable members drawn from other short-term projects), evolutionary (long-term projects where tasks and membership change over time), developmental alliances (set up for learning purposes, e.g., action learning sets), and virtual (geographically dispersed or fuzzy boundaries). Hawkins (2011b) and Clutterbuck (2007) both argue that team coaching needs to be adapted for each team type and specific team situation. How this should be done is, however, an area of difference between them which highlights an important nuance in language. Hawkins (2011b) argues for team coaching where the focus is primarily on the team as a collective, and only of secondary importance is the personal and interpersonal development within the team. Clutterbuck (2007) talks about coaching interventions within a team setting.

## Team leaders

"Teams versus groups" is not, however, the only problem in terminology surrounding coaching teams in organizations. Arguably an even bigger one is assumptions about whether the coach is also the team leader. In some papers the coach refers to the individual who is a member of the team but has special responsibility to help guide team activities (i.e., the team leader is doing the coaching) and this covers much of the work in the wider leadership field, for example Hackman and Wageman (2005) and Fisher (2010). However, in other papers "the coach" refers to an outsider who guides or facilitates the team but is not involved in executing its work.

The coaching behaviors of team leaders has received increasing attention when it comes to team performance. Kozlowski and colleagues (in two 1996 articles) argue that across the course of team development leaders go through a progression of developmental roles: mentor, instructor, coach, and facilitator. Team leaders can also enable the conditions for effective teams and affect the development and motivation of team members, for example, through a supportive organizational context and the deployment of good coaching skills (Burke *et al.*, 2006).

Some management researchers (e.g., Morgeson *et al.*, 2009) suggest that research has tended to focus too much on formally appointed team leaders, despite team leadership often being distributed within and outside the team.

# Definition of Team Coaching

With the rise in popularity and utilization of team coaching, comes the need for clearer clarification on what is meant by the term. The practice of coaching teams in organizations has been conceptualized and described in a variety of ways, which fail to distinguish team coaching from similar but different approaches such as group coaching, teambuilding, team facilitation, process consultancy and so forth. The term has been used to include specific teambuilding and group development activities (Cunha and Louro, 2000); as a day-to-day management skill to continually raise performance standards (Thomas, 2007); coaching individuals within a team as well as the whole team (Carter, 2001) to help the team members be more effective with each other and driving behavioral change across the business (Anderson et al., 2008; Diedrich, 2001); and simultaneous individual coaching, peer coaching, and training in coaching skills followed by cascading back in leaders' workplaces through coaching their own teams (Kets de Vries, 2005).

Hawkins (2011b) offers categorization of different group and team coaching and development processes to try to bring some clarity to the field for the benefit of purchasers, providers, academics, and researchers, so we quote this at length:

1   Group coaching of team members and action learning sets.

   There has been a great deal of confusion, both in the literature and in practice between team coaching and group coaching. Group coaching is the coaching of individuals within a group context, where the group members take it in turns to be the focal client, while the other group members, become part of the coaching resource to that individual. Action learning sets are similar to group coaching where members of a set, often between 4–7 in number, take it in turn to bring real current challenges they are facing to be coached on by the other members of the set and where present, the set facilitator. In group coaching often there is more of an emphasis on the individual; and in action learning sets, more of a focus on the challenge being presented, but this is not always the case and in both instances the focus is on supporting the individual in being the best they can in meeting their work challenges.

   Group coaching can also be carried out in the context of a team, where the individuals being coached are all members of the same team. Kets de Vries (2006, Chapter 11) provides an excellent case example of using group coaching with an intact leadership team. Although group coaching in a team context can be a useful prelude or component of team coaching, it is fundamentally different from team coaching, for in team coaching the primary client is the whole team, rather than the individual team members.

2   Team development is any process carried out by a team, with or without assistance from outside, to develop its capability and capacity to work well together, with its joint task.

   Team development can take many forms, from outward bound exercises, fun activity together to promote bonding, team analysis of its own behavior, reviews of working processes, or away-days. However, research has shown little evidence of team bonding and team activity events having an impact on team performance (Katzenbach and Smith, 1993b; Wageman et al., 2008).

3   Teambuilding is any process used to help a team in the early stages of team development.

   Team building has been defined by Kriek and Venter (2009) as: "A specific intervention to address issues relating to the development of the team. Typically, it consists of a one (or more) day program focused on the improvement of interpersonal relations, improved productivity or better alignment with organizational goals."

Teambuilding aims to assist individuals and groups to examine, diagnose, and act upon behavior and interpersonal relationships (Schein, 1999). Many activities are included under the teambuilding label, such as outdoor team pursuits, social activities, experiential events and simulations. During the 1980s and early 1990s teambuilding was claimed to be one of the most commonly used OD interventions in organizations (Buller and Bell, 1986; Offerman and Spiros, 2001). While there is evidence to show that some teambuilding interventions may have been successful (Mazany *et al.*, 1995), especially in helping team members strengthen collaboration and trust (Klein *et al.*, 2006), there are mixed perceptions of whether this translates into sustained productivity and performance (Klein 2009; Kriek and Venter 2009). Some research has shown little evidence of team bonding or any impact on team performance (Katzenback and Smith, 1993b; Wageman *et al.*, 2008).

Teambuilding can thus be seen as a subcategory of team development, focusing on what Tuckman (1965) would term the *forming* and *norming* stages. Others argue (Wageman *et al.*, 2008; Hackman and Wageman, 2005; Gersick, 1988; and Hawkins, 2011b) that this stage of early team engagement is best achieved by focusing on the mission, goals and expectations of the performance of the team.

4   Team facilitation is when a specific person (or persons) is asked to facilitate the team by managing the process for them so they are freed up to focus on the task.

There is a wide range of areas that a facilitator may be asked to come and facilitate for a team. These include:

(a)   To resolve a particular conflict or difficulty
(b)   To carry out a team review of its ways of operating and relating
(c)   To enable a strategy or planning process
(d)   To run an off-site away-day

Other possible requests usually also focus on enabling the specific process and not to get involved with content or team performance.

5   Team process consultancy is a form of team facilitation where the team consultant sits alongside the team carrying out its meetings or planning sessions and provides reflection and review on "how" the team is going about its task.

Schein (1988, p. 34) defines process consultation as: "A set of activities on the part of the consultant that help the client to perceive, understand, and act upon the process events that occur in the client's environment."

This process consulting may well involve a variety of feedback and inquiry processes before, during, and at the end of meetings, as well as some interventions to enable the team to reflect on its processes as it proceeds.

6   Team coaching.

In recent years a number of key writers have tried to bring clarity to the field and a number of definitions of team coaching have been put forward. In 2005 Hackman and Wageman proposed that team coaching was: "Direct interaction with a team intended to help members make coordinated and task appropriate use of their collective resources in accomplishing the team's work" (2005, p. 269). This clearly indicated that it involved work with the whole team, not just team members, and emphasized the focus on task and best use of resources. Hackman and Wageman (2005) also defined the functions of team coaching in a way that combined the performance and the process. They wrote that team coaching involved: "Interventions that inhibit process losses and foster process gains in each of three performance processes: the effort people put in (motivation), the performance strategies (consultation), and the level of knowledge and skill (education)."

David Clutterbuck (2007, p. 77) defined team coaching as: "Helping the team improve performance, and the processes by which performance is achieved, through reflection and dialogue." He very helpfully shows how team coaching needs to combine a performance and process focus and elsewhere in his book Clutterbuck very usefully elaborates on the continual learning aspects of the team (2007, pp. 123–98).

Hawkins and Smith (2006) defined team coaching as: "Enabling a team to function at more than the sum of its parts, by clarifying its mission and improving its external and internal relationships. It is different therefore from coaching team leaders on how to lead their teams, or coaching individuals in a group setting."

Hawkins (2011b) developed this further to suggest that team coaching needs to focus not just on task and process, and how the team members relate to each other but also on how the team relates to all it stakeholders, creating shared value. He goes on to define what he terms systemic team coaching: "Systemic team coaching is a process by which a team coach works with a whole team, both when they are together and when they are apart, in order to help them improve both their collective performance and how they work together, and also how they develop their collective leadership to engage more effectively with all their key stakeholder groups to jointly transform the wider business."

Thus we would argue that team coaching is distinguished by being a relationship over time between a whole team and a coach in which they jointly work to improve: the collective task achievement; process of operating together; the process of engaging with all their stakeholders and their collective and individual learning and development.

## The "who" of team coaching

Individual coaching has increasingly been delivered in large companies by a mixture of:

- Line managers coaching their own staff with or without any formal coaching training.
- Internal coaches who have undertaken some more extensive coaching training and who often receive supervision, who give a few hour every week to coaching individuals from other departments and functions.
- External coaches brought in to provide specific coaching for senior executives or high potential staff.

The same pattern is also developing more slowly in team coaching. Increasingly, chief executives and other senior leaders are recognizing that coaching their leadership team is a critical aspect of their role (Wageman, 2001; Wageman *et al.*, 2008) and often will use their individual coach to supervise their own coaching of their team. Building and coaching your team is also becoming a more regular part of most senior leadership development programs and a key topic in a senior leader's action learning sets.

A few organizations have created a skilled group of internal coaches who have been trained in team coaching and who can work with teams right across the organization as required. These coaches are sometimes senior managers or HR and OD specialists. Internal coaches are usually expected to carry out their coaching role in addition to or as part of their "everyday" job (Hamlin *et al.*, 2009, Hawkins, 2012).

Some argue that executive team coaching requires externally trained coaches who are not part of the client organization (Grant *et al.*, 2010, p. 6). This is thought to be the case particularly when it comes to coaching top leadership teams; external coaches might be perceived as more credible by the team members. When it comes to teams it is argued an external coach might be more able to focus on how the team is working towards its outcomes because the main stakeholders and team members are too preoccupied with project outcomes (Reich *et al.*, 2009).

Hicks (2010) suggests that organizations do not appreciate the complexity of team coaching, and it is important that they have a full understanding of the time and effort it may take to train their cadres of internal one-to-one coaches and line managers to become effective team coaches. Hicks points to the sheer quantity of studies that explore psychological factors and complex interactions which can have a beneficial or detrimental effect on a team's performance. According to the team effectiveness literature, variances in team performance can come about through: team diversity and the demographic make-up of a team (Jackson and Joshi 2004; Jackson *et al.*, 2003; Jehn and Bezrukova 2004; Kilduff *et al.*, 2000; Kirkman and Shapiro 2001; Li and Hambrick 2005; Timmerman 2000; Webber and Donahue 2001); the team leader's competencies at managing their team (Gilley *et al.*, 2010); the way in which different teams learn (van Dyck *et al.*, 2005; Edmondson *et al.*, 2001; Schippers *et al.*, 2003; Van den Bossche *et al.*, 2006; Van Woerkon 2003); the form and operation of the team; and the membership of the team. Additional considerations that may affect team behavior include member involvement with other teams, social pressure, and team coaching interventions themselves (Rezania, 2009).

Whatever the method organizations use to resource their coaches, most coaching within organizations is conducted in a dyadic (one-to-one) format (Ward, 2008).

There are also serious concerns from within the coaching industry itself over whether coaches trained to deliver coaching in a dyadic format are automatically "qualified" to deliver coaching to teams as well. Coaching practitioner David Sole is quoted in *Personnel Today* magazine as saying has that team coaching "can be like running eight coaching sessions simultaneously" (Sparrow, 2006). Not only does the team coach have to be knowledgeable in their one-to-one coaching skills when working with individual members of the team and the team leader, but they must also be aware of the additional complexities of the team that they will have to manage.

Ward (2008), among others, has argued that a degree of psychological training is essential to deploy the group coaching model developed at INSEAD and presented in his article. He argues: "Group dynamics is a unique differentiator from the usual dyadic coaching relationship. It is a well-researched and documented subject. Skilfully utilised, a good grasp of group dynamics accelerates the transformation process" (p. 71). To practice team coaching is even more demanding as the team coach needs the skills of individual and group coaching and also an understanding of the team's task and systemic context.

## Models of team coaching

The literature suggests that team coaches need to have a clear understanding of when the time is, or is not, propitious to coach the team. Hackman and Wageman (2005) have been leading the way in team coaching by focusing on the functions of the team as a whole and theorizing a new method of team coaching. They focused on four main aims which would enable team coaching to be most beneficial for team performance.

## Coaching functions

Hackman and Wageman (2005) proposed that a coach should move away from the idea that better team performance is brought about by establishing better interpersonal relationships between team members; this is not always the case (Guzzo *et al.*, 1986; Straw 1975; Woolley, 1998). They explored the most beneficial coaching techniques, when exactly to apply them, to what tasks, and to what teams. They propose that, to be successful, a team coach should provide three distinct functions:

1   Motivational coaching: Addresses the effort of the team and encourages process gains such as shared commitment to the group and minimizing process losses such as "social loafing". Coaching by the team leader can motivate members to devote themselves to the teamwork and share workload (Parker, 1994).
2   Consultative coaching: Addresses performance strategy and fosters the invention of new ways of proceeding with the work that is aligned with the task requirements. Denison *et al.* (1996) found that successful leaders facilitate flexible problem-solving and team development.
3   Educational coaching: Fosters the development and appropriate use of team members' knowledge and skill. Team leader coaching increases team psychological safety, which in turn increases learning behaviors and improves members' skills and knowledge (Edmondson, 1999).

Hawkins (2011a) suggests that team coaching can focus on five separate key disciplines, each of which is necessary to create a high performing team. These are:

1   Commissioning – the team being clear about what is being asked of it by those from whom it receives its commission and legitimacy to operate. This includes more senior management or the board, regulators, customers, and other key stakeholders.
2   Clarifying – the team itself being clear about its strategy, goals, collective key performance areas and key performance indicators, and its roles and processes for being effective.
3   Co-creating – how the team functions in relation to each member both in team meetings and outside.
4   Connecting – how the team effectively engages all the team's key stakeholders, including those they lead, to create effective change for the wider system.
5   Core learning – how the team reflects on the other four areas and create collective learning and effective development of all team members.

## Measuring outcomes

From a business management perspective many teams are units of productivity, so one would expect to see numerous outcome studies in respect of team performance, whether these assess measures of productivity, staff retention rates, sales or customer satisfaction. One would also expect comparisons with "control group" teams who have not been coached. But this is not the case. Two of the best studies from among the very few published studies on the relationship between team coaching and team performance had mixed results. Edmondson (1999) found some positive influence, whilst Wageman (2001) showed no influence on team performance.

However, when looking at non-performance aspects, studies have shown that coaching teams positively influences self-management, team member relationship quality, team member satisfaction (Wageman, 2001), team empowerment (Kirkman and Rosen, 1999), and psychological safety (Edmondson, 1999). Burke *et al.* (2006) created a framework and conducted a meta-analysis to examine the relationship between team leadership behaviors and behaviorally based team performance outcomes. They found that empowerment behaviors accounted for nearly 30 percent of the variance in team learning.

There have been advocates for the benefits of executive team coaching. Kets de Vries (2005) argues that durable changes in behavior are more likely in a group setting (where the individuals being coached are all members of the same team) than through one-to one coaching alone. His reasoning is that changing behavior requires a double-pronged approach: dealing with cognition and affect. Based on a case study example of an established leadership team he argues that such a strategy works best in groups, especially "natural" working groups (i.e., teams).

While there is little empirical evidence to state the benefits of team coaching by external coaches a number of practitioners have provided a business case for team coaching, and have published case studies to show how it can work and the benefits it can provide for an organization. Clutterbuck (2007) proposed that team coaching could be used to:

- Improve some specific aspect(s) of team performance: The coach makes sure the team is asking the right questions, at the right time, in order to achieve the shifting requirements. It also helps improve the leader's ability to manage the performance of individuals.
- Make things happen faster: Team coaching can help a team move rapidly through the stages of development, which may be hindered without a coach due to mistrust, poor communication, and avoidance of important but less obvious questions.
- Make things happen differently: Where culture change is accompanied by individual and team coaching, the pace and depth of the change will rapidly increase by supporting people as they come to terms with new attitudes and behaviors.

However, the research of Wageman *et al.* (2008) across 120 leadership teams, and the research of Hackman and Wageman (2005) and Gersick (1988) indicate that the early stages of a team's formation and engagement is better achieved by focusing on the mission, goals, and expectation of the performance of the team, something team coaching typically addresses.

## Discussion and Limitations of the Literature

Although there is now a body of research about coaching at work within organizations, as previously stated the vast majority of this work focuses on one-to-one coaching and then usually at the executive or leadership level. It is unknown whether any of these approaches can be transferred and applied effectively to team coaching and team learning due to the complex dynamics and variances within a team. The literature also provides very little empirical evidence supporting one approach over another.

There is, however, a large body of practitioner expertise and experience in delivering team coaching. As an emerging area of professional expertise, it is expected that practice in organizations will tend to run ahead of research and the development of solid theoretical frameworks and a shared knowledge base. This makes it difficult for those coaching teams to base their practice on evidence. Hackman and Wageman (2005), however, have provided some pointers for team coaching practitioners.

## Timing of coaching

Specific elements of team coaching are most effective when carried out at specific intervals of a team's life cycle. They proposed that motivational coaching is more helpful at the beginning of a performance period, consultative coaching at the mid-point of a performance period, and educational coaching when the performance activities have been completed. Although they agreed that coaching was not irrelevant outside these periods (some coaching to help members coordinate activities or coaching to reinforce good teamwork processes may be beneficial) it would not have as great an impact.

## Team tasks

For coaching to have a positive effect on team performance it needs to focus on the most salient team performance processes for a given task. For example, if a team were assigned to moving materials, then the only process required is the level of physical effort that team members expend. Focusing coaching on other processes, which are not needed or are constrained would be ineffectual and may even decrease team performance as it would redirect employees' time away from the most important process needed to complete the job successfully.

## Team design

Teams need to be well structured and supported in order for competent coaching, which focuses on the three functional areas highlighted above, to be most beneficial. Poor coaching interventions aimed at poorly structured and supported teams will be more detrimental than beneficial for team performance.

Fisher's work (2010) supports the work by Hackman and Wageman. Fisher found that more experienced coaches tended to intervene later on in a team's development and were more likely to use a participative style of coaching (invite member input from the group), whereas less experienced coaches tended to intervene early on in a team's formation, often in response to a perceived negative aspect of group processes, and typically with a directive style. The benefits of intervening at a later stage helped the team learn from their experience rather than trying to immediately improve at the cost of learning, and therefore the participative approach was the most beneficial one to take at this stage. Fisher also set out three functions that a team coach must accomplish if the intervention is to be successful:

1 Team coaches must observe group processes, focusing attention on and perceiving relevant cues (Schein, 1988).
2 They must then interpret the information, diagnosing both whether the team would benefit from, and is receptive to, the intervention.
3 Simultaneously, the coach must decide when to intervene and exactly what to do during the intervention.

A notable study by Chin-Yun Liu *et al.* (2009) has attempted to provide empirical evidence on the links between the coaching intervention, the team process, and the team performance, by applying the Hackman and Wageman theory to research and development teams from industries within Taiwan. They found that not all the team performance processes of effort (motivational), strategy (consultative), and skills and knowledge (educational) impacted the relationship between team coaching and team effectiveness. Team coaching directly affected team members' efforts and skills and knowledge, and therefore influenced how they selected and applied strategy in teamwork. Although the contributions of skills and knowledge of team members did not foster team effectiveness directly, it helped members identify good strategies for team tasks. They found that team coaching improved members' efforts, skills and knowledge, which in turn improved their strategy selection and so enhanced their effectiveness as a team. This is different from Hackman and Wageman's theory, as they believed that team coaching would directly affect all three areas of team performance (effort, strategy, skills and knowledge), which in turn would increase team effectiveness. It is unclear, however, whether these findings can be applied to other types of teams within other cultures.

More recently an exploratory study in an education setting using mixed methods by Reich *et al.* (2009) has attempted to examine the roles (rather than functions) which coaches can play when working with a product development team in an educational setting. The results are empirically tested and it is hoped that they can form the basis of a conceptual framework. Through a mixed method approach of qualitative and quantitative data analysis, Reich distilled five fundamental coaching roles termed: (1) consultant (problem focused intervention due to urgent product or process related needs), (2) supervisor (problem focused intervention due to high authority of the coach), (3) instructor (problem focused guidance to impact knowledge and expertise), (4) facilitator (coaching as a loose, independent relation that focuses on the offer of specialized services by the coach), and (5) mentor (coaching as voluntary, sometimes emotionally related interaction that focuses on mental support, environmental protection, and non-expert task related help).

With three different frameworks being established focusing on the functions (Hackman and Wageman, 2005) of team coaching, the disciplines of high performing teams (Hawkins, 2011b and the role of the team coach (Reich *et al.*, 2009), it has provided a foundation for further academic evidence to build upon and so enlighten the field of team coaching. There is very little mention of supervision for those coaching teams (except in Hawkins (2011b), where it has a separate chapter), even though the complexity of the context and potential for harm is surely greater.

One conceptual problem with the whole team leadership literature is its grounding in traditional leadership theories based on the individual "leader", and this is advanced as if leader relationships exist within a vacuum (House and Aditya, 1997). Some argue (e.g., Burke *et al.*, 2006) that researchers in that field have taken these theories and transposed them into a team setting without going back and customizing the theory-building process for team leadership. There is a risk that coaching teams could go down the same path. Having recently made such progress with coaching in its dyadic form, we need to be mindful that coaching teams may be fundamentally different. Reasons for this include the complexities of teams, stronger effect of wider organizational system and multi-level contextual factors, and multiple stakeholders, each with their own objectives.

# Future Directions for Research

Although there has been an enormous upsurge in papers on coaching in scholarly journals, with English (2006) finding a 300 percent increase in the number of such papers between the period 1994–1999 and the period 2000–2004; the number of research studies is relatively miniscule. According to Garvey *et al.* (2009) a typical coaching paper tends to be an insider account of a retrospective study, with perceptual data collected only from small numbers of coachees, and a narrow focus usually stated in terms of business relevance and improving practice. There are relatively few statistical studies of executive coaching carried out by external coaches that have used pre- and post-coaching ratings, and only a few of these collected data from sources other than the coachee (De Meuse *et al.*, 2009; Grant *et al.*, 2010; Feldman and Lankau, 2005; Kampa-Kokesch and Anderson, 2001; MacKie, 2007; Peterson, 2010).

The review of the research by De Meuse *et al.* (2009) concluded that, although there is a great deal of evidence that coaching does produce improvements in individual effectiveness (across the six studies surveyed 75–95 percent of participants had favorable ratings of their coaching and nearly all studies indicated that the participant's individual effectiveness had improved), fewer reported that it positively impacted on organizational improvement. Parker-Wilkins' research (2006) showed that 41 percent of the respondents indicated that individual coaching had helped them with building their team. Nearly all commentators mention the need for more rigorous, consistent, and multi faceted research that looks at the organizational impact of coaching.

Research on team coaching lags behind the research on individual executive coaching and there needs to be more qualitative and quantative research that explores the benefits of team coaching on team performance. However, the introduction of Hackman and Wageman's theory of team coaching (2005), Wageman *et al.* (2008) and Reich *et al.* (2009), has provided conceptual foundations for understanding the team leader as coach. From this, further studies can be carried out to understand the role of the team coach and the conditions (task, team, contextual, developmental) under which team coaching can meaningfully influence team performance.

We also need more models and theory building for the coaching of teams by external or internal coaches (who are not part of the specific team) that can be tested. Experienced practitioners are sharing what they use, which is very helpful step forward, for example, Hawkins' CID-CLEAR relationship process (2011b), Kets de Vries's (2005) model of group coaching in a team context and Brown and Grant's practical model GROUP (2010).

We would propose a research agenda that tests new team coaching theories, especially:

* the proposed relationships and processes
* that determine their applicability to team learning and outcomes in various organizational settings and contexts
* that determine how sensitive their design is to teams of different types and with different characteristics.

Many organizations now use teams that span countries or use virtual teams to support project work or increasingly to support more family-friendly working practices such as home-based working. All these ways of working mean that teams are increasingly not co-located and many do not speak the same language (Canney Davison and Ward, 1999). Future research could explore a range of moderator variables, including co-located, distributed or virtual teams and cross-cultural teams, which may moderate the relationship between empowering coaching styles of team leadership with team performance outcomes.

# Conclusion

The field of team coaching is still in its infancy, but in a stage of rapid growth and development. In this chapter we have shown how the field is beginning to define itself as different from group coaching, team facilitation, and team development, and to create a craft that brings together skills and models from both the field of coaching and the field of organizational development. Also, it is beginning to define its purpose and the outcomes it sets out to achieve, namely (1) a team more productive at achieving its collective key performance targets, (2) that is better aligned, connected, and motivated, (3) better able to engage its key stakeholders to create shared value, and (4) better able to learn and develop the capabilities and capacities of all its members.

Being clear about its definition and purpose, provides the foundation for more and better quality research, which to date has been sparse, but much is now underway and we expect this area of research and practice to grow exponentially in the next few years.

# References

Anderson, M.C., Anderson, D.L., and Mayo, W.D. (2008) Team coaching helps a leadership team drive cultural change at caterpillar. *Global Business and Organizational Excellence*, Wiley Periodicals, May/June, 40–50.

Banker, R.D., Lee, S., Potter, G., and Srinivasan, D. (1996) Contextual analysis of performance impacts of outcome-based incentive compensation. *Academy of Management Journal*, 39, 920–48.

Bate, P. and Robert, G. (2007) Toward more user-centric OD: Lessons from the field of experienced-based design and a case study. *Journal of Applied Behaviorual Science*, 43, 41–66.

Bazerman, M.H. and Tenbrunsel, A.E. (2011) *Blind Spots – Why We Fail to do What is Right And What to do About it*. Cambridge, MA: Harvard University Press.

Bevan, H., Robert, G., Bate, P., Maher, L., and Wells, J. (2007) Using a design approach to assist large-scale organizational change: 10 high impact changes to improve the *National Health Service* in England *Journal of Applied Behavioural Science*, 43, 135–52.

Brown, D. and Harvey, D. (2006) *An Experiential Approach to Organizational Development* (7th edn). Upper Saddle River, NJ: Pearson Education.

Brown, S.W. and Grant, A.M. (2010) From GROW to GROUP: Theoretical issues and a practical model for group coaching in organizations. *Coaching: An International Journal of Theory, Research and Practice*, 3(1), 30–45.

Buller, P.F. and Bell, C.H. (1986) Effects of team building and goal setting on productivity: A field experiment. *Academy of Management Journal*, 29(2), 305–28.

Burke, C.S., Stagl, K.C., Klein, C., Goodwin, G.F., Salas, E., and Halpin, S.M. *et al.* (2006) What type of leadership behaviours are functional in teams? A meta-analysis. *The Leadership Quarterly.* (2006) 17:288–307.

Canney Davison, S. and Ward, K. (1999) *Leading International Teams*. Maidenhead: McGraw Hill.

Carter, A. (2001) *Executive Coaching: Inspiring Performance at Work.* IES Research Report 379, Brighton UK: Institute for Employment Studies.

Carter, A., Sigala, M., Robertson-Smith, G., and Hayday, S. (2011) *From Financial to Clinical? Perceptions and Conversations in NHS Boardrooms,* IES Research report No 478. Brighton: Institute for Employment Studies.

Clifton, J. (2009) Beyond taxonomies of influence. Doing influence and making decisions in management team meetings. *Journal of Business Communication,* Association of Business Communication, 46(1), January, 57–78.

Clutterbuck, D. (2007) *Coaching the Team at Work.* London: Nicholas Brealey International.

Cunha, P.V. and Louro, M.J. (2000) Building teams that learn. *Academy of Management Executive,* 14(1), 152.

Day, D.V., Gronn, P., and Salas, E. (2004) Leadership capacity in teams. *Leadership Quarterly,* 15, 857–80.

De Meuse, K.P., Dai, G., and Lee, R.J. (2009) Evaluating the effectiveness of executive coaching: Beyond ROI? *Coaching: An International Journal of Theory, Research, and Practice,* 2, 117–34.

Deidrich, R.C. (2001) Lessons learned in and guideleines for coaching executive teams. *Consulting Psychology Journal: Practice and Research,* 53(4), 238–9.

Denison, D.R., Hart, S.L., and Khan, J.A. (1996) From chimneys to cross functional teams: Developing and validating a diagnostic model. *Academy of Management Journal,* 39, 1005–23.

Devine, D.J., Clayton, L.D., Philips, J.L., Dunford, B.B., and Melner, S.B. (1999) Teams in organizations: Prevalence, characteristics, and effectiveness. *Small Group Research,* 30(6) (December), 678–711.

Edmondson, A. (1999) Psychological safety and learning behaviour in work teams. *Administrative Science Quarterly,* 44, 350–83.

Edmondson, A., Bohmer, R., and Pisano, G. (2001) Speeding up team learning. *Harvard Business Review,* October 2001, Reprint R0109.

English, M. (2006) *Business Print Media Coverage of Executive Coaching: A Content Analysis.* Doctoral dissertation, Capella University US.

Feldman, D.C. and Lankau, M.J. (2005) Executive coacing: A review and agenda for future research. *Journal of Management,* 31(6) 829–48.

Fisher, C.M. (2010) The timing and type of team coaching interventions. Unpublished PhD dissertation, Harvard University.

Fisher, S.G., Hunter, T.A., and Macrosson, W.D.K. (1997) Team or group? Managers' perceptions of the differences. *Journal of Managerial Psychology,* 12, 232–42.

Garrow, V., Cox, A., and Higgins, T. (2010) *Large Scale Change: NHS Mobilisation.* UK: NHS Institute for Innovation and Improvement.

Garvey, R., Stokes, P., and Megginson, D. (2009) *Coaching and Mentoring: Theory and Practice.* London: Sage.

Gersick, C.J.G. (1988) Time and transition in work teams: Towards a new model of group development. *Academy of Management Journal,* 31, 9–41.

Gilley, A., Gilley, J.W., McConnell, C.W., and Veliquette, A. (2010) The competencies used by effective managers to build teams: An empirical study. *Advances in Developing Human Resources,* 12–29.

Grant, A.M., Passmore, J., Cavanagh, M.J., and Parker, H. (2010) The state of play in coaching today: A comprehensive review of the field. *International Review of Industrial and Organizational Psychology,* 25, 125–67.

Gratton, L. (2007) *Hot Spots Why Some Companies Buzz with Energy and Innovation – and Others Don't.* London: FT Prentice Hall Financial Times Pearson Education.

Gunnerson, L.H. and Holling, C.S. (eds) (2002) *Panarchy: Understanding Transformations in Human and Natural Systems.* Washington, DC: Island Press.

Guzzo, R.A. and Dickson, M.W. (1996) Teams in organizations: Recent research on performance and effectiveness. *Annual Review of Psychology,* 47, 307–38.

Guzzo, R.A. and Shea, G.P. (1992) *Group Performance and Intergroup Relations in Organizations.* Palo Alto US: Consulting Psychologists Press Inc.

Guzzo, R.A., Wagmer, D.B., Maguire, E., Herr, B., and Hawley, C. (1986) Implicit theories and the evaluation of group process and performance. *Organizational Behaviour and Human Decision Processes*, 37, 279–95.

Hackman, J.R. (2002) *Leading Teams: Setting the Stage for Great Performances.* Boston, MA: Harvard Business School Press.

Hackman, J.R. and Wageman, R. (2005) A theory of team coaching. *Academy of Management Review*, 30, 269–87.

Hamlin, R.G., Ellinger, A.D., and Beattie, R.S. (2009) Toward a profession of coaching? A definitional examination of "coaching", "organizational development" and "human resource development". *International Journal of Evidence Based Coaching and Mentoring*, 7(1), 13–38.

Hawkins, P. (2010) The changing challenge for leadership. In *New World; New Organisations, New Leadership: New Thinking on how Organisations engage with Change.* Henley, UK: Henley Business School White Paper.

Hawkins, P. (2011a) *Beyond the Heroic CEO: The Changing Challenge for Leadership.* Henley White Paper: Henley Business School, University of Reading.

Hawkins, P. (2011b) *Leadership Team Coaching: Developing Collective Transformational Leadership.* London: Kogan Page.

Hawkins, P. (2012) *Creating a Coaching Culture.* London: Open University Press/McGraw Hill.

Hawkins, P. and Smith, N. (2006) *Coaching, Mentoring and Organizational Consultancy: Supervision and Development.* Maidenhead Open University Press/McGraw Hill.

Hicks, B. (2010) *Team Coaching: A Literature Review.* IES HR Network Paper MP88, Brighton UK: Institute for Employment Studies.

House, R.J. and Aditya, R.N. (1997) The social scientific study of leadership: Quo vadis? *Journal of Management*, 23(3), 409–73.

Ireland, D.R. and Hitt, M.A. (1999) Achieving and maintaining strategic competitiveness in the 21st century: The role of authentic. *Academy of Management Executive*, 13.

Jackson, S.E. and Joshi, A. (2004) Diversity in a social context. A multi-attribute, multilevel analysis of team diversity and sales performance. *Journal of Organizational Behaviour*, 25, 675–702.

Jackson, S.E., Joshi, A., and Erhardt, N.L. (2003) Recent research on team and organizational diversity: SWOT analysis and implications. *Journal of Management*, 29, 801–30.

Jehn, K.A. and Bezrukova, K. (2004) A field study of group diversity, group context and performance. *Journal of Organizational Behaviour*, 25, 1–27.

Kampa-Kokesch, S. and Anderson, M.Z. (2001) Executive coaching: A comprehensive review of the literature. *Consulting Psychology Journal: Practice and Research*, 53, 205–28.

Katzenbach, J.R. and Smith, D.K. (1993a) *The Wisdom of Teams: Creating the High Performance Organization.* Harvard, MA: Harvard Business School Press.

Katzenbach, J.R. and Smith, D.K. (1993b) The discipline of teams. *Harvard Business Review*, 71, 111–21.

Katzenbach, J.R. and Smith, D.K. (1999) *The Wisdom of Teams: Creating the High Performance Organization.* London: Harper Business.

Kets de Vries, M.F.R. (2005) Leadership group coaching in action: The Zen of creating high performance teams. *Academy of Management Executive*, 19(1), 61–76.

Kets de Vries, M.F.R. (2006) *The Leader on the Couch: A Clinical Approach to Changing People and Organizations.* San Francisco US: Jossey-Bass.

Kettley, P. and Hirsh, W. (2000) *Learning from Cross-functional Teamwork.* IES Research Report 356, Brighton: Institute for Employment Studies.

Kilduff, M., Angelmar, R., and Mehra, A. (2000) Top management-team diversity and firm performance: Examining the role of cognitions. *Organization Science*, 11, 21–34.

Kirkman, B.L. and Rosen, B. (1999) Beyond self-management: Antecedents and consequences of team empowerment. *Academy of Management Journal*, 42, 58–74.

Kirkman, B.L. and Shapiro, D.L. (2001) The impact of team members' cultural values on productivity, co-operation and empowerment in self-managing work teams. *Journal of Cross Cultural Psychology*, 32, 597–617.

Klein, C., Salas, E., Burke, C.S., Goodwin, G.F., Halpin, S., DiazGranados, D. *et al.* (2006) Does team training enhance team process, performance, and team member affective outcomes? A meta-analysis. In: K.M. Weaver (ed.) *Best Paper Proceedings of the 66th Annual Meeting of the Academy of Management*, Atlanta US: Academy of Management.

Klein, C., DiazGranados, D., Salas, E., Le, H., Shawn Burke, C., Lyons, R. *et al.* (2009) Does team building work? *Small Group Research*, 40, 181–222.

Kozlowski, S.W. and Bell B.S. (2003) Work group and teams in organizations. In: W.C. Borman, D.R. Ilgen and R.J. Klimoski (eds) *Handbook of Psychology: Industrial and Organizational Psychology*, Vol. 12, pp. 333–75. London: Wiley.

Kozlowski, S.W.J. and Ilgen, D.R. (2006) Enhancing the effectiveness of work groups and teams. *Psychological Science in the Public Interest*, 7(3), 77–124.

Kozlowski, S.W.J., Gully, S.M., McHugh, P.P., Salas, E., and Cannon-Bowers, J.A. (1996a) A dynamic theory of leadership and team effectiveness: Developmental and task contingent leader roles. In: G.R. Ferris (ed.) *Research in Personnel and Human Resource Management*, 14, 253–305.

Kozlowski, S.W.J., Gully, S.M., Salas, E., and Cannon-Bowers, J.A. (1996b) Team leadership and development: Theory, principles and guidelines for training leaders and teams. In: S. Beyerlein and D. Johnson (eds) *Advances in Interdisciplinary Studies of Work Teams*. Greenwich US: JAI. pp. 253–92.

Kouzes, J.M. and Posner, B.Z. (2002) *The Leadership Challenge* (3rd edn). San Francisco: Jossey-Bass.

Kriek, H.S. and Venter, P. (2009) The perceived success of team building interventions in South African organizations. *South African Business Review*, 13(1), 112–28.

Li, J.T. and Hambrick, D.C. (2005) Factional groups: A new vantage on demographic faultlines, conflict and disintegration in work teams. *Academy of Management Journal*, 48, 794–813.

Liu, C.-Y., Pirola-Merlo, A., Yang, C.-A., and Huang, C. (2009) Disseminating the functions of team coaching regarding research and development team effectiveness: Evidence from high-tech industries in Taiwan. *Social Behaviour and Personality*, 37(1), 41–58.

Mackie, D. (2007) Evaluating the effectiveness of executive coaching: Where are we now and where do we need to be? *Australian Psychologist*, 42, 310–18.

Manz, C.C. and Sims, H.P. (1987) Leading workers to lead themselves: The external leadership of self-managing work teams. *Administrative Science Quarterly*, 32, 106–28.

Marks, M.A., Mathieu, J.E., and Zaccaro, S.J. (2001) A temporally based framework and taxonomy of team processes. *Academy of Management Review*, 26, 356–76.

Martin, A. and Bal, V. (2006) *The State of Teams*. CCL Research Report, Greensboro US: Centre for Creative Leadership.

Mathieu, J.E., Heffner, T.S., Goodwin, G.F., Salas, E., and Cannon-Bowers, J.A. (2000) The influence of shared mental models on team process and performance. *Journal of Applied Psychology*, 85, 273–83.

Mazany, P., Francis, S., and Sumich, P. (1995) Evaluating the effectiveness of an experiential "hybrid" workshop: Strategy development and team building in a manufacturing organization. *Journal of Management Development*, 14(1), 40–52.

Morgeson, F.P., Scott DeRue, D.S., and Karam, E.P. (2009) Leadership in teams: A functional approach to understanding leadership structures and processes. *Journal of Management*, Southern Management Association, 36(1), 5–39.

Offerman, L.R. and Spiros, R.K. (2001) The science and practice of team development. *Journal of Management Development*, 16(3), 208–17.

Owen, H. (1997) *Open Space Technology: A User's Guide*. San Francisco, CA: Berrett-Koehler.

Paige, H. (2002) Examining the effect of executive coaching on executives. *International Education Journal*, 3(2), 61–70.

Parker, G.M. (1994) *Cross Functional Team: Working With Allies, Enemies and Other Strangers.* San Francisco: Jossey-Bass.

Parker-Wilkins, V. (2006) Business impact of executive coaching: Demonstrating monetary value. *Industrial and Commercial Training*, 38(3), 122–7.

Pearce, C.L. (2004) The future of leadership: Combining vertical and share leadership to transform knowledge work. *Academy of Management Executive*, 19(1), 47–57.

Pedler, M., Burgoyne, J., and Boydell, T. (1991) *The Learning Company: A Strategy for Sustainable Development.* London: McGraw-Hill.

Peterson, D.B. (2010) Executive coaching: A critical review and recommendations for advancing the practice. In: S. Zedeck (ed.) *APA Handbook of Industrial and Organizational Psychology.* Vol. 2. Selecting and Developing Members of the Organization. Washington, DC: American Psychological Association. pp. 527–66.

Plsek, P. (2003) Complexity and the adoption of innovation in healthcare, conference paper for *Accelerating Quality Improvement in Health Care Strategies to Speed the Diffusion of Evidence Based Innovation.* Washington, DC, January, 27–28.

Raelin, J.A. (2005) We the leaders: In order to form a leaderful organization. *Journal of Leadership and Organizational Studies*, 12(2), 18–30.

Rezania, D. and Lingham, T. (2009) Coaching IT project teams: A design toolkit. *International Journal of Managing Projects in Business*, 2, 577–90.

Reich, Y., Ullmann, G., Van der Loos, M., and Leifer, L. (2009) Coaching development teams: A conceptual foundation for empirical studies. *Research of Engineering Design*, 19, 205–22.

Robotham, D. (2009) From groups to teams to virtual teams. *Groupwork: An Interdisciplinary Journal for Working with Groups*, 18, 41–57.

Samra-Fredricks, D. (2002) "Doing boards-in-action" research–an ethnographic approach for the capture and analysis of directors' and senior managers' interactive routines. *Corporate Governance: An International Review*, 8(3), 244–57.

Schein, E.H. (1988) *Process Consultation: Its role in Organizational Development* (2nd edn ). London: Wesley.

Schein, E.H. (1999) *Process Consultation Revisited.* Boston, MA: Addison-Wesley.

Schippers, M.C., Den Hartog, D.N., Koopman, P.L., and Wienk, J.A. (2003) Diversity and team outcomes: The moderating effects of outcome interdependence and group longevity and the mediating effect of reflexivity. *Journal of Organizational Behaviour*, 24, 779–802.

Senge, P. (1990) *The Fifth Discipline: The Art and Practice of the Learning Organization.* New York: Doubleday.

Sparrow, S. (2006) Team coaching: team work. http://www.personneltoday.com/articles/2006/09/19/37309/team-coaching-team-work.html (accessed October 11, 2011).

Srivastava, A., Bartol, K.M., and Locke, E.A. (2006) Empowering leadership in management teams: Effects of knowledge sharing, efficacy and performance. *Academy of Management Journal*, 49(6), 1239–51.

Straw, B.M. (1975) Attribution of the causes of performance: A general alternative interpretation of cross sectional research on organizations. *Organizational Behaviour and Human Performance*, 13, 414–32.

Thomas, M. (2007) *Mastering People Management.* London: Thorogood.

Thompson, L. (2004) *Making the Team: A Guide for Managers.* Upper Saddle River, NJ: Prentice-Hall.

Timmermann, T.A. (2000) Racial diversity, age, diversity, interdependence and team performance. *Small Group Research*, 31, 592–606.

Tuckman, B. (1965) Developmental sequence in small groups. *Psychological Bulletin*, 63(6), 384–99.

Van den Bossche, P., Gisjselaers, W., Segers, M., and Kirschner, P.A. (2006) Social and cognitive factors driving teamwork in collaborative learning environments: team learning beliefs and behaviours. *Small Group Research*, 37, 490–521.

van Dyck, C., Frese, M., Baer, M., and Sonnentag, S. (2005) Organizational error management culture and its impact on performance: A two-study replication. *Journal of Applied Psychology*, 90, 1228–1240.

Van Woerkom, M. (2003) *Critical Reflection at Work: Bridging Individual and Organizational Learning*. PhD dissertation, University of Twente, Netherlands.

Wageman, R. (2001) How leaders foster self-managing team effectiveness: Design choices versus hands on coaching. *Organization Science*, 12, 559–77.

Wageman, R., Nunes, D.A., Burass, J.A., and Hackman, J.R. (2008) *Senior Leadership Teams*. Harvard, MA: Harvard Business School Press.

Ward, G. (2008) Towards executive change: A psychodynamic group coaching model for short executive programs. *International Journal of Evidence Based Coaching and Mentoring*, 6(1), 67–78.

Webber, S.S. and Donahue L.M. (2001) Impact of highly and less job-related diversity on work group cohesion and performance: A meta analysis. *Journal of Management*, 7, 141–62.

Wellins, R.S., Byham, W.C., and Dixon, G.R. (1994) *Inside Teams: How 20 World Class Organizations are Winning Through Team Work*. San Francisco, CA: Jossey-Bass.

Woolley, A.W. (1998) Effects of intervention content and timing on group task performance. *Journal of Applied Behavioural Science*, 34, 30–49.

Yun Liu, C., Pirola-Merlo, A., Yang, C., and Huang, C. (2009) Disseminating the functions of team coaching regarding research and development team effectiveness: Evidence from high-tech industries in Taiwan. *Social Behaviour and Personality*, 37, 41–58.

# Section II
# Mentoring

# 11

# Designing Mentoring Schemes for Organizations

## Paul Stokes and Lis Merrick

## Introduction

In this chapter, we will critically examine the design of mentoring schemes and programs, drawing out the lessons for future practice. In the first section, we will look at the rationale for developing a conceptual framework for mentoring schemes, which will then be followed, in the second section, by an examination of different approaches to mentoring scheme design. In the subsections that follow our consideration of these approaches, we will explore specific issues that emerge from these approaches: mentoring senior stakeholders; clarifying scheme purpose matching; supervision and support for mentoring; review and evaluation. Following this, the importance of context for mentoring schemes will be examined by exploring mentoring scheme design issues in education, diversity programs, and health. The lessons from these areas will then be examined in relation to issues concerning the differents mode of mentoring, in particular electronic and mutual mentoring. Finally, we will draw together some conclusions for the future of mentoring scheme design.

## A Conceptual Framework

In 1994, Stephen Gibb called for the development of a new conceptual framework for thinking about mentoring schemes. This built on earlier work (Gibb and Megginson, 1993) that identified a "new agenda of concerns" within mentoring research. Some of these concerns had focused on the understanding of mentoring as a process but several were around the design of mentoring programs and schemes within organizations: lack of clarity of purpose and the diversity of contexts being two of the main issues. Gibb (1994) argued that a new conceptual framework was necessary in order to "provide the critical perspective necessary to promote debate and analysis about

*The Wiley Blackwell Handbook of the Psychology of Coaching and Mentoring*, First Edition.
Edited by Jonathan Passmore, David B. Peterson, and Teresa Freire.

the potential and limitations of investing in mentoring as a major innovation in employee development, which is arguably capable of meeting a broad range of organizational needs" (Gibb, 1994, p. 48). In an attempt to develop that framework, Gibb (1999) put forward the ideas of communitarian – mentoring happens because people belong to the same community and share the same values around helping each other – and social exchange – people engage in mentoring because there are reciprocal benefits in doing so – to differentiate between different approaches and intentions within mentoring scheme design. In the intervening period there has been considerable change, not least the rise and pre-eminence of the term coaching, but Gibb's (1994) questions still have relevance today. In this chapter, we seek to critically engage with the key writings on mentoring scheme design and to develop a conceptual framework through which such schemes can be examined. We will look at four main areas: the stages of scheme design; the functions of schemes and what they are used to support; the context and processes through which mentoring schemes are delivered; and finally, the future of scheme design.

## The Stages of Scheme Design

Before engaging with the research and literature on mentoring schemes, it is important to consider what we mean by a mentoring scheme. For our purposes in this chapter, we are typically referring to a process set up within an organizational context for the purpose of supporting mentoring conversations. However, following Garvey *et al.*, (2009), we acknowledge that mentoring takes place in wide variety of contexts and modes. This is one of the reasons why writers and researchers have found it difficult to agree on a generic definition of mentoring (or coaching for that matter). Garvey has offered a dimensional framework, which sought to describe the different elements within mentoring relationships (Garvey, 1994). This is summarized in Table 11.1. Whilst these dimensions can be helpful in terms of contracting for mentoring relationships (Garvey *et al.*, 2009), they are also helpful in recognizing the scope of mentoring schemes.

Answering these questions for a particular mentoring scheme may go some way to addressing Gibb and Megginson's (1993) call for clarity of scheme purpose. Whilst different mentoring dyads may differ somewhat in where they position themselves against these dimensions, there is still a need to set the parameters for a mentoring program in order to help participants orientate themselves towards it (Megginson *et al.*, 2006). It is important to remember that Garvey (1994) was clear to point out that these dimensions are continuums, not dichotomies. In other words, it makes more sense, for example, to talk about

**Table 11.1**  Dimensions of mentoring relationship.

| *Dimensions* | *Aspects* |
| --- | --- |
| Open/closed | What is the scope of the conversation and how wide is it? |
| Public/private | Who knows about the relationship and what is talked about within it? |
| Formal/informal | How formal and structured are the conversations? |
| Active/passive | Who takes action in the relationship? |
| Stable/unstable | How predictable and reliable are the behaviors of those involved? |

degrees of formality within a mentoring scheme, rather than labeling a scheme as either formal or informal.

Furthermore, it is also worth noting that it is possible to have an effective, official mentoring program within an organization, whilst still seeing mentoring conversations and relationships as informal; the study by Singh *et al.* (2002) on informal mentoring at Cambridgeshire County Council in the United Kingdom is a good example of this. Hence, the relative formality of an organizational context does not necessarily mean that the mentoring scheme itself will force mentoring conversations to be formal or even to be about work itself. These dimensions, then, hint at the range of possible forms that a mentoring scheme might take.

Megginson *et al.* (2006) have tried to position mentoring schemes within a taxonomy of layers of mentoring, ranging from mentoring moments (key transition points within a mentoring conversation), through to techniques, episodes, relationships; and finally culture. The mentoring scheme is related to the organizational culture and can be seen as an artifact of the culture (Schein, 2010). In our review of best practice in mentoring schemes, Cranwell-Ward *et al.* (2004), Megginson *et al.* (2006), Klasen and Clutterbuck (2002), Sontag *et al.* (2007), and Merrick (2009) have identified some key steps that mentoring scheme designers should pay attention to, these are shown in Table 11.2 below.

**Table 11.2** Comparison of stepped approaches to designing a mentoring program.

| *Cranwell-Ward et al. (2004)* | *Megginson et al. (2006)* | *Klasen and Clutterbuck (2002)* | *Sontag et al. (2007)* | *Merrick (2009)* |
|---|---|---|---|---|
| Identifying and influencing key stakeholders | Scheme purpose | Implementation proposal | Sponsor meeting | Rationale for a program |
| Marketing the scheme | Evaluation | Training | Implementation team planning | Influencing stakeholders |
| Matching | Recruitment and selection | Evaluation | Nominate and recruit mentors/ mentees | Clear recruitment strategy |
| | | | | Communication and publicity |
| Training participants | Training and development | Problem solving | Interview mentors/ mentees | Preparing the participants |
| Maintaining, concluding, and developing the scheme | Matching | | Match mentors/ mentees | Matching process |
| Evaluation and review of the scheme | Supervision | | Mentee and mentor orientation and launch session | Supporting the program |
| | Standards | | 2/4/8 month check point meetings | Review and evaluation |
| | | | Program close and evaluation | Role of the mentoring coordinator |

Whilst these approaches differ to some extent in what they focus on, the US process of Sontag *et al.* (2007) particularly contrasted with the more European stages of design, they have tended to follow a similar practical route in being clear about scheme purpose and buy in from senior stakeholders and then building in appropriate design features to support that purpose, usually covering scheme orientation, skills training, evaluation, and review. We will now use these core principles of mentoring scheme design to examine a number of different approaches that have been taken to mentoring programs.

## Involving Senior Stakeholders

Klasen and Clutterbuck (2002), Cranwell-Ward *et al.* (2004), Megginson *et al.* (2006), and Garvey *et al.* (2009) all recognize the importance of senior management commitment to the success of a mentoring scheme. Klasen and Clutterbuck (2002, p. 190) go as far saying that "unqualified support is needed from all those involved," whilst Cranwell *et al.* (2004, p. 60) point to the dangers of not involving senior stakeholders: "'Why wasn't I asked?' was a question the scheme manager had to address from a number of senior people in the organization, whom it had been assumed would have been too busy to be interested."

Certainly, the importance of senior stakeholder buy-in was seen to be critical in Atterton *et al.*'s (2009) analysis of a UK local government mentoring program, where local councillor involvement and engagement in the process was seen as a critical success factor as they: "Succeeded in prompting greater open mindedness and reflection on the part of previously intransigent councillors, or reaching people other mentors simply could not" (p. 56). This seems to be the case within the US literature, with Allen *et al.* (2006), pointing to the emphasis in the mentoring literature on senior stakeholder validation of successful mentoring programs at the expense of participants' reports of effectiveness. Hegstad and Wentling's (2005) study of mentoring schemes across 17 US companies in the Fortune 500 supports this view: "Without top-level commitment, mentors may view the responsibility negatively because it requires effort beyond regular duties. Management must recognise that developing mentoring relationships requires time, effort and commitment, which could infringe on other responsibilities" (Hegstad and Wentling, 2005, p. 486). Similarly, Wareing's case study of an Australian mentoring scheme within the mining industry (2006, pp. 163–70) calls for the mentoring scheme to be formally linked to management development outcomes in order to build commitment to the scheme.

Using mentoring champions to support different types of mentoring has increased significantly and plays a valuable role in ensuring the success of a program. Cranwell-Ward *et al.* (2004, p. 71) emphasize how instrumental this can be in gaining acceptance of the mentoring scheme by the line and Klasen and Clutterbuck (2002, p. 191) see the role of the champion as perhaps the most important in the design and implementation stage. They stress that the champion should be at a fairly high level in the organization, to possess enough power and experience to get things done.

However, Garvey *et al.* (2009) sound a note of caution here. Sometimes, placing a lot of emphasis on senior stakeholder commitment can bring with it the pressure that attends a formal launch of an initiative within an organization, which can raise expectations too high in terms of what mentoring as a process can achieve within an organizational context. Also, following Gibb (1994, p. 54), such a formal approach to scheme design can be accompanied by functionalist assumptions about cause and effect and the importance of senior management control within organizations. He characterizes such formal schemes as systematic mentoring, contrasting with process mentoring, which he describes as being driven by, "a concern to see mentoring as a relationship continually 'negotiated between partners, rather than defined at the beginning by an external source or the demands of a highly structured system'" (p. 54). Process mentoring seems to be a close fit with what Garvey *et al.* (2009) refer to as the organic approach to mentoring scheme design, which is more low-key, emphasizing a longer term more gradual approach to nurturing mentoring within an organizational context. This also resonates with what Watson (2006) refers to as the contrast between a systems-control view of organizations and a process-relational view, where the former is closer to what Morgan (1986) would describe as viewing the organization as being like a machine. Watson (2006) argues that this perspective can encourage seeing organizational issues in a very rationalist/mechanical fashion, which arguably, might militate against a developmental view of human relationships. However, a process relational view seems closer to what Morgan (1986) would refer to as an organismic view of organizations, seeing them as being like living things that grow and develop.

In conclusion, there may be some dangers in courting senior management commitment, in that this may trigger existing tendencies within some senior managers to submit mentoring programs to crude return on investment analyses, which could place an unbearable burden on a fledgling mentoring scheme.

## Clarifying Scheme Purpose

Megginson *et al.* (2006, p. 8) argue that it is important to have clarity of purpose with regards to a mentoring scheme: "Given that mentoring schemes require resources (finance, effort, time, people) there needs to be a clear understanding of what is intended by the scheme. In other words, it is crucial that people involved understand from the outset what the scheme is there to do."

Similarly, Cranwell-Ward *et al.* (2004) have made much about the importance of a clear objective as it makes a clearer connection with success criteria for the scheme. In the case of Singh *et al.* (2002), in a UK local authority scheme, there was, despite the lack of espoused formality in the scheme, nevertheless an expectation that mentoring might help the authority achieve some of its HR targets: "The council is making it a priority to retain and develop managers to the best of their potential. One source of talent is the pool of female potential managers. While CCC has achieved 32 percent female representation in senior management posts, it has publicly set a target of 42 percent by 2006. Mentoring is one way to help achieve these targets" (Singh *et al.*, 2002, p. 393).

Hence, this is an example of a mentoring scheme with a clear purpose and measurable success factors. Whilst this gives clarity, it is worth pointing out that employing this view of cause and effect evaluation of mentoring schemes might potentially lead to a lack of awareness of other unintended benefits of mentoring programs as well, of course, as any unintended costs or problems that might have been created. For example, Chivers's (2011) study was more exploratory in nature, examining informal learning by traders in investment banks. One of their main conclusions was that peer coaching and mentoring was already working, for some, informally within their businesses and was positively helping some young traders with their development. In contrast to formal training interventions and initiatives, driven by training managers within the businesses, these formal programs were treated with some disdain by the traders. Given this antipathy towards formalizing of training, any coaching and mentoring scheme in this context would need to be communicated carefully to the potential beneficiaries. Similarly, Samujh's (2011) study of micro-business managers in New Zealand revealed a need for such support: "The research revealed the importance of non-business learning, the need to unburden, and the psychological effects of being self-employed. Support for emotional needs and understanding of psychological factors was clearly indicated as an important issue for further research" (Samujh, 2011, p. 24).

However, like Chivers's (2011) study, this study also suggested a likely antipathy towards perceived scheme formality, particularly due to lack of time to devote to non-business related activities. Hence, the launch of a formal scheme with clear outcomes and purposes may, unintentionally, switch off those in most need of support. Interestingly, Hudson-Davies *et al.*'s (2002, p. 251) earlier study of mentoring within the UK retail industry had suggested a similar, " 'negative mindset' associated with structured/formal activities," but still seemed to advocate a formal, focused program with a clear stated purpose and a requirement to formally state expected outcomes. However, it should be noted this study was based on secondary data analysis where it was more difficult to engage with the detail of scheme design.

## Matching Mentors and Mentees Within Schemes

The study by Ragins *et al.* (2000) of 1,162 employees in the United States, using analytical survey techniques, suggests, amongst other things, that the perceived quality of the mentors and the mentoring relationship transcends any element of scheme design. In other words, good mentors in a badly designed scheme were still likely to engender good levels of satisfaction for participants, whereas marginal mentors (to use the Ragins *et al.* terminology) were likely to yield less satisfaction, however well designed the scheme. Nevertheless, as Hedstad and Wentling (2005) have found in their study of US Fortune 500 companies who have mentoring programs, effective matching and selection are seen as a vital element of mentoring scheme design. However, Carver's (2011) analysis draws our attention to the fact that, as mentoring grows in popularity – she states that 70 percent of Fortune 500 companies have one or more mentoring initiatives – the pool of available mentors for one-to-one relationships becomes stretched.

Other US research focuses specifically on matching. Blake-Beard *et al.* (2007) critically examine the importance of matching in successful formal mentoring relationships in the United States. They make connections with several studies that examine formal mentoring schemes (e.g., Allen *et al.*, 2006; Douglas, 1997; Lyons and Oppler, 2004; O'Neill, 2005; O'Reilly, 2001). From their analysis, they are able to identify several common challenges when matching, in their terminology, mentors with protégés in formal mentoring programs. These challenges include:

- dealing with anticipation, awkwardness, and anxiety at the orientation stage;
- the under-utilization of data and participant choice;
- costs of a poor match – reputational risk; and
- making sure that matches support program intent, for example cross-fertilization;

Certainly, in our experience as scheme designers, matching in mentoring programs can present a number of challenges. Following Blake-Beard *et al.* (2007), we have tended to use the "hunch" method (making matches based on personal assessment of compatibility of the dyad) quite often. This seems particularly useful in small schemes where we have had personal knowledge of the mentors and mentees through recruitment, selection, and training (e.g., Megginson and Stokes, 2004). In larger schemes, the designer has to use the best approach they can considering the resources at their disposal.

## Supervision and Support for Mentoring

A key element in mentoring scheme design is supervision and ongoing support for participants. Supervision in formal mentoring programs is a form of supervision that has been minimally researched and there is little evidence of good practice in programs in the United Kingdom. I initial research by Merrick and Stokes (2003), revealed the following common functions of mentor supervision in schemes as understood by participants:

- Being a mentor to the mentors
- Being able to explore techniques and help with problems
- An opportunity to reflect on own practice
- To support a mentor who feels out of their depth
- As a mark of good practice for the profession
- To support with ethical issues
- To be available for the mentor as an emotional safety valve

This echoes Barrett's (2002) work in mentoring, which puts forward the following benefits of being supervised:

- Preventing personal burn-out
- A celebration of what I do
- Demonstrating skill/knowledge
- Helping me to focus on my blind-spot(s)
- Discovering my own pattern of behaviors
- Developing skills as a mentor
- A quality control process
- Providing a different angle on an issue

Barrett's (2002) work aside, there has been relatively little attention focused on mentoring supervision in the literature. However, the widening notion of supervision in other professions has coincided with increasing concerns with how mentors might be developed within the mentoring community (see Garvey and Alred (2000) for a useful discussion of educating mentors). These concerns prompted us following our research in 2003, to develop a heuristic, which linked together the needs of the mentoring supervisee with their development as a mentor. (See Figure 11.1).

The four stages for mentor development can be used as a device for mentoring practitioners to aid reflection on their own practice and the heuristic offers a brief description of each stage, summarizing the benefits and challenges and the role and responsibilities of the supervisor.

**Stages of mentor development**

Increasing mentor development →

| Reflexive mentor | Reflective mentor | Developing mentor | Novice mentor |
|---|---|---|---|
| • Extend range of skills<br>• Reflexive practice<br>• Self-development and improvement<br>• Avoid complacency | • Look at own experience<br>• Critically reflect on own practice in relation to others<br>• Build on skills required | • Process knowledge<br>• Awareness of boundaries<br>• Three stage model<br>• Awareness of skills required | • Need to know the rules<br>• Require scheme knowledge and context knowledge of process |

**Functions of mentor supervision**

| Challenge function | Development function | Training function | Quality assurance/Audit function |
|---|---|---|---|
| • Critical friend to the mentor<br>• Devil's advocacy<br>• Constructive and/or challenging feedback<br>• Spot mentoring | • Opportunity to reflect on practice<br>• Learning from other mentors<br>• Reflecting on skills | • Identifying a mentoring process<br>• Understanding different phases / stages in process | • Audit function, i.e., checking mentor's ability<br>  - Acceptance<br>  - Empathy<br>  - Congruence<br>• Quality assurance to bestow "aura of professionalism" |

**Increasing formality of supervision** →

**Figure 11.1**  A schema for mentor development and supervision.

# Review and Evaluation

Both formative and summative evaluation of mentoring schemes are useful to inform the design and future development of formal programs. However, it is difficult to review what is basically a private developmental relationship between two people and ascertain sufficient information about the activities of and benefits from the mentoring pair to satisfy the organization's expectations and to obtain resources for future mentoring. Cranwell-Ward *et al.* (2004, p.136) state that in order to position mentoring as part of the mainstream of organizational development, a rigorous evaluation process is a key tool, which needs to be in place at the outset of the scheme. Klasen and Clutterbuck (2002) reinforce this message, whilst MacLennan (1995, p. 264) states that if a mentoring system is not systematically evaluated, monitored, and shown to be effective, it will be dropped by design or default. However, Cranwell-Ward *et al.* (2004) and Klasen and Clutterbuck (2002) stress how intangible many mentoring outcomes can be, which is quite a challenge for the evaluator.

# Supporting Different Mentoring Needs

## Mentoring schemes and education

As has already been argued, mentoring schemes, and programs have a broad range of purposes and appear in many different sectors, one of the more established areas for mentoring is in education. A prominent subset of that literature is the research that has been done that looks at the mentoring of teachers and lecturers within schools and higher education establishments. In her study on the mentoring of learner-teachers, Lai (2010) reviews this research. She categorizes existing research into three groups: relational (concerned with the mentoring relationship); developmental (concerned with the professional development of participants); and contextual (concerned with the influence that the organizational/societal context has on mentoring). Lai's aim in her 2010 study was to address all three areas by looking at three key groups: mentors, mentees, and university teachers. The study was conducted in a Hong Kong University, which offered a postgraduate diploma (PgD) in education. The mentees were student teachers who would be supported in school teaching by experienced teachers who were the mentors. The university teachers delivered the PgD to the mentees in the university. The stated goal of the mentoring was, "to help mentees become effective and self improving teachers who possess a good level of professional knowledge, expertise in handling complex classroom situations and a willingness to engage in critical reflection on their practices" (p. 448).

Perhaps unsurprisingly, her study revealed that, for the key players, a key frame of reference was the developmental aspect of the scheme, that is, the development of the mentees' professional practice as teachers. However, the mentors and the university teachers were more aware and focused on the contextual issues surrounding the mentoring, whereas the mentees were much more focused on the relational aspect of the mentoring relationship. Having these three dimensions as part of the study seemed to help Lai (2010) frame her recommendations in terms of improving the mentoring program's efficacy for all key players within it. These three perspectives on the mentoring scheme enabled her to put forward recommendations that helped address some of the weaknesses in it, for example, the weak link between the university and the schools, which militated against a continuous learning experience for all concerned.

Another prominent branch of the education literature is the peer mentoring of students. In the United States, Hughes and Fahy's (2009) study of an undergraduate mentoring scheme examined the mentoring of freshman psychology students by more experienced students. The aim of the study was to help students make the transition from freshmen to feel part of the department of psychology and aid student retention. The findings in this study support earlier work of others (e.g., Asbee and Woodall, 2000; Goodland, 1998) that formal mentoring schemes can be particularly effective in this regard. There is also evidence (Garvey and Langridge, 2006) that mentoring schemes can serve a similar function in UK schools.

## Mentoring schemes and diversity

Another key arena for mentoring programs is that of diversity, particularly those focused on equality of opportunity in terms of race. This sort of mentoring cuts across all sectors but is a common area of focus for mentoring schemes. Hussain (in Megginson *et al.*, 2006, pp. 102–99) and Gerber (in Megginson *et al.*, 2006, pp. 94–101) both discuss schemes where equality of opportunity are central to the scheme. Hussain examined the diversity mentoring program at British Telecom, one of the United Kingdom's largest companies. In his account of the scheme, Hussain (2006) claims the following lessons have been learnt:

- There is a need for robust end-to-end processes with clear roles and responsibilities defined.
- Continual cleansing of the database is essential.
- Expectations particularly of mentees need to be managed very carefully to avoid disappointment.
- The matching needs to be slick and efficient to maintain momentum.
- Every opportunity must be used to promote the program and recruit new mentors and mentees.
- Progression of mentors and mentees through the organization should be tracked to help evaluate the effectiveness of the program.

Whilst these lessons are helpful and pragmatic from the point of view of the scheme designer, Hussain's account does fall into the categories of a practitioner study of mentoring as discussed by Garvey *et al.* (2009). In the chapter on research traditions within coaching and mentoring, they examine the strengths and weaknesses of coaching and mentoring research. One of traditions of both coaching and mentoring practitioner accounts is that they: "Are often insider accounts, written by people who have a stake in the scheme or the relationship... [which] has the advantage of giving insights into the dynamics of the coaching intervention, though it can mean that they do not pay attention to alternative explanations for the phenomena that they observe, and that they tend to emphasize the positive and effective whilst ignoring data that could be seen as negative" (Garvey *et al.*, 2009, p. 50). Applying this to Hussain's case, it is clear that, whilst there is acknowledgement that things can be improved, the author has a vested interest, as program owner, in a positive evaluation of the program and its outcomes.

Gerber's (2006) account, from the same volume of her scheme is more critical in nature. Her account is focused on the career development of black academics in the University of the Witwatersrand, South Africa. In tone it is more similar to the academic tradition that

Garvey *et al.* (2009) attribute to large-scale survey research in mentoring: dispassionate, impartial, and critical in places. She locates the impetus for the mentoring program within the broader struggle against the apartheid regime in South Africa. Her account points to the importance of mentors' understanding of the organizational context and the broader societal issues when selecting mentors, contrasting this with the academic supervision of the mentees when doing higher degrees.

Blake-Beard *et al.* (2007) conducted a comprehensive review of mentoring programs and race in the United States. They conclude that "the study of race and mentoring represents unfinished business for organizational scholars, managers and practitioners" (2007, p. 242). Like Gerber, they see a connection with the broader organizational and societal challenges around social mobility. However, they go further by arguing that advocacy may become a possible strategy, which "moves beyond direct engagement within the relationship, toward engagement in the process of change throughout the organization" (2007, p. 240).

This emancipatory agenda is also reflected in another well researched area for diversity programs, that of mentoring women. In our 2008 article (Merrick and Stokes, 2008a), we reviewed the relevant research and literature on mentoring women to that point and confirmed the existence of issue of a "glass ceiling" that, in the view of many commentators, prevents women from progressing into senior positions within organizations. Mentoring had been put forward as a possible solution to this, but our analysis included the possibility of "androgynous mentoring", which avoids the usual dichotomy of male or female mentors. However, rather than focusing on the mentor's skills as does much of the literature, we called for more attention to be focused on the skills of mentee, because by ignoring mentee agency and autonomy, the discourse disempowers the mentee.

This sentiment is supported also by Ehrich (2008). Her analysis, looking at studies from the United Kingdom, United States, and Australia, concluded that sponsoring women through the glass ceiling can mean that, on the one hand, "certain selected women are granted access to power and resources by their powerful mentors, but on the other, such a practice perpetuates a hierarchical and elitist view of mentoring that reinforces masculine strategies of power" (Ehrich, 2008, p. 479). More recently, Ibarra *et al.* (2010) have further highlighted that dilemma and its impact on the careers of women. They report on a 2008 survey of 4,000 people worldwide who had graduated from MBA programs, showing that women on average get paid $4,600 less in their first jobs and experience less career satisfaction than their male counterparts, despite the fact that more women in the study have mentors than men. This caused them to question the benefit of mentoring schemes for women and to explore the reasons for this in their research. They conducted in-depth interviews with 40 high potential staff (both men and women) who had been selected to be part of their large multinational company's mentoring program. Their main conclusions have some interesting implications for the design of mentoring programs and are neatly summarized in the paragraph below:

> All mentoring is not created equal, we discovered. There is a special kind of relationship – called sponsorship – in which the mentor goes beyond giving feedback and advice and uses his or her influence to advocate for the mentee. Our interviews and surveys alike suggest that high potential women are "over-mentored" and under-sponsored relative to their male peers – and that they are not advancing in their organizations. Furthermore, without sponsorship, women not only are less likely than men to be appointed to top roles but may also be more reluctant to go for them. (Ibarra *et al.*, 2010, p. 82)

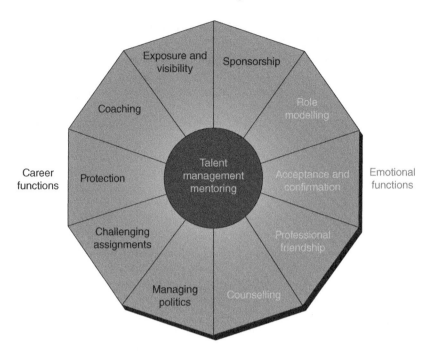

**Figure 11.2** The talent mentoring wheel (Merrick and Stokes, 2008b).

In other words, access to mentoring is not a problem for the women in the study; rather, there is evidence to suggest that is an imbalance in the mentoring that women receive compared with their male counterparts. Sponsorship mentoring appears to have some cultural differences at its roots. Chandler (2009) argues that sponsorship mentoring is more prevalent and accepted in the United States than in Europe, particularly due to the low power distance cultures (Hofstede, 2001) in some of these countries. Interestingly, she argues that the US model of mentoring might be moving towards the more European approach, with its greater focus on pyschosocial support as opposed to an emphasis on career progression (see Kram, 1985). Interestingly, however, our own work on mentoring for talent management (Merrick and Stokes, 2008b) seems to support what Ibarra *et al.* (2010) subsequently found. Several mentees in our small-scale study expressed impatience with their mentor for not helping them in terms of active sponsorship, despite the espoused nature of the mentoring programs being developmental, non-sponsorship mentoring programs. This has led us to explicitly examine sponsorship mentoring behaviors within mentoring programs within mentoring training and development programs (see Figure 11.2). These behaviors include: helping by managing politics, helping to provide exposure and visibility, assistance in getting challenging assignments, and protecting mentees.

## Mentoring and health

There are also a number of mentoring schemes in the health sector that raise some interesting issues in terms of the design of mentoring schemes. It is unsurprising that this is particularly the case in the United Kingdom, given that the UK National Health Service

(NHS) is one of Europe's largest employers. For example, the work by Connor *et al.* (2000) in the 1990s drew together 83 senior doctors from four mentoring programs to examine their understanding of mentoring using a questionnaire design. Interestingly, this study revealed that, although most of the respondents had initially expected primarily to develop mentoring skills, the survey revealed that being part of a network of senior doctors was a key benefit that had emerged for them from the program.

These finding accords with our recent experience of working with Staff Grade and Associate Specialist (SAS) doctors within a UK medical deanery. Although the label used in that context was "coaching", participants saw the value of being able to engage with colleagues within a peer mentoring framework. However, mentoring in the UK NHS context does present some challenges to traditional notions of mentoring due to the common practice of combining traditional mentoring behaviors with that of a manager/assessor. This is well illustrated by Watson's (1999) earlier study where she was trying, in a similar vein to Connor *et al.* (2000), to understand nursing staff's perception of mentoring. She found that, "of the 35 students interviewed, all had similar understanding of the role of mentor, with meaning for them including assessor, facilitator, role model, planning and support in the clinical setting," which fitted well with how the mentors themselves saw the role, except for the planning of learning.

There are two issues here that are of interest when reflecting on designing mentoring schemes. One is the issue of assessment and the power relationships that managerial responsibility brings with it (see Garvey *et al.*, 2009, pp. 111–24) and the other is that of responsibility. In our own experience of designing and developing mentoring schemes, one of the commonest challenges that novice mentors face in mentoring schemes is to resist giving advice to the mentee because the mentor "knows the answer". This is well captured by Hawkins and Smith (2006, p. 41) who state: "The tendency for the untrained mentor is to see the transition of the mentee solely through the lens of their own journey through a similar transition and to give advice according to their own experience alone."

As a result, there may be a tendency for the mentor, particularly where the mentee sees the mentor as the more experienced and capable individual, to project their own experience onto the mentee. In turn, the mentee may therefore assume a more passive role in the relationship, deferring to the mentor as to what they should do next in their learning – these challenges are more fully explored by McAuley (2003) in his article on transference and counter-transference in mentoring relationships. The challenge with this is that this mentee passivity can militate against self-growth and responsibility for one's own learning.

Glimpses of this tendency can be seen in the Watson (1999) study where mentee nurses look to the mentors to plan their learning. As a result it is perhaps unsurprising that the results of the study reveal that participants had mixed feelings about the success of the program, with students feeling that, "when the mentor was available, sometimes very helpful, sometimes unhelpful" (Watson, 1999, p. 260). What constitutes helpfulness and unhelpfulness in a mentoring scheme depends what is understood by mentoring by scheme participants. It is understandable that mentees might see a mentor, who does not see their role as being responsible for the mentee's learning schedule, as being "unhelpful" if they refuse to take responsibility for this. These tendencies have also been recognized in other health studies on mentoring. In their review of mentoring in public health nursing in the United States, Smith *et al.* (2001, p. 103) acknowledged that mentees, "may be inclined to play a blame game when something goes wrong."

**Table 11.3**   Characteristics of a mentoring culture.

| *Supports mentors* | *Supports mentees* |
|---|---|
| Experienced surgeons are expected and encouraged to mentor. | Asking questions is encouraged. |
| Mentoring is seen to be a valued activity. | Trainee evaluations are face to face, with the opportunity for feedback. |
| Time is made available for mentoring. | Making mistakes is an expected part of the training process. |
| Mentoring counts towards promotion. | No one is allowed to fall through the cracks. |
| Time and money are available to train in mentoring skills. | Mentees are able to use a network of mentors to develop different kinds of expertise. |
| | Mentoring is available for older individuals who have become disconnected or lost direction. |
| | Trainees are encouraged to mentor each other. |

Sometimes this responsibility challenge also extends to the mentoring scheme itself. In an Australian study on mentoring nurse managers, Waters *et al.* (2003) largely positive review of a pilot mentoring program did imply that there were some high expectations placed on the mentoring program designers in terms of ensuring high commitment to the program. There is also some evidence of this being important within the United States. Singletary's (2005) review of mentoring surgeons in the United States points to a range of studies where mentoring schemes are seen as being helpful. She argues that, in order to ensure that surgeon mentoring schemes are successful, it is necessary to encourage the development of a mentoring culture. Such a culture is characterized by the characteristics set out in Table 11.3.

Singletary's (2005) approach to mistakes within a medical setting raises some interesting questions about scheme design. Should mentoring schemes have a competency framework built into them so that completion of the mentoring program also constitutes, to some degree, a license to practice. As with education, this conflation of assessment and mentoring raises questions about the purposes of a mentoring program.

## Other mentoring functions

Of course, as the preceding analysis has suggested, mentoring programs feature in all sectors and are designed to address a wide range of purpose. For example, Hansford *et al.* (2002), Gravells (2006), and Megginson and Stokes (2004) examine the prevalence of business-to-business mentoring and the challenges that working with small business owners presents. Colley's (2003) excellent research-based text on mentoring for social inclusion via employment in the United Kingdom draws our attention to the design implications for mentoring schemes in terms of mentee and mentor agency. Furthermore, Simpson (2006), Morgan (2006), and Langridge (2006) draw out the challenges that emerge from community mentoring schemes. However, it is time to begin to draw together the lessons for the design of mentoring schemes. This will be done in two parts: first, we will briefly consider issues around the context and processes of mentoring schemes, after which we will discuss the future of scheme design, addressing the challenge for a conceptual framework for mentoring.

## Context and Processes for Mentoring

As Ragins and Kram have argued, there are many different forms that mentoring can take: peer mentoring, group mentoring, cross-organizational mentoring, diversified mentoring, cross-cultural mentoring, and e-mentoring. Using the metaphor of a garden, they have argued that, the authors, "have planted the seeds for growth for research and innovation in many undernourished areas in the garden of mentoring" (Ragins and Kram, 2007, p. 683). Garvey *et al.* (2009) refer to these different approaches to mentoring as modes, which they contrast with the brands of coaching. The modes they identify include: traditional dyadic mentoring, peer mentoring, co-mentoring, and e-mentoring. We will examine two of the key themes that have the most implications for scheme design: e-mentoring, and peer mentoring and mutuality.

### E-mentoring

When examining e-mentoring in the United Kingdom, Headlam-Wells *et al.* (2006, p. 273) felt that it was a: "Relatively new and under-researched field, particularly from a European perspective." The discussion by Garvey *et al.* (2009) of e-development puts forward a conceptual map of e-mentoring, which positions e-mentoring as a continuum. They argue that mentoring schemes can be purely face-to-face, with relatively little engagement with electronic media, or, on other hand purely web-based, with no face-to-face contact. In our experience of scheme design, most programs fall somewhere in between, although most err towards one end of the spectrum or the other. Emelo's (2011) practitioner article on "open mentoring" is an example of group mentoring which was more virtual than face-to-face in terms of mode. His evaluation of the program suggested that 90 percent of participants found that this blend of face-to-face and virtual mentoring-in groups worked well for them. Garvey *et al.* (2009) report that there are some advantages and disadvantages of e-mentoring as a mode. Advantages include: freedom to be asynchronous with replying to each other (e.g., email); breakdown of geographical barriers; making it easier to access-thus increasing the pool of participants; the ability to capture/record what is said and refer back to it. Disadvantages include: lack of access (depending on the technology used) to body language, etc.; easy to break off – fragile; removal of context and impersonal (see Chapter 26 of this volume for a fuller exploration of virtual and e-mentoring). Ensher and Murphy (in Ragins and Kram, 2007, pp. 299–322) examine e-mentoring in a US context, bringing together the labels online mentoring, virtual mentoring, and telementoring. Their review of studies on e-mentoring is taken from a range of programs in different sectors: company sponsored programs for employees; corporate sponsored programs for students; entrepreneur programs; healthcare; higher education; teaching; public relations; and government. They conclude broadly similar points regarding the lessons for scheme designers. Hence scheme designers must make a decision about how much to engage with electronic mentoring as part of their program and what the blend will look like.

### Peer mentoring and mutuality

Peer mentoring has developed in popularity to rival traditional mentoring as a mode of mentoring in schemes. This has been applied in schools in the United Kinggdom in a number of studies. For example, Pyatt (2002) examined a peer mentoring process between schoolgirls and concluded that this had contributed to towards improvements in behavior of both sets of pupils, affording mutual benefit to both mentors and mentees. Similarly, Knowles and Parsons (2009) reported benefits to mentors in terms of enhanced CVs and skills, as well as improved confidence and behavior on the part of the mentees. In higher education, less mutual learning was experienced in the study by Fox *et al.* (2010) of mentoring in Scottish universities, although some benefits in performance were found in first year accounting undergraduates who were peer mentored as compared with those who were not. Co-mentoring, as understood by Rymer (2002) is a further extension of peer mentoring, but where both parties receive support from the other. This seems to have closer associations with the developmental network perspective offered by Higgins *et al.* (2007), where Rymer (2002) refers to the importance of multiple mutual relationships and the ability of the mentee to make sense of and integrate these perspectives. Higgins *et al.* (2007) argue that organizational schemes should encourage individuals to: "Reflect on their progress toward cultivating a responsive network, engaging in active developmental initiation in developmental relationships and enhancing the mutuality of developmental relationships" (Higgins *et al.*, 2007, p. 363). This blurring of traditional notions of mentor and mentees suggests that scheme design is becoming more about developing a mentoring culture and context for effective mentoring to take place. This, and other implications from the preceding sections will now be drawn together in the final section of the chapter, which will examine the future of scheme design.

## Future Research

At the beginning of this chapter, we took as our starting point Gibb's (1994) call for a new conceptual framework for critically examining mentoring scheme design. Arguably, what we have emerged with, however, is more a set of key principles and questions that should inform scheme design. These will be examined in turn as we look to the future.

*Why have mentoring?* Although this chapter has provided plenty of evidence of how mentoring can benefit individuals and organizations, our experience and this evidence still causes us to be cautious about the amount of hope and expectation that can be thrust towards mentoring schemes. We have argued that it is helpful to have powerful stakeholders bought into the process, this is particularly pertinent at a time of challenging economic circumstances when questions are asked about the added value of a range of activities. Hence, the rationale for investing time and energy in mentoring needs to be clear. However, we are not advocating systems-control view of organizations, with the accompanying assumptions regarding causality and positivistic notions of objectivity. Rather we recognize that other interventions may be more appropriate depending on the need. Nevertheless, in our own practice, we have noticed that, with some of our private sector organization clients, there has been a move towards peer mentoring at the expense of executive coaching during the period 2010–11, due to the perceived cost effectiveness of mentoring.

*Who is it for?* We discussed a number of issues around scheme purpose, followed by recruitment and matching. We recognized, in our analysis of different sectors and purposes, the importance and impact of the context. In this, we explored a number of issues such as the challenge of insider accounts, the importance of the broader social context on the mentoring process, and acknowledged the power and cultural issues that these different influences have on the individuals. Understanding who the mentoring is supposed to affect and in what way is a critical part of making sure that those who are intended to benefit, do so.

Arguably, Gibb's (1999) notions around social exchange versus communitarian approaches, together with Lai's (2010) notions of relational, developmental, and contextual categories give us a more sophisticated set of ideas to work with, which bring together who it is for with notions of scheme purpose. Ragins and Kram's (2007) notion that developmental networks will be an increasingly key area seems to be a useful one, particularly in view of Carver's (2011) challenge regarding the increasingly popularity of mentoring and the pressures that places on the mentoring pool.

*Developing a mentoring culture* Whilst Garvey *et al.* (2009) report on what a mentoring culture might look like, there has been relatively little attention paid to this idea in scheme design. Singletary's (2005) framework for surgeons seems to present a useful starting point as to what this might mean for scheme design in practice and how this might feed into the training and development of mentors and mentees. We see the debates around mutuality and mentoring as being connected to this. If a mentoring culture is developed, the boundaries between formal and informal mentoring may become blurred and those within such cultures may move towards constellations of mentoring networks, as suggested above, where multiple, mutual mentoring occurs as part of the taken-for-granted assumptions (Schein, 2010) within the organization. This will challenge traditional notions of mentoring schemes where one person, who is more experienced, mentors another, particularly when coupled with some of the challenges and opportunities that new communication technology can bring.

## Evaluating mentoring schemes

Given our discussion around the diversity of purposes and the different challenges that mentoring is used to address, it is important to recognize that we will need to be more sophisticated about how we evaluate mentoring. We often seek to evaluate mentoring and coaching initiatives based on a correspondence version of truth (Stokes, 2010) in evaluation; in other words, using a cause and effect scientific model. This model is becoming increasingly problematic to sustain as an approach to evaluation due its limited explanatory power with regards to how scheme sponsors and senior managers make investment decisions. If scheme sponsors persist in applying such models, they may make decisions, which might jeopardize the added value that mentoring programs can bring.

# Conclusion

Mentoring programs – and the needs of those who use them – are diverse and they need to be designed carefully and reflexively to avoid any unintended negative consequences vis-à-vis what was originally intended. Gibb's (1994) research challenge was, and is, a useful one and we have tried in this chapter to engage with the critical perspective necessary to promote debate and analysis about the potential and limitations of mentoring schemes, in order to draw out some lessons for their design and development.

# References

Allen, T.D., Eby, L.T., and Lentz, E. (2006) The relationship between formal mentoring program characteristics and perceived program effectiveness. *Personnel Psychology*, 59, 125–53.

Asbee, S. and Woodall, S. (2000) Supporting access in distance education through student-student mentoring. *Journal of Access and Credit Studies*, 2(2), 220–32.

Atterton, J., Thompson, N., and Carroll, T. (2009) Mentoring as a mechanism for improvement in local government. *Public Money and Management*, January, 51–7.

Barrett, R. (2002) Mentor supervision and development – exploration of lived experience. *Career Development International*, 7(5), 279–83.

Blake-Beard, S.D., O'Neill, R., and McGowan, E.M. (2007) Blind dates? The importance of matching in sucessful formal mentoring relationships.. In: B.R. Ragins and K.E. Kram (eds) *The Handbook of Mentoring at Work: Theory, Research and Practice*. London: Sage. pp. 617–32.

Carver, B.N. (2011) The hows and whys of group mentoring. *Industrial & Commercial Training*, 43(1), 49–52.

Chandler, D. (2009) A United States perspective on coaching and mentoring. In: B. Garvey, P. Stokes, and D. Megginson (eds) *Coaching and Mentoring Theory and Practice*. London: Sage. pp. 205–20.

Chivers, G. (2011) Supporting informal learning by traders in investment banks. Retrived from: www.jessicachivers.com/tag/mentoring/ (accessed June 12, 2012).

Colley, H. (2003) *Mentoring for Social Inclusion: A Critical Approach to Nurturing Mentoring Relationships*. Routledge Falmer: London.

Connor, M.P., Bynoe, A.G., Redfern, N., Pakora, J., and Clarke, J. (2000) Developing senior doctors as mentors: A form of continuing professional development, Report of an initiative to develop a network of senior doctors as mentors: 1994–99. 34, 747–53.

Cranwell-Ward, J., Bossons, P., and Gover, S. (2004) *Mentoring: A Henley Review of Best Practice*. London: Palgrave Macmillan.

Douglas, C.A. (1997) *Formal Mentoring Programs in Organizations: An Annotated Bibliography*. Greensboro: NC Center for Creative Leadership.

Ehrich, L.C. (2008) Mentoring and women managers: Another look at the field. *Gender in Management: An International Journal*, 23(7), 469–83.

Emelo, R. (2011) Creating a new mindset: Guidelines for mentorship in today's workplace. *Training and Development*, 6(1), 44–9.

Ensher, E.A. and Murphy, S.E. (2007) E-mentoring: Next-generation research strategies and suggestions. In: B.R. Ragins and K.E. Kram (eds) *The Handbook of Mentoring at Work: Theory, Research and Practice*. London: Sage. pp. 299–322.

Fox, A., Stevenson, L., Connelly, P., Duff, A., and Dunlop, A. (2010) Peer mentoring undergraduate accounting students: The influence on approaches to learning and academic performance. *Active Learning in Higher Education*, 11(2), 145–56.

Garvey, B. (1994) A dose of mentoring. *Education and Training*, 36(4), 18–26.

Garvey, B. and Alred, G. (2000) Educating mentors. *Mentoring and Tutoring*, 8(2), 113–26.

Garvey, B. and Langridge, K. (2006) *Pupil Mentoring Pocketbook*. Arlesford, Hants, UK: Teachers Pocketbooks.

Garvey, B., Stokes, P., and Megginson, D. (2009) *Coaching and Mentoring Theory and Practice*. London: Sage.

Gerber, H. (2006) Case study 8: Mentoring black junior academics in the University of Witwatersrand. In: D. Megginson, D. Clutterbuck, B. Garvey, P. Stokes, and R. Garrett-Harris (eds) *Mentoring in Action*. London: Kogan-Page. pp. 94–101.

Gibb, S. (1994) Inside corporate mentoring schemes: The development of a conceptual framework. *Personnel Review*, 23(3), 47–60.

Gibb, S. (1999) The usefulness of theory: A case study in evaluating formal mentoring schemes. *Human Relations*, 52(8), 1055–75.

Gibb, S. and Megginson, D. (1993) Inside corporate mentoring schemes: A new agenda of concerns. *Personnel Review*, 22(1), 40–54.

Goodland, S. (ed.) (1998) *Mentoring and Tutoring by Students*. London: BP Educational Service.

Gravells. J. (2006) Case study 13: Mentoring owners of micro businesses in Nottingham. In: D. Megginson, D. Clutterbuck, B. Garvey, P. Stokes, and R. Garrett-Harris (eds) (2006) *Mentoring in Action*. London: Kogan Page. pp. 142–9.

Hansford, B., Tennent, L., and Ehrich, L. (2002) Business Mentoring: help or hindance? *Mentoring and Tutoring*, 10(2), 101–15.

Hawkins, P. and Smith, N. (2006) *Coaching, Mentoring and Organizational Consultancy: Supervision and Development*. Maidenhead: Open University Press.

Headlam-Wells, J., Gosland, J., and Craig, J. (2006) Beyond the organization: The design and management of e-mentoring systems. *International Journal of Information Management*, 26, 272–85.

Hegstad, C.D. and Wentling, R.M. (2005) Organizational antecedents and moderators that impact on the effectiveness of exemplary formal mentoring programs in Fortune 500 companies in the United States. *Human Resource Development International*, 8(4), 467–87.

Higgins, M.C., Chandler, D.E., and Kram, K.E. (2007) Boundary spanning of developmental networks: A social network perspective on mentoring. In: B.R. Ragins and K.E. Kram (eds) *The Handbook of Mentoring at Work: Theory, Research and Practice*. London: Sage. pp. 349–72.

Hofstede, G. (2001) *Cultures Consequences: International Differences in Work Related Values*. Thousand Oaks, CA: Sage.

Hudson-Davies, R., Parker, C., and Byrom, J. (2002) Towards a healthy high street: Developing mentoring schemes for smaller retailers. *Industrial and Commercial Training*, 34(7), 248–55.

Hughes, A. and Fahy, B. (2009) Implementing an undergraduate psychology mentoring program. *North American Journal of Psychology*, 11(3), 464–70.

Hussain, Z. (2006) Case study 9: Diversity mentoring in BT. In: D. Megginson, D. Clutterbuck, B. Garvey, P. Stokes, and R. Garrett-Harris (eds) *Mentoring in Action*. London: Kogan Page. pp. 102–99.

Ibarra, H., Carter, N.M., and Silva, C. (2010) Why men still get more promotions than women. *Harvard Business Review*, 88(9), 80–126.

Klasen, N. and Clutterbuck, D. (2002) *Implementing Mentoring Schemes: A Practical Guide to Successful Programs*. London: Butterworth-Heinemann.

Knowles, C. and Parsons C. (2009) Evaluating a formalised peer mentoring program: Student voice and impact audit. *Pastoral Care in Education*, 27(3), 205–18.

Kram, K. (1985) *Mentoring at Work*. Glenville, IL: Scott Foresman.

Lai, E. (2010) Getting in step to improve the quality of in-service teacher learning through mentoring. *Professional Development in Education*, 36(3), 443–69.

Langridge, K. (2006) Case study 6: JIVE: Tackling gender stereotyping in engineering, construction and technology. In: D. Megginson, D. Clutterbuck, B. Garvey, P. Stokes, and R. Garrett-Harris (eds) *Mentoring in Action*. London: Kogan-Page. pp. 220–4.

Lyons, B.D. and Oppler, E.S. (2004) The effects of structural attributes and demographic characteristics on protege satisfaction in mentoring programs. *Journal of Career Development*, 30, 215–29.

MacLennan, N. (1995) *Coaching and Mentoring*. Farnham, UK: Gower.

McAuley, J. (2003) Transference, counter-transference and mentoring: The ghost in the process. *British Journal of Guidance and Counselling*, 31, 11–24.

Megginson, D. and Stokes, P. (2004) Mentoring for export success. In: J. Stewart and G. Beaver (eds) *HRM in Small Organizations: Research and Practice*. Abingdon: Routledge. pp. 265–85.

Megginson, D., Clutterbuck, D., Garvey, B., Stokes, P., and Garrett-Harris, R. (eds) (2006) *Mentoring in Action*. London: Kogan Page.

Merrick, L. (2009) How to set up a mentoring program. *Coaching at Work*, 3(4), 52–4.

Merrick, L. and Stokes, P. (2003) Mentor development and supervision: A passionate joint inquiry. *International Journal of Mentoring and Coaching* (E-journal), 1(1).

Merrick, L. and Stokes, P. (2008a) Unbreakable? Using mentoring to break the glass ceiling. *International Journal of Mentoring and Coaching* (E-journal), 5(2).

Merrick, L. and Stokes, P. (2008b) *Mentoring for Talent Management*. Conference Paper presented at the 15th European Mentoring and Coaching Council. Amsterdam.

Morgan, G. (1986) *Images of Organization*. London: Sage.

Morgan, J. (2006) Case study 2: Mentoring support for victims of domestic abuse. In: D. Megginson, D. Clutterbuck, B. Garvey, P. Stokes, and R. Garrett-Harris (eds) (2006) *Mentoring in Action*. London: Kogan Page. pp. 47–55.

O'Neill, R.M. (2005) An examination of organizational predictors of mentoring functions. *Journal of Managerial Issues*, 17, 439–60.

O'Reilly, D. (2001) The mentoring of employees: Is your organization taking advantage of this professional development tool? *Ohio CPA Journal*, July–Sept, 51–4.

Pyatt, G. (2002) Cross school mentoring: Training and implementing a peer mentoring strategy. *Mentoring and Tutoring* 10(2), 171–7.

Ragins, B.R. and Kram, K.E. (eds) (2007) *The Handbook of Mentoring at Work: Theory, Research and Practice*. London: Sage.

Ragins, B.R., Cotton, J.L., and Miller, J.S. (2000) Marginal mentoring: The effects of type of mentor, quality of relationship, and program design on work and career attitudes. *Academy of Management Journal*, 43(6), 1177–94.

Rymer, J. (2002) "Only connect": Transforming ourselves and our discipline through co mentoring. *Journal of Business Communication*, 39(3), 342–63.

Samujh, R.H. (2011) Micro-businesses need support: Survival precedes sustainability. *Corporate Governance*, 11(1), 15–28.

Schein, E.H. (2010) *Organizational Culture and Leadership*. San Francisco, CA: Jossey-Bass.

Simpson, J. (2006) Case study 1: Mentoring with the Youth Justice board for England and Wales. In: D. Megginson, D. Clutterbuck, B. Garvey, P. Stokes and R. Garrett-Harris (eds) *Mentoring in Action*. London: Kogan-Page. pp. 40–6.

Singh, V., Bains, D., and Vinnicombe, S. (2002) Informal mentoring as an organizational resource. *Long Range Planning*, 35, 389–405.

Singletary, S.E. (2005) Mentoring surgeons for the 21st century. *Annual of Surgical Oncology*, 12(11), 848–60.

Smith, L.S., McAllister, L.E. and Crawford, C.S (2001) Mentoring benefits and issues for public health nurses. *Public Health Nursing*, 18(2), 101–7.

Sontag, L.P., Vappie, K., and Wanberg, C.R. (2007) The practice of mentoring: MENTTIUM corporation.. In: B.R. Ragins and K.E. Kram (eds) *The Handbook of Mentoring at Work: Theory, Research and Practice*. London: Sage. pp. 593–616.

Stokes, P. (2010) So does coaching have an impact? *Coaching at Work*, 5(3), 57.

Wareing, I. (2006) Case study 16: Weir Warman Ltd mentoring programme in Sydney. In: D. Megginson, D. Clutterbuck, B. Garvey, P. Stokes, and R. Garrett-Harris (eds) *Mentoring in Action*. London: Kogan-Page. pp. 163–70.

Waters, D., Clarke, M., Ingall A., and Dean-Jones, M. (2003) Evaluation of a pilot mentoring program for nurse managers. *Journal of Advanced Nursing*, 42(5), 516–26.

Watson, N. (1999) Mentoring today – the students' views. An investigative case study of pre-registration nursing experiences and perceptions of mentoring in one theory/practice model of the Common Foundation Program on a Project 2000 course. *Journal of Advanced Nursing*, 29(1), 254–62.

Watson, T. (2006) *Organising and Managing Work* (2nd edn). London: Prentice Hall.

# 12

# The Efficacy of Mentoring – the Benefits for Mentees, Mentors, and Organizations

## Chloé Tong and Kathy E. Kram

## Introduction

Theoretical perspectives of the impact of mentoring have evolved greatly from early conceptualizations of a uni-directional influence whereby the protégé is the primary beneficiary of the relationship and the mentor provides support without expectation of reciprocation (Eby *et al.*, 2008; Kram, 1985), "the mentor gives, the protégé gets, and the organization benefits" (Scandura *et al.*, 1996), to an understanding that all stakeholders in the mentoring relationship stand to gain (Hussain, 2006; Ragins and Kram, 2007): the individuals involved in the dyadic relationship and any commissioning organization.

The origins of mentoring can be traced back to the Greek mythology of *The Odyssey* (Baker, 2001). Mentoring has long been a popular means for sharing learning and knowledge from generation to generation (Buhler, 1998). Today mentoring programs are widely used in organizations (Eby *et al.*, 2000) as an individual development strategy to facilitate attainment of a variety of positive outcomes (Atkinson, 2002; Knouse, 2001; O'Reilly, 2001). It is therefore more important than ever that the impacts of mentoring are fully understood (Eby *et al.*, 2006). Empirical research to understand the mentoring phenomenon has only commenced over the past three decades (Allen and Eby, 2007). Developing a solid understanding of the benefits to be gained through mentoring will have a wealth of implications for the advancement of theoretical conceptualization of mentoring, and also application of mentoring in practice (Allen *et al.*, 2004).

This chapter introduces the reader to the various benefits of mentoring, as supported by the literature. First, we will explore the benefits of traditional mentoring relationships for the individual partners: the protégé and the mentor. In the next section we will review the benefits to the the organization. Third, we will review the difficulties with the mentoring literature to date, followed by the variations on traditional mentoring relationships and their unique benefits. Finally, current and future research topics will be suggested.

*The Wiley Blackwell Handbook of the Psychology of Coaching and Mentoring*, First Edition.
Edited by Jonathan Passmore, David B. Peterson, and Teresa Freire.
© 2013 John Wiley & Sons, Ltd. Published 2016 by John Wiley & Sons, Ltd.

# Benefits of Mentoring for the Individual

Mentoring has traditionally been conceptualized as a dyadic relationship between mentor and protégé, where the mentor draws on acquired knowledge and experience to enhance the professional and personal development of the less experienced protégé (Wanberg *et al.*, 2003). The traditional mentoring relationship is usually informal in nature (i.e., naturally evolving, initiated without organizational intervention), existing between two individuals of unequal status in the organization (e.g., Eby, 1997; Higgins and Kram, 2001).

This section will explore the literature pertaining to the benefits of mentoring for the individual, specifically traditional mentoring as defined above, unless otherwise specified. Empirical support for the benefits for the protégé will be examined first, followed by literature relating to the mentor. Finally this section will highlight key research investigating the various negative outcomes that have been associated with mentoring.

## Benefits of mentoring for the protégé

*Career-related outcomes* Much research has been conducted into the proximal or short-term benefits resulting from mentoring, in particular the various career-related advancements and psychosocial support, which are common reported outcomes (e.g., Ragins and Cotton, 1999; Ragins and McFarlin, 1990). More distal benefits of mentoring for protégés have also been identified in the literature, including work, career, and relationship outcomes (Eby *et al.*, 2006).

The predominant focus of research has been on verifying career success of individuals who have experienced mentoring (Allen *et al.*, 2004, e.g., Collins and Scott, 1978; Kram, 1985; Roche, 1979; Zey, 1984), where career refers to all work-related experiences of the individual (e.g., Arnold, 1997; Greenhaus *et al.*, 2000) and career success to accomplishments in the individual's work-life. Stipulated career-related benefits in the literature include having enhanced exposure and visibility to powerful individuals in the organization (Bonzionelos, 2006; Bonzionelos and Wang, 2006) and receiving direct sponsorship and career guidance (Burke and McKeen, 1997; Kram, 1985; Noe, 1988; Scandura, 1992). Research supports, for example, that individuals who have received mentoring demonstrate better job performance, are promoted faster, earn higher salaries, and report greater job and career satisfaction than those who have not (Allen *et al.*, 2004; Chao, 1997; Dreher and Ash, 1990; Fagenson, 1989; Scandura, 1992; Whitely *et al.*, 1992).

Career-related accomplishments are categorized as *extrinsic* or *intrinsic* achievements (Heslin, 2005; Judge *et al.*, 1995; Van Maanen and Schein, 1977). It is important to consider both objective and subjective measures of career success because together these reflect the conventional conceptualization of success as having tangible meaning, and also the individual's more subjective feelings of success relative to their own expectations and goals (Greenhaus *et al.*, 1990; Judge and Bretz, 1994; Judge *et al.*, 1995; London and Stumpf, 1982; Seibert *et al.*, 1999; Turban and Dougherty, 1994).

*Extrinsic career success* Extrinsic achievements indicative of career success are accomplishments that are objectively verifiable against some external criteria, according to societal or organizational definitions of success or failure (Gattiker and Larwood, 1988; Jaskolka *et al.*, 1985). Research has been conducted demonstrating that mentoring is related to various criterions representative of extrinsic career success of protégés (Bonzionelos,

2006). These include: enhanced career advancement and more promotions achieved (e.g., Aryee *et al.*, 1996; Dreher and Ash, 1990; Scandura, 1992; Whitely, *et al.*, 1992), superior income levels (Dreher and Ash, 1990; Turban and Dougherty, 1994; Wallace, 2001), and faster progression through organizational levels (Koberg *et al.*, 1994), for protégés than non-mentored individuals. Johnson and Scandura's (1994) investigation into the influence of mentoring on female accountants' career success and salary, for instance, examined data from 833 males and females; mentoring was associated with a modest increase in the women's earnings.

Explanation for the enhanced performance against these extrinsic criteria has been likened to an *accelerated learning curve* (Torrance, 1984) through which mentored employees get ahead of others who are not receiving mentoring (Baker, 2001). Suggested key functions underpinning this accelerated learning include the knowledge and experience sharing components of the mentoring relationship (Allen *et al.*, 2004), as well as the numerous opportunities provided by mentors to protégés that would not otherwise be available to them (Collie, 1998), such as contacts and networking (Buhler, 1998). Buhler (1998) proposed that mentors aid protégés to set challenging, specific goals for their development, leading to tangible career success.

*Intrinsic career success* Where subjective, internal evaluations are made by individuals regarding their accomplishments these are termed intrinsic achievements (Gattiker and Larwood 1986, 1988; Poole *et al.*, 1993). The most commonly explored measure of intrinsic career success in the literature is that of career satisfaction; protégés self-report increased career satisfaction following mentorship (e.g., Burke, 1984; Dansky, 1996; Fagenson, 1989; Scandura, 1992). Exploration of the mentoring outcomes for a sample of skilled professional and managerial males and females working in a private hospital environment, for example, found protégés reported increased job satisfaction and decreased work alienation (Koberg *et al.*, 1994).

## Psychosocial outcomes

Kram (1985) identified mentoring to fulfill two functions: provision of career-related benefits and provision of psychosocial support. Psychosocial support relates to the interpersonal aspects of the mentoring relationship, "those aspects of a relationship that enhance an individual's sense of competence, identity, and effectiveness in a professional role" (Kram, 1985, p. 32). This refers to aspects of the mentoring relationship such as friendship, role modeling, emotional support, advice, and counseling (Bonzionelos, 2004; Burke and McKeen, 1997; Eby *et al.*, 2000; Kram, 1985; Noe, 1988; Tepper *et al.*, 1996). As a result of this socio-emotional function, protégés are thought to develop their self-confidence, self-esteem, and professional competence (Burke and McKeen, 1997; Kram, 1985).

Bandura's (1977) social learning theory stipulates that learning occurs through the process of modeling, and is linked to the psychosocial outcomes of mentoring (Allen *et al.*, 2004). Social learning occurs in mentoring through protégés modeling the behavior of their more experienced mentors (Manz and Sims, 1981) and learning the behavioral norms of the organization (Bolton, 1980; Dreher and Ash, 1990; Zagumny, 1993). Psychosocial support facilitates the development of the protégé's self-confidence, self-esteem and professional competence, which is fundamental for career success (Kram, 1985).

More recently, Allen *et al.* (2007) defined personal learning as an important outcome of mentoring relationships. Based on a model of career effectiveness defined by Hall (2002), they define personal learning as inclusive of short-term development of personal skills and relational skills, and long-term personal learning as changes in self-views, as well as the capacity to adapt to changing circumstances in the work environment. Their analysis of prior empirical and conceptual work on mentoring provided evidence to support the fact that personal learning outcomes are of equal importance to extrinsic career outcomes.

*Moderating variables*    A number of moderating variables are cited in the literature to affect the outcomes of mentoring relationships. A selection of these are explored briefly here.

First, the term mentoring has traditionally been applied to relationships evolving naturally and spontaneously between two parties, rather than formally arranged by the organization (Baugh and Fagenson-Eland, 2007; Eby, 1997; Higgins and Kram, 2001). Whilst formal mentoring programs can be introduced in the workplace, empirical research suggests these to have differential effects from informal mentoring relationships (e.g., Baugh and Fagenson-Eland, 2007; Fagenson-Eland *et al.*, 1997; Viator, 2001). Formal mentoring provides greater benefit than no mentoring (e.g., Chao *et al.*, 1992; Seibert *et al.*, 1999); however, the efficacy of these relationships is inferior to informal mentoring; protégés gain comparatively greater benefits and positive career outcomes from informal than formal mentoring relationships (Underhill, 2006, e.g., Allen *et al.*, 2005; Chao *et al.*, 1992; Ragins and Cotton, 1999; but see Ragins *et al.*, 2000).

Second, some mentoring literature reports differences in mentoring functions gained by protégés, dependent on the gender of the mentor (Day, 2001). In early research, Dreher and Cox (1996) reported that protégés who had had a male mentor attained higher income levels than those who had had a female mentor. Subsequent research has suggested a more complex interaction between genders of the protégé and mentor leading to differential outcomes. In Ragins and Cotton's (1999) study the pattern of a male protégé and female mentor was found to be associated with lower promotion rates for the protégé, and female protégé and female mentor was related to the lowest financial rewards. Unfortunately only small sample numbers were examined: male protégé–female mentor dyads (N = 23). More recent research into cross-gender and cross-race mentoring relationships indicate mixed empirical findings, highlighting the need for further exploration into how organizational and societal trends shape interpersonal dynamics in diverse mentoring pairs (Blake-Beard *et al.*, 2007; McKeen and Bujaki, 2007).

Third, many studies have failed to examine the characteristics and qualities of mentors in the dyadic relationship, assuming a general level of performance and experience to be offered (Day, 2001). A content analysis conducted on interview data with protégés speculated required characteristics for an ideal mentor: good listening and communication skills, patience, organization and industry-specific knowledge, honesty, and trustworthiness (Allen and Poteet, 1999). The extent to which these specific characteristics influence mentoring outcomes is not yet clear (Day, 2001). However, the proactivity of the mentor (Wanberg *et al.*, 2006), and perceived similarity (Lankau *et al.*, 2005; Wanberg *et al.*, 2006), congruence of cognitive style (Armstrong *et al.*, 2002) and learning goal orientation (Egan, 2005) between protégé and mentor have been linked to differential mentoring outcomes (Chandler *et al.*, 2011).

*Summary of protégé benefits*    A number of reviews of the mentoring literature have been conducted to thoroughly examine existent literature on protégé outcomes (Allen, 2007). The meta-analytic review by Allen *et al.* (2004) was one of the first attempts, exploring objective and subjective career outcomes following mentoring. This generally supports mentoring to lead to career outcomes such as improved compensation and career satisfaction. However, where outcomes were objectively measured, small effect sizes were observed. Underhill's (2006) further meta-analytic research only incorporated research designs where a comparison of career outcomes had been made between mentored and non-mentored individuals. Again, results indicated formal mentoring to enhance career outcomes for protégés. More recently, the meta-analysis by Eby *et al.* (2008) demonstrated a range of mentoring practices (e.g., academic mentoring, workplace mentoring) to have a positive influence on attitudinal, behavioral, and motivational career outcomes. A consistent finding from all studies included, however, was the relatively small effect sizes reported; academic and workplace mentoring effect sizes ranged from 0.11 to 0.36 and 0.03 to 0.19, respectively.

It has been argued that in practical terms, protégés gain more benefit from mentoring on their interpersonal relations (e.g., support), helping behaviors (e.g., organizational citizenship behavior) and situational satisfaction and attachment (e.g., job satisfaction, organizational commitment) than on objective career outcomes such as job performance (Chandler *et al.*, 2011; Eby *et al.*, 2008). This conclusion is drawn based on the relatively small effect sizes found in the literature, which indicates mentoring to only have a small predictive influence on objective career outcomes (e.g., salary), whilst other factors such as education and job tenure have substantial effects. These small effects have led researchers to consider the impact of multiple relationships on career-related outcomes. Higgins and Thomas (2001) found that the effects of a network of supportive relationships are greater than that of a single mentor. These developmental networks – a small set of developers who take an active interest in a focal person's development – have become the focus of contemporary mentoring research (Dobrow *et al.*, 2012; Higgins and Kram, 2001).

## Benefits of mentoring for the mentor

The theoretical perspective of mentoring as a mutually beneficial developmental relationship for both parties in the dyadic relationship is well documented in the literature (e.g., Hunt and Michael, 1983; Kram, 1988; Newby and Heide, 1992), with mentoring hypothesized to lead to growth, self-development and learning for the mentor as well as the protégé (Eby and Lockwood, 2005; Fletcher and Ragins, 2007; Ragins and Verbos, 2007). Until the past decade, however there has been relatively little systematic empirical research (e.g., Allen *et al.*, 1997; Ragins and Cotton, 1993; Ragins and Scandura, 1999) to support these claims (Baker, 2001; Bonzionelos, 2004), with investigation instead focused on exploring the impacts of mentoring for the protégé (Allen, 2007).

*Commonly cited mentoring outcomes for mentors*   There are many claims in the literature of mentoring leading to a variety of benefits for the mentor (Allen *et al.*, 1997; Kram, 1985; Levinson *et al.*, 1978). The substantive qualitative investigation by Allen *et al.* (1997) into perceived outcomes of mentoring for the mentor identified wide-ranging benefits, from subjective feelings of self-satisfaction to tangible gains such as enhanced visibility in the organization. Mentors commonly identify feelings of self-satisfaction, accomplishment and renewed meaning in their working lives, to result from mentoring others (Allen *et al.*, 1997; Clawson, 1980; Kram, 1983, 1985; Levinson *et al.*, 1978; Ragins and Scandura, 1999). In Eby and Lockwood's (2005) study, for instance, mentors reported a sense of personal gratification from providing mentorship. Qualitative literature in general, however, has focused on career-related developments.

Short and long-term objective career benefits have been hypothesized to result from mentoring for the mentor (Collins, 1994; Fletcher and Ragins, 2007; Ragins and Verbos, 2007; Zey, 1984). Mentoring can lead to enhanced job performance (Allen *et al.*, 1997), improved managerial and leadership skills (Eby and Lockwood, 2005; Nykodym *et al.*, 1995), higher levels of job satisfaction (Lentz and Allen, 2009) and updated technical expertise and knowledge (Mullen, 1994; Mullen and Noe, 1999; Newby and Heide, 1992). Mentoring can also provide mentors with an enhanced support network (Allen *et al.*, 1997; Kram, 1985; Mullen, 1994; Ragins and Scandura, 1999), which is beneficial for broadening their potential sources of information and advice (Adler and Kwon, 2002). Through mentoring, the mentor's visibility and base of power has been hypothesized to increase (Hunt and Michael, 1983; Kram, 1985), leading to organizational recognition for their contributions to developing future talent, such as increased promotions (Dreher and Ash, 1990). Various reports have also claimed that the mentoring relationship moderates the mentor's experienced negative feelings resulting from reaching job content plateaus (e.g., Chao, 1990; Elsass and Ralston, 1989; Kram, 1985; Slocum *et al.*, 1985).

Despite these many claims, limited empirical research has been conducted to investigate which, and to what extent, career-related outcomes attributed to mentoring truly result from the mentoring relationship (Eby *et al.*, 2006); research to quantify tangible career benefits such as promotion rates and salary increases is relatively new (Allen, 2007). Whilst most research supports a relationship between acting as a mentor and positive career-related outcomes, the degree to which the outcome is attributed solely to mentoring varies. Allen *et al.* (2006), for example, compared informal mentors with similar others who had no experience in mentoring. After controlling for confounding variables such as age, gender, race, and organizational tenure, they found that mentoring was predictive of current salary, promotion rate, and subjective career success. Bonzionelos (2004), comparably, examined the subjective and objective outcomes of mentoring for 176 mentors who were administrators in educational settings, from a range of managerial grades. Here mentoring was again found to be associated with increased promotions and enhanced career success, consistent with theoretical claims. In this study, however, whilst promotion rate was quantified by controlling for starting grades and job tenure, career success was measured through self-report only. Not all empirical investigation has supported theoretical assertions, for instance, the assumption that mentorship mitigates negative impacts of job plateauing and related constructs (e.g., job satisfaction, intention to leave the organization) was not supported by Lentz and Allen (2005); mentorship does not reduce the impacts of plateauing, although it may lead to less overall job content plateauing when compared with individuals with no experience of mentoring.

In order to further understanding of the impacts of mentoring for the mentor, Eby *et al.* (2006) explored the relationship between short and long-term outcomes of mentorship. Survey results from 218 individuals with mentoring experience supported short-term benefits (e.g., organizational recognition, loyal support base) to predict future work attitudes and intentions to mentor, but not career success (e.g., income level, promotion rate). Eby *et al.* highlighted the fundamental problem associated with attempting to quantify career success as resulting from mentorship; career success is determined by a combination of influences, including age, organizational level, and educational background.

*Moderating variables*   Reports in the literature have identified various factors that are predictive of the benefits reported by the mentor (Allen, 2007). Eby *et al.* (2005) explored mentoring benefits as proposed in Ragins and Scandura's (1999) dimensions of perceived mentor benefits. Results identified personality, motivational variables, and relational behaviors to be predictive of reported mentor benefits. Interestingly, of these variables the personalities of the mentor and protégé had the least influence on reported outcomes. Whilst research popularly indicates the formality of mentoring relationships to lead to differential outcomes for protégés (discussed above), two studies investigating the formality of the mentoring relationship as a potential moderating variable for outcomes for mentors found no evidence to support this (Allen and Eby, 2004; Fagenson-Eland, et al., 1997). Although the study by Fagenson-Eland et al. had limited statistical power due to the small sample sizes involved, these findings are suggestive of differences in moderating variables influencing the impact of mentoring on the protégé and the mentor (Allen, 2007).

*The flip-side: negative outcomes of mentoring relationships* Traditionally research has focused on identifying the positive outcomes of mentoring relationships. However, it has been argued that this presents a somewhat distorted picture of the relational experience (Duck, 1994); mentoring relationships can range from highly satisfying to highly dissatisfying for individuals involved (Allen, 2007). Some mentoring relationships may be, or may become, dysfunctional (Kram, 1985; Scandura, 1998) or inadequate to satisfy their purpose (e.g., Ragins, 2005; Ragins and Verbos, 2007; Ragins et al., 2000) and consequently protégés and mentors in such relationships do not benefit from the outcomes typically associated with mentoring (Bonzionelos, 2006). Interest in developing our understanding of negative outcomes and unhealthy experiences is therefore growing (Allen, 2007; Eby et al., 2000).

Scandura (1998) sought to explore protégés' various negative experiences from mentoring relationships in order to understand "dysfunctional mentoring relationships" (p. 449), or the *dark side*. A content analysis conducted on qualitative protégé self-report data regarding negative experiences found commonly reported experiences including unhealthy relationship dynamics, the mentor claiming undue credit and being deceptive, technically incompetent and self-absorbed. From these, broad themes were identified: match within the dyad, distancing behaviors, manipulative behaviors, level of mentor expertise, and general dysfunctionality. Whilst this taxonomy of negative mentoring experiences is consistent with theorized risks in mentoring relationships (based on psychological-social theory, e.g., Ferris et al., 1989; Kram, 1986; Levinson et al., 1978; Myers and Humphreys, 1985; Noe, 1988; Ragins, 1989; Ragins and Cotton, 1991), it has questionable generalizability as it was developed on a predominantly male sample attending two management development programs. Data collection additionally relied on retrospective, subjective assessments of the protégé's most negative past mentoring experiences.

Whilst traditionally the power differential between mentor and protégé has been conceptualized as a positive force for protégé development, it has also been suggested that this imbalance may be influential in the occurrence of negative mentoring outcomes, such as mentor over-delegation to protégés and credit-taking behaviors (Ragins, 1997; Ragins and Sundstrom, 1989). Similarly, although the close relationship between mentor and protégé has been typically linked to successful outcomes, the potential for overdependence on the part of the protégé, where protégés become too dependent to perform autonomously or are negatively affected if the mentor's reputation falls, has been highlighted (Day, 2001). Some negative mentoring outcomes have been reported in the literature specifically associated with cross-gender mentoring. These include over-protection and paternalism on the part of the mentor, as well as sexual tension between the two parties (Kram, 1985; Noe, 1988; Ragins, 1989; Ragins and Cotton, 1991).

Recent empirical research to examine the prevalence and impact of specific negative experiences has focused on commonly reported mentor behaviors such as credit-taking and sabotage, as well as poor relations within the dyad (e.g., Burk and Eby, 2010; Eby and McManus, 2004; Eby *et al.*, 2004, 2010; Ragins and Scandura, 1997). Findings have revealed negative mentoring experiences to be linked to lower career and psychosocial support from the mentor, diminished job satisfaction and increased reported intentions to leave the organization when compared with positive mentoring experiences (e.g., Eby and Allen, 2002; Eby *et al.*, 2004). Some evidence suggests that negative mentoring experiences have a moderating effect on mentoring outcomes; protégés' self-reported intentions to leave were influenced by the protégé's fear of retaliation from the mentor and perceived mentoring alternatives for the protégé (Burk and Eby, 2010). Eby *et al.* (2010) investigated the predictive validity of good and bad mentoring experiences on protégés and mentors mentoring outcomes. Whilst they found bad experiences to have greater predictive influence for protégés, findings were mixed with respect to mentors.

Literature pertaining to negative mentoring experiences for the mentor is even more limited than that relating to the protégé (Allen, 2007). It consists predominantly of qualitative reports. The qualitative research by Allen *et al.* (1997) reported several negative outcomes, the most commonly cited of which were the high demands made on the time of the mentor. In addition, mentors reported feeling that through provision of mentorship other co-workers may perceive preferential treatment of the protégé, some protégés had unrealistic expectations, and where mentorship was unsuccessful, mentors perceived personal failure. Other qualitative research suggests that "toxic" mentoring relationships can lead to feelings of reluctance to accept future mentorship opportunities (e.g., Feldman, 1999). A content analysis conducted by Eby and McManus (2004) on dysfunctional mentoring relationships from the mentors' perspective revealed themes in experiences, including: protégé unwillingness to learn, exploitation of the relationship, deception, sabotage, harassment, and egocentricity, as well as difficulties in building an interpersonal relationship.

## Benefits of Mentoring for the Organization

The benefits for protégés following mentoring have been hypothesized to subsequently producing tangible benefits for the organization (Baker, 2001; Law *et al.*, 2007; Zey, 1984). Mentoring is typically thought to enable the organization to unleash individuals' potential and talent, thereby facilitating the organization's success (Conway, 1995). A study commissioned recently in the United Kingdom sought to classify the benefits of mentoring, as cited in the literature (Garvey and Garrett-Harris, 2005). Research papers from the United States and Europe pertaining to all sectors (large, medium, and small organizations, in the public and private sector, inclusive of voluntary and not-for-profit businesses) were examined. From over 100 articles, 33 percent cited mentoring to benefit organizations. The authors rank ordered the outcomes cited. The most frequently cited were: enhanced staff retention, improved communication, higher staff morale and motivation, and superior business learning. The outcomes were classified into theorized job-performance benefits, such as enhanced perspective-taking, self-awareness, job satisfaction, loyalty, and opportunities, and business-performance benefits, which included improved staff retention, internal communication, motivation, and organizational learning. These categorizations reflect past research trends, whereby exploration into individual-level variables has revealed job-performance benefits leading to enhanced organizational effectiveness, and exploration into organization-level variables has identified direct business-performance benefits (Chandler *et al.*, 2011).

Some case studies and research articles are available to support these theorized benefits, such as evaluation by Singh *et al.* (2002) of the effects of mentoring relationships at Cambridgeshire County Council, a UK public sector organization, to conclude that mentoring led to positive organizational outcomes. There has generally been little research attention directed towards examining the organizational outcomes of mentoring, however, when compared with the interest aimed towards understanding benefits for individuals in the dyadic relationship (Chandler *et al.*, 2011; Garvey and Garrett-Harris, 2005).

Literature pertaining to individual-level variables will be discussed first, followed by organizational-level variables.

## Individual-level variables

### 1   Organizational attractiveness

Zey's (1988) early research into mentoring purported that mentoring was beneficial for organizations as it enabled them to project the company image of a caring organization, considerate to its workforce's well-being. The key competitive advantage of this was that the organization would attract better job applicants than a similar organization without this positive image, resulting in enhanced recruitment outcomes. Later researchers have echoed this view of enhanced organizational attractiveness (e.g., Allen and O'Brien, 2006; Conway, 1995; Horvath *et al.*, 2008).

### 2   Organizational satisfaction and commitment

A popularly suggested outcome from mentoring is that it will lead to increased organizational satisfaction for those involved (e.g., Burke, 1984; Chao *et al.*, 1992; Fagenson, 1989; Newby and Heide, 1992; Roche, 1979). Empirical evidence comparing the reports of protégés and non-mentored individuals to explore this relationship generally support the claim of greater organizational commitment (e.g., Donaldson *et al.*, 2000; Lankau and Scandura, 2002). Research focusing on the individual receiving mentoring report that protégés' self-reported loyalty to their organization is higher and they perceive organizational justice in the organization to be greater following mentoring (Scandura, 1997; Viator, 2001). A similar effect for mentors has been postulated (Bonzionelos, 2006), with some empirical support (Lentz and Allen, 2009). It has been argued that the act of being a mentor will lead individuals to have more positive attitudes towards their organization (Kram, 1985; Ragins, 1997).

## Organization-level variables

Chandler *et al.* (2011) have argued that to date, there has been little study of how mentoring impacts on organizational outcomes. Their review demonstrates how historically the focus of research has been largely focused on individual level outcomes.

Arguing for a multi-level examination of individual, dyadic, and contextual factors would allow for a more direct examination of the relationship between organizational mentoring and organizational consequences; productivity, for example, can be directly quantified and therefore no inference of organizational impact is necessary. The research conducted by Burke and McKeen (1997), however, did not identify mentoring as affecting work outcomes (such as intention to leave the job). They argued that conclusions regarding the direct impact of mentoring on organizational outcomes should be interpreted with caution, as it is highly likely that a wide range of other influences affect those outcomes also.

## 1   Improved employee efficiency, productivity, and creativity

The claims of enhanced employee efficiency; productivity, and creativity resulting from mentoring processes represent the most popularly cited organizational benefits (e.g., Scandura *et al.*, 1996; Zey, 1988). Some recent reports in the literature stand to support these assertions. Allen *et al.* (2009), for example, revealed the overall performance of abuse treatment agencies to be associated with the proportion of employees receiving mentoring; agencies where the proportion of mentored employees was higher demonstrated better performance.

Various theoretical explanations for the relationship between mentoring and employee efficiency, productivity, and creativity have been suggested. Scandura *et al.* (1996), for example, purported mentoring to foster an organizational culture of individual development, the aggregated whole of which results in superior organizational performance. Alternative explanations include: mentoring relationships provide protégés with reduced role ambiguity and enhanced career progression expectations, causing them to increase individual efforts at work (Kram, 1988; Zey, 1984), and mentoring leads to a heightened intensity of vertical and horizontal communication between individuals in the organization (Baker, 2001; Conway, 1995; Zey, 1988). Enhanced knowledge sharing encourages intellectual capital development and better inter-team working, which results in aggregated benefits for the organization (Allen *et al.*, 1997; Messmer, 1998; Scandura, 1998; Scandura *et al.*, 1996).

This idea of improved organizational communication is supported in mentor and protégé self-reports, such as the UK National Health Service doctor mentoring program, where doctors reported their development of better strategies to deal with specific problems at work to be a direct result of mentoring (Leadership Centre of the NHS and Department of Health, 2004). Others suggest that having a mentor improves integration of new employees (Conway, 1995; Zey, 1984). The protégé adopts organizational norms faster than non-mentored employees and so is socialized into the organization and its culture faster, leading to increased productivity (Buhler, 1998) and enhanced organizational citizenship behaviors (e.g., Le Pine *et al.*, 2002; Meyer *et al.*, 2002). This view of mentoring as enabling faster synergy between the new employee and the organization's culture and values has been reported by organizations. Additionally, future potential of protégés for roles of management or executive positions can be quickly and more accurately recognized as a result of mentoring. This means that training and exposure in the workplace can be tailored to maximize organizational and individual benefit (Buhler, 1998), and succession planning in the organization is improved (Conway, 1995), both contributing to improved organizational performance.

2    Enhanced employee retention

Turnover rates have been suggested as an objectively quantifiable measure of the influence of mentoring on the organization. However, the evidence to support this is lacking and arguably many other factors could influence this outcome. Aryee and Chay (1994) rationalized enhanced retention to result from protégés' improved organizational satisfaction and commitment (described above). This has been theorized to increase feelings of loyalty initially to the mentor, and later to the organization (Buhler, 1998). The idea of a psychological attachment to the organization being fostered through the mentoring relationship (Payne and Huffman, 2005) has been supported through research demonstrating protégés to be less likely to seek employment external to their organization (Scandura and Viator, 1994) and lower employee intentions to leave their organization among protégés than non-mentored individuals (Lankau and Scandura, 2002; Mathieu and Zajac, 1990) and mentors than individuals not involved in providing mentoring (Lentz and Allen, 2009).

## Critical Evaluation of the Literature

In its present state, there is a wealth of published and popularly cited research regarding the positive outcomes and experiences resulting from traditional mentoring relationships (Allen and Eby, 2007; Ragins and Kram, 2007). This research provides reassurance to the organizations and individuals embarking on committed relationships. However, various design and methodology criticisms have been levied at past research, challenging the quality and consistency of conclusions drawn.

Underhill's (2006) meta-analytical review explored the effectiveness of workplace mentoring. A search of scholarly databases for all articles published since 1983, pertaining to adult mentoring in corporate settings revealed 106 articles. Of these, 60 percent drew conclusions solely based on descriptive self-report survey results, 24 percent were theoretical perspectives or reviews of the topic of mentoring rather than research articles, 5 percent relied on interview data only and 5 percent presented longitudinal quasi-experiments involving either pre-test or post-test measures or post-test and non-equivalent control group measures. Whilst the importance of solid empirical research designs is well documented in the scientific literature (e.g., Grant *et al.*, 2010), Underhill reported that only 3 percent of the articles published had involved random allocation of participants to either a mentored or non-mentored condition. Furthermore, and most importantly, less than 22 percent involved comparison of mentored individuals with a non-mentored control group. The absence of a comparison group proves problematic for scientific inferences to be drawn regarding the influence of mentoring on career success.

The quality of research over the past few years has been improving (Allen, 2007); however, awareness of the issues below is crucial for informed practice.

### Common methods bias

Common methods bias (CMB) is concerned with the degree to which the observed correlations in the data are artificially inflated or deflated as a result of the measurement method or instruments employed (Doty and Glick, 1998; Meade *et al.*, 2007). The potential risk of CMB is particularly recognized where a single method (e.g., self-report survey) is used to assess correlations between variables (Meade *et al.*, 2007). This, particularly overreliance on descriptive self-report surveys, is well documented in the literature, (Bonzionelos, 2006; Bonzionelos and Wang, 2006; Underhill, 2006). Attempts to quantify the impact of CMB in organizational research generally (e.g., Doty and Glick, 1998; Meade *et al.*, 2007) conclude that whilst CMB does exist in organizational research, the magnitude is typically small to moderate and thus the potential for CMB to invalidate study conclusions is small. Where possible, however, multi-method research is recommended (Podsakoff *et al.*, 2003).

## Problems intrinsic to self-report measures

There are three critical issues pertaining to self-report measures:

### 1   Lack of objective measurement

Most self-report surveys claiming mentoring to lead to career success have relied exclusively on the perceptions of the mentored individuals to draw conclusions (Underhill, 2006). Consequently, it is difficult to ascertain accuracy of self-reported developments for all individuals. The absence of independent manipulation of variables in self-report approaches means it not possible to refute the possibility that any changes in performance or career-related outcomes resulted from some other influence (Singleton and Straits, 1999). A small number of studies comparing survey responses of mentored and non-mentored individuals are now allowing stronger inferences to be made (Underhill, 2006).

### 2   Percept-percept inflation

Self-report measures may lead to percept-percept inflation: artificial increases in the size of correlations between variables, which can result in falsely concluding relationships to exist between variables where there are none. Crampton and Wagner's (1994) analysis of 42,934 correlations from published articles, however, indicated that artificially inflated correlations were no more likely to be a result of self-report measures than artificially deflated correlations, suggesting that this risk has been widely overstated. Arguably, some constructs of relevance in evaluating the efficacy of mentoring are best measured through self-report (e.g., job and career satisfaction), therefore in the context of mentoring research, multiple methodologies for data collection should be used where possible (Sronce and McKinley, 2006).

### 3   Response bias

Response bias pertains to the representativeness of results obtained. Underhill (2006) reported survey response rates of 22 percent to 75 percent, with a mean response rate of 46 percent. This potentially represents a self-selection bias, whereby one group chose to respond and the other did not, and thus might be lead to challenges regarding sample representativeness and generalizability of results.

## Problems intrinsic to cross-sectional designs

Cross-sectional designs (i.e., correlational designs) suffer from the problem of causality (Chandler *et al.*, 2011; Underhill, 2006); similarly to the conundrum of the chicken and the egg, cross-sectional research can only confirm that there is a relationship between the two groups. Cause and effect can only be resolved through experimental research designs in which the variable of interest (i.e., mentoring) is manipulated. In order to develop a thorough understanding of the benefits of mentoring longitudinal designs are required (e.g., Chao, 1997).

## Scope limitations

Due to the nature of mentoring, much research conducted and published on the outcomes of mentoring has originated from a specific organizational context, industry or group (e.g., professionals, technical specialists). Mentoring experiences, career-related outcomes and socio-emotional effects, however, are influenced by factors external to the mentoring relationship. The structural characteristics of the organization may be one influential factor (Bonzionelos, 2006); commercial organizations with flatter organizational structures and results-orientated cultures may be more supportive to the development of mentoring relationships in the workplace than the public sector. Whilst this as yet remains unexplored in the literature (Allen, 2007) qualitative research indicates that the degree of organizational support to create conditions conducive to mentoring affects mentoring processes (Allen *et al.*, 1997; Billet, 2003). As extrapolation from individual research based on specific mentoring relationships in certain contexts to present a comprehensive account of mentoring benefits is difficult; research should focus on the organizational context in which the mentoring has occurred (Chandler *et al.*, 2011) and the influences of organizational culture and structure ought to be considered during program evaluation (Allen, 2007; Noe *et al.*, 2002).

# Advantages of Variations on Traditional Mentoring

This chapter has focused largely on literature pertaining to outcomes resulting from traditional mentoring relationships. There is variation in how mentoring is conceptualized, however, and therefore differences in the impact that the relationship may have for the individuals and organization concerned (Haggard *et al.*, 2011). Research exploring the impacts of group mentoring, for example, has reported that protégés are more confident, poised, and articulate when dealing with customers and peers following mentoring (Collie, 1998). Research evidence relating to the benefits of peer mentoring and developmental networks is discussed in this section.

## Peer mentoring

Peer mentoring refers to a one-on-one relationship between two employees working at a similar level, where a more experienced employee provides encouragement and support to, and shares their knowledge and skills with, a less experienced employee (Eby, 1997; Kram, 1985). The prevalence of peer mentoring has increased over recent years due to downsizing and changes in organizational structures, resulting in flatter hierarchies with fewer senior managers available to provide traditional mentoring support. Consequently, new employees to the organization may turn to team members who work at a similar level for mentoring (Eby, 1997; Russell and McManus, 2007).

Peer mentoring is thought to result in benefits for the individual, distinct from those associated with traditional mentoring (Allen *et al.*, 1997; Eby, 1997; Ensher *et al.*, 2001). Whilst peer mentors are hypothesized to provide protégés with comparable career-related functions and socio-emotional support as in traditional mentoring relationships (Ensher *et al.*, 2001; Kram and Isabella, 1985), it has also been argued that peer mentoring plays a key role in the social integration of new employees (Allen *et al.*, 1999; Kram, 1985) and also in sharing of valuable information, such as technical or job-related knowledge, that is critical for individual and organizational success (Bryant, 2005; Eby, 1997). Kram and Isabella (1985) provided theoretical explanation for this benefit, suggesting that open communication, collaboration, and mutual support may be easier in a peer-mentoring relationship than a traditional one, due to the absence of hierarchical constraints or influences limiting mentorship outcomes. Indeed, organizations are beginning to establish peer-mentoring programs for the purpose of mutual learning and support (DeLong *et al.*, 2008; Parker *et al.*, 2008).

## Developmental networks

In contrast to traditional mentoring, involving a dyadic relationship between the protégé and the mentor, it has long been hypothesized that an individual's development relies on the support and learning gained from a network of interpersonal relationships (Neugarten, 1975). This was consistent with claims in social psychology that individuals develop their self-concept through a cluster of key relationships (Kram and Isabella, 1985). Kram (1985) proposed that individuals benefit from having a *constellation* of relationships, whilst research into multiple mentors endorsed the idea that having more than one advisor brought enhanced benefits for the individual (Baugh and Scandura, 1999; Crocitto *et al.*, 2005; De Janasz and Sullivan, 2004; De Janesz *et al.*, 2003). Higgins and Kram (2001) suggested that mentoring be considered from the perspective of providing a social network, coining the term *developmental networks* (e.g., Blickle *et al.*, 2009; Cotton *et al.*, 2011; Higgins *et al.*, 2010). Developmental networks re-conceptualize mentoring as a multiple relationship experience involving a portfolio of advisors, rather than the traditional single relationship (Higgins and Kram, 2001). Similarly to the postulated role of peer mentoring in the modern organization, the importance of network resources is evident when considering that organizations increasingly have flattened hierarchies, high levels of work pressure, and low incentives to provide mentorship, all leading to a lack of willing managers and supervisors to act as mentors (Allen, 2003). Colleagues and peers, however, are generally widely available to provide advice and support to focal individuals (De Janasz and Sullivan, 2004). Evidence from educational literature supports this rationale, where the traditional system of having a primary mentor is being replaced by the concept of having a portfolio of mentors to facilitate individuals' development (Baugh and Scandura, 1999; Bonzionelos, 2006; Higgins and Kram, 2001).

Developmental network relationships, which vary in quantity and intensity, may provide the individual with benefits that fall into two broad categories: *instrumental* and *expressive* (Bonzionelos, 2003; Fombrun, 1982). Instrumental functions are those that relate to career advancement of the individual (Adler and Kwon, 2002; Bonzionelos, 2003; Seibert *et al.*, 2001), whilst expressive functions pertain to socio-emotional support resulting from the interpersonal relationships (Eby, 1997; Fombrun, 1982; Kram and Isabella, 1985). Examples of these may include increased information sharing and development of friendships (Ibarra, 1993; Krackhardt, 1992), more optimism (Higgins *et al.*, 2010), and improved career self-efficacy (Higgins *et al.*, 2008).

Compared with the wealth of research available linking the impact of mentoring to career success, the empirical literature exploring the association between network resources and career success is less extensive (Bonzionelos and Wang, 2006). There is growing evidence, however, that network resources do provide instrumental functions (Chandler *et al.*, 2011). Bonzionelos (2006), for example, investigated the relationship with 104 Hellenes bank employees, reporting that having multiple mentors was associated with increased extrinsic career success. Recent research into the significance of network size also suggests support for developmental networks, whereby larger networks are associated with extraordinary career achievement (Cotton *et al.*, 2011), increased work satisfaction (Higgins, 2000), and superior intrinsic career success (Van Emmerik, 2004). Correspondingly, a meta-analysis of factors predicting career success (Ng *et al.*, 2005) found that performance on measures of extrinsic and intrinsic career success was moderated by the individual's self-reported number of acquaintances within their organization. Higgins (2007) has suggested, however, that individuals should develop networks according to their specific developmental needs rather than assuming quantity to be of sole importance. This is supported by literature highlighting that where individuals have networks with more senior-level contacts, they benefit from enhanced positive outcomes such as career opportunities for advancement (Higgins and Thomas, 2001) and higher career satisfaction (Seibert *et al.*, 2001).

An expanding area of investigation is examination of the unique contributions that developmental networks bring, beyond those typically associated with traditional mentoring relationships (Singh *et al.*, 2009a). Research to date is mixed regarding the relative influence of network resources and dyadic mentoring relationships on career outcomes (Chandler *et al.*, 2011; Dobrow *et al.*, 2012). Bonzionelos' (2003) research in British public sector organizations found that network resources provided individuals with enhanced extrinsic and intrinsic career success, incremental to the benefits resulting from traditional mentoring relationships. Other research, however, reported mentoring to have incremental predictive validity for individual promotion and expectations of career advancement, beyond the influence of developmental networks (Singh *et al.*, 2009b).

Similarly to traditional mentoring research, a limited amount of literature has begun to understand the negative outcomes that may be associated with developmental networks (Dobrow, *et al.*, 2012). Dobrow and Higgins (2005), for instance, found that an individual's professional identity might be negatively affected due to having an increasingly complex network. Another study reported that individuals who maintained relationships with contacts from their elite graduate institution had heightened negative perceptions of their own career success because they were continually making comparisons between themselves and other successful people (Higgins *et al.*, 2008). As with traditional mentoring, it is important to understand both positive and negative outcomes of developmental networks in order to appreciate the functioning of the phenomenon.

## Suggestions for Future Research

The field of mentoring research is still developing. A review of the literature highlights several pertinent areas to be addressed in future studies. Four of these will be discussed below.

### Investigate other important outcomes

Much investigative focus has been on the impact of mentoring, particularly with respect to subjective, and more recently objective, career outcomes (Allen, 2007). It is argued, and supported in the literature (e.g., Bonzionelos, 2006), that other important outcomes have been largely neglected. Rather than simply focusing on factors that may be immediately relevant to the career experience, such as income level or promotion rate (Dreher and Ash, 1990), an evolutionary perspective suggests that researchers should also explore the broader impacts of mentoring. This could include the effects of mentoring on reported career satisfaction and career commitment (Aryee and Chay, 1994; Day and Allen, 2003), but also on protégé's and mentor's personal learning (Lankau and Scandura, 2002, 2007), or degree of work-family conflict (Nielson *et al.*, 2001). Recently, for instance, researchers found that informal mentoring provided a buffer from negative personal and work-related attitudes (Ragins *et al.*, 2010).

The impact of mentoring on psychological well-being is one area that could be explored (Bonzionelos, 2006). Due to the changing nature of work and the increase in service-sector jobs, employees are expected to regularly engage in emotional labor (Ashforth and Humphrey, 1993; Hochschild, 1983; Zapf, 2002) and so are being put under increasing emotional strain (Brotheridge and Grandey, 2002). It has been hypothesized that this is a likely contributor to emotional exhaustion (Grandey, 2003; Zapf *et al.*, 2001), which itself contributes to job burnout (Maslach *et al.*, 2001). One function of mentoring, however, is socio-emotional support (Kram, 1985); it is therefore hypothesized that through mentoring protégés may be provided with a means to express their emotions and build self-confidence, as well as learning how to handle customer demands whilst minimizing the impact of this on their emotional well-being (Bonzionelos, 2006). The associations between job burnout and receiving mentoring could be a related area for investigation. Although less researched when compared with emotional exhaustion (Zapf, 2002), this is a factor of high interest for employees and organizations as it may negatively impact on job performance through the effects of depersonalization or reduced personal accomplishment (Judge and Bono, 2001; Schaufeli and Enzmann, 1998). Bonzionelos (2006) hypothesized, for example, that performance feedback and role modeling in mentoring relationships may be effective in enhancing feelings of personal accomplishment and self-worth.

## Investigate alternatives to traditional mentoring

Given the recognition of alternatives to the traditional hierarchical dyadic relationship, it seems important to investigate a range of relationships that occur in dyads and groups or circles. Peer mentoring (Russell and McManus, 2007) and peer coaching (Parker *et al.*, 2008) are already recognized as developmental alternatives, which are increasingly encouraged in organizational settings. In addition, some are experimenting with mentoring circles and group mentoring, both of which rely on a group of peers, the latter often with the presence of a senior mentor, for the primary purpose of supporting the personal and professional development of its members. Thus, developmental networks, comprised of multiple developers who may be senior, junior, or peers of the focal person, as well as group structures dedicated to the learning of individual members, and relational dyads of various kinds provide distinctive functions, benefits, and perhaps unintended consequences, that should be further delineated.

Most recently, there are some who are recognizing the potential value of reverse mentoring, where the junior party serves as a mentor to a senior colleague who lacks expertise that younger adults have already mastered (Meister and Williyerd, 2010). More generally, scholars of relational mentoring (Fletcher and Ragins, 2007; Ragins and Verbos, 2007), as well as high quality connections (Dutton and Heaphy, 2003), are pointing out core relationship characteristics including mutuality, trust, reciprocity, and adaptability, that are required for maximum benefits of growth-enhancing relationship to both individuals and organizations.

## Develop understanding of moderating factors

Early research on the benefits of mentoring assumed a simple relationship between the mentoring relationship and the outcomes of interest, such as career progression and promotion, salary level, and job satisfaction (e.g., Burke, 1984; Fagenson, 1989; Noe, 1988). A review of the literature suggests, however, that the benefits of mentoring may be more limited than claimed in those early reports, as those outcomes are typically determined by a combination of the mentoring and other unquantified personal and situational (e.g., environmental) variables (Burke and McKeen, 1997; Underhill, 2006). It is argued that the current literature fails to provide a thorough understanding of the various mediating factors for the efficacy of mentoring relationships; however, future investigation in this vein is important to inform design of future mentoring initiatives (Chandler *et al.*, 2011).

## Research cultural differences in mentoring efficacy

Most mentoring research to date investigating the impacts of mentoring relationships has been conducted in the United States and other Western economies sharing similar cultural roots (i.e., Anglo-Saxon cultures; see Hofstede, 2001). There has been a significant lack of research conducted in other cultural contexts (Bonzionelos, 2006). This is important because conclusions are drawn regarding the effects of mentoring on protégés' and mentors' career-related outcomes; however, empirical evidence shows human capital factors (e.g., educational level), demographic variables and structural, environmental characteristics (e.g., geographic area, type of industry) to affect performance on measures of career success (Bonzionelos, 2004).

Bonzionelos' (2006) investigation as to the efficacy of mentoring for a Greek sample, for example, found that although mentoring was related to measures of extrinsic career success (as found for Anglo-Saxon populations), there was no association in the Hellenic sample between mentoring received and measures of intrinsic career success. In contrast, investigative research involving a Chinese sample of protégés reported converse findings (Bonzionelos and Wang, 2006); mentoring received was related to measures of intrinsic career success but not extrinsic career success. Similarly, in a study of expatriates working in China and Singapore, Shen (2010) found additional mentoring functions provided in their developmental networks not previously reported. She argued that these are related to the cross-cultural experiences that expatriates navigate. These studies clearly support that national cultural characteristics may affect the benefits of mentoring for protégés and therefore conclusions drawn from accumulated knowledge regarding Anglo-Saxon populations are not necessarily directly transferrable to individuals in other cultures.

Research exploring the experiences and outcomes of mentoring for a broader range of cultures, and among expatriates, particularly those that differ substantially from the Anglo-Saxon culture, is needed to further knowledge in the field.

## Conclusion

This chapter has reviewed the mentoring literature pertaining to the efficacy of mentoring. Theorized outcomes of mentoring for the individual were explored and empirical evidence to support these was evaluated. There is growing evidence to support career-related and socio-emotional benefits of mentoring for the protégé and the mentor. There are also, however, negative aspects to mentoring relationships for both parties in the dyadic relationship, which require further investigation to be fully understood. Whilst originally mentoring was thought to provide sole benefit to the protégé, researchers have demonstrated benefits to mentors, and have hypothesized benefits for the organization as well. These are somewhat supported in the literature. Benefits include individual-level variables such as organizational commitment and organization-level variables such as employee productivity and retention. Problems and difficulties with the mentoring literature were discussed. Outcomes and impacts of alternative forms of mentoring were explored, in particular the efficacy of peer mentoring and developmental networks. Recent literature suggests these to have some incremental benefits over traditional mentoring. These are pertinent avenues to be explored, particularly considering the changes in contemporary organizational contexts. Further future directions for research were proposed; a broader range of mentoring outcomes should be explored and the factors moderating these associations, particularly cultural influences, need to be better understood in order to inform future mentoring initiatives.

# References

Adler, P.S. and Kwon, S. (2002) Social capital: Prospects for a new concept. *Academy of Management Review*, 27, 17–40.

Allen, T.D. (2003) Mentoring others: A dispositional and motivational approach. *Journal of Vocational Behaviour*, 62, 134–54.

Allen, T.D. (2007) Mentoring relationships from the perspective of the mentor. In: B.R. Ragins and K.E. Kram (eds) *The Handbook of Mentoring at Work: Theory, Research, and Practice*. Thousand Oaks, CA: Sage. pp. 123–48.

Allen, T.D., Day, R., and Lentz, E. (2005) The role of interpersonal comfort in mentoring relationships. *Journal of Career Development*, 31, 155–69.

Allen, T.D. and Eby, L.T. (2004) Factors related to mentor reports of mentoring functions provided: Gender and relational characteristics. *Sex Roles*, 50, 129–39.

Allen, T.D. and Eby, L.T. (2007) *Blackwell Handbook of Mentoring: A Multiple Perspectives Approach*. London: Blackwell.

Allen, T.D., Eby, L.T., Poteet, M.L., Lentz, E., and Lima, L. (2004) Career benefits associated with mentoring for protégés: A meta-analysis. *Journal of Applied Psychology*, 89(1), 127–36.

Allen, T.D., Eby, L.T., Scandura, T.A., and Pellegrini, E.K. (2007) Workplace mentoring: Theoretical approaches and methodological issues. In: T.D. Allen and L.T. Eby (eds) *The Blackwell Handbook of Mentoring: A Multiple Perspectives Approach*. Oxford, UK: Blackwell Publishing Ltd.

Allen, T.D., Lentz, E., and Day, R. (2006) Career success outcomes associated with mentoring others: A comparison of mentors and nonmentors. *Journal of Career Development*, 32, 272–85.

Allen, T.D., McManus, S.E., and Russell, J.E.A. (1999) Newcomer socialization and stress: Formal peer relationships as a source of support. *Journal of Vocational Behavior*, 54, 453–70.

Allen, T.D. and O'Brien, K. (2006) Formal mentoring programs and organizational attraction. *Human Resource Development Quarterly*, 17, 43–58.

Allen, T.D. and Poteet, M.L. (1999) Developing effective mentoring relationships: Strategies from the mentor's viewpoint. *Career Development Quarterly*, 48, 59–73.

Allen, T.D., Poteet, M.L., and Burroughs, S.M. (1997) The mentor's perspective: A qualitative inquiry and future research agenda. *Journal of Vocational Behavior*, 51, 70–89.

Allen, T.D., Poteet, M.L., Russell, J.E.A., and Dobbins, G.H. (1997) A field study of factors related to supervisors' willingness to mentor others. *Journal of Organizational Behavior*, 50, 1–22.

Allen, T.D., Russell, J.E.A., and Maetzke, S.B. (1997) Formal peer mentoring: Factors related to protégés satisfaction and willingness to mentor others. *Group and Organization Management*, 22, 488–507.

Allen, T.D., Smith, M.A., Mael, F.A., O'Shea, G., and Eby, L.T. (2009) Organizational-level mentoring and organizational performance within substance abuse centres. *Journal of Management*, 35(5), 1113–28.

Armstrong, S.J., Allinson, C.W., and Hayes, J. (2002) Formal mentoring systems: An examination of the effects of mentor/protégé cognitive styles on the mentoring process. *Journal of Management Studies*, 39, 1111–38.

Arnold, J. (1997) *Managing Careers into the 21st Century*. London: Chapman.

Aryee, S. and Chay, Y.W. (1994) An examination of the impact of career-oriented mentoring on work commitment attitudes and career satisfaction among professional and managerial employees. *British Journal of Management*, 5, 241–49.

Aryee, S., Wyatt, T., and Stone, R. (1996) Early career outcomes of graduate employees: The effect of mentoring and ingratiation. *Journal of Management Studies*, 33, 95–118.

Ashforth, B.E. and Humphrey, R.H. (1993) Emotional labor in service roles: The influence of identity. *Academy of Management Review*, 18, 88–105.

Atkinson, W. (2002) Mentoring programs pick up where training leaves off. *Purchasing*, 131(2), 18–19.

Baker, B.T. (2001) *Mentoring Experiences Among Midshipmen at the United States Naval Academy* (Thesis, Naval Postgraduate School, Monterey, California). Retrieved from http://www.dtic.mil/cgi-bin/GetTRDoc?AD=ADA387834andLocation=U2anddoc =GetTRDoc.pdf.

Bandura, A.L. (1977) *Social Learning Theory*. Englewood Cliffs, NJ: Prentice Hall.

Baugh, S.G. and Fagenson-Eland, E.A. (2007) Formal mentoring programs: A "poor cousin" to informal relationships? In: B.R. Ragins and K.E. Kram (eds) *The Handbook of Mentoring at Work: Theory, Research, and Practice*. Thousand Oaks, CA: Sage. pp. 249–71.

Baugh, S.G. and Scandura, T.A. (2000) The effect of multiple mentors on protégé attitudes toward the work setting. *Journal of Social Behavior and Personality*, 14(2), 503–21.

Billett, S. (2003) Workplace mentors: Demands and benefits. *Journal of Workplace Learning*, 15(3), 105–13.

Blake-Beard, S.D., Murrell, A., and Thomas, D. (2007) Unfinished business: The impact of race on understanding mentoring relationships. In: B.R. Ragins and K.E. Kram (eds) *The Handbook of Mentoring at Work: Theory, Research, and Practice*. Thousand Oaks, CA: Sage. pp. 223–48.

Blickle, G., Witzki, A.H., and Schneider, P.B. (2009) Mentoring support and power: A three-year predictive field study on protégé networking and career success. *Journal of Vocational Behavior*, 74, 181–9.

Bolton, E.B. (1980) A conceptual analysis of the mentor relationship in career development of women. *Adult Education*, 30, 195–207.

Bozionelos, N. (2003) Intra-organizational network resources: Relation to career success and personality. *International Journal of Organizational Analysis*, 11, 41–66.

Bozionelos, N. (2004) Mentoring provided: Relation to mentor's career success, personality, and mentoring received. *Journal of Vocational Behavior*, 64(1), 24–46.

Bozionelos, N. (2006) Mentoring and expressive network resources: Their relationship with career success and emotional exhaustion among Hellenes employees involved in emotion work. *International Journal of Human Resource Management*, 17(2), 362–78.

Bozionelos, N. and Wang, L. (2006) The relationship of mentoring and network resources with career success in the Chinese organizational environment. *International Journal of Human Resource Management*, 17(9), 1531–46.

Brotheridge, C. and Grandey, A. (2002) Emotional labor and burnout: Comparing two perspectives of "people work". *Journal of Vocational Behavior*, 60, 17–39.

Bryant, S.E. (2005) The impact of peer mentoring on organizational knowledge creation and sharing: An empirical study in a software firm. *Group Organization Management*, 30(3), 319–38.

Buhler, P.A. (1998) A new role for managers: The move from directing to coaching: Managing in the 90s. *Supervision*, 59(10), 16.

Burk, H.G. and Eby, L.T. (2010) What keeps people in mentoring relationships when bad things happen? A field study from the protégé's perspective. *Journal of Vocational Behavior*, 77(3), 437–46.

Burke, R.J. (1984) Mentors in organizations. *Group and Organization Studies*, 9, 253–72.

Burke, R.J. and McKeen, C.A. (1997) Benefits of mentoring relationships amongst managerial and professional women: A cautionary tale. *Journal of Vocational Behavior*, 51, 43–57.

Chandler, D.E., Kram, K.E., and Yip, J. (forthcoming) Mentoring at work: New questions, methodologies, and theoretical perspectives. In: J.P. Walsh, and A. Brief (eds) *Academy of Management Annals*.

Chao, G.T. (1990) Exploration of the conceptualization and measurement of career plateau: A comparative analysis. *Journal of Management*, 16, 181–93.

Chao, G.T. (1997) Mentoring phases and outcomes. *Journal of Vocational Behavior*, 51, 15–28.

Chao, G.T., Walz, P.M., and Gardner, P.D. (1992) Formal and informal mentorships: A comparison on mentoring functions and contrast with non-mentored counterparts. *Personnel Psychology*, 45, 619–36.

Clawson, J. (1980) Mentoring in managerial careers. In: C.B. Derr (ed.) *Work, Family, and the Career*. New York: Praeger. pp. 144–65.

Collie, S.V. (1998). Moving up through mentoring. *Workforce*, 77(3), 35.

Collins, E.G., and Scott, P. (1978) Everyone who makes it has a mentor. *Harvard Business Review*, 56(4), 89–101.

Collins, P.M. (1994) Does mentorship among social worker make a difference? An empirical investigation of career outcomes, *National Association of Social Workers*, 413–19.

Conway, C. (1995) Mentoring in the mainstream. *Management Development Review*, 8(4), 27–9.

Cotton, R.D., Shen, Y., and Livne-Tarandach, R. (2011) On becoming extraordinary: The content and structure of the developmental networks of major league Baseball Hall of Famers. *Academy of Management Journal*, 54(1).

Crampton, S.M. and Wagner, J.A. (1994) Percept percept inflation in micro-organizational research: An investigation of prevalence and effect. *Journal of Applied Psychology*, 79, 67–76.

Crocitto, M., Sullivan, S.E., and Carraher, S.M. (2005) Global mentoring as a means of career development and knowledge creation: a learning based framework and agenda for future research. *Career Development International*, 10, 6–7.

Dansky, K.H. (1996) The effect of group mentoring on career outcomes. *Group and Organization Management*, 21, 5–21.

Day, D.V. (2001) Leadership development: A review in context. *Leadership Quarterly*, 11(4), 581–613.

Day, R. and Allen, T.D. (2004) The relationship between career motivation and self-efficacy with protégé career success. *Journal of Vocational Behavior*, 64, 72–91.

De Janesz, S.C. and Sullivan, S.E. (2004) Multiple mentors in academe: Developing a professorial network. *Journal of Vocational Behavior*, 64(2), 263–83.

De Janesz, S.C., Sullivan, S.E., and Whiting, V.R. (2003) Mentor networks and career success: Lessons for turbulent times. *Academy of Management Executive*, 17(4), 78–91.

De Long, T.J., Gabarro, J.J., and Lees, R.J. (2008) Why mentoring matters in a hypercompetitive world. *Harvard Business Review*, 86(1), 115–21.

Dobrow, S.R. and Higgins, M.C. (2005) Developmental networks and professional identity: A longitudinal study. *Career Development International*, 10(6/7), 567–83.

Dobrow, S.R., Chandler, D., Murphy, W., and Kram, K.E. (2012) A review of developmental networks: Incorporating a mutuality perspective, *Journal of Organization and Management*, 38(1), 210–42.

Donaldson, S.I., Ensher, E.A., and Grant-Vallone, E.J. (2000) Longitudinal examination of mentoring relationships on organizational commitment and citizenship behavior. *Journal of Career Development*, 26, 233–49.

Doty, D.H. and Glick, W.H. (1998) Common methods bias: Does common methods variance really bias results? *Organizational Research Methods*, 1, 374–406.

Dreher, G.F. and Ash, R.A. (1990) A comparative study of mentoring among men and women in managerial, professional, and technical positions. *Journal of Applied Psychology*, 75, 525–35.

Dreher, G.F. and Cox, T.H., Jr. (1996) Race, gender, and opportunity: A study of compensation attainment and the establishment of mentoring relationships. *Journal of Applied Psychology*, 81, 297–308.

Duck, S. (1994) Stratagems, spoils, and a serpent's tooth: On the delights and dilemmas of personal relationships. In: W.R. Cupach and B.H. Spitzberg (eds) *The Dark Side of Interpersonal Communication*. Hillsdale, NJ: Erlbaum. pp. 3–24.

Dutton, J.E. and Heaphy, E.D. (2003) The power of high-quality connections. In: K.S. Cameron, J.E. Dutton and R.E. Quinn (eds) *Positive Organizational Scholarship*. San Francisco: Berret-Koehler. pp. 263–78.

Eby, L.T. (1997) Alternative forms of mentoring in changing organizational environments: A conceptual extension of the mentoring literature. *Journal of Vocational Behavior*, 51(1), 125–44.

Eby, L.T. and Allen, T.D. (2002) Further investigation of protégés' negative mentoring experiences: Patterns and outcomes. *Group and Organization Management*, 27, 456–79.

Eby, L.T. and Lockwood, A. (2005) Protégés' and mentors' reactions to participating in formal mentoring programs: A qualitative investigation. *Journal of Vocational Behavior*, 67, 441–58.

Eby, L.T. and McManus, S.E. (2004) The protégé's role in negative mentoring experiences. *Journal of Vocational Behavior*, 65, 255–75.

Eby, L.T., Allen, T.D., Evans, S.C., Ng, T., and DuBois, D.L. (2008) Does mentoring matter? A multidisciplinary meta-analysis comparing mentored and non-mentored individuals. *Journal of Vocational Behavior*, 72(2), 254–67.

Eby, L.T., Butts, M., Durley, J., and Ragins, B. (2010) Are bad experiences stronger than good ones in mentoring relationships? *Journal of Vocational Behavior*, 77, 81–92.

Eby, L.T., Butts, M., Lockwood, A., and Simon, S.A. (2004) Protégés' negative mentoring experiences: Construct development and nomological validation. *Personnel Psychology*, 57, 411–47.

Eby, L.T., Durley, J.R., Evans, S.C., and Ragins, B.R. (2006) The relationship between short-term mentoring benefits and long-term mentor outcomes. *Journal of Vocational Behavior*, 69, 424–44.

Eby, L.T., Durley, J., Evans, S.C., and Shockley, K. (2005). *What Predicts the Benefits of Mentoring for Mentors?* Paper presented at the 20th Annual Conference of the Society for Industrial and Organizational Psychology, Los Angeles, CA (April).

Eby, L.T., McManus, S.E., Simon, S.A., and Russell, J.E.A. (2000) The protégé's perspective regarding negative mentoring experiences: The development of a taxonomy. *Journal of Vocational Behavior*, 57, 1–21.

Eby, L.T., Rhodes, J.E., and Allen, T.D. (2008) Definition and evolution of mentoring. In: T.D. Allen and L.T. Eby (eds) *The Blackwell Handbook of Mentoring: A Multiple Perspectives Approach*. Oxford, UK: Blackwell Publishing Ltd.

Egan, T.M. (2005) The impact of learning goal orientation similarity on formal mentoring relationship outcomes. *Advances in Developing Human Resources*, 7(4), 489–504.

Elsass, P.M. and Ralston, D.A. (1989) Individual responses to the stress of career plateauing. *Journal of Management*, 15, 35–47.

Ensher, E.A., Thomas, C., and Murphy, S.E. (2001) Comparison of traditional, step-ahead, and peer mentoring on protégés' support, satisfaction and perceptions of career success: A social exchange perspective. *Journal of Business and Psychology*, 15, 415–38.

Fagenson, E.A. (1989) The mentor advantage: Perceived career/job experiences of proteges vs. non-proteges. *Journal of Organizational Behavior*, 10, 309–20.

Fagenson-Eland, E.A., Marks, M.A., and Amendola, K.L. (1997) Perceptions of mentoring relationships. *Journal of Vocational Behavior*, 51, 29–42.

Feldman D.C. (1999) Toxic mentors or toxic protégés? A critical re-examination of dysfunctional mentoring. *Human Resource Management Review*, 9, 247–78.

Ferris, G.R., Russ, G.S., and Fandt, P.M. (1989) Politics in organizations. In: R.A. Giacalone and P. Rosenfeld (eds) *Impression Management in the Organization*. Hillsdale, NJ: Erlbaum. pp. 140–70.

Fletcher, J.K. and Ragins, B.R. (2007) Stone center relational theory: A window on relational mentoring. In: B.R. Ragins and K.E. Kram (eds) *The Handbook of Mentoring at Work: Theory, Research, and Practice*. Thousand Oaks, CA: Sage. pp. 373–99.

Fombrun, C.J. (1982) Strategies for network research in organizations. *Academy of Management Review*, 7, 280–91.

Garvey, B. and Garrett-Harris, R. (2005) *The Benefits of Mentoring: A Literature Review, A Report for East Mentors Forum Sheffield*. The Coaching and Mentoring Research Unit, Sheffield Hallam University.

Gattiker, U.E. and Larwood, L. (1986) Subjective career success: A study of managers and support personnel. *Journal of Business and Psychology*, 1, 78–94.

Gattiker, U.E. and Larwood, L. (1988) Predictors for managers' career mobility, success and satisfaction. *Human Relations*, 41, 569–91.

Grandey, A.A. (2003) When "the show must go on": Surface acting and deep acting as determinants of emotional exhaustion and peer-rated service delivery. *Academy of Management Journal*, 46, 86–96.

Grant, A.M., Passmore, J., Cavanagh, M.J., and Parker, H. (2010) The state of play in coaching. *International Review of Industrial and Organizational Psychology*, 25, 125–68.

Greenhaus, J.H., Callanan, G.A., and Godshalk, V.M. (2000) *Career Management*. Fort Worth, TX: Dryden Press.

Greenhaus, J.H., Parasuraman, S., and Wormley, W.M. (1990) Effects of race on organizational experiences, job performance evaluations, and career outcomes. *Academy of Management Journal*, 33, 64–86.

Haggard, D.L., Dougherty, T.W., Turban, D.B., and Wilbanks, J.E. (2011) Who is a mentor? A review of evolving definitions and implications for research. *Journal of Management*, 37(1), 280–304.

Hall, D.T. (2002) *Careers In and Out of Organizations*. Thousand Oaks, CA: Sage.

Heslin, P.A. (2005) Conceptualizing and evaluating career success. *Journal of Organizational Behavior*, 26, 113–36.

Higgins, M.C. (2000) The more, the merrier? Multiple developmental relationships and work satisfaction. *Journal of Management Development*, 19, 277–96.

Higgins, M.C. (2007) A contingency perspective on developmental networks. In: J.E. Dutton, and B.R. Ragins (eds) *Exploring Positive Relationships at Work: Building a Theoretical and Research Foundation*. Mahwah, NJ: Lawrence Erlbaum. pp. 207–24.

Higgins, M.C. and Kram, K.E. (2001) Reconceptualizing mentoring at work: A developmental network perspective. *Academy of Management Review*, 26(2), 264–8.

Higgins, M.C. and Thomas, D.A. (2001) Constellations and careers: Toward understanding the effects of multiple developmental relationships. *Journal of Organizational Behavior*, 22(3), 223–47.

Higgins, M.C., Dobrow, S.R., and Chandler, D. (2008) Never quite good enough: The paradox of sticky developmental ties for elite university graduates. *Journal of Vocational Behavior*, 72(2), 207–24.

Higgins, M.C., Dobrow, S.R., and Roloff, K.S. (2010) Optimism and the boundaryless career: The role of developmental relationships. *Journal of Organizational Behavior*, 31(5), 749–69.

Hochschild, A.R. (1983) *The Managed Heart: Commercialization of Human Feeling*. Berkeley, CA: University of California Press.

Hofstede, G. (2001) *Culture's Consequences: Comparing Values, Behaviors, Institutions, and Organizations across Nations*. Thousand Oaks, CA: Sage.

Horvath, M., Wasko, L.E., and Bradley, J. (2008) The effect of formal mentoring program characteristics on organizational attraction. *Human Resource Development Quarterly*, 19(4), 323–49.

Hunt, D.M. and Michael, C. (1983) Mentorship: A career training and development tool. *Academy of Management Review*, 8, 475–85.

Hussain, Z. (2006) Diversity mentoring in BT. In: D. Megginson, D. Clutterbuck, B. Garvey, P. Stokes, and R. Garrett-Harris (eds) *Mentoring in Action: A Practical Guide*. London, UK: Kogan Page. pp. 102–9.

Ibarra, H. (1993) Personal networks of women and minorities in management: A conceptual framework. *Academy of Management Review*, 8, 56–87.

Jaskolka, G., Beyer, J.M., and Trice, H.M. (1985) Measuring and predicting managerial success. *Journal of Vocational Behavior*, 26, 189–205.

Johnson, N.B. and Scandura, T.A. (1994) The effect of mentorship and sex-role style on male-female earnings. *Industrial Relations*, 33, 263–74.

Judge, T.A. and Bono, J.E. (2001) Relationship of core self-evaluations traits – self-esteem, generalized self-efficacy, locus of control, and emotional stability – with job satisfaction and job performance: A meta-analysis. *Journal of Applied Psychology*, 86, 80–92.

Judge, T.A. and Bretz, R.D. (1994) Political influence behavior and career success. *Journal of Management*, 20, 43–65.

Judge, T.A., Cable, D.M., Boudreau, J.W., and Bretz, R.D., Jr. (1995) An empirical investigation of the predictors of executive career success. *Personnel Psychology*, 48, 485–519.

Knouse, S.B. (2001) Virtual mentors: Mentoring on the Internet. *Journal of Employment Counseling*, 38, 162–9.

Koberg, C.S., Boss, R.W., Chappell, D., and Ringer, R.C. (1994) Correlates and consequences of protégé mentoring in a large hospital. *Group and Organization Management*, 19, 219–39.

Krackhardt, D. (1992) The strength of strong ties: The importance of philos in organizations. In: N. Nohria and R.G. Eccles (eds) *Networks and Organizations: Structure, Form and Action*. Cambridge, MA: Harvard University School Press.

Kram, K.E. (1983) Phases of the mentor relationship. *Academy of Management Journal*, 26, 608–825.

Kram, K.E. (1985) *Mentoring at Work*. Boston, MA: Scott, Foresman.

Kram, K.E. (1986) Mentoring in the workplace. In: Hall & Associates (eds) *Career Development in Organizations*. San Francisco, CA: Jossey-Bass. pp. 160–201.

Kram, K.E. and Isabella, L.A. (1985) Mentoring alternatives: The role of peer relationships in career development. *Academy of Management Journal*, 28(1), 110–32.

Lankau, M.J., Riordan, C.M., and Thomas, C.H. (2005) The effects of similarity and liking in formal mentoring relationships between mentors and protégés. *Journal of Vocational Behavior*, 67, 252–65.

Lankau, M.J. and Scandura, T.A. (2002) An investigation of personal learning in mentoring relationships: content, antecedents, and consequences. *Academy of Management Journal*, 45, 779–90.

Lankau, M.J. and Scandura, T.A. (2007) Mentoring as a forum for personal learning in organizations. In: B.R. Ragins, and K. Kram (eds) *The Handbook of Mentoring at Work: Theory, Research, and Practice*. Thousand Oaks, CA: Sage. pp. 95–122.

Law, H., Ireland, S., and Hussain, Z. (2007) *The Psychology of Coaching, Mentoring and Learning*. Chichester, UK: Wiley.

Le Pine, J.A., Erez, A. and Johnson, D. (2002) The nature and dimensionality of organizational citizenship behavior: A critical review and meta-analysis. *Journal of Applied Psychology*, 87, 522–65.

Leadership Centre of the NHS and Department of Health (September 2004). Mentoring for doctors: Signposts to current practice for career grade doctors. Retrieved from http://www.dh.gov.uk/en/Publicationsandstatistics/Publications/PublicationsPolicyAndGuidance/DH_4089395 (accessed March 5, 2010).

Lentz, E. and Allen, T.D. (2005) *The Link Between Mentoring and the Career Plateau: Addressing the Empirical Gap*. Paper presented at the 2005 Annual Conference of the Society for Industrial and Organizational Psychology, Los Angeles, CA (April).

Lentz, E. and Allen, T.D. (2009) The role of mentoring others in the career plateauing phenomenon. *Group and Organizational Management*, 34(3), 358–84.

Levinson, D.J., Darrow, D., Levinson, M., Klein, E.B., and McKee, B. (1978) *Seasons of a Man's Life*. New York: Academic Press.

London, M. and Stumpf, S.A. (1982) *Managing Careers*. Reading, MA: Addison-Wesley.

McKeen, C.A. and Bujaki, M. (2007) Gender and mentoring: Issues, effects, and opportunities. In: B.R. Ragins and K.E. Kram (eds) *The Handbook of Mentoring at Work: Theory, Research, and Practice*. Thousand Oaks, CA: Sage. pp. 197–222.

Manz, C. and Sims, H.P. (1981) Vicarious learning: The influences of modeling on organizational behavior. *Academy of Management Review*, 6, 105–13.

Maslach, C., Schaufeli, W.B., and Leiter, M.P. (2001) Job burnout. *Annual Review of Psychology*, 52, 397–422.

Mathieu, J.E. and Zajac, D.M. (1990) A review and meta-analysis of the antecedents, correlates, and consequences of organizational commitment. *Psychological Bulletin*, 108, 171–94.

Meade, A.W., Watson, A.M., and Kroustalis, A.M. (2007) *Assessing Common Methods Bias in Organizational Research*. Paper presented at the 22nd Annual Meeting of the Society for Industrial and Organizational Psychology, New York (April).

Meister, J.C. and Williyerd, K. (2010) Mentoring millennials. *Harvard Business Review*, 88(5), 68–72.

Messmer, M. (1998) Mentoring: Building your company's intellectual capital. *HRFocus*, 15(9), 11–12.

Meyer, J.P., Stanley, D.J., Herscovitch, L., and Topolnytsky, L. (2002) Affective, continuance, and normative commitment to the organization: A meta-analysis of antecedents, correlates, and consequences. *Journal of Vocational Behavior*, 61, 20–52.

Mullen, E.J. (1994) Framing the mentoring relationship as an information exchange. *Human Resource Management Review*, 4, 257–81.

Mullen, E.J. and Noe, R.A. (1999).The mentoring information exchange: When do mentors seek information from their protégés? *Journal of Organizational Behavior*, 20, 233–42.

Myers, D.W. and Humphreys, N.J. (1985) The caveats in mentorship. *Business Horizons*, 28, 9–14.

Neugarten, B.L. (1975) Adult personality: Toward the psychology of the life cycle. In: W.C. Sae (ed.) *Human Life Cycle*. New York: Jason Aronson. pp. 379–94.

Newby, T.J. and Heide, A. (1992) The value of mentoring. *Performance Improvement Quarterly*, 5(4), 2–15.

Ng, T.W.H., Eby, L.T., Sorensen, K.L., and Feldman, D.C. (2005) Predictors of career success: A meta-analysis. *Personnel Psychology*, 58, 367–408.

Nielson, T.R., Carlson, D.S., and Lankau, M.J. (2001) The supportive mentor as a means of reducing work-family conflict. *Journal of Vocational Behavior*, 59, 364–81.

Noe, R.A. (1988) An investigation of the determinants of successful assigned mentoring relationships. *Personnel Psychology*, 41, 457–79.

Noe, R.A., Greenberger, D.B., and Wang, S. (2002) Mentoring: A review of the literature and research agenda. In: G.R. Ferris and J.J. Martocchio (eds) *Research in Personnel and Human Resource Management* . Oxford, UK: JAI Press. Vol. 21, pp. 129–73.

Nykodym, N., Freedman, L.D., Simonetti, J.L., and Nielsen, W.R. (1995) Mentoring: Using transactional analysis to help organizational members use their energy in more productive ways. *Transactional Analysis Journal*, 25, 170–9.

O'Reilly, D. (2001) The mentoring of employees: Is your organization taking advantage of this professional development tool? *Ohio CPA Journal*, 60(3), 51–4.

Parker, P., Hall, T.H., and Kram, K.E. (2008) Peer coaching: A relational process for accelerating career learning. *Academy of Management Learning and Education*, 7(4), 487–503.

Payne, S.C. and Huffman, H.A. (2005) A longitudinal examination of the influence of mentoring on organizational commitment and turnover. *Academy of Management Journal*, 48, 158–68.

Podsakoff, P.M., MacKenzie, S.B., Lee, J.Y., and Podsakoff, N.P. (2003) Common method biases in behavioral research: A critical review of the literature and recommended remedies, *Journal of Applied Psychology*, 88, 879–903.

Poole, M.E., Langan-Fox, J., and Omodei, M. (1993) Contrasting subjective and objective criteria as determinants of perceived career success: A longitudinal study. *Journal of Occupational and Organizational Psychology*, 66, 39–54.

Ragins, B.R. (1989) Barriers to mentoring: The female manager's dilemma. *Human Relations*, 42, 1–22.

Ragins, B.R. (1997) Diversified mentoring relationships in organizations: A power perspective. *Academy of Management Review*, 22, 482–521.

Ragins, B.R. (2005) Towards a theory of relational mentoring. Unpublished manuscript, University of Wisconsin-Milwaukee, Milwaukee.

Ragins, B.R. and Cotton, J.L. (1991) Easier said than done: Gender differences in perceived barriers to gaining a mentor. *Academy of Management Journal*, 34, 939–51.

Ragins, B.R. and Cotton, J.L. (1993) Gender and willingness to mentor in organizations. *Journal of Management*, 19, 97–111.

Ragins, B.R. and Cotton, J.L. (1999) Mentor functions and outcomes: A comparison of men and women in formal and informal mentoring relationships. *Journal of Applied Psychology*, 84(4), 529–50.

Ragins, B.R. and Kram, K.E. (2007) *The Handbook of Mentoring at Work: Theory, Research and Practice*. Thousand Oaks, CA: Sage.

Ragins, B.R., Cotton, J.L., and Miller, J.S. (2000) Marginal mentoring: the effects of type of mentor, quality of relationship and programme design on work and career outcomes. *Academy of Management Journal*, 43, 1177–94.

Ragins, B.R., Lyness, K.S., and Winkel, D.E. (2010) Life spillovers: The influence of fear of home foreclosure, diversity and mentoring on work, career and life attitudes. *Under Review: Academy of Management Journal*.

Ragins, B.R. and McFarlin, D.B. (1990) Perceptions of mentor roles in cross-gender mentoring relationships. *Journal of Vocational Behavior*, 37, 321–39.

Ragins, B.R. and Scandura, T.A. (1997) The way we were: Gender and the termination of mentoring relationships. *Journal of Applied Psychology*, 82, 945–53.

Ragins, B.R. and Scandura, T.A. (1999) Burden or blessing? Expected costs and benefits of being a mentor. *Journal of Organizational Behavior*, 20(4), 493–509.

Ragins, B.R. and Sundstrom, E. (1989) Gender and power in organizations: A longitudinal perspective. *Psychological Bulletin*, 105, 51–88.

Ragins, B.R. and Verbos, A.K. (2007) Positive relationships in action: Relational mentoring and mentoring schemas in the workplace. In: J. Dutton and B.R. Ragins (eds) *Exploring Positive Relationships at Work: Building a Theoretical And Research Foundation*. Mahwah, NJ: Lawrence Erlbaum. pp. 91–116.

Roche, G.R. (1979) Much ado about mentors. *Harvard Business Review*, 57(1), 17–28.

Russell, J.E., and McManus, S.E. (2007) Peer mentoring relationships. In B.R. Ragins and K.E. Kram (eds) *The Handbook of Mentoring at Work: Theory, Research, and Practice*. Thousand Oaks, CA: Sage. pp. 273–98.

Scandura, T.A. (1991) Mentorship and career mobility: An empirical investigation. *Journal of Organizational Behavior*, 12, 1–6.

Scandura, T.A. (1992) Mentorship and career mobility: An empirical investigation. *Journal of Organizational Behavior*, 13, 169–74.

Scandura, T.A. (1997) Mentoring and organizational justice: An empirical investigation. *Journal of Vocational Behavior*, 51, 58–69.

Scandura, T.A. (1998) Dysfunctional mentoring relationships and outcomes. *Journal of Management*, 24, 449–67.

Scandura, T.A. and Viator, R. (1994) Mentoring in public accounting firms: An analysis of mentor-protégé relationships, mentoring functions and protégé turnover intentions. *Accounting, Organisations and Society*, 19, 717–34.

Scandura, T.A., Tejeda, M.J., Werther, W.B., and Lankau, M.J. (1996) Perspectives on mentoring. *Leadership and Organization Development Journal*, 17(3), 50–8.

Schaufeli, W.B. and Enzmann, D. (1998) *The Burnout Companion to Study and Practice: A Critical Analysis*. London: Taylor and Francis.

Seibert, S.E., Crant, J.M., and Kraimer, M.L. (1999) Proactive personality and career success. *Journal of Applied Psychology*, 84, 416–27.

Seibert, S.E., Kraimer, M.L., and Liden, R.C. (2001) A social capital theory of career success. *Academy of Management Journal*, 44, 219–37.

Shen, Y. (2010) *Developmental Networks of Expatriates: The Antecedents, Structure, and Outcomes*. Dissertation, Boston University, Boston, MA.

Singh, V., Bains, D., and Vinnicombe, S. (2002).Informal mentoring as an organisational resource. *Long Range Planning*, 35(4), 389–405.

Singh, R., Ragins, B.R., and Tharenou, P. (2009a) What matters most? The relative role of mentoring and career capital in career success. *Journal of Vocational Behavior*, 75, 56–67.

Singh, R., Ragins, B.R., and Tharenou, P. (2009b) Who gets a mentor? A longitudinal assessment of the rising star effect. *Journal of Vocational Behavior*, 74, 11–17.

Singleton, R.A., Jr., and Straits, B.C. (1999) *Approaches to Social Research* (3rd edn). New York: Oxford University Press.

Slocum, J.W., Jr., Cron, W.L., Hansen, R.W., and Rawlings, S. (1985) Business strategy and the management of plateaued employees. *Academy of Management Journal*, 28, 133–54.

Sronce, R. and McKinley, W. (2006) Perceptions of organizational downsizing. *Journal of Leadership and Organizational Studies*, 12, 89–109.

Tepper, K., Shaffer, B.C., and Tepper, B.J. (1996) Latent structure of mentoring function scales. *Educational and Psychological Measurement*, 56, 848–57.

Torrance, E.P. (1984) *Mentor Relationships*. New York: Bearly.

Turban, D.B. and Dougherty, T.W. (1994) Role of protégé personality in receipt of mentoring and career success. *Academy of Management Journal*, 37, 688–702.

Underhill, C.M. (2006) The effectiveness of mentoring programs in corporate settings: A meta-analytical review of the literature. *Journal of Vocational Behavior*, 68(2), 292–307.

Van Emmerik, I.J.H. (2004) The more you can get, the better: Mentoring constellations and intrinsic career success. *Career Development International*, 9(6), 578–94.

Van Maanen, J. and Schein, E.H. (1977) Career development. In: J.R. Hackman and J.L. Shuttle (eds), *Improving Life at Work*. Santa Monica, CA: Goodyear. pp. 30–95.

Viator, R.E. (2001) The Association of Formal and Informal Public Accounting Mentoring with role stress and related job outcomes. *Accounting, Organizations and Society*, 26, 73–93.

Wallace, J.E. (2001) The benefits of mentoring for female lawyers. *Journal of Vocational Behavior*, 58, 366–91.

Wanberg, C.R., Kammeyer-Mueller, J., and Marchese, M. (2006) Mentor and protégé predictors and outcomes of mentoring in a formal mentoring program. *Journal of Vocational Behavior*, 69(3), 410–23.

Wanberg, C.R., Welsh, E.T., and Hezlett, S.A. (2003) Mentoring: A review and directions for future research. In: J. Martocchio and J. Ferris (eds) *Research in Personnel and Human Resources Management*. Oxford,UK: Elsevier Science Ltd., Vol. 22, pp. 39–124.

Whitely, W., Dougherty, T.W., and Dreher, G.F. (1992) Correlates of career-oriented mentoring for early career managers and professionals. *Journal of Organizational Behavior*, 13, 141–54.

Zagumny, M.J. (1993) Mentoring as a tool for change: A social learning perspective. *Organization Development Journal*, 11, 43–8.

Zapf, D. (2002) Emotion work and psychological well-being: A review of the literature and some conceptual considerations. *Human Resource Management Review*, 12, 237–68.

Zapf, D., Seifert, C., Schmutte, B., Mertini, H., and Holz, M. (2001) Emotion work and job stressors and their effects on burnout. *Psychology and Health*, 16, 527–45.

Zey, M.G. (1984) *The Mentor Connection*. Homewood, IL: Dow Jones-Irwin.

Zey, M.G. (1988) A mentor for all reasons. *Personal Journal*, 67(1), 46–51.

# 13

# Training Mentors – Behaviors Which Bring Positive Outcomes in Mentoring

## Robert Garvey and Gunnela Westlander

## Introduction

This chapter is divided into five sections. The first section provides a brief history of mentoring. This demonstrates the historical antecedents of mentoring and helps to explain the current understanding of mentoring. In the second section we offer an overview of how mentors' contributions and needs are described in mentoring research and discuss the research on training courses tailor-made for mentors. It describes how they are designed, and what and who are they aimed at. The third section asks how we know what is going on in mentor education. It addresses this question by exploring the research and evaluation data. The fourth section explores practitioner expert opinion on mentor education. It explores the following questions: What does the term "expert" mean? What behaviors bring positive outcomes in mentoring as presented by "expert" opinion. The final section looks at recent developments in mentor education, including the use of technology and offers a curriculum for mentor education. We then conclude with a summary and a concluding position.

## A Brief History of Mentoring

The first mentor was the Goddess Athena in Homer's epic poem *The Odyssey*. Athena took the form of Mentor, the trusted friend and adviser to Odysseus and worked with Telemachus, the King's son. Athena, in the guise of Mentor, helped Telemachus to learn how to become a king. Her method was essentially experiential learning, dialogue, and reflection.

The mentoring theme was much later developed by Fénélon (1699), tutor to Louis XIV's heir, in his seminal work *Les Aventures de Télémaque*. This is a case history of human development that demonstrates that life's events are potential learning

*The Wiley Blackwell Handbook of the Psychology of Coaching and Mentoring*, First Edition.
Edited by Jonathan Passmore, David B. Peterson, and Teresa Freire.
© 2013 John Wiley & Sons, Ltd. Published 2016 by John Wiley & Sons, Ltd.

experiences. Fénélon shows us that the activity of observing others provides both positive and negative learning opportunities. He suggests that if these events are fully explored with the support and guidance of a mentor, the learner acquires a high-level understanding of "the ways of the world" very quickly. Fénélon implied that leadership could be developed through guided experience and Louis XIV viewed this as a challenge to the divine right of kings and consequently banished Fénélon to Cambrai and cancelled his pension.

In France in 1762, Rousseau, probably the founder of the notion of "experiential learning," produced the educational treatise *Emile*. Rousseau was profoundly influenced by Fénélon's work and Emile, the central character, receives a copy of *Les Aventures de Télémaque* as a guide to his developmental journey. Telemachus is thus employed as a metaphor for learning, growth, and social development.

In 1759, Caraccioli wrote *Veritable le Mentor ou l'education de la noblesse* and it was translated into English in 1760 to become 'The true mentor, or, an essay on the education of young people in fashion'. Caraccioli acknowledges Fénélon's influence on his work as he describes mentoring from the perspective of the mentor. He invites the reader to engage in what we now understand as holistic learning, where the rational and the affective are brought together. This could be regarded as the precursor to the idea of emotional intelligence found in current discourses in mentoring.

Two volumes of the publication *The Female Mentor* by Honoria appeared in the English language in 1793, with a third volume in 1796. Honoria acknowledges Fénélon's influence and provides a recording of conversations about topics of interest among a group of women referred to as "the society". She identifies and describes the characteristics of the female mentor, not as the substance of the book but rather as a commentary and series of asides made throughout the volumes. The mentor, Amanda, seemed to have been a role model for "the society".

These historical writings position mentoring as an educational activity, involving experience and dialogue with the purpose of the mentee learning and developing. These links are maintained in modern writing and the US researcher, Kathy Kram, for example, suggests that mentoring performs a "psychosocial" function (Kram, 1983). Here the mentee is socialized into a specific social context and develops self-insight and psychological well-being through dialogue with an experienced person.

Today, mentoring is found in a range of occupational and social settings. Allen and Eby (2007) argue that when reviewing mentoring research it can sometimes be difficult to assess if the researchers are actually looking at the same thing. They argue that when trying to define mentoring it is necessary to take into account the following:

- Variations in the social contexts
- The formality of the arrangements
- The differences of intention of the organization and the participants
- The expectations of the participants, stakeholders and the organization
- Relationship dynamics (Allen and Eby, 2007).

It is also clear that there are different models of mentoring in use around the world, particularly in the business context. Clutterbuck (2004) suggests that there are two purposes for mentoring, the US "career sponsorship" model and the European "developmental" model. American research (Allen, *et al.*, 2004; Carden, 1990; Ragins, 1989, 1994;

Ragins and Cotton, 1999; Ragins and Scandura, 1999) shows that sponsorship mentoring can bring many benefits for mentee, mentor, and their host organization. For example enhanced:

- Career progression and knowledge development
- Emotional stability and problem solving ability
- Decision making, creativity, and opportunity
- Leadership abilities, organizational morale, and productivity

However, these authors also note that due to inherent power dynamics within sponsorship schemes there is the potential for relationships to become abusive or to breakdown.

Clutterbuck (2004), Garvey (1995), and Rix and Gold (2000) show that developmental schemes offer similar benefits to the sponsorship model with fewer of the negative effects. Therefore, in this section, we have attempted to keep the contexts of the research clear because, as Bruner (1990), a social constructivist psychologist, asserts, it is only really possible to understand human activities if the context in which they happen is also understood.

History shows us that mentoring is a natural and human activity and therefore anyone has the potential to engage in mentoring; however, most writers now suggest that it is also possible to learn how to mentor. Certainly, within formal mentoring schemes, which attempt to replicate the benefits of natural or informal relationships, Megginson *et al.* (2005), Klasen and Clutterbuck (2002), and Allen *et al.*, (2006a, b), for example, recommend and show that mentors should be trained and we raise the question: "So what should inform the training design?"

## The Research

The following is an overview of selected empirical studies about mentoring. These are mostly published in international scientific journals or book chapters and a few are taken from PhD theses. The context of our selected research includes professional, educational (schools and higher education), business, and health settings with various occupations. This suggests that mentorship is a widely applied form of support. Researchers often derive data about mentoring activity by asking the mentees about their mentors, the mentors about what they feel they have done or by asking both parties.

In mentoring research the most common used methods include:

- Large group questionnaire studies
- Smaller group questionnaire studies (about 30 people)
- Combined questionnaire and interview studies
- Small scale in-depth semi-structured interviews

Less common methods include:

- Focus group studies
- Ideographic case studies

## University academic staff

One study defined a mentor as, "an advisor whose guidance focuses on professional issues" and a role model as, "a person who provides an example in a broader context that includes both professional and personal aspects of life" (Levinson *et al.*, 1991, p. 423). They found that having a mentor was linked to:

- Help with research efforts
- Salary benefits
- Gaining time for research
- Encouragement
- Emotional support

Mentoring also correlated with increased research outputs.

However, they also found that having a role model was more associated with life satisfaction and the role model offered more help with personal issues than a mentor.

Pololi and Knight (2005) found that a lack of access to mentors can hinder faculty scholarly productivity and may result in attrition from academia. Their study, within a formal dyadic mentoring program found that some mentees reported that their mentors were inspiring, supportive, and provided psychosocial career support (Kram, 1983). They note that senior people as mentors recognized the benefits of peer support for themselves, but not peer support among lower grades of academics, despite this group benefiting from peer support.

Steiner *et al.* (2004) found that some mentees sought a "caring" mentor which suggests supportiveness. Other mentees reported that their mentors were superficial, exploitive, mediocre, or non-existent, with some reporting that the mentoring felt "forced". Steiner *et al.* (2004) also found that the lack of availability of mentors, sometimes due to time constraints, raised problems for mentees and that the mentor's "good reputation" was an important element for mentees.

## Higher education students

Clark *et al.* (2000) identified the students' perceived benefits of having a mentor in rank order as follows:

- Providing education and training
- Offering support and encouragement
- Acting as a role model

Ninety-one percent evaluated the mentor relationship positively and they cited 1,675 positive and negative qualities observed in their mentors. The six most commonly cited were, in rank order:

- Supportive
- Intelligent
- Knowledgeable
- Ethical
- Caring
- Humorous

Clearly, there are some resonances with the findings above, but the career functions do not seem to feature very highly. Lindgren (2000) offers further support for these findings by noting that mentors seemed to contribute to the doctoral students' developing:

- Self-confidence
- Self-esteem
- Self-awareness

The degree of improvement among the mentees was variable, but both mentors and mentees agreed about *how* the mentees had developed.

In Lindén *et al.* (in press), the issue of "mutuality" within mentoring is raised. Their findings show that the degree of mutuality or reciprocal learning varied and explained this in terms of:

- Different structures of doctoral supervision
- Participation or not in a formal mentoring program
- Access to informal mentors

This study found that "task" learning rather than personal learning was more the norm.

Feiman-Nemser *et al.* (1994; reprinted 2005) in a study of trainee teachers and their mentors found that:

- Mentors dominated the conversation
- Mentors gave praise but without explaining why
- There was no learning about the rationale and sources of mentor's ideas

The paper shows that the training for mentors focused on "technical activity" or "a procedural knowledge derived from research" (p. 6) and the wisdom of practice was downplayed.

In Bray and Nettleton (2007) the mentees were nurses, midwives, and medical doctors in their final training. The researchers looked at the various possible roles and functions of the mentor. In particular:

- Adviser
- Trainer or teacher
- Counsellor
- Supporter
- Role model
- Assessor

The authors found that both mentors and mentees had similar opinions, with the roles of "teacher" and "supporter" being the most important. The assessor role was more often mentioned as the most difficult to understand and perform and mentors who had the dual role of assessor and mentor found them conflicting.

## In schools

The introduction of mentoring in schools is widespread across Europe and the United States. It is often employed as a means to prevent turnover among the teachers in their first jobs. Classroom teaching is often solitary work and a minor part of the working time is devoted to communication and collaboration with other colleagues. Therefore, professional support is a key issue and much research in this area is driven by the question: "Are mentoring programs useful in their efforts to make beginning teachers motivated to stay in their jobs?"

Ingersoll and Kralik (2004) reviewed hundreds of studies on this issue and it was difficult to find clear common features other than, "some empirical support for the claim that assistance for new teachers in form of mentor support have positive impact on teachers and their retention" (p. 14). Lindgren (2003, 2006) found that the mentors offered opportunities to discuss the teacher role in situations with students and parents; they also got advice about handling conflict and lesson planning. Lindgren concludes that the mentors' contributions involved a mix of professional and educational help in different proportions that depended on the individual mentee's requests. The mentees were positive about their mentors and appreciated the opportunity to discuss problems that otherwise would "have been taken home."

Varah *et al.* (1986) found that those with mentors were more satisfied with their choice of profession, more motivated to solve problems, and they had a more distinct professional self-identity than their colleagues in the control group without mentors.

Ganser (1996) found that the most important perceived mentor contributions were:

- Supportive and encouraging
- Helpful with teaching tasks issues
- Helping to avoid learning by trial and error
- Helpful in the transition from college to work
- Inspiring to remain in the job

This study identified reciprocal benefits for mentors, in particular mentors could:

- Reflect on their own teaching
- Learn about new ideas
- Be helpful

However, they also stated that there were obstacles to the mentoring role and these included:

- Lack of time
- Other responsibilities
- Disagreements on teaching ideologies

Hawkey (1998) found contrasting styles between the two mentors in her study despite the subject matter and purpose being the same. One mentor dominated the conversations whereas the other listened and gave equal space to mentees' talking. In a similar study, Feiman-Nemser and Parker (1993) found it was important to take note of the contextual conditions as well as the demographic structure and program philosophy when evaluating the mentor functions.

Bush and Coleman (1995) asked the mentee headteachers to identify key characteristics in their mentors. The following are the conflated responses in rank order:

1  Reciprocal learning and peer support
2  Collaboration
3  Executive succession and socialization
4  Co-counselling

5   Coaching and altruism
6   Career sponsorship
7   Expert-novice

Rowley (1999) suggests the following should ground mentor training within a school-based mentor program, the good mentor is:

* Committed to the role of mentoring
* Accepting of the beginning teacher
* Skilled at providing instructional support
* Effective in different interpersonal contexts
* A model of a continuous learner
* Able to communicate hope and optimism

## In the healthcare sector

In Garvey (1995) the mentees were a mixture of health service managers and clinicians taking an MBA sponsored by the health authority. They looked for the following qualities in their mentors in rank order:

* Good listener
* General experience at executive level
* Previous MBA experience
* Greater health service experience
* Different perspective
* Trust (p. 14)

They felt that their mentors needed:

* Specific training in mentorship
* Opportunities to discuss mentoring with fellow mentors
* Access to background materials on mentoring (p. 14)

The author provided the participants with a framework to help both parties to discuss the expectations of their relationships and to evaluate and review their progress, known as the "dimensions framework" (see Garvey, 1994). The conclusion showed that mentoring worked well and that the tools of learning style inventories and the "dimensions framework" were beneficial.

Nilsson (2000) evaluated a mentor program aimed at recruiting candidates for managerial positions in the public healthcare sector. The fourteen mentees were physicians and dentists. The mentors, recruited from private and public organizations retrospectively believed that they provided psychosocial support and were less career-oriented. Half the mentees believed that their mentors helped to strengthen career ambitions and personal development as well as facilitate open conversations. They believed that their mentors provided a model of future manager positions by giving advice and tips about pitfalls and by developing decision-making capacity. The majority emphasized that the conversations were meaningful and "deep".

## In business

Waters *et al.* (2002) studied mentoring among an unemployed group of people who were training to help them to return to the labor market. The program focused on business planning, conducting risk analyses, learning about financial management, sales, and marketing. Two of the four hypotheses were confirmed, namely:

- Frequency of contact between mentors and protégés will be positively related to career-related support, psychosocial support, and perceptions of business success.
- The career-related function will be more strongly related to business-related outcomes (profit and perceived business success) than the psychosocial function.

In Høigaard and Mathisen (2009) female leaders participated in an evaluation study aimed at obtaining the mentees' picture of:

- Mentor functions and communications
- Listening and communication structures
- The relationship
- The mentoring outcomes for the mentees
- Perceived leader performance
- Job satisfaction and career planning

The mentors received 25 hours of a mentoring skills program focusing on communication, mentor strategies, and functions. The study identified that positive interrelations were found, with one exception. Contrary to other studies (i.e., Ragins and Cotton, 1996) where same-gender mentor relationships in formal mentoring program showed more success than mixed gender partnerships, this study showed that the sex of the mentor was irrelevant.

Westlander (2010a, b) looked at the long-term effects of mentoring experiences with ten middle managers. They completed narrative descriptions of 19 past mentoring relationships 10–20 years ago. The author categorized the analysis in three aspects:

- Early stages of professional career
- Transition to extended managerial responsibility
- Gaining higher management positions

These categories highlighted that mentees had different needs and different work conditions and this created different expectations of their mentors. The study found homogeneity in conversation content, for example:

- More of an organizational socialization in early carrier situations
- More on problem-solving support and situated learning in advanced manager levels

The participants recalled that their discussions with their mentors had lasting effects and were mostly concerned with social competence at work, role-taking, and performance in the "here and now situation", the company culture and possible career paths, but in some cases discussions were more oriented to long-term, work-life values, and occupational adaptability.

## Overall findings

Overall, the selected findings cover three main functions or purposes for mentoring:

- Leadership development
- Educational, learning, and development
- Psychosocial support and development

It is interesting to note that these provide further support for Kram's (1983) observation that mentoring provides a "psychosocial" function in that the mentee is socialized into a specific social context and develops self-insight and psychological well-being through dialogue with an experienced person. However, it is also clear that within each occupational setting, the person of the mentor is defined differently. A further issue relates to Bruner's (1990) assertion that to understand human affairs it is important to understand the social context and these studies were conducted in many different settings.

## Discussion

One issue raised is the extent of role modelling within mentoring. From an historical perspective, role modelling was seen as an aspect of mentoring rather than something separate. This is also the case in modern mentoring literature (Clawson, 1996; Gardiner, 2005; Kram and Chandler, 2005; Ragins and Cotton, 1999). However, the function of role model is not without its difficulties. Moberg and Velasquez (2004, p. 116) consider that the concepts of both role model and mentor within a formalized or semi-formalized scheme is ethically dubious in that it "falls outside the formal system of rules and controls. In the absence of such local normative standards, it is important that such roles come with clear ethical parameters. Otherwise, moral ambiguity and ethical abuse are more likely." This suggests that the design of a mentoring scheme and the training associated with it needs careful consideration.

The design of the mentoring scheme also seems to impact on the participants (Beech and Brockbank, 1999; Colley, 2003; Merrick and Stokes, 2003) and Kram (1985) argue that it is important for the mentor to be clear about his or her role and function within a scheme. In general terms, power differentials may raise issues for mentor training. Habermas (1974) suggests that differences in power and status between people and groups can distort the communication between them. This leads to mutually suspicious interpretations of the other's meaning. Habermas's remedy for distorted communication is the "ideal speech situation". However, the "ideal speech situation" is rarely enacted in practice; it represents a standard to be achieved. Alred and Garvey (2000) suggest that mentoring is a learning relationship and therefore plays an important role within knowledge intensive organizations. This suggests that the main duty of the mentor is to contribute to the mentee's developmental learning. Garvey (1994) goes further and suggests that the development of a "learning culture" is necessary to sustain mentoring as a "normal" organizational activity.

Pololi and Knight (2005) suggest that learning is not necessarily something egalitarian and drawing on Erikson's (1978) concept of "generativity" to explain the power issue in their study they suggest that the notion of peer supported learning conflicts with the mentors' altruistic generativity motive as the mentor discounts collaborative peer support. Generally, in most of the studies, hierarchical structures and power differentials between mentor and mentee are common. Potentially those in power positions have a view that "they know best" or are the "knowledge holders" by virtue of being senior. Colley (2003, p. 2) states that in social mentoring schemes issues of "unacknowledged power dynamics at work such as, class, gender, race, disability, sexuality that may either reduce or reproduce inequalities" are often present and she raises the question of "whose agenda is it?" If it is someone other than the mentee's, there is the potential for difficulties and gratuitous advice giving becomes a norm. A further issue relating to power is the function of a mentor. In one of the studies above the mentor was conflicted in the roles of mentor and assessor.

Beech and Brockbank (1999) explore power issues in their study and note that mentors may see themselves as experienced knowledge holders and advice givers and mentees may react in different ways to these characteristics. McAuley (2003, p. 14) argues that the psychological phenomena of transference and counter-transference are often present but unacknowledged in mentoring conversations. His framework suggest that mentees who are involved with transference may show, "respect for the mentor's expertise and process skills," they may be, "overawed by the mentor" who then, "becomes a parent figure," or they may find, "assertion of personal identity in relation to mentor," or even, "suck the mentor dry, then complain about their incompetence." For the mentor in counter-transference he suggests that the mentor may express "benevolence" and a "desire to be associated with mentee's development," or may make "the mentee stay overawed," or be able to "let go of the" mentee or engage in "victimizing the mentee within the encounter or in the organization." These suggest that training in psychology may be necessary for mentors.

Returning to a central characteristic of mentoring-learning, Garvey (1995) suggests that understanding learning styles can be an aide to mentoring. The view mentors and mentees take about learning may therefore influence the discussions. Eminent scholars of the past, for example Piaget, Jung, Levinson, Buhler, Neugarten, Kegan, Gilligan, and Kohlbergh all positioned learning as something that happens in either stages or phases and arguably, the intellectual movements of the past 200 years have all conspired to make this linear, simplified, and hierarchical model of learning virtually irresistible, and certainly very dominant.

The problem with this view, which constructs practically every curriculum in the educational systems of the developed world, is that it has become part of our everyday outlook and this view of learning implies that it is possible to accelerate people's progress or give them a "leg up the ladder"' of learning. It positions and divides people as achievers or non-achievers, fast learners or slow learners, and it links to the idea that learning can be pre-specified in advance in a cause and effect rational pragmatic world. However, in some contexts, such as learning a specific skill or acquiring some core principle, this may be appropriate but, fundamentally, this approach depends on measurement against the pre-specified pass or fail and it deals with the known world rather than how to cope with uncertainty and complexity. This approach cannot be adequate to develop any awareness of the different kinds of destination available, the speed of travel or the choice of route, nor does it hold out any promise that we will be enriched by the outcome. Mentoring activity that subscribes to this view may distort the communication and change the agenda and this position raises issues as to the purpose and content of mentor education.

The question of what is discussed within mentoring is also part of this issue. Steiner *et al.* (2004) argue that it is important that mentors can provide research training in order to be able to offer support. This raises the question of how subject matter expertise is used within mentoring. Those academic practitioners who critique mentoring activity, often coming from the coaching environment, suggest that mentoring is about gratuitous advice giving (Rosinski, 2003). Studies above seem to suggest that this is the case. However, advice giving is not necessarily a "bad" thing. Knapp *et al.* (1981), Moberg and Velasquez (2004) and Stohl (1986) argue that advice is "potentially transformative"; however, advice should be relevant, address the issue under discussion and be presented as an option for debate.

A further issue of interest raised by the above studies is the issue of "challenge". Many writers, (e.g., Clutterbuck and Megginson, 1999; Colley, 2003; Gibb, 1994) suggest that challenge is an important element within mentoring. Jones (2008) did not find this in her study; "support" was more important, but the mentees expected the mentors to be reactive to this need rather than proactive and as mentees became more independent and self-assured the need for support diminished. However, Colley (2003) suggests that "challenge" can also be part of a power issue and asserts that too strong a challenge can disempower the mentee, particularly if the agenda for mentoring is outside of the relationship.

The nature of the mentoring relationship is also an important element. Neilson and Eisenbach (2003) found that renewal of the relationship through regular feedback and review of the relationship within the relationship played an important part in creating successful outcomes. Healey and Welchert (1990), Fielden *et al.* (2009), and Carden (1990) found, similarly to some of the above studies, that mentoring activity can be mutually beneficial. Levinson *et al.* (1978) and Daloz (1986) argue that mentoring relationships have long been associated with personal transition and change and these studies indicate the same. In one study, "different teaching ideologies" were cited as a problem for mentoring and in another, the "mentor's good reputation". These are about how people are put together. Megginson *et al.* (2005) recommend voluntary matching, but also matching in relation to scheme purpose, and a preference in matching for a small degree of difference between people. "Different ideologies" suggests too large a difference and "good reputation" may link to a sponsorship motive which may also be problematic.

Overall, there are many variations of context and purpose in the above research, but common themes include:

- Identifying the purpose of mentoring within a specific context and articulating it to the participants.
- Understanding the various possible functions of a mentor, including role model.
- Balancing, in context, the importance of personal development and career development.
- Personal qualities; values and skills play an important role.
- Balancing guidance and advice with support, encouragement and challenge.
- Being clear on mutual expectations.
- Considering time, access, and commitment.
- Considering power issues and the potential for these to distort the relationship.

## Empirical Studies on Training Mentors

The subject of mentor training in the literature is limited. However, a number of studies do compare mentors with training, with mentors without training (Giebelhaus and Bowman 2002; Orly, 2008; Pfund *et al.*, 2006). Overall, those with training had statistically significant better results with their mentees than those without. With this in mind we ask:

- What are the aims and purposes of the training?
- What is the content of training?
- What form does the mentor training take?
- When is the mentor training taking place?

## What are the aims and purposes of the training?

Garvey and Alred note that educators in higher education have a variety of aims for teaching their students about mentoring. These are:

- Develop mentoring skills and attributes
- Professional development for the mentor
- Support learners
- Enable mentoring to take place
- Enable people to understand better the concept of mentoring and be better mentors
- Focus on methods and appropriateness of individual development approaches
- Heighten awareness of the role of mentoring
- Aid transition of learning to the workplace
- Part of the knowledge requirement of the course (Garvey and Alred, 2000, p. 115).

Varah *et al.* (1986, p. 32) indicate that the purpose of training was, "to explore the role of the mentor teacher and identify the characteristics of an effective teacher, to develop conference techniques with the inductee in self-evaluation procedures and to become proficient in supervisory methods."

In Pfund *et al.* (2006) the objectives were to train mentors to improve their communication skills, to consider issues of human diversity and discuss various mentoring approaches and Youens *et al.* (2004) indicate the purpose as "quality assurance".

## What is the content of training?

Garvey and Alred (2000, p. 116) note that the content of mentor education is varied and includes, for example, the personal qualities of mentors, skills, and process models. Varah *et al.* (1986) identified two elements of the content of mentor education in a school-based program. The first emphasized the mentor role, the characteristics of an effective teacher, development of conference techniques for self-evaluation, and supervisory methods. The second emphasized effective teaching training procedures and an analysis of teaching through observation. The content therefore was focused on the purpose of the scheme and the tasks the mentor would be expected to work on with their mentees. In Giebelhaus and Bowman (2002) and Feiman-Nemser and Parker (1993), the focus of the mentor training was also on subject matter expertise. Orly's (2008) study focused on different types of mentoring, diversity among students, background characteristics and environment, academic and social difficulties, teaching alternatives, and ending the relationship. The subject of ending relationships is covered in Clutterbuck and Megginson (2004).

Ramani *et al.* (2008, pp. 404–7) identified 12 practical tips for mentor training:

1   Mentors need clear expectations of their roles and enhanced listening and feedback skills.
2   Mentors need awareness of culture and gender issues.
3   Mentors need to support their mentees, but challenge them too.
4   Mentors need a forum to express their uncertainties and problems.
5   Mentors need to be aware of professional boundaries.
6   Mentors also need mentoring.
7   Mentors need recognition.
8   Mentors need to be rewarded.
9   Mentoring needs protected time.
10   Mentors need support.
11   Encouraging peer mentoring unloads the mentor.
12   Continuously evaluate the effectiveness of the mentoring program.

Youens *et al.* (2004) found four main areas of content:

1   Managing the mentees experience
2   Planning
3   Facilitating professional learning
4   Assessing the mentee's performance

In a positive action mentoring program within a UK Police Service (Garvey *et al.*, 2009, p. 183) mentors received training in, "counselling skills, problem-solving, learning styles, conflict management, coaching, motivation theory and action planning."

With the issues of transference and counter-transference raised earlier in the chapter, we could not find any literature that referred to psychological training for mentors, although some mentoring literature draws on developmental psychology (Alred *et al.*, 1998; Johnson *et al.*, 1999; Moberg and Velasquez, 2004). Others (Aryree and Chay, 1994; Beech and Brockbank, 1999; Colley, 2002; Emmerik, 2008; Erdem and Aytemur, 2008; McAuley, 2003; Morgan and Davidson, 2008; Turban and Dougherty, 1994) use various psychodynamic, personality type, and emotional frameworks drawn from psychology to underpin their work and several writers, for example, Johnson *et al.* (1999), Levinson *et al.* (1978), Moberg and Velasquez, (2004), and Ragins and Scandura (1994) link mentoring activity to the psychological concept of "generativity" (Erikson, 1978). However, within the coaching literature the concept of "psychological mindedness" (Lee, 2003) is raised for coach training and rather than full psychological training, it appears that psychological awareness and understanding (Bluckert, 2006) is viewed as appropriate. Perhaps this is also the case for mentors in some circumstances?

## What form does mentor training take?

Orly (2008) included, lectures, group work, presentations during meetings, in-depth studying, library search, and problem solving as approaches to mentor training. Pfund *et al.* (2006) developed an eight-session mentor-training program (equivalent to one day). Garvey and Alred (2000) suggest that such programs need to be delivered in "the mentoring way" in order to mirror mentoring activity. Feiman-Nemser and Parker (1993) evaluated a training program where there were 30 hours in 1–3 hour sessions for mentors, followed by separate workshops on leadership topics. Case studies were also employed with discussions on relevant literature. Youens *et al.* (2004) noted the use of a comprehensive guide for distance learning activities designed to consolidate the new mentor's understanding of mentoring issues.

## When is mentor training taking place?

Giebelhaus and Bowman (2002) investigated mentor training as a preparation for the mentoring role. Others (Orly, 2008) have the mentor training running parallel to the mentoring period and Youens *et al.* (2004) looked at a two training events per year for mentors over two years. In Bush and Coleman (1995) the training preceded the mentoring activities.

Megginson (2000) raised issues on the design of the mentoring scheme. In particular, he highlights the issue of the number of hours needed for people to practice and learn mentoring skills. These seem to range from one-day courses to 1,000 hours. He also asks whether scheme design variables make any difference to the mentoring outcomes. He concludes that the jury is still out.

# Expert Opinion

Given the overall finding in empirical research that skills development for mentors does make a difference to the mentoring activity, we now look at some expert opinion found within practitioner texts. We suggest that an "expert" is someone who has both academic and practitioner-based knowledge and experience. The practitioner element is about continuous professional development and the academic part is about the understanding and practices of research. Both elements develop through critical reflection and critical reflexivity.

With the above description in mind, this limits the field; however, Megginson and Stokes identify three elements in mentor development:

- Skills approach
- Developing a business case
- A conscious seeking-out of the mentor's own way (2004, pp. 94–106).

They suggest that the skills approach focuses on specifically developing appropriate mentoring skills and behaviors within a mentoring conversation. These may include, asking appropriate open questions, checking out assumptions, and active listening.

The business case approach focuses on getting buy-in from the participants in terms of the values of the scheme and helping the participants to make sense of these values in the context of the organization or environment that they operate in. This raises key issues of power, culture, and ownership in most interventions of this type.

The conscious seeking-out approach is learner centered and focuses on drawing out of all participants their existing skills and understanding of mentoring and becoming more aware of these so as to be able to add to them.

They argue that it is likely that all training will contain elements of each, but it is important that conscious decisions are made with regards to the blend of these. It is also important to recognize that, although many mentoring schemes tend to focus primarily on the mentor the skills of the mentee are also important. Skilled mentees are better able to draw what they want and need from mentors and are arguably better equipped to be able to cope with any weaknesses or deficiencies in mentors' skill sets.

Klasen and Clutterbuck (2002) suggest that the quality of the training for mentors is of greater importance than the quantity and offer three key elements necessary for high quality mentor training:

- A clear conceptual model to follow.
- An understanding of the roles and responsibilities.
- An introduction to the relevant skills and techniques of mentoring, with an opportunity to practice and reflect on their performance.

They go on to suggest that: "The objective of training is not mastery of all the skills, but to equip them with the confidence to begin the relationship, the insight to recognize how it should be managed and the tools to identify where the relationship is being least effective and most importantly, how to take appropriate action" (p. 255). They argue that the ideal is for all parties to benefit from some training.

A further consideration are the elements of scheme design. Megginson *et al.* (2005, p. 7) recommend the following:

- Clear link to a business issue, where outcome is measured
- Part of culture change process
- Senior management involved as mentees and mentors
- Link to long-term talent management established
- Mentees (or protégés') in the driving seat
- Light-touch development of individuals and scheme
- Clear framework, publicized, with stories
- Scheme design focused on business issues and change agenda

Alred and Garvey (2010) suggest that voluntarism is necessary. Different organizations deal with this differently, but as a minimum both mentor and mentee should volunteer to participate and there should be a recognition that mentors may need ongoing support and further development during the mentoring period. It is also important that all involved are clear about how the matching process works. There are many different approaches to matching, but nothing can replace people getting together, establishing ground rules, and making an effort to be open and honest. Some experts (Alred and Garvey, 2010; Megginson *et al.*, 2005) recommend the safety net of a "graceful exit" or "no-fault divorce" if a mentoring pair are unable to progress after three meetings and they also suggest that within an organization mentors and mentees need to be matched cross-functionally or inter-professionally. These design elements may help to minimize power problems. Additionally, mentoring is often conceived as the more experienced or older, working with the less experienced and younger and here is the potential heart of the power issue. As Garvey (1997, p. 8) points out in relation to identifying mentors: "We cannot assume that senior people are necessarily the right people."

Additionally, ongoing evaluation of the mentoring is important (Megginson *et al.*, 2005). They recommend a developmental or appreciative enquiry approach to evaluation.

## The Developing Curriculum for Mentors

Taking all the above into account, we look at the future and offer a curriculum for mentor training. We have shown that mentor training is important and does influence the outcomes for mentees. We have also shown that mentoring has various purposes and therefore takes various forms. Mentor training needs to reflect the variety. However, there are also elements upon which those who research and practice mentoring agree, particularly in the area of skills, techniques, and processes. For the future, if mentoring remains an element of organizational and educational development as well as social support, and there is no reason to think that this may change, we ask, what may the future look like?

In Garvey *et al.* (2009), the authors suggest three main themes in the mentoring world that require serious consideration. First, they suggest that one explanation for the rise in interest in mentoring activity across the globe is due, in part, to the social context of the knowledge economy. The concept of the knowledge economy is straightforward, driven by a key question: "How can knowledge be developed and used to add value to goods and services?" (Garvey *et al.*, 2009, p. 221). They argue that this concept is relevant to all sectors of economic activity in capitalist societies, including the voluntary, public and not-for-profit sectors. Learning is central to knowledge acquisition and development and mentoring plays its part in supporting learning through performing a "psychosocial" function (Kram, 1983).

The second theme is "mindset". Mindset is associated with notions of ways of thinking about human affairs. Arguably, mentoring plays its part in working with mindsets within certain communities of practice, again linking to the idea of the "psychosocial". Garvey and Williamson (2002) believe that within Western economies the dominating mindset is pragmatic rationalism. Johnson and Duberley (2000) support this view when they claim that pragmatic positivism dominates management thinking and decision making and added to this, the mentoring literature suggests that mentoring can lead to transformational change among individuals (see, for example, Daloz, 1986; Scandura and Williams, 2004). However, the truth claims about transformational change made by practitioners and the mantra perpetuated by the pragmatic rationalistic mindset of keeping things simple may mean that sometimes, transformational change is not easy because often the issues a mentor is required to discuss may be complex. Allied to this is the idea perpetuated by the rationalistic mindset of "rightness" or the alleged scientific position of "cause and effect". This leads to a belief that there are right answers waiting to be discovered. Clearly, this is the case at certain times and in certain situations, but mentoring does not always deal with the obvious and according to Von Krogh *et al.* (1994, p. 54), "there is no longer a 'right knowledge', but many coexisting conflicting pieces of knowledge."

Extending this line of argument, a further risk of the pragmatic rational mindset is that "simplification" often leads to commodification and this in turn, creates and manufactures language and mentoring becomes a "tool" – an instrument of production. It is not hard to find references in the literature to mentoring as a tool: "Mentoring has been suggested as one tool to assist women in breaking this glass ceiling" (Blake-Beard, 2001, p. 331), and: "Mentoring has been viewed as a crucial tool" (Broadbridge, 1999, p. 338). According to the *Oxford Dictionary*, a "tool" is a device or implement, typically hand-held, used to carry out a particular function or a thing used to help perform a job or, more worryingly, a person exploiting another. A product of the manufacturing language applied in human activities is power or, the misuse of power. The most obvious conflict of interest here is where the mentor acts as both an assessor and a supporter but, generally, we are mindful of Habermas' (1974) notion of the "ideal speech situation" raised earlier in this chapter. For mentoring scheme designers this is an important issue and impacts on the underpinning purpose and philosophy of the mentoring scheme. This is discussed in the section on curriculum in relation to the approach taken to delivery of training.

Third, they suggest that definition is a key issue. As can be seen throughout this chapter, mentoring is an eclectic mix of human activities. This makes definition a problem. The rational pragmatic mindset seeks definition and simplicity; however, mentoring is a social construction and therefore a single and universal definition is simply not possible. However, what is possible is to be clear about the meaning of mentoring within specific contexts. So, the future remains complex and eclectic, but with this understanding, it becomes possible to design appropriate and tailor-made training for specific contexts and purposes.

## Technology

One trend we have observed is that mentor training continues to be developed as an online and distance learning package. While this has the promise of convenience in terms of access, time, and a clear potential to assess knowledge, enabling active situational learning and developing skills through practice and experience is always limited. One of the authors of this chapter was involved in developing an online package for mentors called MentorsByNet. It consisted of a skills-based assessment followed by training packages to help the trainee mentor develop their skills. The cost inhibited full development and the skills elements became simple text-based examples rather than interactive. The program was rolled out across the United Kingdom and its evaluation (Megginson *et al.*, 2003) showed that it was beneficial to the users. A further online training package for mentors within the enterprise environment was developed by one of the authors of this chapter. It involved questions and multiple choice responses, case studies, and voice and filmed activities. However, this was a very expensive program to develop and was inevitably restricted by cost and the medium of the computer resulted in quite a simple program design rather like an online language program. In some ways it served its purpose and its use became extensive despite its limitations. True interactive training programs are expensive to produce and the technology for such products remains inevitably basic.

There are available on the market online mentoring packages. Many of these operate on a "mentoring by numbers" principle, which makes such programs limited. Overall, we have yet to find a mentor training package online that can displace more traditional development.

## A curriculum for mentor and mentee training

The idea of curriculum is central to all debates about education and training and a curriculum is a program or course of study. The educational philosopher Bernstein (1971) raised four key questions in relation to curriculum design and suggested that these need to be addressed in any curriculum design. He asked, what is valid knowledge, a valid pedagogy, a valid evaluation, and a valid realization? In relation to mentor development these also seem relevant. However, the question of pedagogy raises potential power issues and conflicts with Megginson and Stokes' (2004) theory that a mentor needs to find his or her own way. Pedagogy is about teaching and Bernstein (1971) suggests that a high teacher control in education can lead to low autonomy for the learner. In the context of mentoring, where a mentor needs to "consciously seek out their own way" (Megginson and Stokes, 2004, p. 94), an andragogic (Knowles,

1980) approach becomes more appropriate. Knowles (1980) outlined six elements of andragogy, adults:

1 Need to know the reason for learning something.
2 Learn experientially.
3 Need to be responsible and involved in the planning and evaluation of their learning.
4 Are most interested in learning things relevant to themselves.
5 Need a problem-based approach for learning rather than a content-based approach.
6 Tend to be self-motivated rather than need external motivation.

The risk of a pedagogic training program is that it has the potential to disengage the learner and Broad and Newstrom (1992) argued that this approach simply does not deliver. The andragogic approach resonates with the concept of "the mentoring way" (Garvey and Alred, 2000) and is therefore an important element of the curriculum design for mentors. This approach is more empowering for the adult learner and provides an alternative model of learning for potential mentors. This may influence their approach to their subsequent mentoring, potentially reducing the tendency to instruct and advise their mentee and help them to become more andragogic and non-directive in their practice.

Therefore we propose the following content for a mentor-training program:

- Establishing the purpose of the mentoring in the context in which it is employed.
- Mentoring philosophies.
- Exploring a range of possible definitions of mentoring and considering how these apply individually and in the context of the scheme.
- Some psychological education on transference and countertransference.
- Power dynamics and how to work with them in a non-directive way.
- Considering at least two process models of mentoring in relation to the scheme and comparing and contrasting them.
- Skills practice including, listening, questioning, use of summary, challenge and support.
- The importance of establishing ground rules and reviewing them.
- Working with expectations.
- Establishing a good relationship.
- Consider and discuss organizational issues which may impact on mentoring activity.
- Ways of ending the relationship.

We suggest that the minimum time spent on face-to-face development is one day, but it is also important to take into account the variations of experience among mentors. Those with less experience may need more time. Additionally, support for beginner mentors is often important (Alred and Garvey, 2010) and this can take various forms, from one-to-one support to peer group support facilitated by a more experienced mentor.

## Future Research

As shown in the brief history of mentoring at the start, mentoring has had a place as a key element of human intellectual and emotional development for a substantial period. In the last 30 years it has gained momentum throughout industry, commerce, and the public services. Due to this rapid rise in the utilization of mentoring, we believe that its meaning has become confused and altered. There is debate among practitioners and academics as to its true and distinctive nature. Some search for a clear definition of the concept and, in a world of increasing complexity, simplicity has appeal. However, it is probably more appropriate to offer a rich and "thick description" (Geertz, 1974) of mentoring to highlight its complexity rather than attempt to simplify. Therefore, future research must take into account the social context (Bruner, 1990) in which mentoring takes place and the purpose to which it is being employed. In this way the consumers of research develop a great clarity and precision about what is being researched and in what context. Given the wealth of mentoring research extant, perhaps there is now an opportunity for some meta-studies aimed at achieving a genuine "rich description", where patterns and themes may be found and differences explored within the broad and eclectic mix of mentoring activity. This would be with the purpose of fully appreciating the complexity of human developmental relationships.

The paucity of research on mentor training is a cause for concern and perhaps it is time to focus attention on this element as the few papers we employed indicate that training mentors is far from a luxury. How far this is the case, again needs further work.

## Conclusion

This chapter has covered a lot of ground and highlighted the many benefits and pitfalls found within mentoring activity. We have also highlighted the main issues surrounding mentor education and recommended a curriculum for mentors. Clearly, training is a "good thing" and should be undertaken but, it is a complex process and any curriculum for mentors should be developed in line with the scheme's purpose and this should be regularly reviewed in the light of the ever present dynamic changes that occur between mentors and mentees.

## References

Allen, T. and Eby, L. (eds) (2007) *The Blackwell Handbook of Mentoring*. Malden, US: Blackwell Publishing.

Allen, T.D., Eby, L.T., and Lentz, E. (2006a) The relationship between formal mentoring program characteristics and perceived program effectiveness. *Personnel Psychology*, 59, 125–53.

Allen, T.D., Eby, L.T., and Lentz, E. (2006b) Mentorship behaviours and mentorship quality associated with formal mentoring programs: Closing the gap between research and practice. *Journal of Applied Psychology*, 91, 567–78.

Allen, T.D., Eby, L.T., Poteet, M.L., Lentz, E., and Lima, L. (2004) Career benefits associated with mentoring for protégés: A meta-analysis. *Journal of Applied Psychology*, 89(4), 127–38.

Alred, G. and Garvey, B. (2000) Learning to produce knowledge – the contribution of mentoring. *Mentoring and Tutoring*, 8(3), 261–72.

Alred, G. and Garvey, B. (2010) *The Mentoring Pocket Book* (3rd edn). Hants, UK: Management Pocket Book Series – Mentoring Arlesford Press Ltd.

Alred, G., Garvey, B., and Smith, R.D. (1998) Pas de deux – learning in conversations. *Career Development International*, 3(7), 308–14.

Aryree, S. and Chay, Y.W. (1994) An examination of the impact of career-oriented mentoring on work commitment attitudes and career satisfaction among professional and managerial employees. *British Journal of Management*, 5, 241–9.

Beech, N. and Brockbank, A. (1999) Power/knowledge and psychological dynamics in mentoring. *Management Learning*, 30(1), 7–25.

Bernstein, B. (1971) On the classification and framing of educational knowledge. In: M.F.D. Young (ed.) *Knowledge and Control: New Directions for the Sociology of Education*. London: Open University, Collier-Macmillan. pp. 47–69.

Blake-Beard, S. D. (2001) Taking a hard look at formal mentoring programs: A consideration of potential challenges facing women. *Journal of Management Development*, 20(4), 331–45.

Bluckert, P. (2006) *Psychological Dimensions of Executive Coaching*. Maidenhead: Open University Press.

Bray, L. and Nettleton, P. (2007) Assessor or mentor? Role confusion in professional education. *Nurse Education Today*, 27(8), 848–55.

Broad, M.L. and Newstrom, J. (1992) *Transfer of Training: Action-packed Strategies to Ensure High Payoff from Training Investments.*, Reading, MA: Addison-Wesley.

Broadbridge, A. (1999) Mentoring in retailing: A tool for success? *Personnel Review*, 28(4), 336–55.

Bruner, J. (1990) *Acts of Meaning*. Cambridge, MA: Harvard University Press.

Bush, T. and Coleman, M. (1995) Professional development for heads. The role of mentoring. *Journal of Educational Administration*, 33(5), 60–73.

Caraccioli, L.A. (1760) *The True Mentor, or, An Essay on the Education of Young People in Fashion*. London: J. Coote at the Kings Arms in Paternoster Row.

Carden, A.D. (1990) Mentoring and adult career development; the evolution of a theory. *The Counselling Psychologist*, 18(2), 275–99.

Clark, R.A., Harden, S., and Johnson, W.B. (2000) Mentor relationships in clinical psychology doctoral training. Results of a national survey. *Teaching of Psychology*, 27(4), 262–8.

Clawson, J.G. (1996) Mentoring in information age. *Leadership and Organization Development Journal*, 17(3), 6–15.

Clutterbuck, D. (2004) *Everyone Needs a Mentor – Fostering Talent in your Organisations* (4th edn). London: CIPD.

Clutterbuck, D. and Megginson, D. (1999) *Mentoring Executives and Directors*. Oxford: Butterworth Heinemann.

Clutterbuck, D. and Megginson, D. (2004) All good things must come to an end: Winding up and winding down a mentoring relationship. In: D. Clutterbuck and G. Lane (eds) *The Situational Mentor: An International Review of Competences and Capabilities in Mentoring*. Gower: Aldershot. pp. 178–93.

Colley, H. (2002) A "rough guide" to the history of mentoring from a Marxist Feminist perspective. *Journal of Education for Teaching*, 28(3), 247–63.

Colley, H. (2003) *Mentoring for Social Inclusion: A Critical Approach to Nurturing Mentoring Relationships*. London: Routledge Falmer.

Daloz, L.A. (1986) *Effective Teaching and Mentoring*. San Francisco: Jossey Bass.

Emmerik, I.J. (2008) It is not only mentoring. The combined influences of individual-level and team-level support on job performance. *Career Development International*, 13 (7), 575–93.

Erdem, F. and Aytemur, J.O., (2008) Mentoring – a relationship based on trust: Qualitative research. *Public Personnel Management*, 37(1), 55–65.

Erikson, E. (1978) *Childhood and Society*. Harmondsworth, UK: Penguin Books Ltd.

Feiman-Nemser, S. and Parker, M.B. (1993) Mentoring in context: A comparison of two US programs for beginning teachers. *International Journal of Educational Research*, 19(8), 699–718.

Feiman-Nemser, S., Parker, M.B., and Zeicher, K. (1994) (reprinted 2005) Are mentor teachers teacher educators? In: D. McIntyre, H. Hagger, and M. Witkin (eds) *Perspectives on School-Based Teacher Education*. London: Routledge Falmer.

Fénélon De La Mothe F.S. (1699) *The Adventures of Telemachus, 1 and 2*. Trans. St. John's Square 1808. London 1808: Hawkesworth J. Union Printing Office.

Fielden, S.L., Davidson M.J., and Sutherland V.J. (2009) Innovations in coaching and mentoring: Implications for nurse leadership development. *Health Services Management Research*, 22(2), 92–9.

Ganser, T. (1996) What do mentors say about mentoring? *Journal of Staff Development*, 17(3), 36–9.

Gardiner, C. (2005) Learning mentors. In: D. Clutterbuck, D. Megginson, B. Garvey, P. Stokes, and R. Garrett-Harris (eds) *Mentoring in Action*. London: Kogan Page. pp. 56–61.

Garvey, B. (1994) A dose of mentoring. *Education and Training*, 36(4), 18–26.

Garvey, B. (1995) Healthy signs for mentoring. *Education and Training*, 37(5), 12–19.

Garvey, B. (1997) What's in it for me? *The Learning Organization*, 4(1), 3–9.

Garvey, B. and Alred, G. (2000) Educating mentors. *Mentoring and Tutoring*, 8(2), 113–26.

Garvey, B. and Williamson, B. (2002) *Beyond Knowledge Management: Dialogue, Creativity and the Corporate Curriculum*. Harlow, UK: Pearson Education.

Garvey, B., Stokes, P., and Megginson, D. (2009) *Coaching and Mentoring Theory and Practice*. London: Sage.

Geertz, C. (ed.) (1974) *Myth, Symbol and Culture*. New York: W.W. Norton and Company Inc.

Gibb, S. (1994) Evaluating mentoring. *Education and Training*, 36(5), 32–9.

Giebelhaus, C.R. and Bowman, C.L. (2002) Teaching mentors: Is it worth the effort? *Journal of Educational Research*, 95(4), 246–54.

Habermas, J. (1974) *Theory and Practice*. London: Heinemann (first published in 1971 as *Theorie und Praxis*).

Hawkey, K. (1998) Mentor pedagogy and student teacher professional development: A study of two mentoring relationships. *Teaching and Teacher Education*, 14(6), 657–70.

Healey, C.C. and Welchert, A.J. (1990) Mentoring relations: A definition to advance research and practice. *Educational Researcher*, 19(9), 17–21.

Høigaard, R., and Mathisen, P. (2009) Benefits of formal mentoring for female leaders. *International Journal of Evidence Based Coaching and Mentoring*, 7(2), 64–70.

Ingersoll, R and Kralik, J. (2004) The impact of mentoring on teachers retention: What the research says. *University of Pennsylvania: GSE Publications*.

Johnson, P. and Duberley, J. (2000) *Understanding Management Research*. London: Sage.

Johnson, S.K., Geroy, G.D., and Orlando, V.G. (1999) The mentoring model theory: Dimensions in mentoring protocols, *Career Development International*, 4(7), 384–91.

Jones, J. (2008) What makes an effective mentor within the HE sector. *International Journal of Mentoring and Coaching*, VI(3), 12, 1–20.

Klasen, N. and Clutterbuck, D. (2002) *Implementing Mentoring Schemes*. Oxford: Butterworth-Heinemann.

Knapp, M.L., Stohl, C., and Reardon, K.K. (1981) "Memorable" messages. *Journal of Communication*, 31(4), 27–41.

Knowles, M. (1980) *The Modern Practice of Adult Education: From Pedagogy to Andragogy*. Cambridge; Englewood Cliffs: Prentice Hall.

Kram, K.E. (1983) Phases of the mentor relationship. *Academy of Management Journal*, 26(4), 608–25.

Kram, K.E. (1985) Improving the mentoring process. *Training and Development Journal*, April, 40–2.

Kram, K.E. and Chandler, D.E. (2005) Applying an adult development perspective to developmental networks. *Career Development International*, 10(6/7), 548–66.

Lee, G. (2003) *Leadership Coaching: From Personal Insight to Organisational Performance*. London: CIPD.

Levinson, D.J., Darrow, C.M., Klein, E.C., Levinson, M.H., and McKee, B. (1978) *The Seasons of a Man's Life*. New York: Knopf.

Levinson, W., Kaufman, K., Clark, B., and Tolle, S.W. (1991) Mentors and role models for women in academic medicine. *Western Journal of Medicine*, 154(4), 423–6.

Lindén, J., Ohlin, M., and Brodin, E. (in press) Mentorship, supervision and learning experience in PhD education. *Studies in Higher Education.*

Lindgren, U. (2000) *An Empirical Study of Mentorship in Higher Education. Meaning, Design and Effects.* PhD thesis, Didactica Umensis no. 3. Umeå University.

Lindgren, U. (2003) Mentorship for novice teachers. Experiences of a Swedish mentorship program. In: U. Lindgren (ed.) *Mentorship for Learning and Development. Contributions from an International Conference on Mentorship for Beginner Teachers and School Pupils.* Umeå University June 1–4, 2003. Didactica Umensis no. 5. Umeå University.

Lindgren, U. (2006) Towards a professional identity, På väg mot en yrkesidentitet. *Didactica Umensis no. 7.* Uiversity of Umeå.

McAuley, M.J. (2003) Transference, countertransference and mentoring: The ghost in the process. *British Journal of Guidance and Counselling,* 31, 11–24.

Megginson, D. (2000) Current issues in mentoring. *Career Development International,* 5(4–5), 256–60.

Megginson, D. and Stokes, P. (2004) Development and supervision for mentors. In: D. Clutterbuck and G. Lane (eds) *The Situational Mentor: An International Review of Competences and Capabilities in Mentoring.* Aldershot: Gower. pp. 94–107.

Megginson, D., Clutterbuck, D., Garvey, B., Stokes, P., and Garrett-Harris, R. (eds) (2005) *Mentoring in Action* (2nd edn). London: Kogan Page.

Megginson, D., Stokes, P., and Garrett-Harris, R. (2003) *MentorsByNet – an e-mentoring Programme for Small to Medium Enterprises (SME) Entrepreneurs/Managers.* Dronsfield, UK: Mentoring and Coaching Research Group (MCRG).

Merrick, L. and Stokes, P. (2003) Mentor development and supervision: A passionate joint enquiry. *International Journal of Coaching and Mentoring* (e-journal), 1, www.emccouncil.org.

Moberg, D.J. and Velasquez, M. (2004) The ethics of mentoring. *Business Ethics Quarterly,* 14(1), 95–102.

Morgan, L.M. and Davidson, M.J. (2008) Sexual dynamics in mentoring relationships – a critical review. *British Journal of Management,* 19(1), 120–9.

Neilson, T. and Eisenbach, R. (2003) Not all relationships are created equal: Critical actors of high-quality mentoring relationships. *International Journal of Mentoring and Coaching,* 1(1) EMCC, www.emccouncil.org.

Nilsson, L (2000). *Believing in one's Self-Efficacy. The Significance of a Mentor Program for the Managerial Careers pf Fourteen Women.* PhD thesis no. 2000:10. Department of Education and Teaching Methods for Natural and Social Science, Centre for Research in Teaching and Learning, Luleå University of Technology (in Swedish).

Orly, M. (2008) Mentoring mentors as a tool for personal and professional empowerment in teacher education. *International Journal of Evidence Based Coaching and Mentoring,* 6(1), 1–18.

Pfund, C., Pribbenow, C.M., Branchaw, J., Miller Lauffer, J., and Handelsman, J. (2006) The merits of training mentors. *Science,* 311, January, 473–4. With supporting online material.

Pololi, L. and Knight, S. (2005) Mentoring faculty in academic medicine. A new paradigm? *Journal of General Internal Medicine,* 20(9), 866–70.

Ragins, B.R. (1989) Barriers to mentoring: The female manager's dilemma. *Human Relations,* 42(1), 1–23.

Ragins, B.R. (1994) *Gender and Mentoring: A Research Agenda.* Presented at the 40th annual meeting of the South Eastern Psychological Association, New Orleans, LA, April.

Ragins, B.R. and Cotton, J.L. (1996) Jumping the hurdles: Barriers to mentoring for women in organizations. *Leadership and Organization Development Journal,* 17(3), 37–41.

Ragins, B.R. and Cotton, J.L. (1999) Mentor functions and outcomes: A comparison of men and women in formal and informal mentoring relationships. *Journal of Applied Psychology,* 84, 529–50.

Ragins, B.R. and Scandura, T. (1994) Gender differences in expected outcomes of mentoring relationships. *Academy of Management Journal,* 37, 957–71.

Ragins, B.R. and Scandura, T.A. (1999) Burden or blessing? Expected costs and benefits of being a mentor. *Journal of Organisational Behavior*, 20(4), 493–509.

Ramani, S., Gruppen, L., and Krajic Kachur, E.K. (2006) Twelve tips for developing effective mentors. *Medical Teacher*, 28(5), 404–8.

Rix, M. and Gold, J. (2000) With a little help from my academic friend: Mentoring change agents. *Mentoring and Tutoring*, 8(1), 47–62.

Rosinski, P. (2003) *Coaching Across Cultures*. London: Nicholas Brealey.

Rowley, J.B. (1999) The good mentor. *Educational Leadership*, 56(8), 20–2.

Scandura, T. and Williams, E. (2004) Mentoring and transformational leadership: The role of supervisory career mentoring. *Journal of Vocational Behavior*, 65(3), 448–68.

Steiner, J.F., Curtis, P., Landphear, B.P., Vu K.O., and Main, D.S. (2004) Assessing the role of influential mentors in the research development of primary care fellows. *Academic Medicine*, 79(9), 865–72.

Stohl, C. (1986) The role of memorable messages in the process of organizational socialization. *Communication Quarterly*, 34, 231–49.

Turban, D. and Dougherty, T. (1994) Role of protégé personality in receipt of mentoring and career success. *Academy of Management Journal*, 37(3), 688–702.

Varah, L.J., Theune, W.S., and Parker, L. (1986) Beginning teachers: Sink or swim? *Journal of Teacher Education*, 37(1) 30–4.

Von Krogh, G., Roos, J., and Slocum, K. (1994) An essay on corporate epistemology. *Strategic Management Journal*, 15, 53–71.

Waters, L., McCabe, M., Kjellerup, D., and Kiellerup, S. (2002) The role of formal mentoring on business success and self-esteem in participants of a new business start-up program. *Journal of Business and Psychology*, 17(1), 107–21.

Westlander, G. (2010a) When mentoring and coaching leave lasting impressions: Middle managers look back. *The International Journal of Mentoring and Coaching*, VIII(1), June, 24–49.

Westlander, G. (2010b) *När mentorskap och coaching sätter djupa spår* [When mentoring and coaching leave lasting impressions.] Stockholm: GML förlag.

Youens, B. and Bailey, M. (2004) The impact of quality assurance on mentor training in initial teacher education partnerships: A UK perspective. *Canadian Journal of Educational Administration and Policy*, 32(1) (June), 1–18 III, 24–49.

# 14

# Mentoring Programs for Under-represented Groups

Rowena Ortiz-Walters and Lucy L. Gilson

## Introduction

Companies from around the world and across a wide variety of industries are implementing mentoring programs to provide career, leadership, and personal development for employees (Clutterbuck, 2002; Hegstad and Wentling, 2004; Smith *et al.*, 2005). A common theme among many of these programs, whether in the private, public, or non-profit sectors, is that they are designed to assist employees who have limited access to mentoring (Allen *et al.*, 2001). Often, these individuals are members of under-represented groups such as racial or ethnic minorities (Ortiz-Walters and Gilson, 2005; Thomas, 1993). While companies continue to implement formal programs to help those who may not have access to informal mentors, our understanding of the mentoring of under-represented groups remains limited.

As such, we seek to explore in detail the mentoring of under-represented workers primarily in the United States, Europe, and Australia. This sub-sample is selected purely because this is where scholarly research is most readily available; thus the work discussed may not be as relevant to all under-represented groups, although broad themes are likely to be common in many cultures.

We begin our chapter with a review of the most current literature to outline the empirical findings that contribute to the basis of what "we know". Drawing on this body of work, we then identify a number of gaps in existing organizational knowledge. Finally, we pose a number of questions and propose recommendations regarding areas that future research may want to consider. Our aim is to offer a starting point for an in-depth dialogue so that scholars and managers can begin to tease apart these relationships, and in doing so, open the *black box* and understand what mentoring individuals from under-represented groups really means.

*The Wiley Blackwell Handbook of the Psychology of Coaching and Mentoring*, First Edition.
Edited by Jonathan Passmore, David B. Peterson, and Teresa Freire.
© 2013 John Wiley & Sons, Ltd. Published 2016 by John Wiley & Sons, Ltd.

# The Formal Mentoring of Under-represented Individuals and Groups: Setting the Stage

In the past two decades, interest in formal mentoring has continued to grow, as evidenced by the development of institutes such as the European Mentoring and Coaching Council, the Australian Mentor Center, and the amount of research being conducted. Formal mentoring involves a program that is initiated, sponsored, and managed by an organization whereby protégés are matched based upon specific criteria and often for a specified period of time with mentors, who tend to be more senior with regard to position or tenure (Baugh and Fagenson-Eland, 2007; Wanberg *et al.*, 2003). On the whole, mentoring relationships are beneficial to all parties (Baugh and Fagenson-Eland, 2007; Douglas and McCauley, 1999; Seibert, 1999). Not surprisingly therefore, the trend has been that more and more organizations, regardless of industry, size or geographic location are implementing formal mentoring programs at an increasing rate (Clutterbuck, 2002, 2004; Douglas and McCauley, 1999).

While sharing some overarching similarities, there is great variation between formal mentoring programs. Differences have been found between organizations and industries (Allen *et al.*, 2001; Smith *et al.*, 2005), as well as between the United States (Viator, 2001), Australia (Burgess and Dyer, 2009; MacGregor, 2000), and the United Kingdom (Armstrong *et al.*, 2002). In a US-based study of a one-year program established for employees of a federal agency (Lyons and Oppler, 2004), coordinators assigned mentors, taking into consideration protégés' input. In the program examined by Wanberg *et al.* (2007) the mentoring relationships only lasted for nine months and the focus was on personal career development and organizational orientation.

Despite their differences, the purpose of most programs is to provide career and leadership development to employees who may not otherwise have access to mentoring (Allen *et al.*, 2001). Members of under-represented groups, such as racial or ethnic minorities (Blake-Beard *et al.*, 2007; Ortiz-Walters and Gilson, 2005), are often those most likely faced with this challenge. Due to a lack of similar others in senior positions (Ragins, 1997; Thomas, 1990) individuals from under-represented groups frequently lack access to mentors who are, on the surface (i.e., demographically), similar to themselves. The result is that members of under-represented groups are likely to find themselves disproportionately in formal relationships with dissimilar mentors. This is problematic on many levels, and while some research finds mixed results (for a review of recent findings see Blake-Beard *et al.*, 2007; McKeen and Bujaki, 2007), typically individuals in more similar relationships benefit the most from their associations (cf. O'Neill, 2002; Ortiz-Walters and Gilson, 2005; Thomas, 1990).

In light of this, we explore in more detail formal mentoring for individuals from under-represented groups; meaning those in the numerical minority, often with less power and of a marginal or disadvantaged status (Kanter, 1977). Our focus is specifically on members of racio-ethnic minorities (e.g., Hispanics in the United States, indigenous aboriginals in Australia and black or Asian employees in Europe). While under-represented individuals can be defined based upon their sex, sexual orientation, religious background, or physical ability (Ragins, 1997), there is significant variability among these groups and therefore there are benefits from examining them independently of one another. Along with this, the ethnic composition of the workforce continues to change, which has implications for mentoring. For instance, in 2005, 30 percent of the US workforce was non-white, but these numbers are projected to increase to about 48 percent by 2050 (Lee and Mather, 2008). In British organizations black, Asian and minority ethnic (BAME) employees accounted for 8.5 percent of employees in 2007, up from 5.4 percent in 2000 (Kerr, 2008). As in the United States, black and Asian employees are under-represented at management grades, with white employees holding 93 percent of management positions (Kerr, 2008).

## Challenges to Studying Under-represented Groups

While many mentoring programs are developed to help individuals who might have limited access to informal mentors, our understanding of the mentoring of under-represented individuals or groups remains sparse. Although paradoxical, this is really not surprising. Examining the effects of formal mentoring on under-represented groups is rather difficult from a pure numbers perspective. By virtue of being under-represented, the sample size is often too small for meaningful statistical results and thus conclusions, by necessity, have to be based on the sample as a whole, which in most instances tends to be mainly white or Caucasian. This by no means brings into question the validity of the reported results; however, it does mean that our understanding of the under-represented portion of the sample remains unexplored.

For example, Ragins *et al.* (2000) examined mentoring across a diverse set of industries in the United States: social work, engineering, and journalism. Despite their extensive search, 92 percent of protégés were white, so no meaningful conclusions can be made regarding the effectiveness of the mentoring relationships for the 8 percent of the sample that were obviously under-represented. Here, it is simply a lack of statistical power that drives our inability to understand the relationships of the non-white protégés. Similarly, in a study designed to further understand the "career prospects of their female and minority professionals and managers" (Raabe and Beehr, 2003, p. 277), two formal mentoring programs were examined. In one of the firms the program originally had a diversity goal to retain females and minorities. Somewhat ironically, at the time the study took place the program had been expanded to cater to employees, so 62 percent of the mentees were Caucasian, as were 86 percent of the mentors. Of the dyads, 32 percent were Caucasian, two were African-American, and 27 were of mixed-ethnicity. The authors thus stated that, "this study did not provide a subsample big enough to allow sound investigations on matching and non-matching ethnicities" (p. 283).

In contrast to these two examples, many studies simply do not report the racial ethnic compositional mix of the sample. This could be because the sample is homogeneous on these characteristics. For example, in a study of frontline employees at four branches of an Athens bank all respondents are native Hellenes (Greeks) (Bozionelos, 2006). In other instances, the reader is left to assume the sample is homogeneous, as might be the case with a study of the mentoring of Chinese employees working for a state-owned food and beverage company (Bozionelos and Wang, 2006). Lastly, the numbers may not be given simply because they are too small to be meaningful. For instance, Bozionelos (2004) sampled white collar administrators from three universities in the north-west of England. The sample is described as slightly more female (66 percent) and married (57 percent); however, no details are given with regard to race or ethnicity.

We highlighted these examples because of their diverse samples and sampling strategies. Further, they used several industries where census data tells us there are larger proportions of minority employees (i.e., social work, education, banking, etc.). However, it is the simple lack of numbers that makes the groups we are interested in understanding here, under-represented in the workforce. At the same time, however, this limits our ability to draw meaningful conclusions regarding their mentoring. It does need to be stated that in all cases, this is not a limitation of any of these studies, but rather a reality of the phenomena. Finally, when race/ethnicity is provided it is usually treated as an "unexplained variance" (Blake-Beard *et al.*, 2007), further hindering our ability to advance mentoring theory as it relates to under-represented groups.

## Formal and Informal Mentoring: A Comparison

Research comparing informal and formal mentoring describes the dyadic relationships between mentor and protégé (or mentee) as differing on a number of attributes (Chao *et al.*, 1992; Ragins and Cotton, 1999). Differences exist in terms of initiation or how the relationships are initially formed (e.g., Chao *et al.*, 1992; Ragins and Cotton, 1999). Informal relationships develop between individuals who choose to work with one another often because of a perceived sense of similarity, trust, or shared experiences (Kram, 1985). Informal mentoring involves a reciprocal process of identification where mentors see in protégés a more junior version of themselves and protégés see individuals they aspire to be like (Ragins, 1997). In comparison, formal mentoring involves a third party, typically a program coordinator who does the matching based on a set of criteria that can range from demographic characteristics, career goals, and functional area, to just matching people randomly so everyone gets a mentor. The key here is that it is the third party who makes judgments regarding perceived similarity between mentor and protégé (Douglas and McCauley, 1999; Phillips-Jones, 1983).

A second key distinction is that formal relationships usually have a limited timeframe associated with them (Allen and Eby, 2004). This timeframe is also determined by the program manager or organization and is most often about a year in duration. Informal relationships have no time specifications and last as long as both parties feel their association is meaningful (Kram, 1985). Furthermore, with regard to time and structure, formal programs often have meeting guidelines (Wanberg *et al.*, 2003) regarding how often, when and even where mentors and protégés should meet. Given that informal relationships are initiated by one of the parties involved, there is usually no need to set up such a structure. In contrast, because formal programs may match individuals who do not know one another or have little in common, without specifying when they should meet, interaction may never take place. Finally, the location of meetings is often specified in formal programs to ensure that appropriate locations are selected. This is critically important for many under-represented groups where individuals may not be comfortable in certain settings due to religious, ethnic, or other beliefs. Meeting location also may be important to ensure both the appropriateness of the venue and the appearance of propriety in the interaction between individuals who are different from one another.

Whereas formal mentoring programs have been described as the "poor cousin" (Baugh and Fagenson-Eland, 2007, p. 249) of informal relationships, it is important to note that they are not without merit and continue to offer a number of benefits, particularly to individuals who might not otherwise have access to mentoring. From a macro lens, they also offer benefits in that they start to embed mentoring into the organizational culture or climate (Baugh and Fagenson-Eland, 2007). By virtue of organizational backing, formal mentoring programs are more visible than informal ones (Davis, 2005). This increased visibility can result in higher accountability of mentors for their protégés' development (Gilson and Ortiz-Walters, 2005), contributing to a developmental culture. However, visibility also may be a double-edged sword. What might this added level of visibility mean in the case of mentoring protégés from under-represented groups? Does visibility heighten pressure on the relationship and protégés to perform, or is it beneficial in that it places more pressure on the mentor to be accountable for the development of the protégé? Does visibility and accountability make it more or less "acceptable" to work with individuals who are different demographically or from the majority of the organization?

A theme throughout this chapter is that we will leave readers with a number of questions at the end of each section. These are all questions where, despite a great deal of searching, the literature offers no immediate answers, therefore we hope they will spur others to examine them in more detail. While some questions are broad and theoretical in nature, others are more narrow and empirical; however, we believe they all need to be asked if we are going to move this conversation forward.

## What is known about mentoring under-represented groups?

As the discussion above alluded to, formal relationships are much more structured in nature since they are typically part of a career development initiative sponsored by an organization. This necessitates that a project coordinator or human resources manager oversee the implementation of key structural components of the program to ensure that successful, effective formal relationships can form. There are, however, some basic structural attributes that are common across formal mentoring programs in a wide variety of settings (O'Brien *et al.*, 2010). For example, when dealing with the mentoring of a diverse population, thoughtful consideration and planning needs to be given to the composition of the target group; the purpose of the program and developmental needs of the target group, along with key processes such as: selection, matching, training, resource needs, and leadership support. Finally, evaluating the effectiveness of the program in terms of desired outcomes (e.g., amount and types of mentoring support) is also critical (Clutterbuck, 2004; Megginson *et al.*, 2006; O'Brien *et al.*, 2010), especially if funding is required and may need to be justified in the future.

For our purposes, the target group of formal mentoring is predominantly racio-ethnic minorities within organizational settings in the United States, Europe, and Australia. We focus on those components of formal programs mentioned above for which there is some available data highlighting what we know and do not know about how they affect mentoring outcomes. In subsequent sections we address other practices of formal programs, such as selection and training that have received even less attention in the extant literature.

## Access and prevalence of formal mentoring

A great deal of effort has gone into determining if there are differences between minority and majority group members in access to informal mentors, the implicit assumption being that access to formal mentoring is equal across all employees. To examine this, Viator (2001) sampled African-Americans and Caucasians employed at large US public accounting firms. Whereas no significant differences in access to formal mentoring were detected among managerial accountants (39.3 percent for African-Americans versus 35.1 percent for Caucasians), he did find that African-American senior accountants (76.5 percent) reported having an assigned mentor more often than their Caucasian counterparts

(55.4 percent). Furthermore, there appear to be differences in formal mentoring among African-Americans, with senior accountants being more likely to have access to a formal mentor than are higher-level managers. This is an interesting finding because it suggests that African-Americans at the senior accountant level were more likely to have a formal mentor than those at the managerial accountant level. The work of Viator (2001) suggests that for under-represented minorities, at least in the United States, there may well be an interaction between being mentored and the organizational hierarchical level attained.

Another study, as it related to under-represented groups and access to formal mentors, comes from research conducted on the mentoring relationships of high-ranking women across different countries (Argentina, Brazil, Canada, Chile, Mexico, United States, and the West Indies; Monserrat *et al.*, 2009). Across the countries there was significant variation in norms, beliefs, and standards of behavior and, as such, this study paints a more complete picture of what mentoring is and how it is experienced by under-represented groups from diverse cultural backgrounds. Participation in formal mentoring programs was a noted difference based solely on national origin. On average, over 50 percent of the women from Spanish-speaking countries reported having a formal mentor. The women from the United States, on the other hand, were the least likely to participate in formal programs, with only 36 percent reporting obtaining a mentor through formal means; instead they had greater access to informal mentoring. The authors propose that these observed differences might be attributed to variability in cultural norms associated with power and cross-gender relationships. For example, there may be less of a stigma attached to cross-gender work relationships in the United States and therefore greater access to informal mentors, who are typically male since they hold most high-level, influential positions (Ragins, 1997). In Spanish-speaking countries, it could be the case that the only acceptable way for men and women to have a professional relationship is through formal programs that have been sanctioned by the organization and are thus legitimate.

Another plausible explanation offered by the authors as to why there is a greater prevalence of formal mentoring in Spanish-speaking countries is because of a tradition known as "apadrinar" (Monserrat *et al.*, 2009) in which elders are expected to serve in the capacity of godparent to those who are younger and less experienced. Similar research finds that informal mentoring is more prevalent in Chinese and Japanese organizations (Bozionelos and Wang, 2006; Bright, 2005). Here, cultural characteristics such as collectivism, lifetime employment, respect for elders, and a high value placed on duty rather than contractual bonds make mentoring a component of the value system. These cultural characteristics are not as common within English-speaking cultures of Anglo-Saxon origin (Bozionelos and Wang, 2006).

More information about access to formal mentors, in particular cross-race mentoring for under-represented minorities, can be found in work by Thomas *et al.* (2005) who conducted an experiment of formal peer mentoring in a higher education context. Based on fictitious profiles of black college students, it was found that white students were willing to become a formal peer mentor when the black students showed high levels of self-initiative. This finding is akin to what Blake-Beard *et al.* (2007) labeled a "mentoring tax" or an extra hurdle that requires racial minorities to show they have potential. In the high proactive experimental scenario, white participants were also more willing to mentor black women. This may be consistent with the notion that, due to their identities, black women are a "double minority" under-represented in both race and gender and thus, when they show self-initiative, mentors may want to work with them because they are seen as more capable and motivated than black men who are only under-represented with regard to race.

What is clear from these studies is that race plays a significant role in access to formal mentors, but that this association may not be as straightforward as originally thought. In other words, does race impact access to mentoring in the same way for all members of racio-ethnic groups? Our review of the literature seems to indicate that in addition to race, access to a formal mentor also might be dependent on hierarchical position, national cultural background, and initiative. It is critical, therefore, to move away from comparisons only to majority group members because differences may arise within under-represented groups themselves, and given that the group is usually small, these more subtle nuances will get lost.

Beyond access, to begin to understand these developmental relationships more fully and at a deeper level, we next consider the specific experiences of individuals from under-represented groups with formal mentoring. Some of this is gleaned by considering the developmental needs and expectations of protégés of color and, under-represented members themselves in the role of the mentor.

## Needs of the under-represented and their role as mentors

It has been stated, and makes good sense, that the purpose of a formal mentoring program should be driven by the specific needs of the target group for whom it was initiated (Megginson *et al.*, 2006). This is even more important given that somewhere between 30 to 50 percent of programs fail because they do not have a clearly articulated purpose (Clutterbuck, 2002). Many programs targeted at minorities typically seek to increase retention rates, or increase diversity at top levels of the organization (Douglas and McCauley, 1999). It is interesting, therefore, that the existing literature does not appear to provide much in the way of guidance regarding these goals, or consider them as outcomes of interest. Furthermore, it appears that programs are being developed without much knowledge of what the *specific* developmental needs are of the individuals considered to be under-represented. Another area which we know very little about is that of under-represented minorities as mentors. Could race, ethnicity, or cultural heritage influence the readiness (and willingness) of a mentor to provide for the developmental needs of their protégés?

Work by Lewellen-Williams and her colleagues (2006) explored the developmental needs of minority protégés and the readiness of assigned mentors of color to provide for those needs. In the context of academic medicine, protégés of color reported needing the most support in the area of networking. For career-related developmental needs, they expressed needing help in establishing career goals, problem-solving, feedback, and coaching, whereas for more psychosocial needs the list included self-confidence and role modeling. Minority mentors, on the other hand, reported feeling most prepared to help protégés with career-related support, like setting professional goals and providing feedback and coaching, while feeling somewhat comfortable building up protégés' confidence and serving as role models (Lewellen-Williams *et al.*, 2006). With respect to amount of support provided, female mentors of color report giving more psychosocial and career mentoring than they received (Simon *et al.*, 2008). On the whole, formal mentors base their mentoring style on their experiences as a protégé, so in many cases, what is valued as a mentor is what was lacking as a protégé (Smith *et al.*, 2005). Based on these results, it is interesting to note that formal mentors from minority groups appear to be well suited to meet the developmental needs listed as important to minority mentees.

The findings above further highlight the need for clarity around the expectations of under-represented protégés, and the mentoring functions that will help them achieve their developmental goals. Clutterbuck (2004) has highlighted the relevance of expectations in cross-cultural formal mentoring. As an example, mentors-to-be (expatriate managers who were English and Dutch) believed the emphasis should be on stretching protégés for personal learning, thus providing fewer mentoring functions, forcing protégés to be more self-reliant. Protégés-to-be who were from Brunei, on the other hand, expected their mentors to be nurturing and supportive; thus they expected more mentoring functions that would create greater, not less, dependency on mentors. Clearly the expectations of the parties from different cultures were not aligned. More problematic is that when mentee and mentor are demographically similar expectations can be inflated. That is, by virtue of being under-represented in organizational settings, minority protégés may expect more from a minority mentor, such as going out on a limb for them and protecting them, given they have likely shared similar organizational experiences and understand the challenges of being in a minority status (Ragins, 2002). But are these expectations realistic given the limited power base of many minority mentors?

Moving forward, it would seem that assessments and inventories could be a valuable tool to better match both same and cross-race protégés and mentors based on needs and capabilities. This is particularly fascinating given that developmental needs and mentor readiness are not necessarily visible characteristics and may take a deeper-level relationship to be drawn out. In addition, it would be fruitful to assess the extent to which some of the developmental needs expressed by protégés and the capabilities of their formal mentors generalize to other contexts. Since the sample sizes here are very small, drawing conclusions is hard, but as previously discussed they provide a good starting place to move the conversation forward. This leads to the question of matching and whether protégés should in fact be paired with similar or dissimilar mentors and the results in terms of levels and types of support.

## Mentor-protégé match

Once the needs of protégés are assessed, one of the major hurdles to the success of formal mentoring is matching mentees with mentors (Armstrong *et al.*, 2002; Clutterbuck, 2004; Hale, 2000; Megginson *et al.*, 2006). In some formal programs protégés can have a say in mentor selection; in other instances mentors are randomly assigned. Sometimes they are carefully matched based on a set of criteria, or the matching can be done in a format akin to speed-dating (Baugh and Fagenson-Eland, 2007). Therefore, little is known regarding what is actually the best or even a better matching process for under-represented minorities. One salient basis for matching is often race or ethnicity (Lyons and Oppler, 2004). Do protégés from under-represented groups benefit more from being matched with similar versus different mentors – to match or mismatch (Hale, 2000) – or is it other program criteria that matter?

One perspective calls for same-race matching, because there is evidence to suggest under-represented individuals in more similar mentorships typically benefit most strongly from their associations (cf. O'Neill, 2002; Thomas, 1990). This is based on the tenets of most theories of interpersonal relationships that argue matches based on similarity, especially surface-level demographics (Tsui and O'Reilly, 1989), will result in the best fit (e.g., Byrne, 1971). Diversified mentoring theory (Ragins, 1997) further states that the types (i.e., career and psychosocial) and amount of support received differ based upon whether relationships are between individuals who are more similar or different from one another and whether support comes from a mentor of an under-represented group. If the outcome desired is role modeling then trust and interpersonal-comfort are needed, and similarity may be a driver in the matching process. Qualitative data from case studies indicate a same-race approach may be needed when designing formal mentoring for black aboriginals (Burgess and Dyer, 2009). The argument here is that culturally it is beneficial to get to know others on a personal level and have time to "yarn and chat" (Burgess and Dyer, 2009), which allows trust to develop. Research on under-represented groups shows that interpersonal comfort engenders psychosocial support, but is more likely to come from same-race relations (Ortiz-Walters and Gilson, 2005). For example, African-American protégés with African-American mentors (across formal and informal relationships) received more social support than African-American protégés with white mentors (Viator, 2001).

If the desired outcomes are based on power or to expose individuals to different networks, working styles, or groups, then matching individuals who are different to one another may be more desirable. Davis (2005) argues that while individuals are attracted to those with whom they share similarities (e.g., same-race), from a social identity perspective, a match based on dissimilarity could also be attractive in that it allows for an under-represented minority to associate with "in-group" members and in doing so maybe diminish their "out-group" status. This approach advocates for a cross-race matching. Researchers in the United Kingdom add that too much similarity may not support personal learning and growth given that mentoring partners can become too comfortable with each other (Hale, 2000). Research also finds benefits in cross-race relations in that access to white male mentors is associated with higher salaries (Dreher and Cox, 1996).

In contrast to both of these matching techniques, research on a formal program within a US federal agency found no differences based on race or racial composition in terms of satisfaction with the relationship or program satisfaction (Lyons and Oppler, 2004). Instead, it appears that when given input, minority protégés despite being more likely to be paired with racially dissimilar mentors, reported similar levels of satisfaction with the relationship and the formal program as did majority (Caucasian) protégés. A similar finding was obtained in a study of undergraduate students, where 58 percent were white and 40 percent black (Richard *et al.*, 2002). In this work, students assumed the role of protégés in a fictitious diversified management consulting company. As new hires they attended formal mentoring meetings for a year and were paired with a white male mentor. The experimenters varied the levels of voice and input in the mentoring process. Results suggest that under the high-voice condition (i.e., mentor allowed the protégé to express opinions during their interactions) all students perceived the mentoring more positively with regard to satisfaction, amount of career-related help, as well as the mentor's ability to provide assistance.

The findings from these two studies are important because protégés who are highly satisfied with their mentoring relationships exhibit more positive individual (e.g., job satisfaction; satisfaction with promotion opportunities) and organizational attitudes (e.g., commitment, lower intentions to quit), regardless of whether the mentor is formal or informal. For minority protégés, who often find themselves paired with dissimilar mentors, input and being listened to could have the additional benefit of enhancing motivation to participate and thus to make the most out of the relationship, regardless of surface-level differences. We propose that input and voice continue to be examined as variables that have the potential to moderate or attenuate the challenges present in diversified relationships, and to also see whether this holds in different national contexts.

The results of Lyons and Oppler's (2004) study also found that in addition to input, the frequency of meetings with mentors had a direct effect on protégé satisfaction, again regardless of race. This finding suggests that protégés who meet with mentors on a daily, weekly, or even a monthly basis are more satisfied with the relationship and program than protégés who only meet mentors quarterly or never. In a sample of African-American students at four urban US high schools, Linnenham (2001) examined time spent in the program versus simply participating in the program. Results show no significant differences in the academic performance of those who did not participate (non-protégés) and those that participated in the program for a shorter time period (less than half of a school year). Participation for a longer duration (more than half of an academic year), however, was related to improved academic performance such as higher GPA and attendance rates. These results suggest that participation in a formal program alone does not appear to be enough for individuals of under-represented groups to secure the benefits from mentoring, but rather length of time as well as the frequency of meetings may play more prominent roles. These structural components of formal mentoring may potentially serve to mitigate some of the effects in differentiated relationships. This may mean that when mentors and protégés spend more time together, the under-representation becomes less salient, so from a social categorization perspective, the "different" other becomes less of an "out-group" member. This should have implications for the amount and type of mentoring support.

## Mentoring support received

The underlying reason for most mentoring programs is to provide some form of support to protégés. When considering under-represented individuals and groups with regard to the amount of support from formal mentors, we found there are some differences when samples are comprised of protégés from different cultural backgrounds. Being mentored through a formal means was positively related to career development support, but unrelated to the amounts of psychosocial support for successful women, particularly from Brazil, Mexico, and Chile (Monserrat *et al.*, 2009). Minority protégés with formal mentors in the United States have been found to receive less of both social support and career-related support, such as protection and assistance, than white protégés (Kammeyer-Mueller and Judge, 2008; Viator, 2001). Therefore, viewed through a cultural lens (Applebaum *et al.*, 1994) it may be that in Spanish-speaking countries the focus of formal mentoring is overwhelmingly based on career development. Culturally, minimizing the appearance of intimacy or preferential treatment in relationships between men and women (and possibly those who are dissimilar on other characteristics) is seen as the only way that formal mentoring will work. Minimizing behaviors that might be construed as inappropriate is critical, so psychosocial support may be seen as crossing over the divide of what is considered appropriate support for a mentor to give.

Furthermore, expectations of mentor support also might differ based upon protégés' ethnic heritages. For example, Hispanic protégés who receive more career support may be satisfied because this is aligned with their expectations. In contrast, this level of support might appear impoverished to an under-represented protégé who is non-Hispanic. Similarly, a Hispanic mentor may only provide career support to a protégé because this is a cultural expectation. In this instance mentors may truly believe they are fully supporting their protégés, but depending on the cultural lens of the protégé, the relationship might be judged as either effective or lacking in support. Research examining European-based models of mentoring (Clutterbuck, 2002) finds that here, support is often seen as a tool to help empower protégés to be self-reliant. As such, the expectation is typically that mentors will provide more nurturing in the form of emotional or psychosocial (e.g., acceptance, counseling) rather than instrumental or career-related (e.g., protection, visibility, challenging assignments) support.

While it is impossible to draw general conclusions on such a small number of studies, there are some interesting questions that arise based on the results.

Knowledge about mentoring that is rooted in any particular cultural silo may be less applicable to countries with different ethnic and cultural profiles (Bozionelos, 2006; Bozionelos and Wang, 2006). Therefore, when is a protégé from an under-represented group likely to be most satisfied and feel their formal mentor is adequately supporting them? What is the role of national culture or ethnicity in determining satisfaction with support provided by a mentor? Does organizational culture matter here? There is some evidence to suggest that industry or context (e.g., academic, business, military) also significantly influences perceptions of formal mentoring (Smith *et al.*, 2005). Answers to these questions are not easy and further illustrate that there is still a great deal we do not know about effectively mentoring individuals from under-represented groups. From a research perspective, the number of issues previously discussed make it very hard to study these questions; however, we urge researchers to make note of these points, so that over time, with enough samples, some meaningful cross-study analysis can be conducted. In the mean time, in-depth qualitative analysis or case study write ups might be one of the best means to really understand what is taking place at any one point in time. Therefore, we encourage researchers to consider this form of study design as well.

# Future Research

Throughout this chapter we have tried to highlight what we "know" based on the existing research base, and to raise questions to guide future research. This topic is still wide open, especially given that how to define under-representation is so variable and thus, the cultural lens applied will in many instances drive the theoretical one. In this section we close by offering additional questions and a number of recommendations, not designed to be specific propositions of hypotheses, but rather to start the dialogue on how best to mentor and study the mentoring of under-represented groups. Our goal is to pose questions in such a way that academics and practitioners alike are drawn into the conversation.

## Are traditional mentoring supports applicable?

What forms of support are formal mentoring relationships really designed to provide? And more importantly, are the forms of support (career, psychosocial, and networking) as currently examined really those most applicable when we consider the mentoring of individuals from under-represented groups? From the extant literature we know something about the perceptions of blacks and individuals from Hispanic and Anglo-Saxon origins, but there are obviously many other ethnicities. For example, if we consider expatriate employees as under-represented in their host country what other mentoring functions may be needed. Shen (2010) found among a sample of US expatriates in Singapore and China that they needed cultural guidance, home linkage, and facilitating transition; functions aligned to cultural, rather than racial diversity.

Another issue to consider here is whether mentoring is perceived in the same way by members of under-represented groups. That is, do we know how minorities feel about mentoring? Is mentoring of most value as a tool for career advancement, or is it most needed for personal growth and development, or is it in fact an entree into different groups or networks? This is ever more critical in formal programs where organizations are directly targeting minorities. While the numbers who participate are often small, are they smaller than they need be as some individuals *choose* not to participate because they are either not aware of or do not see the value in mentoring?

## Is the mentor-protégé model most relevant?

Some newer work on formal programs has begun to consider mentoring from a variety of perspectives to gain fresh insights and to see what might work best in terms of mentoring for under-represented individuals. One area explored has been termed inter-organizational formal mentoring (Murrell *et al.*, 2008). This method of mentoring may be particularly attractive to individuals from under-represented groups because they can access mentors who are racially and ethnically similar since mentoring is not limited to one's own organization, but rather made available across organizational boundaries. Another alternative model suggested is called the POD (peer-onsite-distance), a formal mentoring program to promote retention and career development for racial minorities (Lewellen-Williams *et al.*, 2006). The POD program involves meeting through a network of mentors to facilitate the development of specific skill sets. Specifically, protégés are paired up with a peer mentor, that is, someone close to their hierarchical level who acts as a confidant and an on-site (traditional) mentor. Finally, work has started to consider mentors who are a part of the larger profession, but who may only meet protégés on occasion or from a "distance".

An interesting question is thus whether these alternatives are "better" than more traditional formal mentoring programs? There are several lessons from these newer models or forms of mentoring that should be instructive for program directors during the planning stages of any new career development initiatives that are targeted for under-represented minorities. First, it appears that restricting the selection of formal mentors to just those within the protégé's own organization may be unintentionally limiting. Thus a wider net could be cast in the selection process. In addition, the needs of under-represented protégés may be varied given their marginal yet visible status within many organizational settings; therefore a "one mentor fits all" approach may not be suitable. Rather, we need research that examines if a multiple mentoring or developmental network approach (Higgins and Kram, 2001; Shen, 2010) might be better suited to meet diverse career and personal developmental needs of the under-represented. For example, Carrater *et al.* (2008) have found among a sample of expatriates the need for both a formal home-country mentor as well as a formal host-country mentor because they provide differing benefits for the protégé.

## Who should be selected to participate?

Selection methods vary significantly between mentoring programs; however, for practitioners there is not much in the form of guidance regarding who may benefit most from participation. The issue of selection is a critical one and one we believe must be addressed given that there are limited organizational resources to implement and support many programs (Clutterbuck, 2002). Another challenge is that if there is an oversupply of protégés (Megginson *et al.*, 2006), then who should participate? Generally speaking, consideration is given based on specified criteria, which can run the gamut from issues of availability of mentors, mentors' interests, protégés' career progression, as well as motivation for participation (Megginson *et al.*, 2006). Three studies in particular (Kim, 2007; Lee *et al.*, 2000; Monserrat *et al.*, 2009) might be useful to the consideration of selection criteria. These works all highlight the use of personality characteristics or traits, which might be related to credibility or differences in commitment and motivation, as potential criteria for the selection of under-represented participants.

Because racio-ethnic minorities are under-represented both numerically and in the top level positions at most organizations, one prominent theme our review has highlighted is that even when formal programs are implemented, minorities are likely to still be paired, assigned or find themselves with a mentor who is dissimilar. We propose this makes "openness to experience" a critical personality variable for use in selection. Lee *et al.* (2000) have argued that protégés should possess high levels of openness (as well as conscientiousness) because those who do are more receptive to new ideas and ways of doing things. In the context of diversified mentoring, the implication is that a protégé from an under-represented group who is high on openness to experience will be more accepting of differences and therefore obtain greater learning from a formal mentor who is different to themselves. This question could also be targeted at mentors where it might be equally if not more important to access their openners to experience when it comes to supporting members of under-represented groups.

Another personality characteristic that holds promise is learning goal-orientation (LGO). It has been suggested that LGO should influence the quality of mentoring relationships (Godshalk and Sosik, 2003) as well as the provision and receipt of support within formal relationships (Kim, 2007). Individuals high on LGO seek challenging assignments, view feedback positively, and are not afraid to make mistakes. Mentors with a high LGO may also provide more support inclusive of career, psychosocial and role modelling, while in the case of protégés, those with a high LGO will seek more developmental assistance (Kim, 2007). Probably more importantly, Monserrat and her colleagues (2009) found the influence of personality on mentoring varies by mentee country of origin. In the United States, for example, an internal locus of control (LOC) was associated with more career and psychosocial support for high-profile female mentees. On the other hand, for Brazilian and Canadian women, LOC, need for achievement and self-efficacy were all important for career and psychosocial functions.

These findings suggest that it might behove program coordinators to consider personality characteristics and traits in the selection process, but more importantly in the success associated with the relevant mentor-protégé matches. We encourage scholars to continue to examine the role of personality in formal and diversified mentoring relationships from both the mentor and mentee perspectives.

## How should under-represented groups be trained?

Training of program participants is another area deserving of attention because it has been suggested that a lack of training and proper understanding of mentoring roles contributes to the failure of corporate programs (see Chapter 13 this volume). The prevailing assumption is that by virtue of being older, more skilled, or experienced, individuals are ready, willing, and able to serve as effective mentors (Hegstad, 1999). While this assumption is clearly an over generalization, does it mean that individuals with less experience holding fewer senior positions are more limited as mentors? Training can help offset some of the lack of experience and help mentors and mentees gain confidence in their roles and develop the appropriate set of skills needed for effective mentoring (Clutterbuck, 2002). Further, if one considers that individuals from under-represented groups tend to have less experience as protégés and opportunities to mentor (Thomas, 1990), they may not only need additional training, but perhaps *differing types* of training. Therefore, in terms of training, there is a need for recommendations to support organizers who are charged with creating and managing mentoring programs for under-represented individuals.

Based on a sample of African-American female administrators in higher education Simon *et al.* (2008) found that participants who had received the least help from their mentors in balancing work and family, also gave little assistance of this kind to their protégés. Moreover, the cross-race mentorships of high-ranking women of color were only able to provide a wide range of psychosocial functions when both mentor and protégé dealt with issues of race in the same manner (i.e., "complementary styles"). Given the potential of these strategies for managing racial dynamics in cross-race mentoring relationships, training may need to incorporate education on interaction strategies. Similarly, in Australia, work-home-community balance has been one of the main challenges for indigenous black aboriginals transitioning back into employment (Dockery and Milsom, 2007). In this setting, training materials should provide guidance and tips so that mentors can support protégés in balancing the demands of work, home and community life.

Finally, Lewellen-Williams and colleagues (2006) add to the conversation with their finding that only about half of the mentors of color in their study reported they could help protégés with networking. Therefore, an area deserving of special attention when training racio-ethnic minority mentors may be developing networking skills. In addition to training for mentors, training here may also benefit protégés. Training members of under-represented groups in the capacity as protégés is relevant because a well-trained protégé might be able to overcome or compensate for the skill and understanding deficiencies of their mentor (Megginson *et al.*, 2006).

## Conclusion

The trend of an increasingly diverse workforce is a reality and organizations will only continue to become more diverse, especially with respect to employees' race, ethnicity, and cultural background. A pressing issue for many, therefore, will be how to deal with career development for members of under-represented groups and how best to prepare these individuals to assume leadership roles. More and more organizations are equipping themselves to deal with this challenge by instituting formal mentoring programs.

In this chapter, we examined the literature on the formal mentoring of employees from under-represented groups mainly in the United States, Australia, and United Kingdom – highlighting both what is known and unknown. Drawing from new literatures, conceptual frameworks and samples, we present numerous questions that we hope will serve to guide future research. From this expanded view, we truly believe our understanding of mentoring outcomes for under-represented individuals and groups will increase and, that going forward, it can aid in the development of more effective mentoring programs and diversified relationships.

# References

Allen, T.D. and Eby, L.T. (2004) Factors related to mentor reports of mentoring functions provided: Gender and relational characteristics. *Sex Roles,* 50, 129–39.

Allen, T.D., Day, R., and Lentz, E. (2001) *Formal Mentoring Programs: A Review and Survey of Design Features and Recommendations.* Paper presented at the 16th Annual Meeting of the Society for Industrial and Organizational Psychology, San Diego, CA (May).

Applebaum, S.H., Ritchie, S., and Shapiro, B.T. (1994) Mentoring revisited: An organizational behavior construct. *The International Journal of Career Management,* 6, 3–10.

Armstrong, S.J., Allinson, C.W., and Hayes, J. (2002) Formal mentoring systems: An examination of the effects of mentor/protégé cognitive styles on the mentoring process. *Journal of Management Studies,* 39, 1111–37.

Baugh, S.G. and Fagenson-Eland, E.A. (2007) Formal mentoring programs: A "poor cousin" to informal relationships. In: B.R. Ragins and K.E. Kram (eds) *The Handbook of Mentoring at Work.* Thousand Oaks, CA: Sage. pp. 249–72.

Blake-Beard, S.D., Murrell, A.J., and Thomas, D. (2007) Unfinished business: The impact of race on understanding mentoring relationships. In B.R. Ragins and K. E. Kram (eds) *The Handbook of Mentoring at Work.* Thousand Oaks, CA: Sage. pp. 223–48.

Bozionelos, N. (2004) Mentoring provided: Relation to mentor's career success, personality, and mentoring received. *Journal of Vocational Behavior,* 64(1), 24–46.

Bozionelos, N. (2006) Mentoring and expressive network resources: Their relationship with career success and emotional exhaustion among Hellenes employees involved in emotion work. *International Journal of Human Resource Management,* 17(2), 362–78.

Bozionelos, N. and Wang, L. (2006) The relationship of mentoring and network resources with career success in the Chinese organizational environment. *International Journal of Human Resource Management,* 17(9), 1531–46.

Bright, M.I. (2005) Can Japanese mentoring enhance understanding of Western mentoring? *Employee Relations,* 27, 325–39.

Burgess, J. and Dyer, S. (2009) Workplace mentoring for indigenous Australians: A case study. *Equal Opportunities International,* 28, 465–85.

Byrne, D. (1971) *The Attraction Paradigm.* New York: Academic Press.

Carrater, S.M., Sullivan, S.E., and Crocitto, M.M. (2008) Mentoring across global boundaries: An empirical examination of home- and host-country mentors on expatriate career outcomes. *Journal of International Business Studies,* 39, 1310–26.

Chao, G.T., Walz, P.M., and Gardner, P.D. (1992) Formal and informal mentorships: A comparison on mentoring functions and contrast with nonmentored counterparts. *Personnel Psychology,* 45, 619–36.

Clutterbuck, D. (2002) Establishing and sustaining a formal mentoring program for working with diversified groups. In: D. Clutterbuck and B.R. Ragins (eds) *Mentoring and Diversity: An International Perspective.* Oxford: Butterworth-Heinemann. pp. 54–86.

Clutterbuck, D. (2004) *Everyone Needs a Mentor: Fostering Talent in Your Organization* (4th edn). London: Chartered Institute of Personnel and Development.

Davis, D.J. (2005) *The Summer Research Opportunity Program (SROP): Mentorship and the Socialization of Under-represented Racial Minorities into the Professoriate.* Ann Arbor, MI: ProQuest Information and Learning.

Dockery, A.M. and Milsom, N. (2007) *A Review of Indigenous Employment Programs.* Adelaide: National Centre for Vocational Education Research.

Douglas, C.A. and McCauley, C.D. (1999) Formal developmental relationships: A survey of organizational practices. *Human Development Quarterly,* 10, 203–20.

Dreher, G.F. and Cox, T.H. (1996) Race, gender, and opportunity: A study of compensation attainment and the establishment of mentoring relationships. *Journal of Applied Psychology,* 81, 297–308.

Gilson, L.L. and Ortiz-Walters, R. (2005) The role of accountability in mentoring relationships. Unpublished manuscript.

Godshalk, V.M., and Sosik, J.J. (2003) Aiming for success: The role of learning goal orientation in mentoring relationships. *Journal of Vocational Behavior*, 63, 417–37.

Hale, R. (2000) To match or mis-match? The dynamics of mentoring as a route to personal and organizational learning. *Career Development International*, 5, 223–34.

Hegstad, C.D. (1999) Formal mentoring as a strategy for human resource development: A review of research. *Human Resource Development Quarterly*, 13, 383–90.

Hegstad, C.D. and Wentling, R.M. (2004) The development and maintenance of exemplary formal mentoring programs in fortune 500 companies. *Human Resource Development Quarterly*, 15, 421–48.

Higgins, M.C. and Kram, K.E. (2001) Reconceptualizing mentoring at work: A developmental network perspective. *Academy of Management Review*, 26, 265–88.

Kammeyer-Mueller, J.D. and Judge, T.A. (2008) A quantitative review of mentoring research: Test of a model. *Journal of Vocational Behavior*, 72, 269–83.

Kanter, R.M. (1977) Some effects of proportions on group life: Skewed sex ratios and responses to token women. *American Journal of Sociology*, 82, 965–90.

Kerr, S. (2008) Race to the top: The place of ethnic minority groups within the UK workforce. *Business in the Community*, 1–14.

Kim, S. (2007) Learning goal orientation, formal mentoring, and leadership competence in HRD: A conceptual model. *Journal of European Industrial Training*, 31, 181–94.

Kram, K.E. (1985) *Mentoring at Work: Developmental Relationships in Organizational Life*. Glenview, IL: Scott Foresman.

Lee, F.K., Dougherty, T.W. and Turban, D.B. (2000) The role of personality and work values in mentoring programs. *Review of Business*, 21, 33–7.

Lee, M.A. and Mather, M. (2008) US labor force trends. *Population Bulletin*, 63, 3–16.

Lewellen-Williams, C., Johnson, V.A., Deloney, L.A., Thomas, B.R. Goyol, A., and Henry-Tillman, R. (2006) The POD: A new model for mentoring under-represented minority faculty. *Academic Medicine*, 81, 275–9.

Linnehan, F. (2001) The relation of a work-based mentoring program to the academic performance and behavior of African-American students. *Journal of Vocational Behavior*, 59, 310–25.

Lyons, B.D. and Oppler, E.S. (2004) The effects of structural attributes and demographic characteristics on protégé satisfaction in mentoring programs. *Journal of Career Development*, 30, 215–29.

MacGregor, L. (2000) Mentoring: The Australian experience. *Career Development International*, 5, 244–49.

McKeen, C.A. and Bujaki, M. (2007) Gender and mentoring: Issues, effects, and opportunities. In: B.R. Ragins and K.E. Kram (eds) *The Handbook of Mentoring at Work: Theory, Research, and Practice*. Thousand Oaks, CA: Sage. pp. 197–222.

Megginson, D., Clutterbuck, D. Garvey, B., and Garrett-Harris, R. (2006) *Mentoring in Action: A Practical Guide*. London: Kogan Page.

Monserrat, S.I., Duffy, J.A., Olivas-Luján, M.R., Miller, J.M., Gregory, A., Fox, S. *et al.* (2009) Mentoring experiences of successful women across the Americas. *Gender in Management: An International Journal*, 24, 455–76.

Murrell, A.J., Blake-Beard, S., Porter, D.M., and Perkins-Williamson, A. (2008) Interorganizational formal mentoring: Breaking the concrete ceiling sometimes requires support from the outside. *Human Resource Management*, 47, 275–94.

O'Brien, K.E., Rodopman, O.B., and Allen, T.D. (2010) Reflections on best practices for formal mentoring programs. In: T.D. Allen and L.T. Eby (eds) *The Blackwell Handbook of Mentoring: A Multiple Perspectives Approach*. MA: Wiley-Blackwell. pp. 369–72.

O'Neill, R.M. (2002) Gender and race in mentoring relationships: A review of the literature. In: D. Clutterbuck and B.R. Ragins (eds) *Mentoring and Diversity: An International Perspective*. Oxford: Butterworth-Heinemann. pp. 1–22.

Ortiz-Walters, R. and Gilson, L.L. (2005) Mentoring in academia: An examination of the experiences of protégés of color. *Journal of Vocational Behavior*, 67, 459–75.

Phillips-Jones, L. (1983) Establishing a formalized mentoring program. *Training and Development Journal*, 37, 38–42.

Raabe, B. and Beehr, T.A. (2003) Formal mentoring versus supervisor and co-worker relationships: Differences in perceptions and impact. *Journal of Organizational Behavior*, 24, 271–93.

Ragins, B.R. (1997) Diversified mentoring relationships in organizations: A power perspective. *Academy of Management Review*, 22, 482–521.

Ragins, B.R. (2002) Differences that make a difference: Common themes in the individual case studies of diversified mentoring relationships. In: D. Clutterbuck and B.R. Ragins (eds) *Mentoring and Diversity: An International Perspective*. Oxford: Butterworth-Heinemann. pp. 161–72.

Ragins, B.R. and Cotton, J.L. (1999) Mentor functions and outcomes: A comparison of men and women in formal and informal mentoring relationships. *Journal of Applied Psychology*, 84, 529–50.

Ragins, B.R. Cotton, J.L., and Miller, J.S. (2000) Marginal mentoring: The effects of type of mentor, quality of relationship, and program design on work and career attitudes. *Academy of Management Journal*, 43, 1177–94.

Richard, O.C., Taylor, E.C., Barnett, T., and Nesbit, M.A. (2002) Procedural voice and distributive justice: Their influence on mentoring career help and outcomes. *Journal of Business Research*, 55, 725–35.

Seibert, S. (1999) The effectiveness of facilitated mentoring: A longitudinal quasi-experiment. *Journal of Vocational Behavior*, 54, 483–502.

Shen, Y. (2010) *Developmental Networks of Expatriates: The Antecedents, Structure, and Outcomes.* Dissertation. Boston University, Boston, MA.

Simon, C., Perry, A.R., and Roff, L.L. (2008) Psychosocial and career mentoring: Female African American social work education administrators' experiences. *Journal of Social Work Education*, 44, 1–12.

Smith, W.J., Howard, J.T., and Harrington, K.V. (2005). Essential formal mentor characteristics and functions in governmental and non-governmental organizations from the program administrator's and the mentor's perspective. *Public Personnel Management*, 34, 31–58.

Thomas, D.A. (1990) The impact of race on managers' experiences of developmental relationships (mentoring and sponsorship): An intra-organizational study. *Journal of Organizational Behavior*, 2, 479–92.

Thomas, D.A. (1993) Racial dynamics in cross-race developmental relationships. *Administrative Science Quarterly*, 38, 169–94.

Thomas, K.M., Hu, C.Y., Gewin, A.G., Bingham, K.L., and Yanchus, N. (2005) The roles of protégé race, gender, and proactive socialization attempts on peer mentoring. *Advances in Human Resource Development*, 7, 540–55.

Tsui, A.S. and O'Reilly, C.A. (1989) Beyond simple demographic effects: The importance of relational demography in superior-subordinate dyads. *Academy of Management Journal*, 32, 402–23.

Viator, R.E. (2001) The association of formal and informal public accounting mentoring with role stress and related job outcomes. *Accounting, Organizations, and Society*, 26, 73–93.

Wanberg, C.R., Welsh, E., and Hezlett, S.A. (2003) Mentoring: A review and directions for future research. In: J. Martocchio and J. Ferris (eds) *Research in Personnel and Human Resources Management*, vol. 22. Oxford: Elsevier Science. pp. 39–124.

Wanberg, C.R., Welsh, E., and Kammeyer-Mueller, J.D. (2007) Protégé and mentor self-disclosure: Levels and outcomes within formal mentoring dyads in a corporate context. *Journal of Vocational Behavior*, 70, 398–412.

# Section III
# Theories and Models With Implications for Coaching

# 15

# Humanistic/Person-centered Approaches

## Jane Brodie Gregory and Paul E. Levy

## Introduction

Humanistic coaching can be defined as the application of the principles of humanistic psychology to the practice of coaching. The goals of coaching are inherently linked with those of humanistic psychology: both take a person-centered approach in emphasizing the needs of the individual and helping the individual realize his/her fullest potential. Some have made the case that coaching and humanistic psychology are "natural bedfellows" (Biswas-Diener, 2010, p. 4), as both are based on the notion that people have the capacity to grow, develop, and reach their highest potential (Joseph, 2006; Linley and Harrington, 2005; Stober, 2006). While the extant research on humanistic coaching is limited, we believe that a great deal of coaching research and practice draws on concepts from humanistic psychology, but does not always refer to it as such.

In this chapter we synthesize and build on this work in order to provide structure and clarity to the notion of humanistic coaching. We explore the general coaching literature to show clear connections to the humanistic school, devoting specific attention to the importance of the coach/client relationship. Finally, we briefly touch on techniques, which are used in coaching and derived from recent research in positive psychology that can be incorporated into the practice of humanistic coaching. In doing so, we hope to lend additional clarity to the meaning of humanistic coaching and provide some new direction for both research and practice.

## The Humanistic Psychology Theory

The inception of humanistic psychology can be traced to the mid-twentieth century, when psychologists like Carl Rogers (1959, 1963), Abraham Maslow (1954, 1962, 1964), and Rollo May (1967, 1969) felt the need for an alternative to then mainstream approaches,

*The Wiley Blackwell Handbook of the Psychology of Coaching and Mentoring*, First Edition.
Edited by Jonathan Passmore, David B. Peterson, and Teresa Freire.
© 2013 John Wiley & Sons, Ltd. Published 2016 by John Wiley & Sons, Ltd.

such as psychoanalytic, behavioral, and biomedical (the "medical model") psychology (Aanstoos *et al.*, 2000). These early leaders of the humanistic movement envisioned an approach to psychology that focused on human potential, growth, and self-actualization, rather than a perspective on humans as damaged, ill or ruled by their unconscious.

As the field began to take shape, some basic principles emerged. For instance, humanistic psychology holds that people are more than simply the sum of their parts, that they exist in a "uniquely human context" (Aanstoos *et al.*, 2000, p. 7), that they are fully conscious and aware, that they have choice and free will, and that they are intentional, goal-oriented, and seek meaning and value in their lives (Aanstoos *et al.*, 2000; Bugental, 1964). Carl Rogers, who is widely considered to be the father of humanistic psychology, put forth the perspective that human beings naturally tend toward growth, development, and reaching their fullest potential, a concept Rogers referred to as the *actualizing tendency* (Rogers, 1959, 1963).

Since those early days, the basic tenets of humanistic psychology and its person-centered approach have been applied beyond the bounds of traditional therapy, to learning and education, conflict resolution, and parenting (Joseph, 2006; Joseph and Bryant-Jefferies; 2007). It is also important to point out that humanistic psychology is not seen as an absolute replacement for other approaches, but can be infused into or combined with other practices. Given the person-centered nature of humanistic psychology and its adaptability to practices beyond therapy, it should come as no surprise that this school of thought found its way into the growing practice and science of coaching.

## Humanistic Coaching

Stober (2006) notes that, at its core, coaching is truly about maximizing human growth and potential. Given humanistic psychology's emphasis on the same ideas, it would be shortsighted to believe that coaching – as a field – does not have strong roots in humanistic psychology. Like humanistic psychology, coaching focuses extensively on growth and development (Downey, 2003; Peterson, 1996; Sherman and Freas, 2004), achieving goals set by the coachee (Gregory *et al.*, 2011; Kilburg, 1996), and maximizing human potential and/or performance (Diedrich, 1996; Gregory, 2010; Kampa-Kokesch and Anderson, 2001; Stober, 2006). As noted previously, a small body of literature on humanistic coaching does exist. One detriment to this work, however, is that it is often referred to by a variety of other names, such as positive psychology coaching (Biswas-Diener, 2010; Biswas-Diener and Dean, 2007; Kaufman, 2006), person-centered coaching (Joseph, 2006; Joseph and Bryant-Jefferies; 2007), and relational coaching (de Haan, 2008), thereby making the subject seem less cohesive and a bit more challenging to investigate. Despite the variability in name, humanistic coaching, positive psychology coaching, person-centered coaching and relational coaching put forth the same basic principles. Thus, throughout the rest of this chapter, we consider these concepts to be synonymous.

Coaching as a field is intriguing for a number of reasons, one of those being the vast assortment of definitions, tools, and best practices. The emergence of humanistic coaching should not further complicate this already dizzying array of options, as humanistic coaching is an approach to coaching that can be easily coupled with other tools and practices (Biswas-Diener, 2010; Joseph, 2006). Therefore, it is important to articulate the unique contributions and core philosophies that make the humanistic approach valuable to the science and practice of coaching. In synthesizing the existing work in humanistic coaching, several key themes become clear. These basic tenets of humanistic coaching include: (1) an assumption that the client can be his/her full or authentic self; (2) a focus on positivity and the client's well-being; (3) an emphasis on the client's growth, development, and maximizing potential; (4) a focus on goal-directed and intentional behavior; (5) the non-directive role of the coach; and (6) the importance of the coaching relationship. In the pages that follow, we will discuss each of these core components in order to provide a clearer picture of what humanistic coaching entails.

## The client is his/her full or authentic self

First and foremost, humanistic coaching begins with a coach adopting a "whole person" approach to working with a client. This stems from humanistic psychology's stance that people are more than merely the sum of their parts, and should be considered "whole" and fully human (Aanstoos *et al.*, 2000). Applied to a coaching context, a client should feel comfortable being his or her true and authentic self when working with the coach (de Haan, 2008; Stober, 2006). This includes attending to all aspects of the client's life, behavior, or current situation (Biswas-Diener, 2010; Kauffman *et al.*, 2009). Optimal functioning, according to positive psychology pioneer Mihaly Csikszentmihalyi, requires that people be "fully involved with every detail of [their] lives, whether good or bad" (1991, p. 2). Humanistic coaching, like positive psychology, does not seek to emphasize only the positive, ignore the negative or advocate hedonistic tendencies (Kauffman *et al.*, 2009; Peterson, 2006). As noted by Biswas-Diener, humanistic coaching focuses on both the positive and negative in a client's life in order to fully address the needs of the "whole" client. Regardless of a client's current issues or challenges, these do not occur in a vacuum, but in the context of the whole person and his or her whole life. Thus, clients' issues cannot be approached unidimensionally (Stober, 2006), but rather as they relate to the whole person.

Coaches may use tools to help a client better understand his or her authentic self, if needed. One popular activity in humanistic coaching is assessing a client's strengths and helping the client identify ways to better leverage those strengths (Biswas-Diener, 2010; Kauffman, 2006; Linley and Harrington, 2006). One frequently used tool is Peterson and Seligman's VIA (values in action) strengths measure (Kaufman *et al.*, 2008; Peterson and Seligman, 2004; discussed in greater detail later in this chapter). The measure uses a series of self-report questions to identify a person's top strengths. Coaches can use the results of this assessment to help clients gain better self-awareness and encourage them to creatively leverage their key strengths in addressing their current challenges. This notion of focusing on strengths, as opposed to weaknesses, originated in the business and consulting world with Peter Drucker (1967), but only recently gained momentum with the rapid growth and popularity of the positive psychology movement (Linley and Harrington, 2006).

## A focus on positivity and the client's well-being

A second key component of humanistic coaching is the focus on positivity and the well-being of the client (de Haan, 2008; Joseph, 2006; Kauffman, 2006; Linley and Harrington, 2005). As noted previously, humanistic psychology as a field emerged largely as a response to psychology's dominant focus on pathology-based approaches (Aanstoos *et al.*, 2000; Kauffman, 2006). As such, humanistic coaching builds on this legacy by focusing on client well-being and positive emotion. Specifically, rather than discussing clients' sources of distress or areas of dysfunction, coaches can facilitate a focus on the client's well-being and optimal functioning (Joseph, 2006; Joseph and Bryant-Jefferies, 2007). Humanistic coaching engagements may focus on helping the client learn how to better care for him/herself (de Haan, 2008), establishing better work/life balance in order to have a higher quality of life (Passmore, 2006), or using tools and activities that foster positive emotions in the coachee (Biswas-Diener, 2010; Kauffman, 2006).

It is important to note here that, like positive psychology, humanistic coaching does not pursue positive emotion simply for the sake of positive emotion, but as a means to numerous ends. As the research of positive psychology continues to expand, we see that positive emotions are strongly linked to such outcomes as better physical health (e.g., improved immune function, lower levels of cortisol, reduced frequency of inflammation) (Davidson *et al.*, 2005; Frederickson and Losada, 2005; Steptoe *et al.*, 2005), higher resilience to adversity and more effective stress response (Fredrickson *et al.*, 2003), better intuition, a wider scope of attention, enhanced creativity, stronger cognitive flexibility, and faster and more accurate decision making (see Kauffman (2006) for a more in-depth discussion). In sum, humanistic coaching is in part defined by its focus on positivity and well-being, which has been demonstrated to have positive outcomes on the client's work and life.

## An emphasis on growth, development and maximizing potential

Positive change is ultimately the driving force in humanistic coaching (Stober, 2006). In addition to focusing on client well-being and positive emotions, humanistic coaching draws on the very foundation of humanistic psychology with its emphasis on the human potential for growth, development, and maximizing potential (de Haan, 2008; Joseph and Bryant-Jefferies, 2007; Stober, 2006). One of the hallmarks of humanistic psychology is the concept of *self-actualization*, or striving to fulfill one's ultimate potential. Self-actualization was a critical element in the work of many early humanistic psychologists, such as Rogers, Maslow, and Horney (Aanstoos *et al.*, 2000). One key role of the coach is to facilitate the client's learning in a way that helps him/her to grow and develop (de Haan, 2008). It is important to note, however, that the coach himself/herself does not drive the client's development, but helps the client to find and utilize his or her own *innate* drive to grow and develop (Biswas-Diener, 2010). Joseph and Bryant-Jefferies (2007) note that the crux of humanistic coaching is the coach's belief that people are "intrinsically motivated towards constructive and optimal functioning" (p. 215). The coach can create a context that helps a client unlock this capacity.

Coaches may use tools and activities to help the client understand what that full potential or desired end state looks like. In other words, it is possible that a client may not fully realize what their ideal self or full potential really entails. By using activities like the "best possible future self" activity (Kauffman *et al.*, 2009), coaches can help clients identify their ideal self and ideal future. If a client is already aware of this desired end state, coaches can use careful, thought-provoking questioning to help the client determine options for working toward that end and maximizing his or her potential (Downey, 2003; Kauffman, 2006). This concept touches on the next key component of humanistic coaching: encouraging goal-directed and intentional behavior.

## A focus on goal-directed and intentional behavior

Without goals, growth, development, and working toward one's maximum potential would be aimless. If no desired end state has been identified, growth, and development may occur at random, and clients may see no meaning in growth simply for the sake of growth. Therefore, effective humanistic coaching relies on clear goals to provide a direction for a client's development and positive change. In the early days of humanistic psychology, Bugental (1964) identified as one of the basic postulates of humanistic psychology the notion that humans act intentionally, are goal oriented, and are aware of their impact on future events. Applied today to humanistic coaching, this suggests that coaches have a responsibility to facilitate clients' goal setting (Kauffman, 2006; Stober, 2006), to ensure that clients have desired end states in mind and to ensure that clients are fully aware that they control their own behavior and can act intentionally to achieve their desired end state or maximize their potential. Recent research has specifically targeted ways in which coaches can facilitate goal setting and help clients use feedback to gauge their progress on goals (Gregory *et al.*, 2011). It is essential to note here that coaches should not identify or assign clients' goals, but that the identification of goals must come from within the client. Coaches can have a significant and positive impact on this process by assuming the stance of a facilitator and using a non-directive approach. This distinction is discussed next.

## The non-directive role of the coach

Inherent in the core concepts of individual growth, development, and positive change is the notion that clients themselves drive this growth in a journey of self-discovery and self-motivated change (Joseph and Bryant-Jefferies, 2007). As a result, the role of a coach in this humanistic framework is that of facilitator. With guidance and support from the coach, the client should be doing the bulk of the "work" in a humanistic coaching engagement (de Haan, 2008). It is imperative that the coachee recognizes that the ability to grow and develop resides solely within him; that positive change is not the result of the coach's "magic" and superior wisdom. Coaches who foster such thinking (e.g., that the coach is the "expert" or problem solver) undermine the value of the humanistic approach by encouraging a sense of dependence on the coach and robbing the client of the gift of ownership and knowledge that the potential for change lies within. As such, effective humanistic coaching relies not on an all-knowing coach who sees himself as an expert or teacher, but on a coach who can use non-directive techniques to foster the coachee's self-development (Joseph and Bryant-Jefferies, 2007; Stober, 2006). This approach is in direct opposition to a perspective of clients as flawed or damaged in which a coach may "work on" the client, rather than work *with* the client (Stober, 2006).

At the core of non-directive coaching is the ability to ask careful and thought-provoking questions (Downey, 2003; Kemp, 2011) and to listen for understanding (Kemp, 2011; Stober, 2006). Coaches can use questioning, active listening, and reflecting a client's responses back to her to help the client set goals, gain self-awareness and insight, and explore options for goal-striving (Downey, 2003; Gregory *et al.*, 2011; Kemp, 2011; Stober, 2006). By facilitating rather than teaching or telling, a coach helps the coachee have a stronger sense of belief, ownership, and commitment to goals and insights that emerge throughout the coaching process. In order for this process to be effective, it is imperative that the coach be able to establish and nurture a strong and genuine relationship with the coachee. This coaching relationship is the sixth and final key theme or component of humanistic coaching discussed in this chapter.

## The importance of the coaching relationship

A strong coaching relationship is arguably the foundation upon which humanistic coaching takes place (Cain, 2002; Gregory, 2010; Gregory and Levy, 2011; de Haan, 2008;

Joseph, 2006; Kauffman, 2006; Passmore, 2006; Stober, 2006). Looking beyond the humanistic approach, the broader coaching literature has consistently emphasized the importance of a genuine relationship between the coach and client in order to have an effective engagement with positive outcomes (Bennett, 2006; Gregory, 2010; Gregory and Levy, 2011; Gyllensten and Palmer, 2007; Hunt and Weintraub, 2002; Kemp, 2011; Smither and Reilly, 2001; Stober and Parry, 2005; Ting and Riddle, 2006). Discussion around the ingredients for an effective coaching relationship have yielded consistent conclusions: coaches must foster trust from their clients (Gregory, 2010; Gregory and Levy, 2011; Gyllensten and Palmer, 2007; Passmore, 2010; Smither and Reilly, 2001; Stober, 2006; Ting and Riddle, 2006), coaches must act with and show empathy for the client (Gregory, 2010; Gregory and Levy, 2011; Kemp, 2011; Kilburg, 2001; Passmore, 2006, 2010; Stober, 2006), coaches must have acceptance/positive regard for their clients (de Haan, 2008; Joseph and Bryant-Jefferies, 2007; Passmore, 2010; Stober, 2006), and the coach must be genuine/authentic in his/her interactions with the client and foster a genuine relationship (Gregory, 2010; Gregory and Levy, 2011; Joseph, 2006; Kemp, 2011; Passmore, 2010; Stober, 2006). Not surprisingly, these components of effective relationships nearly mirror those set forth by Carl Rogers in his discussions of productive relationships for practicing humanistic therapy. Specifically, Rogers (1980) highlighted the importance of empathy, positive regard, and genuineness for creating an effective relationship and, in turn, an optimal climate for facilitating positive change.

In order to be clear on the meaning of these key components of coaching relationships, we offer some basic working definitions. First and foremost, empathy, as defined by Carl Rogers, entails the ability to, "perceive the internal frame of reference of another with accuracy and with the emotional components and meanings which pertain thereto as if one were the person" (Rogers, 1959, p. 210). In other words, empathy includes not only the ability to detect and understand others' emotions, but also to place oneself in the other's shoes and essentially feel what another feels. This ability may come easily or naturally to some, but other coaches may need to work on developing this skill (research has demonstrated that empathy can be trained or developed, e.g., Haynes and Avery, 1979). Though Rogers did not specifically identify trust as one of the key factors in humanistic therapeutic relationships, coaching research has consistently identified trust as essential to effective coaching relationships (Gregory, 2010; Gregory and Levy, 2011; Gyllensten and Palmer, 2007; Passmore, 2010; Smither and Reilly, 2001; Stober, 2006; Ting and Riddle, 2006). We suggest here that both empathy and genuineness/authenticity help to build trust (Gregory, 2010; Stober, 2006), which can therefore be considered an outcome of these other essential factors.

A coach's unconditional positive regard entails his or her ability to fully accept the coachee for who he or she is without judgment (Rogers, 1959). This does not necessarily imply that the coach agrees with or endorses everything about the client, but that he or she is able to hold the client in respectful regard regardless of what the client says or does. This behavior is critical for encouraging the client to bring his or her "whole self" into the coaching engagement. In order to cultivate an effective coaching relationship, the coach must be capable of listening attentively and being fully present and engaged regardless of the client's thoughts or behaviors. Lastly, genuineness or authenticity is essentially the coach's ability to be himself and to be fully present in the context of coaching (Stober, 2006). Just as the client is expected to bring his or her "whole" self to the coaching engagement, so is the coach. Only by showing his or her authentic self to the client can the coach build a genuine and productive relationship. Kemp (2011) suggests that a coach's ability to openly and honestly share his/her own thoughts and experiences contributes to the authenticity of the relationship.

As evidenced by the lengthier discussion of the coaching relationship, the coach's behavior and the environment that the coach creates are clearly the foundation upon which humanistic coaching takes place. While the client will be responsible for doing most of the "work" in the coaching engagement, the coach – through his/her mindset and behavior – sets the stage for how that work will take place and whether or not the coaching engagement will result in positive outcomes for the coachee. Drawing on this knowledge and the previous section, it is therefore safe to say that the coach's primary responsibilities in humanistic coaching are applying the behaviors necessary for fostering a productive, genuine relationship (e.g., showing empathy, being accepting of the client/ holding the client in positive regard, and being genuine in his/her behavior), and building the necessary skills and patience to be an effective non-directive facilitator (e.g., knowing how to ask good questions, having strong listening skills, fighting the urge to teach, tell or give unsolicited advice).

In sum, we suggest that six key components contribute to the uniqueness of humanistic coaching: first, that the client is comfortable bringing his/her full or authentic self into the coaching engagement; second, that the coaching engagement focuses on positivity and the client's well-being; third, that the coaching engagement emphasizes the client's growth, development, and maximizing of his/her potential; fourth, that the coach helps the client focus on goal-directed and intentional behavior; fifth, that the coach adopts a non-directive approach; and sixth, that a strong and authentic relationship is forged between the coach and client. As noted previously, humanistic coaching does not need to be practiced in isolation or replace existing practices, but can be easily combined with other coaching tools and techniques. However, we feel it is necessary to provide a bit more discussion on what makes humanistic coaching unique and also differentiate humanistic coaching from humanistic counseling.

## Distinguishing Humanistic Coaching as a Unique Practice

As noted above, humanistic coaching as an approach to practice is not intended to replace, but rather to complement other established coaching practices (Biswas-Diener, 2010; Joseph, 2006). Coaches who wish to adopt a humanistic approach to their practice can find ways to blend tools and techniques discussed throughout this chapter into their existing coaching strategies. They may find that the humanistic approach works more effectively with some clients than others, depending on their current challenges and personal needs. Overall, what makes humanistic coaching unique is its emphasis on growth, development, and maximizing human potential. Additionally, the behavior of the coach is critical to the effective adoption of a humanistic coaching approach: the coach must be fully prepared to facilitate in a non-directive fashion, and cultivate a genuine relationship through empathy, authenticity, and positive regard for the client.

Kauffman and colleagues (2009) also point out the critical role of the coach's beliefs and expectations, noting potential for self-fulfilling prophecies or a Pygmalion effect (Rosenthal and Jacobson, 1992). Specifically, the coach's expectations for the client's behavior, performance, and development can subtly influence how the client *actually* behaves, performs or develops. A coach's beliefs and expectations will come through in the way he/she interacts with the client – often at a non-conscious level, thereby "causing" those beliefs or expectations to become reality. Therefore, it is essential that the coach truly believes in the client's ability to enact positive change, develop, and strive for his/her maximum potential. While holding negative expectations can result in an unfortunate self-fulfilling prophecy, holding positive expectations can produce a *positive* Pygmalion effect (Kauffman *et al.*, 2009). In other words, if a coach believes his/her client can change and develop, he/she will behave in a way that facilitates the client's growth and development. Kemp (2011) recommends that coaches fully examine their own subjective biases and beliefs to ensure that these are not negatively impacting the coaching relationship and coaching engagement.

Finally, we wish to distinguish humanistic coaching from humanistic counseling. Both Joseph (2006) and Stober (2006) present excellent discussions on this differentiation. While the two practices are similar in terms of their focus on human growth and potential, they are also different in four distinct ways. First, whereas humanistic coaching is forward looking (e.g., what can you do to maximize your potential as you move forward through your life?), humanistic therapy or counseling is more backward looking (e.g., what things have happened in the past that we can discuss in order to make you a more functional person?) (Joseph, 2006; Joseph and Bryant-Jefferies, 2007). Second, Stober points out that humanistic coaching focuses more on *actions* (e.g., what can you do to achieve these goals and enact positive change?), whereas humanistic counseling focuses more on *feelings* (e.g., increased understanding of feelings and sense-making). Similarly, the third difference between the two practices focuses on self-awareness: humanistic coaching uses increased self-awareness as a means to an end (e.g., to gain better self-awareness so you can more accurately determine where you need to make positive change in your life), whereas increased self-awareness can be considered an end in itself in humanistic counseling (e.g., clients may be more challenged in understanding and accurately assessing their own feelings and current situation). Lastly, Stober notes that the type of client (e.g., based on the client's current situation and baseline) differentiates coaching from counseling: humanistic coaching is appropriate for clients who are already high-functioning and wish to live a more *full* life, whereas humanistic counseling focuses more on helping clients to live a more *functional* life. In sum, while humanistic coaching and humanistic counseling share a core philosophy and principles, they meet different needs for clients who are in very different "places" in their lives.

## Research Evidence to Applied Practice

The vast and innovative research on positive psychology that has been conducted over the past decade has much to contribute to the practice of humanistic coaching, where far less research has been done. Here we briefly discuss a few concepts, tools, and techniques that have emerged from the positive psychology literature that could be easily incorporated into a humanistic coach's practice.

Positive psychology researchers have developed a number of unique measures that add value to humanistic coaching practices. First and foremost is the VIA (values in action) strengths assessment (Peterson and Seligman, 2004), which we mentioned earlier in the chapter. Coaches can administer the VIA assessment to their clients (it is available online: http://authentichappiness.org); the results of the assessment will list the client's top five signature strengths (pulled from a series of 24 signature strengths; see Peterson and Seligman, 2004). Coach and client can work through the results of the assessment to help the client gain self-awareness and determine strategies for better leveraging and maximizing those signature strengths. In addition to the VIA Strengths assessment, the Penn Positive Psychology Center (http://authentichappiness.org) offers a host of relevant assessments, including Peterson's Authentic Happiness Questionnaire, Lyubomirsky and Lepper's (1999) General Happiness Questionnaire and measures of "grit", gratitude, and optimism, among many others. While these assessments alone can provide a wealth of information, the real benefit to the client will come from a meaningful and thought-provoking discussion of the results led by his or her coach.

Kauffman (2006) provides a discussion of several other positive psychology techniques that fit nicely into a coaching context. Building on our discussion of the VIA strengths assessment, one of these activities involved finding a new way to use a particular strength. Specifically, Kauffman suggests first having the client choose one of his/her signature strengths, identifying situations in which he/she already applies this strength to activities throughout the day, and then brainstorming new ways or situations in which this strength can be applied. A variation on this activity would be starting with current challenges being faced by the client and brainstorming ways in which his/her top five strengths (as provided by the VIA) could be leveraged or applied to that challenge (Kauffman *et al.*, 2008).

Another useful tool that humanistic coaching can borrow from positive psychology is the "best possible future self" activity (Kauffman *et al.*, 2009), which was mentioned previously. In this activity coaches simply ask their clients to think about what their best future self "looks like" to them. An important part of this exercise is removing constrained thinking; coaches should instruct clients to envision this best future self without any limitations or constraints. For example, a client who worries about an upside-down mortgage on their home and some recurring health challenges should envision their best self in, say, ten years, assuming that the mortgage has been taken care of and the health matters are completely under control. This activity will help clients to understand what reaching their full potential or self-actualizing may entail. By asking the client to look beyond typical constraints, coaches may help clients to realize long-term goals or options that they did not otherwise consider (Downey, 2003).

The activities outlined here barely scratch the surface of what positive psychology has to offer the practice of humanistic coaching. We recommend that coaches interested in practicing from a humanistic perspective make themselves familiar with classic and current work in positive psychology in order to take advantage of the vast array of findings and recommendations available to them, including the positive psychology coaching chapter in this book.

## Future Research

Overall, humanistic coaching has not been particularly well researched. This lack of research is not unlike client-centered therapy, which saw a drop off in research activity in the early 1980s (Joseph and Bryant-Jefferies, 2007). In this chapter we discussed a few key works on humanistic coaching (e.g., de Haan, 2008; Joseph, 2006; Joseph and Bryant-Jefferies, 2007; Kauffman, 2006; Kauffman *et al.*, 2009; Linley and Harrington, 2006;

Stober, 2006), but also draw largely from general coaching literature, positive psychology literature, and humanistic psychology literature. Thus, we strongly recommend that coaching researchers strive to specifically investigate the humanistic approach. Researchers could address such questions as:

- When is the humanistic approach to coaching most effective? Do certain challenges faced by clients lend themselves better to the humanistic approach?
- What tools and techniques from positive psychology are most effective in a humanistic coaching practice?
- What is the most effective way to train coaches on the non-directive approach?
- Can coaches be trained to cultivate a genuine relationship, show their authentic selves, display empathy to their clients and hold the client in unconditional positive regard?
- Can coaches be trained to enact a "positive Pygmalion effect" with their clients?
- Are there characteristics of coaches that make them more likely to be effective humanistic coaches?
- Does humanistic coaching lead to long-term, lasting positive change?

The humanistic coaching literature would also be strengthened by research that shows the direct impact of humanistic coaching on critical outcomes, such as physical health and psychological well-being. Research could also investigate the connection between humanistic coaching and clients' experiences of flow states and self-actualization. In this respect humanistic coaching faces the same challenge that other approaches to coaching currently face: a need for more empirical research that directly links coaching with positive, tangible outcomes and lasting change.

# Conclusion

In this chapter we have sought to synthesize existing work on humanistic coaching (which is often referred to under a variety of other labels: positive psychology coaching (Biswas-Diener, 2010; Biswas-Diener and Dean, 2007; Kaufman, 2006), person-centered coaching (Joseph, 2006; Joseph and Bryant-Jefferies, 2007), relational coaching (de Haan, 2008)), clarify the key themes or concepts of humanistic coaching, address ways in which humanistic coaching as a practice can benefit from drawing on the vast array of research on positive psychology and note the ways in which humanistic coaching is unique from other, similar practices (e.g., humanistic therapy, more directive coaching).

Humanistic coaching is a unique approach to coaching that focuses on helping clients bring out their best selves. With a foundation in the early work of humanistic psychologists, the practice of humanistic psychology is also a natural fit for more recent work in the field of positive psychology (Biswas-Diener, 2010; Kauffman, 2006). Coaches who wish to help their clients strive to maximize their human potential, grow, develop, and nurture positive emotions and well-being would benefit from the application of humanistic coaching in their practice. While good work in this domain has been done, additional empirical support would help to promote humanistic coaching as a prominent approach in the growing field of professional coaching.

# References

Aanstoos, C., Serlin, I., and Greening, T. (2000) A history of division 32 (humanistic psychology) of the American Psychological Association. In: D. Dewsbury (ed.) *Unification Through Division: Histories of the Divisions of the American Psychological Association, Vol. V.* Washington, DC: American Psychological Association.

Bennett, J.L. (2006) An agenda for coaching-related research: A challenge for researchers. *Consulting Psychology Journal: Practice and Research*, 58, 240–9.

Biswas-Diener, R. (2010) *Positive Psychology Coaching: Assessment, Activities, and Strategies for Success.* Hoboken, NJ: John Wiley and Sons.

Biswas-Diener, R. and Dean, B. (2007) *Positive Psychology Coaching: Putting the Science of Happiness to Work for your Clients.* Hoboken, NJ: John Wiley and Sons.

Bugental, J. (1964) The third force in psychology. *Journal of Humanistic Psychology*, 4, 19–25.

Cain, D.J. (2002) Defining characteristics, history, and evolution of humanistic psychotherapies. In: D.J. Cain and J. Seeman (eds) *Humanistic Psychotherapies: Handbook of Research and Practice.* Washington, DC: American Psychological Association. pp. 3–54.

Csikszentmihalyi, M. (1991) *Flow.* New York: Harper.

Davidson, R.J., Kabat-Zinn, J., Schumacher, J., Rosenkranz, M., Muller, D., Santorelli S.F. *et al.* (2005) Alterations in brain and immune function produced by mindfulness meditation. *Psychosomatic Medicine*, 65, 564–70.

Diedrich, R.C. (1996) An iterative approach to executive coaching. *Consulting Psychology Journal: Practice and Research*, 48(2), 61–6.

Downey, M. (2003) *Effective Coaching: Lessons from the Coaches' Coach* (2nd edn). London: Texere.

Drucker, P.F. (1967) *The Effective Executive.* London: Heinemann.

Fredrickson, B.L. and Losada, M. (2005) Positive affect and the complex dynamics of human flourishing. *American Psychologist*, 60(7), 678–86.

Fredrickson, B.L., Tugade, M.M., Waugh, C.E., and Larkin, G. (2003) What good are positive emotions in crises? A prospective study of resilience and emotions following the terrorist attacks on the United States on September 11th, 2001. *Journal of Personality and Social Psychology*, 84, 365–76.

Gregory, J.B. (2010) Employee coaching: The importance of the supervisor/subordinate relationships and related constructs. PhD dissertation, The University of Akron, Akron, Ohio.

Gregory, J.B. and Levy, P.E. (2011) It's not me, it's you: A multi-level examination of variables that impact employee coaching relationships. *Consulting Psychology Journal: Practice and Research*, 63, 67–88.

Gregory, J.B., Beck, J.W., and Carr, A.E. (2011) Goals, feedback, and self-regulation: Control theory as a natural framework for executive coaching. *Consulting Psychology Journal: Practice and Research*, 63(1), 26–38.

Gyllensten, K. and Palmer, S. (2007) The coaching relationship: An interpretive phenomenological analysis. *International Coaching Psychology Review*, 2(2), 168–77.

de Haan, E. (2008) *Relational Coaching: Journeys Toward Mastering One-to-one Learning.* Chichester: John Wiley and Sons.

Haynes, L.A. and Avery, L.W. (1979) Training adolescents in self-disclosure and empathy skills. *Journal of Counseling Psychology*, 26, 526–30.

Hunt, J.M. and Weintraub, J.R. (2002) *The Coaching Manager: Developing Top Talent in Business.* Thousand Oaks, CA: Sage.

Joseph, S. (2006) Person-centred coaching psychology: A meta-theoretical perspective. *International Coaching Psychology Review*, 1, 47–54.

Joseph, S. and Bryant-Jefferies, R. (2007) Person-centered coaching psychology. In: S. Palmer and A. Whybrow (eds), *Handbook of Coaching Psychology: A Guide for Practitioners.* London: Routledge. pp. 211–28.

Kampa-Kokesch, S. and Anderson, M.Z. (2001) Executive coaching: A comprehensive review of the literature. *Consulting Psychology Journal: Practice and Research*, 53, 205–28.

Kauffman, C. (2006) Positive psychology: The science at the heart of coaching. In: D.R. Stober and A.M. Grant (eds) *Evidence-based Coaching Handbook: Putting Best Practices to Work for your Clients*. Hoboken, NJ: John Wiley and Sons. pp. 219–54.

Kauffman, C., Boniwell, I., and Silberman, J. (2009) The positive psychology approach to coaching. In: E. Cox, T. Bachkirova and D. Clutterbuck (eds) *The Complete Handbook of Coaching*. London: Sage. pp. 158–71.

Kauffman, C., Silberman, J., and Sharpley, D. (2008) Coaching for strengths using VIA. In: J. Passmore (ed.) *Psychometrics in Coaching: Using Psycholocial and Psychometric Tools for Development*. London: Kogan Page. pp. 239–53.

Kemp, T. (2011) Building the coaching alliance: Illuminating the phenomenon of relationship in coaching. In: G. Hernez-Broome and L.A. Boyce (eds) *Advancing Executive Coaching: Setting the Course for Successful Leadership Coaching*. San Francisco: Jossey-Bass. pp. 151–76.

Kilburg, R.R. (1996) Toward a conceptual understanding and definition of executive coaching. *Consulting Psychology Journal: Practice and Research*, 48, 134–44.

Kilburg, R.R. (2001) Facilitating intervention adherence in executive coaching: A model and methods. *Consulting Psychology Journal: Practice and Research*, 53, 251–67.

Linley, P.A. and Harrington, S. (2005) Positive psychology and coaching psychology: Perspectives on integration. *The Coaching Psychologist*, 1, 13–14.

Linley, P.A. and Harrington, S. (2006) Strengths coaching: A potential-guided approach to coaching psychology. *International Coaching Psychology Review*, 1, 37–46.

Lyubomirsky, S. and Lepper, H. (1999) A measure of subjective happiness: Preliminary reliability and construct validation. *Social Indicators Research*, 46, 137–55.

Maslow, A.H. (1954) *Motivation and Personality*. New York: Harper.

Maslow, A.H. (1962) *Toward a Psychology of Being*. New York: Nostrand.

Maslow, A.H. (1964) *Religion, Values and Peak-experiences*. Columbus: Ohio State University Press.

May, R. (1967) *Psychology and the Human Dilemma*. Princeton: Van Nostrand.

May, R. (1969) *Love and Will*. New York: Norton.

Passmore, J. (2006) Integrative coaching. In: J. Passmore (ed.) *Excellence in Coaching: The Industry Guide*. London: Kogan Page. pp. 135–52.

Passmore, J. (2010) A grounded theory study of the coachee experience: The implications for training and practice in coaching psychology. *International Coaching Psychology Review*, 5, 48–62.

Peterson, C. (2006) *A Primer in Positive Psychology*. New York: Oxford University Press.

Peterson, C. and Seligman, M. (2004) *Character Strengths and Virtues: A Handbook and Classification*. New York: Oxford University Press.

Peterson, D.B. (1996) Executive coaching at work: The art of one-on-one change. *Consulting Psychology Journal: Practice and Research*, 48(2), 78–86.

Rogers, C.R. (1959) A theory of therapy, personality, and interpersonal relationships as developed in the client-centered framework. In: S. Koch (ed.) *Psychology: A Study of a Science, Vol. 3: Formulations of the Person and the Social Context*. New York: McGraw-Hill. pp. 184–256.

Rogers, C.R. (1963) The actualizing tendency in relation to "motives" and to consciousness. In: M.R. Jones (ed.) *Nebraska Symposium on Motivation*. Lincoln, NE: University of Nebraska Press. Vol. 11, pp. 1–24.

Rogers, C.R. (1980) *A Way of Being*. Boston, MA: Houghton Mifflin.

Rosenthal, R. and Jacobson, L. (1992) *Pygmalion in the Classroom*. New York: Irvington.

Sherman, S. and Freas, A. (2004) The wild west of executive coaching. *Harvard Business Review*, 82, 82–90.

Smither, J.W. and Reilly, S.P. (2001) Coaching in organizations. In: M. London (ed.) *How People Evaluate Others in Organizations*. Mahwah, NJ: Lawrence Erlbaum Associates. pp. 221–52.

Steptoe, A., Wardle, J. and Marmot, M. (2005) Positive affect and health-related neuroendocrine, cardiovascular, and inflammatory responses. *Proceedings of the National Academy of Sciences, US,* 102, 6508–12.

Stober, D.R. (2006) Coaching from the humanistic perspective. In: D.R. Stober and A.M. Grant (eds) *Evidence-based Coaching Handbook: Putting Best Practices to Work for your Clients.* Hoboken, NJ: John Wiley and Sons. pp. 17–50.

Stober, D.R. and Parry, C. (2005) Current challenges and future directions in coaching research. In: M. Cavanaugh, A.M. Grant and T. Kemp (eds) *Evidence-based Coaching.* Brisbane, Australia: Australian Academic Press. pp. 13–19.

Ting, S. and Riddle, D. (2006) A framework for leadership development coaching. In: S. Ting and P. Scisco (eds) *The CCL Handbook of Coaching: A Guide for The Leader Coach.* San Francisco, CA: Jossey-Bass. pp. 34–62.

# 16

# Behavioral Coaching

## Fiona Eldridge and Sabine Dembkowski

## Introduction

In this chapter we explore the influence and impact of behaviorism on developing effective executive coaching practice. Behavioral-based coaching is at the root of some of the most popular coaching models, including the commonly used GROW model. However, all too frequently, coaches and aspiring coaches are unaware of the theoretical basis of the models they learn about and apply, and of the consequences for their practice (Barner and Higgins, 2007; Peel, 2005). In this chapter we aim to redress the balance.

The chapter covers the origins of behavioral approaches, the behavioral approach to coaching, behavioral-based coaching models, effectiveness of behavioral coaching, and future research. We examine the origins of behavioral coaching from the work of behaviorists such as Pavlov, Watson, Thorndike, and Skinner. We also acknowledge the criticisms of the early behaviorists that led subsequently to refinement of theories and development of blended approaches such as Bandura's social learning theory. We will then examine the concepts underpinning many coaching processes that are directly derived from the behaviorist theories.

The popularity of the behavioral-based approach to executive coaching closely relates to the desire of organizational buyers of coaching for a process which uses recognized tools and techniques, which is measurable, and is evidenced by tangible outputs such as action plans (Knights and Poppleton, 2008; Visser, 2010). This has contributed to the development of several different models or frameworks for use by executive coaches. We will describe and compare the models to highlight their similarities, differences, and potential weaknesses. We hope this will give practitioners a better understanding of how the models can be used in their practice.

One of the key questions of any approach to executive coaching must be: "Does it work?" We consider the evidence base for behavioral coaching, although acknowledging that much research into coaching effectiveness is not explicit about the type of coaching

*The Wiley Blackwell Handbook of the Psychology of Coaching and Mentoring*, First Edition.
Edited by Jonathan Passmore, David B. Peterson, and Teresa Freire.
© 2013 John Wiley & Sons, Ltd. Published 2016 by John Wiley & Sons, Ltd.

methodology used. Finally, we conclude by looking at the future direction of behavioral approaches to coaching and how they can continue to offer the coaching profession a sound theoretical base.

## Behavioral Theory

Behaviorism focuses on what people do, how rewards and punishments influence this, and hence how they learn. In its purest form it attempts to explain human behavior without reference to mediating internal influences (Bargh and Ferguson, 2000). The origins of behaviorism lie in the work of Pavlov, Watson, Thorndike, and Skinner in the nineteenth and twentieth centuries (Berg and Karlsen, 2007; de Haan and Burger, 2005; Passmore, 2007a; Peel, 2005; Peltier, 2010; Visser, 2010).

Ivan Pavlov was a Russian physiologist working on understanding reflexive responses to stimuli; that is, those that occur without conscious thought. In his experiments with dogs Pavlov found that he could, over time, modify one of the dog's natural behavioral responses so that they would salivate on hearing a ringing bell. This modification of the response is called classical conditioning.

Watson adapted Pavlov's ideas in a human context and is credited with the first use of the term "behaviorist" (Watson, 1913). His contention was that we should study human behavior by focusing on observable behaviors rather than the internal states that were the focus of Freud's work. Watson suggested that even complex habits could be studied by breaking them down into a series of interlinked conditioned responses. His legacy is that behaviorism today is defined as "an approach to psychology which argues that the only appropriate subject matter for scientific psychological investigation is observable, measurable behavior" (Reber *et al.*, 2009, p. 92). Watson himself only had a short academic career before applying his insights to advertising (Peltier, 2010).

Thorndike was a contemporary of Watson who developed a systematic learning theory. He postulated that strengthening the connection between stimulus and response was at the very heart of learning (Thorndike, 1911). Thorndike's law of effect stated that "behaviors that were rewarded tended to recur, while behaviors that were punished or not rewarded tended to weaken" (Peel, 2005, pp. 20–1). Later Thorndike found that punishment did not weaken the bond between stimulus and response, rather it caused the individual to avoid the activity or to set up a new bond of fear or anxiety (Peel, 2005).

Skinner built on the work of the earlier behaviorists and distinguished between two types of behavior – respondent and operant. Respondent behavior is that which is typical of classical conditioning. Operant behavior is the collection of behaviors which do not stem from a simple, automatic response. It is a voluntary behavior which operates on the environment and includes such things as riding a bicycle, playing football, and going to work. Skinner suggests that such behavior is learned, maybe initially through trial and error, and reinforced and strengthened through the process of operant conditioning in which the desired behavior is rewarded by a successful outcome (Arnold *et al.*, 1998; Passmore, 2007a). Skinner regarded what happened after a behavior as important in determining whether or not a behavior is repeated. So, for example, if an individual volunteers to present back the views of a group in a plenary session and is rewarded by smiles and applause (reinforcement) he or she is more likely to do it again than if faced by stony silence or derision (punishment). The process of operant conditioning can be described using a three-term framework: antecedents (A), behavior (B) and consequences

**Table 16.1**  An ABC functional analysis.

| Individual | Antecedent | Behavior | Consequences |
|---|---|---|---|
| 1 | Individual asked to make presentation and encouraged to see as opportunity to showcase his/her own ideas to the board | Presentation is made with enthusiasm | Successful presentation – boss delighted, individual invited to participate in high level strategic meeting |
| 2 | Individual asked to make presentation and told that he/she is a last minute substitution and that she/he has to present ideas of a competitive colleague | Presentation is made with resignation | Poor presentation – boss disappointed, individual sidelined at next meeting |

(C) (Arnold *et al.*, 1998; Peltier, 2010). Antecedents are the conditions or stimuli that come before the behavior and consequences are what happen following a behavior; this may be either encouraging repetition of the behavior or dissuading the individual from repeating it. Examining what happens before and after a behavior in this way is described as a functional analysis. For example, Table 16.1 compares two different individuals' experiences of making a short presentation to senior stakeholders. In the rather starkly contrasting examples above, individual 1's experience is far more likely to reinforce the desired behavior of presentation.

It was suggested by Premack (1959) that there is a hierarchy of reinforcers and that engaging in one behavior may act as a reinforcer for another, perhaps less personally attractive, behavior. In the example above it could be that individual 1 finds participating in high level meetings so energizing that this is sufficient to stimulate better performance in presentation. This effect of the opportunity to participate in one behavior acting as a reinforcer for another behavior has become known as the Premack principle (Homme *et al.*, 1963). The application and influence of operant conditioning can be seen in both learning and management practices (Arnold *et al.*, 1998; Passmore, 2007a; Peltier, 2010). For example, at work, reinforcement of desired behavior may occur through praise from a manager or more formally through financial incentives of a performance related pay scheme.

In 1957 Skinner published his book, *Verbal Behavior*. Bargh and Ferguson (2000, p. 927) describe this as, "a watershed event in twentieth century psychology because (a) it was the first attempt to extend the S-R [stimulus response] model to higher order processes in humans, and (b) it failed spectacularly." The contention of the early behaviorists that a behavior was simply a response to a given external stimulus was challenged and critiqued by those who were examining the intervening effects of internal processes such as perception and reflection on learning and the development of language (e.g., Chomsky, 1959). Critics thought that reducing all human behavior, particularly higher-order, more complex behavior, to a S-R relationship was both simplistic and reductionist (Bargh and Ferguson, 2000; Peel, 2005) and took no account of the mediating processes occurring internally.

In the late 1960s and 1970s, in response to criticism and to integrate some of the thinking from cognitive approaches (such as acting as a result of beliefs, values, and memories as well as external stimuli) behaviorism was developed further by the work of Bandura (1977a) who introduced the concept of social learning. In this he suggested that people did not need to experience the link between reinforcement and behavior themselves – they could also learn by observing others (Passmore, 2007a; Peel, 2005; Peltier, 2010). From this stem the principles of behavior or role modeling which are often applied in behaviorally based coaching. Peel (2005) suggests that these "terms are used interchangeably" and that modeling uses "techniques such as 'goal setting' and 'self-reinforcement' to help people acquire the characteristics of a competent role model" (Peel, 2005, p. 23).

In social learning theory it is accepted that internal cognitive processes are important in determining behavioral responses. An individual is able to anticipate the consequences of a particular behavior based either on their own or others' past experiences (Bandura 1977a). Such behaviors may have benefits either immediately or in the future. For example, within organizations, new recruits learn the processes and policies (both formal and informal) that reinforce or punish behaviors from observation and interactions with their work colleagues (Abernathy, 2008; Visser, 2010).

A further behavioral concept introduced by Bandura, which influences understanding of behavioral change and coaching, is self-efficacy (Baron and Morin, 2010; Brodie Gregory *et al.*, 2011). Bandura (1977b) explains that an individual's belief about their own abilities to perform a certain activity will affect whether or not they attempt a behavior, even if they believe that completing a certain behavior will produce a desired outcome. Bandura (1977b, p. 194) suggests that "efficacy expectations determine how much effort people will expend and how long they will persist in the face of obstacles." If the individual learns through experience that they can cope in certain previously feared situations, for example public speaking, then they are more likely to repeat the behavior. Later research has shown that there is a strong link between self-efficacy and work performance (Gist *et al.*, 1991; Locke and Latham, 1990; Stajkovic and Luthans 1998). Increasing an individual's self-efficacy is often a desired outcome from coaching (Finn *et al.*, 2007).

The principles of behaviorism were adapted for use within an organizational context during the 1980s by Fred Luthans. He drew on the work of early behaviorists and incorporated it into models of organizational behavior. The basic approach he described was to identify behaviors that are critical for effective work performance and then to use reinforcement techniques to reward and affirm appropriate behaviors by individuals or groups. He described this organizational use of operant conditioning as organizational behavior modification (OB Mod). Luthans and Kreitner (1975) outline a five-step process for using OB Mod techniques:

1　Identify critical behaviors.
2　Measure the critical behaviors.
3　Carry out a functional analysis of the behaviors.
4　Develop an intervention strategy.
5　Evaluate.

At the root of the OB Mod techniques is a reference to Thorndike's law of effect (1911). Organizational behavior modification techniques suggest, therefore, that by controlling the consequences of a particular set of behaviors, an organization can control groups of its employees. This link between the early origins of behavioral coaching and those of performance improvement may explain why organizational buyers of coaching have preferred behavioral based approaches to coaching. There is a commonality of language and a ready understanding of how the coach will be working and an emphasis on observable, measurable change.

# The Behavioral Approach to Coaching

Peltier (2010, p. 81) cautions, "Ignore behavioral principles at risk of great peril." In issuing this note of caution Peltier (2010) is joining Berglas (2002) who emphasized the need for coaches to understand the psychological underpinnings of the techniques that they use, as otherwise, even if well intentioned, coaching can create or exacerbate problems for the client.

In practice, coaches may well draw on several different theoretical backgrounds when working with a client on a coaching assignment, but at the heart of most coaching programs is a behavioral approach to change (Bono *et al.*, 2009; Popper and Lipshitz, 1992; Thach and Heinselman, 1999). Skiffington and Zeus (2003, p. 6) define behavioral coaching as:

> A structured, process-driven relationship between a trained professional coach and an individual or team, which includes: assessment, examining values and motivation, setting measurable goals, defining focused action plans, and using validated tools and techniques to help coaches develop competencies and remove blocks to achieve valuable and sustainable changes in their professional and personal lives.

This approach is a core part of a coach's toolkit and one on which many novice coaches rely heavily (Passmore, 2007b). Peltier (2010, p. 81) states that central to the behavioral approach is the view that, "behavior is a function of its consequences." By understanding the behavioral approach, coaches can assist their clients to make changes through learning what, in their environment, causes them to do one thing instead of another and the consequences of a behavior that either causes them to continue doing something or to do something different (Ting and Hart, 2004).

Coaching is about change; understanding what leads to personal change and how change can be influenced, initiated, and maintained, is at the heart of the link between behaviorism and executive coaching. The model of change used in many coach training programs to assist coaches in learning about how people change is that developed by Prochaska *et al.* (1992). The model is explored in detail in the chapter on motivational interviewing.

Although the model is presented linearly, Prochaska *et al.* (1994) caution that in reality individuals are more likely to follow a spiral pathway moving backwards and forwards through the stages, experiencing setbacks or relapses before moving into the final stages. For coaches working with individuals to effect behavioral change, it is clear that both coach and client need to be aware of which stage the client has reached in the change process. Working on a behavioral intervention will be to no avail if the client is not aware of the need to change. Another influence is that resistance to individual change depends on the strength of the stimulus response bond (Nevin, 1999). The Prochaska model of change emphasizes the client's personal responsibility for change; awareness and responsibility are both key in coaching (Bluckert, 2006; Whitmore, 2009).

Alongside awareness, readiness, and responsibility for change there is also the question of motivation. Why do people choose one form of behavior over another? There is an extensive literature on the field of motivation, particularly in connection with the work environment. Although ostensibly not relevant it does affect an individual's choice of behaviors. Vroom (1964, p. 6) defines motivation as, "A process governing choices, made by persons or lower organisms, among alternative forms of voluntary activity." While helping clients raise self-awareness about their behaviors, coaches may also explore motivation.

Coaches using behavioral approaches will work with clients to understand the impact of their behavior on themselves and others and then help them to make changes to adapt to the demands or expectations of their organizations (Barner and Higgins, 2007; Skiffington and Zeus, 2003). The client will be encouraged to produce an action plan with clearly defined intermediate goals to bring about a desired change. As the client progresses through the plan the coach will hold the client to account and notice the impact of behavior on achieving the desired change.

There is an ongoing debate about the role of genetics and environment on our behavior, but some authors (e.g., Arvey *et al.*, 2006) suggest that approximately 50 percent of an individual's values, attitudes, and behaviors come from genetics and the other half are learned. This is good news for the possibility of change through coaching. "An implication of the 50/50 nature/nurture; born/bred debate is that while the past sets conditions on our behavior, our behavior is not pre-conditioned. Any leader can modify behavior through effective coaching" (Ulrich, 2008, p. 106).

Underpinning behavioral coaching approaches are concepts concerning behavioral control which are derived from the work of the behaviorists described earlier. The key concepts are: stimulus control, reinforcement, modeling, rehearsal, and goal setting.

## Stimulus control

One way to control or modify behavior is to identify the stimulus and then to change it in some way. In human behavior the stimulus may be multifaceted, but the principle of stimulus control suggests that an analysis of the environment can identify which elements of the situation will increase or decrease the likelihood of a particular behavior (Quinn *et al.*, 2010). A simple example of this concept in practice is the exhortation by diet books for individuals to clear the refrigerator of tempting food before beginning a diet. The desired behavior, that is eating appropriate food, is much more likely to occur if the tempting stimulus of cakes is removed. In the coaching context, the coach's feedback or challenge can act as a stimulus to the client.

## Reinforcement

Reinforcement is what happens after a response and will affect whether or not the response is repeated. It is important to understand the principles of reinforcement when considering changing or controlling behavior. To be effective, and to condition the behavior, the reinforcement must occur shortly after the performance of the desired behavior. This is the concept of contiguity. With large gaps between behavior and reinforcement, the effect of the reinforcement will diminish (Ferster and Skinner, 1957).

Another important element is contingency. This means that reinforcement should only be given when the desired behavior occurs. Otherwise you may be reinforcing another, undesired behavior. Reinforcement may be either positive or negative. Positive reinforcement occurs when something desired by the individual is given as a result of the behavior, for example, praise from a line manager. Negative reinforcement occurs when something is withdrawn as a result of the individual performing the desired behavior, for example, the line manager stops shouting at you when you finally get the presentation slides completed. This is not to be confused with punishment, which works by following undesired behavior with something that the individual does not like. For example, if you are late for work, your line manager puts you to work on your least desired task.

Other factors influencing reinforcement are the nature of the reinforcement (intrinsic or extrinsic), the frequency or schedule of reinforcement and individual differences (what is reinforcing to one will not necessarily be the same for others) (Peltier, 2010). Intrinsic reinforcers are those that come from within and are very personal to the individual, such as satisfaction with a job well done. Extrinsic reinforcers are external and include such things as money. Frequency of reinforcement has also been found to be important in conditioning and maintaining behavior. If the reinforcement occurs after each occurrence of the desired behavior, then its effects may wane and the desired behavior may eventually become extinct. However, if the behavior is reinforced intermittently then it is more likely that the behavior will be continued. Sometimes a change is of such a magnitude that it has to be broken down into smaller, more achievable steps. In this case reinforcement, often in the form of feedback, is used to shape behavior as the individual is rewarded for each step he or she takes.

Increasingly, in our practice, we are seeing the use of video feedback in sessions as a means of providing direct, personal evidence which can act as reinforcement (both positive and negative) for client behavior and can help coach and client in the process of change, shaping towards the new desired behavior.

## Modeling

As mentioned above, the concept of modeling was introduced by Bandura's work on social learning (e.g., Bandura, 1977a), sometimes referred to as observational or imitative learning (Peltier, 2010). The model is a person who exhibits the behaviors or skills to which the individual aspires. The behavior of the model (also thoughts and attitudes) acts as a stimulus for the acquisition and performance of new behaviors by the individual. In the coaching relationship the coach may be the model or may encourage the client to seek models within the workplace or personal network. Models may also be symbolic – that is removed from the direct experience of the client – and observed on TV or in films or books. Choosing an appropriate model is important – if the model is too distant in terms of experience, status, or position then the client may simply lack sufficient belief in his or her capacity to act in the same way.

Clients will pick up clues from the behavior of the coach about how they should behave or respond in a particular situation, so coaches need to be aware of their own behavior and guard against being inappropriate models. Conversely, they also need to be aware that their behavior can influence outcomes in a coaching relationship through positive modeling.

Modeling is determined by four processes (Bandura, 1986):

1  Attentional processes – connection or liking of model will determine how much attention is paid to model. So if the client is to model a behavior exhibited by the coach, the coach will need to develop good rapport.
2  Retention – clients have to remember the observed behavior. Therefore practice and actual or mental rehearsal help to embed the changes.

3  Reproduction – just seeing behavior does not mean the client will be able to perform it him/herself so there may need to be some skills training to enable the client to perform the new behavior.
4  Motivation – the client needs to see the benefits of adopting the new behavior.

## Rehearsal

Once the client has determined which behavior to change or which new strategy to adopt, and understood and learned what he or she has to do differently it is useful for him or her to practice or rehearse the new behaviors. The coaching session may be an appropriate place to rehearse as it should be a safe space where the coach can provide feedback either through observation and/or, if appropriate, video or audio recording. Once the client is sufficiently confident with the new approach it can be practiced within the work environment. The client can notice what differences changing behavior has on others and the different outcomes achieved. By noticing these differences (self-monitoring) the client can make adjustments to the new behavioral strategy until the desired outcome is achieved (Bandura, 1969). This is linked to Skinner's early theories of operant conditioning and learning by making successive approximations or changes, which take the individual gradually closer to the desired behavior. The coach can assist the client in this stage by providing additional feedback and also by asking questions which help to clarify what is working and what is not.

## Goal setting

A common component of behavioral approaches to coaching is setting goals. Goal setting focuses attention and generates behavior as it directs thoughts and actions (Ives, 2008). Coaching can help in the process of goal attainment (Grant, 2003). It also stops the coaching process becoming just a conversation and keeps it on track as a learning and growth intervention (e.g., Alexander and Renshaw, 2005; Dembkowski *et al.*, 2006; Passmore, 2003; Starr, 2003). Alexander and Renshaw (2005, p. 239) stress the importance of setting goals to give purpose and direction to the coaching session and to prevent it becoming "a meandering natter". They also emphasize the need for the goal to be set according to SMART principles, that is: specific, measurable, achievable, relevant, and time bound (e.g., Doran, 1981).

The coach can work with the client to monitor progress, reinforce what is working and help the client change or relinquish that which is not. Frequently an overarching goal for executive coaching, whatever the individual's agenda, "is to improve an individual's effectiveness at work in ways that are linked to the organization's business strategy" (Barner and Higgins, 2007, p. 149).

Locke and Latham's (1990) goal setting theory has had a major impact on the understanding of motivation at work. Their theory drew on earlier research by Locke (1968) in developing a theory of task motivation and incentives, combined with Bandura's (1986) work on self-efficacy. Locke and Latham (1990) suggest that an individual's representation of a goal will act as a stimulus to behavior and that performance will be maximized when: (1) the goal is clear and specific, (2) sufficiently challenging and compelling to the individual, (3) the individual also understands what behaviors will lead to the achievement of the goal, and (4) the individual feels competent to execute the behaviors. They also point to the need for feedback on progress towards achievement of the goal and suggest that this feedback is most powerful when self-generated.

Later work builds on this by suggesting the need to break goals down into smaller steps or milestones to assist with monitoring, sense of achievement and self-motivation towards the overall goal (Blanchard and Shula, 1995; Lerner and Locke, 1995). Self-set goals, albeit aligned to organizational priorities, generate more motivation towards the achievement of the goal as the individual feels that he or she then has greater autonomous regulation of his or her behavior (Ryan and Deci, 2000).

## Coaching Models Incorporating Behavioral Approaches

The growth of coaching as an approach to leadership and management development has led to the emergence of coaching models. These models provide a framework for the coaching process and are of benefit in training coaches and explaining the process to clients and their organizations. Several of the models are influenced by the behavioral approach and provide a sequence of steps for performance improvement.

In this section we focus on three models: GROW, Skiffington and Zeus's Behavioral Coaching Model and the Achieve Coaching Model®. Each model is described, followed by a comparison of their similarities and differences.

### GROW model

The GROW model, was developed in the 1980s (Alexander and Renshaw, 2005) and was popularized by Sir John Whitmore (e.g., Whitmore, 2009). Its development was influenced by the inner game approach advocated by Gallwey (1974). Today it is probably the best-known coaching model and the one that is most widely used in coaching assignments in industry (Alexander and Renshaw, 2005, Dembkowski *et al.*, 2006, Passmore, 2007b). GROW stands for: Goal, Reality, Options, Wrap up.

Alexander and Renshaw (2005) describe the process of developing the model via an analysis of audio and video tapes of what was occurring in Graham Alexander's coaching sessions. Prior to this, Alexander had not really thought about the structure of his sessions – he just knew from feedback from the clients that the process was working. The need for a framework or model arose when he began working with a major strategy consultancy, which had engaged him to work on a development program for its consultants and wanted to understand his processes. To complement the analysis of taped sessions he asked neurolinguistic programming practitioners to observe live sessions and provide feedback on what they observed. What emerged was a consistent structure which seemed to occur in each session. After much discussion and debate Alexander settled on the acronym GROW for his model. The GROW model provides a framework of four main stages for a coaching session (see Table 16.2).

The GROW model assists the coach to work with the client to move him or her closer to the goal. This echoes the process of shaping or approximation using a trial and error approach to see which behaviors work and which do not (Passmore, 2007b). The first three stages are all designed to increase the client's awareness of himself, the impact his behavior has on others, his situation and his possibilities for action. The final stage is all about evoking the client's own responsibility to take action.

## Skiffington and Zeus' behavioral coaching model

Skiffington and Zeus' (2003) behavioral coaching model builds on GROW. The model has four stages and seven steps as shown in the table 16.3. In their book, *Behavioral Coaching*, Skiffington and Zeus (2003) also describe five different forms of coaching

**Table 16.2** The GROW model stages.

| **Goal** | **Reality** |
|---|---|
| Agree on topic for discussion. | Invite self-assessment. |
| Agree on specific outcomes. | Offer specific examples of feedback. |
| Set long-term aims if appropriate. | Avoid or check assumptions. |
| | Explore what works and what does not. |
| | Probe beneath surface. |
| **Options** | **Wrap up** |
| Cover the full range of options. | Prepare a plan. |
| Invite suggestions from the client. | Identify possible obstacles. |
| Offer suggestions carefully. | Make steps specific and define timing. |
| Ensure choices are made. | Agree support |

Source: Adapted from Alexander and Renshaw (2005).

**Table 16.3** The behavioral coaching model stages.

| *Stage of individual change* | *Steps of coaching process* |
|---|---|
| Reflection | *Education* <br> Coach explains process of change and coaching and manages client's expectations. |
| Preparation | *Data collection* <br> Coach collects information from wide stakeholder group to help identify client's strengths and areas for development (multi-rater 360-degree feedback, psychometrics, interviews, and appraisals). May complete functional analysis. |
| | *Planning* <br> Coach and client identify specific behaviors for change. Identifies conditions and reinforcers for change to new behavior. Coach and client set goals and build into action plan. |
| Action | *Behavioral change* <br> Work on targeted behaviors by using techniques for change, for example modeling to change antecedents, shaping behavior, and reinforcing consequences. |
| | *Measurement* <br> May involve self-monitoring or direct observation by the coach as client uses new behaviors at work. |
| | *Evaluation* <br> Links the value of the coaching program to business objectives. Evaluation strategy agreed at contract stage. |
| Maintenance | *Maintenance* <br> Coach's role diminishes as client encouraged to be self-maintaining. Coach and client work out critical factors for maintenance of new behaviors. |

Source: Adapted from Skiffington and Zeus, 2003.

which they see as appropriate for use in the different steps. These coaching forms are coaching education, skills coaching, rehearsal coaching, performance coaching, and self-coaching. The aim of the model is to link the stages involved in individual change with the steps of the coaching process.

Skiffington and Zeus (2003) are explicit about the behavioral origins of their model and provide descriptions of how to effect behavioral change through specific techniques. Their model encourages coach and client to identify and then target specific behaviors for change, conduct a functional analysis and use psychometric and other assessments of the client and then formulate goals and develop an action plan. The coach will then work with the client using behavioral change techniques to effect the desired change. Finally coach and client will work on strategies to manage and maintain the change. These stages amplify Goldsmith's process of coaching for behavioral change (Goldsmith, 2000; Jenkins, 2010). Skiffington and Zeus (2003) also draw attention to other dimensions, such as values, emotions, beliefs, and personal and organizational learning which underpin their model. In that sense, although described as the behavioral coaching model, it is perhaps better described as an integrated model of coaching process.

## The Achieve Coaching Model®

The Achieve Coaching Model®, shown in Figure 16.1, provides structure for coaching sessions and ensures that the coaching relationship is purposeful, with clearly defined outcomes, without restricting the flexibility of individual coaches (Dembkowski and Eldridge, 2003, 2008).

The seven-step model was developed in 2002 and is based on analysis of coaching conversations and observation of experienced executive coaches with a reputation for achieving results with their clients (Dembkowski and Eldridge, 2003). It builds on the GROW model by adding new stages, particularly focusing on establishing the current reality and

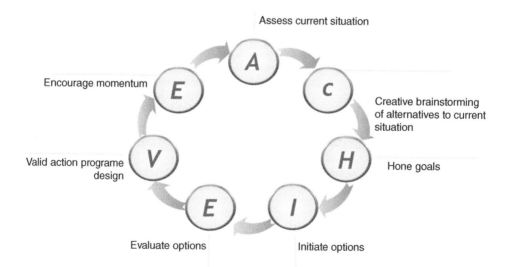

**Figure 16.1**   The Achieve Coaching Model® stages.
Source: Adapted from Dembkowski and Eldridge (2003).

**Table 16.4** The Achieve Coaching Model® – aims of each stage.

| Stage | Aims |
|---|---|
| Assess current situation | Considering the current situation will help the client increase his or her self-awareness and begin to identify areas to work on with the executive coach. |
| Creative brainstorming of alternatives to current situation | This phase is all about the exploration of possibilities. It also aims to increase the choices that a client has when approaching a challenge or specific situation. |
| Hone goals | Helps client to refine his or her aims into a specific goal. The coach's role here is to help the client to specify exactly what they want and formulate clear, SMART goals. |
| Initiate options | The coach works with the client to develop a wide range of ways of achieving the goal. By exploring a range of options the client is expanding choices and breaking away from familiar patterns of behavior. |
| Evaluate options | Having generated a comprehensive list of options, the next step is to evaluate the options systematically to develop an action plan. |
| Valid action plan design | Once the client has a well-developed goal and a preferred set of options for achieving the goal, the next stage is to devise a concrete and practical plan. By breaking the actions needed to achieve the goal into smaller steps the client can begin moving forwards. |
| Encouragement of momentum | The final role for the coach is to assist the client to keep on track through feedback, challenge, and encouragement. This takes place in between each session as well as at the end of a program. |

Source: Adapted from Dembkowski and Eldridge (2003).

helping the client to decide upon and shape their desired outcome. It also provides clients with transparency about the process as the coach can explain what he or she will be doing with the client at each stage (see Table 16.4).

The model places significant emphasis on the development of choice and options, particularly in goal setting. This is essential because if there is only one way to achieve the outcome, any setback is likely to stop all forward movement. However, in developing a well-defined action plan (strategy for behavioral change) coach and client work together to guard against the feeling of overwhelm which clients sometimes experience when presented with options if they cannot see a clear first step towards the outcome. Many organizational sponsors and clients view the production of a written plan as tangible evidence that the coaching program is achieving success. Action planning is not something that just happens towards the end of the coaching program. However, as the end of the program approaches it is useful for the client to have a plan for when the coach has left.

It is important to reinforce even the smallest steps as this helps to build and maintain momentum, shape the behavior and increase the level of confidence and self-efficacy of the client. The small steps add up to the overall change. Sustainable change is easier to achieve with continuous reinforcement and encouragement. The changes that occur through coaching may then act as a stimulus for further development, either with a coach or sustained by the client who has learned how to apply the techniques of change for him or herself.

Table 16.5   A comparison of behavioral coaching models.

| | | *Model* | |
| Steps of behavioral change | GROW | Skiffington and Zeus behavioral coaching model | The Achieve Coaching Model® |
| --- | --- | --- | --- |
| Define focus | Goal | Data collection | Assess current situation/hone goals |
| Conduct a behavior audit | Reality | Data collection | Assess current situation |
| Do a functional analysis | Reality | Data collection | Assess current situation |
| Develop a change strategy or action plan | Options/Wrap up | Planning/behavioral change | Creative brainstorming/ initiate options/ evaluate options/ valid action plan design |
| Collect more data | | Measurement/evaluation | Assess current situation/encourage momentum |

## Comparison of Behavioral Coaching Models

Common to all the models is a framework to guide coaching and a sequential approach to effecting individual change. The underlying steps of behavioral change as suggested by Peltier (2010) and drawn from the OB Mod five-step process of Luthans and Kreitner (1975) is a convenient skeleton against which to compare the models. Table 16.5 relate the stages of the models against these five steps.

One key similarity between the models is that they encourage the use of action plans and the development of measurable objectives. This links clearly to the performance culture of many organizations commissioning coaching. The action plans are then implemented by the client, assisted by the coach using behavioral change techniques.

Of course, action plans are only as effective as the quality of the information used to inform the design of the plan. Two of the models (Skifffington and Zeus, the Achieve Coaching Model®) are explicit in encouraging the coach to collect data from multiple sources from and about the client to raise the client's self-awareness and to begin the process of identifying areas for change. An advantage of reflecting on the current situation is that the coach gains an appreciation of the context for the sessions ahead. However, the most important benefit for the client is that he has time and space to consider the factors which led to the current situation and how their behavior has impacted on others. Some elements of the Skiffington and Zeus (2003) approach appear a little more directive than GROW and the Achieve Coaching Model®, as the authors suggest that the coach should collate and control what information is fed back to the client. The third step of change, conducting a functional analysis is explicit in Skiffington and Zeus and implicit in GROW and Achieve.

The Achieve Coaching Model® encourages coach and client to explore multiple possibilities (creative brainstorming) to get beneath the presenting issue before moving on to focus in on a goal – this is a stage not signposted in the other models. The coach will work with the individual to begin the process of clarifying the individual's desired outcome, that is, what he or she would like to do differently, what are his/her overall professional aspirations and areas for development. This also helps to build the client's ownership and personal responsibility for the outcomes.

All the models emphasize the need for client ownership of goals. In their descriptions accompanying the models, the various authors make it clear that they are intended as frameworks, not straightjackets and that in practice coach and client move backwards and forwards through the stages of the model as needs dictate. Only the Skiffington and Zeus model makes explicit reference to formal evaluation of the coaching process. This, coupled with the education stage at the start of their model, marks it as one which is intended to guide the entire coaching engagement rather than focusing solely on the coaching interaction between the coach and client that leads to behavioral change. The authors of the other models above do refer to issues such as contracting and evaluation, but not within their models.

For some within the coaching community there is a question about whether the behavioral approach may be too directive and manipulative (e.g., Barner and Higgins, 2007). There is also concern that the coach may focus on a narrow range of behaviors to the exclusion of other information that may be affecting the client's behavior. These concerns are not criticisms of any specific model but reinforce the need for coaches to understand how and why the techniques work; coaches should recognize that other approaches or blended approaches may be more appropriate when working on challenges with a client.

Ultimately as Linley (2006) points out, our choice of model is likely to be a reflection of our own preferences and what was available to us when we trained. As coaches develop they grow to understand more about the theoretical underpinnings of approaches and explore alternatives. Linley (2006, p. 5) underlines a coach's responsibility: "Our choice of coaching model is not an idle one, for it influences not only how we work with our clients, and to a small extent the outcomes we may achieve, but it also has a bearing on how we experience our work as coaches on a personal level."

## Effectiveness of the Behavioral Coaching Approach – Outcomes

In the introduction we posed the question – does it work? Conducting literature searches in preparation for writing this chapter quickly led us to the conclusion that there remains a paucity of studies evaluating the effectiveness of coaching. Coaching as an emerging profession has tended to be driven by practice rather than underpinned by theory (Grant *et al.*, 2010). This led Sherman and Freas (2004, pp. 82–4) to comment, "Like the Wild West of yesteryear, this frontier is chaotic, largely unexplored and fraught with risk, yet immensely promising." Indeed, despite more studies beginning to be published (Greif, 2007), as McGurk (2011, p. 70) says, "coaching has an Achilles heel in that its evaluation is largely neglected."

The absence of empirical research into the efficacy of coaching has been noted by many others (e.g., Dembkowski and Eldridge, 2004; Ely *et al.*, 2010; Evers *et al.*, 2006; Feldman and Lankau, 2005; Fillery-Travis and Lane, 2006; Franklin and Doran, 2009; Brodie Gregory *et al.*, 2011; de Haan *et al.*, 2011; Joo, 2005; Kampa-Kokesch and Anderson, 2001; Levenson, 2009; McDermott *et al.*, 2007; Natale and Diamante, 2005; Orenstein, 2006; Passmore and Fillery-Travis, 2011; Passmore and Gibbes, 2007; Sue-Chan and Latham, 2004; Wasylyshyn, 2003). Apart from the limited number of studies on coaching efficacy, an additional barrier for us in answering the question, "do behavioral approaches work?" is that only a very small minority of studies actually consider the approach taken by the coach (e.g., Evers *et al.*, 2006; Grant, 2001; de Haan *et al.*, 2011; Perkins, 2009; Scoular and Linley, 2006).

Much of the research examines the perceived effectiveness from the point of view of the client (de Haan *et al.*, 2011; Moen and Skaalvik, 2009) and many of the studies involve only one measurement at the end of the coaching intervention (Evers *et al.*, 2006; Kochanowski *et al.*, 2010). These retrospective studies attempt to measure whether or not the clients' stated goals have been achieved. In addition, many of these studies are based on data produced through self-report questionnaires, which are well-known for response bias. Often studies are also based on a small sample size of less than 100 participants or where the coaching is of limited duration (Joo, 2005). Another issue is that there are no universally agreed criteria defining a successful outcome (MacKie, 2007). To date, it would appear that only a small number attempt to measure the effectiveness of coaching by examining effects beyond client satisfaction via simple surveys (Baron and Morin, 2009; de Haan *et al.*, 2011; Joo, 2005). These studies are outlined below.

Thach (2002) examined the impact of executive coaching on "leadership effectiveness". A multi-rater 360-degree feedback process (Maloney and Hinrichs, 1959) was administered to 281 participants both before and after the coaching sessions. This both identified the areas for development and provided multi-rater data into the effectiveness of the coaching intervention. Each participant had a total of four coaching sessions over a period of six months. The study showed an increase of 55–60 percent in terms of leadership effectiveness.

Luthans and Peterson (2003) looked at the effect of executive coaching on the integration of data from 360-degree feedback for 67 participants. The study was specifically designed to look at the effects of executive coaching on increasing self-awareness as defined by the degree of difference between self and others' evaluations. The coaching was limited to only two sessions – one to look at the results of the initial 360-degree feedback and one three months later. The study concluded that there was an increase in self-awareness as the gap between self and other evaluations was closed. With so few sessions it is hard to attribute the increase to the effects of coaching. Indeed the differences could be due to a 'Hawthorne effect' – where subjects modify the behavior being measured just as a result of being measured rather than because of any experimental process (e.g., Franke and Kaul, 1978).

Smither *et al.* (2003) is one of the few studies to include a control group and a multi-rater 360-degree feedback both before and after coaching. It is also one of the largest studies, with more than 1000 participants. The control group included over 800 managers, whereas the experimental group was composed of 400 managers. Both groups were from the same multinational corporation. The results of the study indicated that those who received coaching were more likely to set specific goals, ask for suggestions for improvement from their supervisors and gain better evaluations from direct reports and line managers than those who did not receive coaching. Again, the number of sessions was limited to two or three per participant.

Olivero *et al.* (1997) considered the effects of executive coaching on productivity for 23 managers who attended a three-day management skills training program, followed by eight coaching sessions over two months. Training alone improved organizational productivity by 22.4 percent but supplementing with coaching achieved an increase of 88 percent. Productivity was measured by looking at records of historical outputs per employee before the training, then after the training, and finally after the coaching sessions.

Evers *et al.* (2006) looked at the impact of coaching on increasing clients' self-efficacy. It is one of the few studies to include a repeated measures design and also one of only two studies we know of which includes a named coaching model – GROW as the framework for the coaching interventions. The study compared the scores of 30 managers who received 3–4 coaching sessions with 30 managers who received no coaching. Three core areas were measured: setting goals, acting in a balanced way, and a mindful way of living and working. It is important to note that the coaches were the managers' immediate superiors, that is, not professional coaches. The results indicated that coaching had a positive effect on the individuals' self-efficacy relating to setting their own goals and outcome expectancies to act in a balanced way. Again caution is required as the sample size is comparatively small and the measures are self-reported.

The other study to include the GROW model was that conducted by Scoular and Linley (2006). Their study looked at goal setting and personality types and involved 117 coachees and 14 coaches. However, they only reference GROW in passing as the focus of the study was to look at goal setting and performance by comparing the results of two groups, one where coaches used goal setting techniques and the other where they were explicitly instructed not to use the techniques. In common with some of the other studies above, the coaching was very restricted in that coachees only received one 30-minute session. They found that the results showed no difference in performance for those who had been coached in goal setting and those who had not. This is perhaps not totally surprising in that the sessions were very short and were not part of an ongoing coaching relationship, which is important in determining coaching effectiveness (Boyce *et al.*, 2010).

Amongst the small number of studies that actually compare specific approaches to coaching is a study by Grant (2001) on trainee accountants. The study compared the effects of cognitive, behavioral, and cognitive-behavioral coaching on academic performance, study skills, self-regulation, mental health, private self-consciousness, and self-concept. The study had three cohorts of about 20 students, which each received coaching using one of the three approaches and also included a control group. Trainees in the cognitive only cohort reported enhanced study skills and increases in their deep achieving approaches to learning, reduced anxiety and lower levels of depression. However, academic performance declined relative to the control group. In the behavioral only group trainees showed reduced study-related anxiety and improved academic performance. The final group, which received cognitive-behavioral coaching, also demonstrated improved academic performance and reduced anxiety coupled with enhanced study skills, self-regulation and self-concept. Grant (2001, p. 14) concluded that, "it would appear that the combined cognitive and behavioral coaching program is an effective means of enhancing both performance and well-being." Grant (2001) noted that behavioral-based approaches seemed to be essential for enhanced performance, thus supporting the continuing presence of behavioral-based approaches in coach training and coach practice.

## Future Research

As an emerging profession we are beginning to build an evidence base for the effectiveness of coaching in general and for aspects of a behaviorally-based approach. This enables us to answer a tentative "yes" to the question of does it work? However, it is also clear that further rigorous research is needed into specifically which approaches and techniques achieve measurable results.

As practitioners first and researchers second, one of the striking similarities for us of many of the studies is that they are frequently based on student or other specially selected populations for the purpose of the study rather than clients engaged in an ongoing coaching relationship. There are challenges of using "real" case studies, not least the many and various individual outcomes specified by clients, which make controlled comparison difficult (Bowles *et al.*, 2007), although Peterson (2006) suggests that it is possible by using a multi-rater approach. Passmore and Gibbes (2007, p. 122) acknowledge that case studies have their place but suggest that to continue to build the case for coaching, studies should, "be built on control group studies with random selection of participants between the study group and a wait list group."

However, organizations will continue to press coaching practitioners to demonstrate the effectiveness of their processes in real engagements. One of the challenges in executive coaching is that the coaching relationship involves three parties: coach, client, and organization. As Laske (2004, p. 43) says, "coaching practitioners must find ways of showing that 'outcomes' are both organizationally desired and personally beneficial, which for companies viewed long-term, is one and the same thing."

Behavioral approaches clearly have a place in the coach's repertoire and, especially for those from a non-psychological background, form a major part of initial training and practice. Behavioral approaches are also used by coaching psychologists. Whybrow and Palmer (2006) found that just over 60 percent of respondents in their survey of members of the Special Group Coaching Psychology of the British Psychological Society used a behavioral approach. However, this is likely to be in combination with other approaches. As we have outlined, the basic steps of effecting behavioral change underscore formal models of coaching. They are also implicit in coaching approaches to management, particularly in sales driven organizations (Mosca *et al.*, 2010).

## Conclusion

What is the future for behavioral coaching? We think that the approach is likely to remain an important part of the practitioner's toolkit as it is one that can equip the coach with the basic tools needed to conduct a program and achieve results. The approach also resonates with workplace activities, such as performance improvement, quality improvement, bonus targets, and performance appraisals, so coaches, clients, and organizations can operate using a shared language and understanding. In this chapter we have focused on coaching as an individual activity, but we also think that the coach has a role in assisting with organizational cultural change. By explaining behavioral-based approaches the coach can influence beyond the individual client as, applied with care and integrity, the techniques can be used in a range of managerial activities such as performance management and appraisal.

In practice it is likely that coaches combine a range of approaches and that experience helps them select appropriate methodologies for different situations. What is key, in an emerging profession, is that we link theoretical underpinnings to models, tools, and techniques during training, so that coaches in training and practice understand how and why what they are doing is working. To achieve this we will need to research not only coaching effectiveness, but what *specifically* works – which methodologies, tools, and techniques?

## References

Abernathy, W.B. (2008) Implications and applications of a behavior systems perspective. *Journal of Organisational Behavior Management*, 28(2), 123–38.

Alexander, G. and Renshaw, B. (2005) *Super Coaching*. London: Random House.

Arnold, J., Cooper, C., and Robertson, I. (1998) *Work Psychology – Understanding Human Behavior in the Workplace.* London: Pearson Education.

Arvey, R.D., Rotundo, M., Johnson, W., Zhang, Z., and McGue, M. (2006) The determinants of leadership role occupancy: Genetic and personality factors. *The Leadership Quarterly*, 17(1), 1–20.

Bandura, A. (1969) *Principles of Behavior Modification.* New York: Holt, Rinehart and Winston.

Bandura, A. (1977a) *Social Learning Theory.* Englewood Cliffs, NJ: Prentice Hall.

Bandura, A. (1977b) Self-efficacy: Towards a unifying theory of behavioral change. *Psychological Review*, 84(2), 191–215.

Bandura, A. (1986) *Social Foundations of Thought and Action: A Social Cognitive Theory.* Englewood Cliffs, NJ: Prentice Hall.

Bargh, J.A. and Ferguson, M.J. (2000) Beyond behaviorism: On the automaticity of higher mental processes. *Psychological Bulletin*, 126(6), 925–45.

Barner, R. and Higgins, J. (2007) Understanding implicit models that guide the coaching process. *Journal of Management Development*, 26(2), 148–58.

Baron, L. and Morin, L. (2010) The impact of executive coaching on self-efficacy related to management soft-skills. *Leadership and Organization Development Journal*, 31(1), 18–38.

Berg, M.E. and Karlsen, J.T. (2007) Mental models in project management coaching. *Engineering Management Journal*, 19(3), 3–13.

Berglas, S. (2002) The very real dangers of executive coaching. *Harvard Business Review*, June, 3–8.

Blanchard, K. and Shula, D. (1995) *Everyone's a Coach: Five Business Secrets for High-performance Coaching.* New York: Harper Business Books.

Bluckert, P. (2006) *Psychological Dimensions of Executive Coaching.* Maidenhead: McGraw-Hill.

Bono, J.E., Purvanova, R.K., Towler, A.J., and Peterson, D.B. (2009) A survey of executive coaching practices. *Personnel Psychology*, 62, 361–404.

Bowles, S., Cunningham, C.J.L., De La Rosa, G.M., and Picano, J. (2007) Coaching leaders in middle and executive management: Goals, performance, buy-in. *Leadership and Organization Development Journal*, 28(5), 388–408.

Boyce, L.A., Jackson, J.J., and Neal, L.J. (2010) Building successful leadership coaching relationships: Examining impact of matching criteria in a leadership coaching program. *Journal of Management Development*, 29(10), 914–31.

Brodie Gregory, J., Beck, J.W., and Carr, A.E. (2011) Goals, feedback and self-regulation: Control theory as a natural framework for executive coaching. *Coaching Psychology Journal: Practice and Research*, 63(1), 26–38.

Chomsky, N. (1959) Review of verbal behavior by B. F. Skinner. *Language*, 35(1), 26–58.

Dembkowski, S. and Eldridge, F. (2003) Beyond GROW: A new coaching model. *The International Journal of Mentoring and Coaching*, 1(1).

Dembkowski, S. and Eldridge, F. (2004) The nine critical success factors in individual coaching. *The International Journal of Mentoring and Coaching*, 2(2), 1–11.

Dembkowski, S. and Eldridge, F. (2008) Achieving tangible results: The development of a coaching model. In: D.B. Drake, D. Brennan and K. Gørtz (eds) *The Philosophy and Practice of Coaching – Insights and Issues for a New Era.* San Francisco: Jossey-Bass. pp. 195–212.

Dembkowski, S., Eldridge, F., and Hunter, I. (2006) *The Seven Steps of Effective Executive Coaching.* London: Thorogood.

Doran, G.T. (1981) There's a SMART way to write management's goals and objectives. *Management Review*, 70(11), 35–6.

Ely, K., Boyce, L.A., Nelson, J.K., Zaccaro, S.J., Hernez-Broome, G., and Whyman, W. (2010) Evaluating leadership coaching: A review and integrated framework. *The Leadership Quarterly*, 21, 585–99.

Evers, W.J., Brouwers, A., and Tonic, W. (2006) A quasi-experimental study on management coaching effectiveness. *Consulting Psychology Journal: Practice and Research*, 58(3), 174–82.

Feldman, D.C. and Lankau, M.J. (2005) Executive coaching: A review and agenda for future research. *Journal of Management*, 31(6), 829–48.

Ferster, C.B. and Skinner, B.F. (1957) *Schedules of Reinforcement*. East Norwalk, CT: Appleton-Century-Crofts.

Fillery-Travis, A. and Lane, D. (2006) Does coaching work or are we asking the wrong question? *International Coaching Psychology Review*, 1(1), 23–36.

Finn, F.A., Mason, C.M., and Bradley, L.M. (2007) *Doing Well with Executive Coaching: Psychological and Behavioural Impacts*. Presented at the Annual Conference of the Academy of Management, Philadelphia, PA.

Franke, R.H. and Kaul, J.D. (1978) The Hawthorne experiments: First statistical interpretation. *American Sociological Review*, 43(5), 623–43.

Franklin, J. and Doran, J. (2009) Does all coaching enhance objective performance independently evaluated by blind assessors? The importance of the coaching model and content. *International Coaching Psychology Review*, 4(2), September, 128–44.

Gallwey, W.T. (1974) *The Inner Game of Tennis*. New York: Random House.

Gist, M.E., Stevens, C.K., and Bavetta, A.G. (1991) Effects of self-efficacy and post-training intervention on the acquisition and maintenance of complex interpersonal skills. *Personnel Psychology*, 44(4), 837–61.

Goldsmith, M. (2000) Coaching for behavioral change. In: M. Goldsmith, L. Lyons, and A. Freas (eds) *Coaching for Leadership: How the World's Greatest Coaches Help Leaders Learn*. San Francisco: Jossey-Bass. pp. 21–6.

Grant, A.M. (2001) *Coaching for Enhanced Performance: Comparing Cognitive and Behavioral Approaches to Coaching*. Paper presented to 3rd International Spearman Seminar: Extending Intelligence: Enhancements and New Constructs, Sydney.

Grant, A.M. (2003) The impact of life coaching on goal attainment, meta-cognition and mental health. *Social Behavior and Personality*, 31(3), 253–64.

Grant, A.M., Passmore, J., Cavanagh, M.J., and Parker, H. (2010) The state of play in coaching today: a comprehensive review of the field. *International Review of Industrial and Organizational Psychology*, 25, 125–67.

Greif, S. (2007) Advances in research on coaching outcomes. *International Coaching Psychology Review*, 2(3), 222–49.

de Haan, E. and Burger, Y. (2005) *Coaching with Colleagues*. Basingstoke: Palgrave Macmillan.

de Haan, E., Culpin, V., and Curd, J. (2011) Executive coaching in practice: What determines helpfulness for clients of coaching? *Personnel Review*, 40(1), 24–44.

Homme, L.E., Debaca, P.C., Devine, J.V., Steinhorst, R., and Rickert, E.J. (1963) Use of the premack principle in controlling the behavior of nursery school children. *Journal of the Experimental Analysis of Behavior*, 6, 544.

Ives, Y. (2008) What is "coaching"? An exploration of conflicting paradigms. *International Journal of Evidence Based Coaching and Mentoring*, 6(2), 100–13.

Jenkins, S. (2010) What could an executive coach do for an association football manager? *Annual Review of High Performance Coaching and Consulting*, 1–12.

Joo, B. (2005) Executive coaching: A conceptual framework from an integrative review of practice and research. *Human Resource Development Review*, 4(4), 462–88.

Kampa-Kokesch, S. and Anderson, M.Z. (2001) Executive coaching: A comprehensive review of the literature. *Consulting Psychology Journal: Practice and Research*, 53(4), 205–28.

Knights, A. and Poppleton, A. (2008) *Developing Coaching Capability in Organisations*. London: Chartered Institute of Personnel and Development.

Kochanowski, S., Seifert, C.F., and Yukl, G. (2010) Using coaching to enhance the effects of behavioral feedback to managers. *Journal of Leadership and Organizational Studies*, 17(4), 363–9.

Laske, O. (2004) Can evidence based coaching increase ROI? *International Journal of Evidence Based Coaching and Mentoring*, 2(2), 41–53.

Lerner, B. and Locke, E.A. (1995) The effects of goal setting, self efficacy, competition and personal traits on the performance of an endurance task. *Journal of Sports and Exercise Psychology*, 17(2), 138–52.

Levenson, A. (2009) Measuring and maximizing the business impact of executive coaching. *Consulting Psychology Journal: Practice and Research*, 61(2), 103–21.

Linley, P.A. (2006) Coaching research: Who? What? Where? When? Why? *International Journal of Evidence Based Coaching and Mentoring*, 4(2), 1–7.

Locke, E.A. (1968) Toward a theory of task motivation and incentives. *Organizational Behavior and Human Performance*, 3, 157–89.

Locke, E.A. and Latham, G.P. (1990) *A Theory of Goal Setting and Task Performance.* Englewood Cliffs, NJ: Prentice-Hall.

Luthans, F. and Kreitner, R. (1975) *Organizational Behavior Modification.* Glenview, IL: Scott-Foresman.

Luthans, F. and Peterson, S.J. (2003) 360 degree feedback with systematic coaching: Empirical analysis suggests a winning combination. *Human Resource Management*, 42(3), 243–56.

McDermott, M., Levenson, A., and Newton, S. (2007) What coaching can and cannot do for your organization. *Human Resource Planning*, 30, 30–37.

McGurk, J. (2011) Real-world coaching evaluation. *Training Journal*, February, 70–4.

MacKie, D. (2007) Evaluating the effectiveness of executive coaching: Where are we now and where do we need to be? *Australian Psychologist*, 42(4), 310–18.

Maloney, P.W. and Hinrichs, J.H. (1959) A new tool for supervisory development. *Personnel*, 36, 46–53.

Moen, F. and Skaalvik, E. (2009) The effect from executive coaching on performance psychology. *International Journal of Evidence Based Coaching and Mentoring*, 7(2), 31–49.

Mosca, J.B., Fazzari, A., and Buzza, J. (2010) Coaching to win: A systematic approach to achieving productivity through coaching. *Journal of Business and Economics Research*, 8(5), 115–30.

Natale, S.M. and Diamante, T. (2005) The five stages of executive coaching: Better process makes better practice. *Journal of Business Ethics*, 59(4), 361–74.

Nevin, J.A. (1999) Analyzing Thorndike's law of effect: The question of stimulus–response bonds. *Journal of the Experimental Analysis of Behavior*, 72(3), 447–50.

Olivero, G., Bane, K., and Kopelman, R. (1997) Executive coaching as a transfer of training tool: Effects on productivity in a public agency. *Public Personnel Management*, 26(4), 461–9.

Orenstein, R.L. (2006) Measuring executive coaching efficacy? The answer was here all the time. *Consulting Psychology Journal: Practice and Research*, 58, 106–16.

Passmore, J. (2003) Goal-focused coaching. *The Occupational Psychologist – Special Issue Coaching Psychology*, 49, 30–3.

Passmore, J. (2007a) Behavioral coaching. In: S. Palmer and A. Whybrow (eds) *Handbook of Coaching Psychology.* London: Routledge. pp. 73–85.

Passmore, J. (2007b) An integrative model for executive coaching. *Consulting Psychology Journal: Practice and Research*, 59(1), 68–78.

Passmore, J. and Fillery-Travis, A. (2011) A critical review of executive coaching research: A decade of progress and what's to come. *Coaching: An International Journal of Theory, Practice and Research*, 4(2), 70–88.

Passmore, J. and Gibbes, C. (2007) The state of executive coaching research: What does the current literature tell us and what's next for coaching research? *International Coaching Psychology Review*, 2, 116–28.

Peel, D. (2005) The significance of behavioral learning theory to the development of effective coaching practice. *International Journal of Evidence Based Coaching and Mentoring*, 3(1), 18–28.

Peltier, B. (2010) *The Psychology of Executive Coaching: Theory and Application* (2nd edn). London: Routledge.

Perkins, R.D. (2009) How executive coaching can change leader behavior and improve meeting effectiveness: An exploratory study. *Consulting Psychology Journal: Practice and Research*, 61(4), 298–318.

Peterson, D.B. (2006) People are complex and the world is messy: A behavior-based approach to executive coaching. In: D.R. Strober and A.M. Grant (eds) *Evidence Based Coaching Handbook*. Hoboken, NJ: Wiley. pp. 51–79.

Popper, M. and Lipshitz, R. (1992) Coaching on leadership. *Leadership and Organizational Developmental Journal*, 13, 15–19.

Premack, D. (1959) Toward empirical behavior laws: I. *Positive Reinforcement Psychological Review*, 66(4), 219–33.

Prochaska, J.O., Norcross, J.C., and DiClemente, C. (1992) In search of how people change: applications to addicitve behaviors. *American Psychologist*, 47, 1102–14.

Prochaska, J.O., Norcross, J.C., and DiClemente, C. (1994) *Changing for Good*. New York: William Morrow.

Quinn, J.M., Pascoe, A., Wood, W., and Neal, D.T. (2010) Can't control yourself? Monitor those bad habits. *Personality and Social Psychology Bulletin*, 36(4), 499–511.

Reber, A.S., Allen, R., and Reber, E. (2009) *The Penguin Dictionary of Psychology* (4th edn). London: Penguin Group.

Ryan, R.M. and Deci, E.L. (2000) Self-determination theory and the facilitation of intrinsic motivation, social development, and well-being. *American Psychologist*, 55(1), 68–78.

Scoular, A. and Linley, P.A. (2006) Coaching, goal setting and personality type: What matters? *The Coaching Psychologist*, 2, 9–11.

Sherman, S. and Freas, A. (2004) The Wild West of executive coaching. *Harvard Business Review*, 82(11), 82–90.

Skiffington, S. and Zeus, P. (2003) *Behavioral Coaching: How to Build Sustainable Personal and Organizational Strength*. Sydney: McGraw-Hill.

Skinner, B.F. (1957) *Verbal Behavior*. New York: Appleton.

Smither, J.W., London, M., Flautt, R., Vargas, Y., and Kucine, I. (2003) Can working with an executive coach improve multisource feedback ratings over time? A quasi-experimental field study. *Personnel Psychology*, 56, 23–44.

Stajkovic, A.D. and Luthans, F. (1998) Self-efficacy and work-related performance: A meta-analysis. *Psychological Bulletin*, 124(2), 240–61.

Starr, J. (2003) *The Coaching Manual*. London: Prentice Hall.

Sue-Chan, C. and Latham, G.P. (2004) The relative effectiveness of external, peer, and self-coaches. *Applied Psychology: An International Review*, 53(2), 260–73.

Thach, E.C. (2002) The impact of executive coaching and 360 feedback on leadership effectiveness. *Leadership and Organization Development Journal*, 23(4), 205–14.

Thach, L. and Heinselman, T. (1999) Executive coaching defined. *Training and Development*, 53, 34–9.

Thorndike, E.L. (1911) *Animal Intelligence*. New York: Macmillan.

Ting, S. and Hart, E.W. (2004) Formal coaching. In: C.D. McCauley and E. Van Velsor (eds) *The Center for Creative Leadership Handbook of Leadership Development* (2nd edn). San Francisco: Jossey-Bass. pp. 116–50.

Ulrich, D. (2008) Coaching for results. *Business Strategy Series*, 9(3), 104–14.

Visser, M. (2010) Relating in executive coaching: a behavioral systems approach. *Journal of Management Development*, 29(10), 891–901.

Vroom, V.H. (1964) *Work and Motivation*. Wiley, New York

Wasylyshyn, K.M. (2003) Executive coaching: An outcome study. *Consulting Psychology Journal: Practice and Research*, 55(2), 94–106.

Watson, J.B. (1913) Psychology as the behaviorist views it. *Psychological Review*, 20, 158–77.

Whitmore, J. (2009) *Coaching for Performance* (4th edn). London: Nicholas Brealey Publishing.

Whybrow, A. and Palmer, S. (2006) Taking stock: A survey of coaching psychologists' practice and perspectives. *International Coaching Psychology Review*, 1(1), 56–70.

# 17

# Cognitive Behavioral Approaches

## Stephen Palmer and Helen Williams

## Introduction

Cognitive behavioral coaching (CBC) has been defined as: "An integrative approach which combines the use of cognitive, behavioral, imaginal, and problem-solving techniques and strategies within a cognitive behavioral framework to enable clients to achieve their realistic goals" (Palmer and Szymanska, 2007, p. 86). Palmer and Whybrow researched the popularity of coaching psychology models and found CBC to be one of the models most frequently used, based on a sample of largely UK coaching psychologists (Palmer and Whybrow, 2006). Cognitive behavioral coaching has been used across a number of coaching contexts, including skills and performance, life, developmental, executive and leadership, peer, team, career, and health coaching (Williams *et al.*, 2010).

The first section of this chapter will summarize the historical development of the cognitive behavioral approach, detailing its philosophical routes and theoretical foundations in rational emotive behavior therapy (REBT), cognitive therapy, and cognitive behavior therapy (CBT), as well as problem-solving and solution-focused approaches and techniques (Palmer and Neenan, 2000). The second section will summarize the research evidence base of the cognitive behavioral approach. Section three details the development of cognitive behavioral approach in coaching practice, including an overview of the theory of CBC and of the CBC models, tools, and techniques available. Section four provides a review of CBC research, focusing in particular on publications made in 2000–2010. We conclude our analysis with recommendations for future research into the efficacy of CBC across a range of coaching contexts, languages, and measurement outcomes.

*The Wiley Blackwell Handbook of the Psychology of Coaching and Mentoring*, First Edition.
Edited by Jonathan Passmore, David B. Peterson, and Teresa Freire.
© 2013 John Wiley & Sons, Ltd. Published 2016 by John Wiley & Sons, Ltd.

## Theory of the Cognitive Behavioral Approach

The early theoretical underpinnings of the cognitive behavioral approach can be traced back to the first century CE, when a stoic philosopher Epictetus observed how people, "are not disturbed by things but by the view they take of them." Much later, another philosopher, Kant described the four consecutive steps from perception to action: "I see a tiger; I think I'm in danger; I feel afraid; I run." This highlighted the link between the cognitions, emotions, and actions. In 1906 Dubois noted how healthy reflections lead to the healing of functional troubles, demonstrating "the supremacy of the mind over the body" (see Dubois, 1906, p. 58).

From the 1950s onwards psychologists began using behavioral theory in a therapeutic context. Early behaviorism embodied an associative learning philosophy, based on the principles that human beings learn through conditioned associations, and that these associations drive behavior at an unconscious level (Wolpe, 1973; Wolpe and Lazarus, 1966). Key techniques were reciprocal inhibition, desensitization, and exposure. For more information see the work of Eysenck (1959, 1964), Wolpe and Lazarus (Lazarus, 1971, 1981; Wolpe and Lazarus, 1966), Marks (Marks, 1969), and Rachman and Teasdale (1969).

The cognitive perspective was highlighted by the psychiatrist Adler's observation, that people "determine [themselves] by the meaning [they] give to situations" (Adler, 1958, p. 14). Ellis (1962) explored the mechanics of emotional disturbance in developing his approach, later known as rational emotive behavior therapy, in which he observes the intermediary role beliefs play between an activating event and a person's emotional and behavioral responses. Ellis had been influenced by stoic philosophy when he was developing his approach. Beck developed cognitive therapy (1967, 1976), in which emphasis is placed on the role of "internal dialogue" (Beck, 1976) in influencing an individual's subsequent feelings and behavior. Beck found that whilst clients were not always conscious of their internal dialogue, they could learn to identify it, and were then in a position to examine any automatic, emotion-filled thoughts and where useful, replace them (McMahon, 2007). As Neenan observes, "the route to emotional change is through cognitive and behavioral change" (Neenan, 2008a, p. 4). Cognitive therapy adopts a rationalist approach with the underlying assumptions that an individual may first develop metacognitive skills to non-judgmentally observe their own thoughts, and may subsequently think logically and empirically in order to challenge, correct, and replace them (Beck, 1976; Brewin, 2006). Meichenbaum (1977, 1985) also highlighted the importance of self-talk in what he termed cognitive behavior therapy and stress inoculation training (Palmer and Szymanska, 2007).

Cognitions play a central role in CB theoretical frameworks. Judith Beck identifies three levels of cognitions (Beck, 1995): automatic thoughts; intermediate beliefs (attitudes, rules and assumptions); and core beliefs. Negative automatic thoughts and beliefs are believed to directly influence how an individual responds to a situation, in that beliefs tend to determine subsequent emotional, behavioural, and physiological responses to an activating event (Ellis, 1994). Beck's "internal dialogue" (1976) and Meichenbaum's (1977, 1985) "self-talk" describe the critical inner voice that tends to encourage caution and self-doubt, and can over time negatively impact upon self-esteem and self-worth. The theoretical model adopted by CB approaches proposes that this inner voice may first be bought into conscious awareness, and its credibility challenged, before new emphasis is given to an alternative, more constructive, and self-accepting voice.

The term cognitive distortions was taken from cognitive therapy (Beck, 1976), although they are generally referred to as, "thinking errors" in CBC, and are defined as, "errors of processing in which the person cognitively focuses on insufficient or inappropriate data and draws illogical conclusions, makes inaccurate inferences or bases predicted outcomes upon little or no empirical evidence" (Palmer and Szymanska, 2007, p. 99). Where there is a cognitive distortion, or thinking error, this may be about a past, current, or anticipated future event, may be directly related to the issue at hand or be a secondary disturbance in the form of further self-blame (Hauck, 1974). Box 17.1 summarizes the common thinking errors.

---

**Box 17.1** Common thinking errors.

- Mind reading/jumping to conclusions: jumping to foregone conclusion without the relevant information, for example, "If I don't work overtime I'll get sacked."
- All-or-nothing thinking: evaluating experiences on the basis of extremes such as "excellent" or "awful", for example, "She always arrives late."
- Blame: not taking responsibility and blaming somebody or something else for the problem, for example, "It's all her fault. She should have reminded me to post the letter."
- Personalization: taking events personally, for example, "If our team presentation is rejected, it's my fault."
- Fortune-telling: assuming you always know what the future holds, for example, "I know I'll be made redundant next week."
- Emotional reasoning: mistaking feelings for facts, for example, "I feel so nervous, I know this merger will fall apart."
- Labelling: using labels or global ratings to describe yourself and others, for example, "I'm a total idiot," or, "As I failed my exam this proves I'm a complete failure."
- Demands: peppering your narrative with rigid or inflexible thinking, such as "should" and "musts": making demands of yourself and others, for example, "He should have made a better job of that project."
- Magnification or awfulizing: blowing events out of all proportion, for example, "That meeting was the worst I've ever attended. It was awful."
- Minimization: minimizing the part one plays in a situation, for example, "It must have been an easy exam as I got a good mark."
- Low frustration tolerance or "I-can't-stand-it": we lower our tolerance to frustrating or stressful situations by telling ourselves, for example, "I can't stand it."
- Phoneyism: believing that you may get found out by significant others as a phoney or impostor, for example, "If I perform badly, they will see the real me – a total fraud."

© Palmer and Szymanska, 2007.

A number of theoretical models have been proposed to account for the process by which cognitive therapy works (Brewin, 2006):

1.  The accommodation model (Barber and DeRubeis, 1989) proposes that negative memories and corresponding cognitions (thoughts, beliefs, and images) are directly modified through the therapeutic process.
2.  The activation-deactivation model (Barber and DeRubeis, 1989) proposes that negative memories and corresponding cognitions are deactivated whilst positive ones are activated.
3.  The retrieval competition model (Brewin, 1989, 2006) proposes that it is the creation or reinforcement of competing positive memories and cognitions that deactivates or blocks negative ones.

The retrieval competition model provides a possible explanation for relapse following successful therapy, as whilst negative memories and cognitions are deactivated, they are nonetheless still present, and may reoccur given a specific set of contextual cues (Brewin, 2006).

Cognitive therapy and rational emotive behavior therapy are widely recognized under the umbrella term of cognitive behavior therapy, which is also informed by goal setting theory (Locke and Latham, 1990), problem-solving and solution-focused approaches (Palmer and Neenan, 2000), and the multi-modal approach (Lazarus, 1984, 1989; Palmer, 2008a). Recent developments have seen a "third wave" of CBT (Hayes, 2004), including acceptance and commitment therapy (ACT), which focuses on the acceptance of mental events and goal-directed actions (Brewin, 2006; Hayes *et al.*, 1999) and mindfulness-based cognitive therapy (Segal *et al.*, 2002; Singh *et al.*, 2008), which incorporates mindfulness training exercises (Kabat-Zinn, 1990). These approaches adopt a more constructivist philosophy and, drawing on the retrieval competition account of CBT, focus on development of metacognitive skills, and creation and strengthening of positive memories, cognitions, and emotions in order to deactivate or block negative ones (Brewin, 2006; O'Broin and Palmer, 2009). Emphasis is on accepting the present moment as it is, enhancing awareness, attention control, and decentering (observing personal experiences without reacting emotionally) (Claessens, 2010; Segal *et al.*, 2002).

## Research Evidence of the Cognitive Behavioral Approach

Cognitive behavioral therapy has been extensively researched, and is indeed one of the most validated psychotherapeutic approaches available (Neenan, 2008a). Cognitive behavioral therapy has been applied in the treatment of a wide range of disorders (Beck, 1997) and the National Institute for Health and Clinical Excellence (NICE, 2005) recommends CBT for many psychological problems. Cognitive behavioral therapy and REBT have also been widely used with individuals and groups in non-clinical settings (Curwen *et al.*, 2000; DiMattia with Mennen, 1990; Ellis, 1972; Ellis and Blum, 1967; Ellis *et al.*, 1998; Kirby, 1993; Lange and Grieger, 1993; Palmer, 1992, 1995; Palmer and Burton, 1996; Palmer and Ellis, 1995; Richman, 1993).

Numerous papers have been published demonstrating the effectiveness of CBT and REBT for both children and adults across a full range of clinical contexts, including treatment of depression (DeRubeis *et al.*, 1999), anxiety (Hofmann *et al.*, 2008), chronic pain (Morley *et al.*, 1998), personality disorders (Leichsenring and Leibing, 2003), schizophrenia (Pilling *et al.*, 2002), and anger (Beck and Fernandez, 1998). In 2006, Butler and colleagues conducted a review of meta-analyses on treatment outcomes of CBT for a range of psychiatric disorders and found large effect sizes for unipolar depression, generalized anxiety disorder, panic disorder with or without agoraphobia, social phobia, post-traumatic stress disorder, and childhood depressive and anxiety disorder, as well as moderate effect sizes for marital distress, anger, childhood somatic disorders and chronic pain (Butler *et al.*, 2006). The long-term effectiveness of CBT and prevention of relapse have also been researched and reviewed (Simons *et al.*, 1984), and were found to be particularly evident following the application of CBT for treatment of depression, generalized anxiety, panic, social phobia, OCD, sexual offending, schizophrenia, and childhood internalizing disorders (Butler *et al.*, 2006). Butler and colleagues (2006) recommend further meta-analyses investigating the long-term and comparative effectiveness of CBT across an even wider range of disorders (for more information see the 2006 review by Butler *et al.*, 2006).

## The Development of the Cognitive Behavioral Approach in Coaching Practice

Cognitive behavioral coaching began developing in earnest in the 1990s, as practitioners started to adapt cognitive behavior therapy approaches for work with individuals in non-clinical settings, for both personal and workplace coaching (Neenan, 2008a; Palmer and Szymanska, 2007). Dryden and Gordon (1993) have re-positioned REBT and stress management techniques for use by business executives. Palmer and Burton (1996) present Ellis's ABCDE framework and a seven-step, problem-solving model adapted from Wasik (1984). Grant and Greene (2001, 2004) combine solution-focused coaching, goal-setting, and cognitive behavioral coaching approaches, and describe how the latter may be utilized to manage one's thoughts, feelings, and behavior in the face of change, encouraging the reader to dispute negative thoughts and replace them with performance enhancing thoughts. Peltier (2001) effectively considers a wide range of psychotherapeutic theories, including cognitive theory, and applies them to executive coaching with the goal of making "the principles, research, and wisdom of psychology accessible to the practice of executive coaching" (Peltier, 2001, p. xiii). Grant (2001b) provides a detailed review of empirical and theoretical psychological literature on coaching, and proposing a solution-focused, cognitive behavioral framework for a psychology of coaching (Grant, 2001a).

From 2001 onwards, articles, chapters, and books referring directly to cognitive coaching, cognitive behavioral coaching, or rational emotive behavior coaching began to be published in earnest (Auerbuch, 2006; Ellam-Dyson and Palmer, 2010; Good *et al.*, 2009, 2010; Law *et al.*, 2007; McMahon, 2009; Neenan, 2006; Neenan and Dryden, 2002; Neenan and Palmer, 2001; Palmer and Szymanska, 2007), as well as further publications providing accounts of how CBT and REBT principles may be applied in a coaching context (Anderson, 2002; Auerbuch, 2006; Greene and Grant, 2003; Kodish, 2002; Reivich and Shatte, 2002). In 2008 the *Journal of Rational-Emotive and Cognitive-Behavior Therapy* published a special issue on cognitive behavioral coaching (Neenan, 2008b), with a range of contributions from leading CBT and CBC practitioners, covering the adaptation of CBT to CBC (Neenan, 2008a), restructuring metaphors and use of mental re-mapping in cognitive coaching (Smith, 2008), mindfulness training in coaching (Collard and Walsh, 2008), CB, REB, and multi-modal coaching for reduction of work related stress (Palmer and Gyllensten, 2008), and 'Tackling procrastination: an REBT perspective for coaches' (Neenan, 2008c).

There has been a divergence in approaches, with the term cognitive behavioral coaching emerging in the UK and Cognitive Coaching^SM (Costa and Garmston, 2002) in the US. Cognitive Coaching^SM has focused on teacher efficacy for use in teacher training (Sawyer, 2003), and provides a model of supervision for this purpose (Auerbach, 2006). Cognitive Coaching^SM is informed by cognitive theory alongside a number of other theories and models, including humanistic psychology, mediation, systems thinking, and clinical supervision (Auerbach, 2006). The original work of Costa and Garmston (2002) includes a research study in which students of teachers participating in Cognitive Coaching^SM scored better on basic skills, reading, and mathematics. A number of subsequent research papers have considered the effectiveness of Cognitive Coaching^SM, and have found increases in teacher efficacy, focus on student learning, transfer of thinking skills to students, job satisfaction, levels of collaboration, and teacher reflection (Alseike, 1997; Dutton, 1990; Edwards and Newton, 1994, 1995; Edwards *et al.*, 1998; Garmston *et al.*, 1993; Smith, 1997). In the United States, where CBC is being practiced, the term therapy is often still used, as well as alternative terms such as cognitive behavioral executive coaching (CBEC: Good *et al.*, 2010).

## Theory of Cognitive Behavioral Coaching

Cognitive behavioral coaching (CBC) is "time-limited, goal-directed and focused on the here and now" (Neenan and Palmer, 2001, p. 1). It is based on the premise that the way a person thinks about an event will directly and significantly influence how that person feels and behaves in response to the event, and that this in turn will impact upon stress and performance (Palmer and Szymanska, 2007). Cognitive behavioral coaching is based on the same theoretical foundations as CBT, with the main differences being in the severity of the problems the client needs to address (Neenan, 2008a; Palmer and Szymanska, 2007), and the potential to focus on personal growth, leadership flexibility, and attainment of new thinking skills (Good *et al.*, 2009). Cognitive behavioral coaching adopts a dual systems approach, in that both behavioral and psychological interventions are considered important and instrumental in achieving the desired change (Neenan and Dryden, 2002; Palmer and Szymanska, 2007).

Lazarus pioneered the multi-modal approach, acknowledging the significant interplay between behaviour, affect, sensations, imagery, cognitions, interpersonal and biological modalities (Lazarus, 1989; Palmer, 2008a; Neenan, 2008a). This theoretical stance has provided the foundations for a number of multi-modal CBC models (Edgerton and Palmer, 2005; Lazarus, 1989; Neenan and Palmer, 2001; Richard, 1999; Williams and Palmer, 2010). Cognitive behavioral coaching is also often couched in a problem solving, solution-focused and goal setting framework, such that the coach and client first clarify the goal for the coaching session, the problem to be addressed and/or the area for which solutions are to be sought. Grant describes how goal setting provides, "the foundation of successful self-regulation" (Grant, 2001a, p. 30). Locke and Latham's (1990) goal theory is integrated into many CBC approaches, with the coach encouraging the client to identify and work towards specific, measurable, achievable, relevant, and time-bound goals. Principles from the solution-focused approach are also integrated within the CBC framework, placing emphasis on construction of solutions, visioning of future desired states, use of the client's existing resources, and identification of small, achievable next steps (Good *et al.*, 2010; Grant, 2001a; Palmer, 2008b; Palmer and Neenan, 2000).

Early CBC draws on the principles of CBT and REBT are different and take different persperspectives, focusing on alteration and replacement of unhelpful cognitions. Whilst behaviorist principles of experimentation are utilized, this is more for the purpose of collecting data to help the coach and client challenge unhelpful thinking (Brewin, 2006). More recent developments in cognitive behavioral coaching reflect the constructivist philosophy of third wave CBT approaches such as mindfulness based cognitive therapy (MBCT) (Segal *et al.*, 2002; Singh *et al.*, 2008), focusing on the creation and reinforcement of positive memories and cognitions in order to over-ride negative ones (Brewin, 2006). Mindfulness has been described as having four key elements of awareness, attention, time (focus on the present), and acceptance (Passmore and Marianetti, 2007), and may be taught to clients through mindfulness meditation exercises (Kabat-Zinn, 1990). Examples of where mindfulness has been integrated into CBC approaches include Collard and Walsh's (2008) sensory awareness mindfulness training (SAMT) and Spence and colleagues. (2008) mindfulness training in health coaching.

## Cognitive Behavioral Coaching Models

The fundamental aims of cognitive behavioral coaching are to facilitate the client's self-awareness, equip them with thinking skills, build their internal resources, stability and self-acceptance, enhance self-efficacy and enable them to become their own coach (Williams *et al.*, 2010). Cognitive behavioral coaching is perhaps most useful when action models are not working for the client; when there are cognitive or emotional blocks to change; or when stress is impacting on health and/or performance (Williams *et al.*, 2010). A number of CBC models are available, as outlined in Table 17.1. See the respective references listed in Table 17.1 for more information on each model.

**Table 17.1**   CBC models.

| CBC Model | Model steps |
|---|---|
| The PRACTICE model (Palmer, 2007) | Problem identification; Realistic, relevant goals developed; Alternative solution(s) generated; Consideration of consequence; Target most feasible solution(s); Implementation of Chosen solution(s); Evaluation. |
| The ABCDE(F) model (Ellis, 1962; Ellis *et al.*, 1998; Palmer, 2002) | Activating event or Awareness of problem/issue; Beliefs and perceptions about the activating event; Consequences (emotional, behavioral, physiological); Disputing or examining the beliefs; Effective, new response; Future focus. |
| The BASIC ID model (Lazarus, 1981; Palmer, 2008a; Palmer and Burton, 1996) | Behavior; Affect; Sensation; Imagery; Cognition; Interpersonal; Drugs, biology |
| The CABB model (Milner and Palmer, 1998) | Cognition; Affect; Biology; Behavior. |
| The SPACE model (Edgerton and Palmer, 2005) | Social context; Physiology; Action; Cognition; Emotion. |
| ACE FIRST model (Lee, 2003) | Actions, Cognitions, Emotions and Focus, Intentions, Results, System; Tension. |
| The CRAIC model (O'Donovan, 2009) | Control; Responsibility; Awareness; Impetus; Confidence. |
| The INTENT model (Good *et al.*, 2009) | Ideal future; Now; Targeted cognitions and behaviors; Experiment; Nurture; Transition. |
| The CLARITY model (Williams and Palmer, 2010) | Context; Life event or experience; Actions; Reactions; Imagery and Identity; Thoughts/beliefs; Your future choice. |

## Behavioral Tools and Techniques

Models such as the PRACTICE model (Palmer, 2007) encourage goal exploration and setting of SMART objectives – specific, measurable, achievable, relevant, and time-bound (Locke, 1996; Locke and Latham, 1990). Time management strategies may be useful for the client, such as urgent-important prioritization, to-do lists, allowing time for the unexpected and taking small first steps as a way of overcoming procrastination (Palmer and Cooper, 2007, 2010). Assertiveness training can also be a highly effective behavioral intervention, educating the client on the difference between passivity, aggression, and the more assertive ""win-win" approach. Where the client is experiencing significant physiological reactions, relaxation techniques may be effective in alleviating much of the pressure, for example, breathing exercises, relaxation CDs, or more advanced meditation classes.

It is also commonplace within CBC approaches for behavioral strategies to be used to help the client test out their new performance enhancing thoughts (PETS) and core beliefs (Palmer and Szymanska, 2007). In-between session assignments may be agreed, to help maintain the focus of the client on the selected coaching goal, and to collect valuable evidence for the coach and client to review in subsequent sessions. Behavioral experiments may also be instrumental in helping the client to challenge pre-existing and unhelpful automatic thoughts and core beliefs (Palmer and Szymanska, 2007), as they act out a behavior in order to experience the consequences and realize that they are able to cope with these consequences; that they are not the end of the world.

## Cognitive Tools and Techniques

Where the client appears to have a cognitive or emotional barrier to change, cognitive techniques may then be instrumental in facilitating increased self-awareness and personal growth. Socratic questioning is a series of questions aimed at increasing awareness (Neenan and Palmer, 2001). The questions are phrased in a way that stimulates thought and increases awareness, rather than requiring a correct answer (Beck *et al.*, 1993). By raising awareness, Socratic questioning facilitates more rational decision-making (McMahon, 2007). Neenan and Palmer defined the terms "performance interfering thoughts" (PITS) for the unhelpful cognitive distortions, and "performance enhancing thoughts" (PETS) for the new helpful thoughts (Neenan and Palmer, 2001). Additional thinking skills include gaining perspective, persistence, and de-labelling.

The process of inference chaining is used to ascertain the aspect of the problem or activating event (A) that is causing the client most difficulty, otherwise known as the "critical A" (Neenan, 2006; Palmer and Szymanska, 2007). In a similar technique known as the downward arrow technique (Burns, 1990) presenting negative automatic beliefs are explored using questions of the form: "If X were taken to be true, what does that mean to you?" with the aim of eliciting the core negative belief (Palmer and Szymanska, 2007).

Where low self-esteem is an issue for the client, exercises aimed at achieving "greater self-acceptance" (GSA) can be instrumental in reducing levels of anxiety and stress (Neenan, 1997). For the client, self-acceptance is about avoiding global ratings such as: "I'm good/bad/a failure," and "accepting myself, warts and all, with a strong preference to improve myself even though realistically I don't have to" (Palmer and Cooper, 2007, p. 77). The coach encourages the client to rate specific aspects of themselves (e.g., I failed my driving test), as opposed to rating their whole self on only one aspect (e.g., I am a failure) (Neenan, 2006; Palmer and Cooper, 2007, 2010).

Coaching clients often report mental images that they find to be extremely motivating or de-motivating (Palmer and Cooper, 2007, 2010; Peltier, 2001). Palmer and Cooper (2010) describe a range of useful imagery exercises such as motivation imagery, coping imagery, time projection imagery, and relaxation imagery. Collard and Walsh (2008) proposed and researched their sensory awareness mindfulness training (SAMT) approach, including sound meditation, breathing, and body scanning techniques. The SAMT approach integrates cognitive and emotional elements and teaches non-judgmental observation and acceptance of painful experiences, as well as focusing on NOW (Collard and Walsh, 2008).

## Research Evidence of the Cognitive Behavioral Approach in Coaching

Whilst cognitive behavioral coaching initially relied upon the evidence base of cognitive behavioral therapy, there is now a growing body of research publications in direct support of CBC. In 2001 Grant conducted a PsychLIT and PsychINFO® meta-review of coaching psychology research, in which he unearthed only three research papers specifying CBC as part of the coaching program being evaluated (Grant, 2001a).

Strayer and Rossett (1994) conducted a case study exploring the impact of coaching on sales performance for trainee sales persons, involving 20, one-hour coaching sessions targeting cognitive (dealing with fears, rejection, and optimistic outlook) and behavioral measures (lead generation, communication, and selling skills). Improvements were found for measures of handling rejection and the fear of rejection, as well as on the performance measure of reduction in time taken to achieve a first sale (Strayer and Rossett, 1994). Kiel *et al.* (1996) conducted a single case study of a male client "star performer" with interpersonal personal development goals, receiving cognitive behaviorally-based coaching over a period of two years. The participant client reported enhanced self-awareness and behavioral change (Kiel *et al.*, 1996). Richard (1999) similarly conducted a single case study with a female senior executive. Cognitive and behavioral coaching over a ten-month period reportedly resulted in greater productivity, management of stress and conflict at work, and enhanced personal satisfaction (Richard, 1999).

Grant encouraged further research into the effectiveness of cognitive behavioral coaching approaches (Grant, 2001a), and it is since this time that a wealth of research on the efficacy of CBC has been published. Our review, based on a PsychINFO® and Google Scholar search, identified 17 research papers published between 2001 and 2010, summaries of which are presented below.

Grant published a research paper in 2001 comparing cognitive, behavioural, and combined cognitive behavioral coaching programs for trainee accountants, compared to a control group. The programs involved a seven-hour seminar followed by five, two-hour workshops for 20 undergraduate students. Whilst all programs evidenced positive impacts of reduction in test anxiety and increases in academic performance, the latter was only maintained over time for the combined cognitive behavioral program participants (Grant, 2001b). The cognitive and cognitive behavioral programs evidenced additional benefits of increased deep and achieving approaches to learning and enhanced self-concepts relating to academic performance. No program impacted significantly on private self-consciousness, self-reflection, or insight (Grant, 2001b). Grant noted the homogeneity of the participant group, and that this group were particularly motivated, cautioning the extent to which these findings could be generalized to other populations (Grant, 2001b).

Grant (2003) researched the impact of group life coaching utilizing solution-focused, cognitive behavioral techniques. The coaching intervention was delivered for 20 postgraduate student participants over a ten-week period, and found enhanced mental health, quality of life, and goal attainment. No control group was available in this study, a limitation given the motivated nature of the participants (Grant, 2003). Green and colleagues. (2005, 2006) conducted a life coaching intervention based on solution-focused, cognitive behavioral techniques. Fifty-six participants were randomly assigned to either a ten-week life coaching program or a wait list control group. Statistical analysis evidenced enhanced goal striving, positive affect, psychological well-being (personal growth, environmental mastery, positive relations with others, purpose in life, self-acceptance and hope) (Green et al., 2005, 2006). Whilst measures of mental health (depression, anxiety, and stress) decreased, these changes were not statistically significant (Green et al., 2005, 2006). Green and colleagues noted the homogeneity of the participant group and the fact that as volunteers, their motivation to achieve their goals, and to please the researchers, may have been positively skewed (Green et al., 2006). Spence and Grant (2005, 2007) conducted a randomized control group study with 64 participants, evaluating the impact of both professional and peer life coaching using a solution-focused, cognitive behavioral life approach. Both coaching groups showed significant increases in goal-attainment measures. Whilst the professionally, individually coached participants reported enhanced life satisfaction, neither coaching intervention significantly impacted upon measures of mental health or self-reflection; however, the authors noted that the former may be due to ethical pre-selection criteria seeking participants with reported lower levels of psychological distress (Spence and Grant, 2005, 2007). Spence and Grant also noted the possibility that participants had felt an expectation to progress on goal achievement, and that this may have biased self-reports in this area; the recommendation is for future research to minimize the impact of social desirability by including more objective outcome measures (Spence and Grant, 2007).

Libri and Kemp (2006) conducted a single case study to research the effect of cognitive behavioral coaching for a financial sales executive. The 12-week coaching intervention resulted in enhanced sales performance, core self-evaluations (self-esteem, self-efficacy, neuroticism and locus of control), and self-assessed performance (Libri and Kemp, 2006). The authors of this research noted the challenges of collecting robust longitudinal data over longer time lines when conducting research in an applied, commercial setting (Libri and Kemp, 2006). Kearns and colleagues (2007) investigated the effect of cognitive behavioral coaching on perfectionism and self-handicapping for a non-clinical population. The coaching intervention was delivered through a series of workshops to a group of 28 higher education students, utilizing the Multidimensional Perfectionism Scale (MPS: Frost et al., 1990), the Perfectionism Cognitions Inventory (PCI: Flett et al., 1998), and the Self-Handicapping Scale (SHS: Rhodewalt et al., 1984). Perfectionism was found to reduce both immediately following the program, and also at one-month follow-up. Whilst self-handicapping did not reduce immediately following the program, it had done so at one-month follow-up (Kearns et al., 2007). Kearns and colleagues noted the lack of control group in the research study design, and the potential for future research to review the sustainability of the effects of coaching over longer time frames (Kearns et al., 2007).

Green *et al.* (2007) studied the efficacy of a solution-focused, cognitive behavioral life coaching program. The research design was a randomized control study with 56 female senior high school students participating in life coaching or wait list control groups. The results showed significant increases in cognitive hardiness and hope, and significant decreases in levels of depression (Green *et al.*, 2007). The authors of the research noted that future research might compare the effect of the presence of a supportive adult versus participation in a life coaching program, as well as the potential to conduct the research with other educational groups (Green *et al.*, 2007). Grbcic and Palmer (2007) utilized a randomized control trial to evaluate a stress self-manual for 102 middle managers, based on a cognitive behavioral approach, and found significant increases in task, emotion, and distraction-oriented coping styles. Participants reported that discussing the manual with other participants had a positive effect, and as such the authors recommend the manual to be used with groups in organizations (Grbcic and Palmer, 2007). Beddoes-Jones and Miller (2007) conducted a combined quantitative and qualitative case study of eight managers participating in monthly one-hour telephone cognitive behavioral coaching sessions over a three-month period. Whilst the statistical analysis was less conclusive, the qualitative feedback from all participants demonstrated greater meta-cognitive awareness, self-confidence in personal decision making and feeling more authentic (Beddoes-Jones and Miller, 2007).

In 2008 Grant published research looking into the impact of a 10–12-week, five-session solution-focused cognitive behavioral life coaching for 29 coaches-in-training. The results showed reduced levels of anxiety, increased levels of goal attainment, cognitive hardiness, and personal insight, as well as higher end of semester marks than those not receiving coaching (Grant, 2008). The author noted there was no change in levels of psychological well-being (Grant, 2008). Spence and colleagues (2008) investigated integrated mindfulness training and solution-focused, cognitive behavioral coaching in a health coaching context, and found that participants receiving coaching showed significantly greater goal attainment in comparison to a group receiving a series of health education seminars (Spence *et al.*, 2008). Similarly, Collard and Walsh (2008) researched their sensory awareness mindfulness training (SAMT) using the Mindfulness Attention and Awareness Scale (MAAS) (Brown and Ryan, 2003) and found reductions in stress levels and improved mood (Collard and Walsh, 2008). Kearns *et al.* (2008) investigated the effect of cognitive behavioral coaching on levels of innovation in PhD completion, and found participants to have improved their ability to manage time, set specific goals and communicate regularly with their supervisors, which in turn led to reduced stress and improved ability to complete the PhD (Kearns *et al.*, 2008).

Palmer and Gyllensten (2008) present a single case study of a client in therapy for depression, for which they postulate that cognitive behavioral, rational-emotive, or multi-modal coaching may have been offered at an earlier stage to effectively address the client's problem behavior of procrastination (Palmer and Gyllensten, 2008). Yu and colleagues (2008) researched the effectiveness of a workplace coaching program in a healthcare setting. Seventeen managers were selected for the program in a large Australian teaching hospital, participating in individual coaching, group coaching, needs-based coaching skills training, and personal development planning over a period of six months. The researchers made use of an integrated solution-focused, cognitive behavioral approach. The results showed improvements across a number of areas including goal attainment, proactivity, motivation, and core performance. There was less evidence that the coaching positively impacted upon self-reflection, and also global well-being, with most of the well-being sub-measures (with the exception of auto nomy) showing insignificant change pre- and post- coaching intervention (Yu *et al.*, 2008). The authors noted the limitations of the research, including lack of control group, reliance on self-report measures, and the shorter timeframes of the research, meaning that sustainability of outcome measures could not be measured (Yu *et al.*, 2008).

Grant *et al.* (2009) conducted a randomized control study for 41 executives in a public health agency and found enhanced goal attainment, resilience, and workplace well-being, as well as reduced depression and stress, as a result of an executive coaching program including solution-focused, cognitive behavioral coaching delivered by professional coaches (Grant *et al.*, 2009). Karas and Spada (2009) developed and researched a brief cognitive-behavioral coaching program for procrastination. Seven female participants were recruited after responding to a library advert requesting chronic procrastinators. Each participant completed the Decisional Procrastination Scale (DPS: Mann, 1982) and the General Procrastination Scale (GPS: Lay, 1986) before any coaching intervention, after each weekly, one hour coaching session, and at three- and six-month follow-ups. All seven participants showed improvements on both self-report measures of procrastination, and largely maintained these improvements at follow-up (Karas and Spada, 2009). They noted the limitation of the study in its reliance on self-reported outcome measures (Karas and Spada, 2009).

Gyllensten and colleagues (2010) conducted a qualitative study in Sweden, using interpretative phenomenological analysis (see Smith and Osborn, 2003) to investigate the experience of ten individuals participating in cognitive coaching at work. The role of the coach was found to be important, with value placed on confidentiality, the experience and theoretical knowledge of the coach, and their accepting approach. Participants reported benefits in three main areas: increased awareness of self and others, the opportunity to do things in a new way, and development of new cognitive and emotional knowledge (Gyllensten *et al.*, 2010).

From this review it is evident that there is a robust and growing evidence base for the effectiveness of cognitive behavioral coaching across a number of contexts, including work place, life, and health coaching. Whilst more research is needed to establish the impact of CBC on overall psychological well-being (Grant, 2003; Yu *et al.*, 2008), a number of studies have found a significant relationship between CBC and a range of more specific psychological and performance measures, including anxiety and stress reduction, goal attainment, cognitive hardiness, self-awareness and self-confidence, and meta-cognitive skills. There is a growing body of evidence in support of the integration of CBC with other coaching methods, such as solution-focused and mindfulness-based coaching (Spence *et al.*, 2008; Collard and Walsh, 2008). A number of the research authors note the need to continue to conduct research with different participant groups, controlling for levels of motivation and impact of social desirability, to support generalization of findings (Grant, 2001b, 2003; Green *et al.*, 2006, 2007; Spence and Grant, 2007). Specific research papers also noted the need for control groups (Grant, 2003; Kearns and Forbes, 2007; Yu *et al.*, 2008), longer timeframes for measurement of sustainability of outcome measures (Kearns *et al.*, 2007; Libri and Kemp, 2006;) and inclusion of more objective as opposed to self-report outcome measures (Karas and Spada, 2009; Spence and Grant, 2007).

## Future Research

Recent publications reviewing the state of coaching and coaching psychology today, whilst recognizing the progress made, have called for further outcome studies, and in particular both randomized control trials (RCTs) and longitudinal studies (Grant and Cavanagh, 2007; Grant *et al.*, 2010; Neenan, 2006), in order to demonstrate the effectiveness of coaching, "as a methodology for creating and sustaining human change" (Grant and Cavanagh, 2007, p. 243). Within coaching psychology, cognitive behavioral approaches have been relatively well researched (in particular solution-focused, cognitive behavioral approaches), and the research that is there benchmarks reasonably well against the above criteria: in the papers reviewed for this article there are two case studies, with the remaining being a balance of within-subject and between-subject outcome studies. A mix of quantitative and qualitative data is presented, with some of the research study designs being longitudinal. Of the between-subject studies, five were randomized control trials (RCTs) (Grant *et al.*, 2009; Green *et al.*, 2005, 2006, 2007; Grbcic and Palmer, 2007; Spence and Grant, 2005, 2007). It is hoped that research into cognitive behavioral approaches will continue to build in this manner, with even greater emphasis on outcome studies with RCT and longitudinal designs. Whilst pre-post intervention, randomized controlled trials (RCTs) are the preferred method in scientific analysis, Ellam-Dyson and Palmer (2008) discuss the challenges this raises for coaching research, in particular for ethical assignment of individuals to control groups, management of drop-out rates, and measurement of types of coaching used. Wait list control groups tend to be used in order to overcome some of these challenges (Green *et al.*, 2005; 2006).

Grant and colleagues (2010) call for coaching psychology research across a range of coaching contexts (Grant *et al.*, 2010). The 17 research papers reviewed in this chapter have primarily investigated the effects of cognitive behavioral approaches in workplace coaching and life (personal) coaching, as well as executive coaching, health coaching, and education. Grant and colleagues (2010) also call for further research into the impact of coaching for organizations, and clarity on the desired outcome measures. In this respect, further research into the effectiveness of cognitive behavioral approaches across all coaching contexts, but for workplace and executive coaching in particular, may be desirable. The latter would certainly contribute worthwhile evidence for the potential return on investment of management and leadership psychology based coaching at work.

Grant and Cavanagh (2007) noted the difficulty experienced in comparing results of coaching psychology research due to the inconsistency of outcome measures utilized across studies (Grant and Cavanagh, 2007). Within the research evidence base for cognitive behavioral approaches, outcome measures have included:

- Goal attainment and goal striving
- Performance measures (task or job role measures)
- Cognitive, emotional, and physiological (fear, anxiety, rejection, positive affect, optimism, cognitive hardiness, hope)
- Behavioral (procrastination, perfectionism and self-handicapping, communication, interpersonal skills, time management, proactivity, doing things in a new way, conflict management)
- Meta-cognitive (personal insight, self-awareness, cognitive and emotional knowledge, self-reflection, self-evaluations and enhanced self-concepts (self-esteem, self-efficacy), self-confidence, learning approaches, authenticity)
- Mental health (depression, anxiety and stress)
- Psychological well-being (quality of life, life satisfaction, motivation, coping styles, resilience)

Further research into cognitive behavioral approaches might endeavor to review potential outcome measures in order to present an outcome measure framework against which all CBC research may be compared. In relation to specific outcome measures, Grant called for further research into solution-focused, cognitive behavioral life coaching for enhanced well-being (Grant, 2003). Yu and colleagues (2008) similarly noted that there have been variations in findings across research papers as to the impact of coaching on measures of global well-being, and as such called for further research in this area. Whilst some research papers have reported significant positive changes (Grant, 2003; Green *et al.*, 2006), others have not (Spence and Grant, 2007; Yu *et al.*, 2008). Given that, counter-intuitively, research has not yet yielded positive results for the impact of cognitive behavioral coaching on self-reflection (Grant, 2001b; Spence and Grant, 2005, 2007; Yu *et al.*, 2008). Yu and colleagues (2008) called for more research into this outcome measure, investigating the type of coaching provided, and the differences in sample characteristics.

Of the cognitive behavioral coaching models available, the PRACTICE model (Palmer, 2007) has been translated into Portuguese (Dias *et al.*, 2011), and the SPACE model (Edgerton and Palmer, 2005) has been developed into Portuguese and Polish (Dias *et al.*, 2010; Syrek-Kosowska *et al.*, 2010). These developments are in line with the endeavor of the wider coaching industry to become an interconnected and integrated European and international professional network and community. Further translations of CB models into different languages are recommended to facilitate their use across different countries and cultures.

## Conclusion

Cognitive behavioral coaching has been derived from a number of well-established therapeutic frameworks, including cognitive behavioral therapy, which is heralded to be the most well-researched therapeutic intervention available (Neenan, 2006). Cognitive behavioral coaching itself is reported to be one of the most utilized coaching psychology approaches (Palmer and Whybrow, 2006), and within it there are a number of CBC, REB, and multi-modal coaching models available for use by practitioners. Of these models, the PRACTICE model (Palmer, 2007) is available in Portuguese (Dias *et al.*, 2011), and the SPACE model (Edgerton and Palmer, 2005) is available in Portuguese and Polish (Dias *et al.*, 2010; Syrek-Kosowska *et al.*, 2010). The evidence base for CBC approaches is growing, with a clear commitment to research using scientifically approved outcome study designs. Recommendations for further research have been discussed in this chapter for continued investigation into the effectiveness of CBC across coaching contexts, using randomized control trial and longitudinal outcome study designs for the measurement of a breadth of coaching outcomes, and further translations of CB coaching models into different languages for their use across different countries and cultures.

## References

Adler, A. (1958) *What Life Should Mean to You* (ed. A. Porter). New York: Capricorn. (Originally published 1931.)

Alseike, B.U. (1997) Cognitive Coaching^SM: Its influences on teachers. Doctoral dissertation, University of Denver. *Dissertation Abstracts International 9804083.*

Anderson, J.P. (2002) Executive coaching and REBT: Some comments from the field. *Journal of Rational-Emotive Cognitive-Behavior Therapy*, 20(3/4), 223–33.

Auerbach, J.E. (2006) Cognitive Coaching^SM. In: D.R. Stober and A.M. Grant (eds) *Evidence Based Coaching Handbook: Putting Best Practices to Work for your Clients*. Hoboken, NJ: Wiley. pp. 103–27.

Barber, J.P. and DeRubeis, R.J. (1989) On second thought – where the action is in cognitive therapy for depression. *Cognitive Therapy and Research*, 13, 441–57.

Beck, A.T. (1967) *Depression: Clinical, Experimental, and Theoretical Aspects*. Philadelphia, PA: University of Pennsylvania Press.

Beck, A.T. (1976) *Cognitive Therapy and the Emotional Disorders*. New York: New American Library.

Beck, A.T. (1997) The past and future of cognitive therapy. *Journal of Psychotherapy Practice and Research*, 6, 276–84.

Beck, A.T. and Fernandez, E. (1998) Cognitive-behavioral therapy in the treatment of anger: A meta-analysis. *Cognitive Therapy and Research*, 22(1), 63–74.

Beck, A.T., Wright, F.D., Newman, C.F., and Liese, B.S. (1993) *Cognitive Therapy of Substance Abuse*. New York: Guilford Press.

Beck, J. (1995) *Cognitive Therapy: Basics and Beyond*. New York: Guilford Press.

Beddoes-Jones, F. and Miller, J. (2007) Short-term cognitive coaching interventions: Worth the effort or a waste of time? *The Coaching Psychologist*, 3(2), Aug, 60–9.

Brewin, C.R. (1989) Cognitive change processes in psychotherapy. *Psychological Review*, 96, 379–94.

Brewin, C.R. (2006) Understanding cognitive behavior therapy: A retrieval competition account. *Behavior Research and Therapy*, 44, 765–84.

Brown, K.W. and Ryan, R.M. (2003) The benefits of being present: Mindfulness and its role in psychological well-being. *Journal of Personality and Social Psychology*, 84, 822–48.

Burns, D. (1990) *The Feeling Good Handbook*. New York: Plume.

Butler, A.C., Chapman, J.E., Forman, E.M., and Beck, A.T. (2006) The empirical status of cognitive-behavioral therapy: A review of meta-analyses. *Clinical Psychology Review*, 26, 17–31.

Claessens, M. (2010) Mindfulness based – third wave CBT therapies and existential phenomenology: Friends or foes? *Existential Analysis*, 21(2), 295–308.

Collard, P. and Walsh, J. (2008) Sensory awareness mindfulness training in coaching: Accepting life's challenges. *Journal of Rational-Emotional and Cognitive-Behavior Therapy*, 26(1), 30–7.

Costa, A.L. and Garmston, R.J. (2002) *Cognitive Coaching^SM: A Foundation for Renaissance Schools*. Norwood, MA: Christopher-Gordon.

Curwen, B., Palmer, S., and Ruddell, P. (2000) *Brief Cognitive Behavior Therapy*. London: Sage.

DeRubeis, R.J., Gelfand, L.A., Tang, T.Z., and Simons, A.D. (1999) Medications versus cognitive behavior therapy for severely depressed outpatients: Mega-analysis of four randomized comparisons. *American Journal Psychiatry*, 156, 1007–13.

Dias, G., Edgerton, N., and Palmer, S. (2010) From SPACE to FACES: The adaptation of the SPACE model of cognitive behavioral coaching and therapy in to the Portuguese language. *Coaching Psychology International*, 3(1), 12–15.

Dias, G., Gandos, L., Egidio Nardi, A., and Palmer, S. (2011) Towards the practice of coaching and coaching psychology in Brazil: The adaptation of the PRACTICE model to the Portuguese language. *The Coaching Psychologist*, 4(1), 10–14.

DiMattia, D.J. with Mennen, S. (1990) *Rational Effectiveness Training: Increasing Productivity at Work*. New York: Institute for Rational-Emotive Therapy.

Dryden, W. and Gordon, J. (1993) *Peak Performance: Become More Effective at Work*. Didcot, UK: Mercury Business Books.

Dubois, P. (1906) *The Influence of the Mind Over the Body* (trans. L.B. Gallatin). New York: Funk and Wagnails.

Dutton, M.M. (1990) Learning and teacher job satisfaction (staff development). Doctoral dissertation, Portland State University. *Dissertation Abstracts International 51/05-A, AAD90-26940*.

Edgerton, N. and Palmer, S. (2005) SPACE: A psychological model for use within cognitive behavioral coaching, therapy and stress management. *The Coaching Psychologist*, 2(2), 25–31.

Edwards, J.L. and Newton, R.R. (1994) *Qualitative Assessment of the Effects of Cognitive Coaching^SM Training as Evidenced Through Teacher Portfolios and Journals*. (Research Rep. No. 1994–3). Evergreen, CO: Authors.

Edwards, J.L. and Newton, R.R. (1995) *The Effects of Cognitive Coaching*<sup>SM</sup> *on Teacher Efficacy and Empowerment*. Retrieved from: http://eric.ed.gov/PDFS/ED388654.pdf (accessed April 23, 2011).

Edwards, J.L., Green, K., Lyons, C.A., Rogers, M.S., and Swords, M. (1998) *The Effects of Cognitive Coaching*<sup>SM</sup> *and Nonverbal Classroom Management on Teacher Efficacy and Perceptions of School Culture*. Paper presented at the Annual Meeting of the American Education Research Association, San Diego, CA.

Ellam-Dyson, V. and Palmer, S. (2008) The challenges of researching executive coaching. *The Coaching Psychologist*, 4, 79–84.

Ellam-Dyson, V. and Palmer, S. (2010) Rational coaching with perfectionistic leaders to overcome avoidance of leadership responsibilities. *The Coaching Psychologist*, 6(2), 81–7.

Ellis, A. (1962) *Reason and Emotion in Psychotherapy*. New York: Lyle Stuart.

Ellis, A. (1972) *Executive leadership: A rational approach*. New York: Institute for Rational-Emotive Therapy.

Ellis, A. (1994) *Reason and Emotion in Psychotherapy* (revised and expanded ed.) New York: Birch Lane Press.

Ellis, A. (1996) *Better, Deeper and More Enduring Brief Therapy*. New York: Brunner-Mazel.

Ellis, A. and Blum, M.L. (1967) Rational training: A new method of facilitating management labor relations. *Psychological Reports*, 20, 1267–84.

Ellis, A., Gordon, J., Neenan, M., and Palmer, S. (1998) *Stress Counselling: A Rational Emotive Behavior Approach*. New York: Springer Publishing Co.

Eysenck, H.J. (1959) Learning theory and behavior therapy. *Journal of Mental Science*, 195, 61–75.

Eysenck, H.J. (1964) *Experiments in Behavior Therapy*. London: Pergamon Press.

Flett, G.L., Hewitt, P.L., Blankstein, K.R., and Gray, L. (1998) Psychological distress and the frequency of perfectionistic thinking. *Journal of Personality and Social Psychology*, 75, 1363–81.

Frost, R.O., Marten, P., Lahart, C., and Rosenblate, R. (1990) The dimensions of perfectionism. *Cognitive Therapy and Research*, 14, 449–68.

Garmston, R., Linder, C., and Whitaker, J. (1993) Reflections on Cognitive Coaching<sup>SM</sup>. *Education Leadership*, 51(2), 57–61.

Good, D., Yeganeh, R., and Yeganeh, B. (2009) *Cognitive Behavioral Executive Coaching: A Generative Merging of Practices*. Academy of Management Annual Meeting, Chicago, IL.

Good, D., Yeganeh, B., and Yeganeh, R. (2010) Cognitive behavioral executive coaching: A structure for increasing leader flexibility. *ODP Journal*, 42(3), 18–23.

Grant, A.M. (2001a) *Towards a Psychology of Coaching*. Retrieved from: http://www.reframe.dk/Towards_a_Psychology_of_Coaching.pdf (accessed May 31, 2011).

Grant, A.M. (2001b) *Coaching for Enhanced Performance: Comparing Cognitive and Behavioral Approaches to Coaching*. Paper presented at the 3rd International Spearman Seminar: Extending Intelligence: Enhancement and New Constructs, Sydney. Retrieved from: http://www.psych.usyd.edu.au/coach/CBT_BT_CT_Spearman_Conf_Paper.pdf (accessed November 10, 2008).

Grant, A.M. (2003) The impact of life coaching on goal attainment, metacognition and mental health. *Social Behavior and Personality*, 31(3), 253–64.

Grant, A.M. (2008) Personal life coaching for coaches-in-training enhances goal attainment, insight and learning. *Coaching: An International Journal of Theory, Research and Practice*, 1(1), 54–70.

Grant, A.M. and Cavanagh, M. (2007) Evidence-based coaching: Flourishing or languishing? *Australian Psychologist*, 42(4), December, 239–54.

Grant, A. and Greene, J. (2001; 2004) *Coaching Skills: It's your Life – What are You Going to Do With it?* Harlow: Pearson Education Limited.

Grant, A.M., Curtayne, L., and Burton, G. (2009) Executive coaching enhances goal attainment, resilience and workplace well-being: A randomised controlled study. *The Journal of Positive Psychology*, 4(5), Sep, 396–407.

Grant, A.M., Passmore, J., Cavanagh, M.J., and Parker, H. (2010) *The State of Play in Coaching Today: A Comprehensive Review of the Field*. Retrieved from: http://roar.uel.ac.uk/jspui/bitstream/10552/638/1/Grant,%20A%20(2010)%20IRIOP%2025%20125-67.pdf (accessed April 23, 2012).

Grbcic, S. and Palmer, S. (2007) Brief report: A cognitive-behavioral self-help approach to stress management and prevention at work: A randomised control trial. *The Rational Emotive Behavior Therapist: Journal of the Association for Rational Emotive Behavior Therapy*, 12(1), 41–3.

Greene, J. and Grant, A.M. (2003) *Solution-focused Coaching: Managing people in a Complex World*. Harlow: Pearson Education Limited.

Green, S., Grant, A.M., and Rynsaardt, J. (2007) Evidence-based life coaching for senior high school students: Building hardiness and hope. *International Coaching Psychology Review*, 2(1), 24–32.

Green, S., Oades, L.G., and Grant, A.M. (2005) An evaluation of a life-coaching group program: Initial findings from a waitlist control study. In: M. Cavanagh, A.M. Grant and T. Kemp (eds) *Evidence-based Coaching, Vol 1: Theory, Research and Practice from the Behavioral Sciences*. QLD Australia: Bowen Hills. pp. 127–41.

Green, L.S., Oades, L.G., and Grant, A.M. (2006) Cognitive-behavioral, solution-focussed life coaching: Enhancing goal striving, well-being, and hope. *The Journal of Positive Psychology*, 1(3), July, 142–9.

Gyllensten, K., Palmer, S., Nilsson, E., Meland Regner, A., and Frodi, A. (2010) Experiences of cognitive coaching: A qualitative study. *International Coaching Psychology Review*, 5(2), 98–108.

Hauck, P. (1974) *Depression*. London: Sheldon.

Hayes, S.C. (2004) Acceptance and commitment therapy, relational frame theory, and the third wave of behavioral and cognitive therapies. *Behavior Therapy*, 35, 639–65.

Hayes, S.C., Strosahl, K., and Wilson, K.G. (1999) *Acceptance and Commitment Therapy: An Experiential Approach to Behavior Change*. New York: Guilford Press.

Hofmann, S.G. and Smits, J.A. (2008) Cognitive-behavioral therapy for adult anxiety disorders: A meta-analyses of randomized placebo-controlled trials. *Journal Clinical Psychiatry*, 69(4), 621–32.

Kabat-Zinn, J. (1990) *Full Catastrophe Living. How to Cope With Stress, Pain and Illness Using Mindful Meditation*. London: Piatkus.

Karas, D. and Spada, M.M. (2009) Brief cognitive-behavioral coaching for procrastination: A case series. *Coaching: An International Journal of Theory, Research and Practice*, 2(1), 44–53.

Kearns, H., Forbes, A., and Gardiner, M. (2007) A cognitive behavioral coaching intervention for the treatment of perfectionism and self-handicapping in a nonclinical population. *Behavioral Change*, 24(3), 157–72.

Kearns, H., Gardiner, M., and Marshall, K. (2008) Innovation in PhD completion: The hardy shall succeed (and be happy!). *Higher Education Research and Development*, 27(1), 77–89.

Kiel, F., Rimmer, E., Williams, K., and Doyle, M. (1996) Coaching at the top. *Consulting Psychology Journal: Practice and Research*, 48(2), 67–77.

Kirby, P. (1993) RET counselling: Application in management and executive development. *Journal for Rational-Emotive and Cognitive-Behavior Therapy*, 11(1), 51–7.

Kodish, S.P. (2002) Rational emotive behavior coaching. *Journal of Rational-Emotive and Cognitive-Behavior Therapy*, 20(3/4), 235–46.

Lange, A. and Grieger, R. (1993) Integrating RET into management consulting and training. *Journal for Rational-Emotive and Cognitive-Behavior Therapy*, 11(1), 19–32.

Law, H., Ireland, S., and Hussain, Z. (2007) *The Psychology of Coaching, Mentoring and Learning*. Chichester: John Wiley and Sons.

Lay, C.H. (1986) At last, my research article on procrastination. *Journal of Research in Personality*, 20, 474–94.

Lazarus, A.A. (1971) *Behavior Therapy and Beyond*. New York: McGraw-Hill.

Lazarus, A.A. (1981) *The Practice of Multimodal Therapy*. New York: McGraw-Hill.

Lazarus, A.A. (1984) *In the Mind's Eye*. New York: Guilford Press.

Lazarus, A.A. (1989) *The Practice of Multimodal Therapy. Systematic, Comprehensive and Effective Psychotherapy*. Baltimore, MD: Johns Hopkins University Press.

Lee, G. (2003) *Leadership Coaching: From Personal Insight to Organisational Performance*. London: CIPD.

Leichsenring, F. and Leibing, E. (2003) The effectiveness of psychodynamic therapy and cognitive behavior therapy in the treatment of personality disorders: A meta-analysis. *American Journal Psychiatry*, 160, 1223–32.

Libri, V. and Kemp, T. (2006) Assessing efficacy of a cognitive behavioral executive coaching program. *International Coaching Psychology Review*, 1(2), 9–20.

Locke, E.A. (1996) Motivation through conscious goal setting. *Applied and Preventative Psychology*, 5, 117–24.

Locke, E.A. and Latham, G.P. (1990) *A Theory of Goal Setting and Task Performance*. Englewood Cliffs, NJ: Prentice Hall.

McMahon, G. (2006) Cognitive behavioral coaching: Doors of perception. *Coaching at Work*, 1(6), 36–43.

McMahon, G. (2007) Understanding cognitive behavioral coaching. *Training Journal*, January: 53–7.

McMahon, G. (2009) Cognitive behavioral coaching. In: D. Megginson and D. Clutterbuck (eds) *Further Techniques for Behavioral Coaching*. London: Elsevier. pp. 15–28.

Mann, L. (1982) Decision-making questionnaire. In: J.R. Ferrari, J.L. Johnson and W.G. McCown, *Procrastination and Task Avoidance: Theory, Research, and Treatment*, New York: Plenum Press.

Marks, I.M. (1969) *Fears and Phobias*. London: William Heinemann.

Meichenbaum, D. (1977) *Cognitive-behavior Modification: An Integrative Approach*. New York: Plenum Press.

Meichenbaum, D. (1985) *Stress Inoculation Training*. New York: Pergamon.

Milner, P. and Palmer, S. (1998) *Integrative Stress Counselling: A Humanistic Problem-focused Approach*. Cassell: London.

Morley, S., Eccleston, C., and Williams, A. (1999) Systematic review and meta-analysis of randomized controlled trials of cognitive behavior therapy and behavior therapy for chronic pain in adults, excluding headache. *International Association for the Study of Pain*. Elsevier Science B.V. pp. 1–13.

Neenan, M. (1997) Reflections on two major REBT concepts. *The Rational Emotive Behavior Coach*, 4(1), 31–3.

Neenan, M. (2006) Cognitive behavioral coaching. In: J. Passmore (ed.) *Excellence in Coaching: The Industry Guide*. London: Kogan Page. pp. 91–105.

Neenan, M. (2008a) From cognitive behavior therapy (CBT) to cognitive behavior coaching (CBC). *Journal of Rational-Emotive and Cognitive-Behavior Therapy*, 26(1), 3–15.

Neenan, M. (2008b) Introduction to the special issue on cognitive-behavioral coaching. *Journal of Rational-Emotive Cognitive-Behavior Therapy*, 26(1), 1–2.

Neenan, M. (2008c) Tackling procrastination: An REBT perspective for coaches. *Journal of Rational-Emotive and Cognitive-Behavior Therapy*, 26(1), 53–62.

Neenan, M. and Dryden, W. (2002) *Life Coaching: A Cognitive Behavioral Perspective*. Hove: Routledge.

Neenan, M. and Palmer, S. (2001) Cognitive behavioral coaching. *Stress News*, 13(3), 15–18.

NICE (2005) *Clinical Guidelines for Treating Mental Health Problems*. London: National Institute for Health and Clinical Excellence.

O'Broin, A. and Palmer, S. (2009) Co-creating an optimal coaching alliance: A Cognitive Behavioral Coaching perspective. *International Coaching Psychology Review*, 4(2), 184–94.

O'Donovan, H. (2009) CRAIC – a model suitable for Irish coaching psychology. *The Coaching Psychologist*, 5(2), 90–6.

Palmer, S. (1992) Stress management interventions. *Counselling News*, 7, 12–15.

Palmer, S. (1995) A comprehensive approach to industrial rational emotive behavior stress management workshops. *Rational Emotive Behavior Therapist*, 1, 45–55.

Palmer, S. (1997a) Problem-focused stress counselling and stress management: An intrinsically brief integrative approach. Part 1. *Stress News*, 9(2), 7–12.

Palmer, S. (1997b) Problem-focused stress counselling and stress management training: An intrinsically brief integrative approach. Part 2. *Stress News*, 9(3), 6–10.

Palmer, S. (2002) Cognitive and organizational models of stress that are suitable for use within workplace stress management/prevention coaching, training and counselling settings. *The Rational Emotive Behavior Therapist*, 10(1), 15–21.

Palmer, S. (2007) PRACTICE: A model suitable for coaching, counselling, psychotherapy and stress management. *The Coaching Psychologist*, 3(2), 71–77.

Palmer, S. (2008a) Multi-modal coaching and its application to work place, life and health coaching. *The Coaching Psychologist*, 4(1), 21–9.

Palmer, S. (2008b) The PRACTICE model of coaching: Towards a solution-focused approach. *Coaching Psychology International*, 1(1), 4–8.

Palmer, S. and Burton, T. (1996) *Dealing with People Problems at Work*. Maidenhead: McGraw-Hill.

Palmer, S. and Cooper, C. (2007, 2010) *How to Deal With Stress*. London: Kogan Page.

Palmer, S., and Ellis, A. (1995) Stress counselling and management: Stephen Palmer interviews Albert Ellis. *Rational Emotive Behavior Therapist*, 3(2), 82–6.

Palmer, S. and Gyllensten, K. (2008) How cognitive behavioral, rational emotive behavioral or multimodal coaching could prevent mental health problems, enhance performance and reduce work related stress. *Journal of Rational-Emotive and Cognitive-Behavior Therapy*, 26(1), 38–52.

Palmer, S. and Neenan, M. (2000) Problem-focused counselling and psychotherapy. In: S. Palmer and R. Wolfe (eds) *Integrative and Eclectic Counselling and Psychotherapy*. London: Sage.

Palmer, S. and Szymanska, K. (2007) Cognitive behavioral coaching: An integrative approach. In: S. Palmer and A. Whybrow (eds) *Handbook of Coaching Psychology: A Guide for Practitioners*. Hove: Routledge. pp. 86–117.

Palmer, S. and Whybrow, A. (2006) The coaching psychology movement and its development within the British Psychological Society. *International Coaching Psychology Review*, 1(1), 5–11.

Palmer, S., Cooper, C., and Thomas, K. (2003) *Creating a Balance: Managing Pressure*. London: British Library.

Passmore, J. and Marianetti, O. (2007) The role of mindfulness in coaching. *The Coaching Psychologist*, 3(3), 131–7.

Peltier, B. (2001) *The Psychology of Executive Coaching: Theory and Application*. Abingdon: Routledge.

Pilling, S., Bebbington, P., Kuipers, E., Garety, P., Geddes, J., Orbach, G. *et al.* (2002). Psychological treatments in schizophrenia: I. Meta-analysis of family intervention and cognitive behavior therapy. *Psychological Medicine*, 32, 763–82.

Rachman, S. and Teasdale, J. (1969) *Aversion Therapy and Behavior Disorders: An Analysis*. London: Routledge and Kegan Paul.

Reivich, K. and Shatte, A. (2002) *The Resilience Factor: Seven Essential Skills for Overcoming Life's Inevitable Obstacles*. New York: Broadway Books.

Rhodewalt, F., Saltzman, A.T., and Wittmer, J. (1984) Self-handicapping among competitive athletes: The role of practice in self-esteem protection. *Basic and Applied Social Psychology*, 5(3), 197–209.

Richard, J.T. (1999). Multimodal therapy: A useful model for the executive coach. *Consulting Psychology Journal: Practice and Research*, 51(1), 24–30.

Richman, D.R. (1993) Cognitive career counselling: A rational-emotive approach to career development. *Journal for Rational-Emotive and Cognitive-Behavior Therapy*, 11(2), 91–108.

Sawyer, L. (2003) Integrating Cognitive Coaching^SM with a framework for teaching. In: J. Ellison and C. Hayes (eds) *Change into the Culture of an Organization*. Norwood, MA: Christopher-Gordon. pp. 151–6.

Segal, Z.V., Williams, J.M.G., and Teasdale, J.D. (2002) *Mindfulness-based Cognitive Therapy for Depression*. New York: Guilford.

Simons, A.D., Levine, J.L., Lustman, P.J., and Murphy, G.E. (1984) Patient attrition in a comparative outcome study of depression: A follow-up report. *Journal of Affective Disorders*, 6, 163–73.

Singh, N.N., Lancioni, G.E., Wahler, R.G., Winton, A.S.W., and Singh, J. (2008) Mindfulness approaches in cognitive behavior therapy. *Behavioral and Cognitive Psychotherapy*, 36, 569–666.

Smith, J.A. and Osborn, M. (2003) Interpretative phenomenological analysis. In: J.A. Smith (ed.) *Qualitative Psychology: A Practical Guide to Research Methods*. London: Sage. pp. 51–80.

Smith, K.A. (2008) Restructuring metaphors: Using mental re-mapping in cognitive coaching. *Journal of Rational-Emotive and Cognitive-Behavior Therapy*, 26(1), 16–29.

Smith, M.C. (1997) Self-reflection as a means of increasing teacher efficacy through Cognitive Coaching[SM]. Master's thesis, California State University at Fullerton, 1997. *Masters Abstracts International 1384304.*

Spence, G.B. and Grant, A.M. (2005) Individual and group life coaching: Initial findings from a randomised, controlled trial. In: M. Cavanagh, A.M. Grant, and T. Kemp (eds) *Evidence-based Coaching, Vol 1: Theory, Research and Practice from the Behavioral Sciences.* QLD Australia: Bowen Hills. pp. 143–58.

Spence, G.B. and Grant, A.M. (2007) Professional and peer life coaching and the enhancement of goal striving and well-being: An exploratory study. *Journal of Positive Psychology*, 2(3), 185–94.

Spence, G.B., Cavanagh, M.J., and Grant, A.M. (2008) The integration of mindfulness training and health coaching: An exploratory study. *Coaching: An International Journal of Theory, Research and Practice*, 1(2), 145–63.

Strayer, J. and Rossett, A. (1994) Coaching sales performance: A case study. *Performance Improvement Quarterly*, 7, 39–53.

Syrek-Kosowska, A., Edgerton, N., and Palmer, S. (2010) From SPACE to SFERA: Adaptation of the SPACE model of cognitive behavioral coaching and therapy to the Polish language. *Coaching Psychology International*, 3(2), 18–20.

Wasik, B. (1984) Teaching parents effective problem solving: A handbook for professionals. Unpublished manuscript.University of North Carolina, Chapel Hill.

Williams, H. and Palmer, S. (2010) CLARITY: A cognitive behavioral coaching model. *Coaching Psychology International*, 3(2), 5–7.

Williams, H., Edgerton, N., and Palmer, S. (2010) Cognitive behavioral coaching. In: E. Cox, T. Bachkirova, and D. Clutterbuck (eds) *The Complete Handbook of Coaching*. London: Sage. pp. 37–53.

Wolpe, J. (1973) *The Practice of Behavior Therapy*. New York: Pergamon.

Wolpe, J. and Lazarus, A.A. (1966) *Behavior Therapy Techniques*. New York: Pergamon.

Yu, N., Collins, C.G., Cavanagh, M., White, K., and Fairbrother, G. (2008) Positive coaching with frontline managers: Enhancing their effectiveness and understanding why. *International Coaching Psychology Review*, 3(2), July, 110–22.

# 18

# Motivational Interviewing Approach

## Tim Anstiss and Jonathan Passmore

## Introduction

Coaching and mentoring are less about telling people what to do, and more about helping people to learn, grow and develop, to work things out for themselves and to choose what to do within a friendly, supportive, informed, and guiding relationship. This is also very much the purpose of motivational interviewing (MI).

Motivational interviewing has been defined as: "A collaborative, goal-oriented style of communication with particular attention to the language of change. It is designed to strengthen personal motivation for and commitment to a specific goal by eliciting and exploring the person's own reasons for change within an atmosphere of acceptance and compassion." And more briefly as: "A collaborative conversation style for strengthening a person's own motivation and commitment to change" (Miller and Rollnick, in press)

Motivational interviewing has been intensively studied by multiple independent research teams around the world. The evidence clearly demonstrates that MI is effective in helping people to change even very hard-to-change behaviors. The research evidence also sheds light on: (1) why MI is effective; (2) for what types of issues; and (3) what type of training is required for practitioners to become competent. What the research evidence is presently less clear about is whether MI works in coaching, outside the subspecialty of health coaching.

After reviewing the origins, theory, and practice of MI, we hypothesize that the approach will eventually be shown to work in coaching just as it has in other helping domains and we suggest some critical studies to test our hypothesis.

## Theory of Motivational Interviewing

Motivational interviewing originated in 1982 when American Bill Miller took a trip to Norway to talk about the approach he was developing. During his demonstrations his

*The Wiley Blackwell Handbook of the Psychology of Coaching and Mentoring*, First Edition.
Edited by Jonathan Passmore, David B. Peterson, and Teresa Freire.
© 2013 John Wiley & Sons, Ltd. Published 2016 by John Wiley & Sons, Ltd.

hosts would stop him to ask such questions as: "What are you thinking as you say that?" "Why have you taken this line of approach rather than another?" "Why that particular word?" and "What underlying model is guiding your methods?" This forced him to articulate the principles that were guiding him, to make his tacit knowledge explicit (Miller, 1996).

As a result of these discussions Miller wrote a concept paper, which he did not intend to publish but was persuaded to do so to share his developing thinking (Miller, 1983). A growing number of people became curious about the approach, wanted training and wanted to test the approach in good quality research studies – some of which are mentioned in this chapter.

Since these early days motivational interviewing has been described in a growing number of articles and books (e.g., the Applications of Motivational Interviewing series of books published by Guildford Press). These books illustrate how motivational interviewing has been and can be used for a range of problems and with a variety of populations and range from basic guides about MI (Miller and Rollnick, 2002; Rosengren, 2009) to guides to working with people with psychological problems (Arkowitz *et al.*, 2007), and with specific groups such as adolescents (Naar-King and Suarez, 2009).

Motivational interviewing is one of the most rigorously tested approaches to helping people grow, change, and develop. Hypothesises about whether it will work with a particular group, in which circumstances, when delivered by which types of practitioner, with which type of training, delivering which "dose" of the approach have been and are continuing to be tested. Results, both positive and negative, are published in peer reviewed journals in marked contrast to some other approaches such as neuro-linguistic programming which has a very limited supporting research. New hypotheses about the application of MI are being tested, improved measures are being developed, new tools, techniques, and applications tried out, and more and more statistical analyses are being performed, all of which are helping the field of MI to move forward in a controlled, critical, and scientific fashion.

In the beginning, motivational interviewing was "a-theoretical". We knew from a number of research studies that it worked, but we weren't sure how or why. It was an "empirical" approach to helping people, with no well-articulated, theoretical underpinning. Motivational interviewing practitioners could describe how to do it, and knew the approach to be as or more effective than other approaches (and typically more efficient). They knew it helped people change a wide range of different and hard-to-change behaviors (drinking, drug use, physical activity, dietary change, etc.) when delivered in a range of settings (outpatients, in-patients, residential treatment, community, etc.) by a wide range of different trained people (doctors, nurses, psychologists, etc.). But why it worked – that was a mystery.

We now have a better understanding as a result of a series of studies, which have helped flesh out possible causal pathways and mediating mechanisms linking theory with practice. And because motivational interviewing is a scientific approach to helping people to change, this iteration between theory and practice is constantly being checked out and tested by researchers around the world.

Draycott and Dabbs (1998) claimed that the nature, principles, and techniques of motivational interviewing are, "without exception", found to relate to one or more of the principles of cognitive dissonance, whilst Markland *et al.* (2005) proposed that self-determination theory (SDT) (Deci and Ryan, 2008) provides a coherent theoretical framework for understanding motivational interviewing processes and their effectiveness. They outlined and described the parallels between the two approaches and showed how both MI and SDT are based on the assumption that humans have an, "innate tendency for personal growth towards psychological integration" and suggested that motivational interviewing, "provides the social-environmental facilitation factors suggested by SDT to promote this tendency."

Vansteenkiste and Sheldon (2006) also compared the practice of and evidence about motivational interviewing with the theory of, and evidence about, self-determination theory. They showed that SDTs focus on the issues of need satisfaction and the internalization of therapeutic change is entirely compatible with the principles and practice of motivational interviewing, and suggested that basic need satisfaction may be one of the key mechanisms by which MI delivers its helpful effects.

Wagner and Ingersoll (2008) reflected on the fact that MI is commonly described in cognitive and behavioral terms as an approach to helpfully resolve tension in the client resulting from ambivalence about change, making it consistent with a negative reinforcement model in which individuals perform behaviors to escape from aversive or unpleasant states, such as ambivalence and uncertainty about what to do. However, MI could also be described by a positive re-inforcement model where the individual moves towards the positive. The authors describe the role that motivational interviewing can play in helping people to experience such positive emotions and feelings as hope, contentment, interest, and inspiration, helping people to envision a better future, remember past successes, and gain confidence in their ability to change their lives for the better.

Let us look at some of these theoretical frameworks in more detail.

## Self-determination theory

Self-determination theory (SDT) is a wide ranging theoretical framework explaining elements of human motivation, personality development, psychological health, and well-being (Deci and Ryan, 2008). It suggests that there are three basic and universal psychological needs or "nutriments" – the need for autonomy, for competence, and for relatedness. These needs or nutriments are defined as "those supports and satisfactions that are essential and necessary for psychological growth, integrity, and wellness". The fulfilment of these needs is considered necessary for vital, healthy human functioning regardless of human culture or stage of development. The thwarting or frustration of these needs leads to reduced self-motivation and greater ill-being, possibly contributing to psychopathology (Ryan *et al.*, 2006). Self-determination theory also assumes people have deeply evolved tendencies toward psychological growth and development and have innate natural tendencies to seek out challenges, novelty, and opportunities to learn. It distinguishes between different types of motivation – between "autonomous motivation" (which includes intrinsic motivation and forms of extrinsic motivation where people have identified with an activity's value and have integrated it into their sense of self) and "controlled motivation" (where one's behavior is controlled by the external contingencies of reward or punishment, and where one's behavior is energized by such factors as need for approval or the avoidance of shame). Both autonomous and controlled motivation energize and direct a person's behavior, but when people are autonomously motivated they experience more volition, ownership, and self-endorsement of their actions.

Motivational interviewing practitioners seek to discover and build "autonomous motivation" for change within their clients by paying attention to specific aspects of client speech, whilst simultaneously seeking to increase client perceptions and experience of competence and relatedness (Deci and Ryan, 2008; Ryan, 2008).

## Self-discrepancy theory

Self-discrepancy theory suggests that discrepancies, or mismatches, between different ideas about the self are related to different emotions and motivations (Higgins, 1987). It postulates the existence of three different "domains" of the self (actual, ideal, and ought) and two different "standpoints" (own and significant other). A wide range of different gaps or discrepancies can thus exist, for instance between actual/own self and ideal self-states, or between actual/own self and ought self-states. Higgins relates each of these different possible discrepancies to such emotions as "dejection related" (disappointment, dissatisfaction, and sadness), and "agitation-related" (fear, threat, relatedness). Differences in both relative magnitude and the accessibility of a person's self-discrepancies determine a person's level of discomfort with the way things are.

Motivational interviewing practitioners sometimes seek to "develop discrepancy" and talk with a person in a way which increases their sense of discomfort about the way their life currently is. For instance, a client may be spending too much time at work and not enough time at home with their children. Perhaps they have mentioned earlier in the session how much they love their children. The MI practitioner might use an empathic, double-sided reflection to increase motivational discomfort and "develop discrepancy" between the clients actual self and their "ought" or "ideal" self, for instance: "Spending time with your children is important to you, you want to be a dad who is there for their kids, and yet you often find yourself staying behind at work even when you don't really need to." In this way the MI practitioner uses the motivational energy that comes from one or more "discrepancies" to increase the probability that the client will make a helpful behavior change in line with their own goals and values. This possible mechanism of behavior change – of increasing a client's access to pre-existing "self-discrepancies" with a view to tapping into natural occurring change processes – is in harmony with Tyron and Misurell's (2008) bold contention that dissonance induction and reduction is a possible mechanism for explaining why several different therapies are effective.

## Self-efficacy theory

What is the role of a person's beliefs in the regulation of their motivation and behavior? Several large-scale meta-analyses in such domains as academic and work-related performance (Multon *et al.*, 1991; Sadri and Robertson, 1993; Stajkovic and Luthans, 1998), psychosocial functioning in children and adolescents (Holden *et al.*, 1990), health (Holden, 1991), and sports-related performance (Moritz *et al.*, 2000) have shown that "efficacy beliefs" (how confident a person is that they can perform the behavior) predict variations in motivation, effort, performance, and achievement levels and that manipulating these beliefs produce changes in the predicted direction (Bandura and Locke, 2003).

Motivational interviewing practitioners seek to "support self-efficacy" by assessing and building their clients' confidence that they can successfully make the behavior change under consideration. Self-efficacy comes from four main sources (Bandura, 1977): performance accomplishments; vicarious experience; verbal persuasion; and physiological states. Motivational interviewing practitioners work with each of these sources of self-efficacy to increase the probability that their clients will change and stay changed into the future. They may, for instance, use a confidence scaling strategy: "How confident are you, on a scale of 0–10, that you can become and stay more active – where 0 is not at all confident and 10 is very confident?" (assume client says 5); "Why 5, why not a lower number?"

(tapping into the client's existing sources of confidence, including previous experiences); "What would have to happen for your confidence to become 8 or 9?"(getting client to tell you what needs to happen for their confidence to increase).

# Research Evidence for Motivational Interviewing

Over the past two decades MI has built a substantial evidence base. By far the majority of evidence in support of motivational interviewing comes from the field of healthcare and criminal justice. This is understandable as this is where the approach is being used most frequently and reflects its origins. For this chapter we have summarized the research under three main headings:

- Outcome research – does MI work?
- Process research – how does MI work?
- Training effectiveness research – what training is required for competence in MI?

Let us look at each of these types of research evidence in turn.

## Outcome research

Motivational interviewing is one of the best studied ways of helping people, with over 650 outcome studies. When Bricker and Tollison (2011) reviewed the PsychINFO® and PubMed databases they found over 550 peer reviewed publications between May 1999 and April 2009. Motivational interviewing is also the subject (in whole or in part) of over 100 systematic reviews, including 18 meta-analyses (e.g., Burke *et al.*, 2004; Lundahl and Burke, 2009; Lundahl *et al.*, 2010) where the data from several studies is pooled to enable us to be even more confident that an approach works. Few other ways of helping people have been subjected to such rigorous scrutiny. At present MI has mainly been studied in health settings, but each year the approach is being evaluated in new settings and contexts with different groups of people experiencing different issues. We do not think it will be long before MI is rigorously tested as an approach to improve outcomes in organizational coaching and mentoring.

There is good quality research evidence that motivational interviewing is or may be helpful in bringing about beneficial change in the behaviors, conditions, and contexts shown see Table 18.1.

Burke *et al.* (2003) conducted a meta-analysis on controlled clinical trials investigating what they termed "adaptations of motivational interviewing" (AMIs) and found them equivalent to other active treatments – yielding moderate effects compared with no treatment and/or placebo for problems involving alcohol, drugs, and diet and exercise. Overall, the percentage of people who improved following AMI treatments (51 percent) was significantly greater than the percentage who improved (37 percent) with either no treatment or treatment as usual.

Burke *et al.* (2004) subsequently conducted a meta-analytic, qualitative, and process review of the empirical literature for AMIs and once again found them equivalent to other active treatments, yielding moderate effects compared to no-treatment/placebo for problems involving alcohol, drugs, and diet and exercise. They suggested that whilst AMIs are equivalent in efficacy to cognitive behavioral skills training (CBST) approaches,

**Table 18.1** Areas where MI has demonstrated effectiveness.

**Alcohol dependence**
Deas and Clark (2009)
Handmaker and Walters (2002)
Branscum and Sharma (2010)

**Brain injury**
Bell et al. (2005)
Bombardier and Rimmele (1999)
Bombardier et al. (2009)

**Dentistry and oral health**
Freudenthal (2008)
Freudenthal and Bowen (2010)
Skaret et al. (2003)
Weinstein et al. (2004)
Weinstein et al. (2006)

**Domestic violence**
Kistenmacher and Weiss (2008)
Musser et al. (2008)
Rasmussen et al. (2008)

**Heart failure**
Brodie and Inoue (2005)
Meyer et al. (2008)

**Anxiety disorders**
Westra and Arkowitz (2010)
Westra and Dozois (2006)
Westra and Dozois (2008)

**Cancer**
Bennet et al. (2007)
Campbell et al. (2009)

**Diabetes**
Channon et al. (2007)
Dale et al. (2009)
Greaves et al. (2008)
Ismail et al. (2010)
Penn et al. (2009)
Rubak et al. (2009)
Viner et al. (2003)

**Eating disorders**
Cassin et al. (2008)
Dean et al. (2008)
DiMarco et al. (2009)

**HIV risk and prevention**
Cook et al. (2009)
Kiene and Barta (2006)
Kuyper et al. (2009)
Naar-King et al. (2009)
Velasquez (2009)

**Asthma**
Borrelli et al. (2010)
Halterman et al. (2008)
Schmaling et al. (2001)

**Cardiac rehabilitation**
Everett et al. (2008)
Riegel et al. (2006)

**Diet and lipids**
Brug et al. 2007
Campbell et al. (2009)
Hoy et al. (2009)
Resnicow et al. (2005)
Woollard (2003)

**Family**
Cordova et al. (2001)
Runyon et al. (2009)
Slavet et al. (2005)

**Homelessness**
Wenzel et al. (2009)

**COPD**
de Blok et al. (2006)
Soria, et al. (2006)

**Cardiovascular risk**
Groeneveled et al. (2008)
Ogedegbe et al. (2008)

**Dual diagnosis**
Baker et al. (2002)
Barrowclough et al. (2009)
Buckner and Carroll (2010)
Hulse and Tait (2003)
Klag et al. (2009)
Santa Ana et al. (2007)

**Gambling**
Carlbring et al. (2010)
Diskin and Hodgins (2009)
Grant et al. (2009)
Wulfert et al. (2006)

**Injury prevention**
Fernandez et al. (2009)
Johnston et al. (2002)
Schermer et al. (2006)

**Medication taking**
Cook et al. (2008)
Golin et al. (2006)
Heffner et al. (2010)

**Pain**
Ang, D et al. (2007)
Habib et al. (2005)
Rau et al. (2008)

**Sexual health**
Barnet et al. (2009)
Floyd et al. (2007)
LaBrie et al. (2008)
Mausbach et al. (2007)

**Substance use**
Adamson and Sellman (2008)
Kadden et al. (2007)
Scott and Dennis (2009)
Fraser and Solovey (2007)

**Mental health**
Bombardier et al. (2009)
Connel and Dishion (2008)
Kertes et al. (2011)
Merlo et al. (2010)
Swartz et al. (2006)

**Physical activity and
exercise**
Anshel and Kang (2008)
Benbassat et al. (2008)
Hardcastle et al. (2008)

**Screening**
Cutter and Fiellin (2010).

**Tobacco use**
Bolger et al. (2010)
Soria et al. (2006)
Armstrong et al. (2011)

**Obesity prevention**
Flattum et al. (2009)

**Relationships**
Burke et al. (2002)

**Stroke**
Watkins et al. (2007)
Watkins et al. (2011)

**Weight reduction**
Armstrong et al. (2011)
Cavill et al. (2011)
West et al. (2007)

**Offending**
Anstiss B et al. (2011)
Austin et al. (2011)
Farbring and Johnson (2008)
Sinha et al. (2003)

**Safe water behaviors**
Thevos et al. (2000)

**Speech/vocal therapy**
Behrman (2006)

they are commonly briefer, and thus hour for hour are more effective for specific types of presenting issues. Since AMIs focus on developing readiness to change while CBSTs target the change process, they suggested that AMIs can be useful as preludes or additions to CBST.

Rubak *et al.* (2005) conducted a systematic review of the effectiveness of MI in a wide range of disease areas. A search of 16 databases produced 72 randomized controlled trials dating back to 1991. Analysis showed a significant effect for motivational interviewing for changes in body mass index, total blood cholesterol, systolic blood pressure, blood alcohol concentration, and standard ethanol content. Motivational interviewing had significant and clinically relevant effects in approximately three out of four studies, with equal effects on physiological and psychological conditions. Psychologists and physicians obtained an effect in approximately 80 percent of the studies, while other healthcare providers obtained an effect in 46 percent of the studies. Even when motivational interviewing was used in brief encounters of 15 minutes, 64 percent of the studies showed an effect. Further encounters with the patient increased the effectiveness of motivational interviewing. They concluded that motivational interviewing in a scientific setting outperforms traditional advice giving in the treatment of a broad range of behavioral problems and diseases.

Vasilaki *et al.* (2006) examined the effectiveness of MI in reducing alcohol consumption. A literature search revealed 22 relevant studies upon which they performed their meta-analysis. They concluded that brief MI is effective and recommend that future studies of MI explore predictors of efficacy and compare different components of MI to determine which are most responsible for long-term changes in behavior.

Lundahl *et al.* (2009) highlighted the evidence from the three published meta-analyses of MI and a recent meta-analysis of their own. They concluded that MI is significantly more effective than no treatment and generally equal to other treatments for a wide variety of problems ranging from substance use (alcohol, marijuana, tobacco, and other drugs) to reducing risky behaviors and increasing client engagement in treatment. They also found that group-delivered MI appears to be less effective than one-on-one MI, and that delivering MI with "problem feedback" seemed to generate better outcomes for some problems than MI alone.

In the most comprehensive review of MI for smoking cessation conducted to date, Heckman *et al.* (2010) conducted a systematic review and meta-analysis involving 31 smoking cessation research studies for analysis: eight with adolescent samples, eight with adults with chronic physical or mental illness, five with pregnant/postpartum women, and ten with other adult samples, totalling almost 10,000 individual participants. They concluded that MI-based smoking cessation approaches can be effective for adolescents and adults alike, and that more comparative efficacy trials should be conducted.

A similar comprehensive review of MI has also been conducted for weight loss (Armstrong *et al.*, 2011). This study found 3, 540 citations and of the 101 potentially relevant studies, 12 met the inclusion criteria and 11 were included for meta-analysis. Motivational interviewing was associated with a greater reduction in body mass compared to controls (SMD = -0.51 [95% CI 1.04 - 0.01]). There was a significant reduction in body weight (kg) for those in the intervention group compared with those in the control group (difference = -1.47 kg [95% CI - 2.05 - 0.88]). For the body mass index (BMI) outcome, the difference was -0.25 kg m$^{-2}$ (95% CI - 0.50 - 0.01). The research team concluded that MI appeared to enhance weight loss in overweight and obese patients.

Lundahl *et al.* (2010) investigated the unique contribution of motivational interviewing on counseling outcomes and how the approach compared with other interventions. The results from 119 studies were subject to a meta-analysis, with targeted outcomes including substance use (tobacco, alcohol, drugs, marijuana), health-related behaviors (diet, exercise, safe sex), gambling, and engagement in treatment. Across all 132 comparisons they conducted they found that MI interventions were associated with a statistically significant and durable improvement in outcomes and that the added benefits of MI showed no signs of fading up to two years or more after the intervention. Stronger effects were shown when MI was compared to either doing nothing, being placed on a waiting list control group, or being handed a leaflet, compared to when MI was compared to another specific intervention such as cognitive behavioral therapy. Studies incorporating feedback to the client on the results of assessments or screening tests were associated with significantly greater improvement, but therapists trained and instructed to follow a manual achieved less good results than those not so trained or instructed.

To summarize this outcome research, a large number of individual and meta-studies have found that MI is a highly effective approach for bringing about person-centered change in a wide range of contexts. It is as, or more, effective than many other interventions, whilst probably also being more efficient – bringing about more change in shorter periods of time, with less resources. Many of the outcomes achieved appear to be sustained over long periods of time, suggesting that MI is effective at delivering sustained behavior change for even the most challenging and ingrained behaviors.

## Process research

If MI is as effective as the research suggests, why is this so? What factors contribute to these outcomes? A second strand of research has explored these questions, with the aim of identifying the 'active ingredients' which make up MI.

Miller *et al.* (1993) found that problem drinkers randomly assigned to MI versus a confront/direct approach showed 111 percent more "change talk" (speech indicating varying levels of readiness to change) and noted that this was consistent with the findings of the within-subject clinical experiments of Patterson and Forgatch (1985), which also showed how client's use of language changed during MI-based conversations.

Amrhein *et al.* (2003) used psycholinguistic analysis to explore the relationship between the actual language clients used during MI conversations and its relationship with drug use outcomes. They coded 84 videotapes of conversations with drug abusers for the frequency and strength of client utterances expressing commitment, desire, ability, need, readiness, and reasons to change or maintain their habit. Commitment strength predicted outcomes and this in turn was predicted by strength of client statements relating to desire, ability, need, and reasons for change. The authors suggested that commitment strength is a pathway for the influence of client language on subsequent behavior change.

Moyers and Martin (2006) examined 38 motivational enhancement therapy sessions from Project MATCH (Matching Alcoholism Treatments to Client Heterogeneity), using a sequential behavioral coding system to investigate the relationship between therapist behaviors and client speech. They found that MI-consistent practitioner behaviors were more likely to be followed by self-motivational statements, and that MI-inconsistent practitioner behaviors were more likely to be followed by client resistance – lending support to the importance of practitioner behaviors in shaping client speech during MI sessions. They hypothesized that client language in favor of change is a causal mechanism during MI and specific practitioner behavior is recommended for eliciting such speech.

A separate paper (Moyers *et al.*, 2007) explored the role of practitioner behavior in influencing client speech, and the extent to which client speech predicted outcomes in clients receiving treatment for substance abuse. Conversations were coded using the Sequential Code for Process Exchanges (SCOPE) behavioral coding system and the MISC 1.0 behavioral coding system. The authors found that client speech during early sessions appeared to be a powerful predictor of substance abuse outcome and that the pattern of practitioner behaviors and subsequent client language provided support for a causal chain between practitioner behaviors, subsequent client speech, and outcomes. They suggested that aspects of client speech influence the likelihood of behavior change and that the occurrence of such speech is influenced by the practitioner.

Apodaca *et al.* (2009) explored evidence relating to possible within-session mechanisms of change. They examined four aspects of practitioner behavior (MI-spirit; MI-consistent behaviors; MI-inconsistent behaviors; and practitioner use of specific techniques) and five aspects of client behavior (change talk/intention; readiness to change; involvement/engagement; resistance; and experience of discrepancy). They reviewed 152 studies and found that 19 provided data on at least one link in the causal chain model under examination. The most consistent evidence was that client change talk/intention was related to better outcomes, that client experience of discrepancy was related to better outcomes and that practitioner MI-inconsistent behavior was related to worse outcomes.

Vader *et al.* (2010) examined the relationship between language, personalized feedback, and drinking outcomes in a sample of heavy-drinking college students. Motivational interviewing was delivered in a single session with or without a personalized feedback report. They found that MI consistent practitioner language was positively associated with client change talk, that MI with feedback was associated with lower levels of sustain talk, that higher levels of change talk were associated with improved drinking outcomes at three months and that higher levels of sustain talk were associated with poorer drinking outcomes. They highlighted the relationship between practitioner MI skill and client change talk, and the important role of feedback in the change process.

Magill *et al.* (2010) explored whether or not within-session practitioner and client language predicted a client's decision to complete a written change plan in an alcohol-focused MI using data from an ongoing hospital-based clinical trial involving 291 subjects. Analyses showed that practitioner MI-consistent behaviors and client change talk were both positive predictors, and practitioner counter change talk was a negative predictor of the decision to complete a change plan regarding alcohol use.

Where is all this process research leading? After Miller and Rose (2009) "looked under the hood" of motivational interviewing to try to discover what was happening, they described an emergent a testable theory of MI with two main active components: (1) a relational component focused on empathy and the "spirit" of MI, and (2) a technical component involving the differential evocation and reinforcement of "change talk". They described a causal chain model linking practitioner training, practitioner responses during sessions and post-session outcomes. They also suggested that the process research being conducted in MI may also help to clarify more general processes that result in good outcomes in other psychotherapies (Aharonovich *et al.*, 2008; Moyers *et al.*, 2007), see Figure 18.1.

## Training effectiveness research

So if MI works and it works via the pathways described, how does a practitioner become better at the approach? Miller *et al.* (2004) conducted a randomized controlled trial of

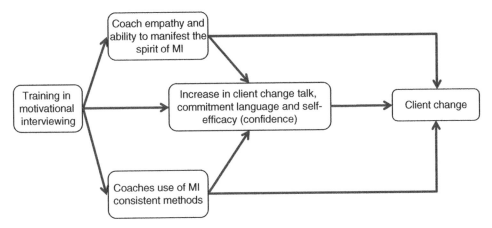

**Figure 18.1** Possible relationships among important variables in MI (adapted from Miller and Rose (2009)).

different methods for learning motivational interviewing. A total of 140 practitioners were randomized to one of five training conditions: (1) a workshop only; (2) a workshop plus practice feedback; (3) a workshop plus individual coaching sessions; (4) a workshop, feedback, and coaching; or (5) a waiting list control group of self-guided training. Audio-taped practice samples were analysed at baseline, post-training, and at 4-, 8-, and 12-month follow-up. All four training groups showed larger gains in proficiency than the control group. Post-training coaching and/or feedback increased proficiency, and post-training proficiency was generally well maintained throughout follow-up. They observed that practitioner self-reports of MI skilfulness were unrelated to proficiency levels in observed practice.

Schoener *et al.* (2006) examined the effectiveness of training practitioners in motivational interviewing (MI) adapted to treat clients with co-occurring disorders. Ten practitioners with high caseloads of culturally diverse clients in two different community mental health settings fulfilled all study requirements. Training consisted of a two-day didactic and experiential workshop followed by bi-weekly small group supervision/coaching sessions for eight weeks. A total of 156 randomly selected sessions involving 28 clients were coded for practitioner fidelity both pre- and post-training. The research team noted significant improvement in MI skill after training on five of six key practitioner ratings, and on the sole client rating (change talk) that was examined.

Martino *et al.* (2008) evaluated the treatment adherence and competence of 35 practitioners from five outpatient community programs delivering either a three-session adaptation of MI or an equivalent number of drug counselling-as-usual sessions to 461 clients. Achievement MI practitioners were carefully prepared to implement the AMI using a combination of expert-led intensive workshop training followed by program-based clinical supervision. Adherence to, and competence in, AMI discriminated between AMI sessions and counseling-as-usual sessions and were significantly related to in-session change in client motivation and some client outcomes (e.g., percentage of negative drug urine screens). They concluded that MI fidelity (how well it is being done) can be reliably assessed and that the combination of expert-led workshops followed by program-based clinical supervision may be an effective method for implementing MI in community settings.

In summary, the evidence suggests that skills development workshops are necessary but not sufficient in and of themselves for proficiency or competence in MI, needing to be followed and supplemented with ongoing practice, practice feedback, and coaching.

# The Spirit, Processes, Principles and Core Skills of Motivational Interviewing

Motivational interviewing has been very well studied and much is known about what constitutes good practice and how good practice or competence can be achieved and maintained (see above). The approach has a well-defined spirit, a set of principles, and some core skills (sometimes called microskills).

## The spirit of the approach

The spirit of motivational interviewing has four aspects: partnership, acceptance, compassion, and evocation. The approach is done collaboratively with a person, in partnership with them – and is not something done "to" them. Practitioner and client work together, jointly and collaboratively viewing aspect of the person's life, their goals, their strengths, their difficulties, their hopes, their concerns, and their ideas for change. When the conversation ceases to become collaborative the practitioner may notice one or more manifestations of resistance, which serve as cues for the practitioner to change tack and re-establish the collaborative, empathic relationship. The conversation should be more like a dance than a wrestle and the practitioner tries not to get too far ahead of the client. If the practitioner overestimates the importance the client places on changing, or their confidence or readiness to change, or talks and acts in ways which reduce the client's sense of control or autonomy then resistance may be triggered. (It should be noted that in the third edition of *Motivational Interviewing*, resistance is broken down into two distinct phenomena – "sustain talk", which is client speech about staying the same, and "discord", which is a problem with an aspect of the relationship).

The approach is evocative in that the practitioner tries to draw things out from the client, rather than put things in. Things evoked from the client include concerns about the current situation, reasons for change, ideas for changing, and ideas for staying changed – including thoughts about barriers and obstacles which might be encountered and ways around them. Reasons for being confident that change is possible may also be evoked. The more the client comes up with ideas, reasons, and arguments, the more likely change will occur – in contrast to the practitioner telling the client why and how to change.

Motivational interviewing is accepting and compassionate – being empathic, affirming, and accepting both of the client's absolute worth and their autonomy or freedom to choose. The approach is autonomy supporting in that the practitioner never forgets that the client is the active decision maker, exploring options and deciding what they want to with their lives (which of course includes the option of not changing and staying the same – letting their life continue in its current direction). These elements of the spirit of MI demonstrate its strong person-centered and humanistic credentials, as the practitioner works hard to create the right conditions for positive change to occur in the client, helping them move naturally towards health, well-being, and the reaching of more of their potential.

*The four processes* Four processes which take place during motivational interviewing are: engaging; focusing; evoking; and planning. Practitioners work on the process of engagement throughout. If engagement is lost or sensed to be lost, then the practitioner works in re-establishing engagement. The focus in MI is change – but what change exactly, and who decides? The focus of the session is influenced by the context (e.g., a cardiac rehabilitation program), the practitioner (a drug and alcohol worker) and the client – but ideally of course the client has the biggest say in the focus of the motivational conversation. Planning, of course, takes place in a wide range of approaches to help people change – but what makes MI distinctive is its emphasis on evoking, especially the eliciting (and strengthening) of "change talk".

*The principles* The principles of MI can be remembered by the acronym RULE:

- Resist the righting reflex.
- Understand and explore the clients motivation.
- Listen with empathy.
- Empower the client, encouraging optimism and hope.

Practitioners also seek to:

- Roll with resistance.
- Develop discrepancy.
- Share information in a neutral way.

The righting reflex is the natural tendency to want to fix things, to put things right, to straighten things out, and make them better. This usually helpful reflex commonly gets in the way of empathic, non-judgmental relationships, and can trigger resistance and reactance as the client feels their autonomy is being undermined by the coach's attempt at being helpful. The righting reflex may prompt practitioners to jump in with such questions as: "Could you try this?" or, "Why don't you do such and such?", which may even prompt the client to do the opposite of the suggested course of action in an attempt to demonstrate their autonomy and freedom.

Motivational interviewing practitioners seek to understand and explore the client's motivation by asking their clients open questions and following these up with empathic listening statements, more questions, affirmations, and the occasional summary. Questions such as: "Why might you want to change?" "What are your three best reasons for doing it?" "What is the best that might happen?" "Looking forwards a few years, when things have improved, what might be going on?" "How important is it for you to change?" and "Why?" often help to get the person sharing their motivation or reasons for changing. Using empathic listening skills helps with the further exploration of these motivations, and listening for and then developing "change talk" may help build and further strengthen client motivation for change.

Motivational interviewing practitioners listen with empathy, really trying hard to imagine what it might be like to be the other person, trying to feel "as if" they were in the other person's shoes, communicating this attempt at understanding with reflective listening statements of varying degrees of complexity and summaries. If nothing else happens in the session, the client should go away feeling heard, listened to, and understood.

Motivational interviewing practitioners seek to empower their clients, encouraging optimism and hope, by working to develop their clients' sense of confidence about being able to change (their self-efficacy), as well as helping them see how change is likely to result in desired outcomes for themselves and others. Open questions such as: "How do you think you might go about it to be successful?" "What do you think would be most helpful here?" "How confident are you that you can change and stay changed for six months?" "Where do you get your confidence from?" "What would have to happen for you to be more confident?" "How can we help you become more confident?" as well as affirmations such as: "You're the kind of person who works hard to be successful," or, "When you set your mind to things, you get results," can all help in empowering people. Helping clients think through the type, volume, and duration of change required for success can build hope, as can reflection on previous mastery experience and discussion about what works for other people.

Motivational interviewing practitioners seek to minimize the manifestation of resistance in the conversation in the first place, and adapt their behavior in the session to reduce resistance as and when it is noticed. They "roll" with resistance, much as a boxer is trained to roll with a punch rather than push their face into it. This rolling may take the form of a reflection: for example, "You really don't want to be here,'" or, "Going for this interview isn't a priority for you a the moment, what with the other things you have going on?" or the form of a reframing or a change of focus: for example, "You're right, perhaps the drinking isn't what we should be focusing right now, but the relationship itself," an apology, for example, "I'm sorry, I think I've rushed ahead a bit, can we go back a little, please forgive me," or a re-emphasizing of client control and autonomy, for example "You're very much the one in charge here, and you will only change this when it feels right for you." All of these methods can help reduce any discord that may have arisen in the relationship and help re-establish good levels of client engagement.

The MI practitioner seeks to develop discrepancy in their clients, helping their clients become more aware of the gap between how things are at the moment and how they would like things to be. This contributes to the "motive force", the desire to change, which the practitioner is trying to develop. Discrepancy can be developed by getting the client to talk about their goals, clarify and talk about their values (what is important to them), getting them to explore "two possible futures", and/or having them "look back" and "look forwards" at how their life was and how they imagine it might be in the future. But whilst discrepancy (or a gap or mismatch) needs to be present before change will occur (why change if everything is perfect and the person is perfectly satisfied?), too much discrepancy may serve to demotivate a client, especially if the person doesn't feel that there is any way they can close the gap. This means raising client awareness about the gap between how things are and how things might to be needs to be done in parallel with building hope and confidence that the necessary changes can be successfully made.

Being an evocative approach, MI practitioners seek to evoke or draw things out from a person. But what if the necessary information just isn't there? In this case the practitioner has to provide the information before the client can reflect on it and come to an informed decision. Things which it might be helpful to share with a client include: what works in managing conflict; how to become more assertive; successful weight loss behaviors; how to prepare for an interview; what other people find helpful when seeking promotion at work; how to become less depressed; aspects of the law or company policy; and so on. Motivational interviewing practitioners may share this information using the

A-S-A (ask, share, ask) format of: asking what the person already knows; asking for permission to share information; sharing the information; and then asking the person what they make of the information. This approach may help the information become more easily "digested" by the client. Compare: "Why don't you consider the following...." or, "You really ought to reduce your risk factors," with: "Can I share with you some things which other people have found helpful?" or, "Can I share with you what we know seems to increase the risk of another episode?" The latter two questions are like laying information out on a table in front of the person and letting them choose, rather than suggesting to them what they should do with the information. This approach may well reduce the emergence of discord and help maintain or increase engagement in the conversation about change.

*The core skills (or micro-skills) – using your OARS*  The MI practitioner seeks to ask skilful Open questions, makes occasional, genuine, and heartfelt Affirmations, uses skilful Reflections or accurate empathy statements and uses occasional Summaries to bring things together, review progress, or as a prelude to moving the conversation in a different direction.

Open questions encourage the client to talk more than closed questions. Rather than ask closed question such as "Could you...?" "Have you thought of...?" MI practitioners prefer such open question as "Why might you want to...?" "What do you think would be most helpful?" "How might you go about this?"

Motivational interviewing practitioners make affirmations – statements recognizing and acknowledging some aspect of client's effort or character, such as: "You're the kind of person who sticks with things once you've made your mind up," "You go out of your way to be kind to people, even when you don't really feel like it," or "I appreciate the fact that you've stuck with this, even though the results are not happening as fast as you wanted."

Motivational interviewing practitioners make a lot of use of reflective listening or accurate empathy statements to check out that they understand the client correctly, help the client feel understood, and perhaps even generate some insight in the client as they hear what they said (and what they think) articulated back to them.

Motivational interviewing coaches use summaries intermittently throughout the session to check and reflect on progress, check for correct understanding, bring several things the client has mentioned together for their benefit (especially change talk), and after one tool or strategy before moving on in the same or a slightly different direction.

# Tools and Techniques Associated With Motivational Interviewing

Motivational interviewing is primarily a style of communication, a way of talking with another person which seeks to create the right conditions for helpful and sustained change to occur. It is not about using a set of tools and strategies with a person in an effort to get them to change. Nevertheless, a range of tools and strategies can help the MI practitioner manifest the spirit and principles of the approach, including: setting the scene; agreeing the agenda; typical day; decisional balance; importance and confident rulers; looking back, looking forwards; two possible futures; the key question; exploring options; and agreeing a plan. Interested readers may wish to consult other texts for details of how to use these tools and strategies in an MI consistent way, for example Rollnick *et al.* (2007) and Rosengren (2009).

# The Development of Motivational Interviewing in Coaching Practice

Despite considerable evidence (see above) of effectiveness in the sub-speciality of health coaching, MI has yet to demonstrate its effectiveness in organizational or executive coaching. At the time of publication, there are a limited number of conceptual papers (see, for example, Anstiss and Passmore, 2011 or Passmore 2007b), a number of technique application papers (e.g., Passmore, 2011a, 2011b; 2012a, 2012b) and no published trials exploring the effectiveness of MI as a coaching intervention within organizational environments or executive populations. We believe it will only be a matter of time before MI-based coaching is properly tested against alternative approaches and the evidence base around effective coaching practice grows.

# Research Evidence of Motivational Interviewing in Organizational or Executive Coaching

A limited number of writers have highlighted the potential of MI as an approach for use with managers and employees to address motivational issues or to support change. The first paper exploring the use of MI in coaching (Passmore, 2007a) considered the use of MI for addressing employee under performance and considered a case study where the approach had been used to increase motivation to engage in a new role with which the employee was unhappy. The potential usefulness and value of MI was subsequently explored in a book chapter (Passmore and Whybrow, 2007), which also considered under what circumstances MI might be preferred to the more popular cognitive and behavioral coaching models used within organizations, and these ideas where developed further in a practice publication (Anstiss and Passmore, 2011).

Passmore *et al.* (2009) also used a practice journal to explore the use of MI with coaching clients through three separate case studies. Each argued that MI offered potential value to organizational clients and should be seen as an approach that was ready to be extended beyond its traditional focus in health contexts into the broad arena of the workplace. Also within the practice sphere has been a series of papers (Passmore, 2011b, 2011c, 2012a) that explored MI techniques for use with managers. These short technique-based papers have included the use of reflective listening, decision balance, and a typical day, each suitably adapted for use with people in organizations, as well as the ethical issues around using MI in an organizational setting where the coach may not have a specific agenda beyond seeking to provoke the motivation to act.

Whilst no organizational studies reviewing the impact of MI coaching have been published, there is growing interest in the technique within the UK following work by Passmore and Anstiss in promoting the approach at conferences and master classes (e.g., see Anstiss and Passmore, 2010).

# Future Research in Motivational Interview Coaching

Given the scarcity of MI coaching-based research in organizational settings there is considerable scope for valuable research. We suggest four main lines of inquiry:

1 To what extent is what coaches currently do in practice actually consistent with MI? This study would involve the coding and analysis of recorded coaching conversations using a validated and reliable measure of MI practice integrity such as the MITI 3.1 (Moyers *et al.*, 2011).

2 Do coaches whose practice is more MI consistent get better outcomes than coaches whose practice is less MI consistent?

3 Does MI-based coaching deliver better client outcomes than cognitive behavioral, systematic, or other coaching approaches? Perhaps in terms of performance, goal achievement, or satisfaction.

4 Does training coaches in MI result in more MI consistent coaching practice and/or improved coach or client outcomes?

It should be noted, however, that the developers of MI do not claim that it should be the sole or exclusive basis of a conversation. Only that it is a helpful way of helping a person to decide whether or not to change, and helping them to change and stay changed. Motivational interviewing is not a cognitive-behavioral skills practice (Miller and Rollnick, 2009) and so it is likely that a balanced approach to coaching – moving in and out of the MI stance – may eventually prove in the best interests of the client. One area where MI may prove particularly helpful is where the client feels stuck, uncertain about what to do, or deeply ambivalent about changing an aspect of their behavior despite other people being concerned. Changing due to external pressure would be considered "controlled" motivation. Motivational interviewing may help the client tap into and develop "autonomous" motivation, which may be good for both themselves and others.

## Conclusion

Motivational interviewing is a powerful, person-focused, respectful, guiding approach to helping people to change, helping to develop and strengthen client autonomous motivation and confidence. It works in a range of settings when delivered by a range of practitioners from a range of different backgrounds, but has yet to be rigorously tested as an approach to organizational coaching.

We hypothesize that once these studies are performed MI will show itself to be as (if not more) effective than other approaches – as has been the case when MI has been subjected to controlled trials in other contexts. This may be because MI works in harmony with natural human decision making processes, helping to supply key psychological nutriments and helping to create the right conditions for healthy and positive psychological growth to occur. Further, MI may represent a distillation of some of the effective ingredients of other approaches.

## References

Adamson, S. and Sellman, J.D. (2008) Five-year outcomes of alcohol-dependent persons treated with motivational enhancement. *Journal of Studies on Alcohol and Drugs*, 69(4), 589–93.

Amrhein, P.C., Miller, W.R., Yahne, C.E. Palmer, M., and Fulcher, L. (2003) Client commitment language during motivational interviewing predicts drug use outcomes. *Journal of Consulting and Clinical Psychology*, 71(5), 862–78.

Ang, D., Kesavalu, R., Lydon, J.R., Lane, K.A., and Bigatti, S. (2007) Exercise-based motivational interviewing for female patients with fibromyalgia: A case series. *Clinical Rheumatology,* 26(11), 1843–9.

Anshel, M.H. and Kang, M. (2008) Effectiveness of motivational interviewing on changes in fitness, blood lipids, and exercise adherence of police officers: An outcome-based action study. *Journal of Correctional Health Care,* 14(1), 48–62.

Anstiss, T. and Passmore, J. (2010) *Using Motivational Interviewing in Your Coaching Practice.* First International Coaching Psychology Congress (16 December). Invited paper: Integrated coaching. City University, London.

Anstiss, T. and Passmore, J. (2011) Motivational interview. In: M. Neenan and S. Palmer (eds) *Cognitive Behavioral Coaching In Practice: An Evidenced-based Approach.* London: Routledge.

Anstiss, B., Polaschek, D., and Wilson, M. (2011) A brief motivational intervention with prisoners: When you lead a horse to water, can it drink for itself? *Psychology, Crime and Law,* 1–22, iFirst.

Apodaca, T.R. and Longabaugh, R. (2009) Mechanisms of change in motivational interviewing: A review and preliminary evaluation of the evidence. *Addiction,* 104(5), 705–15.

Arkowitz, H., Westra, H.A., Miller, W.R., and Rollnick, S. (2007) *Motivational Interviewing in the Treatment of Psychological Problems.* New York: Guilford Press.

Armstrong, M.J., Mottershead, T.A., Ronksley, P.E., Sigal, R.J., Campbell, T.S., and Hemmelgarn, B.R. (2011) Motivational interviewing to improve weight loss in overweight and/or obese patients: A systematic review and meta-analysis of randomized controlled trials. *Obesity Reviews,* 12.

Austin, K.P., Williams, M.W.U., and Kilgour, G. (2011) The effectiveness of motivational interviewing with offenders: An outcome evaluation. *New Zealand Journal of Psychology,* 40(1), 55–67.

Baker, A., Richmond, R., Haile, M., Lewin, T.J., Carr, V.J., Taylor, R.L. *et al.* (2006) A randomized controlled trial of a smoking cessation intervention among people with a psychotic disorder. *American Journal of Psychiatry,* 163(11), 1934–42.

Barnet, B., Liu, J., DeVoe, M., Duggan, A.K., Gold, M.A., and Pecukonis, E. (2009) Motivational intervention to reduce rapid subsequent births to adolescent mothers: A community-based randomized trial. *Annals of Family Medicine,* 7(5), 436–45.

Barrowclough, C., Haddock, G., Tarrier, N., Lewis, S.W., Moring, J., O'Brien, R. *et al.* (2001) Randomized controlled trial of motivational interviewing, cognitive behavior therapy, and family intervention for patients with comorbid schizophrenia and substance use disorders. *American Journal of Psychiatry,* 158(10), 1706–13.

Bandura, A. (1977) Self-efficacy: Toward a unifying theory of behavioral change. *Psychological Review,* 84(2), 191–215.

Bandura, A. and Locke, E.A. (2003) Negative self-efficacy and goal effects revisited. *Journal of Applied Psychology,* 88(1), 87–99.

Behrman, A. (2006) Facilitating behavioral change in voice therapy: The relevance of motivational interviewing. *American Journal of Speech-Language Pathology,* 15(3), 215–25.

Bell, K.R., Temkin, N.R., Esselman, P.C., Doctor, J., Bombardier, C.H., Fraser, R.T. *et al.* (2005) The effect of a scheduled telephone intervention on outcome after moderate to severe traumatic brain injury: A randomized trial. *Archives of Physical Medicine and Rehabilitation,* 86(5), 851–6.

Benbassat, D.O., Dos Reis, P.C., Vandriette, Y.M., De Nutte, N., Corten, P., Verbanck, P. *et al.* (2008) Motivational interviewing increases physical activity in depressed inpatients. *European Psychiatry,* 23(6), S299–S299.

Bennett, J.A., Lyons, K.S., Winters-Stone, K., Nail, L.M., and Scherer, J. (2007) Motivational interviewing to increase physical activity in long-term cancer survivors: A randomized controlled trial. *Nursing Research,* 56(1), 18–27.

de Blok, B.M., de Greef, M.H., ten Hacken, N.H., Sprenger, S.R., Postema, K., and Wempe, J.B. (2006) The effects of a lifestyle physical activity counseling program with feedback of a pedometer during pulmonary rehabilitation in patients with COPD: A pilot study. *Patient Education and Counseling,* 61(1), 48–55.

Bolger, K., Carter, K., Curtin, L., Martz, D.M., Gagnon, S.G., and Michael, K.D. (2010) Motivational interviewing for smoking cessation among college students. *Journal of College Student Psychotherapy*, 24(2), 116–29.

Bombardier, C.H. and Rimmele, C.T. (1999) Motivational interviewing to prevent alcohol abuse after traumatic brain injury: A case series. *Rehabilitation Psychology*, 44(1), 52–67.

Bombardier, C.H., Bell, K.R., Temkin, N.R., Fann, J.R., Hoffman, J., and Dikmen, S. (2009) The efficacy of a scheduled telephone intervention for ameliorating depressive symptoms during the first year after traumatic brain injury. *Journal of Head Trauma Rehabilitation*, 24(4), 230–8.

Borrelli, B., McQuaid, E.L., Novak, S.P., Hammond, S.K., and Becker, B. (2010) Motivating Latino caregivers of children with asthma to quit smoking: A randomized trial. *Journal of Consulting and Clinical Psychology*, 78(1), 34–43.

Branscum, P. and Sharma, M. (2010) A review of motivational interviewing-based interventions targeting problematic drinking among college students. *Alcoholism Treatment Quarterly*, 28(1), 63–77.

Bricker, J.B. and Tollison, S.J. (2011) Comparison of motivational interviewing with acceptance and commitment therapy: A conceptual and clinical review. *Behavioral and Cognitive Psychotherapy*, Feb 22, 1–19.

Brodie, D.A. and Inoue, A. (2005) Motivational interviewing to promote physical activity for people with chronic heart failure. *Journal of Advanced Nursing*, 50(5), 518–27.

Brug, J., Spikmans, F., Aartsen, C., Breedveld, B., Bes, R., and Fereira, I. (2007) Training dietitians in basic motivational interviewing skills results in changes in their counseling style and in lower saturated fat intakes in their patients. *Journal of Nutrition Education and Behavior*, 39(1), 8–12.

Buckner, J.D. and Carroll, K.M. (2010) Effect of anxiety on treatment presentation and outcome: Results from the marijuana treatment project. *Psychiatry Research*, 178(3), 493–500.

Burke, B.L., Vassilev, G., Kantchelov, A., and Zweben, A. (2002) Motivational interviewing with couples. In: W.R. Miller and S. Rollnick (eds) *Motivational Interviewing: Preparing People for Change* (2nd edn). New York: Guilford Press. pp. 347–61.

Burke, B.L., Arkowitz, H., and Menchola, M. (2003) The efficacy of motivational interviewing: A meta-analysis of controlled clinical trials. *Journal of Consulting and Clinical Psychology*, 71(5), 843–61.

Burke, B.L., Dunn, C.W., Atkins, D.C., and Phelps, J.S. (2004) The emerging evidence base for motivational interviewing: A meta-analytic and qualitative inquiry. *Journal of Cognitive Psychotherapy*, 18(4), 309–22.

Campbell, M.K., Carr, C., DeVellis, B., Switzer, B., Biddle, A., Amamoo, M.A. *et al.* (2009) A randomized trial of tailoring and motivational interviewing to promote fruit and vegetable consumption for cancer prevention and control. *Annals of Behavioral Medicine*, 38(2), 71–85.

Carlbring, P., Jonsson, J., Josephson, H., and Forsberg, L. (2010) Motivational interviewing versus cognitive behavioral group therapy in the treatment of problem and pathological gambling: A randomized controlled trial. *Cognitive Behavior Therapy*, 39(2), 92–103.

Cassin, S.E., von Ranson, K.M., Heng, K., Brar, J., and Wojtowicz, A.E. (2008) Adapted motivational interviewing for women with binge eating disorder: A randomized controlled trial. *Psychology of Addictive Behaviors*, 22(3), 417–25.

Cavill, N., Hillsdon M., and Anstiss, T. (2011) *Brief Interventions for Weight Management*. Oxford: National Obesity Observatory.

Channon, S.J., Huws-Thomas, M.V., Rollnick, S., Hood, K., Cannings-John, R. L., Rogers, C. *et al.* (2007) A multicenter randomized controlled trial of motivational interviewing in teenagers with diabetes. *Diabetes Care*, 30(6), 1390–5.

Connell, A.M. and Dishion, T.J. (2008) Reducing depression among at-risk early adolescents: Three-year effects of a family-centered intervention embedded within schools. *Journal of Family Psychology*, 22(4), 574–85.

Cook, P.F., Emiliozzi, S., Waters, C., and El Hajj, D. (2008) Effects of telephone counseling on antipsychotic adherence and emergency department utilization. *American Journal of Managed Care*, 14(12), 841–6.

Cook, P.F., McCabe, M.M., Emiliozzi, S., and Pointer, L. (2009) Telephone nurse counseling improves HIV medication adherence: An effectiveness study. *The Journal of the Association of Nurses in AIDS Care*, 20(4), 316–25.

Cordova, J.V., Scott, R.L., Dorian, M., Mirgain, S., Yaeger, D., and Groot, A. (2005) The marriage checkup: An indicated preventive intervention for treatment-avoidant couples at risk for marital deterioration. *Behavior Therapy*, 36(4), 301–9.

Cutter, C. and Fiellin, D.A. (2010) Integrating screening, brief intervention, and referral to treatment with motivational work. In: P. Levounis and B. Arnaout (eds) *Handbook of Motivation and Change: A Practical Guide for Clinicians*. Arlington, VA: American Psychiatric. pp. 163–80.

Dale, J., Caramlau, I., Sturt, J., Friede, T., and Walker, R. (2009) Telephone peer-delivered intervention for diabetes motivation and support: The telecare exploratory RCT. *Patient Education and Counseling*, 75(1), 91–8.

Dean, H.Y., Rieger, E., and Thornton, C.E. (2008) Group motivational enhancement therapy as an adjunct to inpatient treatment for eating disorders: A preliminary study. *European Eating Disorders Review*, 16(4), 256–67.

Deas, D. and Clark, A. (2009) Current state of treatment for alcohol and other drug use disorders in adolescents. *Alcohol Research and Health*, 32(1), 76–82.

Deci, E.L. and Ryan R. M. (2008) Self-determination theory: A macrotheory of human motivation, development and health. *Canadian Psychology*, 49(3), 182–5.

DiMarco, I.D., Klein, D.A., Clark, V.L., and Wilson, G. T. (2009) The use of motivational interviewing techniques to enhance the efficacy of guided self-help behavioral weight loss treatment. *Eating Behaviors*, 10(2), 134–6.

Diskin, K.M. and Hodgins, D.C. (2009) A randomized controlled trial of a single session motivational intervention for concerned gamblers. *Behavior Research and Therapy*, 47(5), 382–8.

Draycott, S. and Dabbs, A. (1998) Cognitive dissonance 2: A theoretical grounding of motivational interviewing. *British Journal of Clinical Psychology*, Sep, 37, 355–64.

Everett, B., Davidson, P.M., Sheerin, N., Salamonson, Y., and DiGiacomo, M. (2008) Pragmatic insights into a nurse-delivered motivational interviewing intervention in the outpatient cardiac rehabilitation setting. *Journal of Cardiopulmonary Rehabilitation and Prevention*, 28(1), 61–4.

Farbring, C.Å. and Johnson, W.R. (2008) Motivational interviewing in the correctional system: An attempt to implement motivational interviewing in criminal justice. In: H. Arkowitz, H.A. Westra, W.R. Miller, and S. Rollnick (eds) *Motivational Interviewing in the Treatment of Psychological Problems*. New York: Guilford Press. pp. 304–23.

Fernandez, W.G., Winter, M.R., Mitchell, P.M., Bullock, H., Donovan, J., St. George, J. *et al.* (2009) Six-month follow-up of a brief intervention on self-reported safety belt use among emergency department patients. *Academic Emergency Medicine*, 16(11), 1221–4.

Flattum, C., Friend, S., Neumark-Sztainer, D., and Story, M. (2009) Motivational interviewing as a component of a school-based obesity prevention program for adolescent girls. *Journal of the American Dietetic Association*, 109(1), 91–4.

Floyd, R.L., Sobell, M., Velasquez, M.M., Ingersoll, K., Nettleman, M., Sobell, L. *et al.* (2007) Preventing alcohol-exposed pregnancies: A randomized controlled trial. *American Journal of Preventive Medicine*, 32(1), 1–10.

Fraser, J.S. and Solovey, A.D. (2007) Substance abuse and dependency. In: J.S. Fraser and A.D. Solovey (eds) *Second-order Change in Psychotherapy: The Golden Thread that Unifies Effective Treatments*. Washington, DC: American Psychological Association. pp. 223–44.

Freudenthal, J.J. (2008) Motivational interviewing (MI) as an intervention for early childhood caries risk-related behaviors. *Journal of Dental Hygiene*, 82(5), 67–67.

Freudenthal, J.J. and Bowen, D.M. (2010) Motivational interviewing to decrease parental risk-related behaviors for early childhood caries. *Journal of Dental Hygiene*, 84(1), 29–34.

Golin, C.E., Earp, J., Tien, H.C., Stewart, P., Porter, C., and Howie, L. (2006) A 2-arm, randomized, controlled trial of a motivational interviewing-based intervention to improve adherence to antiretroviral therapy (ART) among patients failing or initiating ART. *Journal of Acquired Immune Deficiency Syndromes*, 42(1), 42–51.

Grant, J.E., Donahue, C.B., Odlaug, B.L., Kim, S.W., Miller, M.J., and Petry, N.M. (2009) Imaginal desensitisation plus motivational interviewing for pathological gambling: Randomised controlled trial. *British Journal of Psychiatry*, 195(3), 266–7.

Greaves, C.J., Middlebrooke, A., O'Loughlin, L., Holland, S., Piper, J., Steele, A. *et al.* (2008) Motivational interviewing for modifying diabetes risk: A randomised controlled trial. *British Journal of General Practice*, 58(553), 535–40.

Groeneveld, I.F., Proper, K.I., van der Beek, A.J., van Duivenbooden, C., and van Mechelen, W. (2008) Design of a RCT evaluating the (cost-) effectiveness of a lifestyle intervention for male construction workers at risk for cardiovascular disease: The health under construction study. *BMC Public Health*, 8.

Habib, S., Morrissey, S., and Helmes, E. (2005) Preparing for pain management: A pilot study to enhance engagement. *The Journal of Pain*, 6(1), 48–54.

Halterman, J.S., Borrelli, B., Fisher, S., Szilagyi, P., and Yoos, L. (2008) Improving care for urban children with asthma: Design and methods of the school-based asthma therapy (SBAT) trial. *Journal of Asthma*, 45(4), 279–86.

Handmaker, N.S. and Walters, S.T. (2002) Motivational interviewing for initiating change in problem drinking and drug use. In: S.G. Hofmann and M.C. Tompson (eds) *Treating Chronic and Severe Mental Disorders: A Handbook of Empirically Supported Interventions*. New York: Guilford Press. pp. 215–33.

Hardcastle, S., Taylor, A., Bailey, M., and Castle, R. (2008) A randomised controlled trial on the effectiveness of a primary health care based counselling intervention on physical activity, diet and CHD risk factors. *Patient Education and Counseling*, 70(1), 31–9.

Heckman, C., Egleston, B., and Hofmann M. (2010) Efficacy of motivational interviewing for smoking cessation: A systematic review and meta-analysis. *Tobacco Control*, 19, 410–16.

Heffner, J.L., Tran, G.Q., Johnson, C.S., Barrett, S.W., Blom, T.J., Thompson, R.D. *et al.* (2010) Combining motivational interviewing with compliance enhancement therapy (MI-CET): Development and preliminary evaluation of a new, manual-guided psychosocial adjunct to alcohol-dependence pharmacotherapy. *Journal of Studies on Alcohol and Drugs*, 71(1), 61–70.

Higgins, E. (1987) Self-discrepancy: A theory relating self and affect. *Psychological Review*, 94(3), 319–40.

Holden, G. (1991) The relationship of self-efficacy appraisals to subsequent health-related outcomes: A meta-analysis. *Social Work in Health Care*, 16, 53–93.

Holden, G., Moncher, M.S., Schinke, S.P., and Barker, K.M. (1990) Self-efficacy of children and adolescents: A meta-analysis. *Psychological Reports*, 66, 1044–46.

Hoy, M.K., Winters, B.L., Chlebowski, R.T., Papoutsakis, C., Shapiro, A., Lubin, M.P. *et al.* (2009) Implementing a low-fat eating plan in the women's intervention nutrition study. *Journal of the American Dietetic Association*, 109(4), 688–96.

Hulse, G.K. and Tait, R.J. (2003) Five-year outcomes of a brief alcohol intervention for adult in-patients with psychiatric disorders. *Addiction*, 98(8), 1061–8.

Ismail, K., Maissi, E., Thomas, S., Chalder, T., Schmidt, U., Bartlett, J. *et al.* (2010) A randomised controlled trial of cognitive behavior therapy and motivational interviewing for people with type 1 diabetes mellitus with persistent sub-optimal glycaemic control: A diabetes and psychological therapies (ADaPT) study. *Health Technology Assessment*, 14(22), 1–101, iii–iv.

Johnston, B.D., Rivara, F.P., Droesch, R.M., Dunn, C., and Copass, M.K. (2002) Behavior change counseling in the emergency department to reduce injury risk: A randomized, controlled trial. *Pediatrics*, 110(2), 267–74.

Kadden, R.M., Litt, M.D., Kabela-Cormier, E., and Petry, N.M. (2007) Abstinence rates following behavioral treatments for marijuana dependence. *Addictive Behaviors*, 32(6), 1220–36.

Kertes, A., Westra, H.A., Angus, L., and Marcus, M. (2011) The impact of motivational interviewing on client experiences of cognitive behavioral therapy for generalized anxiety disorder. *Cognitive and Behavioral Practice*, 18(1), 55–69.

Kiene, S.M. and Barta, W.D. (2006) A brief individualized computer-delivered sexual risk reduction intervention increases HIV/AIDS preventive behavior. *Journal of Adolescent Health*, 39(3), 404–10.

Kistenmacher, B.R. and Weiss, R.L. (2008) Motivational interviewing as a mechanism for change in men who batter: A randomized controlled trial. *Violence and Victims*, 23(5), 558–70.

Klag, S., O'Callaghan, F., Creed, P., and Zimmer-Gembeck, M. (2009) Motivating young people towards success: Evaluation of a motivational interviewing-integrated treatment program for COD clients in a residential therapeutic community. *Therapeutic Communities*, 30(4), 366–86.

Kuyper, L., de Wit, J., Heijman, T., Fennema, H., van Bergen, J., and Vanwesenbeeck, I. (2009) Influencing risk behavior of sexually transmitted infection clinic visitors: Efficacy of a new methodology of motivational preventive counseling. *AIDS Patient Care and STDS*, 23(6), 423–31.

LaBrie, J.W., Pedersen, E.R., Thompson, A.D., and Earleywine, M. (2008) A brief decisional balance intervention increases motivation and behavior regarding condom use in high-risk heterosexual college men. *Archives of Sexual Behavior*, 37(2), 330–9.

Lundahl, B. and Burke, B.L. (2009) The effectiveness and applicability of motivational interviewing: A practice-friendly review of four meta-analyses. *Journal of Clinical Psychology*, 65(11), 1232–45.

Lundahl, B.W., Kunz, C., Brownell, C., Tollefson, D., and Burke, B.L. (2010) A meta-analysis of motivational interviewing: Twenty-five years of empirical studies. *Research on Social Work Practice*, 20(2), 137–60.

Magill, M., Apodaca, T., Barnett, N., and Monti, P. (2010) The route to change: Within sessions predictors of change plan completion in a motivational interview. *Journal of Substance Abuse Treatment*, 38(3), 299–305.

Markland, D., Ryan, R.M., Tobin, V.J., and Rollnick, S. (2005) Motivational interviewing and self-determination theory. *Journal of Social and Clinical Psychology*, 24(6), 811–31.

Martino, S., Ball, S.A., Nich, C., Frankforter, T.L., and Carroll, K.M. (2008) Community program therapist adherence and competence in motivational enhancement therapy. *Drug Alcohol Dependance*, 96(1–2), 37–48.

Mausbach, B.T., Semple, S.J., Strathdee, S.A., Zians, J., and Patterson, T.L. (2007) Efficacy of a behavioral intervention for increasing safer sex behaviors in HIV-negative, heterosexual methamphetamine users: Results from the fast-lane study. *Annals of Behavioral Medicine*, 34(3), 263–74.

Merlo, L.J., Storch, E., Lehmkuhl, H.D., Jacob, M.L., Murphy, T.K., Goodman, W.K. *et al.* (2010) Cognitive behavioral therapy plus motivational interviewing improves outcome for pediatric obsessive-compulsive disorder: A preliminary study. *Cognitive Behavior Therapy*, 39(1), 24–7.

Meyer, C., Muhlfeld, A., Drexhage, C., Floege, J., Goepel, E., Schauerte, P. *et al.* (2008) Clinical research for patient empowerment – a qualitative approach on the improvement of heart health promotion in chronic illness. *Medical Science Monitor*, 14(7), CR358–CR365.

Miller, W.R. (1983) Motivational interviewing with problem drinkers. *Behavioral Psychotherapy*, 11, 147–72.

Miller, W.R. (1996) Motivational interviewing: Research, practice, and puzzles. *Addictive Behaviors*. 21(6), 835–42.

Miller, W.R. and Rollnick, S. (2002) *Motivational Interviewing: Preparing People For Change* (2nd edn). New York: Guilford Press.

Miller, W. R. and Rollnick, S. (2009) Ten things that motivational interviewing is not. *Behavioural and Cognitive Psychotherapy*, 37(2), 129–40.

Miller, W.R. and Rollnick, S. (in press) *Motivational Interviewing* (3rd edn). New York: Guilford Press.

Miller, W.R. and Rose, G.S. (2009) Toward a theory of motivational interviewing. *American Psychologist*, 64(6), 527–37.

Miller, W.R., Benefield, R.G., and Tonigan, J.S. (1993) Enhancing motivation for change in problem drinking: A controlled comparison of two therapist styles. *Journal of Consulting and Clinical Psychology*, 61(3), 455–61.

Miller, W.R., Yahne, C.E., Moyers, T.B., Martinez, J., and Pirritano, M. (2004) A randomized trial of methods to help clinicians learn motivational interviewing. *Journal of Consulting and Clinical Psychology*, 72(6), 1050–62.

Moritz, S.E., Feltz, D.L., Fahrbach, K.R., and Mack, D.E. (2000) The relation of self-efficacy measures to sport performance: A meta-analytic review. *Research Quarterly for Exercise and Sport*, 71, 280–94.

Moyers, T. and Martin T. (2006) Therapist influence on client language during motivational interviewing sessions. *Journal of Substance Abuse Treatment*, 30(3), April, 245–251.

Moyers, T.B., Martin, T., Christopher, P.J., Houck, J.M. Tonigan, J.S., and Amrhein, P.C. (2007) Client language as a mediator of motivational interviewing efficacy: Where is the evidence? *Alcoholism: Clinical and Experimental Research*, 31, Issue Supplement s3, 40s–7s.

Moyers, T., Martin, T., Manuel, J., Miller, W., and Ernst D. (2011) MITI 3.1.1. Revised Global Scales: Motivational Interviewing Treatment Integrity 3.1.1. Retrieved from: http://casaa.unm.edu/download/MITI3_1.pdf (accessed July 17, 2011).

Multon, K.D., Brown, S.D., and Lent, R.W. (1991) Relation of self-efficacy beliefs to academic outcomes: A meta-analytic investigation. *Journal of Counseling Psychology*, 38, 30–38.

Musser, P.H., Semiatin, J.N., Taft, C.T., and Murphy, C.M. (2008) Motivational interviewing as a pregroup intervention for partner-violent men. *Violence and Victims*, 23(5), 539–57.

Naar-King, S. and Suarez, M. (2009) *Motivational Interviewing with Adolescents and Young Adults*. New York: Guilford Press.

Naar-King, S., Parsons, J.T., Murphy, D.A., Chen, X., Harris, D.R., and Belzer, M.E. (2009) Improving health outcomes for youth living with the human immunodeficiency virus: A multisite randomized trial of a motivational intervention targeting multiple risk behaviors. *Archives of Pediatric and Adolescent Medicine*, 163(12), 1092–8.

Ogedegbe, G., Chaplin, W., Schoenthaler, A., Statman, D., Berger, D., Richardson, T. *et al.* (2008) A practice-based trial of motivational interviewing and adherence in hypertensive African Americans. *American Journal of Hypertension*, 21(10), 1137–43.

Passmore, J. (2007a) Addressing deficit performance through coaching: Using motivational interviewing for performance improvement in coaching. *International Coaching Psychology Review*, 2(3), 265–79.

Passmore, J. (2007b) Integrative coaching: A model for executive coaching. *Consulting Psychology Journal: Practice and Research*, 59(1), 68–78.

Passmore, J. (2011a) Motivational interviewing – a model for coaching psychology practice. *The Coaching Psychologist*, 7(1), 35–9.

Passmore, J. (2011b) MI techniques – reflective listening. *The Coaching Psychologist*, 7(1), 49–52.

Passmore, J. (2011c) MI techniques – balance sheet. *The Coaching Psychologist*, 7(2).

Passmore, J. (2012a) MI techniques – typical day. *The Coaching Psychologist*, 8(1).

Passmore, J. (2012b) MI techniques: Recognising change talk. *The Coaching Psychologist*, 8(2).

Passmore, J. and Whybrow, A. (2007) Motivational interviewing: A specific approach for coaching psychologists. In: S. Palmer and A. Whybrow (eds) *The Handbook of Coaching Psychology*. London: Brunner-Routledge. pp. 160–73.

Passmore, J., Anstiss, T. and Ward, G. (2009) This way out: Motivational interviewing. *Coaching at Work*, 4(2), March, 38–41.

Patterson, G.R. and Forgatch, M.S. (1985) Therapist behavior as a determinant for client noncompliance: A paradox for the behavior modifier. *Journal of Consulting and Clinical Psychology*, 53(6), 846–51.

Penn, L., White, M., Oldroyd, J., Walker, M., Alberti, K.G., and Mathers, J.C. (2009) Prevention of type 2 diabetes in adults with impaired glucose tolerance: The European diabetes prevention RCT in Newcastle upon Tyne, UK. *BMC Public Health*, 9, 342.

Rasmussen, L.A., Hughes, M.J., and Murray, C.A. (2008) Applying motivational interviewing in a domestic violence shelter: A pilot study evaluating the training of shelter staff. *Journal of Aggression, Maltreatment and Trauma*, 17(3), 296–317.

Rau, J., Ehlebracht-Konig, I., and Petermann, F. (2008) Impact of a motivational intervention on coping with chronic pain: Results of a controlled efficacy study. *Schmerz*, 22(5), 575–8, 580–5.

Resnicow, K., Davis, R.E., Zhang, G., Konkel, J., Strecher, V.J., Shaikh, A.R. *et al.* (2008) Tailoring a fruit and vegetable intervention on novel motivational constructs: Results of a randomized study. *Annals of Behavioral Medicine*, 35(2), 159–69.

Resnicow, K., Jackson, A., Blissett, D., Wang, T., McCarty, F., Rahotep, S. *et al.* (2005) Results of the healthy body healthy spirit trial. *Health Psychology*, Jul, 24(4), 339–48.

Riegel, B., Dickson, V.V., Hoke, L., McMahon, J.P., Reis, B.F., and Sayers, S. (2006) A motivational counseling approach to improving heart failure self-care: Mechanisms of effectiveness. *Journal of Cardiovascular Nursing*, 21(3), 232–41.

Rollnick, S., Miller, W.R., and. Butler., C.C. (2007) *Motivational Interviewing in Health Care: Helping Patients Change Behavior*. New York: Guilford Press.

Rosengren, D.B. (2009) *Building Motivational Interviewing Skills: A Practitioner Workbook*. New York: Guilford Press.

Rubak, S., Sandbaek, A., Lauritzen, T., and Christensen, B. (2005) Motivational interviewing: A systematic review and meta-analysis. *British Journal of General Practice*, 55(513), 305–12.

Rubak, S., Sandbaek, A., Lauritzen, T., Borch-Johnsen, K., and Christensen, B. (2009) General practitioners trained in motivational interviewing can positively affect the attitude to behavior change in people with type 2 diabetes. One year follow-up of an RCT, ADDITION Denmark. *Scandinavian Journal of Primary Health Care*, 27(3), 172–9.

Runyon, M.K., Deblinger, E., and Schroeder, C.M. (2009) Pilot evaluation of outcomes of combined parent-child cognitive-behavioral group therapy for families at risk for child physical abuse. *Cognitive and Behavioral Practice*, 16(1), 101–18.

Ryan, R.M., Deci, E.L., Grolnick, W.S., and LaGuardia, J.G. (2006) The significance of autonomy and autonomy support in psychological development and psychopathology. In: D. Cicchetti and D. Cohen (eds) *Developmental Psychopathology: Theory and Methods* (2nd edn, vol 1, pp. 295–849). New York: John Wiley and Sons.

Sadri, G. and Robertson, I.T. (1993) Self-efficacy and work-related behavior: A review and meta-analysis. *Applied Psychology: An International Review*, 42, 139–52.

Santa Ana, E.J., Wulfert, E., and Nietert, P.J. (2007) Efficacy of group motivational interviewing (GMI) for psychiatric in-patients with chemical dependence. *Journal of Consulting and Clinical Psychology*, 75(5), 816–22.

Schermer, C.R., Moyers, T.B., Miller, W.R., and Bloomfield, L.A. (2006) Trauma center brief interventions for alcohol disorders decrease subsequent driving under the influence arrests. *Journal of Trauma*, 60(1), 29–34.

Schmaling, K.B., Blume, A.W., and Afari, N. (2001) A randomized controlled pilot study of motivational interviewing to change attitudes about adherence to medications for asthma. *Journal of Clinical Psychology in Medical Settings*, 8(3), 167–72.

Schoener, E.P., Madeja, C.L., Henderson, M.J., Ondersma, S.J., and Janisse, J.J. (2006) Effects of motivational interviewing training on mental health therapist behavior. *Drug and Alcohol Dependence*, 82(3), 269–75.

Scott, C.K. and Dennis, M.L. (2009) Results from two randomized clinical trials evaluating the impact of quarterly recovery management checkups with adult chronic substance users. *Addiction*, 104(6), 959–71.

Sinha, R., Easton, C., Renee-Aubin, L., and Carroll, K.M. (2003) Engaging young probation-referred marijuana-abusing individuals in treatment: A pilot trial. *American Journal of Addiction*, 12(Jul-Sep, 4), 314–23.

Skaret, E., Weinstein, P., Kvale, G., and Raadal, M. (2003) An intervention program to reduce dental avoidance behavior among adolescents: A pilot study. *European Journal of Paediatric Dentistry*, 4(4), 191–6.

Slavet, J.D., Stein, L.A., Klein, J.L., Colby, S.M., Barnett, N.P., and Monti, P.M. (2005) Piloting the family check-up with incarcerated adolescents and their parents. *Psychological Services*, 2(2), 123–32.

Soria, R., Legido, A., Escolano, C., Lopez Yeste, A., and Montoya, J. (2006) A randomised controlled trial of motivational interviewing for smoking cessation. *British Journal of General Practice*, 56(531), 768–74.

Stajkovic, A.D. and Luthans, F. (1998) Self-efficacy and work-related performance: A meta-analysis. *Psychological Bulletin*, 124, 240–61.

Swartz, H.A., Zuckoff, A., Frank, E., Spielvogle, H.N., Shear, M.K., Fleming, M.A.D. *et al.* (2006) An open-label trial of enhanced brief interpersonal psychotherapy in depressed mothers whose children are receiving psychiatric treatment. *Depression and Anxiety*, 23(7), 398–404.

Thevos, A., Quick, R., and Yanduli, V. (2000) Motivational interviewing enhances the adoption of water disinfection practices in Zambia. *Health Promotion International*, 15(3), 207.

Tyron, W. and Misurell, J. (2008) Dissonance induction and reduction: A possible principle and connectionist mechanism for why therapies are effective. *Clinical Psychology Review*, 28, 1297–309.

Vader, A.M., Walters, S.T., Prabhu, G.C., Houck, J.M., and Field, C.A. (2010) The language of motivational interviewing and feedback: Counselor language, client language, and client drinking outcomes. *Psychology of Addictive Behaviors*, 24(2), 190–7.

Vansteenkiste, M. and Sheldon, K.M. (2006) There's nothing more practical than a good theory: Integrating motivational interviewing and self-determination theory. *British Journal of Clinical Psychology*, 45(1), 63–82.

Vasilaki, E.I., Hosier, S.G., and Cox, W.M. (2006) The efficacy of motivational interviewing as a brief intervention for excessive drinking: A meta-analytic review. *Alcohol and Alcoholism*, 41(3), 328–35.

Velasquez, M.M., von Sternberg, K., Johnson, D.H., Green, C., Carbonari, J.P., and Parsons, J.T. (2009) Reducing sexual risk behaviors and alcohol use among HIV-positive men who have sex with men: A randomized clinical trial. *Journal of Consulting and Clinical Psychology*, 77(4), 657–67.

Viner, R.M., Christie, D., Taylor, V., and Hey, S. (2003) Motivational/solution-focused intervention improves HbA1c in adolescents with Type 1 diabetes: A pilot study. *Diabetic Medicine*, 20(9), 739–42.

Wagner, C. and Ingersoll, K. (2008) Beyond cognition: Broadening the emotional base of motivational interviewing. *Journal of Psychotherapy Integration*, 18, 191–206.

Watkins, C.L., Auton, M.F., Deans, C.F., Dickinson, H.A., Jack, C.I., Lightbody, C.E. *et al.* (2007) Motivational interviewing early after acute stroke: A randomized, controlled trial. *Stroke*, 38(3), 1004–9.

Watkins, C.L., Wathan, J.V., Leathley, M.J., Auton, M.F., Deans, C.F., and Dickinson, H.A. (2011) The 12-month effects of early motivational interviewing after acute stroke: A randomized controlled trial. *Stroke*, Jul, 42(7), 1956–61.

Weinstein, P., Harrison, R., and Benton, T. (2004) Motivating parents to prevent caries in their young children: One-year findings. *Journal of the American Dental Association*, 135(6), 731–8.

Weinstein, P., Harrison, R., and Benton, T. (2006) Motivating mothers to prevent caries: Confirming the beneficial effect of counseling. *Journal of the American Dental Association*, 137(6), 789–93.

Wenzel, S.L., D'Amico, E.J., Barnes, D., and Gilbert, M.L. (2009) A pilot of a tripartite prevention program for homeless young women in the transition to adulthood. *Womens Health Issues*, 19(3), 193–201.

West, D.S., DiLillo, V., Bursac, Z., Gore, S.A., and Greene, P.G. (2007) Motivational interviewing improves weight loss in women with type 2 diabetes. *Diabetes Care*, 30(5), 1081–7.

Westra, H.A. and Arkowitz, H. (2010) Combining motivational interviewing and cognitive behavioural therapy to increase treatment efficacy for generalized anxiety disorder. In: D. Sookman and B. Leahy (eds) *Resolving Treatment Impasses with Resistant Anxiety Disorders*. Abingdon: Routledge. pp. 199–232.

Westra, H.A. and Dozois, D.J. (2006) Preparing clients for cognitive behavioral therapy: And randomized pilot study of motivational interviewing for anxiety. *Cognitive Therapy and Research*, 30, 481–98.

Westra, H.A. and Dozois, D.J.A. (2008) Integrating motivational interviewing into the treatment of anxiety. In: H. Arkowitz, H.A. Westra, W.R. Miller, and S. Rollnick (eds) *Motivational Interviewing in the Treatment of Psychological Problems.* New York: Guilford Press. pp. 26–56.

Woollard, J., Burke, V., Beilin, L.J., Verheijden, M., and Bulsara, M.K. (2003) Effects of a general practice-based intervention on diet, body mass index and blood lipids in patients at cardiovascular risk. *Journal of Cardiovascular Risk*, 10(1), 31–40.

Wulfert, E., Blanchard, E.B., Freidenberg, B.M., and Martell, R.S. (2006) Retaining pathological gamblers in cognitive behavior therapy through motivational enhancement: A pilot study. *Behavior Modification*, 30(3), 315–40.

# 19

# Psychodynamic Approach

## Michael A. Diamond

## Introduction

Psychodynamic executive coaching takes into account three major perspectives arising from three theoretical traditions – classical, object relations, and systems. This chapter explains many elements of these three frameworks as represented by three leaders in executive coaching – Levinson, Kets de Vries, and Kilburg. Also included are discussions of organizational role analysis and Bion's theory of group dynamics. Each of these theories illuminates different dimensions of what executive coaches encounter relative to leadership, groups, and organizational dynamics, the context in which executives experience a sense of self, actions, and outcomes.

Contemporary psychoanalysis is predicated on the value of authenticity and the idea of a true self hidden behind the veil of a false self. The false self, like the ego, is a stable and recurring, continuously operative structure. Pediatrician and psychoanalyst D.W. Winnicott (1971) observed that some individuals suffer a false self-disorder – a particular way of viewing the schizoid character – but he repeatedly asserted that this separation of self into true and false is also normal. True and false thus refer not to a moral order, but to qualities in self-other experiences that support spontaneous expression (true self) or reactive living (false self) (Moore and Fine, 1990). Authenticity is an element of the idea of true self, which requires self-consciousness and attentiveness to the executive's own impact on others and in turn others effect on the executive in role. Thus, psychodynamic executive coaching is, at its core, about self-understanding and truth. These truths include the ideas of psychological (or psychic) reality and sense of self (consciousness, awareness) in the world of work.

Psychological (or psychic) reality, which is synonymous with the terms inner reality and subjective reality, is a cornerstone of executive consultation. The relational and experiential disposition of the executive in the context of his or her organization becomes the pivotal point of investigation and consciousness. The concept of self (or self-organization)

*The Wiley Blackwell Handbook of the Psychology of Coaching and Mentoring*, First Edition.
Edited by Jonathan Passmore, David B. Peterson, and Teresa Freire.
© 2013 John Wiley & Sons, Ltd. Published 2016 by John Wiley & Sons, Ltd.

refers to the individual's manner of cognitively and emotionally organizing experience and perceptions of self and others at work (Diamond and Allcorn, 2009).

This notion of self is a critical concept in attending to executive dispositions, psychological defenses, and anxieties, and in promoting conscious and reflective practice. Psychodynamic approaches to executive coaching focus on unconscious (emotional and cognitive) processes, and relational and group dynamics in the executive's mind. Articulation between consultant/coach and clients about unconscious dynamics facilitate deeper understanding of the meaning of actual interpersonal exchanges and influences in the external world of work. The psychodynamic process moves the consultant's and client's attentiveness beyond behavioristic observations and toward the defensive sources of inattention and deficiency in (false, inauthentic, compliant, and reactive) self and other relations at work. As noted above, the development of psychodynamic coaching is explored by describing and explaining approaches to executive coaching and consultation in the writings of Levinson (1962, 1968, 1970, 1972, 1981, 2002), Kets de Vries (1984, 1991, 2006, 2007, 2010), and Kilburg (2000, 2004a, 2004b, 2004c, 2005). These three approaches were chosen due to their overall influence on psychodynamic coaching and consultation and their use of different psychoanalytic schools of thought – classical ego psychology, object relational, and an integrated and cross-disciplinary systems model, respectively. Organizational role analysis (Newton *et al.*, 2006) originating with the group relations traditions of Tavistock and A.K. Rice Institutes is also briefly discussed. In the following, psychodynamic theories and concepts are applied to understanding organizations and to practicing coaching and consultation. Finally, a summary of psychodynamic approaches to coaching and recommendations for future research are presented.

# The Theoretical Development of Psychodynamic Coaching

Psychodynamic approaches to organizations have evolved most visibly over the Past 25 years or so. This evolution and emergence is rooted in the clinical paradigm of psychoanalysis and in particular the psychoanalytic study of organizations (Czander, 1993; Diamond, 1993; Gabriel, 1999; Kets de Vries *et al.*, 1991; Sievers, 2009). Within psychoanalysis there are a number of competing schools of thought that are also represented in the work of psychoanalytically-oriented consultants to organizations, which is reflected in a multiplicity of psychodynamic approaches to executive coaching and consultation.

Psychoanalytic theory is comprised of at least three major schools of thought: classical psychoanalytic theory (and ego psychology) rooted in the Freudian drive and structural model, psychoanalytic object relations theory rooted in the (Kleinian and Winnicottian) relational (object-seeking) model, and (Kohutian) self-psychology rooted in a mixed model with a particular focus on the developmental lines of narcissism and self-organization. One of the better overviews of the evolving psychoanalytic paradigms and schools of thought is *Object Relations in Psychoanalytic Theory* (Greenberg and Mitchell, 1983). Contemporary approaches to executive coaching take a pluralistic approach relying primarily on object relations theory, but not exclusively. Thus, most psychodynamic approaches integrate ideas and concepts from all three schools of thought. And, while these three schools of psychoanalytic thought are predominant, it ought to be mentioned that Lacanian psychoanalytic theory and other postmodern and poststructuralist approaches are also applied to social and organizational phenomena as well (Arnaud, 2003; Driver, 2009). In the following section, the works of Levinson, Kets de Vries, Kilburg, and Newton *et al.* are discussed. However, a wide number of others have also contributed to the development of the approach (e.g., Brunning, 2006; Lee, 2009, 2010; Peltier, 2010). The contributions of organization psychologist Harry Levinson and his introduction of the idea of a psychological contract are reviewed.

## Psychodynamic models

*A focus on desires, needs, and expectations in context*   Levinson *et al.* (1962) introduced the concept of a *psychological contract* where he explained how a particular dialogue between employer and employee might shape mutual expectations as a key ingredient to successful organizational membership and affiliation. Levinson's notion of a psychological contract encompassed an acknowledgement of conscious and unconscious human needs and desires as well as the complexity of authority relations. Employees are emotionally invested in their relationship to the organization and its leadership – a *transference* of emotions tie individuals and their identities to their work organizations. In psychoanalytic theory, transference dynamics represent the degree to which past experiences from childhood shape and influence perceptions of others particularly those in positions of authority in the present moment, often projected emotions from the past may distort present relationships. Transference dynamics are often characterized by mirroring, on the one hand, and idealizing, on the other. Mirroring transference refers to the individual unconscious desire for others to reinforce a need to be seen as omnipotent and grandiose, the narcissistic leader who requires admiring and adoring followers and who views him- or herself as god-like. Idealizing transference is the opposite side of the coin in which followers are in search of leaders to idealize and admire – the unconscious need for an all-powerful leader where followers feel safer and grander simply by being in his or her proximity. Unless management is psychologically aware of and attentive to these manifest and latent dimensions of worker motivation, it is highly unlikely that employees will feel adequately taken care of by their employers. For Levinson, this managerial oversight and deficiency can lead to demoralization and poor performance.

The psychological contract became a valuable conceptual tool for managers, consultants, and executive coaches as they considered failures of supervision and communication between supervisors and subordinates, executives, and their staff. Application of the psychological contract between employer and employee requires perpetual dialogue between the parties, acknowledging the dynamics of mutual emotional needs and expectations, conscious and unconscious. Levinson highlighted the significance of the ego ideal for individual motivation. He came to view the management of the ego ideal as crucial to successful mentoring and central to the psychological contract. He simply defined the idea of the ego ideal as one's image of oneself at one's future best. The value of this concept was shaped by his earliest thinking about motivation, career development, mentoring, and emotional well-being at work. Most fundamentally, his emphasis on the ego ideal acknowledged the nature of emotional attachments to organizations and the world of work.

Levinson (1964) observed that supervisors had difficulty managing. In particular, he saw a problem for managers that some individuals understood intuitively yet had no psychological basis for articulation and correction. Managers often felt conflicted, that is *guilty*, about evaluating subordinate performance, especially when the evaluation required negative and critical feedback of the employee's work.

Levinson not only explained the psychodynamics of guilt, he emphasized the human compassion inherent in and necessary for providing subordinates with unambiguous, direct, and honest feedback in performance evaluation. From the notion of "management-by-guilt" supervisors came to better appreciate their ambivalent feelings surrounding the act of subordinate evaluations. They also came to appreciate the value of sincere feedback in the development of subordinate career opportunities. Consultants and executive coaches learned to pay attention to these difficulties of supervision and provide help to their clients. Out of these insights surrounding the individual ego ideal of workers, managers, and executives, Levinson came to stress the leadership's role in mentoring and educating workers and managers.

In his book *Executive*, Levinson (1981) directs managers to pay attention to three primary human drives: ministration, maturation, and mastery. In the caretaking practice of *ministration* needs for gratification, closeness, support, protection, and guidance are served. In supporting human developmental requirements, *maturation* needs for creativity, originality, self-control, and reality testing are supplied. And, given the demands for self-competence and confidence, *mastery* needs that encompass individual demands for ambitious striving, realistic achievement, rivalry with affection, and consolidation are satisfied. With these human needs in mind, executive coaches and consultants might assist executives by engaging in more thoughtful and reflective dialogues with their managers and workers, thereby establishing management systems more responsive to individual potential and desire for advancement. Motivation could be understood as multidimensional and leaders with the assistance of coaches might facilitate growth and maturation in their own executive careers and the careers of their employees. One cannot help but reflect on how challenging such sensitivity to human needs of workers has become in our contemporary global economy of volatility, downsizing, and re-engineering.

In *Executive*, Levinson (1981 revised) provides a psychoanalytic framework for problem diagnosis. The framework is designed to assist executives and managers in problem solving focused on personnel conflicts and performance issues, providing a template for analyzing troublesome human relations at work and a practical application of a psychodynamic approach to executive coaching.

Starting with the concept of the ego ideal in the work setting, the executive coach or consultant might consider the degree to which the individual executive feels he or she has lived up to their ideal self-image, and the degree to which that ideal maybe within or may be out of reach of what is plausible for them given their current self-image and the organizational realities they must contend with. Many consultants and executive coaches can appreciate the frequency with which executives, managers, and workers feel they fall short of their personal goals or are not working at their level of competency and training. A large gap between one's self-image and ego ideal may produce low self-esteem according to Levinson. It also might produce anger and resentment as a consequence of disappointment.

Next, individual needs for *affection* and the desire to develop closer ties with colleagues and fellow workers ought to be considered. One might reflect on the value of attending to human needs for affection among workers and their relations to executives. This might entail taking into account an executive's proclivity to "move toward or away from" others such as his staff and fellow workers. Paying attention to the emotional tensions of *transference and counter-transference* dynamics as evidenced by the executive's patterns of relationships at work is critical to accessing insights into what is happening to feelings of affection in the workplace.

Next, how the individual executive copes with *aggression* at work is considered. Here the influences of classical psychoanalytic drive theory and ego psychology come through in an implicit acknowledgement of the role of work as a form of sublimation. As executive coaches or consultants we might look at the degree to which the individual executive "moves against" others in a manner that might be experienced as intimidating, hostile, abrasive, or intrusive to employees. Opportunities to observe, discuss, and reflect on these destructive proclivities is a constructive dimension of executive coaching and consultation. Fostering awareness of *transference and counter-transference* dynamics as evidenced and contextualized in patterns of behavior and conflicts between executives and their colleagues is critical to self and other awareness.

Finally, Levinson's model encourages paying attention to how executives (managers and workers) manifest human *dependency* needs (1981, p. 33). Given the hierarchic structure of most organizations, the phenomenon of dependency enables executive coaches and consultants to examine once again the psychodynamics of *transference and counter-transference* in the context of super- and subordinate relationships. Is the degree of dependency appropriate or inappropriate, constructive or destructive, progressive or regressive? Co-dependencies can emerge as well in which executives provoke, often unconsciously, subordinate behavior that renders adult workers in un-adult-like roles – what in psychoanalytic theory is called psychological *regression*.

Levinson (1964) formulated a framework for problem analysis that remains helpful to executive coaches and consultants. In the context of a comprehensive consultation (including organizational diagnosis and assessment) with the leader and her organization, the executive coach or consultant considers the following general questions: Who is in pain? When did it begin? What is happening to this individual's needs for aggression, affection, and dependency? What is the nature of their ego ideal? Is the problem solvable? How? In so doing, Levinson illustrates how one can arrange and interpret data (in a psychodynamically-informed way) around problems and conflicts that might otherwise leave executives and their managers perplexed and seemingly without recourse.

Levinson (1972, 2002) depicts the complexity of diagnosing and assessing organizations with the mishmash of data: factual, historical, genetic, and interpretive (narrative), which taken together comprise open systems as integrative and adaptive processes of operation. This diagnostic/clinical framework is an adaptation of an open systems model for the purpose of studying and analyzing organizations. If properly contextualized, strategies of intervention and change such as executive coaching ought to be governed in part by organizational diagnosis and assessment. In the case of executive coaching, the organizational diagnosis provides needed context for examining relational and experiential psychological dynamics. As a product of organizational diagnosis, the organizational story with its thematic patterns and points of urgency is significant and proffers concrete examples of the executive's key relationships and cognitive-emotional schema. Levinson's legacy for executive coaching is one that seriously questions coaching without context, and context for reflectivity produces more thoughtful and humane leadership. This emphasis on context in the form of independent organizational diagnosis and assessment adds validity, greater opportunities for reality testing, client ownership, claimed action and personal responsibility, depth, and richness of understanding to the examination of *transference and counter-transference* dynamics between executives and staff, as well as between psychodynamically-oriented executive coaches and their clients.

*A focus on character and the inner theater of leaders*   In contrast with Levinson's application of psychoanalytic ego psychology to executive coaching, and his emphasis on the management of human needs and expectations, Manfred Kets de Vries (2006) takes psychoanalytic object relations theory (and, to a lesser degree, self-psychology) as the clinical paradigm for interpreting executive character and individual dispositions. He writes: "Character is the sum of the deeply ingrained patterns of behavior that define an individual" (p. 52).

Psychoanalytic object relations theory starts from the maturational premise of healthy, primary narcissism as a by-product of good enough parenting during infancy and early childhood. In this developmental schema, the emerging sense of self evolves from a state of attachment and total dependency. Thus, the infant begins life from a symbiotic and dedifferentiated position, one in which the child is in fact at the center of the parent-child universe. In this primitive state, cognitive capacity, nascent brain and emotional development, are signified by part object relationships where the other is experienced and perceived in simplistic absolutes such as either all good or all bad, always loving or always hating, only accepting, or only rejecting. In developmental transition the young child eventually and ambivalently moves physically, cognitively, and emotionally, away from primary caregivers and toward a more independent, holistic, and integrated sense of self. For example, the child's early mobility in crawling away from the parent and simultaneously turning back toward the parent for cues to see if all is OK. Assuming a positive and reassuring signal, the child continues onward in exploration of the external yet unknown object world. Developmental experiences of separation, differentiation, and individuation confront the child with a jumble of contrary emotions. These maturational realities of separation and loss include acknowledging paradox and an imperfect and depressive object (self and other) world of pain and pleasure, acceptance and rejection, love and hate.

Kets de Vries's clinical paradigm is shaped by several psychoanalytic and developmental theorists, starting with John Bowlby's attachment research. Bowlby's developmental stages of attachment, separation, and loss, are critical ideas for interpreting the psychodynamics of significant (self and other) adult relationships. Highlighted in these clinical and developmental findings and also found in Levinson's work is the treatment of change as emotional loss – a concept important to working empathically with participants undergoing organizational transitions. Also, Kets de Vries's clinical paradigm is shaped by the ground-breaking theories of (pediatrician and psychoanalyst) D.W. Winnicott, who like Melanie Klein emphasizes the emotional and developmental significance of self and other (internalized object relations) concepts from infancy and early childhood. Winnicott's transformational childhood highlights of "good enough mothering" and "holding environments" signify object (self and other) relationships that at their best facilitate and nurture psychological safety, interpersonal security, emotional bonding, and maturation – attributes at the core of self-cohesion and integrity. For Winnicott, good enough mothering and adequate holding environments are characterized as *transitional and potential spaces* for playing and creativity and are represented in childhood by *transitional objects* such as teddy bears and blankets. Correspondingly, in adulthood, individuals engage in playing and creative imagination through music, art, entertainment, and culture. These activities serve as transitional objects – objects of our creative efforts derived from the psychological and experiential space located between fantasy and reality. Ideally, work and vocation serve as transitional, if not transformational, objects. In addition, Winnicott's ideas of true (authentic) and false (compliant) self shape Kets de Vries's emphasis on the value of authenticity between leaders and followers, and with the organizational cultures they promote and reproduce. These values of true and false self and their relevance are revisited later in the chapter. Next, analysis of leaders and followers requires an understanding of group psychodynamics.

Kets de Vries's clinical paradigm is also shaped by W.R. Bion's writings on the experiences of groups. In particular, his conceptions of work groups (primary task group) operating in parallel with underlying (unconscious) basic assumption groups, such as fight-flight groups, dependency groups, and the phenomenon of pairing or utopian groups. Bion's theory of groups is discussed in relation to organizational role analysis later in the chapter. This interpretive framework for group dynamics is particularly instructive in identifying psychologically-regressive interpersonal dynamics within organizations under stressful conditions. Both Levinson and Kets de Vries stress that it is important to keep in mind that groups and organizations are the context in which executive coaching and consultation take place. Next, I discuss the vital concept of narcissism followed by a brief description of leaders' and followers' dispositions as presented in the clinical theory of Kets de Vries. He writes: "The aim of clinically informed leadership coaching is not a temporary high, but lasting change. They [leaders] want to move beyond reductionistic formulas to sustainable transformation" (Kets de Vries *et al.* 2007, p. Li).

In *The Leader on the Couch: A Clinical Approach to Changing People and Organizations*, Kets de Vries (2006) reviews narcissism in leaders, and in particular examines the nuance of constructive versus reactive narcissism. In the psychoanalytic literature the degree to which narcissism is constructive or destructive is frequently identified by the idea of "primary narcissism" typical of early life and "malignant narcissism" as defining compensatory and pathological forms of narcissism in adulthood. Ironically, narcissism is a relational concept and therefore it ought to be seen through the lens of a two-person psychology such as object relations theory and self-psychology. A key concept in the interpretation of narcissism is the psychoanalytic idea of *transference* – what Kets de Vries (2006) calls the "t-word".

In his clinical application of object relations theory to organizations and their leaders, Kets de Vries (1984, 2006) draws on Melanie Klein's (1946, 1959) important discovery of the infantile roots of adulthood paranoid-schizoid and depressive positions and on Heinz Kohut's (1977) notion of the prevalence of narcissistic personalities through *mirroring and idealizing transference* dynamics. On the matter of *mirroring* Kets de Vries (2006) writes:

> Within organizations, the mirroring process between leaders and followers can become collusive. Followers use leaders to reflect what they want to see, and leaders rarely resist that kind of affirmation. The result is a mutual admiration society. Leaders... tend to take actions designed to shore up their image rather than serve the needs of the organization. In times of change, embedded mirroring processes can be fatal to the organization. (pp. 43–4)

While, on the complementary matter of *idealizing transference* he writes:

> Through this idealizing process, we hope to combat feelings of helplessness and acquire some of the power of the person admired. Idealizing transference is a kind of projective shield for followers. Reactive narcissists are especially responsive to this sort of administration, often becoming so dependent upon it that they can't function without the emotional fix. It's a two-way street, of course: followers project their fantasies onto their leaders, and leaders mirror themselves in the glow of their followers. (p. 44)

Mirroring and idealizing transference dynamics represent an inescapable paradox of narcissism and leadership. Leaders require followers who legitimize their power and authority (real or imagined), and of course followers need leaders who direct and inspire them. Mirroring and idealizing transference is a dyadic relationship in which the leader defines the character and emotionality of the follower and vice versa. In sum, narcissistic leaders demand idealizing and adoring followers who reinforce their defensive and compensatory need for idealization and grandiosity. Whether leaders are constructive or reactive narcissists depends on the nature and quality of these transference dynamics, and the degree to which organizational strategies and structures minimize unilateral, expansive, and grandiose leadership style.

In particular, the degree to which the personality of the narcissistic leader is driven by infantile narcissistic injuries and associated rage and hostility matters when it comes to the character of executives in role. Discovering leaders with flexibility and the capacity to openly reflect and consider change as opposed to leaders who react with rigidity and inflexibility as manifested in persistent resistance distinguishes constructive from reactive narcissists. Constructive narcissistic leaders are transformational and inspiring role models. They are capable of assuming responsibility for their actions and less prone to blaming others. Their vision extends beyond themselves. In contrast, reactive narcissists are troubled by inadequacies, bitterness, anger, depressive thoughts, lingering feelings of emptiness, and deprivation. Attempting to master feelings of inadequacy and insecurity, they construct an exaggerated sense of self-importance and self-grandiosity along with an associated desire for admiration. Reactive narcissists lack empathy and are unable to understand what others feel and experience. This latter observation may be critical in one's expectations about the value of executive coaching and consultation with "reactive" narcissists. If empathy is seemingly absent in our executive clients, one might ask whether or not it is sufficient and helpful to engage in coaching rather than recommending psychotherapy. Similar to arguments made by psychoanalyst Otto Kernberg who has written on the subject of regression in leadership and organizations (1998), Kets de Vries (2006) suggests "downsizing" the negative and potentially destructive impact of narcissistic leaders on workers and organizations. Writing specifically of boards of directors, he states:

> Organizations need not be helpless in the face of reactive narcissistic leadership. They can take action, both preemptive and follow-up. Strategies include distributing decision-making and erecting barriers against runaway leadership; improving the selection, education, and evaluation of board members; and offering coaching and counseling to executives showing signs of excessive narcissism. (p. 46)

In working with varying degrees of narcissism in leaders, executive coaches and consultants might consider the following questions: How dependent is this executive on the admiration of his staff through the mirroring transference? To what degree are staff dependent on their need to admire and aggrandize their leaders through idealizing transference? To what degree are followers responsible for projecting omnipotent qualities onto their executives? To what extent do leaders move against or away from followers as opposed to moving toward followers in the form of cooperation and collaboration as opposed to unilateralism and deception?

Finally, on the spectrum of personalities in the dispositions of leaders and followers Kets de Vries (2006) writes: "Prototypes aren't depictions of mental disorders: each one includes a range of human behavior, from normal to dysfunctional, because normality and pathology are relative concepts, positions on a spectrum" (p. 57). Reflecting on their proclivities for leadership and followership, eleven prototypes on a continuum of personalities include: (1) the *narcissistic* disposition with very high leadership tendencies and low follower tendencies; (2) the *dramatic* disposition with medium leadership tendencies and high follower tendencies; (3) the *controlling* disposition with high leadership tendencies and high follower tendencies; (4) the *dependent* disposition with very low leadership tendencies and high follower tendencies; (5) the *self-defeating* disposition with very low leadership tendencies and high follower tendencies; (6) the *detached* disposition with medium leadership tendencies and medium follower tendencies; (7) the *depressive* disposition with low leadership tendencies and low follower tendencies; (8) the *abrasive* disposition with medium leadership tendencies and low follower tendencies; (9) the *paranoid* disposition with high leadership tendencies and medium follower tendencies; (10) the *negativistic* disposition with very low leadership tendencies and medium follower tendencies; and (11) the *antisocial* disposition with high leadership tendencies and low follower tendencies.

In this approach to executive coaching and consultation, these dispositions or core conflictual relational themes not only have consequences for relations between leaders and followers, but also for productive and counter-productive strategizing, decision making, delegating and structuring, and organizational dynamics. In the end, beyond individual proclivities and character, and when true to the ethic of psychoanalytic theory, psychodynamic approaches to executive coaching and consultation value authenticity and truth. In that spirit practitioners of psychodynamic approaches are engaged in the removal of individual and organizational defensive screens, which typically distort the quality and reality of cooperative relationships at work. Next, an integrated and comprehensive approach to psychodynamic executive coaching by Kilburg (2000) is examined.

*A focus on complexity and chaos: Systems, psychodynamics, and reflective containment*    Kilburg's (2000) *Executive Coaching: Developing Managerial Wisdom in a World of Chaos* is a detailed and relatively comprehensive articulation of psychodynamic executive coaching. His model is complimentary to Levinson's focus on needs and expectations and Kets de Vries's focus on the character and inner theatre of executives and their organizations. In contrast, Kilburg places greater emphasis on systemic chaos and complexity in addition to internal psychodynamics. Kilburg constructs a 17-dimension model of systems and psychodynamics, which is an elaborate conceptual framework joining external components of systems with internal components of psychodynamics. This linkage between systems and psychodynamics is supported by the notion of the executive character as a complex self-organizing adaptive system. Here is a model for executive coaching grounded in psychodynamic and systemic processes, which incorporates the conceptual and contextual complexity of leadership in contemporary organizations, public and private, along with the challenges of helping executives become more reflective and thereby better at adapting to changing and unpredictable environments.

For Kilburg, psychodynamic executive coaching demands a "fully connected" (2000, p. 44) overarching dimensional model, linking open systems and psychodynamic processes. Awareness of these connected components of people and systems, consultants and coaches, means paying attention to organizational structure, input, process, output, content, and throughput, along with psychodynamic components such as psychological and social defenses, relational dynamics (past and present), transference of emotions, instinctual dynamics, conflicts, idealizing dynamics, focal relationships, cognition, and conscience. Ultimately, Kilburg is after what he calls a "foci for executive coaching" (p. 61) in which the mutual spotlight on open systems (structure, process, content, input, throughput, and output) and reflective, self-aware executives (rational self, conscience, idealized self, instinctual self, cognition, emotion, defenses, conflict, knowledge, skills, abilities, personality styles, jobs, roles, and tasks) produces a mediated focal point on relationships (past, present, focal) and behavior (system, whole organization, subunit, organizational work unit, group, individual). It is in this intervening hub of relationships that the work of executive coaching and consultation occur in practice.

Kilburg's notion of a mediated focus is rooted in contemporary psychoanalytic object relations theories. These psychodynamic theories are presently shaped to some extent by attachment research, theories of postmodernism and complexity, as well as findings in neuroscience and brain research. Fundamentally, Kilburg's mediated focus shares much in common with concepts in object relations theory literature (Benjamin 2004; Diamond 2007; Ogden 2004; Winnicott 1971) such as transitional objects, intermediate areas, intersubjectivity, thirdness, potential, and transitional space. For Winnicott (1971) these concepts signify a psychological reality embedded in the mother and baby dyad. "Good enough mothering" means adequate holding and containment of the baby's toxic feelings and emotions. Under these optimal circumstances, the child learns to adapt to the coming and going of mother and the shifting emotions of love and hate, good and bad, acceptance and rejection. Maturation for the child requires containment of projected emotions displaced from the "contained" infant onto the "container" mother (Bion 1967). Holding and containing are considered critical caregiving object functions of the parent in the emotional and cognitive development of the child.

Winnicott's (1971) notion of a "facilitative holding environment" as characteristic of "good enough mothering" provides the child with the interpersonal security and safety necessary for healthy separation and individuation. The critical nature of the quality of earliest attachments is supported by research in attachment theory and neuroscience (Fonagy 2001; Fonagy and Target 1997; Leffert 2010; Siegel 2001). Winnicott refers to a "facilitative environment" that fosters a transitional and potential space for the emergence of play and imagination, curiosity, and reflectivity. Transitional and potential space so vital to infant development, represents according to Winnicott the psychosocial location of culture. Culture as derived from play and imagination. Culture as the area of human experience situated in-between reality and fantasy – the source of imagination and creativity, art and music, the reflective practices of theorizing and problem solving. The effectiveness of Kilburg's comprehensive model of open systems and psychodynamics depends on seeing and working with the executive as a self-organizing complex system. Consistent with the ideas and functions of containment and transitional or potential space in object relations theory, Kilburg's concept of "reflective containment" is at the core of his method of psychodynamic executive coaching (p. 72).

Next, awareness of one's sense of self in the world of work requires paying attention to the affect of organizational roles, which is briefly reviewed next.

*Psychodynamic coaching and organizational role analysis* The genesis of organizational role analysis (ORA) stems from the Tavistock and A.K. Rice traditions of group relations education and training, where the analysis of authority, responsibility, and roles in groups, and the combination of open systems theory and psychodynamics, are prominent features of method and application. Organizational role analysis is influenced by the original thinking of W.R. Bion (1959) and his book *Experiences in Groups and Other Papers*. His psychodynamic model for understanding groups emphasizes the parallel processes of work groups. Bion's hypothesis is that groups operate on two levels, conscious and unconscious. At the manifest level of group activity is the task of the group – the group's purpose or mission. Concurrently, at the latent level of group activity are three basic underlying assumptions of fight-flight, dependency and pairing (or utopia). This model provides analysts, consultants, coaches, and facilitators with a richer and deeper appreciation of the complexity of group psychology. For instance, it is observed that groups come together behind a leader to engage in fight against or flight from some designated scapegoat or enemy. It is also observed that groups emerge behind a leader whose members collectively believe they can depend upon and feel comforted and safe in following his or her lead. Finally, it is observed that within groups, individual members are frequently attracted to pairings of members who offer hope and a sense of a better future for members in contrast to a disturbing or disappointing present. These are Bion's basic assumptions, which in some instances support the primary task of the work group and in other instances contradict or pull groups into unproductive, destructive, and psychologically regressive, psychodynamics.

Newton *et al.* (2006), in *Coaching in Depth: The Organizational Role Analysis Approach*, proffer a collection of papers on the theory and practice of ORA. Practitioners stress the value of staying in role and on task by expanding their awareness of underlying basic assumptions. Many of the proponents of ORA claim the approach is intended to focus on the role, not an individual's character. Thus, ORA is a process for clarifying roles within organizations. It is a peer driven inquiry that focuses on the systemic dimension of work problems and role performance. It is a psychodynamic approach that "assists clients in examining the dynamic process of finding, making, and taking up their organizational roles." Organizational role analysis attends to the interaction between psychological and social pressures on the individual-in-role, "by the consultant assisting the client to discern his or her organization in mind and test this against the goals of the system." It is a process of coaching-in-depth and exploring how the organization becomes, "an object of the inner world of a client, entangled with authority structures derived from childhood experience and made accessible through the use of work drawings within the ORA process" (Newton *et al.*, 2006).

It appears that roles are peculiarly shaped by character and therefore one can imagine conflicted and ambivalent relationships to organizational roles. Thus, one might expect frequent tensions between the external organizational demands for belonging, affiliation, adaptation, and compliance, and the internal individual needs for independence, autonomy, self-identity, and authenticity (Diamond, 1991). The idea of authenticity is a critical theme of the self-narrative in psychodynamic executive coaching and consultation.

In the section to follow, a review is offered of important articles and issues considered on the matter of research evidence in psychodynamic approaches to executive coaching.

## Research Evidence

Executive coaching has roots in the "development counseling" of the 1940s and emerged as a widespread practice in the 1980s (Kampa-Kokesh and Anderson, 2001). The study of executive coaching falls into three distinct categories: psychological, training and development, and management (Kampa-Kokesh and Anderson, 2001). Empirical studies of the efficacy of executive coaching date back to the mid-1990s (Passmore and Fillery-Travis, 2011). However, there are relatively few in comparison to domains such as counseling or leadership development (see Grant *et al.*, 2010). Of the papers which have been published few have adopted a psychodynamic orientation, partly as psychodynamic approaches lend themselves less well to scientific methods of evaluation in favor of case study methods.

Executive coaching has been empirically shown to increase executive productivity and the effectiveness of the organization as a whole primarily through executive learning and self-awareness (Kilburg, 2004b). Most executives seek coaching to help them change their relational patterns, cope better with change and build trust (Kampa-Kokesh and Anderson, 2001). These motivations are especially well-suited to a psychodynamic approach. The push for empirical research follows an increased demand for executive coaching services. Executive coaching is intended to assist executives with the pressure to do more while facing increasingly complex environments and rapid change (Blattner, 2005).

As noted above, research supporting the efficacy of psychodynamic consulting is based primarily in case studies. The case study approach has an extensive and respectful history in developing the theory and practice of organizational assessment and consultation (Lowman, 2001). Case studies are significant because they provide a foundation from which generalizable truths are developed (Lowman, 2001). Case studies offer a way to examine theory in practice and generate hypotheses that are then subject to quantitative analysis. The apparent lack of quantitative approaches to understanding executive coaching, especially from a psychodynamic point of view, stems from the difficulty of quantifying relational phenomena and predicting human behavior. Quantification and prediction of human behavior is difficult because much of it lies outside of conscious awareness.

Executive coaching is uniquely based in psychological theory, especially systems and psychodynamic theory. Kilburg (2004c) argues that events, feelings, thoughts, and patterns of behavior that are outside the conscious awareness of executives can significantly influence what they decide and how they act. Highlighting the importance of consciousness and awareness of self and others (what some might call emotional intelligence) in the practice of executive coaching, Kilburg's article offers an overview of conflict and object relations approaches to understanding psychodynamics. Conflict here refers to intrapersonal conflict or tension between the forces of id, ego, and superego as indicative of the classical Freudian drive model. So the conflict approach may be considered synonymous with carrying over some of the key concepts and clinical experiences of the classical psychoanalytic model into the contemporary object relational model. Kilburg suggests in his work that he also embeds the material (emotional and cognitive) of executive coaching in, "scientific reviews of unconscious mental and emotional phenomena." Research evidence linking psychoanalytic object relations theory, attachment research, and neuroscience, is considerable, which might surprise coaches and consultants unfamiliar with brain research and contemporary psychoanalytic findings (e.g., Edelman, 2006; Fonagy, 2001; Jurist *et al.*, 2008; Kandel, 2006; Karen, 1998; Modell, 2003; Siegel, 2007; Stern, 2004).

In his critique of the existing literature on executive coaching, Kilburg (2004c) calls for detailed case studies that describe the *process* of executive coaching; Lowman (2001) also supports the practice of executive coaching moving towards the path of scientific psychology, a "deficit-repair model" (Kilburg, 2004c, p. 205). Despite the rise of scientifically validated treatments in clinical psychology and psychotherapy, it is difficult to pin down what actually causes those positive outcomes (Blattner, 2005; Kilburg, 2004c; Rosenzweig, 1936; Wampold, 1997). There are almost as many psychological therapies as disorders, and the empirical findings show little difference across therapies although they indicate positive outcomes (Wampold, 2001).

Lowman argues that the lack of a "scientific" base may result in executive coaching going the way of the dodo bird. In other words, non-empirical approaches can only go so far, and the narrative, self-report case study approach on which the bulk of the coaching literature is based has created a slippery slope for practitioners. Similarly, in an earlier article Kilburg (2004a) suggests that, "the traditional routes that psychologists take from their scientist-practitioner models may lead us to the land of 'Dodoville' in which everything is equally valid and everyone is entitled to a prize" (p. 91). Kilburg wonders, at least by implication, if it is worth "trudging to Dodoville" if all we find when we get there is non-specific effects that presumably would not match the available theory-driven approaches (p. 91). Others (Passmore and Fillery-Travis, 2011) have argued that while nonspecific effects may be identified in general, specific approaches or interventions may emerge as more effective when addressing specific presenting problems.

It seems that the nonspecific characteristics of the coaching process and psychotherapy may be the most meaningful in general, that aside from technique the intense involvement of coach with the client, the interpersonal connection is at the core of the success of coaching as an intervention. Empirical approaches to understanding the truth about executive coaching reflect this assessment of its success and reaffirm what psychotherapists and clinical psychologists have reported for over 100 years (Kilburg, 2004c).

Lowman (2005) notes we cannot have it both ways, we cannot be, "exempt from the rules of scientific psychology while also laying claim to the mantle of psychology" (p. 92). He suggests that there is no reason to suppose that executive coaching is valid or has specific effects, or even which techniques work and under what circumstances. Empirical findings about the effectiveness of executive coaching are too broad to be the basis for drawing any firm conclusions. He argues that "scientific" approaches to understanding the outcomes of executive coaching are a needed partner for case study findings. Lowman's purpose is not to offer one approach over another, but simply to suggest that both "logico-deductive" and "constructivist-narrative" approaches have something to offer the theory and practice of executive coaching. On the one hand, case studies are important for generating hypotheses, and on the other hand empirical analysis is important for validating the self-reported successes and favorite techniques of the authors of case studies. "In the grip of this eternal dialectic between the narrative and paradigmatic modes of thought and study, we surely will continue to grow and hopefully prosper" (Kilburg, 2004c).

Wasylyshyn's (2005) case study of a long-term coaching relationship illustrates several clinical principles important to the practice of executive coaching, along with several "meta-principles" of executive coaching: traction, trust, and truth-telling. The case also addresses role management for both the coach and the client. Key psychological elements of the case include anxiety, narcissism, attachment, leader-follower dynamics, and transference dynamics.

Blattner's (2005) study of an executive over the course of job change illustrates additional concepts that are important aspects of a psychodynamic approach to coaching, such as the importance of the perception of self, coping mechanisms, and emotional intelligence. In this case the coach takes a strengths-based approach and emphasizes the awareness of the emotional states of self and others, especially as a tool for developing behavioral and supervisory strategies that enhance the effectiveness of employees and thus the executive.

Schnell (2005) presents a case study of long-term coaching to a leadership pair in a rapidly changing organization. Psychodynamic aspects of this case include identification and attachment between members of the leadership pair, leader-follower dynamics, and the effects of leadership style on organizational performance, and transference dynamics as the emotional experiences of each executive are processed within the coaching session. Schnell (2005) points to executive coaching as contextualized within a broader array of consultative interventions. The case also discusses the important aspects of the contracting phase of the coaching intervention. A systems approach is also illustrated in light of the pair and their interactions with the organization as a whole. While (Kralj, 2001) also demonstrates the systems approach, it does not present individual coaching interventions.

Finally, Wasylyshyn's (2005) coaching as a successful support for leadership succession is illustrated. This section concludes with a note of reservation on the matter of "research evidence".

Social and human science theories of psychodynamic executive coaching are rooted in what Aristotle in *The Nicomachean Ethics* called *phronesis* or practical wisdom. Phronesis differs from *episteme* (epistemology as basic science and predictive theory) and *techne* or technical skills and crafts. Phronesis is the reflective practitioner's ability to deliberate between the universal and the particular by drawing from a wealth of universal knowledge, which is then practiced in everyday situations. "The goal of the phronetic approach becomes one of contributing to society's capacity for value-rational deliberation and action" (Flyvbjerg, 2001, p. 167). The study of organizations and individuals who lead and reproduce systems, and who are in turn shaped by these very same cultures, is the study of reflective human subjects, not of dead objects (2001). Constructing meaning and mutual understanding, not prediction, is the aim. The goal of self-consciousness by attending to what Bollas (1987) calls the "unthought known" or unconscious thoughts and emotions, distinguishes psychodynamic executive coaching. Developing cognitive and emotional capacity for reflective action on behalf of executives and leaders are at the heart of this enterprise of organizational intervention.

Case examples and qualitative approaches to the study of organizations and their leaders are critical to advancing the psychodynamic paradigm in executive coaching and consultation as they are important to more deeply understanding human organizations and their executive leaders in pursuit of value-laden action, power, and interests.

## The Development of Psychodynamic Approaches in Coaching

The development of psychodynamic approaches in coaching has been discussed in the earlier section on psychodynamic models with reviews of Levinson, Kets de Vries, Kilburg, and others. This reflection continues with the subsequent discussion below that addresses the heart of psychodynamic executive coaching in theory and practice, and by further articulating its paradigmatic origins in object relations theory and the contributions of D.W. Winnicott as mentioned at the beginning of this chapter, in particular the ideas of true and false self systems and transitional phenomena such as the ideas of holding environment, potential, and transitional space discussed elsewhere.

However, it is critical at this juncture to articulate the following epistemological position. Executive coaching is a form of organizational intervention. It is a step in a larger process of working with systems and individuals. Executive coaching is an idea situated within a larger conceptual framework that links theory and practice. And, while there are varied approaches to executive coaching, the psychodynamic approach as presented here combines psychoanalytic theory and practice with systems and group relations theory. Psychoanalytic theory is over 100 years old and continues to experience evolution rooted in clinical, historical, cultural, and global tensions – one might say it has advanced despite and because of internal and external pressures.

Earlier on in this chapter the emergence of object relations theory was discussed. Yet, psychoanalytic theory is a school of thought with competing paradigms. Many scholars and practitioners believe this state of affairs represents a healthy and productive paradigmatic tension. Beyond the paradigmatic conflicts and tension, all of the psychodynamic approaches discussed in this chapter concern themselves with minimizing defensiveness, enhancing awareness of self and others, and promoting authenticity. Levinson's approach emphasizes the value in understanding executives' desires, needs, and expectations, not in isolation but in the context of organizational diagnosis and assessment. Kets de Vries's approach debunks the rational economic man model and proffers categories of character dispositions and individual executive proclivities rooted in the realities of the workplace. His extensive typology of dispositions provides insights into the characteristics that shape key relationships, organizational strategies, decision making, and performance. Kilburg's systemic approach to psychodynamics and organizations stresses complexity and chaos, and the challenges of self-organizing adaptive systems. Finally, organizational role analysis highlights the significance of analyzing roles over individual character, and stresses the importance of the group (over individual) level of analysis. An integration of these approaches may be preferable.

From a psychodynamic perspective, executive coaching and consultation is often an exercise in reflecting upon conflict and character, which is why Winnicott's notion of authenticity, true and false self, is addressed in the following section.

## The challenge of authenticity: True versus false self

Winnicott's (1965) theory of infancy and childhood development describes a nascent self of potential spontaneity and authenticity. This emerging true self, however, fades away behind the defensive forces of an acquiescent and reactive false self where inadequate, "not good enough" parenting and holding are present. This phenomenon of false self normally occurs in adulthood and in particular is commonplace among narcissistic executives unconsciously defending themselves against the pain and discomfort of conflict (internal and external) and against the threat of rejection by underlings who might question the "wisdom" of their leadership, thus losing subordinates' idealization and reinforcement of their need for aggrandizement.

Employees are frequently required, implicitly and explicitly, by managers and executives to be submissive and obedient. This compliance requires that subordinates function psychologically from behind the fortress of a false self. Simultaneously, managers and executives shun personal responsibility for their actions and tend to blame subordinates for failed or flawed organizational strategies whenever necessary and convenient. Workers under these stressful and alienating conditions will experience demoralization and become disgruntled.

Under conditions of stress and demands for change, executives find with the assistance of psychodynamically-oriented executive coaches and consultants that reactive and defensive solutions to anxiety are no longer manageable or acceptable. They may also find that secrecy and withholding of information is ineffective and that it further deflates workers' sense of self-confidence and competence. Rigid dispositions of executives' character are challenged by circumstances in which resilience and openness to change in the status quo are imperative yet seemingly absent. Profound change can come about with mutual authenticity, respect, and shared responsibilities among leaders and followers (executives, managers, and workers). Followers (or subordinates) despite having limited power and authority need to assert themselves as well. They need to acknowledge their shared responsibility for perpetuating inauthentic and defensive leadership and culture. Executive coaches and consultants help by supporting and facilitating a *transitional space* or *reflective containment* for participants engaged in change. To reiterate, transitional space refers to the need to provide a safe and creative emotional and psychological, virtual room for people in their attempt to produce radical change and solve complex problems. By directing feedback to address unconscious reactive and defensive behavior patterns and dispositions that block positive change, executive coaches work to enhance participants' self-awareness and emotional intelligence. Heightened self-awareness and consciousness in executives is the first step toward minimizing the toxic consequences of reactive narcissism and giving voice to the true self of authentic leaders and followers while limiting the prevalence of the false self and the negative impact of excessively defensive operations on organizational culture.

In the concluding section, the advancement of psychodynamic executive coaching is addressed by promoting organizational ethnographic and action research.

## Psychodynamic Executive Coaching and Future Research

The study of psychodynamic executive coaching and consultation is advanced by qualitative and idiographic approaches to the study of organizations and leadership, and by the interpretive power of case examples. Not simply more, but better case illustrations of psychodynamic coaching in theory (conceptual frameworks) and practice (concrete applications) are required. Reconstructing narratives between coaches and clients with a better understanding and illustration of what psychodynamically-oriented coaches and consultants are thinking and precisely what sorts of questions they are asking and at what times they seem most effectively and appropriately asked. In what manner and to what degree do psychodynamic coaches take into consideration the importance of organizational culture, diagnosis, and assessment? If they do so, examples depicting the influence of independent organizational diagnoses on executive coaching sessions and the sorts of psychological issues and dynamics discussed would be helpful. How do they manage the anticipated transference and counter-transference dynamics? Psychodynamic executive coaching and consultation differ from psychoanalytic psychotherapy. These differences and commonalities need to be better clarified and further explored.

While some might argue that the practice of psychodynamic executive coaching ought to be grounded in current organizational circumstances supported and informed by organizational diagnoses and assessments; other practitioners might argue about this requirement and might articulate the value added for clients in processes in which organizational assessments are not a precondition. Psychodynamic executive coaching, and for that matter other forms of executive coaching, are intervention strategies that can increase reflective learning among executives, managers, and workers, and therefore can contribute to positive organizational change. However, when executive coaching is not a component of comprehensive organizational change efforts, there might be a tendency to take executive-client issues and psychodynamics out of context, providing little assistance to the collective whole of the organization, its members and executives. Without the benefits of independent organizational diagnoses, some argue, executive coaching efforts carry serious limitations and at best ought to carry modest expectations.

Psychodynamic approaches to executive coaching and consultation as principally influenced by the works discussed in this chapter and other works referenced are abundant with case examples and illustrations. Works by Zaleznik (1984a, 1984b, 1989, 1991), Sievers (2009), Stapley (2002), Diamond (1993, 2007), Diamond and Allcorn (2009), and Stein (1994, 2001) offer case illustrations and vignettes that support conclusions drawn and interpretations espoused. These examples are instructive and could benefit from more elaborate organizational ethnographies and case narratives that better depict and account for the actual interpersonal dynamics between executive coaches/consultants and clients in particular organizational interventions. Psychodynamic theories and approaches to organizational consultation and executive coaching are not intended as theories for prediction; rather, they are designed for more deeply understanding and interpreting the significance and meaning of complex human relationships and work roles, groups, and organizations. The psychodynamic approaches to executive coaching outlined and briefly discussed in this chapter offer consultants a more profound understanding and consideration of the impact of psychological reality on organizational roles and working relationships; it is intended to help leaders and executives by engaging them in authentic and reflective dialogue that expands awareness and consciousness of self and others in the workplace.

# References

Aristotle (1976) *The Nicomachean Ethics* (translated by J.A.K. Thomson). Hammondsworth: Penguin.

Arnaud, G. (2003) A coach or a couch? A Lacanian perspective on executive coaching and consultation. *Human Relations,* 56 (9), 1131–54.

Benjamin, J. (2004) Beyond doer and done to: An intersubjective view of thirdness. *The Psychoanalytic Quarterly,* 73 (1), 5–46.

Bion, W.R. (1959) *Experiences in Groups.* New York: Basic Books.

Bion, W.R. (1967) *Second Thoughts.* London: Karnac Books (reprinted 2003).

Blattner, J. (2005) Coaching: The successful adventure of a downwardly mobile executive. *Consulting Psychology Journal: Research and Practice,* 57 (1), 3–13.

Bollas, C. (1987) *The Shadow of the Object: Psychoanalysis of the Unthought Known.* New York: Columbia University Press.

Bowlby, J. (1969) *Attachment,* vol.1. New York: Basic Books.

Bowlby, J. (1973) *Separation,* vol. 2. New York: Basic Books.

Bowlby, J. (1980) *Loss,* vol. 3. New York: Basic Books.

Brunning, H. (2006) *Executive Coaching: Systems Psychodynamic Perspective.* Karnac: London.

Czander, W.M. (1993) *The Psychodynamics of Work and Organizations.* New York: Guilford Press.

Diamond, M.A. (1991) Stresses of group membership: Balancing the needs for independence and belonging. In: M.F.R. Kets de Vries and associates, *Organizations on the Couch.* San Francisco, CA: Jossey-Bass Publishers.

Diamond, M.A. (1993) *The Unconscious Life of Organizations.* Westport, CT: Quorum Books, Greenwood Publishing.

Diamond, M.A. (2007) Organizational change and the analytic third: Locating and attending to unconscious organizational psychodynamics. *Psychoanalysis, Culture and Society,* 12, 142–64.

Diamond, M.A. and Allcorn, S. (2009) *Private Selves in Public Organizations.* New York: Palgrave Macmillan.

Driver, M. (2009) Struggling with lack: A Lacanian perspective on organizational identity. *Organization Studies,* 30(1), 55–72.

Edelman, G.M. (2006) *Second Nature: Brain Science and Human Knowledge.* New Haven, CT: Yale University Press.

Flyvbjerg, B. (2001) *Making Social Science Matter.* New York: Cambridge University Press.

Fonagy, P. (2001) *Attachment Theory and Psychoanalysis.* New York: Other Press.

Fonagy, P. and Target, M. (1997) Attachment and reflective function: Their role in self-organization. *Development and Psychopathology,* 9, 679–700.

Gabriel, Y. (1999) *Organizations in Depth,* London: Sage.

Grant, A.M., Passmore, J., Cavanagh, M., and Parker, H. (2010) The state of play in coaching. *International Review of Industrial and Organizational Psychology*, 25, 125–68.

Greenberg, J. and Mitchell, S. (1983) *Object Relations in Psychoanalytic Theory*. Cambridge, MA: Harvard University Press.

Jurist, E.L., Slade, A., and Bergner, S. (eds) (2008) *Mind to Mind: Infant Research, Neuroscience, and Psychoanalysis*. New York: Other Press.

Kampa-Kokesch, S. and Anderson, M.Z. (2001) Executive coaching: A comprehensive review of the literature. *Consulting Psychology Journal: Practice and Research*, 53 (4), 205–28.

Kandel, E.R. (2006) *In Search of Memory: The Emergence of a New Science of Mind*. New York: W.W. Norton.

Karen, R. (1998) *Becoming Attached*. New York: Oxford University Press.

Kernberg, O.F. (1998) *Ideology, Conflict, and Leadership in Groups and Organizations*. New Haven, CT: Yale University Press.

Kets de Vries, M.F.R. (ed.) (1984) *The Irrational Executive: Psychoanalytic Explorations in Management*. New York: International Universities Press.

Kets de Vries, M.F.R. (ed.) (1991) *Organizations on the Couch: Clinical Perspectives on Organizational Behavior and Change*. San Francisco, CA: Jossey-Bass Publishers.

Kets de Vries, M.F.R. (2001) *The Leadership Mystique*. New York: Financial Times/Prentice Hall.

Kets de Vries, M.F.R. (2006) *The Leader on the Couch: A Clinical Approach to Changing People and Organizations*. Chichester: John Wiley and Sons, Ltd.

Kets de Vries, M.F.R. and Miller, D. (1984) *The Neurotic Organization*. San Francisco: Jossey-Bass Publishers.

Kets de Vries, M.F.R., Guillen, L., Korotov, K., and Florent-Treacy, E. (2010) *The Coaching Kaleidoscope: Insights from the Inside*. New York: Palgrave Macmillan.

Kets de Vries, M.F.R., Korotov, K., and Florent-Treacy, E. (2007) *Coach and Couch: The Psychology of Making Better Leaders*. New York: Palgrave Macmillan.

Kilburg, R.R. (1996) Toward a conceptual understanding and definition of executive coaching. *Consulting Psychology Journal: Practice and Research*, 48, 134–44.

Kilburg, R.R. (2000) *Executive Coaching*. Washington, DC: American Psychological Association.

Kilburg, R.R. (ed.) (2004a) Trudging toward Dodoville – Part I: Conceptual approaches in executive coaching (Special issue). *Consulting Psychology Journal: Practice and Research*, 56(4).

Kilburg, R.R. (2004b) Trudging toward Dodoville: Case studies and conceptual approaches in executive coaching. *Consulting Psychology Journal: Practice and Research*, 56, 203–13.

Kilburg, R.R. (2004c) When shadows fall: Using psychodynamic approaches in executive coaching. *Consulting Psychology Journal: Practice and Research*, 56, 246–68.

Kilburg, R.R. (ed.) (2005) Trudging toward Dodoville—Part II: Case studies in executive coaching (Special issue). *Consulting Psychology Journal: Practice and Research*, 57(1 and 2).

Klein, M. (1946) Notes on some schizoid mechanisms. *International Journal of Psychoanalysis*, XXVII, 99–110.

Klein, M. (1959) Our adult world and its roots in infancy. *Human Relations*, 12, 291–303.

Kohut, H. (1977) *The Restoration of the Self*. New York: International Universities Press.

Kralj, M. M. (2001) Coaching at the top: Assisting a chief executive and his team. *Consulting Psychology Journal: Research and Practice*, 53(2), 108–16.

Lee, G. (2010) Psychodynamic approaches to coaching. In: E. Cox, T. Bachkirova and D. Clutterback, (eds) *The Complete Handbook of Coaching*. London: Sage.

Lee, G. and I. Roberts (2009) *Coaching for Authentic Leadership*. In: J. Passmore (ed.) *Leadership Coaching*. London: Kogan Page.

Leffert, M. (2010) *Contemporary Psychoanalytic Foundations: Postmodernism, Complexity, and Neuroscience*. New York: Routledge, Taylor and Francis Group.

Levinson, H. (1964) *Emotional Health and the World of Work*. New York: Harper & Row.

Levinson, H. (1968) *The Exceptional Executive*. Cambridge, MA: Harvard University Press.

Levinson, H. (1970) *Executive Stress*. New York: Harper and Row.

Levinson, H. (1972) *Organizational Diagnosis*. Cambridge, MA: Harvard University Press.

Levinson, H. (1981) *Executive*. Cambridge, MA: Harvard University Press.

Levinson, H. (2002) *Organizational Assessment: A Step-by-step Guide to Effective Consulting*. Washington, DC: American Psychological Association.

Levinson, H., Mandl, H.J., Solley, C.M., Munden, K.J., and Price, C.R. (1962) *Men, Management, and Mental Health*. Cambridge, MA: Harvard University Press.

Lowman, R.L. (2001) Constructing a literature from case studies: Promise and limitations of the method. *Consulting Psychology Journal: Practice and Research*, 53(2), 119–23.

Lowman, R.L. (2005) Executive coaching: The road to Dodoville needs paving with more than good assumptions. *Consulting Psychology Journal: Practice and Research*, 57(1) 90–6.

Modell, A.H. (2003) *Imagination and the Meaningful Brain*. Cambridge, MA: MIT Press.

Moore, B.E. and Fine, B.D. (1990) *Psychoanalytic Terms and Concepts*. New Haven, CT: Yale University Press.

Newton, J., Long, S., and Sievers, B. (eds) (2006) *Coaching in Depth: The Organizational Role Analysis Approach*. London: Karnac Books.

Ogden, T.H. (2004) The analytic third: Implications for psychoanalytic theory and technique. *The Psychoanalytic Quarterly*, 73(1), 167–96.

Passmore, J. and Fillery-Travis, A. (2011) A critical review of executive coaching research: A decade of progress and what's to come. *Coaching: An International Journal of Theory, Practice and Research*, 4(2).

Peltier, B. (2010) *The Psychology of Executive Coaching: Theory and Application* (2nd edn). New York: Routledge.

Rosenzweig, S. (1936) Some implicit common factors in diverse methods of psychotherapy. *American Journal of Orthopsychiatry*, 6(3), 412–15.

Schnell, E.R. (2005) A case study of executive coaching as a support mechanism during organizational growth and evolution. *Consulting Psychology Journal: Practice and Research*, 57(1), 41–56.

Siegel, D. (2001) Toward an interpersonal neurobiology of the developing mind: Attachment relationships, "mindsight" and neural integration. *Infant Mental Health Journal*, 22(1–2), 233–47.

Siegel, D. (2007) *The Mindful Brain*. New York: W.W. Norton & Company.

Sievers, B. (ed.) (2009) *Psychoanalytic Studies of Organizations: Contributions from the International Society for the Psychoanalytic Study of Organizations (ISPSO)*. London: Karnac Books.

Stapley, L.F. (2002) *It's an Emotional Game: Learning about Leadership from the Experience of Football*. London: Karnac.

Stein, H.F. (1994) *Listening Deeply*. Boulder, CO: Westview Press.

Stein, H.F. (2001) *Nothing Personal, Just Business: A Guided Journey into Organizational Darkness*. Westport, CT: Quorum Books, Greenwood Publishing Group.

Stern, D.N. (2004) *The Present Moment in Psychotherapy and Everyday Life*. New York: W.W. Norton.

Wampold, B.E. (1997) Methodological problems in identifying efficacious psychotherapies. *Psychotherapy Research*, 7, 21–43.

Wampold, B.E. (2001) *The Great Psychotherapy Debate: Models, Methods, and Findings*. Mahwah, NJ: Erlbaum.

Wasylyshyn, K.M. (2005) The reluctant president. *Consulting Psychology Journal: Practice and Research*, 57(1), 57–70.

Winnicott, D.W. (1965) *The Maturational Processes and the Facilitating Environment*. Madison, CT: International Universities Press, Inc.

Winnicott, D.W. (1971) *Playing and Reality*. London: Tavistock Publications.

Zaleznik, A. (1984a) Charismatic and consensus leaders: A psychological comparison. In: M.F.R. Kets de Vries (ed.) *The Irrational Executive*. New York: International Universities Press.

Zaleznik, A. (1984b) Power and politics in organizational life. In: M.F.R. Kets de Vries (ed.) *The Irrational Executive*. New York: International Universities Press.

Zaleznik, A. (1991) Leading and managing: Understanding the difference. In M.F.R. Kets de Vries and Associates (ed.) *Organizations on the Couch: Clinical Perspectives on Organizational Behavior and Change*. San Francisco, CA: Jossey-Bass Inc., Publishers.

Zaleznik, A. (1989). *The Managerial Mystique*. New York: Harper and Row, Publishers.

# Acknowledgements

I wish to thank C. Mindy Duncan, Seth Allcorn, and the editor Jonathan Passmore for their reviews and recommendations of earlier drafts of this chapter.

# 20

# Gestalt Approach

## Juliann Spoth, Sarah Toman, Robin Leichtman, and Julie Allan

## Introduction

Although the gestalt approach to psychotherapy has been in existence for decades, the application of gestalt theory concepts to coaching is more recent. Gestalt theoretical concepts, including relational and dialogic stance, emphasis on awareness, contact, phenomenology, paradox, polarities, resistance, unit of work, levels of systems, and use of experiment have been incorporated into the coaching process, creating a unique gestalt approach to coaching. The purpose of this chapter is to highlight aspects of gestalt theory and methodology that provide the foundation for gestalt coaching and to describe the distinct contributions of gestalt theory to the coaching field.

This chapter begins with an overview of applicable gestalt theory concepts, followed by a description of the development of gestalt coaching. Next, gestalt coaching methods are featured, followed by a review of research and implications from the coaching literature. The chapter closes with suggestions for future research and development of gestalt coaching.

## Gestalt Theory

In this section, a brief review of gestalt theory concepts is offered, outlining the traditional and contemporary applications particularly relevant to gestalt coaching. While Simon (2009) and Allan and Whybrow (2007) have described several gestalt concepts core to gestalt coaching, for this chapter the gestalt concepts of (1) working from a relational stance, (2) dialogue, (3) gestalt cycle of experience, (4) awareness and contact, (5) blocks to awareness and change, (6) the paradoxical theory of change, (7) figure and ground, (8) field theory, (9) here and now, and (10) experiment are defined. These gestalt concepts, with a particular emphasis on the notion of working within a relational stance, establish the context for applications to gestalt coaching.

*The Wiley Blackwell Handbook of the Psychology of Coaching and Mentoring*, First Edition.
Edited by Jonathan Passmore, David B. Peterson, and Teresa Freire.
© 2013 John Wiley & Sons, Ltd. Published 2016 by John Wiley & Sons, Ltd.

## Working from a relational stance

Beginning with the work of Buber (1958) and the notion of I-Thou, there remains a focus in the gestalt approach on the quality of the relationship between client and coach. The in-between, or the relationship, is a place of meaningful contact, growth, and change. From an I-Thou stance, no power differential is experienced; there is no expert but rather an opportunity for mutuality and collaboration.

Crocker (2005) explained that caring, openness, being with the client, respect for the client's perspective, all help to create an I-Thou relationship. From another theoretical stance, Carl Roger's person-centered therapy (1951), the development of the therapeutic relationship relies on building trust, empathy, and unconditional positive regard. These relationship qualities are valued by the gestalt coach as much as the content of the session. The gestalt coach intentionally builds trust and rapport through dialogue as he and the client partner to co-create the relationship.

Dialogue

A vital tool for building a quality coaching relationship is dialogue. Dialogue does not mean teaching, or guiding or recommending, but being in conversation around the other's story and experience. As the dialogue unfolds, new awarenesses, meanings, energy, and contact emerge. A gestalt theory description of the developmental phases of experience can be explained through the concept of the gestalt cycle of experience: sensation, awareness, mobilization of energy, action, contact, and withdrawal.

## The cycle of experience

The cycle of experience or contact cycle (Figure 20.1) offers a representation of the human experience of person-environment contact. Beginning with a sensation, the person moves to an awareness that mobilizes energy; action is taken and contact is made, concluding with withdrawal.

Clarkson (2004) provided additional descriptors of the cycle phases which coaches may find useful: Sensation, she described as "fore-contact", awareness as "emerging

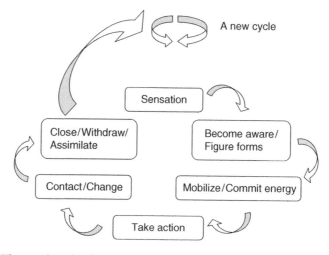

**Figure 20.1**  The gestalt cycle of experience.

social or biological need", mobilization as "excitement phase of contact", action as "choice of and implementation of appropriate action", final contact as "full and vibrant", adding "satisfaction or post-contact and gestalt completion", and finally withdrawal as "organism at rest" (p. 35).

The cycle phases can assist coaches with understanding experiences from their clients' perspectives, strengthening the mutuality of the I-Thou relationship, and provide a structure or system for explaining growth, change, movement, resistance, and blockages.

The awareness and contact phases of the cycle of experience (COE) are rich phases for joining with the client for the purpose of development, growth, or movement and for mobilizing energy for action or change. Simon (2009) suggested that, "it is Gestalt theory's focus on awareness that may differentiate it from other approaches to coaching" and that, "the Gestalt practitioner understands that there is a direct relationship between the degree of awareness and the potential for new choices of behavior" (p. 237).

From experiencing a sensation, an accompanying awareness becomes figural. Once the awareness becomes known, it can be like walking through life with new clarity and meaning. One simple example might be the sensation of restlessness during a staff meeting that could lead to an awareness of not getting enough sleep the night before that could evolve to having a fundamental opposition to the topic of the meeting. With increased awareness of the experience there comes a tipping point where change is inevitable.

Simon (2009) explained the value of the contact phase of the COE as, "a foundational Gestalt belief ... growth and development occur as a result of contact with the environment" (p. 233). Making contact with one's sleepiness or opposition during a meeting could be understood as an environmental and an internal contact. The gestalt coach is interested in the quality of a person's contactfulness as it indicates how available the person is to participate in the coaching relationship and the change process.

## Blocks to awareness and change

As explained by Perls *et al.* (1951), "every healthy contact involves awareness (perceptual figure/ground) and excitement (increased energy mobilization). Every block conversely necessitates the performance of actual work to prevent contact" (p. 365). At any point along the gestalt cycle of experience, energy can be blocked or resisted and forward movement thwarted. Resistance, as defined by the gestalt coach, is not necessarily negative, as is the defense mechanism in other theoretical approaches. A blocking mechanism to ward off awareness, contact, or change can be in place for a reason, it may be a "normal response to that which feels too new or too different" (Simon, 2009, p. 235). As explained by Mauer (2005), "we see resistance as 'the energy,' not the 'enemy' ... resistance is a creative adjustment to a situation" (p. 252). Resistances are appreciated as energetic blocks and the purposes they serve in and for an individual's experience is respected. Working with, rather than through, a resistance can promote change.

## The paradoxical theory of change

Yontef (2007) stated that a "central question" is: "How do individuals and their societies, including psychotherapists, influence and support change in the direction of healing, growth, and wholeness?" (p. 82). Central to change theory from a gestalt perspective is the paradoxical theory of change (Beisser, 1970). From this stance, the gestalt coach assists the coachee to be more of who they already are, until additional awareness is gained, resistance is encountered, and energy builds to the inevitable point of change – something has to give and movement is accomplished. The change or difference may create new choices, awarenesses, or figures.

## Figure and ground

When attending to the content presented during a coaching session, the gestalt coach takes note of those topics that easily rise to the surface out of the background of possibilities. The gestalt psychologists of the early 1900s offered many perceptual images, which later became the core principle of figure/ground in gestalt theory. The famous face/vase image clearly illustrates how at one time we can perceive the image as a face emerging out of the background of a vase, while at another moment in time the perceived image flips to a vase. The gestalt practitioner attends to the figural experience, content, thought, or feeling, yet understands that with change, new experiences and new meanings occur, so the figure will inevitably shift. This shift is noticed while also attending to the background, for awareness of both can assist with developing new meaning or understanding that goes beyond acknowledging figure without the context or field.

## Field theory perspective

Field, in its simplest form, may be understood as the context out of which figure emerges. O'Neill (2010) noted that even within the field of gestalt theory, there is controversy about the definition and application of the term field. McConville (2003) explained that inner and outer human experience merges and includes, "the genetic and physiological givens, the familial, social, cultural, political and geographical contexts of development, and the experiential domains of thought, need, fantasy, feeling and personality organization" (p. 217). Awareness can be enhanced, blocks to awareness and contact understood, the complexity of the ground recognized and change and growth promoted when putting all in the perspective of a person's field.

## The here and now

The application of the above gestalt theory concepts occur within the timeframe of the here and now. The person's past history is part of the ground or field, yet is explored within the moment of now; the effects and perceptions of history are experienced in current time. It is within the here and now that current awareness arises, and contact, growth, and change emerge. Experiments or interventions are created in the immediacy of the session to further the impact of the here and now experience.

## A gestalt intervention or experiment

A gestalt experiment, or intervention is designed to offer the client an alternative perspective, awareness, understanding, meaning, and so on, through enactment in the here and now, enhanced by the support of the coach. As Stevenson (2005) stated, experiment, "leads to an awareness of what might be, or how things could be better in the future" (p. 39). Gestalt experiments could easily be misunderstood as merely a technique or intervention, yet the distinction is that experiments are co-created, are derived from the here and now work of the session, and emerge from the client's field of experience. This process ends with dialogue about the here and now experience of the experiment and any contributions to insight or awareness.

The preceeding paragraphs briefly summarized several primary gestalt theory concepts. These same principles, with slight adaptations, can be applied when coaching at any level of system: individuals, pairs, teams, and the organizational level. This chapter continues with applications of the basic gestalt therapy constructs to coaching.

## The Development of Gestalt Coaching

Gestalt coaching emerged from the rich and fertile ground of gestalt theory, the essence of which is existential, experiential, and experimental (Perls, 1978). Contemporary gestalt theory is derived from the psychological and philosophical theories that evolved during the period 1930–1965 (Nevis, 1997). These were varied and birthed in a liberal, dynamic, and revolutionary era, making the originators of gestalt therapy, Fredrick (1893–1970) and Laura Perls (1905–1990), and the early years of gestalt therapy the source of considerable controversy.

These theories included the Freudian notion of the power of unconscious, Smuts' (1926/1996) holistic perspective, Horney's (1937) and Reich's (1945) emphasis on the impact of the socio-cultural environment, the gestalt psychologists' focus on perception of wholes, Koffa's (1935) organization of perception by figure and ground, Goldstein's (1939/1995) emphasis on phenomenology and his expansion of Gestalt psychology to a holistic, person-oriented perspective, Rank's (1941) focus on the here and now, Goodman's (1945/1977) idea of self-organizing regulation, Jung's (1961) polarities concept, and Moreno's (1959) psychodrama and experiential theater (Gillie, 2010; Bowman, 2005; Wulf, 1996).

Philosophical treatises were also infused into gestalt theory. The existential philosophies of Buber (1958) gave rise "to Gestalt therapy's values of presence, authenticity, dialogue and inclusion" (Bowman, 2005, p. 12) and those of Kierkegaard, Heidegger, and Husserl underscored that "passionate choices, strong convictions and personal experience compose an individual's truth" (Bowman, 2005, p. 12). Eastern philosophy's emphasis on awareness, and Lewin's (1951) field theory and the concept of unfinished business further influenced gestalt theory (Wulf, 1996). Despite the controversy and critiques, gestalt theory became mainstream with the increase in gestalt therapy books, journals, training at gestalt institutions, and inclusion in large associations for therapists (Bowman, 2005).

As gestalt theory continued to evolve, many of the new therapeutic applications came from the Gestalt Institute of Cleveland (GIC; Bowman, 2005). In the late 1950s the innovative culture of GIC spawned the most radical departure from traditional gestalt theory; the application of gestalt concepts and methodology to organizational development (OD; Nevis, 1997). In 1959 the first documented gestalt organizational consulting project included leadership development (Nevis, 1997). This foreshadowed the emergence of gestalt coaching as it legitimized using gestalt concepts with non-clinical individuals and groups in an arena particularly relevant to coaching-organizations.

Gestalt coach training entered the public arena in Europe when P. Barber (personal communication, July 24, 2011) introduced a gestalt coaching in a Master's program at the University of Surrey in the early 1990s and offered public workshops on "Emergent coaching: A gestalt approach". Similarly in 1996 D. Siminovitch and J. Carter created a gestalt coaching workshop at GIC that eventually became a multi-week international training program. Siminovitch and Van Eron (2006) described this approach which included traditional gestalt concepts and incorporated newer concepts honed by the OD faculty such as self-as-an-instrument of change, resistance as a creative adjustment, unit of work as an organizing structure and attending to different levels of system.

At the same time another perspective, the gestalt coaching stance, was introduced by Stevenson at GIC. Derived from the OD work of Nevis (1987), Stevenson outlined the unique characteristics of the stance which "distinguishes Gestalt from other forms of coaching" (Stevenson 2005, p. 35) and described the underlying assumptions as well as the critical skills needed by a gestalt coach.

More recently the Gestalt International Study Center (GISC) at Cape Cod, Massachusetts began Gestalt coach training programs adapted from the gestalt OD model pioneered by Nevis in the late 1950s (Nevis *et al.*, 2008). Many concepts and methodologies are common to the other gestalt coaching approaches; however, there are notable differences in orientation and their approach to interventions (Carr, 2009; Simon, 2009; Walk, 2009). These distinctions are described later in this chapter.

Bowman (2005) observed that in keeping with their anarchistic roots, gestalt training institutes invariably, "differentiate into new organizations as a result of theoretical differences, practical considerations, or personality conflicts" (p. 17). Certainly in some cases this explains the development of similar, but differentiated gestalt approaches to coaching that mirror the approach of the gestalt training institution that spawned them. There may be earlier instances when gestalt coaching and training were publicly introduced and other variations in its practice but if so it is not currently reflected in publications written in English.

## The Development of Gestalt Coaching Around the World

While gestalt therapy is practiced in many countries, it has not been uniformly introduced nor embraced throughout the world as reflected in the distribution of gestalt therapy training institutions. Currently, the majority of gestalt training programs are in North America and Europe, followed by Australia and New Zealand and then South America. There are fewer institutes in South Africa, Mexico, and Central America and the least in Russia, the Middle East, and Asia (Gestalt Training Institutes and Associations, 2011). As many gestalt coach training programs are offered at these institutions or by their graduates, it is not surprising that gestalt coaching also has not been uniformly introduced or practiced around the world. For example, today in South Africa only 8.3 percent of coaches surveyed use the gestalt approach (Steenkamp *et al.*, 2011), yet in Europe it has been common for OD practitioners to integrate gestalt into their organizational and coaching work since the mid-1990s (Gillie, 2010).

Other factors have affected its distribution worldwide. In the UK there were no legal constraints on a psychotherapist also being a coach, so it was a natural transition for many gestalt psychotherapists to become gestalt coaches. Today, it is not uncommon for OD practitioners to seek gestalt psychotherapy training to prepare them for becoming gestalt consultants and coaches (personal communication; J. Leary-Joyce, March 21, 2011). The evolution of gestalt coaching within a country also affects how it may be practiced. For instance, coaching supervision, a process akin to clinical supervision for therapists, is a common practice in the UK and Australia (Armstrong and Geddes, 2009; Gillie, 2010), but uncommon in the US. Unfortunately, it is difficult to trace the emergence of gestalt coaching internationally due to the lack of related literature. At this time most differences in the international practice of gestalt coaching are discovered through experience, deduction from articles and conference presentations, or discussions with gestalt coaches from other countries.

## Gestalt Coaching Today

Gestalt coaching is not a preferred or popular coaching methodology as indicated in a survey of coaching psychologists (Palmer and Whybrow, 2007) and coaches (Grant and le Roux, 2011). The results suggest this trend may continue, as unlike gestalt coaching, the favored approach in the surveys was structured and goal oriented, with defined, concrete, measurable outcomes. These characteristics suit many workplace cultures and the emphasis on measurement helps the organization determine the return on investment. It is also a more familiar and therefore comfortable process for individuals facing the uncertainty of change. While pursuing clients' goals is not uncommon in gestalt coaching, pre-determined goals are held lightly. Consistent with gestalt coaching's more emergent and phenomenological approach a goal is viewed as a figure of interest that may evolve into a different figure to become a new goal.

The gestalt coach also values exploring the interplay of forces within an individual and between the individual and their environment. This holistic discovery process gives the client a better understanding of all the dynamics involved and more options for the focus of the work. This robust coaching approach is more likely to support sustainable change; however, it is also more complex and demanding of the coach. Hopefully the accumulating evidence that individuals must learn to thrive in ever increasing ambiguity, complexity, and uncertainty along with the recognition that emotional and social intelligence is vital to success and health will increase receptivity for the gestalt approach to coaching.

Additional issues that limit the spread of gestalt coaching are the difficulty explaining it and the lack of related publications. Concisely explaining to the uninitiated what gestalt coaching is and how it differs from other coaching models is cumbersome at best and confusing at worse. Even the word "gestalt" requires an immediate translation. The absence of a common definition compounds the problem and is a challenge especially when writing about it (Allan and Whybrow, 2007). In lieu of a definition, a typical gestalt coaching article describes its principles and/or uses a case study for illustration (Chidiac, 2008; Daley, 2009; Gillie, 2010; Grant and le Roux, 2011; Siminovitch and Van Eron, 2006; Simon, 2009; Stevenson, 2002). The underlying message is that the best way to understand and appreciate gestalt coaching is through experience. While true, it restricts gestalt coaching to a small select population.

In some cases gestalt practitioners add to the confusion. For instance, in a journal issue dedicated to gestalt coaching, Carlson and Kolodny (2009) explained that they use the term consulting instead as "coaching is one kind of consulting work" (p. 199). This is incongruent with the emphasis in the coaching field on differentiating the two.

To be fair, coaching itself is hard to define (Grant, 2007). Citing various authors, Grant (2007) reported that coaching "definitions vary considerably and have been the subject of much debate" (p. 25). Daley (2009) stated, "coaching is a slippery word right now" (p. 31).

The lack of gestalt coaching publications is the other barrier to the expansion of gestalt coaching. Simon (2009) commented that: "Gestalt theory can offer a significant contribution to the field of professional coaching" (p. 230). However, he found only six gestalt coaching articles, published between 2000 and 2008. During the same eight-year period Grant (2011) documented 227 scholarly articles on coaching and none of these were the publications identified by Simon (2009). As a consequence gestalt coaches look to the gestalt therapy literature to deepen theoretical understanding and for innovative practices.

The collective impact of these barriers is a limited body of shared knowledge among gestalt coaches worldwide and little stimulation for evolving the theory and creating innovative practices specifically for gestalt coaching. However, the literature search indicated there has been some increase in gestalt coaching publications since 2009, lending credence to Gillie's (2009a) assessment that the interest in gestalt coaching is accelerating.

Ironically, even though gestalt coaching is not widespread, it has had an impact on the coaching world. Several principles originally unique to gestalt coaching have been integrated into other coaching approaches; for example self-as-an-instrument. While this is a tribute to the power of gestalt it also gives the false impression that gestalt coaching is no longer distinctive; however, the synergistic effect of its concepts and methods cannot be duplicated. These principles and methodologies are reviewed next.

## Gestalt Coaching Methodology

Theory, models, methods, and principles build a fundamental platform for any coaching practice. They influence coaches' perceptions, meaning making, expectations, interactions, intentions, and interventions. Gestalt coaching practice sets on a foundation informed by a theoretical and methodological base that has withstood the test of time for over 50 years. One reason for this resilience is that gestalt is a process oriented theory offering ways to practice rather than dictating specific steps or what one has to do. Melnick and March-Nevis (2005) stressed that this focus on process is "of prime importance" (p. 23).

While there are others, the four core processes of gestalt coaching are: co-creating the relational field, using self as an instrument of change, using the present moment, mobilizing energy for learning and growth, and experimentation. The heart of all gestalt coaching, however, is increasing awareness of and contact with self and self-in-the-environment and increasing self-acceptance. This is grounded in "a deceptively simple yet immensely profound notion" (Bluckert, 2009; p. 91) that self-awareness and self-acceptance in themselves create change. This notion and the fact that awareness expands the ground of possibilities for intentional choice are the reasons increasing awareness and contact is a major part of gestalt coaching. It is a meta-process and the gestalt coach uses the four processes as ways to facilitate awareness, contact, and growth in themselves and their clients. These processes are reviewed next.

## Co-creating the Relational Field

Gestalt coaching is relationship-centered, as differentiated from client-centered (Leary-Joyce, 2007). The gestalt approach has always emphasized the emergent, contextual, and relational nature of change. Nonetheless, there is increasing emphasis on the intersubjective nature (Jacobs, 2009) of relationships in which no objectivity is possible;

the relationship is mutually constructed through verbal and non-verbal interactions. These non-verbal interactions in combination with dialogue are the vehicles through which change occurs within the gestalt coaching relationship (Critchley 2010; Gillie, 2010). The gestalt coach understands that this relational field supports or diminishes the possibility of change and that the coach's entire being, known and unknown, affects the nature of the relationship.

The gestalt coach also recognizes that partnering with the person to co-create the relationship heightens the coach's impact. Knowing this the gestalt coach maintains healthy boundaries and takes an accepting stance. Gestalt coaches hold that their reality is no more valid than the other's (Yontef, 2008) and do not try to resolve the tension of multiple co-existing realities by determining which one is "right". Holding this creative tension in the service of self-discovery requires a strong trusting relationship cultivated by the coach's transparency, empathy, collaboration, respect, and accepting presence.

For the gestalt coach the relational field is more than just two people; it is a complex triadic system of self, the other and the coach-person-environment system. The gestalt coach is aware of the qualities of each and attends to their dynamics and impact on moving forward. The principle means of achieving this insight is through observation, dialogue, and the artful use of self as an instrument tuned to these levels of system.

## Using Self as an Instrument of Change

The degree and consistency of gestalt's emphasis on the use of self, also differentiates gestalt coaching from other coaching orientations (Stevenson, 2005). The use of self as an instrument means how the coach "shows up" in the relationship affects the other's change process regardless of how aware the coach is about what she brings to the relationship. The coach's ability to use self effectively, however, is highly dependent on what is known about oneself. The more the coach is self-aware, the more she can use herself choicefully and with intention in service of the person's learning and growth.

Presence is a quality of self that also impacts the coaching relationship. The gestalt coach provides a presence wherein the coach is energetically available and has a fluid responsiveness (Chidiac and Denham-Vaughan, 2007). Some characteristics contributing to one's presence, like height, are fixed. However, some qualities of presence, like posture and carriage can be altered and change perceptions of the fixed characteristic. In either case gestalt coaches are expected, "to be aware of, to accept, to own and to be responsible for the presence they establish in the interactive field" (Siminovitch and Van Eron, 2006, p. 40). At times a gestalt coach intentionally alters some aspect of his presence to provide a quality that is otherwise missing in the relationship (Stevenson, 2005).

One aspect of presence is being able to "hold space" wherein the coach's sheer presence, not actions, creates a psychologically safe environment for the person's explorations. It is a quality of being and "not doing". Holding space requires the gestalt coach to contain his reactions for a time and "to 'fill' each moment with positive silence and relaxed attentiveness" (Stevenson, 2005, p. 46). This space becomes a velvet void, pregnant with possibility.

Exercises, experiments, experience, and coaching supervision in combination with reflection and feedback help develop the coach's self-awareness and presence. The use of self, however, "cannot be taught in a prescriptive or normative manner, since each coach will draw on unique personal experiences and knowledge, and each coaching encounter will present unique constellations of opportunity for the coach's use of self" (Siminovitch and Van Eron, 2006, p. 39).

The capacity to know oneself, consciously notice one's experience, and bring all one is to bear in the moment does not come easily. The lifelong pursuit of personal mastery is essential to the use of self in gestalt coaching and may not appeal to every coach (Bluckert, 2009).

## Using the Present Moment

In reality the only place where growth is possible is the ever present here and now. Latner (1986) emphasized that: "The present contains everything. Memories, dreams, reflections are all present activities … remembering is done in the present, planning is done in the present, reflecting is done in the present. It cannot be done otherwise" (pp. 16–17).

A gestalt coach uses the present moment as an opportunity to bring the, "usual, the habitual, and the unconscious … into our present awareness where they can be re-constructed, re-experienced and re-examined at length" (Stevenson, 2002, p. 35). Gestalt coaches have an expanded sense of the here and now (Parlett, 2005), which does not exclude reflecting on past experiences. The past contextualizes the present and sets the stage for exploring what is alive now as a result of the past. The coach traces the threads among the person's past and present stories to discover persistent patterns and styles.

## Mobilizing for Learning and Growth

The gestalt coach notices how the person moves through the cycle of experience (Figure 20.1) from sensation and awareness to mobilizing resources, taking action, assimilating, and withdrawing. Typically, this cycle has been described as a circular process and more recently as a continuous wave of energy. In either case the coach notices the quality of the contact with self and self-in-environment (Harris, 1999; Stevenson, 2005) and the flow of energy within the cycle.

Difficulties occur when interruptions slow or halt movement through the cycle. Traditionally, gestalt identifies six types of interruptions or resistances. Allan and Whybrow (2007) provide a robust description of each interruption, what it is, where it interrupts the cycle and examples of how each might manifest in coaching.

Working with these resistances is a core skill in gestalt coaching. Gestalt coaches respect resistance as a protective, adaptive function vital to self-regulation (Maurer, 2011), which contains both the desire to stay the same and to change. The coach brings a lively curiosity about the form resistance takes, the embedded polarities and the impact on movement through the cycle. The coach raises awareness of resistance so it is contextually appropriate and consciously chosen, enabling the person to use the resistance when needed and make other choices when it is dysfunctional.

Tracking the movement through the COE gives the gestalt coach, "a way of identifying more precisely where processes become 'stuck,' thereby preventing learning and change, and for creating interventions that help clients recognize for themselves the habitual locations and patterns of becoming stuck" (Siminovich and Van Eron, 2006, p. 42). Noticing the quality and degree of available energy is especially important in working with resistance. It indicates the strength of the resistance and likelihood of being able to working through it at that time. Walk (2009) stated: "Coaching is only successful when a client believes that the output is worth the energy expended to get through the resistance in order to change" (p. 252). When resistance does dissipate, the released energy becomes available to fuel movement through the cycle.

Noting where the movement in the cycle slows or stops is one side of the polarity; noting where it is moving too fast is the other. Typically, the gestalt coach discourages moving to action too quickly as it diminishes contact with self and awareness of the context (Melnick and March-Nevis, 2005), and the power of the coaching relationship and dialogue (Denham-Vaughan and Chidiac 2010), reducing the possibility of meaningful change.

While tracking the ebb and flow of energy is most commonly associated with the COE, gestalt coaches are attuned to energy in the relational field. Noticing the level of energy helps identify the quality of the contact, figures of interest, the uppermost figure, when and how to grade experiments, the scope and depth of the work that is possible, and what might be needed to help the coach and/or person manage the energy level. There is more to working with energy than just noticing its ebb and flow. As examples, Karp (2006) describes how hyperactive or inhibited energy may manifest and gives coaching tips for intervening with each type and Spoth (2006) provides a model for working with energy and examples of interventions for building and releasing energy.

## Experimentation

Co-creating coaching experiments is a potent process the gestalt coach uses to raise awareness and increase contact with self and self-in-environment. Melnick and March-Nevis (2005) emphasized that a gestalt experiment is not a technique as it, "is crafted to fit the individual as he or she exists in the here and now" (p. 108). An experiment is an active discovery process with an unknown outcome. They range from simple experiments, for example asking the person to substitute words such as "and" instead of "but" or "I" instead of "it" to complex ones, such as acting out both sides of a polarity. The gestalt coach suggests an experiment based on what has emerged and then co-creates it with the person so it is challenging yet possible. The experiment offers an opportunity to try new behaviors in a relational field where the person is less vulnerable and susceptible to shame (Lee, 1996) and learn something that enables him to take the next step forward (Melnick and March-Nevis, 2008). The gestalt coach follows a process for co-creating an experiment which includes identifying the theme or emerging figure, suggesting an experiment and getting agreement, developing the experiment and grading it for the appropriate level of challenge, doing the experiment and adjusting it as needed, debriefing the experience emphasizing what is new and lastly, helping the client integrate it. Experiments can also be crafted for exploration outside the session. In either case the intent of the experiment is not merely to actively engage the person, but to create a temporary arena that welcomes learning and change.

While some differences in individual practice are natural occurrences among gestalt practitioners (Leahy and Magerman, 2009), two published gestalt coaching models and their methodologies have notable differences (Nevis *et al.*, 2008; Siminovitch and Van Eron, 2006; Simon, 2009; Stevenson, 2005). For the purposes of the review each model is referred to by the gestalt institute where it originated; the Cleveland model from the Gestalt Institute of Cleveland, and the Cape Cod model from the Gestalt International Study Center (GISC) at Cape Cod. Both models have influenced gestalt coaching worldwide.

**Table 20.1** A unit of work (UOW): The architecture of gestalt coaching.

| Beginning | Transition | Middle | Transition | Ending |
|---|---|---|---|---|
| *Assessing and heightening the current "what is"* | *Choosing what to attend to* | *Acting on the choice* | *Closing out an activity* | *Closing out the session* |
| • Get grounded/centered/ present<br>• Establish/revisit confidentiality or other agreements as needed<br>• Explore the initial figure (expressed goal) and emerging figures of interest<br>• Increase awareness of self/ other/environment (verbalized and non-verbalized)<br>• Begin co-creating a trusting relationship | • Confirm uppermost figure<br>• Explore and fatten the figure | • Discuss potential directions of work<br>• Select a direction and recheck uppermost figure/emergent theme<br>• Articulate the resistance; the forces for change and for staying the same<br>• Co-create an experiment, exercise or another way of working with the resistance/theme<br>• Enact and adjust as needed | • Reflect, make meaning, identify learnings or conclusions (mini-closure)<br>• Identify what is new<br>• Generalize to "out there" and how it might impact the situation<br>• Another figure may emerge in the debrief, and the transition-middle-transition phases may be repeated if there is interest, time, and energy. | • Summarize and appreciate the work done in the session as a whole and the new "what is"<br>• Agree on tasks/an experiment to do in between sessions to further learning and movement<br>• Withdraw from the session for further assimilation and integration |

## The Cleveland Coaching Model and Methods

As mentioned previously, the Cleveland coaching model was initially articulated with the advent of GIC's first gestalt coaching workshop in 1994. In addition to the classical gestalt concepts and methods, the model included adaptations developed at GIC from the late 1970s through the 1990s (Nevis, 2004). These included Lewinian field theory and system theory (Stevenson, 2002) as well as new methodologies developed for work settings (Carter, 2004; Tolbert-Rainey, 2004). One tool especially useful in coaching is the unit of work (UOW). It provides a lens for shaping a coaching conversation, a session or a segment of work within a session. The UOW describes the flow of activities in the beginning, middle, and end phases of a gestalt coaching interaction. It guides the coach through the COE and at the same time suggests where work with polarities, resistance, and thematic experiments are most likely to occur. The UOW phases and the activities in each are outlined in Table 20.1.

Another unique aspect of the GIC coaching model is the concept of levels of system. The levels include the intrapersonal, interpersonal, subgroup, group, organization, and beyond. Each level is a part of the person's field and is a context containing constraints and possibilities for change. Each level is embedded in the level above, thus each level of system is a microcosm of the others. When working with an individual the gestalt coach can help the person understand the dynamics within and among these levels as they play out in the person's life. This understanding can inform what actions may be needed at the different levels of system and which are most likely to produce the desired change.

In addition to the levels of system, the gestalt coaching stance is also particular to GIC. It describes the values, attitudes, and competencies of a gestalt coach. Originally described by Stevenson (2005), this coaching stance has since been expanded and updated (Table 20.2) and is used to set coaching standards for students in GIC's coach certification program.

The holistic approach of Gestalt theory has always included a strong emphasis on somatic process. In the 1980s Kepner (1999), a member of GIC's faculty, refined and expanded working with physical process emphasizing the impact of the physical self on contact and relationships. Around 2003, a group of graduates from Kepner's therapeutic training adapted his work for OD and coaching. Known as physical process work, it can range from increasing physical awareness through voicing simple observations such as the person's posture to more complex physical experiments. Embracing the physical aspects of self is important for the coach as well. Embodiment, physical presence, and a person's energy signature (Spoth, 2006) are important aspects of self as an instrument. Furthermore, the quality of embodied resonance between the coach and client has been shown to be one of the main factors of effective coaching (Critchley, 2010).

## The Cape Cod Coaching Model and Methods

The Cape model originated from Sonia March-Nevis's pioneer work in gestalt therapy for couples and families which was adapted for organizational settings and coaching. There are many similarities in both models as Sonia and Ed Nevis were GIC faculty when they began evolving their model; however, its notable differences are in the coaching orientation and approach to interventions.

**Table 20.2**   The gestalt coaching stance.

| Category | Stance-competency |
|---|---|
| Cultivating the relational field | • Committing to dialogue with curiosity, inquiry, and suspension of judgment<br>• Cultivating meaningful contact<br>• Managing multiple realities<br>• Providing what is missing in the relationship |
| Empowering the person | • Using the person's interest and energy to guide the coaching conversation<br>• Reinforcing the person's ownership and accountability for his/her experience and work<br>• Building on the person's resources and strengths<br>• Acknowledging and respecting resistance and differences |
| Cultivating awareness | • Building awareness of self, other, and the relational field<br>• Seeing the person and his/her environment as a whole<br>• Attending to the whole of oneself and the other; body-mind, body-emotions, spirit, and relationships<br>• Taking an experimental stance |
| Focusing on the present and presence | • Embodying a mindful presence<br>• Attending to what is emerging in the moment<br>• Being choiceful in the use of self as an instrument of change |
| Embracing an ethical practice | • Adhering to GICs and the International Coach Federation's ethical guidelines<br>• Having an ethical compass |

© Gestalt Institute of Cleveland. Revised by Juliann Spoth, PhD 2009, 2011.

While all gestalt coaching starts from the proposition that a person is healthy and is doing the best they know how, this model has a greater emphasis on an optimistic orientation (Melnick and March-Nevis, 2005). The focus is always on the person's strengths (Melnick and March-Nevis, 2005) to the extent that even overtly dysfunctional behavior is reframed as an over-developed strength. Additionally, regardless of the observed patterns, the coach always focuses on the positive pattern first.

The notion of relaxed waiting wherein the coach does not look for anything in particular, says very little and waits for patterns to emerge also sets this model apart. The emphasis is on listening so the coach can discover what is not known in the belief that when the coach speaks it is about what she already knows (Nevis *et al.*, 2008).

The Cape Cod model also has a particular approach to coaching interventions. Interventions are intended to be useful, brief, and bold, specifically describing what has been heard, seen or felt so the person can recognize his behavior. Boldness is defined as staying with the intervention until there is a clear response, saying what others are avoiding, sharing the coach's experience of the other and using rich language such as metaphors (Nevis *et al.*, 2008). Interventions are either intentionally strategic (i.e., helping the person achieve a goal) or intimate (i.e., enhancing connection and bonding; Nevis *et al.*, 2003). Lastly, the word "experiment" is recast as "let's try this" and the practice is repeated until it becomes habitual (Nevis *et al.*, 2008).

Both models make important contributions to gestalt coaching and their continuing evolution strengthens the body of work available for the practice of gestalt coaching.

# The Art and Practice of Gestalt Coaching

In gestalt coaching the whole is truly greater than the sum of its parts. The power of gestalt coaching lies in the synergistic effect of using gestalt principles and methods in tandem and in tune with one's self, the moment, the person, and the context. This gives gestalt coaches the "ability to work at a deeper, more psychological level" (Gillie and Shackleton, 2009, p. 173) without doing therapy. Because of this potential, a gestalt coach needs to know when to engage and fully explore or when to acknowledge, support the client in the moment, and then move on.

As the primary gestalt coaching skills are embodying the gestalt coaching stance and the artful blending of gestalt methodologies in service of the other, gestalt coaching can best be described as a craft and the skillful gestalt coach a master craftsperson. The gestalt coach co-creates every session according to the person's needs within the context and nature of the desired change and the unique qualities the coach brings. The gestalt coach has "permission to be creative" (Zinker, 1977, p. 3) and as a result: "How we practice gestalt, how we bring these concepts into action very much differs from one practitioner to the next" (Leahy and Magerman, 2009, p. 136). While the gestalt coach may use some tools, the emphasis on process takes precedence over tools and techniques. Gestalt coaching does not ask, "a coach to fit into a mold or to learn a set of tools and techniques to operate on someone" (Bluckert, 2009, p. 91) rather it cultivates, "a way of being and engaging with the world" (Gillie and Shackleton, 2009, p. 173). The embodiment of gestalt values, principles, and coaching stance gives gestalt coaches the freedom to introduce other compatible method or tools and still practice "the gestalt way". For example, the mapping process used in immunity to change (Kegan and Lahey, 2009) can be used in working through resistance as it identifies a competing commitment which interferes with mobilizing energy.

The principles and methods used in gestalt coaching have been mentioned throughout this chapter. These include dialogue, the choiceful use of self, heightening awareness of what is happening in the moment; facilitating fuller contact with self and one's environment, cultivating presence, using a unit of work to shape a coaching conversation, expanding the ground, tracking figures of interest, identifying the uppermost figure, skillful tracking of the COE, monitoring and working with energy, identifying and naming resistances and themes, working with polarities, using descriptive and bold language including analogies and metaphors, trying on new language, creating experiments, working with the physical self, and encouraging reflection and integration. Unfortunately, there is no one gestalt coaching resource that outlines how to do each of these. Examples of the principles and methods used, however, are illustrated in the various gestalt coaching case studies, coaching practice descriptions, and the articles describing the gestalt coaching models. The references for these are cited elsewhere in this chapter. While this chapter has focused on coaching individuals, with slight adaptations these principles and methods can also be used when coaching teams.

Ironically, the most comprehensive and practical explanations of how to use gestalt methods are found in counseling books (Joyce and Sills, 2001; Mackewn, 1997; Passons, 1975). However, readers must discriminate between therapeutic and coaching applications. Unfortunately, while gestalt coaches experience and tout the efficacy of these methods, there is no outcome research to validate this.

# Gestalt Coaching Research

A theme throughout the coaching literature is the need for more coaching research (Drake, 2009; Grant and Cavanagh, 2007; Leedham, 2005; Linley, 2006; Stober, 2005). Despite coaching's popularity, there is limited evidence that coaching works (Grant, 2003, 2007). This can be attributed to the fact that "coaching is still at the stage of an emerging discipline, and the development of coaching-specific theory and evidence-based practice is a major challenge" (Grant and Cavanagh, 2007, p. 241). The core questions of what works, how it works, why it works, how well it works, how we know what works, when and with whom it works, and what may work better (Drake, 2009; Linley, 2006) need to be answered. While evidence of coaching's effectiveness is beginning to accumulate, much still needs to be done (Stober, 2005).

If "coaching research is in its infancy" (Stober, 2005, p. 13) then gestalt coaching research has yet to be born. To date, there is no outcome research in gestalt coaching literature nor does the literature reflect any urgency to validate its efficacy. The compilation of scholarly coaching publications from 1937 to May 2009 listed only one gestalt coaching article (Grant, 2007). In this article (Karp, 2006) gestalt therapy theory was used to identify problematic behavioral patterns and perspectives and tactics for coaches and counselors were proposed when working with these problems. Another study not included in the Grant's (2007) list interviewed gestalt coaches and clients to discover what the coaching experience was like, what successful gestalt coaching looked like and whether gestalt coaching was different from other coaching approaches (Leahy and Magerman, 2009). They identify five core aspects of a gestalt coaching experience, their characteristics and the outcome of each. Three of the five aspects that emerged reflected classical gestalt concepts: that is, the coach-client relationship, experiencing and experimenting, and becoming aware. The successful outcomes for each aspect were, respectively, a better relationship with oneself and others, getting beyond self-judgments, and expanded awareness of self and self-in-environment. Two of the aspects reflected a goal orientation: a person with a goal and realizing the person's desired results. Unfortunately, this exploratory study did not reveal the answer to the most important research question: "Is gestalt coaching different from other approaches to coaching?" (Leahy and Magerman, 2009, p. 83).

While there is no outcome research on gestalt coaching, there is some evidence that the theory informing gestalt coaching has a positive impact on successful change. Elliot (2002) conducted a meta-analysis of 86 humanistic therapy studies, including those related to gestalt therapy. He concluded there is substantial evidence that humanistic therapy clients show substantially more change over time than comparable untreated clients in randomized clinical trials. It can be hypothesized that coaching based on a humanistic psychology, such as gestalt, may show substantially more change over time. Coaching using a psychological theory base has another advantage. Grant (2007) proposes that coaches whose practice is based on a psychological theory, such as gestalt, can develop coaching interventions that are theoretically grounded and use evidence-based processes and techniques. Less than 5 percent of 2,529 professional coaches surveyed had a psychology background (Grant and Zackon, 2004), suggesting that gestalt coaches operate from a more substantial foundation than most coaches.

In lieu of outcome research, gestalt coaches document their impact through case studies (Allan and Whybrow, 2007; Gillie and Shackleton, 2009; Meulmeester, 2009), anecdotes (Leahy and Magerman, 2009), examples from their gestalt coaching practices (e.g., Chidiac, 2008; Gillie, 2009b, 2010) and heuristic inquiry (Barber, 2009).

While case studies are often dismissed by researchers, they have value. They "fulfill an exploratory purpose in coaching research where they point out relevant constructs for further study" (Stober, 2005, p. 3). In an emerging field such as coaching they are often the first stage towards controlled studies (Grant, 2007). Their main drawback is the limited ability to generalize, which also limits confidence in the results (Brownell, 2010). Thus, for gestalt coaching exploratory research is a logical starting place.

Although there is no empirical research to back their claims, gestalt coaches are not shy about asserting that gestalt coaching methods have a positive outcome. For example, Stevenson (2005) maintained that experiment, "leads to an awareness of what might be, or how things could be better in the future" (p. 39). Additionally, gestalt authors have stressed the importance of different qualities and skills for gestalt coaches, including self-awareness (Allan and Whybrow, 2007; Simon, 2009), experimenting in the "here-and-now" (Du Toit, 2007) and being able to use the COE and UOW to guide the effective use of self (Siminovitch and Van Eron, 2006). In all cases no empirical evidence exists to support their statements. Research on gestalt coaching has not yet caught up with the field's need for documented, evidence-based practices and skill profiles.

One contributing factor to the lack of research is that gestalt theory was first introduced in the late 1940s when there was no demand for empirical and evidence-based research. This seems to have continued, as even today there is not a great demand for research among gestalt practitioners. Some reasons for this may parallel the barriers to coaching research in general: a lack of funding (Bennett, 2006; 2008 Global Convention on Coaching); lack of agreement about the definition of coaching (Grant, 2007); underestimating the importance for a professional coaching practice (2008 Global Convention on Coaching); few university-based gestalt programs to support research; and differences in the interests of and resources between academic researchers and gestalt practitioners (Stober, 2003).

The nature of gestalt theory may also contribute to the lack of research. According to Crocker (2005) phenomenology discourages interpretation, avoids explanations about which elements are more important than others, and maintains that any theoretical construct has only transitory validity. Other than favoring impartial data collection, phenomenology belies the intent of research. Likewise, the nature of relationality poses a problem. When everything is subjective and related to everything else, no causal relationship can be claimed.

So, too, conducting efficacy studies is difficult when practices are not uniform or comparable. Gestalt itself is inherently creative (Zinker, 1977) and gestalt coaching sessions can vary greatly, depending on choices about use of self, what is of interest to the client, what emerges in the moment, and the experiments crafted. The artistic aspect of gestalt coaching makes it difficult to predict which ideas will emerge and how they will be implemented (Drake, 2009). Given this nature, the type of practitioners attracted to gestalt coaching are more likely to be attracted to creating than predicting or measuring.

Despite all the barriers to conducting gestalt coaching research, it must be done. Gestalt coaching research is needed to document what gestalt coaches have always claimed; gestalt coaching is a potent and efficacious coaching methodology.

## Future Research in Gestalt Coaching

The theoretical literature for the gestalt approach is historically vast and ever growing. The lure of the gestalt approach attracts excellent theorists and practitioners, yet fails to attract those who conduct empirical research. Given this void, the opportunity for research conducted by gestalt coaches is limitless.

Empirical research needs to be conducted that measures specific gestalt theoretical concepts and methodologies with particular populations of clients in particular settings. For example, assessing an increase in awareness following specific interventions may guide practitioners in choosing those interventions that produce the most impact. No researcher has studied the conditions of self-awareness or measured its impact on mobilizing energy towards action steps. Doing this research would require measures that quantitatively assess the degree of awareness and the impact on beliefs and assumptions. Longitudinal research which documents the effects of increased awareness over time could then follow. Such investigative research could be considered for each gestalt concept and application. For example, comparing the here and now approach with other foci.

Qualitative research is particularly suited to studying the phenomenological aspects of gestalt coaching and the results can be used to design further empirical research. For example, survey protocols could be used to gather qualitative information on the conditions of self-awareness. Dialogue and narrative could be analyzed for themes on the impact of increased awareness on beliefs and assumptions. This information could then be used to generate hypotheses and measurements for empirical research.

The coaching community could also benefit from comparative studies on the efficacy of different coach training and models. Gestalt coaching training programs could be compared and contrasted for their effectiveness in preparing coaches, as opposed to those trained in other methods and theories. The gestalt coaching model also could be compared with other coaching models for their impact on change and clients' satisfaction.

To remain relevant and contemporary, gestalt coaching must continue its development. Gestalt coaching is a robust process with firm roots. It has the capacity to embrace the best thinking and practice of the day just as gestalt therapy originally did. Some examples of current theories and methodologies that could add value to gestalt coaching are neurobiology (Rock and Page, 2009; Spoth, 2010; Wheeler, 2009), positive psychology/appreciative inquiry (Gordon, 2008; Seligman, 2007), immunity to change (Kegan and Lahey, 2009), deliberate practice (Colvin, 2008), and the energetics of coaching (Spoth, 2006). More infusion of intersubjectivity, the relational field, and gestalt development theory (Gillie, 1998; Wheeler, 1998) could also advance coaching practice.

Gestalt coaching clients' experience and the concepts and methodology need further study and description in the literature. It is time for gestalt coaches to stop being one of the best kept secrets in the coaching world.

# Conclusion

Gestalt coaching is a robust process with firm roots in a psychological theory and methodology that arose from some of the most dynamic and revolutionary theorists and philosophers of the twentieth century. Its application to coaching enables gestalt coaches to work at a deeper level and bring about powerful shifts (Daley, 2009; Gillie and Shackleton, 2009). The current challenge for gestalt coaches is to evolve the theoretical base and methodologies as gestalt pioneers have done for over 50 years. The next, and equally important challenge, is publishing.

In this chapter an overview of the theoretical foundations of gestalt coaching and a historical account of the development of gestalt coaching has been provided. Furthermore, a call was made for the continued development of gestalt coaching through research and publishing. It is hoped that readers will be energized to pursue an even greater understanding of the theory, practice, and power of gestalt coaching.

# References

Allan, J. and Whybrow, A. (2007) Gestalt coaching. In: S. Palmer and A. Whybrow (eds) *Handbook of Coaching Psychology: A Guide For Practitioners*. London: Routledge. pp. 133–59.

Armstrong, H. and Geddes, M. (2009) Developing coaching supervision practice: An Australian case study. *International Journal of Evidence Based Coaching and Mentoring*, 7(2), 1–15.

Barber, P. (2009) The nature of gestalt coaching and therapy. Retrieved from http://www.gestaltinaction.com/articles.html.

Beisser, A.R. (1970) The paradoxical theory of change. In: J. Fagan and I. Shepherd (eds) *Gestalt Therapy Now*. Palo Alto: Science and Behavior Books. pp. 77–80.

Bennett, J.L. (2006) An agenda for coaching-related research: A challenge for researchers. *Consulting Psychology Journal: Practice and Research*, 58(4), 240–9.

Bluckert, P. (2009) The Gestalt approach to coaching. In: E. Cox, T. Bachkirova, and D. Clutterbuck (eds) *The Complete Handbook of Coaching*. Thousand Oaks, CA: Sage. pp. 80–93.

Bowman, C. (2005) The history and development of Gestalt therapy. In: A. Woldt and S. Toman (eds) *Gestalt Therapy: History, Theory and Practice*. Thousand Oaks, CA: Sage. pp. 65–81.

Brownell, P. (2010) *Gestalt Therapy: A Guide to Contemporary Practice*. New York: Springer.

Buber, M. (1958) *I and Thou* (trans. R.G. Smith). New York: Charles Scribner's (original work published in 1923).

Carlson, C. and Kolodny, R. (2009) Have we been missing something fundamental to our work? *The International Gestalt Journal*, 32(11), 199–227.

Carr, A.A. (2009) Commentary I: Applying Gestalt theory to coaching. *Gestalt Review*, 13(3), 241–6.

Carter, J. (2004) Carter's cube and a Gestalt/OSD toolbox. *OD Practitioner*, 36(4), 11–17.

Carter, V. (2004) Gestalt OSD and systems theory: A perspective on levels of system and intervention choices. *OD Practitioner*, 36(4), 6–10.

Chidiac, M. (2008) A Gestalt perspective of coaching: A case for being more yourself. *Development and Learning in Organizations*, 22, 15–16.

Chidiac, M. and Denham-Vaughan, S. (2007) The process of presence: Energetic availability and fluid responsiveness. *British Gestalt Journal*, 16(1), 9–19.

Clarkson, P. (2004) *Gestalt Counseling in Action* (3rd edn). London: Sage.

Colvin, G. (2008) *Talent is Overrated*. New York: Penguin.

Critchley, B. (2010) Relational coaching: Taking the coaching high road. *Journal of Management Development*, 29(10), 851–63.

Crocker, S. (2005) Phenomenology, existentialism, and eastern thought in Gestalt therapy. In: A. Woldt and S. Toman (eds) *Gestalt Therapy: History, Theory and Practice*. Thousand Oaks, CA: Sage. pp. 65–81.

Daley, N. (2009) Coaching and Gestalt, the circle is complete. *The International Gestalt Journal*, 32(11), 19–33.

Denham-Vaughan, S. (2005) Will and grace. *British Gestalt Journal*, 14(1), 5–14.

Denham-Vaughan, S. and Chidiac, M. (2010) Dialogue goes to work. In: L. Jacobs and R. Hycner (eds) *Relational Approaches to Gestalt Therapy*, Santa Cruz., CA: Gestalt Press.

Drake, D.B. (2009) Evidence is a verb: A relational approach to knowledge and mastery in coaching. *International Journal of Evidence Based Coaching and Mentoring*, 7(1), 1–12.

Du Toit, A. (2007) Making sense through coaching. *Journal of Management Development*, 2(3), 282–91.

Elliott, R. (2002) The effectiveness of humanistic therapies: A meta-analysis. In: D.J. Cain and J. Seeman (eds) *Humanistic Therapies: Handbook of Research and Practice*. Washington, DC: American Psychological Association. pp. 57–81.

Fillery-Travis, A. and Lane, D. (2007) Research: Does coaching work? In: S. Palmer and A. Whybrow (eds), *Handbook of Coaching Psychology: A Guide for Practitioners.* London: Routledge. pp. 133–59.

Gestalt Training Institutes and Associations (2011) *Gestalt Global EJournal.* Retrieved from: http://www.g-gej.org/gestaltbookmarks/associate.htmll.

Gillie, M. (1998) Daniel Stern: A developmental model for Gestalt. *British Gestalt Journal,* 8(2), 107–117. *The International Gestalt Journal,* 32(11), 173–196.

Gillie, M. (2009a) Applying Gestalt theory to coaching: Commentary. *Gestalt Review,* 13(3), 254–60.

Gillie, M. (2009b) Coaching approaches derived from Gestalt. In: D. Megginson and D. Clutterbuck (eds) *Further Techniques for Coaching and Mentoring.* Amsterdam: Elsevier. pp. 29–48.

Gillie, M. (2010) The Gestalt supervision model. Retrieved from: www.the GilliePartnershop.co.uk.

Gillie, M., and Shackleton, M. (2009) Gestalt coaching or gestalt therapy: Ethical and professional considerations on entering the emotional world of the coaching client. *The International Gestalt Journal,* 32(11), 173–96.

Global Convention on Coaching, Working group on a research agenda for the development of the field. (2008) White paper: Research agenda for the development of the field. Retrieved from http://www.instituteofcoaching.org/images/pdfs/State-of-Coaching-Research.pdf.

Goldstein, K. (1995) *The Organism: A Holistic Approach to Biology Derived from Pathological Data in Man.* New York: Zone (original work published 1939).

Gordon, S. (2008) Appreciative inquiry coaching. *International Coaching Psychology Review,* 3(1), 9–31.

Grant, A.M. (2007) Past, present and future: The evolution of professional coaching and coaching psychology. In: S. Palmer and A. Whybrow (eds) *Handbook of Coaching Psychology: A Guide for Practitioners.* London: Routledge. pp. 23–39.

Grant, A.M. (2011) *Workplace, Executive and Life Coaching: An Annotated Bibliography from the Behavioural Science and Business Literature* (Jan 1). Coaching Psychology Unit, University of Sydney, Australia.

Grant, A. and Cavanagh, M. (2007) Evidence-based coaching: Flourishing or languishing? *Australian Psychologist,* 42(4), 239–254.

Grant, F. and le Roux, A.R. (2011) *A Gestalt Approach to Coaching: Optimising Individual and Team Wellness.* Paper presentation at the 1st Congress of Coaching Psychology 2010–2011, Southern Hemisphere (May).

Grant, A.M. and Zackon, R. (2004) Executive, workplace and life-coaching: Findings from a large-scale survey of International Coach Federation members. *International Journal of Evidence Based Coaching and Mentoring,* 2(2), 1–15.

Harris, J. (1999) A Gestalt approach to learning and training. Retrieved from: http://www.123webpages.co.uk/user/index.php?user=mgc&pn=10723.

Horney, K. (1937) *The Neurotic Personality of our Time.* New York: W.W. Norton and Company.

International Congress of Coaching Psychologists. (2010–2011) Welcome. Retrieved from: http://www.coachingpsychologycongress.org/.

Jacobs, L. (2009) Relationality: Foundational assumptions. In: D. Ulman and G. Wheeler (eds) *Co-Creating The Field: Intention and Practice in the Age of Complexity.* New York: Routledge, Taylor and Frances. pp. 45–72.

Joyce, P. and Sills, C. (2001) *Skills in Gestalt Counseling and Psychotherapy.* London: Sage.

Jung, C.G. (1961) *Memories, Dreams, Reflections.* New York: Vintage.

Karp, H.B. (2006) Greasing the squeaky wheel: A Gestalt perspective to problem behavioral patterns. *Gestalt Review,* 10(3), 249–59.

Kegan, R. and Lahey, L. (2009) *Immunity to Change.* Boston: Harvard Business School.

Kennedy, D. (2005) The lived body. *British Gestalt Journal,* 14(2), 109–17.

Kepner, E. (1980) Gestalt group process. In: B. Feder and R. Ronall (eds) *Beyond the Hot Seat.* New York: Brunner/Mazel. pp. 5–24.

Kepner, J. (1999) *Body Process: A Gestalt Approach to Working with the Body in Psychotherapy.* Santa Cruz, CA: GestaltPress.

Koffka, K. (1935) *Principles of Gestalt Psychology.* NY: Harcourt Brace.

Latner, J. (1986) *The Gestalt Therapy Book.* Highland, NY: Gestalt Journal Press.

Leahy, M. and Magerman, M. (2009) Awareness, immediacy, and intimacy: The experience of coaching as heard in the voices of gestalt coaches and their clients. *International Gestalt Journal,* 32(1), 81–144.

Leary-Joyce, J. (2007) To be or not to be: A gestalt approach to coaching. *Coaching at Work,* 2(5). Retrieved from: www.aoec.com/articles/Gestalt Coaching article.pdf.

Lee, R. (1996) Shame and the Gestalt model. In: L. Robert and G. Wheeler (eds) *The Voice of Shame: Silence and Connection in Psychotherapy.* Philadelphia: San Francisco. pp. 3–21.

Leedham, M. (2005) The coaching scorecard: A holistic approach to evaluating the benefits of business coaching. *International Journal of Evidence Based Coaching and Mentoring,* 3(2), 30–44.

Lewin, K. (1951) *Field Theory in Social Science.* New York: Harper.

Linley, P. (2006) Coaching research: Who? What? Where? When? Why? *International Journal of Evidence Based Coaching and Mentoring,* 4(2), 1–7.

McConville, M. (2003) Lewinian field theory: Adolescent development and psychotherapy. *Gestalt Review,* 7(3), 213–38.

Mackewn, J. (1997) *Developing Gestalt Counseling.* London: Sage.

Mauer, R. (2005) Gestalt approaches with organizations and large systems. In: A. Woldt and S. Toman (eds) *Gestalt Therapy: History, Theory and Practice.* Thousand Oaks, CA: Sage. pp. 237–56.

Maurer, R. (2011) The gestalt approach to resistance in coaching. *IJCO,* 8(4), 91–98.

Melnick, J. and March-Nevis, S. (2005) The willing suspension of disbelief: Optimism. *Gestalt Review,* 9(1), 10–26.

Melnick, J. and March-Nevis, S. (2007) Gestalt therapy methodology. In: A. Woldt and S. Toman (eds) *Gestalt Therapy: History, Theory and Practice.* Thousand Oaks, CA: Sage. pp. 101–15.

Meulmeester, F. (2009) Dealing with conflicts in organizations: A gestalt approach. *The International Gestalt Journal,* 32(11), 229–47.

Moreno, J.L. (1959) *Psychodrama: Foundations of Psychotherapy.* Beacon, NY: Beacon.

Nevis, E. (1987) *Organizational Consulting: A Gestalt Approach.* Cambridge, MA: GestaltPress.

Nevis, E. (1997) Gestalt therapy and organizational development: A historical perspective, 1930–1996. *Gestalt Review,* 1(2), 110–30.

Nevis, E. (2004) Origins of gestalt-oriented organizational development consulting. *OD Practitioner,* 36(4), 3–5.

Nevis, S., Backman, S. and Nevis, E.C. (2003) Connecting strategic and intimate interactions: The need for balance. *Gestalt Review,* 7(2), 134–46.

Nevis, E., Melnick, J., and March-Nevis, S. (2008) Organizational change through powerful micro-level interventions: The Cape Cod model. *OD Practitioner,* 40(3), 4–8.

O'Neill, B. (2010) Being present to the emergent creation of the field: Wordsworth, Buber, and gestalt therapy. *Gestalt Review,* 14(2), 171–86.

Palmer, S. and Whybrow, A. (2007) Coaching psychology: An introduction. In: S. Palmer and A. Whybrow (eds) *Handbook of Coaching Psychology: A Guide for Practitioners.* London: Routledge. pp. 1–20.

Parlett, M. (2005) Contemporary Gestalt field theory. In: A. Woldt and S. Toman (eds) *Gestalt Therapy: History, Theory and Practice.* Thousand Oaks, CA: Sage, Inc. pp. 41–63.

Passons, W. (1975) *Gestalt Approaches in Counseling.* New York: Holt, Rinehart and Winston.

Perls, L. (1978) Concepts and misconceptions of gestalt therapy. *Voices,* 14, 31–5.

Pearls, F., Hefferline, R., and Goodman P. (1951) *Gestalt Therapy: Excitement and Growth in the Human Personality.* New York: Julian Press.

Rank, O. (1941) *Beyond Psychology.* Philadelphia: Dover.

Reich, W. (1945) *Character Analysis* (trans. T.P. Wolfe). New York: Farr, Straus and Giroux.

Rock, D. and Page, L. (2009) *Coaching with the Brain in Mind: Foundations for Practice.* New York: John Wiley and Sons.

Rogers, C. (1951) *Client-centered Therapy: Its Current Practice, Implications and Theory.* London: Constable.

Seligman, M. (2007) Coaching and positive psychology. *Australian Psychologist,* 42(4), 266–7.

Siminovitch, D. and Van Eron, A. (2006) The pragmatics of magic: The work of Gestalt coaching. *The OD Practitioner,* 38, 50–5.

Simon, S. (2009) Applying gestalt theory to coaching. *Gestalt Review,* 13(3), 230–40.

Smuts, H. (1996) *Holism and Evolution.* New York: Macmillan (original work published 1926).

Spoth, J. (2006) Working with energy in organizations. In: B. Jones and M. Brazzel (eds) *The NTL Handbook of Organizational Development and Change.* San Francisco: Pfeiffer. pp. 424–39.

Spoth, J. (2010) *The Neurophysiology of Coaching for Change.* Presentation at the National Training Laboratory (NTL) National Conference (August).

Steenkamp, H., Odendaal, A., and le Roux, A.R. (2011) *Profiling the Coaching Industry in South Africa.* Presentation at the 1st Congress of Coaching Psychology 2010–2011, Southern Hemisphere, University of Johnnesburg (May).

Stevenson, H. (2002) Chapter one: Gestalt principles. Unpublished manuscript. Retrieved from: http://www.herbstevenson.com/book-chapters.php.

Stevenson, H. (2005) Gestalt coaching. *OD Practitioner,* 37(4), 35–40.

Stober, D. (2003) *Current Challenges and Future Directions in Coaching Research.* Fort Collins, Co: Coaching Research Consortium.

Stober, D. (2005) Approaches to research on executive and organizational coaching outcomes. *International Journal of Coaching in Organizations,* 3(1), 6–13.

Tolbert-Rainey, M. (2004) What is Gestalt organization and systems development? All about the O, the S, the D and of course Gestalt. *OD Practitioner,* 36(4), 41–5.

Walk, M. (2009) Commentary II: Applying gestalt theory to coaching. *Gestalt Review,* 13(3), 247–53.

Wheeler, G. (1998) Towards a gestalt developmental model. *British Gestalt Journal,* 7(2), 115–25.

Wheeler, G. (2000) *Beyond Individualism: Toward a New Understanding of Self, Relationship, and Experience.* Hillsdale, NJ: Analytic Press.

Wheeler, G. (2009) New directions in gestalt theory: Psychology and psychotherapy in the age of complexity. In: D. Ulman, and G. Wheeler (eds) *Co-creating the Field: Intention and Practice in the Age of Complexity.* New York: Routledge, Taylor and Frances. pp. 3–44.

Wulf, R. (1996) The historical roots of gestalt therapy theory. *Gestalt Dialogue.* Newsletter for the Integrative Gestalt Centre, 1–7.

Yontef, G. (2007) The power of the immediate moment in Gestalt therapy. *Journal of Contemporary Psychotherapy,* 37, 17–23.

Yontef, G. (2008) Relational gestalt therapy: What it is and what it is not: Why the adjective "relational". *The International Gestalt Journal,* 37(1), 92–112.

Zinker, J. (1977) *Creative Process in Gestalt Therapy.* New York: Random House.

# 21

# Narrative Approaches

## Reinhard Stelter

## Introduction

Narrative coaching is representative of the new wave, or third generation, of coaching practice[1]. The theory and practice of narrative coaching takes into account the social and cultural conditions of late modern society, and must be seen as intertwined with them. Some initial conceptualizations of narrative coaching were developed by David Drake (2006, 2007, 2008, 2009a) in the United States and Australia, by Ho Law in the UK (Law *et al.*, 2006, 2007), and by Reinhard Stelter (2007, 2009; Stelter and Law, 2010) in Denmark. In this chapter the aim is to present coaching as a narrative-collaborative practice, an approach that is based on phenomenology, social constructionism, and narrative theory. Seeing narrative coaching as a collaborative practice also leads to reflecting on the relationship between coach and coachee(s) in a new way, where both parts contribute to the dialogue equally and sometimes even symmetrically.

The practice of narrative coaching will be examined in relation to the concrete experiences gained in a related field of practice, that is, narrative therapy (White, 1997, 2007). Narrative coaching is to be understood as a reflective space, either of an individual or of a group or team, where the main focus is on values and on providing opportunities for meaning-making. Problematic experiences or events are reframed by the unfolding of alternative narratives; these are based on re-experience and recollection, as well as on the process of co-creation between coach and coachee. The conceptual framework will be tested by presenting central results of a research

---

[1] Law and Stelter (2010) characterize three generations of coaching by focusing on the *intentional orientation* of the coach, which only partly reflect specific theoretical positions: (1) Coaching with a problem or goal perspective, (2) Coaching with a solution and future perspective, and (3) Coaching with a reflective perspective.

*The Wiley Blackwell Handbook of the Psychology of Coaching and Mentoring*, First Edition.
Edited by Jonathan Passmore, David B. Peterson, and Teresa Freire.
© 2013 John Wiley & Sons, Ltd. Published 2016 by John Wiley & Sons, Ltd.

project. The ideas discussed in this chapter expand upon earlier concepts of the narrative approach (mainly formulated by White in 2007) by integrating ideas from phenomenology and experiential approaches with collaborative and social constructionist thinking.

# Theory of Narrative Coaching

Narrative coaching is based on a theoretical framework influenced by narrative and cultural psychology, as well as theories of narrativity. The coaching community is showing a growing interest in narrative coaching because this approach allows the coach to apply techniques that foster personal and social meaning-making. As a result, the coach is better equipped to deal with the societal, organizational, and cultural changes faced by coachees.

## The narrative approach

The emergence of narrative approaches in social science can be traced to the last decades of the twentieth century when a shift in epistemological understanding became increasingly obvious – a shift away from a notion of truth to a notion of significance or meaning (Rorty, 1981). This understanding has gained importance in therapy, counselling, and psychology (of which Howard, 1991 is an early example). When the therapist is helping and developing the psyche, the dialogue does not focus on the historical truth, but rather on the formation and elaboration of stories.

Bruner (1996) spoke about narratives (truth or fiction) that are based on *coda*, a specific morale, by "restoring teller and listener to the here and now" (p. 96). Stories have to make sense and be meaningful – both for the teller and the listener, who share a life context but see the world from different angles. Storytelling is always a cultural activity, central for the understanding and the forming of the culture and context people live in. Acting in specific contexts and telling tales about them are integrated and co-dependent constituents to the narrative approach.

According to Sarbin (1986), one of the founders of narrative psychology, a story is a: "Symbolized account of actions of human beings that has a temporal dimension. The story has a beginning, middle, and an ending. The story is held together by recognizable patterns of events called plots. Central to the plot structure are human predicaments and attempted resolutions" (p. 3).

The important perspective in storytelling is the selection of events that help to shape the plot of the narrative (Polkinghorne, 1988). In storytelling people are always selective and motivated. Sometimes they stick to specific stories, even though they might hurt and make the teller feel sorry and sad. Stories reach a status of truth for the individual. By changing dialogues – as in coaching (or therapy) – the coach helps the client create new, uplifting, alternative stories, stories that have significance and value for the individual and present the world from new angles and encourage other forms of behavior.

The three following concepts are central to the narrative approach: agency, intentionality, and deconstruction. *Agency* is a term that describes the human capacity to choose among various possibilities, to make choices, to mobilize energy, to pursue goals based on own reflections and earlier experience. This concept presupposes human beings as proactive in the way they relate to their environment: human beings are able to take an initiative and take their lives into their own hands. They do not react to specific impulses or stimuli, but are guided by their intentions, via values, purposes, or goals which are based on their interaction with the social and material environment. When individuals talk about their activities and their ways of acting, their stories take a starting point in specific events which are coupled through a plot. In the process of storytelling, events become meaningful for the teller and, it is hoped, also for the listener. In narrative coaching we speak about *landscapes of action*, a term originally developed by the literary theorists Griesmas and Courts (1976), and transferred to psychology by Bruner (1990) and to narrative therapy by White (2007).

*Intentionality* describes the individual's continuous directedness towards his or her environment. This directedness finds expression in the intentional orientation that the individual/coachee has towards others, specific tasks or situations. Because individuals are rooted in a social and material environment, their intentions express their values and form the basis for meaningful behavior. In coaching dialogues, values are conveyed by the aspirations or commitments the coachees express when referring to their work or a possible future that they have in mind. In narrative coaching these reflections about values lead to conversations about the coachee's identity and the meaning a specific activity might have for the coachee. This is clearly different from first-generation coaching methodologies (e.g., the GROW model), where the starting point of the coaching conversation often aimed at getting a grasp of the goals that the coachee wished to achieve (see also Stelter and Law, 2010). As the complementary metaphor to the term *landscape of action* mentioned earlier, the term *landscape of consciousness*, or better – *landscape of identity* – is used to describe the narrative practice that casts light on the coachee's thoughts and feelings that are related to his or her self-understanding and identity (Bruner, 1986). A narrative coach puts special emphasis on the interplay and interconnectedness between the coachee's *landscape of action* on the one hand, and the *landscape of identity* on the other. The exploration of this interrelationship deepens the dialogues and helps the coachee understand why certain actions are meaningful and valuable.

*Deconstruction* expresses the concept that reality is constructed in specific relationships and contexts and can always be deconstructed and rearranged, an idea originally presented as a reaction to idealistic philosophy and structural literary theory. Deconstructionists (e.g., Derrida, 1978) have turned against a structural text reduction where the intention was to eliminate inner contradictions and differences that persist in text or speech. This deconstructionist perspective invites a multitude of interpretations and thereby realities which are inherent in certain stories. In a narrative coaching conversation, the coach invites the coachee to re-tell stories and thereby seek a new understanding of earlier challenging, complicated, or unbearable events. New aspects, a changed focus or a renewed highlight on the players in the story may change the plot and thus encourage the teller to come forward with a narrative that differs from the original one. According to White (2007), deconstruction applies procedures that undermine the teller's reality and practices, which are being taken for granted. Referring to Bourdieu (1983), White spoke about making the familiar exotic, causing the teller to depart from intimate relationships and explore other ways of thinking and living, with the aim of producing a new plot and a renewed narrative.

When storytelling is used in coaching, specific events must be connected to form a coherent story (Gergen, 1994; McAdams, 1993; Polkinghorne, 1988; Stelter and Law, 2010). The telling – also in the coaching dialogue – takes place in a *well-defined context*: The coach supports the coachee by anchoring the story in a recognizable environment, with situations and events placed on a timeline. The various players in the story are described; character traits are attributed to them, thereby shaping their *identity*. A well-established narration includes players and objects that are formed in the course of the story and that keep the same identity. Only as an exception can the identity and character of a person change, but this will have major implications for the plot. The identity of selected players can also be described as a developmental process.

Often the story begins with an *opening event*, which gives the story its dynamic: "Monday morning I came to work, and the day started with a very important meeting with my boss." The story is shaped by the *intentions* and *aspirations* that drive the players. In the coaching dialogue, the coachee expresses *intentions* concerning the further development of the coaching process. Intentions build on convictions, beliefs, and values, which should be elaborated on in the dialogue and will help to form the narration and describe the functions of the different parties. In that sense it is also vital to bring to light convictions, beliefs, and values of others, which might differ from those of the coachee, and could result in tensions and conflicts.

The narration is formed by highlighting the *consequences* and ensuing *reactions*. In general, every narration has a *climax* where the whole is brought to a head and possibly to a conclusion. In the coaching dialogue it is important to elucidate the climax as a possible basis for initiating actions and processes of change. The interconnectedness and interplay between the events and the patterns of action taken by the players form the narrative *plot*. The teller expresses his or her intentions by telling the story in a certain way. The plot knits events together in a unique storyline so that the narration gives meaning and makes sense. Therefore a narration about a situation or context may differ greatly when told by another speaker. And therein lies the possibility for coaches as listeners and co-authors to come forward and contribute to the process of storytelling. During the coaching dialogue, the original storyline of the coachee is deconstructed and reshaped in the coordinated process of meaning-making between coach and coachee.

Narrative coaching is a fairly new approach in the field of coaching and only a limited number of (practitioner) researchers have contributed to its development. Nevertheless, a growing interest in this approach is evident, probably due to the growing changes and demands engendered by societal and cultural developments that will be presented in the following section.

## The societal and cultural foundation of narrative coaching

A strong argument for the formation of narrative coaching is based on the awareness of societal changes. Narrative coaching takes these changes into account by focusing on processes of meaning-making and by reflecting on values as central issues in the coaching process. Since the 1980s, our society has evolved fundamentally and radically and these changes have had a major influence on professional and private lives, and more specifically, on the way we generate knowledge, construct self and identity, and make sense of our lives.

A number of social scientists, using diverse approaches, have done major research work in the area of social change and its impact on the human condition. Coaching psychologists can greatly enrich their work by taking a closer look at the socio-psychology underlying the understanding of the key challenges individuals are confronted with in today's world. The following presentation – tracking from global to more individual aspects – offers a brief outline.

*A world of globality*    The first aspect that has an influence on the current forms and future development of coaching and coaching psychology is related to the changes in our world caused by growing globality. Ulrich Beck (2000, p. 10), the famous German sociologist, described globality as living, "in a world society, in the sense that the notion of closed spaces has become illusory. No country or group can shut itself off from others." The financial crisis of the years 2008–2010 presented clear evidence of the impact of globality on the life of almost every person. Climate change, migration, media coverage are further examples of how globality invades every workplace and household. Beck (2000, p. 11) discussed some consequences: "Globality means that from now on nothing which happens on our planet is only a limited local event; all inventions, victories and catastrophes affect the whole world, and we must reorient and reorganize our lives and actions, our organizations and institutions, along a 'local-global' axis."

Local and global are interconnected. Some of the challenges we are faced with and that should be dealt with in a coaching dialogue must be seen in the light of globality. We may have to adapt to a reality where progressively fewer elements of our lives can be controlled locally. Even the idea of control may be devalued by the influence of globality on individual lives.

*Hypercomplex society*    In our late or postmodern society, the individual is faced with a growing diversity of social spheres, each with its own autonomous "developmental logic". Social settings shape their own forms of organization and culture, and their members develop suitable ways of communicating, as befitting the local culture. But society in general has lost its inner coherence. The German sociologist Luhmann (1998) put it like this: "The system tends towards 'hypercomplexity', towards a multitude of opinions and interpretations about its own complexity" (p. 876; own translation). Following this line of thought it seems to be quite impossible to achieve a uniform and consistent sense of understanding about specific social contexts that people share. Furthermore, we are faced with a growing challenge in regard to handling social diversity and the interaction between various social spheres, where everyone speaks their own language and has different interpretations of the same events.

To become a member of a dynamically changing culture (e.g., an organization), the individual must have the competence to assimilate, adapt, and negotiate. Furthermore, employees will have varying understandings of a working situation; husband and wife will each have different views of their marriage. As long as they are not in conflict with one another, these differences will not matter much, but if the two parties try to convince each other of their views, disagreement will grow.

*A society of reflectivity*    The English sociologist Anthony Giddens asked how people's everyday lives are affected by the massive social changes of late modernity. Giddens (1991) regarded self-reflexivity and self-identity as a kind of permanently running, individual project where coaching can contribute in a positive manner, as a tool for self-reflection. Giddens (1991) said: "The reflexivity of modernity extends into the core of the self. Put in another way, in the context of a post-traditional order, the self becomes a reflexive project. ... The individual feels bereft and alone in a world in which she or he lacks the psychological supports and the sense of security provided by more traditional settings" (pp. 32–3).

How might this social analysis influence our work as coaches and coaching psychologists? The prevalent trend in the coaching industry has been to offer solutions or to be goal-oriented (e.g., Jackson and McKergow, 2007; King and Eaton, 1999; Pemberton,

2006). But following Giddens' analysis, coaching should not (only) strive towards solution. Coaching cannot function as the *quick fix*. Our social world has become so complex that there might be greater value in offering a reflective space where coach and coachee have time for self-reflection; such a thoughtful pause might, in the end, allow for new ways of acting in specific and sometimes challenging situations.

*Self and identity*   Self and identity have become central psychological issues in our late or postmodern societies. Gergen (1991), a leading social constructionist, has set the stage for a new understanding of the individual in contemporary life. He describes the postmodern being as "a restless nomad" (p. 173). The postmodern self is overwhelmed by innumerable possibilities and ways of acting on the one hand, and disoriented about what to do and how to behave on the other.

The Norwegian psychiatrist Skårderud (1998) defined the psychological state of many individuals in our time as "unrest" – a state of mind which has led to forms of experimentation in search of purity, control, and meaning. He described how one group of individuals finds expression through socially accepted behavior such as marathon running and extreme sports; others end up with psychological or psychiatric "dysfunctions" like eating disorders, cutting, stress, and depression.

## Coaching – reflecting on values and meaning-making

On the basis of this societal analysis, we can define the main focus and guiding question to be: How can coaches help to develop a reflective space in coaching dialogues? Two aspects serve as guiding principles for the reflective dialogue between coach and coachee, and for narrative coaching in general: (1) reflecting on values, (2) providing opportunities for meaning-making.

Both terms are placed at the highest level of intentional orientation and are interrelated with one another (Figure 21.1). This hierarchy of intentions makes clear that simply focusing on goals with regard to a specific situation or task – representing the lowest level of intentional orientation – narrows the perspective and can make it more difficult to allow for new understandings.

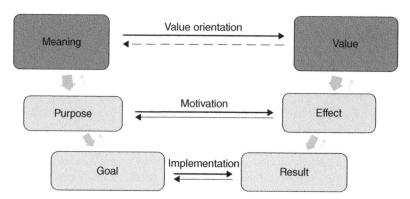

**Figure 21.1**   Levels of intentional orientation: Meanings and values as central in the concept of intentionality (Stelter, 2009; originally presented by Nitsch, 1986). The broken line arrow indicates that a focus on values (using the protreptic approach, see p. 413) can be a decisive factor in the process of meaning-making.

*Reflecting on values* In our society, which is characterized by a growing diversity in social and organizational values, we must encourage coachees to reflect on values as guiding markers to help them organize their private and professional lives. Many of these values are no longer timeless and universal, but are often grounded in the practices and events of local communities or working teams. The ultimate aim is to facilitate and improve communication, leadership, personal and social understanding, not by focusing on specific goals, but by reflecting on key values as a feature of the human condition. Putting values in the pivotal position of the coaching dialogue is inspired by *new protreptic*-based ideas of the Danish philosopher and leadership theorist Ole Fogh Kirkeby (2009). Protreptic, or meta-coaching, is a Greek idiom for the art of turning oneself and others towards the heart of one's life, a philosophically oriented coaching that focuses exclusively on the reflection on values and not on current and future action patterns. Protreptic is a method of self-reflection and dialogic guidance of others and has been applied in the Greek executive academies for "top managers" and commanders since 500 BCE.

In this phase the dialogue between coach and coachee tends to be *symmetrical*, meaning that both are equally engaged. The idea is to establish conditions for a reflective space and create moments of understanding by forming the dialogue into a number of events where the focus is on a different level of self-consciousness; together, coach and coachee create "something new" for one another. The basic idea of a coaching dialogue – inspired by the protreptic approach – is: both participate in the dialogue and reflect on terms or concepts such as "responsibility", "freedom", "cooperation", and so forth. Coach and coachee do not try to understand themselves as "empirical" persons, but strive to get in touch with what is "universal" in their nature. Unlike the usual (asymmetrical) coaching dialogue, this symmetry is important; both coach and coachee are involved and interested in the investigation of specific values, especially those of general interest for all human beings. In a narrative coaching framework we can speak about being a "fellow human" (Stelter and Law, 2010), where both coach and coachees (e.g., in a group session) resonate about one another's comments. It is the discussion about values followed by reflections from the other that the listener seems to find meaningful. Some central thoughts about values, partly inspired by Kirkeby (2009), are presented below.

Values are a major part of our selves and provide an entrance into the landscape of identity. Focusing on values leads to reflecting on the essence of an individual´s life. Values represent "a possible mode of certainty" as Kirkeby (2009, p. 155) stated. And he continued: "A value is an 'I can' based on knowledge, knowledge of what we have done, and will be able to do, and guided by ethical imagination by both deliberate and intuitive judgment" (p. 156).

Strengthening the landscape of identity will boost the development of landscapes of action and the coachee's competence (White, 2007). Values serve as guides for our knowledge and practical wisdom (in Greek *phronesis*). In that sense they help individuals establish their own purposeful and desirable way of acting. In an organizational context, values are meant to guide the employee to act purposefully, meaningfully, and with commitment to the organization. In order to have impact, values need to reflect personal aspirations.

*Providing opportunities for meaning-making* Meaning-making is considered one of the main approaches to facilitating the coaching dialogue (Stelter, 2007). Meaning is fundamental, because we ascribe specific values to our experiences, actions, our interplay with others and to our life and work. Things become *meaningful*, when we understand our own way of sensing, thinking and acting, for example, by telling stories about ourselves and our world. In the process of meaning-making, the individual or groups of people holistically integrate past and present experiences as well as ideas about the future. Meaning evolves in the interplay between sensing, reflecting, speaking, and acting.

Meaning-making is an integration of individual and socio-cultural processes. In the following, two lines of meaning-making are analytically distinguished; in an authentic dialogue these two dimensions flow into each other, are coupled:

1   *Personal meaning* is formed through the *actual experiences and (implicit) knowledge* that the individual acquires in various contexts in life. Individuals know – or better, sense – a lot about their practices, but rarely reflect upon the practical or implicit knowledge which guides their way of acting.
2   *Social meaning* is shaped through *social negotiation and narratives* that describe the life practice of the person or group in focus. From a *social constructionist* standpoint, meaning is negotiated between the participants in specific social settings.

## Theoretical orientation of coaching as narrative-collaborative practice

The theoretical basis of the narrative approaches arise*s mainly from social c*onstructionism and a non-naturalistic position (e.g., White, 2007). This theoretical stand has been extended in the following because social constructionism leaves out some elements which are fundamental for narrative thinking. In the following presentation of how the author has applied the theory to practice, three lines of thought will be coupled: *Social constructionism and phenomenology as central positions, and narrative psychology which joins them.*

The lines of thought presented differ in some of their basic assumptions, but there are specific epistemological similarities which make it feasible to integrate them as coherent intervention theory. Social constructionism, phenomenology, and narrative psychology are epistemologically linked by the following two concepts:

1   *The concept of reality.* In all three approaches, reality is not something definite and final. Reality can be constructed socially in relationships with others (social constructionism), or in the present moment of experiencing and will therefore change from one situation to another (phenomenology). Reality is also constructed by including or excluding specific events in a storyline and telling the story by following a specific plot that shapes reality in a specific way (narrative psychology).
2   *The concept of meaning.* Meaning can be based on social negotiation (social constructionism), on personal and embodied experiences (phenomenology) and on a specific discourse and storyline (narrative psychology).

With regard to this epistemological stance, let us take a closer look at the following three lines of thought as the foundation of intervention theory and as the framework for the application of coaching as a narrative-collaborative practice.

*Social constructionism*   Social constructionism deals with discourses between people and the implications of relationships and culture on the construction of the individual's reality. It is not the individual with specific traits upon whom the intervention will focus. The social reality of individuals and groups is understood as being shaped in relationships between various individuals and through specific social contexts (Gergen, 2009). It is therefore crucial for the developmental outcome of the coaching intervention *how* the coachee(s) talks about the challenges experienced in professional and everyday life. It is through language that reality is constructed, and the construction of this reality – formed jointly by coach and coachee – may lead to a readiness for change and preparation for action. Two interventional approaches inspired by the epistemology of social constructionism are *appreciative inquiry* and *solution-focused coaching*. Certain elements of these approaches can help the coachee form renewed and alternative stories. The coach will focus on aspects of success, strengths, and possible solutions that the coachee has, has had, or will find in specific situations and events (Cooperrider and Sekerka, 2003; Orem *et al.*, 2007; De Jong and Berg, 1997).

*Phenomenology*   Phenomenology has developed as a genuine "science of experience", with its main focus on how individuals create their own world. Husserl (1985), the founder of phenomenology, spoke about a "descriptive psychology", where the point of departure for psychological investigation is phenomena as *perceived by the subject*. In that sense phenomenology begins with a kind of empirical observation directed at the whole field of possible experiential phenomena, as Ihde (1977) stated: "Ideally, this stance tries to create an *opening* of a particular type towards things; it wishes to capture the original sense of wonder which Aristotle claimed was the originating motive for philosophy. Thus, its first methodological moves seek to circumvent certain kind of predefinition" (p. 31).

Phenomenologists have developed an empirical method for that open approach to phenomena called *epoché*, meaning suspension of judgement. In epoché, the individual attempts to grasp the pure subjectiveness of the world – the individual's world in itself. In that sense we can speak about an *individual, experiential construction of reality*. There are a number of strategies that allow an individual's perceived experience to be explored in depth (Stelter, 2007, 2008). A link to mindfulness is more than sensible (Spence, 2008). To counter the accusation of subjectivism, phenomenologists draw a sharp line between themselves and rational, empiricist traditions in philosophy and psychology, as represented by the method of introspection, a process of "looking within" one's own mind, that is, thoughts, emotions, and sensations are explored through a method of reflective self-observation.

*Narrative psychology*   From an epistemological perspective, narrative psychology can be seen as an expansion and adjustment of certain social constructionist positions by reintroducing experiential and embodied dimensions (Crossley, 2000; Polkinghorne, 1988; Stam, 2001; Stelter 2008) that are highlighted in phenomenology. Crossley (2003), as a narrative psychologist, expressed a need for a different kind of psychology that retained the ability of appreciating the linguistic and discursive structuring of "self" and "experience" on the one hand, and also included a sense of the essentially personal, coherent and "real" nature of individual subjectivity. Arguing for a narrative structure Crossley (2003) saw everyday activities being based on people's practical, embodied, and affective orientation within the world and concluded: "The whole process of narration and the implicit orientation towards narrative structure operates to transform a person's physical, emotional, and social world (p. 297).

Shotter and Lannaman (2002), Stam (1990), and Sampson (1996) all saw the possibility of linking phenomenological with social-constructionist thinking by establishing a narrative position. They are far from taking a naturalistic standpoint by, for example, regarding personality as anchored in more or less stable traits. Instead, they strive towards a culturally oriented psychology, where experiences and emotions are the basis for forming narratives shaping the personal and communal values of self and others. As Bruner (1990) has stated: "[values] become incorporated in one's self identity and, at the same time, they locate one in a culture" (p. 29). Telling stories to one another and developing and sharing narratives and accounts, either in a coach-coachee relationship or in a group setting, is fundamental for the process of social meaning-making; the grounding of an individual in a cultural context is always based on specific values and meanings. The narrative work in the coaching process can be regarded as a process of "the 'doing' of identity" (Kraus, 2006). Through forming alternative, more uplifting stories about events and situations, new connections between the coachee's self-understanding, values, intentions, purposes, and goals on the one hand and the coachee's readiness and possibility to act on the other, will be formed (White, 2007).

## Towards coaching as a narrative-collaborative practice

From the theoretical point of view, meaning-making is regarded as the essential factor of orientation in the coaching dialogue. Meaning-making integrates two theoretical lines, one from phenomenology and the other from social constructionism. In the actual dialogue these two lines of meaning-making are interwoven.

### 1   *Individual experiences and meaning-making*

In the first stream, the focus of coaching intervention is on *individual experience and personal meaning-making. The coach can* help the coachee(s) *to put words on this tacit dimension.* From a predominantly phenomenological point of view, "meaning is *formed in the interaction* of experiencing and something that functions as a symbol" (Gendlin, 1997, p. 8). This symbolization often takes a verbal form (at best through metaphors), but could also be expressed by other means, such as painting, dramatic movement, or writing. Together with the coach, coachees strive to understand their subjective reality or a subjective experience of their culture. Their focus is on the implicit, embodied dimensions of their being. As the starting point of the conversation, the coachees study detailed descriptions of certain activities and recount how they feel at the time (Gendlin, 1997; Stelter, 2000), in order to better understand their thoughts, feelings, and behavior. Gendlin (1997), a leading practitioner-researcher in this field, defined the felt sense as a form of inner aura or physical feeling about a specific situation, event or person. But this felt sense is often pre-reflective, namely pre-conscious and not verbalized. The coach's sensitive questioning helps the coachees get in touch with these implicit, embodied, and pre-reflective dimensions of their being. But this form of inquiry remains a challenge, because it is difficult to find words for experiences that are personal and embodied. Stevens (2000) mentioned that it depends on "how articulate, how skilled and expressive" people are in speaking about their experiences. Another challenge for Stevens is, "that the words used relate to a diffuse network of semantic assemblies both for the speaker and the listener" (p. 115), meaning that both speaker and listener must together create their universe of meaning.

One of the best ways to articulate experience is through metaphors (Parkin, 2001; Stelter, 2007). From a narrative perspective, White (2000, 2007) spoke about revisiting the absent but implicit, thus emphasizing the importance of personal meaning-making. His idea was to relate to forgotten experiences and episodes and join them with a storyline that is more uplifting than the training story the coach may have presented in the beginning of the session. By revisiting the absent but implicit reality, for example, by remembering the importance of a teacher in one's first school years, the coachees have a chance to re-tell and enrich their stories on the basis of their cultural background and life history. This opportunity may lead them to modify story plots and join events in a new way, thus leading to the creation of a more uplifting storyline and a positive, encouraging reality.

## 2 *Co-creation of meaning – developing alternative stories*

In the second dimension of meaning-making – which is integrated with the first in the actual coaching conversation – the focus is on the *socially* co-constructed reality. This constructive process takes place in the dialogue between coach and coachee, but more significantly in dialogues among a group of coachees. In a coaching dialogue, social meaning is formed in two different contexts: coach and coachee(s) co-create meaning in their dialogue (on the basis of questions, reflections, or mutual responses). Furthermore, the coachee can reinterpret situations and events that become the focus of the coaching dialogue, letting the coach and coachee together create new stories. Ideally, coachees realize that their position and opinion exist among many possibilities, and provide only one view of the world. Hence, open-mindedness and curiosity about whether others see the world in different ways or how they relate to things, is extremely helpful in the negotiation process or social discourse. The views of others may inspire an individual's personal or professional growth.

The dialogues are initiated by the coach through a form of intervention called outsider witnessing (White, 2007). In a group-coaching session, outsider witnesses are participants who reflect on a conversation by expressing what has been important and valuable from *their* perspectives. Their positions may help the coachees to see certain challenges or events from a new perspective. In a one-on-one session, the coach functions both as the reflective partner and witness – as a fellow human – of reflections and thoughts presented by the coachee. In that sense, we find, from time to time, a form of symmetry between coach and coachee.

This social dimension of meaning-making derives from social constructionists (e.g., Gergen, 2009) and narrative psychologists (e.g., Bruner, 1991), who suggested that reality is shaped in a process of co-action and in a social and linguistic discourse. This form of discourse is comprised of collections of statements and other verbal constructs which, in a given context, form the basis for development of meaningful linguistic systems. In these discourses, knowledge, understanding, and concepts are shaped in a way that meets acceptance in the social context and verifies the context itself. One of the central aspects of the discourse between coach and coachee or among various coachees is the co-creation of values and meaning: Which values do we find central and meaningful? Why do we do the things we do? Can we do things differently so that our activities are more fun, more efficient, or beneficial to our performance? The coach's questions or the contribution of others – singly or in a group – can enrich the current reality of every participant in the dialogue and thus make space for new meanings and the unfolding of new and alternative narratives. It is through relating to one another in words and actions that we create meaning and our ever-changing social reality.

## Narrative-collaborative practice: Some assumptions and guidelines

Narrative coaching is a process of art and co-creation, and the course of the dialogue cannot be predicted. In Box 21.1, a number of assumptions and guidelines are presented that might provide orientation for novice coaches interested in applying narrative coaching in their practice.

**Box 21.1 Assumptions and guidelines of coaching as narrative-collaborative practice.**

- Both coach and coachee(s) are conversational partners. Every participant contributes to the joint process of meaning-making and the production of knowledge.
- All participants strive to be flexible and willing to change, thereby making mutual development possible and allowing them to redefine their perspective and position.
- Being attentive to others and to differences can be very fruitful for one's own development and learning.
- All participants value the contribution of others to the dialogue and the knowledge that unfolds co-creatively, but at the same time they value possible and enduring differences.
- Generous listening is central for mutual inquiry, where interested and sometimes naive wondering helps to develop generative conversations.
- Paraphrasing of remarks or reflections made by the coachee and interpreting or shaping these reflections on own premises, including associative comments on specific reflections ("When you say that, it makes me think of ...").
- Flexible attitudes make it possible to redefine own and other positions; one is thereby open for further development and for learning from others.
- Using questions (as the coach) that invite the participant(s) to a change of perspective. Employing different types of circular questions, as used in systemic coaching.
- Inviting the coachee to use metaphors, and using metaphors as coach to unfold sensuous reflections and expand the dimensions of actions, perceptions, and thoughts through language.
- Coupling of landscapes of action (perspective on purpose, goals and action) and landscapes of consciousness (values, focus on identity, aspiration, dreams and wishes) and vice versa.
- Coupling of specific values to individuals who are or might have been important to the coachee. In this process the stories grow in richness and complexity, and can develop in a new direction (alternative storyline). This lets the coach strengthen the coachee's sense of identity, for example, by using the process of scaffolding to bridge the coachee's learning gap by recruiting lived experiences.
- Encouraging the use of narrative documents – a poem, short essay, concrete reflection or retelling of a story either by the coach or the coachee(s).
- Outsider witness procedure: others reflect on a story told by a coachee in order to cast light on its value and meaning for the storyteller and listeners.

In narrative-collaborative practice the outsider witness procedure is very central. In a narrative group coaching context the following steps are taken:

- Identifying/highlighting an expression or phrase used by the coachee: "What expression or phrase caught your attention as you listened to the story?"
- Ask others to imagine the coachee: What kind of picture do you have about the coachee's life, identity or mode of relating to things in general? What does this

expression or phrase reveal about the coachee's intentions, values, attitudes, aspirations, hopes, dreams, or commitments?

- Relating an expression or phrase to your own life: How does that expression/phrase resonate with your own reality? What kind of ideas about own intentions, values and attitudes struck you while listening to the story? How might elements of this story be important to your life, career, etc., and why?
- Description of own response to the story: How are you touched by the expression, phrase, or story as a whole? Where do your own experiences with the story lead you? What kind of changes in yourself do you notice?

In a one-on-one session these questions can be part of a reflective process where the coach functions as a dialogical partner, rather than the more traditional neutral facilitator of the coaching process. In these moments the coach–coachee relationship becomes almost symmetrical.

## Research Evidence of Narrative Coaching

Narrative coaching has a very brief history as a field of practice, so it is not surprising that little research has been done in the area. Even in the field of narrative therapy – which is closely related to narrative coaching – empirical research is rather limited. Probably the first and only randomized control study is Stelter *et al.* (2011).

The aim of the study was to investigate the influence of narrative-collaborative group coaching on career development, self-reflection, and the general functioning of young sports talents with the goal of achieving integration of their sports careers, educational demands, and private lives. Participating in elite sports is often a stressful endeavor. The participants in this study were all in high school and consequently had lessons, homework, and exams to handle, as well as coping with a potentially difficult transition to adult life. In addition, they faced a great many training hours and the pressure of performing well in competitions. Such a palette of challenges has been recognized as a major cause of stress in elite sports participants (Cohn, 1990).

A randomized control design with a total of 77 participants (N = 31 in the intervention group, N = 46 in the control group) including a pre-, intermediate, and post-assessment, where a questionnaire measuring recovery/stress, motivation, and action control was applied. For a minor qualitative interview study, six participants were selected for an intermediate and post-intervention interview.

The intervention was based on the theoretical framework and methodology presented in this chapter. Eight group-coaching sessions with 4–6 participants (age 16–19) were held in a time period of 12 weeks. The goal of the intervention was to involve the participants in a group dialogue, where the individual was in focus and where all participants in a process of collaboration and co-creation could shape meaning and consider the value of their actions. This would be done by forming stories about certain events and challenges and, if necessary, reformulating them into alternative (more uplifting) stories.

What did the statistical results of this intervention show? The quantitative analysis dealt with the 77 athletes who had filled in the questionnaires at both baseline and after 12 weeks. There were no differences in the baseline mean scores of the dependent variables, namely general well-being or social recovery. Prior to the repeated-measures analysis of these two factors, an internal consistency test was performed and revealed acceptable

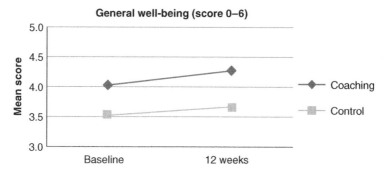

**Figure 21.2**    The group coaching participants scored higher on general well-being after the end of the intervention.

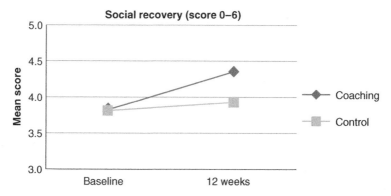

**Figure 21.3**    The group coaching participants scored higher on social recovery after the end of the intervention.

levels. The Cronbach's alpha on the scales for general well-being was 0.821 at baseline and 0.798 after 12 weeks; for social recovery it was 0.759 at baseline and 0.757 after 12 weeks.

The results (see Figures 21.2 and 21.3) demonstrate that the 12 weeks of coaching intervention had an impact on the levels of general well-being and social recovery. After the 12 weeks of coaching, the intervention group's score for general well-being was 0.311 (95% CI: 0.013–0.635, p = 0.029) higher than that of the control group when adjusted for baseline scores. This corresponds to an intervention effect of medium size (r = 0.22). Participants in the coaching intervention also developed a 0.381 (95% CI: 0.022–0.739, p = 0.019) point higher score for social recovery than the control group after adjusting for differences in baseline levels, reflecting a medium effect (r = 0.24) of the intervention in this aspect.

The qualitative study (see Stelter *et al.*, 2011) showed that narrative-group coaching had a strong influence on the identity of the interviewed subjects. Support and reflections from others helped clarify their thoughts about themselves, their daily lives, and especially their involvement in training and competition. The coaching group was experienced as a community of practice and as a context for social learning, giving the young athletes the opportunity to learn from the experiences, thoughts, ideas, and perspectives of others. By listening to others, they learned new ways of handling the challenges they met in daily life, in school, and in their sports careers. These strategies were formulated and further developed in collaboration with the coaching group.

The interviewed participants experienced an increased intrinsic motivation towards focusing on these new action strategies. This result could not be documented in the quantitative analysis and might therefore only be valid for specific participants. A reason for this might be that the participants in both the intervention and control groups (all young sports talents) were generally very motivated and high achievers.

Furthermore, the participants were encouraged by the other group members to continue behaving in ways which they experienced as meaningful and valuable – a process where the interviewees strongly emphasized the benefit of being supported by the others in the group-coaching context. In the group-coaching intervention, the athletes got in touch with implicit, embodied, and pre-reflective dimensions of their doing. Turning this embodied knowledge or felt senses into words led them to a greater understanding of themselves and others.

The qualitative study provided insight into ways of handling certain challenging situations; these ways were further developed during the course of the group-coaching process. The athletes realized that focusing on the present moment is highly valuable as a means of coping with stress and handling time constraints. They each developed their own way of being aware of, and concentrating on, the present moment. With regard to their participation in sports, they appeared to have improved their abilities to stay focused. In relation to everyday life, they have enhanced their abilities to avoid distractions from extraneous factors.

## The Development of the Narrative Approach in coaching

In the social sciences there has been a growing interest in the narrative approach during the last two decades (Lieblich *et al.*, 1998). The general understanding is that narratives help to build identity, both for oneself when telling them, and for the listener or reader who shares the story and relates it to one's own experiences and life situations. Stories develop strength by reciprocally influencing all participants (Sluzki, 1992). The stories of others can be a bearing compass for the listeners, which can help them form and revise their own narratives, and thereby make their own way of living (more) intelligible.

In the theory and practice of coaching, the narrative approach has recently found entrance to the field, often inspired by authors of narrative therapy (especially White, 1997, 2000, 2007). Because of the non-labelling approach to the client and the focus on best intentions and future possibilities, narrative therapy in its theory and practice is not fundamentally different from narrative coaching. It is only the clientele and the focus of the conversation that transforms narrative coaching into something different.

In narrative coaching a number of conceptual and theoretically-based articles have been produced; for example by Drake (2007, 2008, 2009). His primary research interest has been the role of stories in understanding and shaping identity, development, and change. To assist the teaching of his work and to provide basic orientation for the narrative coaching practice, Drake (2007) has developed the so-called *narrative diamond*. The model helps to establish links between the four corners of the *diamond* in the narrative field: the narrator, the listener, the characters, and the story, which is embedded in a larger context of a specific community or organization.

Recently, Drake tried to combine narrative thinking with the psychodynamic-oriented attachment theory which is based on the study of the patterns of connection and communication between parents and infants, and how they shape the latter's cognitive, emotional, and social development (Drake, 2009). Here some narrative thinkers would say that Drake has moved too far from the original social construction framework. Drake's attempt to broaden the perspective of narrative coaching to more than just social construction and deconstruction is commendable, but the move towards essentialist thinking diverges too far from fundamental narrative positions. In the theoretical foundation presented in this chapter, the intention of broadening the perspective has been similar (see also Stelter, 2007), but the path is different. Here the focus is on the inclusion of a phenomenological and experiential perspective.

It seems that coaches in a number of countries show special interest in narrative coaching. Denmark has become a vital ground for the development of narrative coaching and consulting. In recent years several books that give a good introduction to narrative thinking have been published (Nielsen *et al.*, 2010; Schnoor, 2009). In Australia – through the work of Drake and the Dulwich Centre in Adelaide – and in South Africa (Royston, 2011), there is a growing interest in narrative coaching as well. Evidently there is a special affinity for community orientation in these countries, which supports a narrative approach.

## Future Research

The lack of research in narrative coaching provides significant opportunities for researches to explore this area of practice through both quantitative research and qualitative inquiry. Stelter's research (Stelter *et al.*, 2011) needs to be further explored. One option would be to repeat the study within an organizational context, or with a sample of individuals seeking coping with career transition – a similar high stress period. Furthermore, the narrative approach should be applied and evaluated in the health and social sector, where the potential of the intervention to develop social capital and social coherence, especially in group settings, could be further explored and documented.

Other key questions, too, need to be understood, in common with other approaches. For example, what presenting issues is narrative coaching best suited to address. We might hypothesize that issues where the focus is on fundamental meaning and value issue in work and life may be well suited to a narrative approach. Further, given the successful outcomes from the only RCT narrative study, it will be interesting to explore the active ingredients which produce the positive effect. Which ingredients does narrative coaching have in common with other approaches, and which aspects are distinctive and unique? Here, it seems to be important not only to focus on statistics, but to go in depth and investigate the subjective experiences of coachees participating in narrative coaching, and compare these results with similar studies of other approaches. Finally, it seems to be worthwhile to focus on the role of the narrative coach and the coach-coachee(s) relationship that can be unfolded in narrative-collaborative dialogues. Here, linguistically-based research could give a totally new perspective to coaching research.

## Conclusion

When we consider the chaotic time we live in and the social changes we all are faced with, narrative coaching can be regarded as a promising form of intervention. The central perspective of this approach focuses less on specific goals right from the beginning of the course of coaching, but rather on meeting challenges by means of reflection and the exploration of values and on meaning-making – meanings that help to explain personal and professional aspirations and ways of relating to the world. Coach and coachee are co-creators of renewed stories that help the coachees to see things from a different angle. But this new perspective is more than just a new idea or solution; it is already embedded in a narration that links relevant events to one another and connects past, present and future. Meaning is embedded in the plot of the renewed or alternative story; life then appears to make more sense.

Current theory-based research has formed a complex, more or less coherent conceptual frame, and the first empirical study on narrative coaching indicated that the approach can have a significant impact on social recovery and general well-being. Using coaching as a narrative-collaborative practice in group contexts seems to be promising, because it helps to develop social capital (Bourdieu, 1983), a theoretical concept that highlights the importance of others as a central social anchor and leads to personal well-being and social integration.

# References

Beck, U. (2000) *What is Globalization?* Oxford: Policy.

Bourdieu, P. (1983) Forms of capital. In: J.C. Richards (ed.) *Handbook of Theory and Research for the Sociology of Education.* New York: Greenwood Press.

Bruner, J. (1990) *Acts of Meaning.* Cambridge, MA: Harvard University Press.

Bruner, J. (1991) The narrative construction of reality. *Critical Inquiry,* 18(1), 1–21.

Bruner, J. (1996) *The Culture of Education.* Cambridge, MA: Harvard University Press.

Cohn, P.J. (1990) An exploratory study on sources of stress and athlete burnout in youth golf. *The Sport Psychologist,* 4(2), 95–106.

Cooperrider, D.L. and Sekerka, L.E. (2003) Elevation of inquiry into appreciable world – toward a theory of positive organizational change. In: K. Cameron, J. Dutton, and R. Quimm (eds) *Positive Organizational Scholarship.* San Fransisco: Berrett-Koehler, pp. 225–40.

Crossley, M. (2000) *Introducing Narrative Psychology.* Buckingham, UK: Open University Press.

Crossley, M.L. (2003) Formulating narrative psychology: The limitations of contemporary social constructionism. *Narrative Inquiry,* 13, 287–300.

De Jong, P. and Berg, I.K. (1997) *Interviewing for Solutions.* Pacific Grove, CA: Brooks/Cole.

Derrida, J. (1978) *Writing and Difference.* Chicago: University of Chicago.

Drake, D.B. (2006) Narrative coaching: The foundation and framework for a story-based practice. *Narrative Matters International Conference.* Wolfville, Nova Scotia.

Drake, D.B. (2007) The art of thinking narratively: Implications for coaching psychology and practice. *Australian Psychologist,* 42(4), 283–94.

Drake, D.B. (2008) Thrice upon a time: Narrative structure and psychology as a platform for coaching. In: D.B. Drake, K. Gortz and D. Brennan (eds) *The Philosophy and Practice of Coaching: Insights and Issues for a New Era.* London: John Wiley and Sons. pp. 55–71.

Drake, D.B. (2009a) Narrative coaching. In: E. Cox, T. Bachkirova and D. Clutterbuck (eds) *The Sage Handbook of Coaching.* London: Sage. pp. 120–31.

Drake, D.B. (2009b) Using attachment theory in coaching leaders: The search for a coherent narrative. *International Coaching Psychology Review,* 4(1), 49–58.

Gendlin, E.T. (1997) *Experiencing and the Creation of Meaning.* Evanston: Northwestern University Press (original from 1962).

Gergen, K.J. (1991) *The Saturated Self – Dilemmas of Identity in Contemporary Life.* New York: Basic Books.

Gergen, K.J. (1994) *Realities and Relationships – Soundings in Social Construction.* Cambridge, MA: Harvard University Press.

Gergen, K.J. (2009) *Relational Being. Beyond Self and Community.* Oxford: Oxford University Press.

Giddens, A. (1991) *Modernity and Self-identity – Self and Society in Late Modern Age.* Oxford: Polity.

Greismas, A.J. and Courtès, J. (1976) The cognitive dimension of narrative discourse. *New Literary History,* 7(3), 433–47.

Howard, G.S. (1991) Culture tales: A narrative approach to thinking, cross-cultural psychology and psychotherapy. *American Psychologist,* 46(3), 187–97.

Husserl, E. (1985) Encyclopaedia Britannica. In: E. Husserl (ed.) *Die phänomenologische Methode I* (pp. 196–206). Stuttgart: Reclam.

Ihde, D. (1977) *Experimental Phenomenology: An Introduction.* New York: Putnam's Sons.

Jackson, P.Z. and McKergow, M. (2007) *The Solutions Focus: Making Coaching and Change Simple* (2nd edn). London/Boston: Nicholas Brealey.

King, P. and Eaton, J. (1999) Coaching for results. *Industrial and Commercial Training,* 31(4), 145–51.

Kirkeby, O.F. (2009) *The New Protreptic – the Concept and the Art.* Copenhagen: Copenhagen Business School Press.

Kraus, W. (2006) The narrative negotiation of identity and belonging. *Narrative Inquiry,* 16(1), 103–11.

Law, H.C. (2007) Narrative coaching and psychology of learning from multicultural perspectives. In S. Palmer, and A. Whybrow, (2007 Ed). *Handbook of Coaching Psychology.* London: Routledge.

Law, H.C. and Stelter, R. (2009) Multi story – coaching narrative. *Coaching at Work,* 5(2), 28–33.

Law, H.C., Aga, S., and Hill, J. (2006) "Creating a 'camp fire' at home" – narrative coaching – community coaching and mentoring network conference report and reflection. In: H.C. Law (ed.) *The Cutting Edge,* 7(1), 2, Peterborough, School of Arts Publication.

Law, H.C., Ireland, S., and Hussain, Z. (2007) *Psychology of Coaching, Mentoring and Learning.* Chichester: John Wiley and Sons.

Lieblich, A., Tuval-Mashiach, R., and Zilber, T. (1998) *Narrative Research: Reading, Analysis and Interpretation.* Thousand Oaks, CA: Sage.

Luhmann, N. (1998) *Die Gesellschaft der Gesellschaft (The Society of Society).* Frankfurt/M: Suhrkamp.

McAdams, D.P. (1993) *The Stories We Live By: Personal Myths and the Making of the Self.* New York: Guilford Press.

Nielsen, K. S., Klinke, M., and Gregersen, J. (2010) *Narrative Coaching – en ny fortælling (Narrative Coaching – a New Narrative).* Virum: Dansk Psykologisk Forlag.

Orem, S.L., Binkert, J., and Clancy, A.L. (2007) *Appreciative Coaching – a Positive Process for Change.* San Francisco, CA: Jossey-Bass.

Parkin, M. (2001) *Tales for Coaching: Using Stories and Metaphors with Individuals and Small Groups.* London: Kogan Page.

Pemberton, C. (2006) *Coaching to Solutions: A Manager's Toolkit for Performance Delivery.* Oxford: Butterworth-Heinemann.

Polkinghorne, D.P. (1988) *Narrative Knowing and the Human Sciences.* Albany, NY: SUNY Press.

Rorty, R. (1981) *Philosophy and the Mirror of Nature.* Princeton, NJ: Princeton University Press.

Royston, V. (2011) *The Opportunities and Challenges of Applying a Narrative Coaching Methodology to an Executive Population Within South Africa.* Paper presented at the 1st International Congress for Coaching Psychology Southern Hemisphere event, May 27, 2011.

Sampson, E.E. (1996) Establishing embodiment in psychology. *Theory Psychology,* 6, 601–24.

Sarbin, T.R. (ed.) (1986) *Narrative Psychology: The Storied Nature of Human Conduct.* New York: Praeger.

Schnoor, M (2009) *Narrative Organisationsudvikling (Narratively Based Organizational Development).* Virum: Dansk Psykologisk Forlag.

Shotter, J. and Lannamann, J.W. (2002) The situation of social constructionism: Its "imprisonment" within the ritual of theory-criticism-and-debate. *Theory and Psychology,* 12(5), 577–609.

Skårderud, F. (1998) *Uro (Unrest) – en reise i det moderne selv.* Olso: Aschehoug.

Sluzki, C.E. (1992) Transformations: A blueprint for narrative changes in therapy. *Family Process,* 31, 142–58.

Spence, G. (2008) *New Directions in Evidence-Based Coaching: Investigations into the Impact of Mindfulness Training on Goal Attainment and Well-Being.* Saarbrücken: VDM Verlag Dr. Mueller.

Stam, H.J. (1990) Rebuilding the ship at the sea: The historical and theoretical problems of constructionist epistemologies in psychology. *Canadian Psychology*, 31, 239–53.

Stam, H. (ed.) (2001) Social constructionism and its critics. *Theory and Psychology*, 11, 3.

Stelter, R. (2000) The transformation of body experience into language. *Journal of Phenomenological Psychology*, 31, 63–77.

Stelter, R. (2007) Coaching: A process of personal and social meaning making. *International Coaching Psychology Review*, 2(2), 191–201.

Stelter, R. (2008) Learning in the light of the first-person approach. In: T.S.S. Schilhab, M. Juelskjær, and T. Moser (eds) *The Learning Body* (pp. 45–65). Copenhagen: Danish University School of Education Press.

Stelter, R. (2009) Coaching as a reflective space in a society of growing diversity – towards a narrative, postmodern paradigm. *International Coaching Psychology Review*, 4(2), 207–17.

Stelter, R. and Law, H. (2010) Coaching – narrative-collaborative practice. *International Coaching Psychology Review*, 5(2), 152–64.

Stelter, R., Nielsen, G., and Wikman, J. (2011) Narrative-collaborative group coaching develops social capital – a randomized control trial and further implications of the social impact of the intervention. *Coaching: An International Journal of Research, Theory and Practice.* 4(2), 123–37.

Stevens, R. (2000) Phenomenological approaches to the study of conscious awareness. In: M. Velmans (ed.) *Investigating Phenomenal Consciousness* (pp. 99–120). Amsterdam/Philadelphia: John Benjamins.

White, M. (1997) *Narratives of Therapists' Lives.* Adelaide: Dulwich Centre Publications.

White, M. (2000) *Reflections on Narrative Practice. Essays and Interviews.* Adelaide: Dulwich Centre Publications.

White, M. (2007) *Maps of Narrative Practice.* New York: Norton.

# 22

# Positive Psychology Approaches

## Teresa Freire

## Introduction

There is growing consensus regarding the development of coaching as a scientific discipline, although it still appears to be in an early stage of theory development. As highlighted by Grant *et al.* (2010), a coherent body of knowledge supporting coaching is lacking. In fact, coaching interventions have been used in a variety of populations and issues (Grant, 2006) and have grown significantly since the 1990s (Palmer and Whybrow, 2005), but further research must be conducted to obtain a widely agreed upon definition and to investigate the professional training techniques that have thus far varied significantly (Biswas-Diener and Dean, 2007). Kauffman and Scoular (2004) argue that there is currently a second generation of coaches (researchers and professionals) who must focus their attention on the development of theories related to human development and on research designs to study the efficacy of coaching.

Within this movement, psychological theories and models contributed to a relevant and fruitful scientific field in improving coaching processes and products (Grant, 2001). More recently, "many have claimed that the emerging area within psychology known as positive psychology holds a great promise for advancing knowledge about optimal human functioning and improving the quality of life in modern societies" (Donaldson, 2011, p. 3). Scientific knowledge based on positive psychology has been strongly applied by many researchers and professionals toward improvements in many important aspects of modern life, including improvements in societies and in the lives of individuals. Some of the main topics in positive psychology are now well known and defined, and this background facilitates the definition of core areas in research and practice in new and emergent fields. These areas include well-being and happiness, positive emotions, and character strengths (cf. Donaldson *et al.*, 2011).

The aim of this chapter is to discuss how positive psychology science can be applied to coaching conceptualization and practices, considering existing theoretical and empirical literature.

*The Wiley Blackwell Handbook of the Psychology of Coaching and Mentoring*, First Edition.
Edited by Jonathan Passmore, David B. Peterson, and Teresa Freire.
© 2013 John Wiley & Sons, Ltd. Published 2016 by John Wiley & Sons, Ltd.

## Positive Psychology Approaches and Coaching

Coaching is one of the applied fields that can benefit from this science of positive psychology, specifically in relation to questions regarding work life and organizations. The science of positive psychology is being applied to improve workplace coaching practices, leadership and organizational development efforts, organizational virtuousness, psychological capital, and work flow. As stated by Ko and Donaldson (2011), during the past decade, an increasing number of organizational scholars have attempted to determine how positive psychology can be used to improve organizational effectiveness and employee well-being. Their efforts in this domain led to the emergence of a substantial body of literature that presents diverse information regarding how to improve the context of work through the science of positive psychology within the new perspective that work involves life and that life must have meaning, resulting in better work.

The first coaching movement was focused on leadership or executive coaching. However, since the 1980s, the executive coaching field has exploded in popularity and entered a new era of services from top management to other client groups. As a consequence, a large number of people who call themselves coaches provide executive, performance enhancement, and life coaching for an ever-growing segment of the population (Kauffman and Scoular, 2004). In this process, coaching psychology has been one of the most important contributors to the development and growth of the field and has contributed to the emergence and development of both executive and life coaching. Sharing the perspective of other authors, Grant (2001) stated that the aim of executive or life coaching is sustained cognitive, emotional, and behavioral changes that facilitate goal attainment and performance enhancement either in one's work or in one's personal life.

Scholars who are interested in the world of work and organizational settings realize that the work world is embodied in daily life and that daily life is also defined by work life. Thus, work and organizations are two of the main applied contexts for positive psychology. Some scholars claim that positive psychology is a fresh lens through which we can focus research on human and organizational behavior to improve positive institutions and organizations, work effectiveness, and employee well-being, which represented some of the initial concerns and goals to achieve in the development of the coaching field (Donaldson, 2011; Kauffman, 2009; Seligman, 2007).

In the past two decades, positive psychology emerged with a new focus on the study of human functioning and condition, and posited that little is known about how normal people flourish under benign conditions (Seligman and Csikszentmihalyi, 2000). According to these authors (who initiated the movement for this new scientific field), the new focus is on enhancing resources, strengths and competencies, and building positive qualities rather than resolving problems, eliminating weaknesses, or only repairing the worst things in life. In their formal presentation of what positive psychology entails in the 2000 positive psychology special issue of the *American Psychologist*, these authors demonstrated how this movement should progress along different levels, such as subjective, individual, group, and organizational/institutional levels.

The emergence of coaching is associated with the recognition that individuals can be encouraged to seek positive things in life, "harnessing the best in people and inspiring them to live out their potential" (Biswas-Diener and Dean, 2007, p. 2). For these authors, coaching is naturally directed toward positivity, growth, and optimism, although such elements are not yet strongly developed concerning the potential of coaching as a scientific field.

Thus, the combination of positive psychology and coaching psychology is currently a consensual scientific position of some coaching researchers. The movement is designed to facilitate an understanding of the core concepts of positive psychology and to apply these concepts to the coaching field to create a well-defined, empirically valid body of knowledge. In the literature, this new field is known as positive psychology coaching (cf. Biswas-Diener and Dean, 2007) or positive coaching psychology (Kauffman and Linley, 2007).

Several authors highlight the similarities between positive psychology and coaching psychology and suggest that coaching psychology is a form of applied positive psychology (Grant and Cavanagh, 2007; Ko and Donaldson, 2011; Linley and Kauffman, 2007; Linley *et al.*, 2009) or that coaching provides one of the natural mechanisms through which positive psychology can be translated into action (Peterson, 2006). Authors in positive psychology attempt to show the commonalities between the two fields by stating that positive psychology combined with a strength-based orientation provides a more appropriate model for coaching because both are based on the assumption that individuals possess everything that they need to address challenges (Kauffman and Scoular, 2004). Generally, positive psychology appears to offer a robust framework for coaching in several areas (Kauffman *et al.*, 2009); therefore, positive psychology constitutes one of the solutions to the lack of a theoretical framework in the coaching field because positive psychology can provide theories, interventions, and assessments that are lacking, to attain coaching objectives.

According to Linley and Harrington (2005), there are three important commonalities between coaching psychology and positive psychology: both areas focus on performance enhancement, concentrate on the positive aspects of human nature and are concerned with the strengths of individuals. In fact, the emphasis on the improvement of the positive aspects of human experience has generated increased attention for the concept of strengths or character strengths, which may be used as a tool in practical situations (Govindji and Linley, 2007; Linley and Joseph, 2004).

Many definitions of strengths exist, but according to Linley and Harrington (2006), the concept should include the process and outcome of using strengths. Therefore, these authors define strength as, "a natural capacity for behaving, thinking or feeling in a way that allows optimal functioning and performance in the pursuit of valued outcomes" (p. 39). Many studies seem to demonstrate that characteristics such as bravery, curiosity, and leadership are important for people independently of their cultures/countries (Biswas-Diener and Dean, 2007). Linley and Harrington (2006) stated that focusing on strengths in coaching interventions promotes the use of strengths in innovative ways that can lead to the promotion of higher levels of engagement, energy, and motivation as well as increases in happiness and significant decreases in depression (Govindji and Linley, 2007; Seligman *et al.*, 2005). According to Biswas-Diener and Dean (2007) coaches can offer interventions with regard to two types of strengths: interpersonal strengths (social strengths) and intrapersonal strengths (time orientation, savoring, appreciating the present, and optimism). These authors claim that both types of strengths are equally important in the coaching field. From Kauffman's perspective (2009), four main important areas can be highlighted when studying the positive psychology of executive coaching: positive emotion, flow, hope, and strengths. Similarly, Biswas-Diener and Dean (2007) focused their attention on happiness, positivity, and character strengths.

Concerning emotions, one of the objectives of positive psychology is to understand how positive emotions work; in contrast, other psychological orientations focus on understanding how individuals cope with negative emotions, such as anxiety and sadness. The positive emotions are associated with competences that are necessary in daily life and useful for coaching intervention goals. Fredrickson (2001) provided insight into this topic and stated that positive emotions enhance certain psychological functions, such as empowerment, and that it is possible to measure the role of this type of emotion in enhancing the resources of individuals. Her research shows that positive emotions seem to improve immune function, resilience, and resistance to infections, and appear to be a predictor of longevity and well-being. In addition, these emotions also appear to have a positive effect on the functioning of work teams and a great influence on productivity. Fredrickson and Kurtz (2011) claim that opportunities to experience positive emotions abound but must be noticed, explored, and amplified as a method of providing alternatives for applying positive psychology to improve society. Coaching can be an efficient way to take advantage of these opportunities.

One important positive emotion that has been the focus of positive psychology researchers is *happiness*, which is considered to be an important component of healthy functioning. The literature shows that happy individuals are more helpful, creative, prosocial, and altruistic than unhappy individuals (Biswas-Diener and Dean, 2007). Happiness is a concept that can be studied scientifically, and studies have shown that this emotion is beneficial in several life domains (Biswas-Diener and Dean, 2007).

In this area, two researchers have offered important contributions: the studies of Diener (2000) with regard to subjective well-being and the studies of Csikszentmihalyi (1990) that are dedicated to this subject, including his notion that happiness depends on each individual's quality of subjective experience. Through these studies, it is possible to understand some of the variables that are associated with happiness and the stability of this emotion over time.

Although happiness is seldom an explicit objective for coaching clients, this emotion is often an indirect goal. Within this new perspective that intends to prepare people for life challenges and daily events, happiness can be an intervention target in coaching because coaches can take some actions to increase the positive emotions of their clients. One of the best approaches to promoting happiness is the establishment of realistic expectations regarding happiness rather than expectations of intense or permanent fulfillment (Biswas-Diener and Dean, 2007). In addition, only small increases of happiness are necessary to have a positive effect on one's life (Kauffman, 2006).

Biswas-Diener and Dean (2007) suggest that two important variables of happiness can be used in coaching: goals and social relationships. Having strong relationships is essential to emotional well-being and happiness. In coaching sessions, it could be beneficial to discuss the importance of social relationships and the rewarding feeling of helping others. The promotion of strong social relationships can be especially important for coaching in working environments. With regard to goals, coaches can assist clients in establishing goals in life. The use of this construct is now being extensively studied in different coaching situations.

The study of the subjective experience of *flow* has shown how it is directly associated with being fully engaged in life and related activities of work or leisure (Freire, 2011). Flow is a positive experience in which an individual's activity demands match his or her abilities and skills. In addition, a person who is engaged in a flow activity may experience some loss of self-consciousness, a sense of control over the activity, an altered sense of time and high levels of intrinsic motivation and may describe the experience in terms of cognitive, affective, and motivational dimensions (Csikszentmihalyi, Abuhamedh, and Nakamura, 2005). Considering the importance of flow and the positive quality of the experience with which it is associated, it seems worthwhile that coaching practices seek to promote these conditions to their clients to achieve these high performance states, which in turn have significant consequences on the promotion of higher levels of subjective and psychological well-being (Kauffman, 2006; Wesson, 2010; Wesson and Boniwell, 2007). This concept of flow has been used in coaching, and its underlying processes have been studied to identify methods of improving the occurrence of this positive subjective experience in both work settings or tasks and daily life moments.

The concept of daily life is critical when applied to coaching processes. Coaching aims to assist clients in leading good lives by contributing to optimal human functioning and improving the quality of life in modern societies. Within daily life, people find their own sources of strengths, happiness, and involvement in order to build new and worthy lives.

There is also significant scientific interest in the concept of *hope*. Individuals with higher levels of hope seem to report better physical and psychological health, academic achievement, and interpersonal competences, among other benefits (Snyder, 2000). These benefits arise because individuals with greater hope seem to have better responses to obstacles as a result of their tendencies to seek alternatives and maintain a sense of agency (Kauffman, 2006). According to Snyder (2000), there are two important variables of hope: pathway thinking (finding alternatives) and a sense of agency (a sense that it is possible to achieve goals). Both of these components of hope can be cultivated in coaching theories and practices to increase the relevance of coaching interventions in improving the lives of individuals.

Nakamura (2011) highlights the importance of a focus on intentional action or human agency in the coaching field from a positive development perspective. The author states that a shared premise in positive psychology is that individuals possess a measure of control over their own flourishing, and this premise defines the science of positive functioning that is applied in several areas throughout the lifespan. For this construct of human agency to be effective, one must consider different levels of analysis. According to this, Nakamura discusses the need to articulate simultaneously the continuous efforts to increase the well-being of individuals through the building of their personal resources and the powerful influences that are realized by the environments in which they live. This intersection defines the author's concept of positive development, which involves flourishing, thriving, and increasing in complexity over the lifespan rather than focusing on a dichotomous perspective that attempts to define and differentiate the positive as opposed to the negative. Nakamura (2011) demonstrates how this perspective of positive development in adults can be responsible for new applications of human functioning; specifically, she presents her innovative perspective regarding good work and good mentoring, which will be presented later in this chapter.

Together, these positive concepts highlight the perspective of interaction between different scientific domains, which lend clarity to the link between positive psychology and coaching psychology. This link requires a new label that reflects the aim and core of this new field. Scholars who are interested in this issue have suggested different terminologies for this new area of study. Biswas-Diener and Dean formulated the expression "positive psychology coaching," which is also the title of their 2007 book. The underlined perspective was the desire to employ the science of happiness (positive psychology) to work for clients, and it showed how positive psychology could be the solution to the coaching paradox (Biswas-Diener and Dean, 2007). However, in the same year of 2007, a special issue on "positive psychology and coaching psychology" was published by the *International Coaching Psychology Review*. This special issue, edited by Michael Cavanagh and Stephen Palmer (co-editors) and P. Alex Linley and Carol Kauffman (guest editors), used the expression "positive coaching psychology" to reflect the purpose of integrating the science of positive psychology with the practice of coaching psychology. Although these terms are similar and understood as synonymous, the two expressions must be analyzed and discussed because they may be focused on different (but equally relevant) issues.

For the purpose of this chapter, and considering the conceptual similarity between the two expressions, we will use "positive coaching psychology" as it is shared by several leading figures in positive psychology, including Biswas-Diener (who spoke about positive psychology coaching). This terminology will be used to name this new field (positive coaching psychology), although the structure of this chapter integrates some additional perspectives to those perspectives with which it was initially associated.

## Positive Coaching Psychology Approaches and Models

The literature contains several models that show the interface of positive psychology and coaching. These models will be presented in this section independently of their degree of conceptual development and application. Our aim is to describe what is available in the related literature and what is still needed in order to continue to achieve a greater level of scientific development in coaching theory and practice.

### Authentic happiness coaching

Seligman (2002) created authentic happiness coaching (AHC), which is the application of positive psychology to coaching with the objective of fostering happiness. According to Seligman, there are three components of happiness (i.e., pleasure, engagement, and meaning) based on three different theories of what happiness is: hedonism, desire theory, and objective list theory (Sirgy and Wu, 2009). Considering these theories, Seligman and Royzman (2003) defined three types of happiness: the pleasant life (pleasure), the good life (engagement), and the meaningful life. To promote higher levels of happiness, interventions such as authentic happiness coaching should consider these three types of happiness, which include positive emotions, understanding what is intrinsically rewarding, and finding meaning.

The application of this approach to coaching highlights the need for coaches to promote the strengths of their clients and to increase positive emotions with regard to the present, past, and future. This approach should also aim to enhance flow and involvement and to encourage clients to adopt a sense of purpose in their lives (Kauffman, 2006).

### The flow-enhancing model

To explore the applications of flow theory to coaching psychology, Wesson and Boniwell (2007) proposed the flow-enhancing model of coaching. Considering the benefits of experiencing a state of flow, which includes feelings of pleasure, satisfaction and happiness, as demonstrated in the literature, the model presents a step-by-step pathway to increase opportunities to experience flow during both coaching sessions and daily activities and to increase awareness of external sources to ensure that clients can improve their time and energy management. The authors consider that the coaching process involves conditions for "goal-setting progressions" and conditions for "identifying and addressing additional issues." In these two areas, coaches can assist in improving the experience of flow for clients. During a goal-setting progression, it is important to have clear goals, which a coach should prompt clients to establish by encouraging divergent thinking; to balance challenges and skills, which a coach can promote by encouraging gradual increases in the difficulty of goals or subdividing such goals into smaller parts to facilitate their achievement; to emphasize the importance of doing well to assist clients in understanding the importance of a specific activity; to maintain goal congruence, which is primarily important when goals are changed; and to provide clear and immediate feedback to assist clients in achieving their goals. In addition, regarding the conditions that are important for identifying and addressing additional issues, it is important to increase autonomy, which a coach can encourage by promoting the exploration of a client's interests, and to increase absorption, in which it is important to increase a client's awareness of situations and activities that promote optimal experiences.

## The co-active coaching model

Regarding the relationship between coaches and coachees, a positive approach is present in the co-active coaching model that was developed by Whitworth *et al.* (2007). The concept of "co-active" is highlighted in that both coaches and clients are active participants in the process of coaching and thus form an alliance with the objective of answering the needs of clients. The agenda of the client is the cornerstone of this model. This agenda can be regarded from two perspectives. The first perspective considers a more general picture that includes the client's life and focuses the principles of fulfillment, balance, and progress. The second perspective involves specific issues that the client wishes to address during coaching sessions. Considering these perspectives, which are centered on the agenda of the client, the coach conducts coaching sessions in five different contexts, which are the points of contact with the client: listening, using intuition, forwarding/deepening, self-managing, and expressing curiosity. The relationship between coaches and clients is viewed as a triangle. Both coaches and clients yield power to the coaching relationship, which in turn empowers clients. In this model, all of the power in the coaching relationship is intended to serve clients.

## Positive organizational psychology

Several researchers and professionals have applied positive psychology to the organizational field. Within this perspective, Ko and Donaldson (2011) summarized the state of the science and practice of what they have termed applied "positive organizational psychology" (POP) (Donaldson and Ko, 2010; Ko and Donaldson, 2011). These authors have been working on a theory-driven perspective of how to improve research in this area and to develop and evaluate positive interventions to improve organizational effectiveness and the quality of work life.

These authors suggested that this approach includes the positive organizational behavior (POB) and positive organizational scholarship (POS) areas of study. Positive organizational behavior is defined as, "the study and application of positively oriented human resource strengths and psychological capacities that can be measured, developed, and effectively managed for performance improvement in today's workplace" (Luthans, 2002a, pp. 59, 2002b), and POS is, "concerned primarily with the study of especially outcomes, processes, and attributes of organizations and their members" (Cameron *et al.*, 2003, p. 4; Cameron, 2011). According to

Ko and Donaldson (2011), both POB and POS are based on positive psychology and highlight the importance of scientific process in the development of knowledge. Despite this commonality, the two approaches are distinguishable in three main aspects: their core topics of interest, their degree of emphasis on performance improvement, and their level of analysis. As the POP approach integrates the other two approaches, the POB and POS approaches will not be developed in this chapter; for more information refer to the studies of Ko and Donaldson (2011) and Cameron (2011).

Positive organizational psychology (POP) is defined as, "the scientific study of positive subjective experiences and traits in the workplace and positive organizations, and its application to improve the effectiveness and quality of life in organizations" (Donaldson and Ko, 2010, p. 178). Through POP, it is possible to improve work life and organizations and increase the relevance of the following topics: strengths, coaching, positive leadership, positive organizational development and change, organizational virtuousness, psychological capital, and work flow. Therefore, coaching becomes a relevant issue that is integrated into this broad perspective of applied positive psychology.

## Good work and good mentoring approach

Beginning with a positive perspective of human development focused on flourishing, thriving, and increased complexity during the lifespan, Nakamura (2011) describes how these processes are concerned with life contexts and recognizes that development occurs through the reciprocal interaction of multiple systems. To understand flourishing or thriving over the course of life, one must study positive contexts of development, which the author defined as those contexts that have the potential to facilitate and support optimal development across the course of life.

One important stage of adult development that has received scant attention is the process through which a young person prepares for and enters full-time working life. Some studies on this topic show that mentoring can be one of the positive contexts for adult development. Nakamura (2011) defines mentoring as a, "relationship with a more experienced member of the profession during training and/or the early career that has a significant, positive impact on the young adult's professional formation" (p. 191). Her investigation of this issue demonstrated the necessity of considering both positive and negative influences to obtain a better understanding of developmental relationships during professional formation; in fact, this view corresponds to her broader perspective regarding the core of positive psychology in terms of scientific focus. Subsequently, she presents a taxonomy of mentoring that shows the relationship between behavior and its effect on novices. Four types of developmental relationship are defined and serve as a frame of reference that permits a discussion regarding the manner in which good mentoring creates a positive context for development during early adulthood.

Within this conceptual framework, the author developed the concepts of good work and good mentoring and thus contributed to the academic knowledge regarding working life and organizational life to understand how to create organizations in which workers will flourish and in which these workers will help their organizations to thrive. The creation of contexts that facilitate good work and the identification and promotion of societal conditions that support those contexts is a primary direction of applied positive psychology.

The notion of good mentoring (Nakamura, 2011; Nakamura *et al.*, 2009) reflects this perspective by highlighting the role of context in positive development, including three main aspects: the interpersonal relationships between the participants who are involved, the cultural meme pool to which the mentor exposes the student, and the community in which mentoring is situated. Within these processes, context and agency interact to foster development.

All of the different approaches that are presented in this section illustrate that psychological concepts and models from positive psychology can be the basis for thinking about new coaching issues and can contribute to the emergence of new and applied models and approaches. Several existing studies illustrate how this articulation is useful for the enhancement of scientific knowledge in coaching. The combination of positive psychology and coaching creates a new range of topics that assists us in understanding the human condition while simultaneously improving new lines of research that enable the possibility of new coaching practices and assessments. The following section discusses some empirical studies in the positive coaching psychology field.

## Research Evidence and Positive Coaching Psychology in Coaching Practice

The coaching field has been concerned with the development of a framework that consists of a theoretical background that is sustained in a consistent body of research. Hence, Linley (2006) stated that coaching researchers must ask five questions to establish a high-quality research foundation: (1) Who? Who is participating in the investigation, and for whom is the investigation designed? (2) What? Which approach yields the best results, and what are the commonalities among different approaches? (3) Where? What different locations of coaching sessions can influence the methodology? (4) When? Should we give priority to longitudinal designs with pre- and post-test measures when possible to understand the process of coaching? and (5) Why? "Why" is the fundamental question with which every researcher should begin his or her study. Coaching research has been focused on efficacy (i.e., the variables that can predict successful outcomes), as was psychotherapy during previous decades (Linley, 2006).

Considering the positive variables applied to coaching that were discussed previously, a growing body of studies has been attempting to understand the effects of these variables and their relevance for a coaching conceptual framework and practice (Grant and Cavanagh, 2007).

As stated previously, coaching reflects one of the most evident fields of applied positive psychology. This applied emphasis creates a fruitful domain for the link between research and intervention: research serves to create better interventions, and interventions create the need for new research developments. This relationship illustrates the difficulty of presenting coaching studies that are related only to the research domain or only to the intervention domain. Therefore, this section intends to discuss studies in this applied positive coaching psychology field not by demonstrating the boundary between research and intervention but by discussing how these two domains overlap to create scientific knowledge that is empirically based and validated.

Only studies that are explicitly identified as being associated with positive psychology issues will be presented. However, it is recognized that numerous studies and investigations are not labeled accordingly. Rather, the authors of such studies produce significant knowledge and results that are directly or indirectly connected with positive psychology.

Studies of positive psychology have been fundamental for the development of new and valid instruments of measurement or methodologies that are adequate for coaching purposes. The new focus on strengths rather than weaknesses increased the relevance of the assessment of human strengths. For example, Peterson and Seligman (2004) developed the values in action (VIA) instrument, which assesses strengths using six categories of primary strengths and subcategories to obtain a total of 24 potential strengths. This instrument has been used and proven to be useful in coaching practices (Kauffman, 2009) and has produced new results pertaining to the human condition and new ways of improving performance in a flourishing pattern. The identification of strengths allows a higher level of understanding with regard to a client's profile; moreover, a coach can also select more adequate interventions according to a client's specific profile. In addition, the identification of a client's strengths is only the first step in the coaching process. The final aim is to assist clients in understanding how they can use their strengths to improve their performance in different domains of their lives.

This emphasis on the improvement of the daily lives of clients increases the relevance of the use of new research methodologies, such as the "experience sampling method" (ESM). This methodology aims to collect data throughout daily moments within the same subject to facilitate the study of the conditions that are associated with the fluctuation of subjective experience, especially those conditions that are associated with flow states (Csikszentmihalyi, 1990). At the present, coaching research also includes the use of this methodology in coaching sessions, in order to study how various factors might interact to produce flow experience (Wesson, 2010).

In general, this relationship between positive psychology and coaching provides valid instruments and methods with which to assess a coachee's strengths, well-being, life satisfaction, positive emotions, and the potential to improve performance, among other areas.

According to literature, there are two major areas of intervention and research in the coaching field: executive coaching and life coaching (Grant, 2001). As stated previously, executive coaching was the prime goal of the development of a coaching framework. Currently, coaching has spread to other areas with the single but complex goal of promoting a worthy life for clients. Thus, even in the world of work, knowledge pertaining to a person and all of his or her strengths and powerful resources are of interest. Therefore, executive and life coaching are currently two sides of the same coin. Both types of coaching influence scientific knowledge production, benefit from research in coaching, and allow intervention to be supported by serious research and theories.

Executive coaching can be considered as the meeting between a coach and an executive; the objective of this individual engagement is to create personalized goals and explore how to achieve these goals (Coutu and Kauffman, 2009). This type of coaching is characterized as aiming to develop the competences of a high-potential executive or to facilitate individual or organizational transitions and improve well-being and performance (Grant, 2005). Executive coaching themes range from enhancing strategic planning and presentation skills to stress management, team building, and leadership development (Grant, 2005).

Although the evidence is limited, it appears that executive coaching is effective. Early qualitative works showed that this type of coaching can help promote leadership skills (Grant *et al.*, 2009). Literature reviews have revealed that the studies concerned with the effect of this type of coaching are scarce (Kampa-Kokesch and Anderson, 2001). Other reviews (Passmore and Gibbes, 2007) have shown that more studies have been published with the conclusion of several benefits for coaches: improved skills, relationships, problem solving, and motivation; improved leadership and charismatic behavior; and increases in self-efficacy beliefs. Research regarding such benefits provides important information for coaches with regard to coaching practices in their sessions, particularly the need to adapt coaching styles to the preferences of clients, the need to manage a sense of collaboration in work, the importance of the experience of coaches from the perspective of coachees, the importance of the selection of homework tasks, and the relationship between coaches and coachees (which is rated highly by coachees).

An executive coaching program that was implemented by Grant *et al.* (2009) was effective in assisting clients in achieving their goals; this outcome is consistent with past research on enhancing resilience and workplace well-being. Several programs have been tested concerning their efficacy in terms of achieving objectives. For example, the Leadership Development Program (Grant *et al.*, 2009), which focused on enhancing and developing leadership capability, was applied to executives and senior managers. At the end of the program, goal attainment and resilience were enhanced, and levels of workplace well-being were higher. Another study that evaluated the effects of coaching within companies showed that the most significant result of coaching was stress management (Gyllensten and Palmer, 2006).

A consensus exists among scholars that life coaching involves a collaborative process that is underlined by a holistic perspective, focused on solutions and results in the objective of promoting life experience, goal attainment, well-being, and personal growth (Green *et al.*, 2007). This definition identifies the importance of an action-oriented collaborative relationship in which the coach is the facilitator (Spence and Grant, 2007). Life coaching seems to be used by individuals who intend to attain important personal and/or professional goals (Grant and Green, 2001) and to enhance their well-being (Naughton, 2002). In this type of coaching, clients evaluate and attempt to change and improve their lives (Grant, 2005).

The results of studies pertaining to the effect of this type of coaching show increases in goal attainment, satisfaction with life, and perceived control, as well as greater openness toward new experiences (Spence and Grant, 2005). In general, life coaching appears to increase quality of life; reduce depression, anxiety, and stress; facilitate goal attainment; and improve mental health, quality of life, and general life satisfaction as a general effect of life coaching, sometimes beyond the defined objectives of a program (Grant, 2003).

Research on positive emotions highlights the importance of manager optimism because of its influence on employee well-being and engagement (Arakawa and Greenberg, 2007). However, strengths have been associated with several benefits for individuals, including employee engagement (Harter *et al.*, 2002) and significant increases in happiness if such strengths are used in innovative ways (Seligman *et al.*, 2005); in addition, these strengths are associated with subjective well-being, psychological well-being, and subjective vitality (Govindji and Linley, 2007). These data highlight the relevance of including strengths in coaching practice. Strength-based coaching programs have been proven to produce fewer days of absence and higher grade point averages in students, and to produce greater employee engagement, higher levels of hope, and other benefits (Hodges and Clifton, 2004).

An evidence-based life coaching program (Green *et al.*, 2007) that aimed to enhance cognitive hardiness and hope in senior female high school students showed that it was possible to significantly increase levels of cognitive hardiness and hope as well as decrease levels of depression. Another intervention (Burke and Linley, 2007) with students (athletic college students) with the objective of fostering hope as well as athletic and academic performance showed that the participants possessed higher levels of hope after the program. An intervention program about peer tutoring and coaching has been implemented with Portuguese college students, showing how adaptation to university context can be positively achieved if tutoring and coaching become intentional strategies to improve optimal functioning among students (Freire, 2010). Life coaching programs have also been applied in general communities as an intervention that aimed to enhance goal striving and well-being (Spence and Grant, 2007). The results of this program showed that life coaching had a minimal effect on the well-being of the participants. In contrast, a different life coaching program in the community showed increases in goal striving, subjective well-being, psychological well-being, and hope (Green *et al.*, 2005). For example, Kauffman (2006) discussed how coaches can promote or improve the experience of flow in coaching for the improvement of performance in the daily lives of coachees. For this purpose, the author suggests that coaches integrate the aspects that are associated with flow into coaching sessions to facilitate its generalization for daily life.

## Future Research

The majority of papers and chapters that are presented in the literature in the expanding scientific field of positive coaching psychology describe a vast number of future research directions. In fact, the authors of such works are concerned with the development of new and innovative ways of effective coaching that can affect the quality of life of clients.

In any type of applied scientific field, research is a dynamic process that serves the present purpose and facilitates the emergence of new and important topics for future studies and research projects. The current state of positive coaching psychology is in a creative stage, in which what has been studied is not sufficient but justifies the continuation of the process of rendering the field as stronger and more scientifically valid. The majority of the studies that are presented in the literature highlight these demands and future directions that are associated with positive coaching research, including several areas that investigators consider to be essential for the field.

The fundamental questions are related first to the concept of coaching and second to the concept of positive psychology coaching. There is a need for a clear and unanimous definition of coaching and its specific areas of application (Biswas-Diener and Dean, 2007) for use by coaches and this scientific community. The accuracy of the definition of coaching can also assist in distinguishing this area from other areas, such as counseling and psychotherapy, particularly in terms of competences and practices (Grant, 2006).

In addition to obtaining a definition and theoretical background, it is essential to define and refine adequate methodologies. According to several authors, the development and validation of psychological-based coaching methodologies are necessary in the immediate future (Grant, 2006), and research protocols for coaches to include in their assessments are also critical (Kauffman and Scoular, 2004). These potential studies can assist in determining which methodologies are more adequate for coaching research.

Concerning specific variables of positive psychology, Govindji and Linley (2007) focus on the potential positive effect of the use of strengths, especially in coaching psychology interventions, because the use of strengths has the potential to promote optimal functioning; thus, the use of strengths should constitute a future research topic. However, happiness can also be critical for coaching interventions, and future research regarding the conditions that affect the happiness of individuals is essential for coaches to intervene in the quality of life of such individuals. Finally, flow also has the potential to produce important information for the coaching field. Wesson and Boniwell (2007) indicate the necessity of understanding the importance of the coaching relationship, particularly in situations in which one of the individuals who is involved in a coaching relationship acts as a trigger of a flow experience. Furthermore, given that coaching uses a variety of interaction media, such as the Internet, it is important to study how these types of media can affect the experience of flow in coaching sessions and to question whether the lack of physical presence in specific cases affects the experience of flow.

As a synthesis of research demands and directions in coaching, the work of Strober and Parry (2005) suggest that particular attention be devoted to different areas and define what they have termed, "a framework of coaching research agendas." These authors describe several key aspects of the establishment of a framework for coaching research. They highlight the main step of finding a standard definition of coaching and developing appropriate measures for coaching research because most concepts and measures that the social sciences offer are viewed from a clinical perspective, which must be differentiated from a coaching perspective. Strober and Parry also refer to the need to evaluate the effectiveness of coaching using comparison studies to obtain measurable outcomes and understand the effect of coaching interventions on clients. The evaluation of the effectiveness of coaching is related to the development of theories of the coaching process. Finally, these authors also consider the importance of studying the characteristics of coaches, clients, and organizations and their associations with successful or unsuccessful outcomes, such as personality characteristics, readiness for change, and environmental factors. Although this framework is not elaborated for the domain of positive coaching psychology, it serves as an agenda for issues that can be shared between positive psychology and coaching psychology to create a fruitful scientific field of psychological studies.

# Conclusion

This chapter began by presenting evidence that positive coaching psychology is still at an early stage in its conceptual development. At the end of this chapter (and with a broad view of the entire book), it is now possible to offer conclusions with regard to the expansion of the coaching psychology field and its potential for growth as a scientific field with strong and promising research and intervention areas.

This movement toward scientific complexity inside the coaching field has been possible because of two strategies of scientific development: the relationship of coaching to different scientific fields and the relationship between different types and domains inside the coaching field. According to the first strategy, the emergent conceptual enrichment that was obtained by crossing different scientific domains was illustrated in this chapter using positive psychology and coaching psychology. The commonalities and differences between these two types of psychology allow for the definition of this new discipline of positive coaching psychology. The second strategy, although it was not developed in this chapter, highlights the necessity and importance of articulating different coaching areas that can each contribute to emergent validated knowledge regarding coaching processes and outcomes. For example, studies of coaching processes in the sports, educational, or clinical domains facilitate the generalization of outcomes that are developed or promoted by coaching processes. As stated by the majority of researchers in the field, positive coaching psychology is a specific applied approach that benefits from the intersection of positive psychology and coaching in terms of research, intervention, and methodologies.

Positive psychology introduces and complements coaching with new questions and offers well-validated theories, methodologies, and measurements. However, studies about specific coaching contexts, situations and practices, relationships, and associated goals, also contribute to positive psychology by offering a better understanding of the core concepts and applications of positive psychology and by contributing to a better discussion of new emergent fields. As stated by Shane Lopez (2007), "positive psychology theory and research has a great deal to contribute to people living better lives. My concern about applying positive psychology to coaching is that only the best coaches take the time to learn the in depth aspects of positive psychology science. Applying popularized notions of positive psychological principles do little to improve the lives of people" cited (in Kauffman and Linley, 2007, p. 90).

# References

Arakawa, D. and Greenberg, M. (2007) Optimistic managers and the influence on productivity and employee engagement in a technology organization: Implications for coaching psychologists. *International Coaching Psychology Review*, 2, 78–89.

Biswas-Diener, R. and Dean, B. (2007) *Positive Psychology Coaching: Putting the Science of Happiness to Work for Your Clients*. Hoboken, NJ: John Wiley.

Burke, D. and Linley, P.A. (2007) Enhancing goal self concordance through coaching. *International Coaching Psychology Review*, 2, 62–9.

Cameron, K.S. (2011) Effects of virtuous leadership on organizational performance. In: S.I. Donaldson, M. Csikszentmihalyi, and J. Nakamura (eds) *Applied Positive Psychology: Improving Everyday Life, Health, Schools, Work, and Society*. New York: Routledge. pp. 171–84.

Cameron, K.S., Dutton, J.E., and Quinn, R.E. (2003) *Positive Organizational Scholarship*. San Francisco: Berrett-Koehler.

Coutu, D. and Kauffman, C. (2009) *The Realities of Executive Coaching*. Harvard Business Review Research Report.

Csikszentmihalyi, M. (1990) *Flow: The Psychology of Optimal Experience*. New York: Harper Row.

Csikszentmihalyi, M., Abuhamdeh, S., and Nakamura, J. (2005) Flow. In: A.J. Elliott and C.S. Dweck (eds) *Handbook of Competence and Motivation*. New York: Guilford Press. pp. 598–608.

Diener, E. (2000) Subjective well-being: The science of happiness and a proposal for a national index. *American Psychologist*, 55, 34–43.

Donaldson, S.I. (2011) Determining what works, if anything, in positive psychology. In: S.I. Donaldson, M. Csikszentmihalyi, and J. Nakamura, J. (eds) *Applied Positive Psychology. Improving Everyday Life, Health, Schools, Work, and Society*. New York: Routledge. pp. 3–11.

Donaldson, S. and Ko, L. (2010) Positive organizational psychology, behaviour and scholarship: A review of the emerging literature and evidence base. *Journal of Positive Psychology*, 5, 177–91.

Donaldson, S., Csikszentmihalyi, M., and Nakamura, J. (2011) *Applied Positive Psychology: Improving Everyday Life, Health, Schools, Work and Society*. New York: Routledge.

Fredrickson, B. (2001) The role of positive emotions in positive psychology: The broaden-and-build theory of positive emotions. *American Psychologist*, 56, 218–26.

Frederickson, B.L. and Kurtz, L.E. (2011) Cultivating positive emotions to enhance human flourishing. In: S.I. Donaldson, M. Csikszentmihalyi, and J. Nakamura, J. (eds) *Applied Positive Psychology. Improving Everyday Life, Health, Schools, Work, and Society*. New York: Routledge. pp. 35–47.

Freire, T. (2010) Peer tutoring and coaching. A program for college students. University of Minho (unpublished report).

Freire, T. (2011) From flow to optimal experience: (Re)searching the quality of subjective experience throughout daily life. In I. Brdar (Ed.), The Human Pursuit of well-being: a cultural approach. Dordrecht: Springer.

Govindji, R. and Linley, P.A. (2007) Strengths use, self-concordance and well-being: Implications for strengths coaching and coaching psychologists. *International Coaching Psychology Review*, 2, 143–53.

Grant, A. (2001) *Towards Coaching Psychology*. Sydney: Coaching Psychology Unit, University of Sydney.

Grant, A. (2003) The impact of life coaching on goal attainment, metacognition and mental health. *Social Behaviour and Personality*, 31, 253–63.

Grant, A. (2005) What is evidence-based executive, workplace and life coaching? In: M. Cavanagh, A. Grant, and T. Kemp (eds) *Evidence-based Coaching: Theory, Research, and Practice from the Behavioural Sciences*. Bowen Hill: Australian Academic Press. pp. 1–12.

Grant, A. (2006) A personal perspective on professional coaching and the development of coaching psychology. *International Coaching Psychology Review*, 1, 12–20.

Grant, A. and Cavanagh, M.J. (2007) Evidence-based coaching: Flourishing or languishing? *Australian Psychologist*, 42, 239–54.

Grant, A. and Greene, J. (2001) *Coach Yourself: Make Real Change in Your Life*. London: Momentum Press.

Grant, A., Curtayne, L., and Burton, G. (2009) Executive coaching enhances goal attainment, resilience and workplace well-being: A randomized controlled study. *The Journal of Positive Psychology*, 4, 396–407.

Grant, A.M., Passmore, J., Cavanagh, M., and Parker, H. (2010) The state of play in coaching. *International Review of Industrial & Organizational Psychology*, 25, 125–68.

Green, S., Grant, A., and Rynsaardt, J. (2007) Evidence-based life coaching for senior high school students: Building hardiness and hope. *International Coaching Psychology Review*, 2, 24–32.

Green, L.S., Oades, L.G., and Grant, A. (2006) Cognitive behavioural, solution-focused life coaching: Enhancing goal striving, well-being and hope. *Journal of Positive Psychology*, 1, 142–9.

Gyllensten, K. and Palmer, S. (2006) Experiences of coaching and stress in the workplace: An interpretive phenomenological analysis. *International Coaching Review*, 1, 86–98.

Harter, J.K., Schmidt, F.L., and Hayes, T.L. (2002) Business-unit-level relationship between employee satisfaction, employee engagement, and business outcomes: A meta-analysis. *Journal of Applied Psychology*, 87, 268–79.

Hodges, T.D. and Clifton, D.O. (2004) Strengths-based development in practice. In: A. Linley and S. Joseph (eds) *Handbook of Positive Psychology in Practice*: John Wiley. Hoboken, NJ: pp. 256–68.

Kampa-Kokesch, S. and Anderson, M.Z. (2001) Executive coaching: A comprehensive review of the literature. *Consulting Psychology Journal: Practice and Research*, 53, 205–28.

Kauffman, C. (2006) Positive psychology: The science at the heart of coaching. In: D. Stober and A. Grant (eds) *Evidence Based Coaching Handbook*. Hoboken, NJ: John Wiley. pp. 219–54.

Kauffman, C. (2009) Positive psychology and coaching: Moving from theory to intervention. In: T. Freire (ed.) *Understanding Positive Life: Research and Practice on Positive Psychology*. Lisboa: Climepsi Editores. pp. 305–22.

Kauffman, C. and Linley, A. (2007) The meeting of minds: Positive psychology and coaching psychology. *International Coaching Psychology Review*, 2, 90–6.

Kauffman, C. and Scoular, A. (2004) Toward a positive psychology of executive coaching. In: P.A. Linley and S. Joseph (eds) *Positive Psychology in Practice*. Hoboken, NJ: John Wiley. pp. 287–302.

Kauffman, C., Boniwell, I., and Silberman, J. (2009) The positive psychology approach to coaching. In: E. Cox, T. Bachkirova, and D. Cutterbuck (eds) *The Complete Handbook of Coaching*. London: Sage. pp. 158–71.

Ko, I. and Donaldson, S.I. (2011) Applied positive organizational psychology: The state of the science and practice. In: S.I. Donaldson, M. Csikszentmihalyi, and J. Nakamura, J. (eds) *Applied Positive Psychology: Improving Everyday Life, Health, Schools, Work, and Society* (pp. 137–54). New York: Routledge.

Linley, P.A. (2006) Coaching research: Who? What? Where? When? Why? *International Journal of Evidence Based Coaching and Mentoring*, 4, 1–7.

Linley, P.A. and Harrington, S. (2005) Positive psychology and coaching psychology: Perspectives on integration. *The Coaching Psychologist*, 1, 13–14.

Linley, P.A. and Harrington, S. (2006) Strengths coaching: A potential-guided approach to coaching psychology. *International Coaching Psychology Review*, 1, 37–45.

Linley, P.A. and Joseph, S. (2004) *Positive Psychology in Practice*. Hoboken, NJ: John Wiley.

Linley, P.A. and Kauffman, C. (2007) Positive psychology and coaching psychology (special issue). *International Coaching Psychology Review*, 2(1), 5–8.

Linley, P.A., Woolston, L., and Biswas-Diener, R. (2009) Strengths coaching with leaders. *International Coaching Psychology Review*, 4, 37–48.

Luthans, F. (2002a) Positive organizational behavior: Developing and managing psychological strengths. *Academy of Management Executive*, 16, 57–72.

Luthans, F. (2002b) The need for and meaning of positive organizational behavior. *Journal of Organizational Behavior*, 23, 695–706.

Nakamura, J. (2011) Contexts of positive adult development. In: S.I. Donaldson, M. Csikszentmihalyi, and J. Nakamura, J. (eds) *Applied Positive Psychology. Improving Everyday Life, Health, Schools, Work, and Society*. New York: Routledge. pp. 185–201.

Nakamura, J., Shernoff, D.J., and Hooker, C.H. (2009) *Good Mentoring: Fostering Excellence Practice in Higher Education*. San Francisco: Jossey-Bass.

Naughton, J. (2002) The coaching boom: Is it the long-awaited alternative to the medical model? *Psychotherapy Networker*, 42, 1–10.

Palmer, S. and Whybrow, A. (2005) *The Proposal to Establish a Special Group in Coaching Psychology*. Lexington: International Coaching Federation.

Passmore, J. and Gibbes, C. (2007) The state of executive coaching research: What does the current literature tell us and what's next for coaching research? *International Coaching Psychology Review*, 2, 116–28.

Peterson, C. and Seligman, M. (2004) *Character Strengths and Virtues: A Handbook and Classification*. Washington, DC: American Psychological Association.

Peterson, D. (2006) People are complex and the world is messy: A behavior-based approach to executive coaching. In: D. Stober and A. Grant (eds) *Evidence-based Coaching Handbook*. Hoboken, NJ: John Wiley. pp. 51–76.

Seligman, M. (2002) *Authentic Happiness*. New York: Free Press.

Seligman, M. (2007) Coaching and positive psychology. *Australian Psychologist*, 42, 266–7.

Seligman, M. and Csikszentmihalyi, M. (2000) Positive psychology: An introduction. *American Psychologist*, 55, 5–14.

Seligman, M. and Royzman, E. (2003) Happiness: The three traditional theories. *Authentic Happiness Newsletter*, July. Retrieved from: http://www.authentichappiness.sas.upenn.edu/newsletter.aspx?id=49.

Seligman, M., Steen, T. A., Park, N., and Peterson, C. (2005) Positive psychology progress: Empirical validaton of interventions. *American Psychologist*, 60, 410–21.

Sirgy, M. and Wu, J. (2009) The pleasant life, the engaged life and the meaningful life: What about the balanced life? *Journal of Happiness Studies*, 10, 183–96.

Snyder, C.R. (2000) *Handbook of Hope: Theory, Measures, and Applications*. San Diego: Academic Press.

Spence, G.B. and Grant, A. (2005) Individual and group life-coaching: Initial findings from a randomised, controlled trial. In: M. Cavanagh, A. Grant, and T. Kemp (eds) *Evidence-based Coaching: Theory, Research and Practice from the Behavioural Sciences*. Bowen Hill: Australian Academic Press. pp. 143–58.

Spence, G. and Grant, A. (2007) Professional and peer life coaching and the enhancement of goal striving and well-being: An exploratory study. *Journal of Positive Psychology*, 2, 185–94.

Strober, D. and Parry, C. (2005) Current challenges and future directions in coaching research. In: M. Cavanagh, A. Grant, and T. Kemp (eds) *Evidence-based Coaching: Theory, Research, and Practice from the Behavioural Sciences*. Bowen Hill: Australian Academic Press. pp. 13–20.

Wesson, K.J. (2010) Flow in coaching conversation. *International Journal of Evidence Based Coaching and Mentoring*, 4, 53–65.

Wesson, K. and Boniwell, I. (2007) Flow theory: Its application to coaching psychology. *International Coaching Psychology Review*, 2, 33–43.

Whitworth, L., Kimsey-House, K., Kimsey-House, H., and Sandahl, P. (2007) *Co-active Coaching: New Skills for Coaching People Toward Success in Work and Life*. Palo Alto: Davies-Black Publishing.

# Section IV
# Issues in Coaching and Mentoring

# 23

# Conducting Organizational-Based Evaluations of Coaching and Mentoring Programs

## Siegfried Greif

## Introduction

One of the basic questions of coaching and mentoring programs in organizations is how can their effects be evaluated? Without answering this question, organizations are unable to make clear investment decisions. The primary aim of this chapter is to inform the reader about evaluation models and methods that meet high standards of quality and can be recommended for use in program evaluation studies.

What kinds of data can be used for evaluation within HR interventions? This question has prompted long-standing debates and research in the field of training. For coaching and mentoring, however, this is a relatively new question. Nevertheless, we can draw on solutions from training evaluation models to aid our understanding of what might work well in studies on coaching and mentoring.

The chapter begins with an overview of general program evaluation taxonomies. After this, specific evaluation models of coaching and mentoring and basic literature on quantitative measures will be presented. Qualitative evaluation methods will then be introduced that can also be applied and that are often seen as an alternative approach to quantitative methods. Following on from this, the challenging question of future evaluation research will be discussed, and finally in the last section the conclusions will be summarized.

## Standard Evaluation Concepts and Taxonomies

The following section describes basic characteristics of "evaluation", on which there is much consensus between practitioners and scientists. It shows how evaluations are used in organizational decisions on the implementation of the evaluation of coaching or mentoring programs. The last part of the section provides an introduction to the classical taxonomy

*The Wiley Blackwell Handbook of the Psychology of Coaching and Mentoring*, First Edition.
Edited by Jonathan Passmore, David B. Peterson, and Teresa Freire.
© 2013 John Wiley & Sons, Ltd. Published 2016 by John Wiley & Sons, Ltd.

of data by Kirkpatrick (1976), which has been applied widely in the evaluation of HR-interventions.

## Definition and standards of evaluation

In their classic book, Rossi and Freeman (1993, p. 5) define evaluation research as the, "systematic application of social research procedures in assessing the conceptualization and design, implementation and utility of social intervention programs." However, evaluation of interventions like coaching and mentoring is not restricted to scientific research methods. The general meaning of the term "evaluation" is the appraisal or assessment of interventions, including their preconditions, costs, processes, and especially their outcomes.

For many clients and mentees the coaching or mentoring experience is novel. A summary of surveys of coaching shows that they are usually satisfied or very satisfied with the intervention (Greif, 2008, p. 215), and sometimes they are even enthusiastic (Wasylyshyn, 2003). However, we also find skeptical practitioners who doubt the usefulness of mentoring or coaching programs (Bachmann and Spahn, 2004). "I don't need coaching," is a sentence that is often heard. It implies that coaching is about deficit deduction rather than development fulfillment. Organizations contribute to this kind of implicit discrimination when they target coaching programs towards problem employees ("coaching as the last chance before dismissal"). Which employee when knowing this would voluntarily participate in a coaching program? To argue against coaching and mentoring as an intervention is easy. Both are sensitive, complex and intangible services. If nobody, except the two people in the room engaged in the process, really knows what has happened in the confidential coaching conversation, it is easy to spread negative rumors about it.

Coaching and mentoring, more so than other services, needs rational evaluation in order to avoid prejudice and false information. Professional associations in both fields therefore strongly advocate scientific methods of evaluation and make use of evaluation studies for their marketing. In the discussion at the end of the chapter we will come back to examine the interesting relations between evaluation and marketing.

Personnel managers or other decision makers who select human resources (HR) interventions for their organization may evaluate their cost and benefit and ask for data on the economic return on the investment. Number-oriented reviewers may ask for additional quantitative data, for example, the satisfaction ratings of the coachees or mentees, or improvement of leadership behavior assessed by leadership scales. However, in organizations we also find decision makers who are skeptical as to whether it is possible to evaluate all HR investments by means of economic data or quantitative measures. The majority of deciders probably follow the personal recommendations of their colleagues, based on practical experience or reports on the outcome of similar applications. The advantage of such qualitative information is their authenticity and credibility. The results of a recent survey (Stephan and Gross, 2011, p. 168) show that recommendations by word-of-mouth communication or opinions within the network are preferred by 58 percent of personnel managers when seeking a coach. Other types of information such as Internet searches (17 percent) or internal databases (5 percent) are used much less frequently.

The general purpose of evaluation that goes beyond word-of-mouth recommendations is to obtain an objective, reliable, and valid information basis for decisions on investments. Scientific methods and evaluation studies that are performed and interpreted independently and without regard to preconceived opinions are often seen as the best information basis for making rational decisions. As Wottawa and Thierau (1998) emphasize, the practitioner or scientist who is conducting an evaluation study carries a high moral responsibility to follow the standards of quality of science in a transparent and checkable way. The standards apply when planning the design of the study and also to the selection of instruments. The realization, statistical data processing, interpretation, and presentation of the results have to comply with these standards. The management is also meeting a clear corporate policy decision when it passes part of its influence over for independent analysis. The results are uncertain and may have important consequences.

Wottawa and Thierau (1998, p. 14) outline three basic characteristics of evaluations:

1  "Evaluation" implies an appraisal of alternative measures and serves as a basis for planning and decision making.
2  "Evaluation" is a goal and purpose oriented activity and aims primarily at a review or improvement of measures and decisions about measures.
3  "Evaluations" have to meet and be adapted to the current requirements of scientific techniques and methods.

Scriven (1980, 1996) has introduced the differentiation between *formative* and *summative evaluation*. Formative evaluation refers to the analysis of the preparation, implementation, and processes of an evaluation object. Its purpose is often to shape and improve the quality of the measures, if possible in the course of the processes. Summative evaluation focuses on the results or outcomes of an intervention in relation to its goals. This chapter concentrates more on the latter, but as shown below, extended evaluation models in addition to outcome criteria also embrace the antecedents, processes, and organizational context of coaching and mentoring.

## The classical taxonomy of Kirkpatrick

Kirkpatrick (1976) published a taxonomy of different kinds of data that can be used in evaluating training programs in organizations as well as other HR-interventions like coaching and mentoring. While 40 years old, the model is still considered the benchmark evaluation model for training. Kirkpatrick differentiates between four levels of evaluation criteria or "segments" of the evaluation process:

1  Reaction: How do the participants feel about the program they attended? To what extent are they 'satisfied customers'?
2  Learning: To what extent have the trainees learned the information and skills? To what extent have their attitudes been changed?
3  Behavior: To what extent has their job behavior changed as a result of attending the training program?
4  Results: To what extent have results been affected by the training program?

(Kirkpatrick, 1977, p. 9)

Questionnaires are the most common examples of a *reaction* measure, for example, the satisfaction of the participants with the program content or the trainer's delivery style. Kirkpatrick (1977) advocates anonymous surveys in order to get honest reactions. Such reaction evaluations are widely distributed in organizations. The results of such surveys reflect a moment in time response, but normally the program goals go beyond making participants happy.

The relationship of data from the next level to program goals – *learning* – is normally more meaningful. In order to detect learning improvements, the participants may be assessed on their learning from the program. More objective evidence could be found by means of knowledge tests, administered before and after the intervention.

The third level suggested by Kirkpatrick is to assess the *behavior* change of the participants. Simple methods of getting evidence here are open questions, asking the participants to describe what they eventually did differently after the program, or asking their bosses. A better but much more complex method mentioned by Kirkpatrick (1977) is observing and measuring participants' behavior changes before and after the intervention.

Examples of data from the fourth level, the *results* (mentioned by Kirkpatrick (1977, p. 9) are profits, return on investment, sales, production quality, quantity, schedules being met, costs, turnover, grievances, and morale. The examples show that this level refers to the more long-term organizational outcomes of the program. These data are often very important and relate directly to central organizational goals.

Kirkpatrick's essential message is that it is not sufficient to use only subjective reaction data after the intervention as evidence for its effectiveness. He demands the utilization of data from multiple sources and encourages pragmatic assessment methods. As Kirkpatrick (1977) discusses in his paper, it is relatively easy to find "evidence" of changes for each level by comparing pre- and post-assessments. However, it is difficult to obtain "proof" that the changes have been caused by the program. Many other possible factors that could have influenced the changes have to be eliminated. As the best solution, he advocates comparison of the program participants with randomized control groups (see also Grant in Chapter 2 of this book). However, he argues, especially with regard to the evaluation of results that it is often impossible or impractical to prove that the changes have been caused by the program alone. He describes a good example in which he helped a friend to convince his boss that it is impossible to prove, "in dollars and cents that a certain leadership training program was achieving more benefits than it was costing" and that "evidence" in the case was good enough (Kirkpatrick, 1977, p. 12).

Kirkpatrick's four-level evaluation taxonomy remains the international standard. It has inspired others to offer alternative models, but the Kirkpatrick model remains the benchmark for organizational evaluations. However, aspects of the model require improvement or modification. Kraiger *et al.* (1993) propose a modification of the *learning level*. They differ between: (1) cognitive outcomes (verbal knowledge, knowledge organization, and cognitive strategies), (2) skill-based outcomes (skill compilation and automaticity), and (3) affective (attitudinal and motivational) outcomes. Similarly, the remaining levels of Kirkpatrick's taxomony could be systematized. The "results" level in particular seems to be very heterogeneous.

Holton (1996) criticized, more fundamentally, the fact that Kirkpatrick and his followers called the concept a "model". As he argues, the system does not meet any of the standard criteria for scientific models (e.g., definition of constructs, assumptions about their relations, propositions and hypotheses and predictions). He suggests calling it a "taxonomy of outcomes". In his reply, Kirkpatrick (1996) accepts that his system is not a model in the conventional meaning and does not mind calling it a taxonomy. Holton (1996) recommends developing a more comprehensive evaluation model in the narrower meaning of the term that would contain preceding, intervening, and outcome variables, together with assumptions about their relations. The open question is whether his or other evaluation models can be generalized for use with all kinds of specific HR-interventions. In the following, two evaluation models are presented that refer more specifically to coaching and mentoring.

# Program Evaluation Models and Measures of Coaching and Mentoring Outcomes

The role relationship between mentor and protégé is very different from that between coach and individual coachee. The mentor is often a senior in the occupational field and has rarely received any specific training. The coach has normally received a professional education, but does not necessarily come from the occupational field of the coachee. Additionally, the expected outcomes of both interventions differ. Mentoring aims at career development and building social networks. Individual coaching is broader in its scope. It can support the coachee in a variety of goals, for example, improvement of leadership behavior, effective self- and stress management, team communication, conflict resolution, better work-life balance, and in some cases also career developmental. The following evaluation models mirror these differences. However, there are also similarities. In both, intimate supportive relationships are important that are based on mutual trust. The outcomes of coaching and mentoring on the reaction-level of Kirkpatrick's taxonomy can be measured by satisfaction questionnaires. On the learning-level, increases in knowledge on social interactions are expected in both fields. Desired outcomes on the behavior-level are self-efficacy and occupational performance improvement, and on the result-level eventually an increase in organizational productivity.

Both of the sub-sections in the following section will commence with a description of the evaluation models. Then a summary of criteria and exemplary evaluation studies will be presented. The presentation focuses on the outcome measures of organizational programs that were implemented in individual and not group coaching and mentoring. The evaluation models mainly refer to quantitative measures. As mentioned in the introduction, qualitative evaluation methods also provide important, sometimes very convincing, evidence of coaching outcomes. Exemplary methods will be described later in another sub-section.

## How to evaluate coaching programs

Since the turn of the century, the number of reviews on coaching evaluation research and recommendations for future studies has increased substantially (Bachkirova and Kauffman, 2008; Cornett and Knight, 2009; De Meuse *et al.*, 2009; Ellam-Dyson and Palmer, 2008; Feldman and Lankau, 2005; Fillery-Travis and Lane, 2008; Grant, 2006, 2009; Grant *et al.*, 2010; Greif, 2007, 2011a; Künzli, 2006, 2009; Latham, 2007; Levenson, 2009; Linley, 2006; Passmore and Fillery-Travis, 2011; Passmore and Gibbes, 2007; Smither *et al.*, 2001). A common theme is a plea for more and better research on the effectiveness of coaching that would provide a valuable foundation for the profession. In their review of leadership coaching studies Ely *et al.* (2010; Ely and Zaccaro, 2011) refer to the four-level taxonomy by Kirkpatrick (1976) and the supplement by Kraiger *et al.* (1993) as a framework. In their conclusions for future program implementations and evaluation studies they demand that a greater focus is placed on the antecedents' influence on coaching outcomes. They especially mention the organizational stakeholders and actors involved, their relationship, and the process of coaching. As many of the reviewers of the list above also emphasize, the effectiveness of the program depends much on the quality of the antecedents and processes.

The coaching evaluation model presented in Figure 23.1 gives a broad overview of *antecedents, organizational context*, and *process variables* that are assumed to influence

| Antecedents | Coaching process | Proximal outcomes — General measures | Proximal outcomes — Specific to coaching | Distal outcomes — Individual |
|---|---|---|---|---|
| **Coach characteristics**<br>• Professional skills and credibility<br>• Advance clarification of expectations of coachee | **Relationship**<br>• Mutual respect and trust<br>• At eye level<br>• Coach does not have hierarchical authority over the coachee<br>• Confidentiality | **Coachee**<br>• Satisfaction<br>• Goal attainment and goal satisfaction<br>• Reduction of negative affect, anxiety, stress, and depression<br>• General well-being or health<br>• Self-esteem | **Coachee change**<br>• Goal clarity and concreteness<br>• Structure, process, and result quality<br>• Emotional clarity<br>• Result-oriented problem and self-reflection<br>• Self-efficacy beliefs<br>• Perspective taking capacity<br>• Performance improvement<br>• Skills and traits | **Coachee outcomes**<br>Extrinsic:<br>• Promotions<br>• Compensation<br>Intrinsic:<br>• Job satisfaction<br>• Career satisfaction and commitment<br>• Work-life balance<br>• Life satisfaction |
| **Coachee characteristics**<br>• Change motivation and readiness<br>• Persistence | **Coach behavior**<br>• Esteem and emotional support<br>• Affect calibration<br>• Result-oriented problem- and self-reflection<br>• Clarification of goals<br>• Activation of client's resources<br>• Support of transfer into practice | **Coach**<br>• Satisfaction<br>• General well-being<br>• Self-esteem | **Coach change**<br>• Self-reflections<br>• Practical knowledge<br>• Professional skills | **Coach outcomes**<br>• Income<br>• Occupational success<br>• Professional credibility<br>• Satisfaction of rescuer needs |
| **Program antecedents**<br>• Expected costs and time expenditure<br>• Program announcement<br>• Acceptance of the program<br>• Selection and matching of coaches<br>• Participation of high potentials | **Coachee**<br>• Optimism and self-efficacy<br>• Openness<br>• Reflectiveness<br>• Self-motivation<br>• Persistence | | **Organization change**<br>• Team performance<br>• Conflict management | **Organization**<br>• Org. climate and culture<br>• Org. leadership behavior<br>• Productivity/performance<br>• Efficiency<br>• Cost reduction<br>• Economic return |
| **Organizational context**<br>• Organizational culture<br>• Transfer climate | | | | |

*proximal* and *distal outcomes.* This is an updated version of coaching outcome research with a particular focus on studies that applied randomized control groups (Greif, 2007), a recent coaching research review by Grant *et al.* (2010), and scales mentioned by Ely and Zaccaro (2011). The model was inspired by the mentoring model by Wanberg *et al.* (2003) which is presented later. The revised model embraces antecedent and the context variables, as well as a differentiation between proximal or short-term and distal or long-term outcomes. The figure contains many variables. Not all of them will be described in detail. The presentation concentrates instead on measures and scales with previously tested reliability and validity, and which have demonstrated their value in several outcome studies.

Important *antecedents* of successful coaching interventions are acceptance of the program by organizational stakeholders and participation of people with high potential and not just so-called "problem cases". Positive transfer climate, for instance, is a relevant *organizational context* variable. Examples of *process variables* are mutual respect and trust in the *coaching relationship* or skilled behaviors of the coach, like activation of the client's resources.

We start with a description of the model and the recommended measurement scales and instruments that can be applied both in the organizational and scientific evaluation projects. Companies evaluate the efficiency of their structures, processes, and output by means of comparing multiple measures with the best practices of other companies. They do this by *benchmarking* and investing money and time in order to improve their performance in comparison with their competitors (Boxwell, 1994). In order to compare the improvement in investments and outcomes of coaching and mentoring programs, it would be necessary to use the same or at least similar standard benchmark criteria and measurement scales. This would also be of great advantage to research. Only when different research studies apply comparable scales will it be possible to derive general conclusions on the efficiency of coaching. We will therefore pay special attention in the following passages to criteria and scales that have approved reliability and validity, have been applied frequently in evaluation studies and can be recommended as future standard benchmark measures both for research and practice.

*Proximal outcomes* Typically, the short-term outcomes of coaching programs are evaluated by the *satisfaction ratings* of the coachees (Peterson and Kraiger, 2003). The use of such scales is not restricted to coaching evaluation. They are therefore classified in Figure 23.1 as *general measures.* Five-point Likert scales (1 = not satisfied to 5 = very satisfied) are common. Satisfaction ratings are reaction-level data and subject to the so-called "Hello-good-bye-effect", a positive feeling of gratefulness or leniency or a way of saying thank you. Positive satisfaction ratings do not imply that the coaching has produced concrete results. They can be interpreted as a standard feedback-reaction from the customers. They are useful for marketing and to motivate other potential coachees (Ely and Zaccaro, 2011).

It is somewhat disappointing that in many organizations coaching programs are evaluated merely by means of simple ratings and seldom rigorously (Fillery-Travis and Lane, 2008). One example is the coaching implementation conducted in the worldwide leading ERP-Software company SAP in Germany (Grafe and Kronig, 2011). The outcomes were evaluated by means of four satisfaction ratings (satisfaction with the coaching results, satisfaction with the coaching process, willingness to participate again in coaching, and willingness to recommend the coaching). The company won second place in the German

Coach Federation's coaching award 2010 for best practice project. They were specifically complimented on their selection of qualified coaches with the program. It is an especially good model for successful bottom-up implementation strategies: the employees, for example, need not ask their supervisor for permission if they want coaching. A continuous rise in demand shows the acceptance of the strategy. The jury that decided on the award therefore evaluated the implementation by means of the program antecedents and the management of the process of implementation.

It does not make much sense for companies to construct homemade satisfaction scales for the outcome evaluation of HR-programs. *Benchmark-comparison* of coaching programs in different organizations or between different types of HR-interventions are only possible if the outcomes are measured by standard scales that have been applied in many different organizations and evaluation studies.

An example of a diffused and very simple rating of customer satisfaction that has proved practical is the Net Promoter Score® (NPS) (Reichheld, 2003). The coachee would have to answer only one, nevertheless very revealing, question: "How likely is it that you would recommend participation in the coaching program to a friend or colleague?" An 11-point scale is presented for the answers that range from 0 ("not at all likely") to 10 ("extremely likely"). An open-ended question follows, where the person may elaborate on or explain their rating. Customers who give a rating of 9 and 10 are classified as "promoters", and those with ratings of 0–6 as "detractors". The promoter score is calculated by subtracting the percentage of the detractors from that of the promoters. It can vary between -100 and +100. The answers to the open questions can be used to improve the services. One of the advantages of the NPS is its simplicity. Nobody could argue that this scale generates too much work for the company. Due to the long 11-point scale it is possible to identify enthusiastic customers: something that would be impossible with five-point scales.

A more sophisticated standard satisfaction measurement instrument, and one which has been applied in numerous production and service branches, is the American Customer Satisfaction Index (ACSI) (Fornell *et al.*, 1996). It uses ten-point scales. The index is based on weightings of the importance of standard quality attributes of the service and comparison with competitors. It is not purely a low-level measure of emotional reactions, since it also predicts customer behavior and correlates with economic return. Notably, up to the present day there have been no published studies that have applied either the NPS or ACSI in the field of coaching.

The second group of frequently used outcome criteria consists of subjective *goal attainment* or *goal satisfaction* ratings. Again, we often find simple five-point ratings or open responses with estimated percentages. Such ratings may also be classified as reaction level data if they are based merely on the spontaneous impressions and feelings of the coachee. However, if they are assessed by means of more refined methods they can reach the behavior level.

Spence (2007) recommends a refined method of goal attainment scaling (GAS) to reduce subjective distortions or biases. He obtains a score by asking the respondents to rate their success for each goal on a five-point Likert scale (e.g., $1 = 0$–$20$ percent successful, to $5 = 80$–$100$ percent successful). A direct estimation of the percentages is also possible. To obtain a mean value, these ratings are summed up and divided by the total number of goals. In addition, he recommends assessing the ratings of difficulty of reaching the goal for each goal (e.g., $1 =$ very easy, to $4 =$ very difficult). The goal attainment formula (Spence, 2007):

$$goal\,attainment = \frac{\left(goal\,1\,difficulty \times attainment\right) + \left(goal\,2\,difficulty \times attainment\right) + \left(\ldots\right)}{total\,number\,of\,goals}$$

In this formula the attainment of difficult goals is weighted more highly than that of easy goals. Spence recommends assessing such scores at different times (e.g., at least at the beginning and the end of the coaching). The scoring approach has been applied especially by the researchers of the Coaching Psychology Unit of the University of Sydney, Australia.

Similarly, in the research at the University of Osnabrück, Germany, it is standard to assess ratings of goal attainment and difficulty (or probability of reaching the goals). Before the ratings, the coaches are asked to define their goals and to describe sub-goals and possible steps by means of open-ended questions. In addition, Likert scale ratings are used that refer to the importance of the goals, goal attainment satisfaction, determination to reach the goals, disappointment if the goals cannot be reached, concreteness of the steps planned, persistence in pursuing the goals, favorable or unfavorable context conditions, and finally the chances of reaching the goals. The differentiated ratings provide valuable information for the subsequent coaching. It is also taken into account that goal and other attributes may change. If the initial goals change during the intervention process or if the client realizes that it is impossible to reach the goal 100 percent, goal attainment satisfaction seems to be a more valid rating than the percentage of goal attainment.

Additional scales showing effects of coaching in several outcome studies using random or not-random control groups (Ely *et al.*, 2010; Grant, 2009; Grant *et al.*, 2010; Greif, 2007, 2011a) are: *affect scales*, for example PANAS (Watson *et al.*, 1988) or similar instruments, The Depression, Anxiety and Stress Scale (DASS; Lovibond and Lovibond, 1995), and the scales of Psychological Well-being (Ryff and Keyes, 1995), or Cognitive Hardiness (Nowack, 1990). The results of several studies support a reduction in *negative affect*, *anxiety*, *stress*, and *depression* after coaching, as well as an improvement in *general well-being* and *health*. Some studies found an increase in *hardiness* of *self-esteem* or *hope*. The standard scales that are used here are reliable and valid and have proven their worth in many different fields of application. If they are used in parallel with training programs that aim at similar goals, then benchmark-comparison between coaching and training interventions is possible. Normally we would expect that the outcomes are significantly better for coaching since it is more individualized and intensive. Contrary to expectation, the necessary expenditure of time and the investment costs of coaching can be lower than the costs of training. This applies if the expense of providing substitutes for the participants in the company's training programs are high, as has been demonstrated in the cost analysis of a case study (Greif and Scheidewig, 1998).

If we consider the hypothetical *short-term general outcomes* of the *coaches*, we would expect that *satisfaction, general well-being*, and *self-esteem* would improve if the coaching were rated as a success by the coachees and organization. However, to date there are no published studies that assess proximal outcomes of this sort for the coach.

Figure 23.1 also presents *outcomes* that are *specific to coaching* (coachee, coach, and organization). Goal-oriented coaching, for example, is expected to result specifically in an improvement of *goal clarity* or *concreteness* that can be assessed by goal attainment scaling. In contrast to such elementary ratings, Runde (2004) has validated a holistic questionnaire instrument (S-C-Eval, German version only). Confirmatory factor analysis confirmed three basic *quality dimensions of coaching*: structure, process, and result-quality by means of retrospective evaluation of the coachees. The short but reliable scales have so far been used for coaching program evaluation in the German police force (Runde *et al.*, 2005), individual leadership coaching (Sass, 2006), a randomly controlled coaching program with business administration and law students (Schmidt and Thamm, 2008), and also in an adapted version by a mentoring program (Klien, 2011). It would be prudent to translate and test it in other countries.

A questionnaire scale that seems particularly suitable for coaching evaluation is the Insight Scale by Grant *et al.* (2002). It assesses the perceived clarity of the participant's own feelings. The items of the scale are similar to the items of the Emotional Clarity subscale of the Trait Meta-Mood Scale (TMMS, Mayer *et al.*, 2004; Salovey *et al.*, 1995). Emotional clarity is an important component of emotional intelligence. According to several studies emotional insight improves after coaching (Greif and Berg, 2011).

According to Grant (2006, pp. 153f.), coaching not only means facilitating the coachees in setting goals, developing plans of action and beginning to act. It also implies strengthening their self-monitoring and *self-awareness* of their performance when evaluating the results. A synonym term that is often used in the field is *self-reflection*. Self-reflection is seen as a basis for modifying coachees' actions in order to better reach their goals. Grant refers to the self-regulation theory of Carver and Scheier (1998), who regard cycles of such processes as the core of all goal-directed actions. Ely and Zaccaro (2011) mention self-awareness as an important outcome of coaching, but demand more rigorous measurements. There have been several approaches to developing scales for assessing self-awareness as a positive outcome of coaching. However, an increase is not always positive. Self-awareness or self-reflection may be confounded with rumination and correlate with depression (Greif and Berg, 2011). Therefore, in our integrative process theory of coaching (Greif, 2008, 2010), we differentiate between circular rumination and result-oriented problem and self-reflection. Further, we assume that in the majority of cases coaching stimulates merely those reflections that are salient to the specific coaching intervention for a short period of time. A coaching session that focuses on goal clarification, for example, will intensify goal reflections. In contrast, self-management coaching will result in more reflections on self-management. We have constructed validated specific scales that assess *result-oriented problems* and *self-reflection* of goals and self-management and are not biased by rumination. Several randomly controlled studies have shown the expected specific short-term improvements (Greif and Berg, 2011).We therefore recommend the application of these scales in evaluation studies.

Figure 23.1 lists improvements in *self-efficacy beliefs* as hypothetical proximal results in coaching. The concept and basic theory was developed by Bandura (1977). He assumes that self-efficacy expectations (e.g., "I am able to perform the desired behavior") are a central source of motivation and are, among other variables, good predictors of behavior changes. It is possible to differ between global self-efficacy beliefs (e.g., "If I want, I can solve all problems"), situation oriented ("I am very good at communicating with people") and task-specific beliefs ("I am very good at leading discussions in my team"). Global scales of self-efficacy have been applied in several studies and have often shown the expected increases (Ely *et al.*, 2010; Greif, 2007). They belong to the group of general measures. We assume that more specific self-efficacy beliefs, which relate to the themes of coaching, will result in even stronger effects. Webers (2008) has supported this hypothesis in her evaluation study.

One example of a high quality randomized control trial in the field of coaching was a project completed by a team at Sydney University, Australia (Cavanagh, 2010). The study involved 270 participants (lawyers and hospital managers). They were assigned to three groups at random: training with coaching, training only, and wait list control. Assessments by means of a set of standard scales were performed before, directly after, and one year after the intervention. In the outcome evaluation the team applied goal attainment scaling and standard scales as mentioned above, as well as qualitative interviews. A very interesting specific outcome scale that they developed was a questionnaire concerning perspective taking capacity (PTC). They assumed that this capacity is required when managing complex organizational changes. In order to manage such changes successfully, it is advantageous to perceive and integrate the different perspectives of the people involved in them. The results of the study confirm the assumption that coaching strongly improves this capacity.

Figure 23.1 mentions *performance improvements* as proximal outcomes. Without doubt, the assessment of changes on the individual behavior level that relate to the goals of the coaching program would be very important evidence. However, there are only very few studies that have applied behavior observation methods and "hard" performance measures (e.g., of improvements in productivity or in meeting performance goals), when assessing coaching outcomes (Ely and Zaccaro, 2011; Ely *et al.*, 2010; Levenson, 2009). One example is a study by Sue-Chan and Latham (2004). They developed and applied a team behavior observation method and used MBA-grades for appraising performance.

Often, 360-degree ratings of performance by different sources, especially supervisors, colleagues, subordinates, and the persons themselves, are employed as substitutes for laborious behavior observation systems. An example of best practice implementation of coaching combined with before-after 360-degree feedback assessments has been described by Kaufel and his colleagues (Kaufel, 2009; Kaufel *et al.*, 2006). However, the feedback ratings often disagree (especially among subordinates). The methodological aspect of the problem is that the disagreement reduces inter-rater reliabilities of such measures substantially (Conway and Huffcutt, 1997). The psychological problem is the low acceptance of inconsistent negative feedback. According to a meta-analysis of Kluger and DeNisi (1996) most 360-degree feedback appraisal systems are effective, but more than a third are ineffective and lower subsequent performance. DeNisi and Kluger (2000) recommend individual coaching in order to help the recipients interpret the differences in the feedback, cope with negative feedback, and develop a strategy for performance improvement (see also Luthans and Peterson, 2003). In summary, 360-degree feedback assessments are possible – but somewhat knotty – outcome measures, since these measures elicit positive or negative reactions depending on their differences and direction. If in addition the quality of the coaching has an influence on the quality of the resulting measurement of the performance changes, the values of the control groups without coaching are not comparable.

As an alternative for outcome studies of leadership coaching we would recommend reliable and validated leadership behavior scales. A well-established example is the MLQ-scale by Bass and Aviolo (1990). It measures transformational leadership and is therefore particularly suitable for evaluation studies on coaching leaders managing organizational changes. As will be discussed below, a review of meta-analysis studies on leadership development interventions (Avolio *et al.*, 2010) shows that in most cases leadership development programs improve the economic benefit of the organization.

It is a complex question as to which proximal improvements belong to the learning level and which to the behavior level of Kirkpatrick's taxonomy, since learning can be defined by behavior changes. The allocation of variables therefore depends on the background theory. We assume that *skills and traits* are hierarchical superordinate constructs that imply concrete behavior changes. We would therefore prefer to classify them as a distinct level above behavior changes and have added this in Figure 23.1. Examples are communication

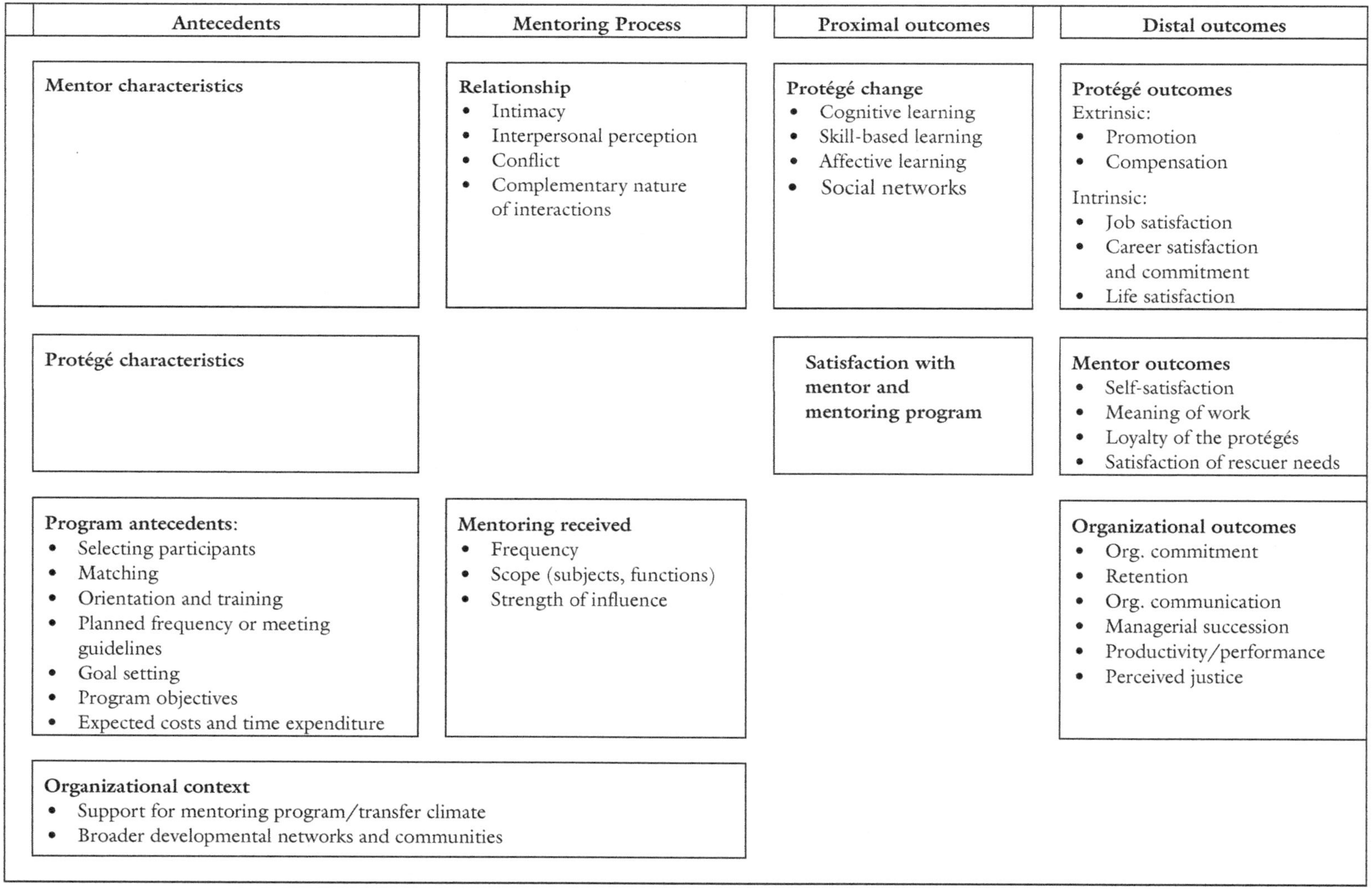

**Figure 23.2** Mentoring evaluation model (modified from Wanberg *et al.*, 2003, p. 92)

or leadership skills. Improvement of cognitive flexibility, as mentioned by Ely and Zaccaro (2011), would also be classified here. Emotional insight, self-reflection, and PTC could also be grouped here. It might even make sense to integrate learning and behavior change to form a combined category.

Figure 23.1 summarizes a short list of specific *coach changes* and the *organization changes*. However, this is speculative since studies that apply such measures are missing in the field (Ely and Zaccaro, 2011; Ely *et al.*, 2010).

*Distal outcomes* Coaching research has, until now, mostly been restricted to proximal outcomes. There are only a few studies that cover longer periods of time, for example, that of Finn *et al.* (2006) who assessed self-ratings of changes directly after the coaching and after three months. They found that the ratings of openness to new behaviors and developmental planning showed proximal changes and additional distal improvements. In the field experiment mentioned before, Cavanagh (2010) collected long-term changes after one year. He observed expected increases after coaching, but also unexpected long-term improvements in the wait list control groups. These effects could be attributed to interventions by the organizations that were not anticipated in the planning of the study. Outside the laboratory it is difficult to establish control groups that are not subject to other influences that may have an impact on the outcome measures.

In Figure 23.2, as examples of hypothetical distal *coachee outcomes*, we imported several variables from the mentoring model such as promotion, compensation, and career satisfaction. Life satisfaction is a distal outcome that is known not only in mentoring but also in coaching outcome studies. The Life Satisfaction scale by Diener *et al.* (1985) is a standard scale that has been used in several coaching studies.

Examples of long-term *coach outcomes* that are assumed are income, occupational success, and professional credibility. The latter is again, in accordance with Sue-Chan and Latham's (2004) study, an antecedent of coaching outcomes. Kets de Vries (2010) provokes the profession by assuming that coaching satisfies the *rescuer needs of the coaches*. A mild need tendency may in his opinion be all right. However, he found that many coaches show problematic rescuer syndrome scale values and behaviors in his questionnaire.

There is a lack of studies that apply measures that evaluate the *long-term outcomes* for the *organization* (Ely *et al.*, 2010), such as organizational climate, productivity, and efficiency. This is a severe deficit. However, one exception seems to exist. Several studies estimate the economic return on investment (ROI) of coaching. The most cited estimation has been published in a report by the consulting firm MetrixGlobal and Cylient by McGovern *et al.* (2001). It amounts to an ROI after coaching of an incredible 545 percent. Anderson (2004) similarly found a value of 689 percent ROI-improvement through coaching. Anderson and Anderson (2005) show how to estimate the ROI for a "coaching that counts" (see also Anderson, 2011). The simple formula applied here is in principle acceptable (ROI percent = (estimated financial benefit from coaching – costs of coaching/ costs of coaching) x 100). However, a problem is that the coaching benefit is estimated directly by executives and other experts of the organization, who are involved in the coaching program. Typical are direct estimations of the proportion of the total economic profit of a company that are attributed to coaching. Grant *et al.* (2010) criticize the estimations by using the following example: the overall monetary benefits for the company are large (e.g., US$ 10 million). The executives attribute a high proportion to the coaching (around 50 percent). The coach's fee is low (e.g., US$ 5,000). If we insert these values into the formula, the result would be a ROI of 99,000 percent!

The big question is whether any expert is able to make a fair estimation of the proportion of the ROI that is caused by coaching. The overall ROI of a company is influenced by many complex factors. There may be cases where it is possible to isolate coaching clearly as an initial cause: for example, a brilliant solution that later increased the profit of a company may have emerged in a coaching conversation. Also, a problem reflection could have resulted in efficient measures that prevented great economic risks. However, even if coaching may have been the spark of the solution here, much more has to be done and many more people have to be involved to turn an idea into money.

A more refined and cautious estimation approach of ROI has been applied in the field of leadership training by Avolio *et al.* (2010); this could be used as a model for future research in the field of coaching. The authors have used the methodology of Cascio and Boudreau (2008). The model evaluates HR-interventions over multiple points and therefore allows the endurance and sustainability of their effects to be estimated. The authors have chosen more conservative estimations for transforming performance into dollar benefits. Notably, the basic estimated economic value of the interventions is based on a meta-analysis of 133 studies that had compared the effects with randomly and not randomly controlled groups (Avolio *et al.*, 2009). Instead of using subjective estimates, they analyze the strength of the statistical relationship between the interventions and subsequent improvement in leadership effectiveness, so-called "effect sizes". The results show that the expected ROI from leadership development interventions – with a conservative confidence interval of 95 percent – range from a low negative return to the organization (US$ 460,588) to highly positive returns (US$ 5,811,600 or over 200 percent). Its magnitude depends on the type and duration of the intervention and the management level. On average, the authors expect a substantial positive dollar return for the organization, but the range is very wide and in some cases even extends into the negative range. We might expect that leadership coaching similarly contributes to leadership effectiveness. Since comparable studies and meta-analyses are missing, this has remained until now a merely speculative assumption.

As in the model by Wanberg *et al.* (2003), we assume that economic outcomes and other changes on the organizational level are normally distal outcomes (on the result-level of Kirkpatrick's taxonomy). In our evaluation model the proximal changes (e.g., individual improvements in skills, leadership behavior and style, more efficient self-management, better team leadership, and incorporation of more perspectives in complex change management tasks or conflict management) are intermediate variables that are assumed to have a possible distal impact on economic return and other criteria of organizational outcomes. In the last section of the chapter we will return to the subject.

As has been shown before in a review of evaluation studies in the field of classic group dynamic trainings (Greif, 1976), we should not assume that all outcomes are fully predictable. Coaching is a broadband intervention with many unpredictable adaptations and changes in the process. We should not be surprised if some of the improvements predicted cannot be found. As a consequence, evaluation studies should embrace a broad band set of outcome measures. If unexpected effects are to be expected in evaluation studies, we can apply statistical tests in a different way. Instead of testing the statistical significance of all the single variables, the test model estimates the probability of the distribution frequency of effects in our set of outcome variables. The test should show that the frequency of significant improvements is the result of more than chance.

## How to evaluate mentoring programs

In mentoring evaluation studies the discussion about providing evidence for the economic return of organizational investments seems to be less intensive in comparison with the field of coaching. There are three possible reasons that might explain the difference. First, as mentioned in the introduction, coaching is performed by psychological experts in confidential conversations and provokes negative, sometimes even discriminatory reactions in some people. Second, mentoring is a voluntary activity and an honorary job often performed by occupational successful mentors. Third, the program costs of mentoring are very low in contrast to coaching. This may therefore be the reason why almost nobody complains that organizational mentoring programs are often evaluated simply by means of protégé satisfaction surveys. However, as we can deduce from more sophisticated evaluation studies, it is useful to analyze the intervention by means of additional criteria.

This section will commence with a description of a comprehensive evaluation model of formal mentoring programs. Second, measures of the model's variables and some exemplary studies will be presented. Many of the measures behind the variables in the model are the same or similar to those presented in the coaching field. This allows the following presentation to be abbreviated by naming and explaining only those variables of the model that have not been described above. Also, for a detailed review of the literature on measures applied in studies on the efficacy of mentoring we can refer to Chapter 12 by Kram and Tong in this book.

Figure 23.2 shows a modified version of the mentoring model by Wanberg *et al.* (2003), who tried to summarize over 90 studies of mentoring outcomes. Since mentoring focuses on facilitation of long-term career development, longitudinal studies are very important and cover longer periods than typical coaching studies.

We modified the original figure by Wanberg *et al.* (2003, p. 92) and organized it in a similar structure to our model in Figure 23.1 (the original contains arrows symbolizing hypothetical relations between the variables). Wanberg *et al.* (2003) did not specify *antecedent mentor* and *protégé characteristics* in their model. A longitudinal study by Blickle *et al.* (2010) analyzes the perceived barriers to mentoring. They found that protégé characteristics such as low socioeconomic origin and a dispositionally low positive affect reduce participation in mentoring. This reduces the chances of positive outcomes for mentoring programs. Prior positive experiences with mentoring predict positive outcomes. A possible explanation is a better participant knowledge about strategies concerning how to obtain mentoring support and how to surmount possible barriers. These variables could be added to the model as well as further variables from our coaching model in Figure 23.1.

*Program antecedents* that refer to the quality of the planned mentoring are specified very precisely in the model. This mirrors the fact that evaluation studies show that the outcome depends on the quality of the program. It seems to be a waste of time to implement mentoring programs without detailed advance design of meeting manuals and of plans as to how to ensure the quality of the mentoring meetings. The mentors should be prompted, instead of merely talking extensively about their life experience, to focus in the meetings on the needs of the protégé. In Figure 23.2, we have added the costs and time expenditure of the program, since we would expect that if they were very low, then they would indicate low quality and effort.

According to the evaluation research summarized by Wanberg *et al.* (2003), the *organizational context*, especially a favorable organizational culture and support for the mentoring program, also influences the outcomes. Blickle *et al.* (2010) found in their study that a low culture of organizational learning and embeddedness (e.g., low encouragement of relationship building), was a barrier to success. In Figure 23.2, we append "transfer climate", a technical term from the field of organizational psychology that indicates the organizational support of the program.

The model presented in Figure 23.2 includes variables that belong to the *mentoring process*, such as the *relationship* (intimacy, interpersonal perception, conflict, and complementary nature of interactions). In the coaching process, a positive relationship is also referred to by attributes that are similar in parts. The different terminology mirrors a more professional role relationship in contrast to mentoring. We have included process factors in the coaching evaluation model that implicate aspects of specialized professional behavior of the coach, which we would not expect in a mentor.

Wanberg *et al.* (2003) name three variables that characterize the *mentoring received: frequency of the meetings* (number and duration of the conversations), *scope* (breadth of subjects and mentoring functions, e.g., learning about other parts of the organization, how to get recognition or career strategies), and *strength of influence* (of the protégé by information that meets his or her needs in contrast to superficial ideas). Mentoring relationships may fail if only one or two meetings are held and if the scope is narrow or if the content of the conversations has no relevance for the protégé.

According to the model, the *proximal outcomes* are *protégé changes* and *satisfaction with mentor and mentoring program*. A collection of short questionnaire forms and interview questions has been published by Saito (2001). It can be applied in the evaluation of youth mentoring programs and may be adapted to other target groups. Wanberg *et al.* (2003) refer to the classification by Kraiger *et al.* (1993) mentioned above, who differentiated between the "learning" level of Kirkpatrick's taxonomy and also distinguish between *cognitive, skill-based,* and *affective learning.* Kram and Tong mention research in Chapter 12 of this book, which supports the theory that mentoring can improve performance and short-term development of personal skills or relational skills learning. Since mentoring is about developing networks, Wanberg *et al.* (2003) add *social networks* to their model. As mentioned in Chapter 12, developmental networks are a focus of contemporary mentoring research.

Karcher *et al.* (2006) propose a model of the causal relationship between proximal outcomes (e.g., increased social support or improvement) and distal results (e.g., gains in achievement). They assume that their relationship is mediated by enabling intermediate outcomes (e.g., increased self-esteem). Typical focal *distal outcomes* that have been assessed in many mentoring evaluation studies are career success indices, especially promotion and compensation (see Chapter 12 for a review of the literature). In the model they are classified as extrinsic outcomes. Blickle *et al.* (2010) in their longitudinal study assess yearly gross income, reported by the protégé as an outcome measure. Similarly to the coaching model, Figure 23.2 lists improvements in the job and life-satisfaction of the protégés and specifically career satisfaction, which are classified here as intrinsic outcomes.

Since the mentor is a volunteer and is not normally compensated for the mentoring activity, an obvious question is what might his or her alternative short- and long-term outcomes be. Wanberg *et al.* (2003) assume that, similar to informal mentoring, the benefit is *personal satisfaction.* Qualitative research supports the view that mentors perceive feelings of self-satisfaction, accomplishment, and renewed meaning in their working lives, or the personal loyalty of the protégés. In addition, we might assume that, similar to coaching, mentoring could satisfy the rescuer needs of a proportion of the mentors.

Assumed distal *organizational outcomes* of formal mentoring programs include improvements in organizational commitment, loyalty and retention, organizational communication, managerial succession, productivity and performance, and perceived justice.

Outcome variables such as promotion, retention, managerial succession, and perceived justice are specific to mentoring, but there are similarities to our evaluation model of coaching. It is therefore possible to apply the same standard scales of satisfaction, goal attainment, negative affect, and adapted versions of general and specific self-efficacy and result-oriented problem- and self-reflection, as Klien (2011) shows in her evaluation study (control group not randomized) of a mentoring program for university students. Again, the advantage is that if we use standard scales, we are able to benchmark and compare the outcome with other mentoring or coaching program implementations.

# Qualitative Evaluation

The evaluation models and research literature presented above concentrate on variables that have been assessed by quantitative methods. However, in the field of coaching, there is a debate about their value. Many researchers prefer qualitative methods (Fatzer, 2008) and some favor a combination (Greif, 2011b). As mentioned in the introduction, qualitative evaluations and reports of successful programs can have an important influence on the decision to start coaching or mentoring programs. They provide concrete observations that are more comprehensible and convincing than scale numbers.

In the following section a short summary of recommended qualitative evaluation methods will be presented. They can be applied to both coaching and mentoring. The section will start with a short introduction to phenomenological analysis and its difference to methods of grounded theory development. Second, narrative interview methods will be introduced that can be used to produce rich stories of experiences. Then, a standard evaluation method will be described that combines qualitative interviews, structure analysis, and quantitative ratings. Finally, recent evaluation approaches will be referred to, that apply linguistic micro-analysis to transcripts of interactions between coach and coachee.

## Interpretive phenomenological analysis and grounded theory development

Qualitative phenomenological analysis has a long tradition in the social sciences. It goes back to the German philosopher and phenomenologist Edmund Husserl (1859–1938). He claimed that it is possible to grasp the essence of phenomena by means of intuitive but "objective" contemplation, the so-called "Wesensschau" (perception of the essential meaning). Recently, Jonathan Smith (1996) introduced a modern method of interpretive phenomenological analysis (IPA). It has since become popular as an approach to analyzing and interpreting narratives of individual experiences from interviews and also diaries or focus groups (Smith *et al.*, 2009). After transcription of the narratives, the interpreter reads the text several times. He or she makes notes and a record of the words of the participants and his or her interpretations of the text, focusing on the perspectives of the participants. Repeating patterns that emerge in a bottom-up exploration and interpretation process are called "themes". Finally, the clustering of the themes is organized in a hierarchical table.

Gyllensten and Palmer (2007) give an example of the application of IPA to the analysis of nine interviews on workplace coaching experiences. They identified "the coaching relationship" as a main theme, with three subthemes: valuable coaching relationship, trust, and transparency. Other themes are "working toward goals" and "improving performance". They conclude that it is important that coaches are aware of and work with these themes.

The method of grounded theory (GT) is also a bottom-up approach that can be applied when analyzing qualitative interview data. The first version was published by Glaser and Strauss (1967). The basic idea was to design an alternative research strategy to mainstream top-down hypothesis-testing science and to develop more local theories that are "grounded" in qualitative data. Similar in part to IPA, the interview data are analyzed and categorized bottom-up. However, the theoretical categories from the beginning of the analysis are checked between different participants. The research strategy also permits additional studies to be performed that review, refine, or even reform the emerging theory. Later, Glaser and Strauss designed different versions of GT. For an overview we refer to Coolican (2009, p. 231).

Wilkins (2000) interviewed 22 coaches by telephone. In her GT analysis, a theoretical process model emerged. It characterized the essentials of the coaching process as an interaction between coach and coachee, seeking to develop the coachees to their fullest potential. Passmore (2010) also analyzed transcripts of semi-structured interviews by means of a GT approach. He identified multiple key behaviors and attributes of executive coaches, for example, confidentiality, being collaborative, setting take-away tasks, stimulating problem-solving and helping develop alternative perspectives that use of a variety of focusing tools and "self as a tool".

## Narrative interviews

Understandable descriptions of experience with concrete cases or successful program implementations are useful for substantiating the practical value of coaching or mentoring. Narrative interviews are methods that can be applied in order to assess and analyze the experiences of coaches or protégés and the managers who implemented the programs. Gold *et al.* (2003) discuss the applicability of narrative interviews with managers in the field of mentoring. They claim that they are more appropriate than questionnaire evaluation in small businesses and industry. They provide illuminating stories with rich context information, which help to convince the managers of the value of the intervention.

König (2005) designed a *construct interview*, which is a further interesting example of qualitative coaching evaluation, since here the interviewer not only asks the coach to describe his or her experiences with a coaching case, but also to explicate his or her subjective assumptions about the coaching processes and outcome. Only 4–6 open core-questions are determined in the interview guideline (e.g., the start and development of the coaching process, outcomes, and factors that have led to them). The interviews should not be performed in a standardized form, but rather in a way that provides open space for a reconstruction of experiences.

## Change explorer interview

The change explorer is a theory-based evaluation method that combines semi-standardized interview and rating scales. The purpose is to assess and reflect the subjective reconstruction of the evaluation models of the interview partners. This is used as a basis for making concrete improvement suggestions. It assesses the personal ratings of the success or failure of an intervention or change and goal attainment of its sub-goals. The interviewees are requested to describe perceived outcomes as concretely as possible. In addition, they are asked to evaluate the methods or other measures used in the coaching sessions and to explicate the subjective causes of all specified outcomes.

Originally, the methods were applied widely as an instrument for the evaluation and improvement of organizational change processes (Greif and Seeberg, 2007; Jacobs *et al.*, 2006). Adapted versions can be used in the field of coaching (Greif, 2008, S. 239 ff.; Greif *et al.*, 2005; Rhebergen, 2011) and mentoring (Qualbrink and Zengin, 2004).[1] A download of the guideline of how to apply it as a self-evaluation and reflection tool between coach and coachee in the closing session of an individual coaching session, is available (see Greif *et al.*, 2011). The feedback protocols of the interviews show that the common reflection, stimulated by the method, facilitates a deep common understanding between coachee and coach of the intangible processes, and possible causes and outcomes of coaching. Moreover, it helps the coachee and coach to explicate and communicate concrete results, and also how coaching works, to other people. We therefore recommend it as a standard qualitative evaluation method for coaching and mentoring.

## Linguistic analysis

Graf *et al.* (2010) have published an exemplary qualitative linguistic analysis of transcripts from authentic coaching narratives. They analyze and interpret two short excerpts from the dialogues between coach and coachee in which the coach explains his or her coaching concept. Characteristic of the method of conversation analysis is a detailed transcript of all verbal and para-verbal interactions. Subsequently, the micro-process is described and abnormalities are identified (e.g., hesitant talking, vague formulations or dominant behavior by the coach, when he or she started to explain the coaching concept). The conversations are interpreted theoretically as common negotiations and constructions of the identities of the coach and coachee. The practical goal is to stimulate a critical exchange between practitioners and scientists from different disciplines on authentic micro-processes of coaching and, in the long run, to develop common standards for the evaluation of coaching narratives.

# Challenging Questions of Evaluation Research

Coaching and mentoring are complex and intangible services. The outcomes can be very concrete, but it is difficult for customers to understand how they are co-constructed in conversations. As Schneider and Bowen (1995, p. 93) recommend, it is essential to help the customer clarify his or her co-production role: "Providing customers with realistic service previews (RSPs) can help them to make informed decisions about whether they want a co-production role and how they could perform in it." Schneider and Bowen (1995, p. 95) emphasize that such information enhances the quality of the service and also customer esteem and loyalty. Evaluation models and methods contain the relevant information that can be utilized here. As a conclusion, practitioners of coaching and mentoring are encouraged to employ evaluation models as guidelines as to how to inform their customers. Knowledge of the results of qualitative and quantitative evaluation studies can be used to help customers develop realistic expectations regarding the expected value of the intervention. This would be a profitable marketing investment.

---

[1] The program, based on this evaluation, won the award "Diversity as an Opportunity" of the Federal Commissioner for Migration and Integration of Germany.

A large variety of quantitative and qualitative methods can be applied when planning and conducting program evaluation studies. The discovery of the results of coaching or mentoring programs depends on the selection of adequate outcome measures and qualitative assessment methods. When planning an evaluation project, how can we select the relevant variables and evaluation methods pragmatically? The first step is to decide on an evaluation model, which embraces the variables that are relevant according to the theoretical assumptions of the evaluators and the demands of the organization. The second step is to answer three questions that will help us to select adequate methods and outcome criteria: (1) Are reliable and valid standard qualitative and qualitative methods available? (2) Are the scales and methods specific and sensitive enough to assess the effects of our concrete intervention? (3) Will the results be comprehensive, relevant, and convincing for the clients?

Once again, we recommend selecting reliable and valid standard quantitative measurement instruments and combining them with standard qualitative methods wherever possible. Most of them are very short and there are not many reasons that speak against them. Why develop homemade scales of goal attainment, stress, well-being, or leadership behavior, if tested and tried scales exist and we have neither time nor money to test the reliability and validity of our homemade scales before we apply them in our study? For benchmarking we need methods with tested quality. In addition, we recommend using standard qualitative methods for qualitative benchmarking.

However, even where similar measures have been applied in randomly controlled evaluation studies, the results are not consistent (Grant *et al.*, 2010). One study shows this result while the next shows another, and other studies even show no statistically significant results. As mentioned above, the outcomes are not fully predictable. Possible reasons are heterogeneity of the goals and context conditions or differences between the concepts and quality of the coaching or mentoring interventions and programs. Therefore, it is advantageous to expect unexpected outcomes. It would be wise to allow for a broad band of criteria and to include qualitative methods that are open for exploring new evidence bottom-up. Another conclusion is not only to evaluate the outcomes, but at the same time also to compare the quality of the program and the interventions, as listed in our evaluation models.

The high road for improving low outcome is to use evaluation studies as feedback and to improve the quality of the interventions until the results are in the desired range. This is not only true for practical evaluations, but also for scientific research studies, where the quality of the intervention is often low. Sue-Chan and Latham's (2004) study, for example, the "education" of the "coaches" took less than half a day and the coaching was very short. I like the study because it is one of the few that assesses and provides evidence that coaching improves observable behavior change and the final grades of MBA-education, but actually for me it still remains a miracle that such a "mini-coaching" can do that.

The second question is more intriguing. Discovery often requires the development of specific measurement instruments. For example, in order to detect nuclear radiation, specific measurement instruments had to be developed. Without a Geiger counter people exposed to radiation cannot sense the magnitude and believe that they are safe. I expect that one of the reasons why we do not detect consistent outcomes of coaching and mentoring is that we have not invented the requisite methods that are specifically sensitive to discovering all relevant outcomes. Methods applied in today's generation of coaching and mentoring evaluation research are in my view a bit like poking around with a rod in the fog. One conclusion, as mentioned above, is to develop methods that are able to assess such specific outcomes. Simple examples are scales of specific efficacy beliefs that relate specifically to the interventions or to specific result-oriented problems and self-reflections (Greif and Berg, 2011). The PTC scale (Cavanagh, 2010) is an example of a more complex methodological innovation. In the future, we should encourage and invent further evaluation methods that are adapted to the fields of coaching and mentoring.

The answer to the third question from a practical perspective is perhaps the most important. As in the example of Kirkpatrick mentioned above, who helped his friend to convince his boss, it is not an easy task to sell an evaluation study to customers. To test whether our evaluation model and the methods selected are comprehensible, relevant, and convincing to our customers, we may try to explain the concept to a practitioner friend and ask for feedback. If he or she is not convinced, it would be better to improve the message and/or the measures!

Critics challenge coaching by demanding proof of its utility. An evaluation of the return on investments (ROI) is often judged as the ultimate measure of success of organizational coaching programs (Grant *et al.*, 2010, p. 142). As discussed above, existing studies estimating the ROI are open to criticism since they are based on assailable subjective estimations. They would not convince intelligent critics. In the change explorer interviews described above, we routinely ask whether the coaching resulted in measurable economic outcomes. Only in a few exceptions were the professional coaches able to explicate concrete examples.

Return on investments or other economic criteria are not the most important outcomes and are often even irrelevant measures of the success of coaching and mentoring. Like Kirkpatrick and his friend, we have to explain this to the customers. As the evaluation model shows, coaching is a broadband intervention, which can be adapted to many different purposes and goals. It can lead to a broad variety of very useful results. Examples are improvements in individual behavior and performance, development of skills and potentials, stress reduction, a better work-life balance, well-being and life-satisfaction, and organizational commitment and productivity. The open question is whether these important changes have a direct or long-term effect on the economic return on the organization's investment. Mentoring is more specific. It can promote the career and raise individual income, but it can also improve a broad range of further outcomes. This broadness and variety of outcomes is the major return of investing time and money in coaching and mentoring programs.

## Conclusion

The general purpose of the evaluation of HR-investments is to obtain an objective, reliable, and valid information basis for decision making. Investment decisions should not rely on subjective evaluations alone: data from multiple methods and different levels have to be included. This chapter presents comprehensive evaluation models of organizational coaching and mentoring programs, which show how to evaluate relevant antecedents, organizational context, processes, and the expected short- and long-term outcomes of successful program implementations. These models provide a basis for planning and managing evaluation studies as well as for program improvement.

This chapter reviews and discusses a variety of quantitative measures, including estimations of economic return, which can be recommended for the evaluation of programs in organizations and in scientific research. Standard scales that meet scientific criteria and have proven their value in several evaluation studies are highly advisable. It is favorable to combine them with qualitative methods in order to incorporate rich context information and case histories. These models and methods can then be used to inform customers as to how complex and intangible coaching and mentoring services work, as well as how they can be adequately evaluated and optimized.

# References

Anderson, D.L. and Anderson, M.C. (2005) *Coaching That Counts – Harnessing the Power of Leadership Coaching to Deliver Strategic Value.* Amsterdam: Elsevier Butterworth-Heinemann.

Anderson, M.C. (2004) Executive briefing: The business impact of leadership coaching at a professional services firm. Retrieved from: http://www.google.de/search?sourceid=chromeandie=UTF-8andq=http://www.cylient.+com/images/pdfs/MetrixGlobalROIofCoachingProfSvsExec Brief.pdf.+Anderson August 8, 2010.

Anderson, M.C. (2011) Evaluating the ROI of coaching: Telling a story, not just producing a number. In: G. Hernez-Broome and L.M. Bohon (eds) *Advancing Executive Coaching – Setting the Course for Successful Leadership Coaching.* San Francisco: Jossey-Bass. pp. 352–69.

Avolio, B.J. Avey, J.B., and Quisenberry, D. (2010) Estimating return on leadership development investment. *The Leadership Quarterly,* 21(4), 633–44.

Avolio, B.J., Reichard, R.J., Hannah, S.T., Walumbwa, F.O., and Chan, A. (2009) A meta-analytic review of leadership impact research: Experimental and quasi-experimental studies. *Leadership Quarterly,* 20(5), 764–84.

Bachkirova, T. and Kauffman, C. (2008) Many ways of knowing: How to make sense of different research perspectives in studies of coaching. *Coaching: An International Journal of Theory, Research and Practice,* 1(2), 107–13.

Bachmann, T. and Spahn, B. (2004) Wie Führungskräfte über Coaching denken: Coaching – Brauche ich das? Berlin: artop, Retrieved from: http://www.artop.de/5000_Archiv/5000_PDF_und_Material/artop percent20- percent20Was percent20Fuehrungskraefte percent20 ueber percent20Coaching percent20denken.pdf (accessed March 31, 2011).

Bandura, A. (1977) Self-efficacy: Toward a unifying theory of behavioral change. *Psychological Review,* 84(2), 191–215.

Bass, B.M. and Avolio, B.J. (1990) *Manual for the Multifactor Leadership Questionnaire (MLQ).* Palo Alto: Consulting Psychologist Press.

Blickle, G., Schneider, P.B., Meurs, J.A., and Perrewé, P.L. (2010) Antecedents and consequences of perceived barriers to obtaining mentoring: A longitudinal investigation. *Journal of Applied Social Psychology,* 40(8), 1897–920.

Boxwell, R.J. (1994) *Benchmarking for Competitive Advantage.* New York: McGraw-Hill.

Carver, C.S. and Scheier, M.F. (1998) *On the Self-regulation of Behavior.* New York: Cambridge University Press.

Cascio, W.F. and Boudreau, J.W. (2008) *Investing in People: Financial Impact of Human Resource Initiatives.* New Jersey: Financial Times Press.

Cavanagh, M.J. (2010) *The Four Factor Model of Leadership: Empirical Foundations and Practical Application.* Paper presented at the International Conference of Applied Psychology (ICAP 2010), July 13, 2010, Melbourne, Australia.

Conway, J.M. and Huffcutt, A.I. (1997) Psychometric properties of multisource performance ratings: A meta-analysis of subordinate, supervisor, peer, and self-ratings. *Human Performance,* 10(4), 331.

Coolican, H. (2009) *Research Methods and Statistics in Psychology* (5th edn). London: Hodder Education.

Cornett, J. and Knight, J. (2009) Research on coaching. In: J. Knight (ed.) *Coaching: Approaches and Perspectives.* Thousand Oaks, CA: Corwin Press. pp. 192–216.

De Meuse, K.P., Dai, G., and Lee, R.J. (2009) Evaluating the effectiveness of executive coaching: Beyond ROI?, *Coaching: An International Journal of Theory Research and Practice*, 2(2), 117–34.

DeNisi, A.S. and Kluger, A.N. (2000) Feedback effectiveness: Can 360-degree appraisals be improved? *Academy of Management Executive*, 14(1), 129–39.

Diener, E., Emmons, R.A., Larsen, R.J., and Griffin, S. (1985) The satisfaction with life scale. *Journal of Personality Assessment*, 49(1), 71.

Ellam-Dyson, V. and Palmer, S. (2008) The challenges of researching executive coaching. *The Coaching Psychologist*, 4(2), 79–84.

Ely, K. and Zaccaro, S.J. (2011) Evaluating the effectiveness of coaching – a focus on stakeholders, criteria, and data collection methods. In: G. Hernez-Broome and L. A. Boyce (eds) *Advancing Executive Coaching – Setting the Course for Successful Leadership Coaching*. San Francisco: Jossey-Bass. pp. 319–49.

Ely, K., Boyce, L.A., Nelson, J.K., Zaccaro, S.J., Hernez-Broome, G., and Whyman, W. (2010) Evaluating leadership coaching: A review and integrated framework. *Leadership Quarterly*, 21(4), 585–99.

Fatzer, G. (2008) Nachhaltige Veränderungen in Organisationen. Erfolgsforschung bei Veränderungsprozessen: Organisationsentwicklung, Coaching und Supervision. *Profile*, 15, 129–40.

Feldman, D.C., and Lankau, M.J. (2005) Executive coaching: A review and agenda for future research. *Journal of Management*, 31(6), 829–48.

Fillery-Travis, A. and Lane, D. (2008) Research: Does coaching work? In: S. Palmer and A. Whybrow (eds) *Handbook of Coaching Psychology: A Guide for Practitioners*. New York: Routledge/Taylor and Francis Group. pp. 57–69.

Finn, F., Mason, C., and Griffin, M. (2006) *Investigating Change Over Time – the Effects of Executive Coaching on Leaders' Psychological States and Behaviour*. 26th International Congress of Applied Psychology, Athens, Greece. Paper retrieved from (accessed May 5, 2012) http://eprints.qut.edu.au/10125/.

Fornell, C., Johnson, M.D., Anderson, E.W., Cha, J., and Bryant, B. (1996) The American customer satisfaction index: Description, findings, and implications. *Journal of Marketing*, 60(4), 7–18.

Glaser, B.G. and Strauss, A.L. (1967) *The Discovery of Grounded Theory: Strategies for Qualitative Research*. Chicago: Aldine.

Gold, J., Devins, D., and Johnson, A. (2003) What is the value of mentoring in a small business? Using narrative evaluation to find out. *British Journal of Guidance and Counselling*, 31(1), 51.

Graf, E.-M., Aksu, Y., and Rettinger, S. (2010) Qualitativ-diskursanalytische Erforschung von Coaching-Gesprächen. *Organisationsberatung Supervision Coaching*, 17(2), 133–49.

Grafe, K. and Kronig, R. (2011) Internes Coaching bei SAP. *Coaching Magazine*, 1, 24–8.

Grant, A.M. (2006) Workplace and executive coaching: A bibliography from the scholarly business literature. In: D.R. Stober and A.M. Grant (eds) *Evidence Based Coaching Handbook*. New York: Wiley. pp. 367–88.

Grant, A.M. (2009) Workplace, executive and life coaching: An annotated bibliography from the behavioural science literature. Scholarly Coaching Publications from 1937 to 1st May 2009 (N = 518) Retrieved from: http://www.coachfederation.org/includes/docs/110-Coaching-Biographies-(GRANT).pdf (accessed May 11, 2011).

Grant, A.M., Franklin, J., and Langford, P. (2002) The self-reflection and insight scale: A new measure of private self-consciousness. *Social Behavior and Personality: An International Journal*, 30(8), 821–36.

Grant, A.M., Passmore, J., Cavanagh, M.J., and Parker, H.M. (2010) The state of play in coaching today: A comprehensive review of the field. *International Review of Industrial and Organizational Psychology*, 25, 125–67.

Greif, S. (1976) Effekte gruppendynamischer Trainingsprogramme. *Zeitschrift für Sozialpsychologie*, 7, 327–39.

Greif, S. (2007) Advances in research on coaching outcomes. *International Coaching Psychology Review*, 23, 220–47.

Greif, S. (2008) *Coaching und ergebnisorientierte Selbstreflexion*. Göttingen: Hogrefe.

Greif, S. (2010) A new frontier of research and practice: Observation of coaching behaviour. *The Coaching Psychologist*, 6(2), 21–9.

Greif, S. (2011a) Die wichtigsten Erkenntnisse aus der Coachingforschung für die Praxis aufbereitet. In: M. Loebbert and R. Wegener (eds) *Coaching entwickeln. Forschung und Praxis im Dialog*. Göttingen: Vandenhoeck and Ruprecht. pp. 34–43.

Greif, S. (2011b) Qualitative oder quantitative Methoden in der Coachingforschung – Methodenstreit zwischen unversöhnlichen Wissenschaftsauffassungen? In: Y. Aksu, E.-M. Graf, I. Pick, and S. Rettinger (eds), *Beiträge zur Beratungsforschung - multidisziplinäre Perspektiven "sprachwissenschaftlich kommentiert"*. Wiesbaden: VS Verlag für Sozialwissenschaften.

Greif, S. and Berg, C. (2011) Coaching and result-oriented self-reflection – construct validation of theory-based scales. *Internatonal Coaching Psychology Review*, (under revision).

Greif, S. and Scheidewig, V. (1998) Selbstorganisiertes Lernen von Schichtleitern. In: S. Greif and H.-J. Kurtz (eds) *Handbuch Selbstorganisiertes Lernen* (2nd edn). Göttingen: Verlag für Angewandte Psychologie. pp. 347–62.

Greif, S. and Seeberg, I. (2007) Der Change Explorer – Ein Instrumentarium zur Exploration und Beratung von Veränderungen in Organisationen. *Gruppendynamik und Organisationsberatung*, 38(4), 371–86.

Greif, S., Runde, B., and Seeberg, I. (2005) Change explorer. In: C. Rauen (ed.) *Coaching-Tools* (2. Aufl. edn). Bonn: ManagerSeminare. pp. 317–21.

Greif, S., Seeberg, I., and Santaniello, K. (2011) The change explorer interview for coaching – a self-evaluation and reflection tool Retrieved from: http://www.home.uni-osnabrueck.de/sgreif/veroeffentlichungen.html (accessed May 23, 2011).

Gyllensten, K. and Palmer, S. (2007) The coaching relationship: An interpretative phenomenological analysis. *International Coaching Psychology Review*, 2(2), 168–77.

Holton, E.F., III. (1996) The flawed four-level evaluation model. *Human Resource Development Quarterly*, 7(1), 5–21.

Jacobs, G., Keegan, A., Christe-Zeyse, J., Seeberg, I., and Runde, B. (2006) The fatal smirk: Insider accounts of organizational change processes in a police organization. *Journal of Organizational Change Management*, 19(2), 173–91.

Karcher, M.J., Kuperminc, G.P., Portwood, S.G., Sipe, C.L., and Taylor, A.S. (2006) Mentoring programs: A framework to inform program development, research, and evaluation. *Journal of Community Psychology*, 34(6), 709–25.

Kaufel, S. (2009) *Verhaltensentwicklung bei Führungskräften: Empirische Untersuchungen zur Wirkung von Coaching*. Saarbrücken: Südwestdeutscher Verlag für Hochschulschriften.

Kaufel, S., Scherer, S., Scherm, M., and Sauer, M. (2006) Führungbegleitung in der Bundeswehr - Coaching für militärische Führungskräfte. In: W. Backhausen and J.-P. Thommsen (eds) *Coaching. Durch systemisches Denken zur innovativen Personalentwicklung*. Wiesbaden: Gabler. pp. 419–38.

Kets de Vries, M. (2010) *Leadership Coaching and the Rescuer Syndrome: How to Manage both Sides of the Couch*. Working paper. INSEAD.

Kirkpatrick, D.L. (1976) Evaluation of training. In: R.L. Craig (ed.) *Training and Development Handbook. A Guide to Human Resource Development*. New York: MacGraw-Hill. pp. 181–91.

Kirkpatrick, D.L. (1977) Evaluating training programs: Evidence vs. proof. *Training and Development Journal*, 31(11), 9–12.

Kirkpatrick, D.L. (1996) Invited reaction: Reaction to Holton article. *Human Resource Development Quarterly*, 7(1), 23–5.

Klien, A. (2011) Evaluation des Expertenmentoring-Programms an der Universität Osnabrück. unpublished thesis, University of Osnabrück, Work and Organizational Psychology Unit.

Kluger, A.N. and DeNisi, A. (1996) Effects of feedback intervention on performance: A historical review, a meta-analysis, and a preliminary feedback intervention theory. *Psychological Bulletin*, 119(2), 254–84.

König, E. (2005) Das Konstruktinterview: Grundlagen, Forschungsmethodik, Anwendung. In: E. König and G. Volmer (eds) *Systemisch denken und handeln*. Weinheim: Beltz. pp. 83–117.

Kraiger, K., Ford, J.K., and Salas, E. (1993) Application of cognitive, skill-based, and affective theories of learning outcomes to new methods of training evaluation. *Journal of Applied Psychology*, 78(2), 311–28.

Künzli, H. (2006) Wirksamkeitsforschung im Führungskräftecoaching. In: E. Lippmann (ed.) *Coaching Angewandte Psychologie für die Beratungspraxis*. Berlin: Springer. pp. 280–93.

Künzli, H. (2009) Wirksamkeitsforschung im Führungskräfte-Coaching. *Organisationsberatung Supervision, Coaching*, 16(1), 4–16.

Latham, G.P. (2007) Theory and research on coaching practices. *Australian Psychologist*, 42(4), 268–70.

Levenson, A. (2009) Measuring and maximizing the business impact of executive coaching. *Consulting Psychology Journal: Practice and Research*, 61(2), 103–21.

Linley, P. A. (2006) Coaching research: Who? What? Where? When? Why? *International Journal of Evidence Based Coaching and Mentoring*, 4(2), 1–7.

Lovibond, S.H. and Lovibond, P.F. (1995) *Manual for the Depression Anxiety Stress Scales*. Sydney: Psychology Foundation of Australia.

Luthans, F. and Peterson, S.J. (2003) 360 degree feedback with systematic coaching: Empirical analysis suggests a winning combination. *Human Resource Management*, 42(3), 243–56.

Mayer, J.D., Salovey, P., and Caruso, D.R. (2004) Emotional intelligence: Theory, findings and implications. *Psychological Inquiry*, 15, 197–215.

McGovern, J., Lindemann, M., Vergara, M., Murphy, S., Barker, L., and Warrenfeltz, R. (2001) Maximizing the impact of executive coaching: Behavioral change, organizational outcomes, and Return on Investment. *Manchester Review*, 6, 1–9.

Nowack, K.M. (1990) Initial development of an inventory to assess stress and health risk. *American Journal of Health Promotion*, 4(3), 173–80.

Passmore, J. (2010) A grounded theory study of the coachee experience: The implications for training and practice in coaching psychology. *International Coaching Psychology Review*, 5(1), 48–62.

Passmore, J. and Fillery-Travis, A. (2011) A critical review of executive coaching research: A decade of progress and what's to come. *Coaching: An International Journal of Theory, Practice and Research*, 4(2 eval.).

Passmore, J. and Gibbes, C. (2007) The state of executive coaching research: What does the current literature tell us and what's next for coaching research? *International Coaching Psychology Review*, 2(2), 116–28.

Peterson, D.B. and Kraiger, K. (2003) A practical guide to evaluating coaching: Translating state-of-the-art techniques to the real world. In: J.E. Edwards, J.C. Scott, and N.S. Raju (eds) *The Human Resources Program-evaluation Handbook*. London: Sage. pp. 262–82.

Qualbrink, C. and Zengin, H. (2004) Mentoring für Mitarbeiter mit Migrationshintergrund unpublished thesis. University of Osnabrück, Wortk and Organizational Psychology Unit.

Reichheld, F.F. (2003) The one number you need to grow. *Harvard Business Review*, 81(12), 46–54.

Rhebergen, P. (2011) A review on coaching effectiveness and an exploration of coaching effectiveness offered by SSR in the Dutch judiciary (Master thesis. VU University Amsterdam) Retrieved from: http://www.ubvu.vu.nl/scripties/ft/27_1419633.pdf (accessed May 23, 2011).

Rossi, P.H. and Freeman, H.E. (1993) *Evaluation: A Systematic Approach* (5th edn). Thousand Oaks, CA: Sage.

Runde, B. (2004) Der Fragebogen S-C-Eval In: C. Rauen (ed.) *Coaching-Tools* Bonn: ManagerSeminare. pp. 337–40.

Runde, B., Bastians, F., and Weiss, U. (2005) Coaching– und Supervisionsmaßnahmen des Sozialwissenschaftlichen Dienstes der Polizei NRW – erste Evaluationsergebnisse. *Polizei and Wissenschaft*, 3, 40–53.

Ryff, C.D. and Keyes, C.L.M. (1995) The structure of psychological well-being revisited. *Journal of Personality and Social Psychology*, 69(4), 719–27.

Saito, R.N. (2001) *What's Working: Tools for Evaluating Your Mentoring Program.* Minneapolis, MN: Search Institute.

Salovey, P., Mayer, J.D., Goldman, S.L., Turvey, C., and Palfai, T.P. (1995) Emotional attention, clarity, and repair: Exploring emotional intelligence using the Trait Meta-Mood Scale. In: J.W. Pennebaker (ed.) *Emotion, Disclosure, and Health.* Washington, DC: American Psychological Association. pp. 135–54.

Sass, K. (2006) Den Erfolg von Coaching messbar machen. *Wirtschaftspsychologie aktuell,* 13(2–3), 18–21.

Schmidt, F. and Thamm, A. (2008) Wirkungen und Wirkfaktoren im Coaching – Verringerung von Prokrastination und Optimierung des Lernverhaltens bei Studierenden. Diploma thesis, Work and Organizational Psychology Unit, University of Osnabrück, Germany.

Schneider, B. and Bowen, D.E. (1995) *Winning the Service Game.* Boston, MA: Harvard Business School Press.

Scriven, M. (1980) *The Logic of Evaluation.* Pt. Reyes, CA: Edgepress.

Scriven, M. (1996) Types of evaluation and types of evaluator. *American Journal of Evaluation,* 17(2), 151–61.

Smith, J.A. (1996) Beyond the divide between cognition and discourse: Using interpretative phenomenological analysis in health psychology. *Psychology and Health,* 11(2), 261–71.

Smith, J.A., Folwers, P., and Larkin, M. (2009) *Interpretative Phenomenological Analysis: Theory Method and Research.* London: Sage.

Smither, J.W., Reilly, S.P., and London, M. (2001) *Coaching in Organizations: How People Evaluate Others in Organizations.* Mahwah, NJ: Lawrence Erlbaum Associates. pp. 221–52.

Spence, G.B. (2007) GAS powered coaching: Goal Attainment Scaling and its use in coaching research and practice. *International Coaching Psychology Research Review,* 2(2), 155–67.

Stephan, M. and Gross, P.-P. (eds) (2011) *Organisation und Marketing von Coaching: Beiträge des Marburger Coaching Symposiums 2010.* Wiesbaden: VS Verlag für Sozialwissenschaften.

Sue-Chan, C. and Latham, G.P. (2004) The relative effectiveness of external, peer, and self-coaches. *Applied Psychology: An International Review,* 53(2), 260–78.

Wanberg, C.R., Welsh, E.T., Hezlett, S.A., Martocchio, J.J., and Ferris, G.R. (2003) *Mentoring Research: A Review And Dynamic Process Model. Research in Personnel and Human Resources Management,* vol. 22. Oxford England: Elsevier Science Ltd. (pp. 39–124).

Wasylyshyn, K. M. (2003) Executive coaching: An outcome study. *Consulting Psychology Journal: Practice and Research,* 55(2), 94–106.

Watson, D., Clark, L.A., and Tellegen, A. (1988) Development and validation of brief measures of positive and negative affect: The PANAS scales. *Journal of Personality and Social Psychology,* 54, 1063–70.

Webers, G. (2008) D*ie Untersuchung der Selbstwirksamkeitserwartungen, Selbststeuerungskompetenzen und Selbstreflexion im Kontext eines Coachings zum Thema Procrastination.* Diplomarbeit im Fachgebiet Arbeits- und Organisationspsychologie der Universität Osnabrück.

Wilkins, B.M.A. (2000) A grounded theory study of personal coaching. Dissertation Abstracts International Section A: Humanities and Social Sciences Retrieved from: http://search.ebsco host.com/login.aspx?direct=trueanddb=psyhandAN=2000-95021-108andsite=ehost-live (accessed May 25, 2011).

Wottawa, H. and Thierau, H. (1998) *Lehrbuch Evaluation.* Bern: Huber.

# 24

# The Role of Emotions in Coaching and Mentoring

## Kate Hefferon

## Introduction

What role does positivity play in your coaching sessions, and indeed within your own life? The relatively new area of positive psychology has facilitated new insight into the powerful effects of positive emotions on individual well-being and development. This chapter focuses on the area of emotion research and its role in coaching, from both the coach and client perspective. Major concepts such as happiness, compassion, empathy, and emotional intelligence will be explored, in addition to major theoretical models such as the broaden-and-build theory of positive emotions. Furthermore, this chapter will provide practical exercises to complete with clients as well as yourself.

## Positive Psychology

To understand the importance of emotions and their role within coaching, we need to first review the burgeoning field of positive psychology (Linley, 2009). Until the last two decades, happiness and emotions have been regarded as luxuries, irrelevant and selfish endeavors in a world of chaos and suffering. However, research supporting the study of happiness, emotions and well-being demonstrates mounting evidence for the individual and societal benefits of creating flourishing individuals (Carr, 2011; Diener 1984, 2009; Diener and Biswas-Diener, 2008; Hefferon and Boniwell, 2011). Emotions are no longer a "wish-washy" topic area (Cohn and Fredrickson, 2009).

The good news is that, as individuals, we have a considerable amount of control over whether or not we become happy. Known as the "40 percent solution", researchers postulate that after genetics (50 percent) and life circumstances (10 percent) we have control over approximately 40 percent of our happiness levels (Lyubomirsky, 2006, 2008). Positive psychology researchers and practitioners have therefore focused on developing

*The Wiley Blackwell Handbook of the Psychology of Coaching and Mentoring*, First Edition.
Edited by Jonathan Passmore, David B. Peterson, and Teresa Freire.
© 2013 John Wiley & Sons, Ltd. Published 2016 by John Wiley & Sons, Ltd.

this 40 percent as one of the keys to flourishing. In order to harness the "power" of the 40 percent solution, we can use positive psychological interventions (also known as PPIs), which have been found to have a significant positive effect on well-being (Seligman *et al.*, 2005; Sin and Lyubomirsky, 2009).

Positive psychology can, and has had, a favorable impact on the coaching area (Hefferon, 2011; Kauffman, 2006; Kauffman and Scouler, 2004), the most important being the provision of scientific discoveries. Building on the research studies and the redevelopment of validated assessment tools, the area of positive psychology has enabled the coaching world access to new interventions, and developments of traditional approaches (Grant, in press; Grant and Spence, In press).

However, within coaching, the target of happiness as a desired outcome is often over-looked in exchange for searching for answers to a person's problem or their goals for the future (Biswas-Diener, 2010). Biswas-Diener argues that in order to lay the foundation for achievement and personal best, one must start with their client's level of positivity or happiness first. The benefits of experiencing frequent positive emotions include becom-ing: more curious; more sociable; more creative; healthier (physically); more likely to persevere; more self-accepting; more social support; more purposeful; and more masterful (Biswas-Diener, p. 41; Cohen *et al.*, 2003).

In terms of "positive psychology coaching" (PPC), Biswas-Diener (2010, pp. 11–12) proposes three important elements when pairing the disciplines:

- A positive focus
- The benefits of positive emotions
- The science of strength.

Ultimately, positive psychology coaching would not only focus on developing the individual (as opposed to fixing), but have a strong emphasis on happiness and positive emotions. Furthermore, Biswas-Diener argues that it is a coach's role to help their clients understand how positive emotions are important, how they can be cultivated and when it is appropriate to evoke them.

The next section of the chapter will review the *what, where, why,* and *how* of emotions to help navigate coaches through this topic area with a rich and complicated history.

## The "what" of emotions

An emotion can be regarded as a, "psychological state defined by subjective feelings but also characteristic patterns of physiological arousal thought and behaviors" (Peterson, 2006, p. 73)[1]. The difference between emotions and mood is conceptualized as: emotions tend to be focused and relating to a specific event either in the past present or future (Hefferon and Bonwell, 2011); whereas moods are longer lasting and less tied to an exact event. Individuals vary on their levels of affectivity (affective style), with some experiencing more positive or negative emotions than others (DeNeve and Cooper, 1998; Peterson, 2006; Shiota *et al.*, 2006; Wheeler *et al.*, 1993) as well as differing intensities of these emotions (Larsen and Diener, 1992; Russell, 1980).

Humans are complex creatures with a rich mixture of emotions that appear to be universally binding (interest, joy, surprise, shame, fear, guilt, distress, disgust, anger, and

---

[1]    Feelings tend to be used interchangeable with emotions (Fredrickson, 2001).

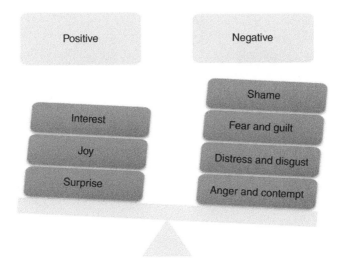

**Figure 24.1** Basic universal emotions (based on Eckman, 2003).

contempt) (Eckman, 2003) (Figure 24.1). When researchers began to identify and study these emotions, they focused on the obviously useful emotions – negative emotions – that kept us alive and safe.[2] Evolutionary psychologists postulate that any emotions, thoughts, and behaviors that exist today must have had some adaptive element to remain within our species today. Thus, the reason for fear and anger and disgust are clear – they have certain specific action tendencies, which provide adaptive responses and promote survival (e.g., fear = run; anger = defend).

From decades of research, conducted across many populations, there exist ten main positive emotions. In order of occurrence, these include: joy, gratitude, serenity, interest, hope, pride, amusement, inspiration, awe and, love (Figure 24.2) (Fredrickson, 2009).

*The 3:1 ratio*   Positive psychology has suggested a 3:1 positivity ratio. The positivity ratio is the result of mathematical analysis on team performance and positive to negative interaction. Mathematician Losada (Fredrickson and Losada, 2005) found that for every negative interaction, a team must engage in six positive interactions (asking about others' opinions, talking about others rather than themselves) for each negative interaction (6:1 ratio). The results from this experiment were then transferred and adapted to see if the same ratio might exist in everyday life. A consistent ratio for daily optimal human functioning did indeed exist at 2.9 positive emotions to 1 negative (rounded up to 3:1 for simplicity's sake). Of course this does not mean that one seeks out a negative event or situation to even out the balance. However, the ratio recognizes that one must balance the positive with the negative in a healthy equilibrium.

## The "why" of emotions

Why do we have, need, and like positive emotions? The broaden-and-build theory of positive emotions has been proposed to explain the lingering existence of positive emotions within human consciousness. Fredrickson's positive emotions lab has repeatedly

---

[2]   Interestingly enough, notice how the number of positive to negative emotions is slightly unequal (Figure 24.1).

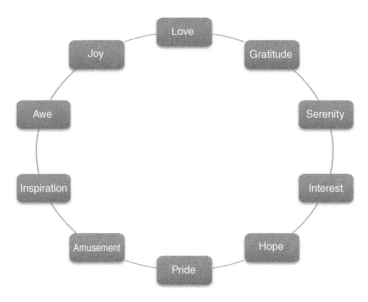

**Figure 24.2**　Top ten positive emotions (based on Fredrickson, 2009).

tested the broadening, building, and undoing effects of positive emotions (Fredrickson *et al.*, 2008).

The research findings suggest that when we experience one of the main positive emotions (Figure 24.2) our minds tend to open up – or broaden – and we are able to think "outside the box". This is important because when we broaden our thinking patterns we tend to get a bird's-eye view of our situation, which can help generate alternative solutions to the tasks at hand. We also become more creative, with positive emotions being found to enhance overall scores on verbal creativity tasks.

Positive emotions do not only open our mind to alternative strategies – research has shown that the experience of positive emotions coupled with the broadening effect has the ability to build personal resources, which we are able to dip into when needed (Fredrickson, 2001). These include intellectual resources (problem solving, being open to learning), physical resources (increased cardiovascular health, increased coordination), social resources (we can maintain relationships and create new ones), and psychological resources (resilience, optimism, sense of identity, and goal orientation). As these develop, they induce more positive emotions that continue building resources in an upward spiral (see Figure 24.3).

In addition to this, there is evidence to show that the experience of positive emotions can, "quell or undo cardiovascular after-effects of negativity" (Fredrickson, 2009, p. 105). Thus, when we feel anxiety or stress or any other negative emotions, experiencing positive emotions can help our bodies return to normal physiological functioning significantly faster than any other types of emotion (Fredrickson and Levenson, 1998).

## The "how" of emotions

The next section will review several main theories on emotions and where they come from. Of course, each culture has certain "display rules", which govern how much one

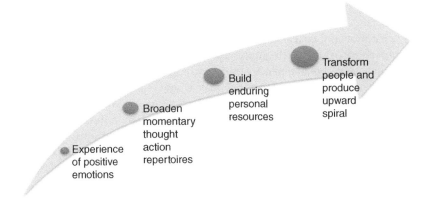

**Figure 24.3**  Broaden and build theory of positive emotions.

displays or expresses emotions in social situations (Passer and Smith, 2004). These theories date back to the 1800s, linking behavior, cognition, and the brain in the role of emotions.

*James-Lange somatic theory* proposes that physiological changes within our bodies force us to interpret these changes, thereby feeling associated emotions and producing behavior (Passer and Smith, 2004). The major component of their theory is that the physiological component happens first, signaling to the person what is going on (James, 1879, 1950). For example, we cry (physiological), and then we know/ interpret that we are sad (emotion). Another example regards facial feedback theory, that movement in the facial muscles that signals to the brain that we are feeling good or bad (Adelmann and Zajonc, 1989). The critiques of this theory stem from the fact that different emotions can produce the same physiological responses. For example, humans cry when sad and when happy, thus, psychologists have concluded that physiological changes are not solely responsible for creating emotions (Passer and Smith, 2004).

*Cognitive appraisal theory* is the direct opposite of the James-Lange theory, stating that emotions arise from our cognitive appraisal of the situation as having either or negative or positive effect on our selves. This appraisal therefore results in us experiencing what we would call emotions. Another example of this is the Schacter-Singer theory of emotion which posits that a person's interpretation or perception of the situation comes before feeling emotions. Thus, if someone has acted in a kind way (e.g., opening the door for you), you feel happy (Schacter, 1966).

The *Canon-Bard theory* of emotions provides a balanced perspective of the sequencing of emotions. It posits that the physiological changes and the brain's interpretation of the situation happen at the same time (Cannon, 1929, as cited in Passer and Smith, 2004).

Now that we have reviewed some of the social psychological theories of emotion formation (see Hefferon and Boniwell, 2011 for a detailed review of contemporary theories of emotion formation) the next section will review how you can develop certain emotional skills (e.g., compassion, empathy, and emotional intelligence) to enhance your abilities as a coach as well as enable clients to reach their full potential.

## Harnessing emotions

The integrative model of coaching relies on six components melded together to create a holistic approach to coaching (Passmore, 2006, 2007). The first two components focus on the development and maintenance of the coaching relationship. As we know, the relationship is at the heart of successful therapy and coaching outcomes (Messer and Wampold, 2002). In order to develop and maintain a healthy relationship with clients, a coach must learn certain emotion-based fundamentals, such as developing empathy (for trust) and compassion, as well as understanding and managing their own emotions. In this sense the coach needs to have emotional intelligence, be able to read and understand the emotions of their coachee, be able to interpret and manage their own emotions, and adjust their behavior appropriately to help their coachee move forward.

## Developing compassion and empathy for your clients

Taking another's perspective is a uniquely human specific ability, which is argued to motivate individuals towards pro-social and altruistic behaviors. Empathy is therefore thought of as a basic evolutionary adaptation, most likely for the parental relationship and survival of the species (de Waal, 2010).

Compassion is defined as, "the concern we feel for another's welfare" (Keltner, 2010, p. 8). When we see/feel love for others, we experience an overwhelming sense of positive emotions, as objectively established via FMRI scanning (Keltner, 2010). Furthermore, when we hear or see harm to others, known or unknown to us, we feel immediate negative emotions.

Coaches need to walk a fine line between empathic connections and appropriate displays of professionalism, which may at times appear stand-offish and removed (Goleman, 2010). Coaches can also convey compassion through non-verbal accounts, such as a specific facial expression, requiring "oblique eyebrows and a concerned gaze" (p. 11).

Researchers believe that although we may have this propensity to be compassionate, it can depend on our genes and our social context. Some components have been found to enhance the compassion instinct more than others (secure attachment, authoritative parenting styles, and modeling) (Keltner, 2010). From the recent scientific discoveries of mirror neurons, we know that monkeys who see another performing an act will experience the same brain activity in relevant sections as if they had done it themselves. Thus, coaches offering compassion and empathy can potentially create a modeling situation for their clients. Goleman (2010) proposes three major pathways to empathizing with others, which coaches can employ in order to enhance their client-coach relationship:

1 Cognitive empathy: This is simply acknowledging how another person (your client) feels and/or thinks about the situation they are currently experiencing. Coaches need to take on their client's perspective in order to truly reach their client.
2 Emotional empathy: This pathway asks you to physically "feel" what the client is experiencing internally. This type of empathy differs from the above mentioned, since it asks you to not just intellectualize the other situation, but sense it as well.
3 Compassionate empathy: The final addition to truly engaging in empathy is to not just think and feel empathy, but be motivated to action to help. Your clients will need to feel these three from you in order to build trust and experience positive emotions from your interactions.

## Developing the emotion of gratitude

A useful exercise which coaches can use with clients is the act of savoring, or more specifically gratitude (Bryant and Veroff, 2007). A well-researched concept, gratitude, has been documented to have a large and long-lasting positive effect on an individual's well-being (Emmons and McCullough, 2003; Seligman *et al.*, 2005).

Why is gratitude so important? Leading researcher Robert Emmons concluded that: "Gratitude serves as a key link between receiving and giving: it moves recipients to share and increase the very good they have received" (Emmons, 2010, p. 77). There are several emotional, psychological, and physical benefits to engaging in gratitude, such as higher levels of happiness, social connections, physical abilities, and health behaviors.

In one well-documented experiment, individuals were asked to write down three good things that happened to them each day, for one week. Researchers found that this had a significant impact on reported levels of well-being and depression (Seligman *et al.*, 2005). This exercise is a simple, easy to do project that you can set your clients for the week. After one week, try and reduce recording to only once a week.

## Developing elevation and inspiration

Another area of positive emotion research relevant to coaching is that of inspiration or "elevation". Researchers have found that people felt an overwhelming sense of awe and warmth after seeing someone act out of the ordinary in order to complete a "good deed". Common side effects of witnessing heroic or kind deeds include feelings of "joy, love, admiration and social connectedness" (Haidt, 2010, p. 90). Coaches can enable powerful feelings within their clients by asking them to think of a moment when they witnessed, "a manifestation of humanity's higher or better nature" (Haidt, 2010, p. 89). In applying these techniques the coach can build on this by asking them to describe what they felt when they saw this and what they wanted to do after. This can then be linked to future goals, by asking the client to reflect on how they can make a small change to help others that day (Haidt, 2010).

## Developing emotional intelligence

Stemming from the concept of multiple intelligences (Gardner, 1993), emotional intelligence (EI) is defined as the, "ability to monitor one's own and other's feelings and emotions, to discriminate among them, and to use this information to guide one's thinking and action" (Salovey and Mayer, 1990, p. 189). Emotions are therefore signals to the self to notify, alert, or interpret the environment and people within in it (Davidson 2003; Mayer and Salovey, 1993; Mayer *et al.*, 2001, 2004; Waugh *et al.*, 2008). Passmore (2007) has argued that coaches need a developed level of emotional intelligence in order to maintain their alliance with the client.

Emotional intelligence seems to predict several outcomes, such as: well-being, self-esteem, more pro-social behaviors, less smoking and alcohol-use, enhanced positive mood, less violent behavior, greater academic eagerness, and higher leadership performance (Brackett *et al.*, 2009; Salovey *et al.*, 2002).

There are now two separate models of emotional intelligence, including the ability EI models and mixed EI models (see Passmore *et al.*, 2011, for a fuller discussion with respect to coaching). The ability model and its subsequent standardized tool (MSCEIT) were developed by leading EI researchers John Mayer, Peter Salovey, and David Caruso. This tool was created using hundreds of leading experts, so that it could objectively "test" individuals on their level of EI, unlike the mixed models, which use subjective scoring (Day and Carroll, 2008; Goleman, 1996; Grubb and McDaniel, 2007; Mayer *et al.*, 2003). The ability model includes four stages of competencies or mental skills (Bracket *et al.*, 2009):

1   The first branch is "perceiving", which encompasses the ability to recognize emotions either in oneself or in others. Some individuals are very good at "reading faces" or "feeling a room". Ultimately, in order to understand people you need first to be able to perceive the correct emotions in order to deal with the individuals.

2   The second stage of the model is "using", which is the ability to use or manipulate emotions to facilitate your mood. Research has shown that certain moods facilitate better performance during certain tasks. Thus, when editing a research paper or performing surgery, you will need to manipulate your emotions to reduce arousal, and mood. Likewise, when you need to be creative or are performing easy tasks high levels of arousal are necessary for peak performance.

3   The third branch is "understanding" emotions, again, a very important skill needed for coaching. This branch focuses on an individual's ability to understand that emotions are extremely complex and can exist in blends and chains. If coaches have a limited emotional vocabulary, they will be unhelpful in empathizing and understanding their client's situations.

4   Finally the last branch is "managing" emotions and this is the ability to manage, or self-regulate, your emotions. One of the fundamental skills needed for successful coaching is regulating your emotions, especially when in a coaching session. An inability to control your emotional expression may fracture the trusted relationship.

## Further Coaching Activities

So how can we use this research and theory within coaching practice? We know that positive emotions are not frivolous indulgences. They are real, productive, and can help us move from simply existing to thriving. When working with clients, the coach can invite the coachee to engage in a different savoring exercise or work with reminiscing. If they are interested in strengthening their own emotional repertoire, coaches can invite clients to explore the emotions (see Figure 24.2), for example, when these are triggered, how they manage the emotion, and what impact it has on their performance. For positive emotions the coach may be asking the client to consider how they might evoke such emotions at appropriate times to increase their work satisfaction, well-being, as well as their task performance.

### Strengths exercises

Strengths are defined as, "positive traits that a person owns, celebrates and frequently exercises" (Lewis, 2011, p. 43). The strengths approach (in business, life, or coaching) focuses on what's right, what's working, what's strong. Strengths are basic human nature, everyone has them. Furthermore, our greatest areas of potential are in our greatest strengths and we succeed by addressing weaknesses in addition to strengths: "Using our strengths is smallest thing we can do for the biggest change" (Lewis, 2001, p. 46).

## Measuring emotions

Some clients and coaches like to have an objective record of change. The satisfaction with life scale (SWLS) is a free to use measure that assesses the level of your client's subjective well-being (overall life satisfaction, experience of positive versus negative emotions). The SWLS contains five statements scored on a seven-point Likert scale. See Box 24.1.

---

**Box 24.1**   Satisfaction with life scale: Statements.

1   In most ways my life is close to my ideal.
2   The conditions of my life are excellent.
3   I am satisfied with life.
4   So far I have gotten the important things I want in life.
5   If I could live my life over, I would change almost nothing.

See: http://www.ppc.sas.upenn.edu/lifesatisfactionscale.pdf.

---

A second tool which can be useful for clients is the positive and negative experiences, the SPANE (Diener *et al.*, 2009). This tool invites clients to think about what they have been doing and experiencing during the past four weeks. They are then asked to select a number from 1 to 5 (very rarely/never – very often/always) to indicate whether they have felt: positive, negative, happy, and so on. This is a new scale developed by some of the authors of the satisfaction with life scale (SWLS) (Diener *et al.*, 1985).

## Future Research

Both coaching and emotional research within positive psychology are developing rapidly. However, little work has been published showing the application of these researched techniques within the organizational coaching relationships. We would encourage researchers to partner with coaching practitioners to explore the application of these techniques within organizational contexts, and specifically explore the impact of these emotional techniques on the wider workplace, such as the impact on organizational bullying and harassment, as well as the impact on issues such as employee turnover, absenteeism, and productivity.

Other avenues to explore would involve qualitative research on the employee experience of working within an organizational culture where coaching that has an emotional focus has been widely used, in contrast to a goal focus. With the growth in organization-wide mentoring programs and the development of in-house coaches, the potential for a more central role for emotionally informed coaching is now available.

## Conclusion

In conclusion, emotions are a critical element within the coach and coachee relationship. Understanding one's own emotions and how to use them is central for the coach seeking to build an effective alliance. Furthermore, this chapter highlights the importance of happiness in the development of fulfilled individuals, with some suggestions about how the coach, drawing on research, may bring these aspects into the coaching conversation.

# References

Adelmann, P. and Zajonc, R. (1989) Facial efference and the experience of emotion. *Annual Review of Psychology*, 40, 249–80.

Biswas-Diener, R. (2010) *Practicing Positive Psychology Coaching: Assessment, Activities and Strategies for Success*. Malden, MA: John Wiley & Sons.

Brackett, M., Crum, A., and Salovey, P. (2009) Emotional intelligence. In: S. Lopez (ed.) *The Encyclopedia of Positive Psychology*. Chichester: Blackwell Publishing Ltd. pp. 310–15.

Bryant, F.B. and Veroff, J. (2007) *Savoring: A New Model of Positive Experience*. Mahwah, NJ: Lawrence Erlbaum Associates.

Carr, A. (2011) *Positive Psychology: The Science of Happiness and Human Strengths* (2nd edn). London: Routledge.

Cohen, S., Doyle, W.J., Turner, R.B., Alper, C.M., and Skoner, D.P. (2003) Emotional style and susceptibility to the common cold. *Psychosomatic Medicine*, 65(4), 652–7.

Cohn, M. and Fredrickson, B. (2009) Broaden-and-build theory of positive emotions. In: S. Lopez (ed.) *The Encyclopedia of Positive Psychology*. Chichester: Blackwell Publishing Ltd. pp. 105–10.

Davidson, R.J. (2003) Affective neuroscience and psychophysiology: Toward a synthesis. *Psychophysiology*, 40(5), 655–65.

Day, A. and Carroll, S. (2008) Faking emotional intelligence (EI): Comparing response distortion on ability and trait-based EI measures. *Journal of Organizational Behavior*, 29, 761–84.

DeNeve, K.M. and Cooper, H. (1998) The happy personality: A meta-analysis of 137 personality traits and subjective well-being. *Psychological Bulletin*, 124(2), 197–229.

Diener, E. (1984) Subjective well-being. *Psychological Bulletin*, 95, 542–75.

Diener, E. (2009) The science of well-being: The collected works of Ed Diener. New York: Springer.

Diener, E. and Biswas-Diener, R. (2008) *Happiness: Unlocking the Mysteries of Psychological Wealth*. Malder, MA: Blackwell Publishing.

Diener, E., Emmons, R.A., Larsen, R.J., and Griffin, S. (1985) The satisfaction with life scale. *Journal of Personality Assessment*, 49(1), 71–5.

Diener, E., Suh, E.M., Lucas, R.E., and Smith, H.L. (1999) Subjective well-being: Three decades of progress. *Psychological Bulletin*, 125, 276–302.

Diener, E., Wirtz, D., Tov, W., Kim-Prieto, C., Choi. D., Oishi, S., *et al.* (2009) New measures of well-being: Flourishing and positive and negative feelings. *Social Indicators Research*, 39, 247–266.

Eckman, P. (2003) *Emotions Revealed: Recognizing Faces and Feelings to Improve Communication and Emotional Life*. New York: Henry Holt and Company, LLC.

Emmons, R. (2010) Pay it forward. In: D. Keltner, J. Marsh, and J. Smith (eds) *The Compassionate Instinct*. New York: W.W. Norton and Company Inc.

Emmons, R.A. and McCullough, M.E. (2003) Counting blessings versus burdens: An experimental investigation of gratitude and subjective well-being in daily life. *Journal of Personality and Social Psychology*, 84(2), 377–89.

Fredrickson, B. (2009) *Positivity: Groundbreaking Research Reveals How to Embrace the Hidden Strength of Positive Emotions, Overcome Negativity, and Thrive*. New York: Crown Publisher.

Fredrickson, B. (2001) The role of positive emotions in positive psychology – the broaden-and-build theory of positive emotions. *American Psychologist*, 56(3), 218–26.

Fredrickson, B.L. and Levenson, R.W. (1998) Positive emotions speed recovery from the cardio-vascular sequelae of negative emotions. *Cognition and Emotion*, 12(2), 191–220.

Fredrickson, B. and Losada, M.F. (2005) Positive affect and the complex dynamics of human flourishing. *American Psychologist*, 60(7), 678–86.

Fredrickson, B.L., Cohn, M.A., Coffey, K.A., Pek, J., and Finkel, S.M. (2008) Open hearts build lives: Positive emotions, induced through loving-kindness meditation, build consequential personal resources. *Journal of Personality and Social Psychology*, 95, 1045–62.

Gardner, H. (1993) *Frames of Mind: The Theory of Multiple Intelligences* (2nd edn). New York: Basic Books.

Goleman, D. (1996) *Emotional Intelligence: Why It Can Matter More Than IQ*. London: Bloomsbury.

Goleman, D. (2010) Hot to help. In: D. Keltner, J. Marsh, and J. Smith (eds) *The Compassionate Instinct*. New York: W.W. Norton and Company Inc.

Grant, A. (2012) Coaching and positive psychology. In: K.M. Sheldon, T.B. Kashdan, and M. Steger (eds) *Designing the Future of Positive Psychology*. Oxford: Oxford University Press.

Grant, A. and Spence, G.B. (2011) Using coaching and positive psychology to promote a flourishing workforce: A model of goal-striving and mental health. In P.A. Linley, S. Harrington, and N. Page (eds) *Oxford Handbook of Positive Psychology and Work*. Oxford: Oxford University Press.

Grubb, W. and McDaniel, M. (2007) The fakability of Bar-On's emotional quotient inventory short form: catch me if you can. *Human Performance*, 20, 43–59.

Haidt, J. (2010) Wired to be inspired. In: D. Keltner, J. Marsh, and J. Smith (eds) *The Compassionate Instinct*. New York: W.W. Norton and Company Inc.

Hefferon, K. (2011) Positive psychology and coaching. In: L. Wildflower and D. Brennan (eds) *Theories, Concepts and Applications of Evidence Based Coaching: A User's Manual*. San Fransisco: Jossey-Bass.

Hefferon, K. and Bonwell, I. (2011) *Positive Psychology: Theories, Research and Applications*. London: McGrawhill/Open University Press.

James, W. (1879) Are we automata? *Mind*, 4, 1–22.

James, W. (1890) *The Principles of Psychology*, vol. 2. New York: Dover Publications.

Kauffman, C. (2006) Positive psychology: The science at the heart of coaching. In: D.R. Stober and A.M. Grant (eds) *Evidence Based Coaching Handbook: Putting Best Practices to Work for your Clients*. Hoboken, NJ: John Wiley. pp. 219–53.

Kauffman, C. and Scouler, A. (2004) Towards a positive psychology of executive coaching. In: A. Linley and S. Joseph (eds) *Positive Psychology in Practice*. New York: Wiley Press.

Keltner, D. (2010) The compassionate instinct. In: D. Keltner, J. Marsh, and J. Smith (eds) *The Compassionate Instinct*. New York: W.W. Norton and Company Inc.

Larsen, R. and Diener, E. (1992) Promises and problems with the circumplex model of emotion. In: M.S. Clark (ed.) *Review of Personality and Social Psychology*, vol. 13. Newbury Park, CA: Sage. pp. 25–59.

Lewis, S. (2011) *Positive Psychology at Work: How Positive Leadership and Appreciative Inquiry Create Inspiring Organizations*. Chichester: John Wiley & Sons.

Linley, A. (2009) Positive psychology (history). In: S. Lopez (ed.) *The Encyclopedia of Positive Psychology*. Oxford: Blackwell Publishing Ltd. pp. 742–6.

Lyubomirsky, S. (2006) Happiness: Lessons from a new science. *British Journal of Sociology*, 57(3), 535–6.

Lyubomirsky, S. (2008) *The How of Happiness: A Practical Guide to Getting the Life You Want*. London: Sphere.

Mayer, J.D. and Salovey, P. (1993) The intelligence of emotional intelligence. *Intelligence*, 17(4), 433–442.

Mayer, J.D., Salovey, P., and Caruso, D.R. (2004) Emotional intelligence: Theory, findings, and implications. *Psychological Inquiry*, 15(3), 197–215.

Mayer, J.D., Salovey, P., Caruso, D.R., and Sitarenios, G. (2001) Emotional intelligence as a standard intelligence. *Emotion* (Washington, DC), 1(3), 232–42.

Mayer, J.D., Salovey, P., Caruso, D.R., and Sitarenios, G. (2003) Measuring emotional intelligence with the MSCEIT V2.0. *Emotion* (Washington, DC), 3(1), 97–105.

Messer, S.B. and Wamplod, B.E. (2002) Let's face the facts: Common factors are more potent than specific therapy ingredients. *Clinical Psychology: Science and Practice*, 9(1), 21–5.

Passer, M. and Smith, R. (2004) *Psychology: The Science of Mind and Behavior* (2nd edn). Boston, MA: McGraw-Hill.

Passmore, J. (2006) Integrative coaching. In: J. Passmore (ed.) *Excellence in Coaching*. London: Kogan Page. pp. 135–52.

Passmore, J. (2007). Integrative coaching: A model for executive coaching. *Consulting Psychology Journal: Practice and Research, America Psychology Association*, 59(1), 68–78.

Passmore, J., Tong, C., and Wildflower, L. (2011) Theories of intelligence. In: D. Brennan and L. Wildflower (eds) *The Handbook of Knowledge-Based Coaching: What We Really Do When We Coach*. New York: Wiley.

Peterson, C. (2006) *A Primer in Positive Psychology*. New York: Oxford University Press.

Russell, J.A. (1980) The circumplex model of affect. *Journal of Personality and Social Psychology*, 39, 1161–78.

Salovey, P. and Mayer, J. (1990) Emotional intelligence. *Imagination, Cognition and Personality*, 9, 185–211.

Salovey, P., Caruso, D., and Mayer, J.D. (2004) Emotional intelligence in practice. In: P.A. Linley and S. Joseph (eds) *Positive Psychology in Practice*. Hoboken, NJ: John Wiley and Sons. pp. 447–63.

Salovey, P., Mayer, J., and Caruso, D. (2002) The positive psychology of emotional intelligence. In: C.R. Snyder and S.J. Lopez (eds) *Handbook of Positive Psychology*. New York: Oxford University Press. pp. 159–71.

Schachter, S. (1966) The interaction of cognitive and physiologcial determinants of emotional state. In: C.D. Speilberger (ed.) *Anxiety and Behavior*. New York: Academic Press.

Seligman, M., Steen, T.A., Park, N., and Peterson, C. (2005) Positive psychology progress – empirical validation of interventions. *American Psychologist*, 60(5), 410–21.

Shiota, M.N., Keltner, D., and John, O.P. (2006) Positive emotion dispositions differentially associated with Big Five personality and attachment style. *Journal of Positive Psychology*, 1(2), 61–71.

Sin, N.L. and Lyubomirsky, S. (2009) Enhancing well-being and alleviating depressive symptoms with positive psychology interventions: A practice-friendly meta-analysis. *Journal of Clinical Psychology*, 65(5), 467–87.

de Waal, F. (2010)The evolution of empathy. In: D. Keltner, J. Marsh, and J. Smith (eds) *The Compassionate Instinct*. New York: W.W. Norton and Company Inc.

Wheeler, R.E., Davidson, R.J., and Tomarken, A.J. (1993) Frontal brain asymmetry and emotional reactivity: A biological substrate of affective style. *Psychophysiology*, 30(1), 82–9.

# 25

# Cross-cultural Working in Coaching and Mentoring

## Geoffrey Abbott, Kate Gilbert, and Philippe Rosinski

## Introduction

This chapter focuses on the interplay between the intellectual and practical fields of coaching and mentoring, and the cultural contexts in which they operate. Our starting position is that all forms of knowledge creation and dissemination are culturally influenced and mediated. Even knowledge "about" culture cannot be claimed to be free of the influences of culture. It is with this awareness that this chapter seeks to critically review the literature in this field.

The theoretical foundations and evidence base for each of these aspects are presented and critically examined. The extent to which mentoring and coaching are seen to differ in the "cultural" literature is also explored. Could coaching, for example, be said to be more a manifestation of a particular cultural worldview than mentoring? There have been suggestions that coaching has a comfortable fit with the predominantly Western characteristic of cultural individualism, focused as it seems to be on individual goals and achievement; whereas mentoring might have a better fit with less individualistic cultures of the southern and eastern hemispheres, which often also tend to encourage relationships in which an "elder" passes on his or her wisdom to foster the development of someone younger or less experienced. There are always pitfalls in generalization, though, and the danger that cultural relativism might slide into stereotyping.

In writing this chapter we are aware that turning the lens of critical scrutiny onto the cultural assumptions and biases of coaching and mentoring practice risks exposing a theoretical and practical minefield. One introductory example illustrates the complexity of the task. Bozionelos and Wang (2006) examine the link between mentoring and social capital in China. They found that the amount of mentoring received by protégés in their study had a positive impact on the intrinsic career success of those individuals. However, there was no particular impact on extrinsic career success, suggesting that while Guanxi, or network ties, in the Chinese system are extremely important, it would be mistaken to

*The Wiley Blackwell Handbook of the Psychology of Coaching and Mentoring*, First Edition.
Edited by Jonathan Passmore, David B. Peterson, and Teresa Freire.
© 2013 John Wiley & Sons, Ltd. Published 2016 by John Wiley & Sons, Ltd.

assume that they necessarily have an instrumental *raison d'être*. We proceed with caution and are mindful that our tentative conclusions are open to other possibilities.

Regardless of the difficulties, it is an important area to explore. As Abbott (2010) has noted, in the early twenty-first century, it is endemic in organizational life that cross-cultural situations are encountered on a daily basis, and yet many coaches, perhaps the majority, lack theories, frameworks, and models to inform their work in a cultural context. Parallels will be drawn with the fields of counseling and therapy, particularly in relation to cross-cultural working and diversity, in which the hegemony of a mono-cultural knowledge base has been challenged from many quarters in recent years (Laungani, 1997; Pedersen, 1999).

## The Theoretical Foundations

One of the first tasks of the cultural theorist is to define the scope of the term "culture". As with coaching and mentoring, there are almost as many definitions as there are authors, and there has been much contention and debate (Guirdham, 1999; Jandt, 2010), but the picture is further complicated by the multidimensionality of culture in the social world. We think of human behavior as having three levels influencing it – the universal, the collective, and the individual (Cornes, 2004). The universal level consists of "human nature", or the "operating system", such as the urge to find a mate and reproduce, or the general value placed on reciprocating kindness. Peterson and Seligman's (2004) catalogue of strengths and values draw from this universal level of human values. The individual level, that mix of nature and nurture that makes us unique, consists of genetic programming and the influence of our life's experiences. The collective level is behavior specific to particular groups or categories of people. It is shared, and passed on from one generation to the next. It consists of systems and habits of behavior in certain circumstances, such as ritual and "etiquette". It also operates at a deeper level in ways of bringing up children, ways in which the sexes relate to one another, and ways in which power operates in relationships and organizations. This is the level of culture.

National culture is often the focus of attention for coaches and mentors – particularly in international organizational contexts. Writers on national cultures emphasize that they are deeply rooted in the soil of centuries-deep history, and conditioned by natural constraints of geography and climate (Hofstede, 1999; Schein, 1988). There are elements in each country's history and culture that make it distinctive and unique (Luthans *et al.*, 1993); and any cultural changes represent changes in whole social cultural systems whose roots stretch back down the centuries. This means that globalization is having seismic repercussions in cultures all around the world, and these are playing out in people's daily lives. The idea of a culture conjures up images of cultural differences and similarities at the level of the country or entire society, but the term is also used to embrace group, organizational, and professional cultures. Recent writers have apparently become increasingly uncomfortable with conceptualizations of culture that focus solely on national identities and national boundaries (Rosinski, 2003).

Executive coaching in its earliest manifestations had little direct relationship with culture, particularly with the often subtle influences of national culture and identity, and the complexities of cross-border corporate activity. The "foundational" coaching texts that have guided much of the practice and training of executive coaching (most of which have had several updates) make limited references to culture. Although one might argue about which books are foundational, we refer here to texts such as Kilburg (2000), and Whitmore (1992). Where culture is given attention, it is usually at the organizational level. Kilburg's (2000, p. 67) oft-quoted definition of executive coaching illustrates the general approach that does not give attention to culture:

> A helping relationship formed between a client who has managerial responsibility in an organization and a consultant who uses a wide variety of behavioral techniques and methods to assist the client to achieve a mutually identified set of goals to improve his or her professional performance and personal satisfaction and consequently to improve the effectiveness of the client's organization within a formally defined coaching agreement.

In practice, executive coaches seeking to leverage value from culture in the coaching relationship were forced to look elsewhere and to design their own approaches in context. The usual first port of call has been the work of Hofstede (1980, 2001). Once this work became known in coaching circles via its promulgation through cross-cultural training and organizational development interventions, it provided a new language and structure for introducing culture into executive coaching conversations. His later and more accessible work (Hofstede, 1997) gave specific attention to how cultural orientations were relevant at the organizational culture level. Hofstede's (2001) five-dimensional model of culture is arguably the most influential, the most widely-used of its type, not least because the concepts underlying the dimensions are deceptively straightforward, and have compelling face validity. It would be fair to say that the impact of culture in executive coaching was primarily driven by the language of Hofstede's dimensions and by the philosophy and assumptions that underpin it. While this dimensional approach is open to challenge on several grounds, we present the framework in detail here for the reason that many coaches will first enter into dialogue about culture within the sphere of international business (particularly HR), where the vocabulary of these dimensions has acquired considerable currency in the field, through its promulgation within business schools and by institutions such as the UK's Chartered Institute of Personnel and Development (French, 2010; Gardenswartz and Rowe, 2001).

Based on factor analysis of a huge data set of attitudinal questionnaire responses from IBM employees around the world (Hofstede, 2001), it proposed that national cultures differ along four dimensions or indices; power distance, uncertainty avoidance, masculinity/femininity, and individualism/collectivism. Following work carried out in the Far East, Hofstede added a fifth dimension, Confucian dynamism, or short-term/long-term time orientation.

The first dimension, power distance (PD), is defined as, "the degree of inequality among people which the population of a country considers as normal" (Hofstede, 1980), summed up in the Orwellian borrowing, "all societies are unequal, but some are more unequal than others." Canada and the United States have low PD, relative to many other countries (e.g., in Latin America). However, power distance in the United Kingdom appears to be lower still. Given that coaching is predicated essentially on principles of equality typical of the "Anglo" cultures, this raises the question of whether a mentoring model of mentor and protégé might be deemed more appropriate to power relations in developing countries, in which power distance seems to be greater. To what extent is an apparent preference for an autocratic boss a reflection of historical tradition, a legacy that people should be ready to shake off? The question relates to coaching and mentoring not only in respect of the relationships between coach and coachee, mentor and mentee, and how power moves in the space between them, but also relating to the concept of the "coaching culture", the logic of which is that power relationships are turned on their heads, leaders and managers seeking to learn from those they lead and manage.

The second dimension, the individuality/collectivism continuum, relates to the extent to which members of a culture identify themselves as individuals, rather than as members of a group. For Hofstede (1997, 2001) individualism is correlated with latitude, "countries with moderate and cold climates tend to show more individualist cultures; in such countries ... people's survival depends more on personal initiative, which supports individualist cultures." In the current maelstrom of change that newly emerging leaders in the global economy are experiencing, the concept of collectivism presents problems (Schwartz, 1994). These countries are the so-called "BRIC" nations, Brazil, Russia, India, and China, all either "southern" or "eastern" in relation to the previously dominant axis of the United States and Western Europe. It is noticeable that as one moves from west to east across the map of the world with the Greenwich meridian at its centre, and from northern to southern hemisphere, the grip of individualism becomes generally weaker The executives who are leading the economic transformations of these countries may themselves be strong individualists atypical of their "home" cultures, and this may in itself be a factor in interpersonal issues that surface in coaching.

The masculinity/femininity dimension is another source of ambiguity. "[M]asculinity pertains to societies in which social gender roles are clearly distinct ... femininity pertains to societies in which social gender roles overlap" (Hofstede, 2001, pp. 82–3). Masculinity implies a tendency towards large-scale organizational structures, an emphasis on formal and extrinsic goals and rewards, and high levels of internal competition. On the societal level, masculine cultures will tend to emphasize materialism and economic growth over environmental conservation. There are relatively few areas of the world where "femininity" can be said to be a strong feature of cultural life. Perhaps a more comfortable way of thinking about this dimension (for today's sensibilities that is) is to use the concept of *yin and yang* from oriental philosophy – the idea of opposite forces both repelling and attracting each other in endless dynamism, seeking balance and equilibrium (Kim, 2001). Masculinity as a cultural characteristic would then be represented by hard, thrusting, competitive *yang*, and femininity, by the softer, yielding, immanent force of *yin*.

The fourth dimension is uncertainty avoidance, the extent that, "members of a culture feel threatened by uncertain or unknown situations" (Hofstede, 2001, p. 113). High uncertainty avoidance is evinced in cultures that seek assurance of the hereafter through religious observance, but also seek short payback times in business investment. Low uncertainty avoidance may be interpreted simplistically as a willingness to take risks, but the concept is actually more subtle than this, and critics who attack Hofstede and his ilk for being simplistic would do well to give the original works more careful reading.

Using the dimensions, people, organizations, and societies can be mapped on a scale with the underlying premise that the scores are relatively stable and can be used by executives as valuable data for understanding behavior and making decisions in culturally diverse situations. Although this is a very simplified interpretation, the aim of the executive is to accept that differences occur and to work with that understanding to ensure that culture does not become a barrier for successful practice. The language and the thinking behind Hofstede's work (particularly regarding the individualism/collectivism dichotomy) are still embedded in the relationship between executives and culture in organizational contexts. Hofstede has made a huge contribution in providing theory and language around culture to enable conversations and to validate culture as a major variable in executive and organizational life.

The work of Fons Trompenaars and Charles Hampden-Turner (1998) expanded Hofstede's scope. Based on questionnaire data from 15,000 managers in 47 countries, Hampden-Turner and Trompenaars's (1997) study derived a seven-dimensional model of the differences between national cultures. Inevitably, coaches who worked with executives have turned to the same body of thinking and writing for their information, with many attending training courses from this tradition and embedding elements in their coaching work (including set readings for executive clients). This is still the case.

As well as the orientation to time (past, present, and future) Trompenaars's framework shares the individualism/collectivism dimension with Hofstede. A close examination of his work demonstrates how research into culture can itself be colored by cultural preconceptions and assumptions. For example, after the fall of the Communist Bloc 20 years ago, when it became possible for the first time to carry out comparative cultural studies in those countries, there was a general expectation in the West that these countries would demonstrate collectivist tendencies in their cultures (Gilbert, 2001). Contrary to expectations, Trompenaars's results showed a surprising level of individualism in the respondents; those from Hungary, Czechoslovakia, Poland, Bulgaria, Romania, and Russia all scoring in the top quartile for individualism. Given that other studies have tended to support (or assume) an inherent and deep tendency towards collectivism, at least in Bulgaria, Romania, and Russia, it is open to speculation that there may be something unsafe about the validity of the questionnaire items. The manager cohort surveyed may be extremely untypical for the populations at large, or situational factors operating at the time of the study skewed the results. Regarding individualism, the questionnaire results could be interpreted either way. Trompenaars asked his respondents whether they preferred to make decisions alone or in a group, where everybody, "has a say in the decisions that are made". Given that the respondents were managers, a marked preference for individual decision making is empirical evidence of the tradition of one-man management. Similarly, the response to a second item, whether responsibility for faults and mistakes should be borne by the individual or by the group, showed a strong preference to punish the miscreant. However, once we recognize the cultural tendency to work on the basis of "in-groups" that by definition have to isolate and eject deviants, the result could be interpreted to support collectivism, rather than individualism. Another cultural dimension identified by Trompenaars and Hampden-Turner, that of whether status and respect are endowed upon people by virtue of their achievements or by the fact of their age or seniority (ascription), may be useful in indicating where and why informal mentoring arrangements may have an easier "fit" in certain cultures than formal coaching arrangements (Okurame, 2008).

There is no doubt that the work of Hofstede, Trompenaars, and Hampton-Turner has been of great value for the coaches and mentors who have accessed this knowledge. However, the major criticism of this positivistic and "dimensional" approach to dealing with culture is that it promotes unhelpful stereotyping and depicts culture as a rigid and static force that must be worked around to avoid problems. It raises the conundrum that theoretical and empirical research on culture has generally been at the level of a whole population (or grouping within a population), whereas coaching and mentoring are by their nature focused on the individual. This is one of the paradoxes explored by Abbott (2010). To what extent can an individual be understood to represent or (still more) "embody" their culture? Though Hofstede (2001, p. 17), warns of applying the concept of culture to the individual level, stating that, "Cultures are not king-size individuals," in practice that is exactly what tends to happen – giving rise to assumptions about individuals based upon their nationality. The caution against "sophisticated stereotyping," put forward by Osland *et al.* (2000), provides compelling reasons why cultural dimensions need to be treated with care. As Charles Hamrick (2008, p. 142) cautions: "The derivation of cultural theories and frameworks can lead to erroneous conclusions, and the results themselves are often not fine-grained enough to offer possible solutions to intercultural dilemmas." At the same time, he highly recommends the work of Hofstede and Trompenaars. We are left with an uneasy tension where the frameworks are both useful and dangerous at the same time.

As noted earlier, culture is most conspicuous by its absence from mainstream literature and discourse on coaching and mentoring. There are various possible reasons for this. The first is that coaching and mentoring, over the past three decades, have become popularized primarily as *organizational* interventions. The English-speaking world has grown used to its hegemony over organizational and management knowledge and as a result expects that "Western" ideas, along with "democracy", will somehow effortlessly permeate across geographical and linguistic borders (Gilbert and Gorlenko, 1999). The second is a related idea – that "globalization" and the connectedness that goes with it, is making the world more and more similar – smoothing out the contours of cultural diversity. This assumption merits close investigation; are cultures really converging, or is this "evidence" superficial? Is it that people's outward behaviors change, while the values and beliefs underlying those behaviors are changing much more slowly, if at all? Third, the spread of coaching and mentoring practice across the world is as yet patchy, so research in non-Western and non-English-speaking contexts has yet to reach critical mass. Finally, knowledge of the impact of culture on learning habits and styles, and on values and goals, has yet to penetrate into the knowledge base of mainstream coaching and mentoring. "Cross-cultural" working is seen as something of a niche. However, there are exceptions to these generalizations.

The work of Rosinski (2003, 2010) and Abbott (2010) has raised awareness of the importance of culture and the potential for incorporating culture into a broader "global" approach to coaching. Rosinski (2003) provided the first integrated set of methodologies for mobilizing culture as a positive and crucial element in coaching, though the target audience of the book reached beyond executive coaching. Rosinski moved away from Hofstede's positivist premise towards a social constructivist position where people are encouraged to view cultural "orientations" as fluid and subject to self-determined change (using an expanded and less rigid set of orientations that draw on multiple intercultural researchers and theorists, and thinkers from multiple disciplines). Executive coaches were presented with a methodology that could inform conversations with a rich glossary of terms and concepts. These could then be applied to leveraging and expanding the cultural repertoire of the individuals, teams, and organizations in focus.

Hawkins and Smith (2006) have included a rare example of good practice in supervision that presents cross-cultural awareness as a tool for deeper engagement, both by the supervisor and the supervisee, while Passmore (2009) made a major contribution to awareness-raising with the publication of an edited work bringing under one cover contributions from all around the world. To date, there has been relatively little large-scale empirical research carried out in the field of culture and cross-cultural practice in coaching and mentoring. The scholar and the committed practitioner thus have to draw on small-scale studies and work in related areas to mine the deeper structure of our emerging knowledge.

An example of the way the coaching literature is expanding to encompass culture in different ways is in the field of expatriate management (i.e., coaching with managers working on overseas assignment). Salomaa (2011) in reviewing literature specifically relating the intersection of coaching with expatriate management found three empirical studies on expatriate coaching (Abbott, 2006; Herbolzheimer, 2009; McGill, 2010), which all support the idea that coaching seems to be an efficient intervention in the expatriate context. Abbott (2011) explored evidence-based executive coaching as a means of supporting and developing expatriate executives through the facilitation of cognitive complexity and meta-cognition. He provided evidence from three coaching case studies conducted in Central America, interpreted in the light of knowledge from a "cognitive revolution" (Thomas, 2010) in international management research, specifically global mindset (GM) and cultural intelligence (CQ). Coaching seemed to operate to enhance CQ and GM though cognitive complexity and meta-cognition respectively, providing unique opportunities for expatriates to navigate the interrelationship of situational, cognitive, emotional, and behavioral domains.

## A four-fold model of culture in coaching and mentoring

This section explores the extent to which "culture" has been recognized as a "special" or "niche" area of knowledge in the field of coaching and mentoring. It suggests a four-fold framework for conceptualizing the ways in which the concept of culture has penetrated coaching and mentoring practice:

1 Cultural diversity within the practice of coaching and mentoring, particularly on the international level.
2 Coaching and mentoring in a cross-cultural context (e.g., working with executives on expatriate assignments).
3 Coaching and mentoring in diversity and inclusion (working to celebrate and work with diversity as a resource, rather than dealing with diversity as a "problem").
4 Culture as part of a "global" holistic approach, encompassing "cultural intelligence" as a resource and dimension of learning for coaching and mentoring situations.

## Cultural diversity within the practice of coaching and mentoring

It has become fairly commonplace to speak of the East-West divide, as a convenient way of differentiating between types of cultures. A few authors have investigated this (e.g., Nangalia and Nangalia, 2010). They carried out a small-scale interview survey of coaches working in Asia and revealed a consensus that emphasis on social hierarchy in "Eastern" cultures means that coaches have to moderate their techniques with Asian coachees. They concluded that coaches have to act more like "mentors" in some circumstances. Their data seem to confirm the ideas that emerged from their literature review. However, Nangalia and Nangalia's study focused on coaches' perceptions of coachees' needs, rather than on collecting data from coachees about their own perceptions and preferences.

Law (2010) proposed that coaching in Asia, or with Asian clients, is distinctively "different" from coaching in "the West" and has a kind of *prima facie* validity. The nature of any fundamental difference is undoubtedly extremely complex. For one thing, the "Western" world increasingly manifests great cultural diversity, and this diversity evidences itself in different approaches to coaching, particularly the dynamics of the coaching relationship (Bresser, 2009).

One of the issues to be taken into account is: "Who are the coachees?" Palmer and Arnold (2009) in their report on their coaching in the Middle East, are at pains to emphasize that their clients were a "subset" of the general population, that is, overwhelmingly Arab (in a multi racial Middle East), male, fluent in English, and accustomed to spending their working lives in a "Western" organizational environment. It is arguable that in emerging economies, the people most likely to be pioneer leaders and *ergo* most likely to seek coaching, are precisely the "outliers" who are least representative of their "home" cultures (Gilbert and Cartwright, 2008). Therefore it can be misleading to take cultural characteristics of whole populations and assign them to particular groups, still less to individuals. Hofstede himself was at pains to point out that, in the case of individuals, personality differences will always be more salient than cultural differences (Hofstede, 2001).

But with this caveat, there are some illuminating and interesting differences that align with different cultures. One "given" of coaching in the Anglo world is the emphasis on strengthening the internal locus of control (Roland, 2001), a belief that the individual is the author of his or her own fate, can write his or her own "script", and is capable of making internal change that will have an effect on the "outside". But this in itself is a cultural bias and not reflected to the same extent, for instance, in the Arab world. This may not sit so well with coachees who have grown up in cultures where an external locus of control is dominant and real, "the sense that things are done to me, that I'm the passive recipient of life ... that what will be, will be" (Palmer and Arnold, 2009). The evidence base for significant variation in the practice of coaching and mentoring around the globe is small and often based on individual case study evidence (Sood, 2009; Tanaka, 2009).

Schein's (1969) model of culture has three levels: the upper "visible" level of artifacts and behaviors, an underlying level of attitudes, and a deeper level of fundamental assumptions and beliefs about the world and the purpose of human existence. This is often presented by the metaphor of the iceberg (Jenkins, 2006). The upper level can change quite quickly – witness the way that the mobile phone has spread all over the globe at an amazing rate. This might give a misleading impression that cultures are converging into a kind of mono-cultural globalized blur, that the iceberg has melted, and that "culture" as a variable is no longer important. According to Schein, while changes might occur quite rapidly across a whole population in terms of visible culture, changes at the deeper level may take as long as two generations. If we think of a generation renewing itself every 35 years or so, it is rather intriguing to think that it might take 70 years for the underlying values inherent in a culture to begin to shift. So the implication of this is that behaviors that appear the same on the surface may have very different meanings. This challenges attempts to introduce standardized systems of coach/mentor accreditation across the world (Griffiths and Campbell, 2008).

Culture should not be viewed in isolation. Gilbert and Cartwright (2008), in a study of cross-cultural consultancy interventions, developed a framework in which culture is conceived as a "field" of influence on individuals and their interactions, along with environment, organization, interpersonal (including language), and intrapersonal factors. This framework is also useful in coaching and mentoring. The idea of culture as a "field" or as patterns (Adams and Markus, 2001) helps us to avoid reifying culture merely into sets of habits and behaviors – those "artifacts" in the top layer of Schein's model. Attention to cultural patterns can make a contribution to understanding cross-cultural coaching interactions between "Western" coaches and coachees from other cultural backgrounds, but cannot by and of itself tell the whole story. The wider environment and organizational fields, as well as the interpersonal field, also have at least as important a role in exploring and explaining what makes these interactions more or less successful. This concept of integrating culture into a broader picture is also consistent with the concept of "global" coaching.

The idea of a reified culture, that can be defined, measured, and packaged into convenient dimensions, resists capture. One may look for culture and find only circumstance, a reaction to a particular situation that is bounded in time and space, whereas culture is by its definition continuous and capable of being shared across boundaries of time and space. One cannot make sense of culture today without also having an acute understanding of the environment in which businesses and people are struggling to survive and develop.

In some areas of the world undergoing massive change in their industrial and social environments, such as in the BRIC economies (Brazil, Russia, India, China), in order to cope with the environmental pressures within and beyond the organization, executives are expected to be strong, even authoritarian leaders. Leaders have "their people" around them at all times and demand long hours and complete loyalty. To some extent, the dominant paradigm of coaching within management development assumes that coaching is about developing and extending the autonomy of the coachee, growing capabilities to take on increased responsibility and become more proactive in leading change at his or her level within the organization. To some extent this notion of coaching conflicts with the reality of power and hierarchy in organizations, particularly those in high power distance cultural settings. The leader seeks absolute loyalty and dependability from his protégé managers (for it is usually, though not always, a he), and autonomy may be far from what is actually required (although the rhetoric may be otherwise).

## Coaching and mentoring in a cross-cultural context

Coaching in this area is often tailored to expatriate managers – those on sojourns with companies that have international operations. There are many well-established practitioners in this field, which is becoming more sophisticated as the nature of international work changes with increased virtual work and a more complex global economy. Hampden-Turner and Trompenaars (2000) provided early suggestions for "leveraging difference" and thus creating value out of cultural diversity. More recently, Abbott *et al.* (2011) and Miser and Miser (2011) have provided specific coaching-related models and theoretical foundations for coaches working with expatriates. This practice has matured as different models of international work have emerged with shorter sojourns, greater use of local hires, and increased use of information communications technologies (ICTs). Coaching approaches are also emerging to meet the technological realities of this changing market (e.g., the work by Abbott *et al.* (2011) on coaching with global virtual teams).

The knowledge base that supports the practice of coaching in cross-cultural contexts (and interculturalism more generally) has become more sophisticated. An example of this is the GLOBE project which has produced some quite specific knowledge about global leadership practice The GLOBE project engaged 70 researchers who worked together for ten years collecting and analyzing data on cultural values and practices and leadership attributes from over 17,000 managers in 62 societal cultures (House *et al.*, 2004). This work, in turn, has led to the development of constructs such as global mindset (Javidan *et al.*, 2010a) and cultural intelligence (CQ; Earley and Ang, 2003; Thomas, 2010).

Global mindset suggests that global functioning requires a particular set of psychological, intellectual, and social competences, which can be measured (Javidan *et al.*, 2010b). The intellectual competences are "global business savvy", "cognitive complexity", and "cosmopolitan outlook". Psychological competences are "a passion for diversity", "thirst for adventure", and "self-assurance". Social capital within "the global mindset" consists of "intercultural empathy", "interpersonal impact", and "diplomacy". Javidan *et al.* (2010a) suggest that the resulting three-by-three model can be used by executives with a simple self-scoring system to measure their own grasp of the global mindset. As with many apparently simple models, it provides a wealth of potential for the skilful and mindful coach to use with a client.

The related construct of cultural intelligence taps into meta-cognition (thinking about thinking) and the need for navigating and channelling interactions across the behavioral, cognitive and affective domains if one is to be an effective global executive. Global mindset and CQ are useful emergent constructs contributing to efforts to isolate variables that predict intercultural leadership competence. As such, they are entering the "mainstream" of business education. At the same time, there exists scant evidence-based knowledge on how to grow an executive's GM and CQ. Coaches who label themselves as "global coaches" are utilizing this knowledge and coaching practices have emerged that aim to increase executive capabilities and competencies in these areas (e.g., Abbott *et al.*, 2006, 2011). The research and theoretical literature behind this connection is not well developed, though it is emerging. While this research direction is important, it is very unlikely that a "final" model will emerge. More likely, GM and CQ will be better positioned as useful heuristics to promote more rigorous and high impact coaching engagements in intercultural contexts.

There remain numerous unanswered questions about the way in which "cross-cultural coaching" is practiced and developing, though some knowledge is emerging. Plaister-Ten (2009) has examined how 25 coaches conceptualize and operationalize culture in coaching and raised various questions that require further attention. To what extent is it appropriate to refer to cross-cultural coaching as a "genre" within coaching? What do cross-cultural coaches do? What are the contexts in which they work? What evidence is there for a distinctive knowledge or skills base for coaches and/or mentors working with clients "outside their own culture"? What is the evidence that coaching and/or mentoring are effective in supporting the success of international assignees?

Foreign "sojourners" in a complex environment need to be aware that they carry within themselves their own cultural "baggage" (St Claire-Ostwald, 2007). An understanding of one's own preconceptions and expectations may be the soundest protection against culture shock when it strikes the migrant in a new country. But more than a protective function, awareness of one's own cultural field and its interactions with other aspects of the self can be a tool in the coach's toolkit, providing heightened sensitivity to nuances in interpersonal communication. Culture shock (Ward *et al.*, 2001), however serious or mild, tends to set up defence mechanisms in the self. Above all, cultural awareness is a key to effective reflexivity in an unknown environment.

The process of adjustment to living and working in a new culture, whether for the voluntary migrant or the expatriate assignee, is challenging, and more challenging the greater the level of cultural "toughness" in the new culture, as a measure of the difference from the "home" culture. Cross-cultural coaches are often hired to support a new assignee once settled into the new environment. However, coaching that focuses on the external details of the culture, rather than the internal processes of adjustment, may miss the mark. The concept of the "diaglogical self" may be useful here. This concept was developed by Hermans (1999) as a model for explaining the psychology of internal transition, and developed both by him (2001) and others (Bhatia and Ram, 2001; Konig, 2009) specifically in relation to the internal dialogues between a person's initial cultural "position" and their new "cultural position". This concept presents the potential for use as a tool within cross-cultural coaching and mentoring.

## Coaching and mentoring in diversity and inclusion

Over the past 30 years or so, the issue of equal opportunities for people of different ethnic and cultural backgrounds has become ever more salient, and has developed to encompass dimensions of sexuality, gender, age, religious observance, and disability, as well as culture and ethnicity. The discourse of equal opportunities within organizations emphasizes the uniqueness of the individual and the imperative to foster respect and appreciation. The antithesis of respect for the uniqueness of the individual is the stereotype, and so there is a justifiable horror of stereotyping individuals and groups (Alexis, 2005; Allan, 2010). But paradoxically, this fear of stereotyping might lead coaches and mentors to underestimate or disregard evidence of the influence of culture on learning and personal change.

Any modern organization in the developed world will have diversity among its people, and this is becoming more and more an important part of working life for people operating in "global virtual teams". Such teams may never meet face to face, so cultural differences may be accompanied by differences in time zones, working conditions, environments, language, and perceptions of role. An assumption here is that individuals have, as well as personality differences, differences in cultural orientation that will give them unique combinations of orientation towards time, space, personal and working relationships, motivation, and so forth. The increasing use of culturally diverse teams through virtual teaming should therefore provide opportunities. Typically though, diversity issues have been seen as a challenge or "problem" to people introducing coaching and mentoring schemes. A defensive stance has been necessary, particularly in ensuring equality and equity (Alexis, 2005; Allan, 2010; Bruner, 2008; Clarkson and Nippoda, 1997; Parvis, 2003), and often in the context of leadership development to ensure better representation in leadership positions of people from disadvantaged groups (often with different cultural heritages).

Various issues have emerged for coaching. Culturally-conditioned ways of approaching perceived authority figures (and the coach or mentor might be seen as an authority figure), of orienting towards time and space (for instance use of "personal" space) will need to be taken into account by the coach (Gilbert and Rosinski, 2008); in some cultural settings the gender of the coach and/or coachee may be an issue. How can a coach, mentor, or "coaching manager" use an understanding of these cultural dimensions in such a way as to enrich organizational life and enhance individual experience? To what extent do coaching and mentoring have an "emancipator" responsibility towards people who may be suffering from exclusion, or experiencing forms of oppression, because of their cultural background or orientation? What is the evidence that, using cultural orientation as a resource for learning, with coaching and mentoring as the medium, diversity can be harnessed as a resource for the individual and organization, rather than being a "problem" to be tackled through ameliorating measures?

## Culture as part of a "global" holistic approach

The need for integration keeps increasing in a world that is becoming more and more connected and complex. This section examines the extent to which cultural awareness and understanding can penetrate mainstream coaching and mentoring, using a dynamic definition and approach to culture that aims to embed it in an integrated approach to individual learning and change.

Rosinski (2003), drawing on cultural theorists including Kluckhohn and Strodtbeck (1961), Hall (1976), Hofstede (2001), and Hampden-Turner and Trompenaars (1997), developed the cultural orientations framework. Use of the framework in coaching has been developed through a series of international seminars, and has been encapsulated in an online assessment tool. The purpose of obtaining, for the coachee, an individual cultural orientations profile is not so much to justify existing positions and preferences, but to provide insights into the possible positions and preferences of others, and help the coachee discover new ways to look at things and do things that previously seemed constrained (Gilbert and Rosinski, 2008).

The social constructivist and pragmatic humanist positions that are inherent in Rosinski's approach are consistent with some contemporary movements generally in psychology and philosophy, and specifically in management thinking. Wilber's integral model (2000) introduces culture as one of the four domains of human endeavor. Bolman and Deal's (2008) framing methodology for organizational leadership includes culture as one of four frames that leaders needed to take into account in making decisions. Both models are very helpful for introducing culture as a variable if the coach notices that the language of the executive and the direction of the coaching dialogue is not giving attention to culture, or is not integrating cultural influences into the bigger picture. The role of the coach is to ask insightful questions that shift the client's thinking towards mobilizing culture as a positive force. Armstrong (2011) has written specifically on how to use the integral and framing models in international business coaching.

Since the release of Rosinski's work, various extensive handbooks and edited texts aimed at the executive coaching market have been published (e.g., Cox *et al.*, 2010; Palmer and Whybrow, 2007; Passmore, 2006; Peltier, 2010; Stober and Grant, 2006). Most of these have included chapters dedicated to cross-cultural or intercultural coaching. Palmer and Whybrow (2007) subsume culture under the mantle of "diversity". This trend recognizes the establishment of a discrete executive coaching genre that links coaching and culture, and continues with this chapter. Also, there is a now a growing body of literature on coaching global leaders (e.g., Morgan *et al.*, 2006) and this has developed into a consolidated body of work on global coaching (Rosinski, 2010). A Google search of global coaching reveals an array of global coaching practices and models, of varying quality. Much of the practice of coaching in this area is directed at expatriate managers. There are many well-established practitioners in this field, which is becoming more sophisticated as the nature of international work changes with increased virtual work and a more complex global economy. Abbott and Stening (2011) and Miser and Miser (2011) have provided models and theoretical foundations for coaches working with expatriates.

Within coaching practice, awareness of culture can lead to insights about hidden biases in frequently used psychometric instruments. For example, items on "problem-solving" in the Bar-On Emotional Quotient Inventory (Bar-On, 2002) favor adopting a "step-by-step" approach. This in itself reveals an inbuilt bias towards linear thinking, which has a distinct cultural element. Many of the major psychometric tools have their roots in Western cultures – usually the United States. This is not to say that instruments derived from and carrying cultural biases should not be used by coaches – far from it. "Appropriate use with knowledge" and "adaptation in context" are suggested as guiding principles.

Recent coaching texts have endeavored to integrate culture into coaching practice rather than separate it out (e.g., Law and Yueng, 2009; Law *et al.*, 2007; Moral and Abbott, 2011; Rosinski, 2010; Stout Rostron, 2009). These approaches work from the assumption that culture is part of the executive coaching landscape that must be integrated, leveraged, and synthesized if coaching is to be truly effective for executives working in complex global environments. Although there has been movement in the right direction, the issue remains that for executive coaching culture is often perceived as a separate issue to be integrated only when the client is presenting with an explicit cultural issue or situation. In the organizational context, cross-cultural issues tend to be swept up in minority issues and diversity, with a view that they are outside the "mainstream" of organizational life and power. The shift of power in the global economic landscape means that such sidelining is no longer acceptable. With Asian and Latin American companies moving into traditionally "Western" domains, there is a shifting in the reality of corporate life that places cross-cultural coaching in the boardroom rather than, "down the corridor, third door on the left."

In looking into the future of culture in coaching on a global level, we cannot fail to be struck by a contemporary phenomenon, that of the "third culture kid", noted first in educational research (Pollock and van Reken, 2001), that is sure to have an impact on leadership and organizations In the field of psychology, attempts to measure cultural awareness, as "world-mindedness" go back to the 1950s (Sampson and Smith, 1957). There is now a generation of young professionals and potential leaders who have spent all their formative years in a globalized environment – "third culture kids" (Fail *et al.*, 2004), the children of expatriates, who have grown up in cultures different from their parents, often living nomadic lives as their parents moved, or were moved, around the globe and attending international schools, rubbing shoulders with other third culture kids of many races and backgrounds. This is different from the previous experiences of, for example, the children of middle-class British diplomats and military families of the nineteenth and twentieth centuries, who had the experience of living abroad, but a schooling and social conditioning that was firmly rooted in a controlled environment of boarding schools and closely monitored social interaction. For these contemporary young people, having an international perspective is core to their being in that they are liberated from a single-parent culture and have no sense of "home country". They are "world citizens" who, unlike their former counterparts, are untrammelled with any sense of imperialistic obligation or entitlement. This gives an undeniable advantage in the global arena, giving rise to capabilities to deal with increased "integrative complexity" (Tadmor and Tetlock, 2006). The downside may be a sense of rootless "liminality" – feeling always on the edge of social interactions, superficially at home anywhere, but belonging nowhere. Coaches and mentors need to be aware of the particular psychological factors that may affect the "third culture kid" in adulthood.

The knowledge base that supports the practice of interculturalism – including in coaching and mentoring – is becoming more sophisticated and more "'global". Importantly, research is increasingly being conducted by multicultural research teams. An example of this is the GLOBE project, which has produced some quite specific knowledge about global leadership practice. The GLOBE project engaged 70 researchers who worked together for ten years collecting and analyzing data on cultural values and practices and leadership attributes from over 17,000 managers in 62 societal cultures (House *et al.* 2004). This work, in turn, has led to the development of constructs such as global mindset (Javidan *et al.*, 2010b) and cultural intelligence (Earley and Ang, 2003; Thomas, 2010). Global mindset suggests that global functioning requires a particular set of psychological, intellectual, and social competences. Cultural intelligence taps into meta-cognition and the need for navigating and channeling interactions across the behavioral, cognitive, and affective domains if one is to be an effective global executive. Niitamo (2011) emphasizes in particular the behavioral domain by urging a focus on behavioral competences in the form of sets of desired behaviors in the globalizing world of work. He proposes a move away from an emphasis on cultural differences (as do the "global coaching" proponents) towards an emphasis on commonalities in people processes in order to enhance intercultural exchange. Global mindset and CQ represent current efforts to isolate variables that predict intercultural leadership competence and are entering the "mainstream" of business education. Coaches who label themselves as "global coaches" are utilizing this knowledge and coaching practices have emerged that aim to increase executive capabilities and competences in these areas (Abbott and Stening, 2011; Abbott *et al.*, 2006,). The research and theoretical literature behind this connection is not well developed, though it is emerging (e.g., Abbott, 2011). Significantly more needs to be done to move cultural development and its associated literature forward in this area.

## Future Research

As noted earlier, research that examines the influence of culture in coaching and mentoring is emerging and growing more sophisticated in its scope. Also, studies into the impact of coaching are studying interventions with coaching models that systematically integrate culture, thereby making it more likely that associated findings will provide further knowledge about the coaching/culture relationships. As the practice of intercultural and global coaching increases – particularly through executive coaching programs in multinational companies, more knowledge is needed about what is being done now and what is possible. The vehicles for creating and disseminating such knowledge are increasing. Academic institutions such as the Academy of Management are beginning to accept coaching as a legitimate field of study and academic journals from multiple disciplines are publishing research about coaching. Various journals dedicated to coaching are well established (such as the *International Journal of Evidence Based Coaching and Mentoring*). What is needed is a focus on the cultural influences that addresses research questions such as:

- Do coaching and mentoring interventions that mobilize knowledge about culture make a difference to the leadership effectiveness of international executives – and if so, how?
- What is the current state of "global coaching"?
  - Who is doing it, and who with?
  - What do they say/think they are doing?
  - What is the impact?
- What scope is there for global/intercultural coaching and mentoring programs to be utilized to empower those who are currently outside of the impact of executive coaching interventions funded by large corporations?

## Conclusion

In summary, the coaching/mentoring-culture relationship has matured since 1990 and the literature and practice continue to develop. Now, there is recognition by rigorous coaching practitioners, trainers, and writers that culture needs to be a variable for consideration in executive coaching interventions. This is evident in the emergence of executive coaches whose work is primarily in cross-cultural coaching, dedicated courses on coaching and culture, and related books and book chapters. A parallel process is the integration of culture as a variable within established coaching and mentoring practice, such as models based on Wilber's integral model and related frameworks. As this chapter has indicated, the coaching/mentoring-culture relationship is by no means simple and it is unlikely that firm and fast recommendations will emerge for coaches and mentors on the "how to" of working with culture. More likely, coaches and mentors will be provided with a better idea of the complexity of the landscape and the need for them to be equally sophisticated in their interventions.

# References

Abbott, G.N. (2006) Exploring evidence-based executive coaching as an intervention to facilitate expatriate acculturation: Fifteen case studies. Unpublished dissertation, Faculty of Economics and Commerce, Canberra: Australian National University.

Abbott, G.N. (2010) Cross cultural coaching: A paradoxical perspective. In: E. Cox, T. Bachkirova, and D. Clutterbuck (eds) *The Complete Handbook of Coaching*. London: Sage. pp. 324–40.

Abbott, G.N. (2011) *Executive Based Coaching With Expatriates: Evidence from the Field Revisited in the Light of a Cognitive Revolution in International Management*. Proceedings of the 2011 Annual Conference of the European Academy of Management, Tallinn, June 1–4, 2011.

Abbott, G.N. and Stening, B.W. (2011) Coaching expatriate executives: Working in context across the affective, behavioral and cogntive domains. In: M. Moral and G.N. Abbott (eds) *The Routledge Companion to International Business Coaching*. Milton Park: Routledge. pp. 181–202.

Abbott, G.N., Stening, B.W., Atkins, P.W.B., and Grant, A.M. (2006). Coaching expatriate managers for success: Adding value beyond training and mentoring. *Asia Pacific Journal of Human Resources*, 44(3), 295–317.

Adams, G. and Markus, H.R. (2001) Culture as pattern: An alternative approach to the problem of reification. *Culture and Psychology*, 7. 283–98.

Alexis, O. (2005) Managing change: Cultural diversity in the NHS workforce. *Nursing Management – UK*, 11(10), 28–30.

Allan, H. (2010) Mentoring overseas nurses: Barriers to effective and non-discriminatory mentoring practices. *Nursing Ethics*, 17, 603–13.

Armstrong, H. (2011) Integral coaching: Cultivating a cultural sensibility through executive coaching. In: M. Moral. and G.N. Abbott (eds) *The Routledge Companion to International Business Coaching*. Milton Park: Routledge. pp. 34–44.

Bar-On, R. (2002) *Bar-On EQi Inventory (short) Technical Manuel*. Toronto: MHS.

Bhatia, S. and Ram, A. (2001) Locating the dialogical self in the age of transnational migrations, border crossings and diasporas. *Culture and Psychology*, 7, 297–311.

Bolman, L.G. and Deal, T.E. (2008) *Reframing Organizations: Artistry, Choice, and Leadership*. San Francisco: Jossey-Bass.

Bozionelos, N. and Wang, L. (2006) The relationship of mentoring and network resources with career success in the Chinese organizational environment. *International Journal of Human Resources Management*, 17, 1531–46.

Bresser, F. (2009) *The State of Coaching Across the Globe — the Results of the Global Coaching Survey 2008/2009*. Cologne: Frank Bresser Consulting.

Bruner, D.Y. (2008) Aspiring and practicing leaders addressing issues of diversity and social justice. *Race, Ethnicity and Education*, 11, 483–500.

Clarkson, P. and Nippoda, Y. (1997) The experienced influence or effect of cultural/racism issues on the practice of counselling. *Counselling Psychology Quarterly*, 10(4), 415.

Cornes, A. (2004) *Culture from the Inside Out*. Yarmouth, UK: Intercultural Press.

Cox, E., Bachkirova, T., and Clutterbuck, D. (eds) (2010) *The Complete Handbook of Coaching*. London: Sage.

Earley, P.C. and Ang, S. (2003) *Cultural Intelligence: Individual Interactions Across Cultures*. Stanford: Stanford University Press.

Fail, H., Thompson, J., and Walker, G. (2004) Belonging, identity and third culture kids: Life histories of former international school students. *Journal of Research in International Education*, 3, 319–38.

French, R. (2010) *Cross-Cultural Management in Work Organizations*. London: McGraw-Hill/CIPD.

Gardenswartz, L. and Rowe, A. (2001) Cross-cultural awareness. *HR Magazine*, 46(3), 139–42.

Gilbert, K. (2001) Management change in Central and Eastern Europe. In: S. Cartwright, C. Cooper, and C. Earley (eds) *International Handbook of Organizational Culture and Climate*. London: John Wiley and Sons. pp. 207–28.

Gilbert, K. and Cartwright, S. (2008) Cross-cultural consultancy initiatives to develop Russian managers. *Academy of Management Learning and Education*, 7 (4), 504–18.

Gilbert, K. and Gorlenko, E. (1999) Transplant and process approaches to Western assistance to management development in Russia. *Human Resource Development International*, 2(4), 335–54.

Gilbert, K. and Rosinski., P. (2008) Accessing cultural orientations: The online Cultural Orientations Framework Assessment as a tool for coaching. *Coaching: An International Journal of Theory, Research and Practice*, 1(1), 81–92.

Griffiths, K. and Campbell, M. (2008) Regulating the regulators: Paving the way for international, evidence-based coaching standards. *International Journal of Evidence Based Coaching and Mentoring*, 6(1), 9–31.

Guirdham, M. (1999) *Communicating Across Cultures*. London: Macmillan.

Hall, E.T. (1976) *Beyond Culture*. New York: Anchor Books.

Hampden-Turner, C. and Trompenaars, F. (1997), *Riding the Wave of Culture: Understanding Diversity in Global Business*. New York: McGraw-Hill.

Hampden-Turner, C. and Trompenaars, F. (2000) *Building Cross Cultural Competence. How to Create Wealth from Conflicting Values*. London: John Wiley and Sons.

Hamrick, C. (2008) Focus on cultural elements in coaching: Experiences from China and other countries. In: D. Drake, D. Brennan, and K. Gortz (eds) *The Philosophy and Practice of Coaching*. Chichester: John Wiley and Sons.

Hawkins, P. and Smith N. (2006) *Coaching, Mentoring and Organizational Consultancy: Supervision and Development*. Maidenhead: Open University Press.

Herbolzheimer, A. (2009) *Coaching Expatriates. The Practice and Potential of Expatriate Coaching for European Executives in China*. Kassel: Kassel University Press.

Hermans, H.J.M. (1999) Dialogical thinking and self-innovation. *Culture and Psychology*, 5(1), 57–87.

Hofstede, G. (1980) *Culture's Consequences*. Beverly Hills, Sage.

Hofstede, G. (1997) *Cultures and Organizations: Software of the Mind*. New York, McGraw-Hill.

Hofstede, G. (1999) Software of the mind. *Human Resource Development International*, 4(6), 227–35.

Hofstede, G. (2001) *Culture's Consequences* (2nd edn). London: Sage.

House, R.J., Hanges, P.H., Javidan, M., Dorfman, P.W., and Gupta, V. (2004) *Culture, Leadership and Organizations: The GLOBE Study of 62 Societies*. Thousand Oaks, CA: Sage.

Jandt, F. E. (2010). *An Introduction to Intercultural Communication: Identities in a Global Community* (6th edn). Thousand Oaks, CA: Sage.

Javidan, M., Teagarden, M.B., and Bowen, D.E. (2010a) Making it overseas: Developing the skills you need to succeed as an international leader. *Harvard Business Review*, April, 109–13.

Javidan, M., Hough, L., and Boullough, A. (2010b) *Conceptualizing and Measuring Global Mindset: Development of the Global Mindset Inventory*. Technical Report. Thunderbird Global Mindset Institute, Glendale, Thunderbird School of Global Management.

Jenkins, J. (2006) Coaching meets the cross-cultural challenge. *Leadership in Action*, 26(5), 23–4.

Kilburg, R. R. (2000) *Executive Coaching: Developing Managerial Wisdom in a World of Chaos*. Washington, DC: American Psychological Association.

Kim, E. (2001) *The Yin and Yang of American Culture: A Paradox*. New York: Intercultural Press.

Kluckhohn, F.R. and Strodtbeck, F.L. (1961) *Variations in Value Orientations*. Evanston, IL: Row, Peterson.

Konig, J. (2009) Moving experience: Dialogues between personal cultural positions. *Culture and Psychology*, 15, 97–121.

Laungani, P. (1997) Replacing client-centred counselling with culture-centred counselling. *Counselling Psychology Quarterly*, 10(4), 343–51.

Law, H. (2010) An Asian perspective on leadership coaching – Sun Tzu and the art of war. In: J. Passmore (ed.) *Leadership Coaching; Working with Leaders to Develop Elite Performance*. London: Kogan Page. pp. 93–114.

Law, H. and Yeung, L. (2009) Cross cultural coaching psychology: A fruitful dialogue. *Coaching Psychology International*, 2(1), 17–19.

Law, H., Ireland, S., and Hussain, Z. (2007) *The Psychology of Coaching, Mentoring and Learning*. Chichester: John Wiley and Sons.

Luthans, F., Welsh, D.H.B., and Rosenkrantz, S.A. (1993) What do Russian managers really do? An observational study with comparisons to US managers. *Journal of International Business*, 24(1), 741–61.

McGill, J.O. (2010) *The Impact of Executive Coaching on the Performance Management of InternationalManagers in China*. A thesis submitted in partial fulfillment of the requirements for PhD. Work and organizational studies, University of Sydney, Australia.

Miser, A.L. and Miser, M.F. (2011) Couples coaching for expatriate couples: A sound investment for international businesses. In: M. Moral and G.N. Abbott (eds) *The Routledge Companion to International Business Coaching*. Milton Park: Routledge. pp. 203–18.

Moral, M. and Abbott, G. (eds) (2011) *The Routledge Companion to International Business Coaching*. Milton Park: Routledge.

Morgan, H., Harkins, P., and Goldsmith, M. (eds) (2006) *The Art and Practice of Leadership Coaching*. Hoboken, NJ: John Wiley and Sons.

Nangalia, L. and Nangalia, A. (2010) The coach in Asian society: Impact of social hierarchy on the coaching relationship. *International Journal of Evidence Based Coaching and Mentoring*, 8(1), 51–66.

Niitamo, P. (2011) Intercultural work competence. People with people: Views of corporate social responsibility. *Alto University Publication Series, Crossover*, 1, 39–45.

Okurame, D. (2008) Mentoring in the Nigerian academia: Experiences and challenges. *International Journal of Evidence Based Coaching and Mentoring*, 6(2), 45–56.

Osland, J.S., Bird, A., Delano, J., and Jacob, M. (2000) Beyond sophisticated stereotyping: Cultural sensemaking in context. *Academy of Management Executive*, 14(1), 65–79.

Palmer, T. and Arnold, V. (2009) Coaching in the Middle East. In: J. Passmore (ed.) *Diversity in Coaching: Working with Gender, Culture, Race and Age*. London: Kogan Page. pp. 110–26.

Palmer, S. and Whybrow, A. (2007) *The Handbook of Coaching Psychology*. Hove: Routledge.

Parvis, L. (2003) Diversity and effective leadership in multicultural workplaces. *Journal of Environmental Health*, 65(7), 37–8.

Passmore, J. (ed.) (2006) *Excellence in Coaching: The Industry Guide*. London: Kogan Page.

Passmore, J. (ed.) (2009) *Diversity in Coaching: Working with Gender, Culture, Race and Age*. London: Kogan Page.

Pedersen, P. (1999) *Hidden Messages in Culture-Centered Counseling: A Triad Training Model*. Thousand Oaks, CA: Sage.

Peltier, B. (2010) *The Psychology of Executive Coaching* (2nd edn). New York: Routledge.

Peterson, C. and Seligman, M. (2004) *Character Strengths and Virtues: A Handbook and Classification*. Oxford: Oxford University Press.

Plaister-Ten, J. (2009) Towards greater cultural understanding in coaching. *International Journal of Evidence Based Coaching and Mentoring, Special Issue*, 3: 64–81.

Pollock, D.C. and van Reken, R.E. (2001) *Third Culture Kids: The Experience of Growing Up Among Worlds*. London: Nicholas Brealey.

Roland, A. (2001) Another voice and position: Psychoanalysis across civilizations. *Culture and Psychology*, 7, 311–22.

Rosinski, P. (2003) *Coaching Across Cultures: New Tools for Leveraging National, Corporate and Professional Differences*. London: Nicholas Brealey Publishing.

Rosinski, P. (2010) *Global Coaching: An Integrated Approach for Long-Lasting Results*. London: Nicholas Brealey.

Salomaa, R. (2011) Expatriate management. *Conference Proceedings, European Academy of Management*. Tallinn, June 1–4 2011.

Sampson, D.L. and Smith, H.P. (1957) A scale to measure world-minded attitudes. *The Journal of Social Psychology*, 45, 99–106.

Schein, E. (1969) The mechanisms of change. In: W.G. Bennis, K.D. Benne, and R. Chin (eds). *The Planning of Change*. New York: Holt, Rinehart and Winston. pp. 98–108.

Schein, E. (1988) *Process Consultation: Its Role in Organization Development* (2nd edn). Reading: Addison-Wesley Publishing Company, Inc.

Schwartz, S.H. (1994) Beyond Individualism/Collectivism – New Dimensions of Values. In: U. Kim, H.C. Triandis, C. Kagitçiabasi, S.C. Choi, and G. Yoon (eds) *Individualism and Collectivism: Theory Application and Methods*. Newbury Park: Sage.

Sood, Y. (2009) Coaching in India. In: J. Passmore (ed.) *Diversity in Coaching*. London: Kogan Page.

St Claire-Ostwald, B. (2007) Carrying cultural baggage: The contribution of socio-cultural anthropology to cross-cultural coaching. *International Journal of Evidence Based Coaching and Mentoring*, 5(2), 45–52.

Stober, D.R. and Grant, A.M. (eds) (2006) *Evidence Based Coaching Handbook: Putting Best Practices to Work for Your Clients*. Hoboken, NJ: John Wiley and Sons.

Stout Rostron, S. (2009) *Business Coaching International: Transforming Individuals and Organizations*. London: Karnac.

Tadmor, C.T. and Tetlock, P.E. (2006) Bi-culturalism: A model of the effects of second culture on acculturation and integrative complexity. *Journal of Cross Cultural Psychology*, 37(2), 173–9.

Tanaka, T. (2009) Coaching in Japan. In: J. Passmore (ed.), *Diversity in Coaching*. London: Kogan Page.

Thomas, D.C. (2010) Cultural intelligence and all that jazz: A cognitive revolution in international management research? In: T. Devinney, T. Pederson and L. Tihanyi (eds). *The Past, Present and Future of International Business and Management*. Bradford: Emerald Group Publishing. 169–87.

Trompenaars, F. and Hampden-Turner, C. (1998) *Riding the Waves of Culture: Understanding Cultural Diversity in Global Business*. New York: McGraw Hill.

Ward, C., Bochner, S. and Furnham, A. (2001) *The Psychology of Culture Shock*. Hove: Routledge.

Whitmore, J. (1992) *Coaching for Performance*. London: Nicholas Breadley.

Whitmore, J. (2002) *Coaching for Performance: GROWING People Performance and Purpose*. London: Nicholas Brealey.

Wilber, K. (2000) *Integral Psychology: Consciousness, Spirit, Psychology, Therapy*. Boston: Shambhala.

# 26

# Virtual Coaching and Mentoring

## Niloofar Ghods and Camala Boyce

## Introduction

Virtual work, working with those not co-located in the same space and/or, working with technology to engage in communication (e.g., telephone, email, text), has become nearly ubiquitous. The individual who doesn't engage in some form of virtual work or virtual work relationship might be the rare exception. Our personal lives, too, reflect a more virtual nature with connections other than face-to-face via electronic-mediated means such as video conferencing/calling (e.g., Skype or WebEx), social network sites (e.g., Facebook), and broadcast or personal communications (via Twitter and cell/mobile phone). Perhaps, then, it should not be too surprising to see the growing popularity of virtual coaching. Popular press and anecdotal evidence view these modalities as a practical, creative, and cost-effective alternative to face-to-face development for coaching (Goldsmith and Lyons, 2006; Hagevik, 1998; Hakim, 2000; Hudson, 1999; Kilburg, 2000), as it reduces travel and time expenses, and increases productivity and knowledge (Hakim, 2000; Rossett and Marino, 2005). However, aside from anecdotal praise and a few recent publications that examine virtual coaching more in-depth (Boyce and Clutterbuck, 2011; Clutterbuck and Hussain, 2010), only a limited number of studies have researched virtual coaching (Berry, 2005; Bowles and Picano, 2006; Charbonneau, 2002; Ghods, 2009; Wang, 2000; Wilson et al., 2006a; Young and Dixon, 1996). The intent of this chapter is to review the literature of virtual coaching, as well as disciplines involved in virtual work relationships, specifically virtual or e-mentoring, as well as tele-work, virtual counseling, and relevant technology-assisted communications research. Across these bodies of literature, themes will be identified relevant to virtual coaching, while critiquing the literature and identifying areas for future research within the virtual development arena.

*The Wiley Blackwell Handbook of the Psychology of Coaching and Mentoring*, First Edition.
Edited by Jonathan Passmore, David B. Peterson, and Teresa Freire.
© 2013 John Wiley & Sons, Ltd. Published 2016 by John Wiley & Sons, Ltd.

# The Prevalence of Virtual Coaching

Coaching is considered one of the fastest growing professions over the past decade and is predicted to continue developing significantly in the near future (Driscoll and Cooper, 2005). Although coaching in-person has been the primary method of delivering coaching, virtual coaching is prevalently used. According to the 2011 Sherpa Executive Coaching survey, 39 percent of nearly 700 participants, which included coaches, human resources, and training professionals, indicated using the telephone or webcam in coaching. Adding to this, Berry (2005) found that 100 percent of the 102 coaches in her study reported some use of the telephone in communicating with clients and 25 percent reported rarely or never meeting in-person with the clients. Similarly, Frazee (2008) found 26 percent of her sample of 191 coaches engaged clients primarily or exclusively at a distance, with little or no face-to-face interaction. In terms of geography, both studies' participants that conducted virtual coaching were heavily United States based (78 percent from the continental United States), posing an opportunity for researchers to scientifically compare the prevalence of virtual coaching across the globe.

# Empirical Review of Virtual Helping Relationships

This section reviews several bodies of literature related to virtual coaching, such as virtual therapy, virtual counseling, and telepsychiatry. In terms of therapeutic modalities offered via technology assisted means, Mallen *et al.* (2005a) have conducted one of the most comprehensive reviews. The authors review outcome studies, relevant process, and intervening variables to effective outcomes and the telephone, specifically, as a medium for delivering services. Overall, the outcome studies revealed online counseling as beneficial for clients. In reviewing the studies on computer-mediated therapy, the authors speculate as to whether some participants may not have received services otherwise, as face-to-face means may be challenging due to physical limitations, geographic distance or the aspect of perceived hidden identity when dealing in a virtual environment. In addition to the Mallen *et al.* (2005b) comprehensive review, several books have been published on the topic of online counseling (Kraus *et al.*, 2004; Maheu *et al.*, 2005). The book by Maheu discussed the many advantages of "psychotechnologies". In comparing studies of psychotechnologies and face-to-face therapies, they concluded that clients felt comparably satisfied with the process and their treatment gains.

One of the most robust studies in the virtual counseling literature is by Day and Schneider (2002). Day and Schenider examined how media may potentially influence coach-client interaction. In this experimental design, clients experienced short-term therapy in either face-to-face, audio, or video therapy modalities. The tapes of these sessions were reviewed by a group of trained raters that evaluated the sessions on the strength of the relationship, that is, the working alliance, as well as extent the client improved, that is, problem resolution. No significant differences were observed in terms of outcomes across the modalities. One of the most salient findings was that clients in the technology-facilitated conditions participated more than those in the face-to-face condition; this included aspects such as client initiative, trust, spontaneity, and disinhibition. The authors suggested the clients may have taken more responsibility and tried harder to communicate when they perceived a barrier between them and the therapist. Other potential explanations included more ease due to a feeling of greater anonymity via the technology, thereby creating more disinhibition. Overall, these findings seem to suggest that the media, itself, may be interdependent with the actors.

Meta-analytic and literature reviews of the telepsychiatry profession from 1965 to 2007 agreed that telepsychiatry was feasible, increased access to care, enabled specialty consultation, allowed reliable evaluations, yielded positive outcomes, reported few negative aspects of communication and was generally satisfactory to both patients and doctors (Hilty *et al.*, 2004; Monnier *et al.*, 2003). In addition, when researchers compared telepsychiatry to in-person services, no significant differences in attendance, clinical status, and improvement were found (McLaren *et al.*, 2002; Rohland *et al.*, 2000). These research findings clearly demonstrated that tele-psychiatric services could become additional options for patients and practitioners. Moreover, these findings gave credence to the coaching profession's move to offer virtual coaching to a wider range of clients.

Another avenue of virtual relationship research is occurring via immersive technologies, whereby a virtual human representing the self (referred to as an avatar) interacts with other virtual humans in simulated activity and real-time conversation via voice-over-Internet. These virtual environments have been utilized for therapeutic applications such as post-traumatic stress disorder treatment via virtual reality immersive or exposure therapy (Difede *et al.*, 2006; Rizzo *et al.*, 2007). Within the context of virtual coaching, the Center for Creative Leadership, a global coaching organization based in the United States, is currently conducting research within a virtual reality application, Second Life. The intention of this in-progress study is to compare coaching outcomes across face-to-face versus a virtual environment (Torres *et al.*, 2009).

## Introduction to E-mentoring Literature

Another arena of virtual helping relationship is e-mentoring. Ensher and Murphy (2007) offer a definition of e-mentoring, compiling across other definitions (Bierema and Merriam, 2002; Ensher *et al.*, 2003; Hamilton and Scandura, 2003; Headlam-Wells, 2004), "as a mutually beneficial relationship between a mentor and a protégé which provides new learning as well as career and emotional support, primarily through email and other electronic means (e.g., instant message, chat rooms, social networking spaces, etc.)" (p. 300). This section provides a summary of prior e-mentoring literature reviews, as well as a critical review of qualitative and quantitative empirical e-mentoring studies.

E-mentoring programs are abundant as evidenced by a number of prior reviews (Bierema and Merriman, 2002; Ensher *et al.*, 2003; Hamilton and Scandura, 2002; Single and Single, 2005). Clutterbuck and Hussain (2010) devote much of their book to virtual mentoring, discussing implementation, technology and special populations, among other topics. Single and Single (2005) conduct a review of the literature, detailing the history of e-mentoring and one of the first large-scale e-mentoring projects. The authors point out that e-mentoring is particularly suited for addressing social inequities by affording mentoring to those who may not otherwise receive it due to costs, geography, or physical limitations. This review also highlights two primary advantages of e-mentoring, perhaps unique from face-to-face mentoring, as impartiality due to the distance, as well as facilitating inter-organizational connections. Ensher *et al.* (2003) review the e-mentoring literature and provide a listing of several large e-mentoring projects with the corresponding websites. From the literature reviewed, the authors propose new directions for future research. Bierema and Merriman (2002) review the literature and classify e-mentoring projects by the populations served, including K-12 programs, teachers, university-sponsored, corporate-sponsored, women and girls, as well as disadvantaged and special populations. They highlight advantages of e-mentoring to include the egalitarian nature due to its ability to cross hierarchies, as well as the boundary-less exchange via reduction of geographical constraints.

Several reviews have been conducted to explore specific populations and applications (Bierema and Hill, 2005; Columbaro, 2007; Cravens, 2003; Gentry *et al.*, 2008; Perren, 2003; Smith and Israel, 2010). In one of the most scientifically rigorous reviews, Gentry *et al.* (2008) conduct a comprehensive examination of empirical studies pertaining to in-service teachers. The authors identify 14 studies meeting the review's criteria and critique each study on design, technologies employed, variables studied, as well as other factors. In another systematic review, Perren (2003) examines literature within the e-mentoring arena as applied to the population of entrepreneurs examining effectiveness outcomes, as well as findings suggesting best practices. Cravens (2003) presents a review of all known online virtual mentoring projects via the Virtual Volunteers project whereby the programs, practices, and effectiveness are reviewed, as well as providing an appendix of all known online mentoring projects and the corresponding website addresses. Columbaro (2007) reviews studies examining e-mentoring for online doctoral students. Bierema and Hill (2005) review the literature exploring studies from the perspective of benefits and challenges within the context and application by human resources development professionals. Smith and Israel (2010) review research studies relevant to e-mentoring for beginning special education teachers.

## Review of e-mentoring research

The body of literature on e-mentoring is much more extensive than virtual coaching, especially with respect to qualitative studies and it was necessary to define parameters for this review. This e-mentoring review was restricted to include published empirical research where the primary purpose was studying some aspect of an e-mentoring relationship. Studies were excluded where the mentoring relationship was a paid professional allocated a set number of hours of support to the mentee (e.g., Thompson *et al.*, 2010), where the sole or primary goal was to report on a mentoring network or community (Thoresen, 1997) and where the primary goal was distance learning. For example, Angulo and Alegre De La Rosa's (2006) report on a six-week online distance learning course that also included an e-mentoring component for mentees located in the Canary Islands was excluded for this reason.

The e-mentoring research studies meeting the criteria for inclusion in this review varied in terms of the qualitative and quantitative methods. A number of studies used a more robust design of either a quasi-experimental, experimental, and/or a pre-post measurement (Cascio and Gasker, 2001; Hixenbaugh *et al.*, 2008; Kasprisin *et al.*, 2003; Miller *et al.*, 2008; Penny and Bolton, 2010). However, the bulk of studies were primarily qualitative although they may have presented some quantitative results consisting primarily of frequencies and means (Brown and Kysilka, 2005; Buche, 2008; Davies, 2005; Headlam-Wells, 2004; Headlam-Wells *et al.*, 2006; de Janasz *et al.*, 2008; Paul, 2006; Plummer and Omwenga Nyang'au, 2009; Rickard and Rickard, 2009; Shrestha *et al.*, 2009; Shpigelman *et al.*, 2008; Stewart, 2008; Wadia-Fascetti and Leventman, 2000).

The studies can also be examined by the targeted population of mentees. Categories identified include health professionals (Miller *et al.*, 2008; Paul, 2006; Stewart,

2008; Stewart and Carpenter, 2008), women (Buche, 2008; Headlam-Wells, 2004; Wadia-Fascetti and Leventman, 2000), academicians and/or pre-service teachers (Brown and Kysikla, 2005; Penny and Bolton, 2010; Plummer and Omwenga Nyang'au, 2009; Shrestha *et al.*, 2009), disadvantaged individuals (Davies, 2005; Shpigelman *et al.*, 2008), students (Cascio and Gasker, 2001; Hixenbaugh *et al.*, 2006; De Janasz *et al.*, 2008; Kasprisin *et al.*, 2003), and small business leaders (Rickard and Rickard, 2009).

Among the studies with quantitative results, there have been a number of positive outcomes from e-mentoring programs for both mentors and mentees. Results have been demonstrated for increased professional identity compared to a control group, as well as pre-post comparisons (Cascio and Gasker, 2001), improved social integration and satisfaction with the organization compared to a control group (Hixenbaugh *et al.*, 2006) and improved professional confidence by the mentors (Miller *et al.*, 2008), and further improved attitudes on the part of mentors toward working in an inner city school compared to a control group (Penny and Bolton, 2010).

Cascio and Gasker (2001) examined the impact of e-mentoring on professional identity development for undergraduate social work mentees paired with graduate students in social work as mentors. The design consisted of pre- and post-measurement of professional identity for the mentors, mentees, and comparison control groups consisting of non-mentors and non-mentees. Findings revealed only the mentored students showed significant increases in professional identity development as measured by the self-report survey at post-measurement. Qualitative analyses were also conducted identifying themes of mentor-mentee dialogue. This study is significant in that it included a pre-post comparison control design for both mentors and mentees; however, the sample size was limited (N = 12 for mentees).

Hixenbaugh *et al.* (2006) studied the self-reported outcomes of seven variables: self-esteem, self-efficacy, academic ambition, confidence/anxiety, financial concerns, social integration, and satisfaction of mentored students, comparing the results to a control group of non-mentored students. Measurements in this quasi-experimental design were made at three points across the year for both mentored and non-mentored students. The first-year students were mentored by more senior undergraduates over the course of the school year, primarily via email, with some face-to-face meetings and telephone contact. The results showed two variables, social integration and satisfaction with the university, were significantly different in the comparison of groups as well as across time. The mentored students reported greater social integration and satisfaction at time 3 compared to time 1, as well as compared to the non-mentored control group. While the other five variables did not reveal significant differences, some of the variables are less malleable to the influence of a mentor (e.g., financial concerns, general self-esteem). This study is important in that it used a strong design of a comparison control group as well as repeated measures. However, the measurement did not include triangulation; all measures were sole-source, self-report measures.

While continuing to examine mentoring outcomes, some studies have explored the impact of e-mentoring on the mentor (Miller *et al.*, 2008; Penny and Bolton, 2010). Miller *et al.* (2008) found e-mentoring improved mentors' confidence in the nursing practice and profession, perceived ability to mentor and other mentoring-related skills as determined by a self-rated survey delivered prior to and following the mentoring program. This study illustrates that the mentee may not be the only beneficiary of the mentoring relationship; mentors, and their associated organizations, may also receive benefits. A challenge of this study was that the pre- and post-measure assessment of the skills was retrospectively completed and solely self-reported, resulting in response bias.

In another study examining mentor outcomes, Penny and Bolton (2010) conducted a quasi-experimental design to explore the impact of e-mentoring on mentors' attitudes towards working in an urban district school. The student-teachers were assigned to: a control condition of no mentoring, e-mentoring without a visit to an urban district school, or e-mentoring with a visit to a school in the urban district. The authors found a significant effect such that those mentors that also visited the urban school reported more favorable attitudes toward working in an urban school than either the control or e-mentoring alone conditions. The authors' controlled for pre-experimental attitudes, as well as other factors. This study, like Miller *et al.* (2008) illustrates the reciprocal nature of e-mentoring. Further, this study's findings suggest the importance of a blended approach, that is, mentoring was more effective when it involved more than one modality (e.g., face-to-face visit as well as computer mediated) in creating positive outcomes. This study's findings are limited by the quasi-experimental design.

While outcome studies are important in illustrating that mentoring is effective in a virtual environment, it is also important to explore intervening variables, such as process and relationship variables that result in the positive benefits of e-mentoring. One such study exploring mentor-mentee match, was conducted by de Janasz *et al.* (2008). In this study consisting of 183 business students mentored by business managers, it was found that perceived similarity (e.g., values and attitudes), but not demographic similarity, predicted e-mentoring effectiveness (as rated by the mentees). The authors suggest the findings are the result of reduced emphasis on observable differences due to the lack of face-to-face interaction. The authors speculate that focusing on value similarity benefits those groups (e.g., minorities, women) that may be normally disadvantaged by such observable differences. This study illustrates there may be unique advantages for mentoring in a virtual compared to a face-to-face environment, although there was no control group of face-to-face participants. Additionally, a confounding factor was that not all interactions were virtual and, the mentees selected their own mentors, rather than via assignment. Further, it is not possible to make causal linkages in this correlation-based design.

De Jansz *et al.* (2008) found a positive relationship between the amount of time spent connecting with the e-mentor and the perceived support, as well as overall satisfaction with the relationship. The authors report the average amount of time spent interacting by the mentees was 5.5 hours per month. This is in contrast to a study in the virtual coaching literature (e.g., Bowles and Picano, 2006) where time in the relationship had no impact on outcomes.

In addition to the findings by de Jansz *et al.* (2008) regarding how to increase the impact of e-mentoring, Kasprisin, *et al.* (2003) conducted a study to explore how e-training may positively impact e-mentoring outcomes such as satisfaction, involvement, and value. In this study, the authors employed an experimental control group comparison design. Undergraduate science majors were randomly assigned to either a control (no e-training) or experimental (e-training) condition with both groups receiving e-mentoring. The data collected were as part of a larger project, MentorNet where technical and science students were paired with professionals working in technical fields. The mentee-reported outcomes consisted of involvement, satisfaction, and value. Analyses of the control group participants ($N = 60$) compared to the experimental group mentees ($N = 50$) showed involvement was significantly greater for the e-training mentees compared to those mentees that did not receive e-training. There were no significant differences in perceived value or satisfaction for either group. This study is important as it helps to clarify the factors that may assist in increased positive outcomes from an e-mentoring program.

The next section reviews studies that were primarily qualitative in design or consisted of minimal quantitative analyses, such as frequencies and means. Paul (2006) provides a case study of 10 e-mentoring projects in which 74 semi-structured interviews of key informants (e.g., IT personnel, clinicians, program administrators) were conducted in this telemedicine study. Projects were selected through meeting a specified set of criteria and selected across three health networks contracted to provide health knowledge to remote clinical sites (e.g., teleradiology, teleconsultation, and distance learning for the remote healthcare facility). Informants provided estimations of effectiveness across three indicators, cost, quality, and access to healthcare, resulting in an overall effectiveness score. The studies had a range of effectiveness scores and the author examined the type of knowledge exchange as a possible related factor. The studies were categorized as predominantly: knowledge transfer, knowledge creation, and knowledge discovery. In the first, knowledge transfer, the communication tends toward didactic; knowledge creation and discovery are more collaborative in nature. Although no inferential statistics were calculated, a cross-tabulation revealed a relationship between effectiveness and the type of e-mentoring knowledge. More specifically, there was greater effectiveness for the knowledge discovery and creation projects than the knowledge transfer. This study also explored communication modalities of still media (e.g., radiologists' X-rays), video-conferencing, and mixed media interactions (e.g., multiple modes of communication). Similar to the previous finding, effectiveness scores were greater for video-conferencing and the mixed media projects. This study is significant in its exploration of the impact of media type on outcomes. Further, this study points to a possible criteria for selection of media; that is, the nature of the task as per the type of knowledge sharing. Although this study brings new awareness, it was challenged in its methodology. As is inherent in case study reviews, the variables were confounded such that knowledge type (e.g., transfer) was confounded with the media type (e.g., X-ray review). Additionally, the outcome measures were ratings completed by those heavily involved in the implementation and administration of the e-mentoring, thereby limiting objectivity.

While Paul's (2006) research was a multiple case study design and was limited in sample size, it was useful in adding to the limited body of literature including some quantitative analysis (e.g., cross tabulations). Similarly, Headlam-Wells *et al.* (2006) adds to this literature by detailed inclusion of frequency data of 122 female participants formed into mentor-mentee pairs between professional women and disadvantaged women seeking employment. The purpose of the case study was to explore the implementation of an e-mentoring web-based system from social (e.g., mentor-mentee matching) as well technological (e.g., usage of web-based features) aspects. The matching process was based on mentee self-rated needs across 11 factors deemed important by prior mentoring research. Outcomes were measured by mentees' self-rated pre- and post-assessments of employability skills such as networking, self awareness, and self-promotion. Results demonstrated that the skill areas varied widely in terms of self-rated improvements with several showing dramatic increases. Quantitative data was collected on a number of factors, by both mentors and mentees, including mentor match, satisfaction with the mentoring, and e-mentoring as a medium for mentoring. Results indicated approximately half felt they had a good match. In terms of satisfaction, more than half of mentors and almost two-thirds of mentees reported that the mentoring experience had greatly met their expectations. However, 42 percent of mentors and 34 percent of mentees felt their expectations had not been fully met. While the vast majority of mentors and mentees rated mentoring via e-mentoring as effective, 15 percent of mentors and 25 percent of mentees felt it was not very effective. The majority reported a blended approach, with approximately 20 percent having at least one face-to-face meeting. Additionally, comments revealed the initial face-to-face meeting was highly beneficial for beginning the mostly online relationship. This study is important for several reasons, primarily, in that it reports quantitative results of satisfaction and outcome data. While there are many e-mentoring projects, few of these studies are published, making access difficult and, fewer still, actually report quantitative results. From this study, it can be observed that mentee-mentor matching can be a challenging aspect, even with the assistance of an objective formula as used in this study. Also, while receiving very positive praise by the majority, some mentees and fewer mentors prefer an alternate medium. This study is limited by the self-reported nature of outcomes by mentees, yet, overall results suggested general improvement as a result of e-mentoring.

Continuing with the focus on women mentees, there have been a number of e-mentoring studies (Boule, 2008; Headlam-Wells, 2004; Wadia-Fasctti and Leventman, 2000). In another study by Headlam-Wells (2004), qualitative analyses were conducted by studying 24 mentor-mentee pairs of women as part of a management development program for women. The mentees were categorized as either (1) aspiring to management or (2) returning from career breaks, and each was paired with a professional woman manager. The study included a mix of media for communication including email, telephone, face-to-face meetings, and a chat room on the website supporting the system. Email was the most frequently reported media, while face-to-face meetings were lengthier than other modes of communication. Self-reported outcomes included positive changes in career aspirations for a third of the women, and, two of the five mentees in group, returning from a career break, gained new employment. This study was limited due to the small sample size and lack of triangulation of data.

In another qualitative study focused on females, Wadia-Fasctti and Leventman (2000) explored mentor clubs of 3–6 females consisting of professional working engineers, female college students in engineering, and pre-teen girls. The purpose was to promote females in technical careers. There were several identified themes to the mentor conversations, including informal and social communication as well as career advice. The study identified participation and commitment to the program as challenges as well as a desire for more face-to-face meetings.

Additionally, Boule (2008) conducted a qualitative study of a focus group of five female mentors and in-depth interviews with another five women involved in mentoring. From this, Boule identified the themes of e-mentoring, including miscommunication, convenience, maintenance of the relationship, imposed media choice, and impact on trust. From there, the author develops a model whereby trust is depicted as the mediator between communication modalities and satisfaction with the mentorship.

In addition to studies on women, other authors have focused on teachers and students (Brown and Kysilka, 2005; Shrestha *et al.*, 2009). Brown and Kysilka (2005) conducted a qualitative study of ten undergraduate pre-service teachers each paired with two teacher mentors enrolled in a doctorate level class. One stated purpose was to expand the mentees' thinking of curriculum development. Qualitative analyses revealed several themes regarding relationship development. One challenge was with respect to the pre-established agenda. The mentees were perceived as eager to get to personalized, individualized concerns rather than the curriculum development requirements. Another stated challenge was the lack of any face-to-face meetings.

Shrestha *et al.* (2009) conducted a qualitative study consisting of interviews of 21 university student mentors paired with first year student mentees. The program was a blend of communication modalities, including face-to-face and email as well as an online forum. The mentors reported the email allowed for convenience and reduction of status differences, as well as allowing the mentors to reach out without stigmatizing mentees.

In addition to students, disadvantaged populations have been studied for e-mentoring application (Davies, 2005; Shpigelman *et al.*, 2008). In one email-based mentoring study, Shpigelman *et al.* (2008) paired five special needs students with undergraduate mentors, also with a disability. The qualitative data reports positive results by mentors and mentees as well as identified themes of the communications such as development of the relationship, and roles of the mentoring. During the phase of e-mentoring, coined "deepening" by the researchers, both mentors and mentees complained of not having vocal or visual feedback. This study is unusual in that it appears mentoring occurred solely through electronic means (e.g., email), whereas most other studies use a blended approach (e.g., some face-to-face or telephone meetings).

The Brightside Trust is a program to help disadvantaged populations make informed choices about education and employment (Davies, 2005). Davies (2005) provides a brief evaluation of the e-mentoring component of this program. Reported results showed that more than two-thirds of mentees indicated e-mentoring as an excellent way to get to know the mentoring partner and more than half indicating that e-mentoring reinforced the desire for further schooling. This brief summary report does not provide a complete description of the methods or instrumentation.

Focusing on small business leaders as mentees, Rickard and Rickard (2009) reported on the qualitative analysis derived from in-depth interviews and a post-program survey from 20 mentees and 5 mentors. The experiences of participants were classified as effective or ineffective based on a post-program questionnaire overall effectiveness score. From this dichotomization, comments were analyzed by themes such as quality of the program, quality of the relationship, and overall impact. The authors note the overwhelming majority were categorized as effective and thus the bulk of the comments fall into that category. Unfortunately, the authors do not provide adequate description of the sample and the overall research design. They do, however, reference an unpublished doctoral dissertation (Rickard, 2007) where more complete data may be found.

Two case studies reviewed included the authors as participant observers (Plummer and Omwenga Nyang'au, 2009; Stewart, 2008). Focusing on health professionals, Stewart (2008) and (also featured in Stewart and Carpenter, 2008) described a case study of a mentor (the author) with two mentees, new to the profession of being a midwife. This New Zealand-based study analyzed the frequency of the emails and themes from mentor and mentee perspectives. The themes of the email communications centered on de-briefing and reflection, clinical inquiries, and provision of information. The mentor reported being challenged in asking critical thinking questions while maintaining a supportive tone. The two mentees both reported the format suited their communicative styles allowing for reflection via writing.

Plummer and Omwenga Nyang'au (2009) described a case study of a reciprocal mentoring relationship where one half of the partnership consisted of a US university professor and the other half consisted of a director of a non-governmental organization (NGO) in Kenya. The two authors (also the two participants in the case study) analyzed their email communications over the course of two years for themes which included: mutual support, funding, academic research projects, relationship building, and knowledge exchange. While this case study adds to the findings of mutual benefit by both mentor/mentee, it is limited by inherent challenges of a case study design with participant-observers.

In this section, e-mentoring has been reviewed for exploration of findings that may be relevant to virtual relationship development. Commonalities revealed the paucity of outcome studies in this arena, yet, overall, demonstrate generally positive results (de Janasz *et al.*, 2008; Paul, 2006). Further, these studies suggest the quality of the relationship, the relationship strength, may be more salient in a virtual context as measured by perceived similarity and match (de Janasz *et al.*, 2008; Headlam-Wells *et al.*, 2006). These studies also suggest the nature of the work may impact the over-all effectiveness in a given modality (de Janasz *et al.*, 2008; Paul, 2006). Finally, while reporting mostly positive results from e-mentoring, several of the studies indicated more face-to-face communication was desired (Brown and Kysilka, 2005; Shpigelman *et al.*, 2008; Wadia-Fascetti and Leventman, 2000).

## Virtual Coaching Empirical Literature

The arenas of e-mentoring and virtual therapy provide some guidance that may be relevant to virtual coaching. This is important because, although traditional coaching is continuing to build its research base, researchers have only begun to examine virtual coaching. The literature of virtual coaching consists of many articles devoted to theory, concepts, and anecdotal reviews and only recently more comprehensive works have been published that help evolve thinking around virtual coaching. Clutterbuck and Hussain (2010), for example, provide an overview of current knowledge and theory of good virtual coaching and mentoring practices that include case studies of individuals and programs. Boyce and Hernez-Broom (2010) provide a framework for leadership coaching in virtual environments that highlight critical issues and alternative considerations for virtual coaching. Finally, Boyce and Clutterbuck (2011) provide a foundation for thinking about virtual coaching, review practical considerations, and provide guidance on incorporating virtual coaching practices. These new publications provide great insights that help understand the benefits, challenges, and implications of virtual coaching. However, more extensive research is required to support the practice of these recommendations.

The research-based virtual coaching literature, however, only includes eight studies: one peer-reviewed study (Bowles and Picano, 2006), two industry publications (Wilson *et al.*, 2006a; Young and Dixon, 1996), and five unpublished dissertations (Berry, 2005; Charbonneau, 2002; Frazee, 2008; Ghods, 2009; Wang, 2000). The studies are vastly varied, yet, some broad categories can be created in examining this limited body of research. While none of these studies fits entirely into any one categorization, several of these studies focused on the change in outcomes as a result of coaching (e.g., Wilson *et al.*, 2006b; Young and Dixon, 1996), while others focused on the process, that is, what happens between the coach and client that results in positive outcomes (e.g., Berry, 2005; Bowles and Picano, 2006; Ghods, 2009; Wang, 2000) and a third group focused on the media (e.g., virtual and face-to-face) and its differential impacts on the relationship and outcomes (e.g., Charbonneau, 2002; Frazee, 2008).

The first peer-reviewed study on virtual coaching was by Bowles and Picano (2006). They examined the impact of coaching on 19 US Army recruiter-managers over six months on both quality and quantity objectively measured indicators (e.g., number or recruits and quality of recruits as measured by a standardized military test). Unfortunately, the study results do not report results on pre- and post-differences on these objective outcomes measures. Instead, the study explores the impact of self-reported goal type (quality and quantity) on the objective outcomes, as well as coaching intensity and client commitment on the goals and outcome measures. The study found an inverse relationship between quantity and quality self-reported goal attainment such that progress toward quantity goals decreased attainment of quality goals. As for coaching intensity, defined as the number of interactions/sessions by the length of the interactions, no significant relationships were found either with self-reported goals or objective outcomes. Clients' perceived commitment as measured by the coaches also did not demonstrate significant relationships with goals and outcomes. However, the study found that one aspect of client involvement, the extent to which the coach perceived the client applied his/her advice, was positively related to work and life satisfaction. The researchers speculate the impact of the coaches' background may provide a partial explanation for the outcomes; coaches in this study were subject matter experts (SMEs) and not trained psychologists. The study reports an average of 15 sessions across the six months and the total length of session averaged to 30 minutes. The length of the sessions, on the whole, may have not have reached a threshold to delve into deeper process and interpersonal growth issues. Additionally, the nature of the job, recruiting, may have a longer life cycle than the time allotted for the study (e.g., six months). Further, while this study provides a contribution to the literature of virtual coaching, no comparisons are possible either between pre- and post-outcomes (due to the nature of the reported data), as well as coaching modalities (all coaching was conducted via telephone).

The next five studies were unpublished dissertations retrieved from *Dissertation Abstracts International* (Berry, 2005; Charbonneau, 2002; Frazee, 2008; Ghods, 2009, Wang, 2000). Berry's (2005) unpublished dissertation consisted of comparisons of face-to-face and virtual coaching as perceived by the coach. Fifty-one coaches that had a recent client in both a face-to-face condition, as well as a virtual condition were involved in the primary part of this study. The coaches were asked to recall a recent client where services were provided in one of the two modalities (e.g., coaching in primarily virtual and primarily face-to-face settings) and to rate the client's perceived outcome via a problem resolution survey, as well as the perceived strength of the coach-client relationship, called the working alliance. Analyses revealed no significant differences in outcomes or the working alliance across the modes of delivery. However, a significant relationship was found between the working alliance and the level of client change in the virtual modality, but not in the face-to-face coaching. When evaluating the differences between face-to-face and virtual contexts, neither the number of meetings nor the coach's experience appeared to affect the working alliance or client change. In interpreting these findings, Berry speculated that it was critical to develop a stronger working relationship in virtual scenario due to the absence of visual cues. This idea supports the common belief held by coaching experts that a strong, trusting coach-client relationship leads to more successful coaching engagements despite the physical distance they maintain (Blattner, 2005; Brotman *et al.*, 1998; Bush, 2004; Diedrich, 1996; Kilburg, 1996, 2001; Lowman, 2005; Luebbe, 2005; Peterson, 1996; Wasylyshyn, 2003).

Although Berry's (2005) study contributed significantly to the coaching literature, several critical limitations weakened it. First, the coaches' perspectives were retroactive; therefore, potential error in their memory recall might have seriously compromised the accuracy of their observations. Using coaches as the sole assessors of coaching outcomes was also problematic because they did not hold an objective position in the coach-client relationship. Additionally, coaches only had limited interactions with clients, so they could not observe them in non-coaching contexts. Their perspective was constrained by what clients reported about their performance. Even if coaches were to observe change firsthand, these changes might only be temporary and unsustainable once coaching reached completion. Because coaches are invested in the relationship, they may subconsciously want to see changes, which may not necessarily or directly be attributable to the coaching engagement. In contrast, coaches may not report real change because they may be too close to the situation to notice it. Finally, a possible confound may be coaches' vested interest in reporting changes for reasons of self-interest (e.g., promoting their coaching business). Therefore, it is imperative to accompany a coach's report with the reports of other, more objective observers.

Charbonneau's (2002) qualitative dissertation investigated the differential experiences and meanings of media selection for executive coaches and their clients using different coaching modalities: face-to-face, telephone, email, and video conferencing. Unlike Berry (2005), after conducting 20 semi-structured interviews with ten executive coaches and ten clients, Charbonneau found that coaches and clients generally perceived face-to-face coaching to be more effective than telephone coaching. Charbonneau found that telephone coaching was especially ineffective in the first session, when it is necessary to establish trust, and in feedback sessions, when critical and sensitive information is shared with the client.

Despite the limitations of telephone coaching, Charbonneau (2002) described several positive aspects of this modality. Coaches can use it to conveniently access clients, provide accountability, focus clients, and promote follow-through. It is also a cost- and time-effective alternative to meeting face-to-face. Moreover, Charbonneau proposed that good telephone coaches compensate for a lack of visual cues, ask powerful questions, and verbalize the process to the client. Finally, Charbonneau highlighted the importance of coach-client-media fit, as it alone can be critical to the success of coaching. Three necessary fits were suggested: "The fit between the coach and his/her preferred coaching medium ... the fit between the client and that medium ... and the fit between the coach and the client as people" (p. 122). According to Charbonneau, each component is essential to effective coaching.

Charbonneau's (2002) study provided rich information about several elements of virtual coaching from the perspectives of coaches and their clients. One, being the importance of having comfort with and knowledge about the technology used for coaching that in itself can dictate the success of a virtual coaching process. Therefore, Charbonneau's study is pioneering in uncovering several components of virtual coaching that to this date were assumed versus formally researched. Nevertheless, the study was limited by its small sample size that restricted the study's generalizability and its qualitative nature which lacks empirical support.

Frazee's (2008) exploratory study examined how virtual coaching is being used in organizations now, its projection for the future, technologies and practices involved in virtual coaching, factors that influenced their use, and the conditions that are most favorable for successful implementation of virtual coaching in organizations. Frazee surveyed 191 organizational professionals from professional organizations and communities of practice for workplace learning and performance professionals and coaches. Frazee also conducted 20 semi-structured interviews with coaches that used virtual coaching in their practice.

Frazee found most coaching was conducted face-to-face and that virtual coaching was more used as an alternative to coaching face-to-face. Consistent with opinions of experts in the field, the primary reasons for virtual coaching included cost, scheduling issues, geographic distance, need for real-time support, and access to expertise and perspectives (Goldsmith and Lyons, 2006; Hagevik, 1998; Hakim, 2000; Hudson, 1999; Kilburg, 2000; Rossett and Marino, 2005). The primary technologies used for virtual coaching included email, phone, sharing of electronic files, and video conferencing. Like Berry's (2005) study, video conferencing was the least modality used for coaching and instead was part of a formal or blended learning or development program. Furthermore, consistently with Charbonneau's emphasis of the coach-client-media fit, Frazee found that the compatibility and ease of technology use was most important for coaches when choosing what technology to use for coaching. Other predictors of virtual coaching included certain coaching topics, purposes and coach's beliefs about the usefulness of virtual coaching. For example, similar to Charbonneau's study, Frazee found that many participants felt coaching in-person was necessary for providing sensitive feedback or addressing deeper issues, while the use of technology-based tools supported connecting coaching clients with resources and peers, providing just-in-time support and tracking progress.

Frazee's study validated Charbonneau (2002) and Berry's (2005) findings by having similar empirical results. Frazee had a large sample of professionals that represented internal and external coaches. The large and diverse sample size helps generalize these findings to the broader coaching population. Finally, the study provided both quantitative and qualitative data on virtual coaching, providing both empirical support and rich information about the intricacies of virtual coaching. Like Berry, Frazee's study shared the limitation of only providing the coach's perspective on the use, preference, and effectiveness of virtual coaching. Furthermore, like both Charbonneau and Berry's studies, this study involved retrospective reflections of coaches, which can limit the accuracy of the participant's perceptions of virtual coaching.

Ghods' (2009) quantitative dissertation investigated the coach-client relationship and its correlation to observed virtual coaching outcomes, defined as: (1) behavioral changes in daily work, (2) overall job performance, (3) increased openness to feedback, and (4) overall leadership effectiveness, as measured by and compared to client self-report and multi-rater feedback. Multi-raters included the clients' immediate supervisors/bosses, peers, and direct reports. The study also examined whether coaching outcomes were sustained over time via self-report. Finally, the study examined whether a relationship existed between client satisfaction with virtual coaching and the strength of their coach-client relationship. The virtual coaching program included six telephone coaching sessions that entailed: (1) 360-degree feedback from multi-raters (e.g., immediate supervisor/boss, peers and direct reports), (2) coach-facilitated multi-rater feedback interpretation, (3) a socialized developmental plan, (4) support and guidance from the coach, (5) individualized recommendations for resources for self and team, (6) intervention techniques and tools used by the coach, and (7) inclusion of an immediate supervisor/boss in the structured coaching process. One-hundred and fifty two clients provided self-reports of their satisfaction level with virtual coaching and observed coaching outcomes immediately after their coaching was completed. Six months later, 99 of the same 152 clients provided self-reports of observed coaching outcomes again. During the same time, 252 multi-raters of 84 clients reported observed coaching outcomes.

Ghods (2009) found that the majority of clients were satisfied with being coached at a distance and observed positive coaching outcomes, both immediately after coaching ended and six months after its cessation. However, the level of self-observed outcomes were lower six months after virtual coaching ceased in comparison to immediately after end of coaching. Multi-raters of clients also reported witnessing positive coaching outcomes six months after coaching ended. Therefore, not only did virtual coaching posi tively impact the client, but also clients' direct observers. Ghods also found empirical support for clients and their coaches developing and maintaining a strong coaching relationship solely from a distance. Furthermore, this relationship was related to positive coaching outcomes observable to the client immediately and six months after coaching ended.

Ghods' (2009) findings are striking for several reasons. First, with 404 participants, this study is the largest empirical study on virtual coaching. This study also used the largest homogeneous sample of virtual coaching clients within the same organization, not to mention the largest homogenous sample of observers who rated them in the same organization. Second, this study provided empirical evidence that virtual coaching yields change observable to clients and their co-workers. This study also empirically confirmed the findings from previous multi-rater studies that self-ratings are inflated in comparison to observer ratings (Church, 1997; Podsakoff and Organ, 1986; Van Velsor *et al.*, 1993) and that coaching results attenuated over time. Third, this study demonstrated that a positive coaching relationship can be established solely at a distance, without any prior face-to-face introduction. This information is critical in allaying many coaches' fears that distance inhibits both the relational aspects of the coaching relationship (e.g., development of rapport, trust, communication) and its goal-oriented aspects (e.g., development of and working towards coaching goals). Furthermore, clients' satisfaction with virtual coaching provides the coaching profession with the first empirical barometer about clients' reactions to virtual coaching. Finally this study validated the instrument that measured the coach–client relationship, which included assessment of both the coach–client rapport and the extent to which coach and client collaboratively develop and work toward coaching goals. This finding empirically supports the current conceptualization of the working alliance theory (Bordin, 1979), which Berry's (2005) study originally employed in this framework to coaching.

Ghods' (2009) study did have several limitations. First, it did not have a pre-test or a control group, and was therefore unable to conclude that distance coaching yielded lower or higher outcomes than face-to-face coaching. Second, all clients received 360-degree feedback as part of their coaching and most attended a one-day leadership development training workshop before, during, or after their coaching was completed. Therefore, like other research (Wang, 2000; Wilson *et al.*, 2006a; Young and Dixon, 1996), this study was unable to parse out the influence of the 360-degree feedback or training which may have impacted the results. Finally, this study was unable to provide the coaches' perspectives on this virtual coaching program.

Lastly, Wang's (2000) unpublished dissertation differs from the others in examining the relationship between a six-month post-training virtual coaching strategy and training transfer after 28 participants received on-site professional development training. The purpose of virtual coaching was to provide trainees with ongoing follow-up to aid their effective application of new knowledge and skills in their home organizations. Coaching entailed emailing, asynchronous web-board postings, asynchronous text chat space, a progress report database, an online consultant archive, a digital archive, and a help desk. The study found a positive relationship between supportive virtual coaching activities such as the relationship and interaction with the coach, the coach's encouragement and provision of resources to participants, and the transfer of training. These findings are congruent with those found by Berry (2005), Charbonneau (2002), and Ghods (2009), among other coaching researchers, who examined the importance of having a strong coaching relationship (Blattner, 2005; Brotman *et al.*, 1998; Bush, 2004; Diedrich, 1996; Kilburg, 1996, 2001; Lowman, 2005; Luebbe, 2005; Murphy, 2005; Peterson, 1996; Wasylyshyn, 2003).

Although Wang's (2000) findings are consistent with those of Berry (2005), Charbonneau (2002), and Ghods (2009), several elements of the study differed in fundamental ways.

First, virtual coaching was used to enhance the transfer of knowledge gleaned from the training to participants' home organizations. Unlike Charbonneau and Ghods who examined executive coaching, or Berry, who studied executive and personal coaching, the content of Wang's coaching was specific to the training. Second, it was part of a larger training program; therefore, the specific aspect of the training program that generated the outcomes was unclear. Third, the method of virtual coaching only entailed online coaching, which excluded telephone use. Fourth, online coaching was conducted by six facilitators who had also provided in-person training prior to the time coaching began; thus, the strength of the coach–client relationship prior to establishing online coaching was unclear. Finally, both Charbonneau's and Wang's studies were partially or entirely qualitative, which means they lacked empirical support and the results cannot be generalized to the wider population. Although Wang's study added value to the virtual coaching literature, it was limited because it did not control for various aspects of coaching. In addition, since its methodology vastly differed from the other two studies, it was difficult to adequately compare their results.

The last two studies to investigate virtual coaching modalities were industry publications from the Center for Creative Leadership (CCL). The first study only entailed a small component of virtual coaching. Wilson *et al.* (2006a) investigated the impact of a coaching program as part of a multiple leadership development initiative for corporate staff and high-potential managers across business units. The coaching program entailed classroom instruction and follow-up coaching sessions on two separate occasions (six months apart), as well as during quarterly conference calls with CCL coaches, which were the only virtual coaching aspects of this program. The study found positive changes such as integration of learned information in daily work and improvement in leadership performance, relationships with others, knowledge sharing, and job performance.

Furthermore, Wilson *et al.* (2006b) provided several perspectives on positive outcomes through a program that incorporated a component of virtual coaching. Because the virtual coaching component was limited to quarterly conference calls with coaches, it was unclear if it was the virtual coaching component, or other components of the program, that mainly led to the study's results. Furthermore, it was unclear if specific components of the program, or the program as a whole, generated these results. The study's two limitations were its relatively small sample size and the fact that virtual coaching calls were conducted with coaches whom the clients had previously met in face-to-face coaching sessions. As a result, it was unclear how well this study truly assessed a measure of virtual coaching.

The second study by CCL (Young and Dixon, 1996) involved a multi-pronged developmental intervention. Young and Dixon examined the impact of coaching on 29 participants of a six-month CCL leadership program with classroom and coaching components. Participants received coaching both during classroom training sessions and telephonically while on the job. By the end of 12 months, participants and co-worker reports showed significant positive change in participants on all but one subscale of the CCL questionnaire; therefore, multiple raters reported positive change. Additionally, when Young and Dixon compared the program participant group with a control group of 38 non-participants, the leadership program participants also presented positive change on all subscales of the instrument and significant change on more than half of the subscales. The participant group clearly benefited more from participating in the program than did non-participants. When asked to rate which component of the program was most helpful to their learning, the participants reported coaching versus feedback and classroom activity.

Results from this study (Young and Dixon, 1996) demonstrated that coaching as a component of a leadership development program produced significant observable change, that change was perceived by various observers, and that observable change was significantly different between the experimental and control groups. These findings added much value to the coaching and virtual coaching literatures. Despite these valuable findings, several critical limitations need to be addressed. Each group had a small number of participants, which limited the study's statistical power and generalizability. Second, although the participants reported that the coaching component of the program was the most helpful component in their learning, Young and Dixon did not test this data empirically. Third, as in Wang's (2000) study, some of the coaches taught the in-person training prior to beginning coaching. The perceived efficacy of the coaching process may have differed depending upon whether or not clients had established a prior, face-to-face relationship with their trainer-coaches. Finally, since an industry sponsored this study, potential unintended biases or influences may have affected the results. Caution is warranted when generalizing the significance of this research.

In summary, the virtual coaching literature is limited. Still, there are several studies that measure outcomes (Berry, 2005; Ghods, 2009; Young and Dixon 2006) and overall, virtual coaching appears to provide promising positive outcomes. However, all of these studies contain methodological challenges; either the outcomes are not clearly indicated by virtual coaching due to the integration of a training component and/or the outcome measures may be biased due to rating sources. The virtual coaching literature has adopted the working alliance theory from the therapeutic realm, and, this concept of a strong coach–client partnership appears to be an important component with respect to outcomes and satisfaction (Berry, 2005; Ghods, 2009). Research in the virtual coaching arena is just beginning to explore how the media may be interdependent with the coach–client interactions as well impacting outcomes (Charbonneau, 2002; Frazee, 2008).

Although a few studies on virtual coaching share certain commonalities, most vary vastly, primarily in terms of their methodology, approach, and findings. As a group, these studies suggested that coaching at a distance has advantages and disadvantages. The primary advantages are that it is practical, accessible, and cost effective. Disadvantages include its level of complexity, such as the need for coaches to develop a trusting relationship, provide critical feedback and manage other interpersonal issues from a distance. Most often, these issues are critical and/or central to the purpose of having a coach; thus, most think face-to-face coaching is preferable to virtual coaching. However, if the purpose of coaching is more concerned with maintaining certain behaviors or tasks, then virtual coaching appears to be more cost effective and practical. This context may also be more useful for clients who hold less senior leadership roles. Clearly, more research is needed before valid conclusions can be drawn about this modality of coaching.

## Future Research: Evolving Empirical Guidance From Virtual Domains

Most studies in virtual work (e.g., virtual teams, virtual coaching, computer-mediated communication, e-mentoring, virtual therapy) conduct the research within the context of undifferentiated virtual media (e.g., a blend of telephone, email, text) or, the research is comprised of a comparison of media modalities (e.g., face-to-face or telephone) (e.g., Day and Schenider, 2002). However, this notion of "either/or" likely does not reflect the way work relationships are conducted. Indeed, in many of the studies that are comparisons of virtual versus face-to-face, the virtual condition consists of a blended approach of usually at least one face-to-face meeting (e.g., Frazee, 2008). Based on this, some researchers are now calling for research that examines relationships and work within the context of the degree of virtualization (Chudoba *et al.*, 2005; Workman, 2007). By this, the researchers suggest that virtual work is characterized by the amount of distance in terms of frequency of work in non-face-to-face contexts, across time zones, as well as culture. These researchers suggest that the field of virtual relationships and virtual work needs to move beyond a simple categorization (e.g., virtual or not), and move toward a continuum approach of considering virtualization or virtuality (Gibson and Gibbs, 2006; Lojeski, 2006; Scott and Timmerman, 1999). To support this arena of research, Chudoba *et al.* (2005) developed an index of virtuality.

Additionally, Workman (2007) studied the impact of virtuality on performance and found a curvilinear relationship such that teams working more proximally, as well as teams working more distally, performed more poorly than those with moderate amounts of virtualization, that is, a blend of distant and face-to-face work. Exploring the relationship more robustly, Gajendra and Harrison (2007) conducted a meta-analysis of 46 tele-communicating studies involving more than 12,000 employees. Relevant to the concept of virtualitiy, the authors examined the moderating relationship between tele-communicating intensity (high intensity as mostly homebased and low-intensity being mostly office based) on manager and co-worker relationship quality. The results did not support a significant moderator for the supervisory relationship but did for co-workers such that those engaging in high intensity tele-communicating had less positive relationships with co-workers. This suggests that moderate amounts of virtualization may be optimal.

While research suggests that working in a blended manner may yield higher work outcomes, the capability to work in technology-assisted environments may depend on important individual difference variables. Workman (2007) found individuals that are more task-orientated compared to relationship-oriented, as well as more technical compared to social, outperformed as virtualization increased. Colquitte *et al.* (2002) found that teams comprised of individuals higher in the personality variable, openness, were more quickly and adeptly able to navigate between technologies (face-to-face and computer-mediated) and discern when and how to make best use of them.

Taken together, these studies suggest that the extent of virtuality or virtualization may impact on performance (Workman, 2007), as well as some relationships (Gajendra and Harrison, 2007), and that individuals may differ in their ability to adapt to virtual or blended approaches (Collquitte *et al.*, 2002; Workman, 2007). Perhaps most importantly, these studies suggest virtualization and individual differences within the context of technology as considerations for future research for virtual coaching.

In addition, future research in virtual coaching should address the interdependence between communication media and communicators and how these factors interact in a reciprocally influential manner. Morris *et al.* (2002) conducted a set of laboratory experiments involving a negotiation task, revealing how communication is different depending on media. The authors suggested that in email, the participants "tell" each other the relationship is important whereas in face-to-face they "show" each other it is important by engaging in rapport building. The authors found negative tactics were much more detrimental in the computer-mediated condition and that offers were more complex in the computer-mediated condition. This study revealed two findings about virtual relationship development that may be important to virtual coaching. First, it illustrated the way in which we engage, specifically, in building relationships, may be different in different media – it was more direct and explicit in the email condition. Other research indicates similar findings; using communications via texting, Spagnolli and Gamberini (2007) revealed how unique behavior patterns within this media convey rapport-building. Second, this study illustrated certain strategies of influencing may be less effective in text-based contexts. More specifically, strategies that were competitive (vs. collaborative) were less effective. This raises questions as to how various coaching strategies such as challenging, probing, and supporting may differentially convey given different media and is an important avenue for future research.

Naquin *et al.* (2010) found differences across media such that participants were more likely to deceive, and, to feel justified in doing so, in a negotiation exercise when communicating via email rather than writing. The authors speculate that the social norms for this relatively newer media are more ambiguous. Also studying email, Kruger *et al.* (2005) found participants were likely to be over-confident (and inaccurate) in conveying emotional and/or ambiguous messages. Further investigation is needed to explore the implications of such findings and how they may impact a virtual developmental relationship, such as virtual coaching.

Given the paucity of quantitative rigorous studies on virtual coaching, more extensive exploration is warranted. More research is needed on outcome studies, as well as important intervening variables like the working alliance in virtual coaching. The field would benefit from exploring which individual difference factors may create greater comfort with specific technology. Perhaps more importantly, research should focus on how the coach/mentor and client, together, can determine which media to use for which purpose and at what point in the developmental cycle of the coaching. Virtual coaches/mentors would benefit from a greater understanding of how the interaction can be expected to vary across differing media, as well as guidance on how to build social presence and intimacy across differing media (Morris *et al.*, 2002).

The field would benefit from the use of control groups for comparison to the treatment group, as well as pre-intervention measurements, along with multiple measurements of outcomes (e.g., objective, observer ratings, coach ratings, client self-report). Rigorous empirical studies containing these elements would add significantly to the coaching and mentoring fields.

# Conclusion

This chapter has critically reviewed the virtual coaching and mentoring literatures, primarily focusing on published and unpublished research studies in order to better understand the prevalence and effectiveness of virtual coaching and mentoring. Related literatures of virtual helping relationships were also reviewed and relevant information discussed in order to inform the practice of virtual coaching and mentoring. From our review, it is our general recommendation for practitioners to thoroughly access and evaluate the unique needs and requirements of the coaching/mentoring engagement prior to choosing a virtual modality. Some considerations include: being aware of the context, nature, and purpose of the coaching/mentoring engagement; understanding client/ mentee and coach/mentor comfort with and competency in the technology deployed; evaluating availability, functionality, and feasibility of technology used; setting ground rules around desired behaviors during coaching/mentoring e.g., not multi-tasking during the session; assessing client/mentee motivation for change and readiness for coaching/ mentoring; and evaluating the overall client/mentee-coach/mentor-technology fit. It is hoped that this chapter provides the level of guidance that leads to more successful virtual coaching and mentoring engagements.

# References

Angulo, L.M. and Alegre De La Rosa, O.M. (2006) Online faculty development in the Canary Islands: A study of e-mentoring. *Higher Education in Europe*, 31, 65–81.

Berry, R.M. (2005) A comparison of face-to-face and distance coaching practices: The role of the working alliance in problem resolution. Unpublished doctoral dissertation, Georgia State University, Atlanta, GA.

Bierema, L.L. and Hill, J.R. (2005) Virtual mentoring and HRD. *Advances in Developing Human Resources*, 7, 556–68.

Bierema, L.L. and Merriam, S.B. (2002) E-mentoring: Using computer mediated communication to enhance the mentoring process. *Innovative Higher Education*, 26, 211–28.

Blattner, J. (2005) Coaching: The successful adventure of a downwardly mobile executive. *Consulting Psychology Journal: Practice and Research*, 57, 3–13.

Bordin, E.S. (1979) The generalizability of the psychoanalytic concept of the working alliance. *Psychotherapy: Theory, Research, and Practice*, 16, 252–60.

Boule, M. (2008) Development of trust in electronic mentoring relationships. *International Journal of Networking and Virtual Organisations*, 5, 35–50.

Bowles S.V. and Picano, J.J. (2006) Dimensions of coaching related to productivity and quality of life. *Consulting Psychology Journal: Practice and Research*, 58, 232–39.

Boyce, L.A. and Clutterbuck, D. (2011) E-coaching: Accept it, it's here, and it's evolving! In: G. Hernez-Broome and L.A. Boyce (eds) *Advancing Executive Coaching: Setting the Course for Successful Leadership Coaching*. San Francisco: Jossey-Bass. pp. 285–315.

Boyce, L.A. and Hernez-Broome G. (2010) E-coaching: Consideration of leadership coaching in a virtual environment. In: D. Clutterbuck and Z. Hussain (eds) *Virtual Coach, Virtual Mentor*. Charolotte, NC: Information Age Publishing, Inc. pp. 139–74.

Brotman, L.E., Liberi, W.P., and Wasylyshyn, K.M. (1998) Executive coaching: The need for standards of competence. *Consulting Psychology Journal: Practice and Research*, 50, 40–6.

Brown, S.C. and Kysilka, M.L. (2005) Investigating telementoring with preservice and professional teachers: Exploring the issues and challenges. In: F.K. Kochan and J.T. Pascarelli (eds) *Creating Successful Telementoring Programs*. Information Age Publishing. pp. 185–206.

Buche, M.W. (2008) Development of trust in electronic mentoring relationships. *International Journal of Networking and Virtual Organisations*, 5, 35.

Bush, M.W. (2004) Client perceptions of effectiveness in executive coaching. Unpublished.

Cascio, T. and Gasker, J. (2001) Everyone has a shining side: Computer-mediated mentoring in social work education. *Journal of Social Work Education*, 37, 283–94.

Charbonneau, M.A. (2002) Participant self-perceptions about the cause of behavior change from a program of executive coaching. Unpublished doctoral dissertation, Alliant International University, Los Angeles, CA.

Chudoba, K.M., Wynn, E., Lu, M., and Watson-Manheim, M.B. (2005) How virtual are we? Measuring virtuality and understanding its impact in a global organization. *Information Systems Journal*, 15, 279–306.

Church, A.H. (1997) Managerial self-awareness in high-performing individuals in organizations. *Journal of Applied Psychology*, 82, 281–92.

Clutterbuck, D. and Hussain, Z. (2010) *Virtual Coach, Virtual Mentor*. Charolotte, NC: Information Age Publishing, Inc.

Colquitt, J.A., Hollenbeck, J.R., Ilgen, D.R., Lepine, J.A., and Sheppard, L. (2002) Computer-assisted communication and team decision-making performance: The moderating effect of openness to experience. *Journal of Applied Psychology*, 87, 402–10.

Columbaro, B.N.L. (2007) E-mentoring possibilities for online doctoral students: A literature review. *Adult Learning*, 20, 9–15.

Cravens, J. (2003) Online mentoring: programs and suggested practices as of February 2001. *Journal of Technology in Human Services*, 21, 85–109.

Davies, S. (2005) The brightside trust: A dynamic e-mentoring tool. *Education and Health*, 23, 8.

Day, S.X. and Schneider, P.L. (2002) Psychotherapy using distance technology: A comparison of face-to-face, video, and audio treatment. *Journal of Counseling Psychology*, 49, 499–503.

Diedrich, R.C. (1996) An iterative approach to executive coaching. *Consulting Psychology Journal: Practice and Research*, 48, 61–6.

Difede, J., Cukor, J., Patt, I., Giosan, C., and Hoffman, H. (2006) The application of virtual reality to the treatment of PTSD following the WTC attack. *Annals of the New York Academy of Sciences*, 1071, 500–1.

Driscoll, J. and Cooper, R. (2005) Coaching for clinicians. *Nursing Management*, 12, 18–23.

Ensher, E. and Murphy, S. (2007). E-mentoring: Next generation research strategies and suggestions. In B.R. Ragins and K.E. Kram (eds) *The Handbook of Mentoring at Work: Theory, Research and Practice*. Los Angeles: Sage.

Ensher, E., Heun, C., and Blanchard, A. (2003). Online mentoring and computer-mediated communication: New directions in research. *Journal of Vocational Behavior*, 63, 264–88.

Frazee, R.V. (2008) E-coaching in organizations: A study of features, practices, and determinants of use. Unpublished doctoral dissertation, University of San Diego, San Diego, CA.

Gajendran, R.S. and Harrison, D.A. (2007) The good, the bad, and the unknown about telecommuting: Meta-analysis of psychological mediators and individual consequences. *Journal of Applied Psychology*, 92, 1524–41.

Gentry, L.B., Denton, C.A., and Kurtz, T. (2008) Technologically-based mentoring provided to teachers: A synthesis of the literature. *Journal of Technology and Teacher Education*, 16, 339–73.

Ghods, N. (2009) Distance coaching: The relationship between the coach-client relationship, client satisfaction, and coaching outcomes. Unpublished doctoral dissertation, Alliant International University, San Diego, CA.

Gibson, C.B. and Gibbs, J.L. (2006) Unpacking the concept of virtuality: The effects of geographic dispersion, electronic dependence, dynamic structure, and national diversity on team innovation. *Administrative Science Quarterly*, 51, 451–95.

Goldsmith, M. and Lyons, L.S. (2006) *Coaching For Leadership: The Practice of Leadership Coaching From the World's Greatest Coaches* (2nd edn). San Francisco, CA: Pfeiffer.

Hagevik, S. (1998) Choosing a career counseling service. *Journal of Environmental Health*, 98(4), 31–2.

Hakim, C. (2000) Virtual coaching: Learning, like time, stops for no one. *Journal for Quality and Participation*, 23(1), 42–4.

Hamilton, B.A. and Scandura, T.A. (2002) Implications for organizational learning and development in a wired world. *Organizational Dynamics*, 31, 388–402.

Headlam-Wells, J. (2004) E-mentoring for aspiring women managers. *Women in Management Review*, 19, 212–18.

Headlam-Wells, J., Gosland, J., and Craig, J. (2006) Beyond the organisation: The design and management of E-mentoring systems. *International Journal of Information Management*, 26, 372–85.

Hilty, D.M., Marks, S.L., Urness, D., Yellowlees, P.M., and Nesbitt, T.S. (2004) Clinical and educational telepsychiatry applications: A review. *Canadian Journal of Psychiatry*, 49, 12–23.

Hixenbaugh, P., Dewart, H., Drees, D., and Williams, D. (2006) Peer e-mentoring: Enhancement of the first year experience. *Psychology Learning and Teaching*, 5, 8–14.

Hudson, F.M. (1999) *The Handbook of Coaching: A Comprehensive Resource Guide For Managers, Executives, Consultants, and Human Resource Professionals.* San Francisco, CA: Jossey-Bass.

de Janasz, S., Ensher, E., and Heun, C. (2008) Virtual relationships and real benefits: Using e-mentoring to connect business students with practicing managers. *Mentoring and Tutoring: Partnership in Learning,* 16, 394–11.

Kasprisin, C.A., Single, P.B., Single, R., and Muller, C. (2003) Building a better bridge: Testing e-training to improve e-mentoring programmes in higher education. *Mentoring and Tutoring,* 11, 67–78.

Kilburg, R.R. (1996) Toward a conceptual understanding and definition of executive coaching. *Consulting Psychology Journal: Practice and Research,* 48, 134–44.

Kilburg, R.R. (2000) *Executive Coaching: Developing Managerial Wisdom in a World of Chaos.* Washington, DC: American Psychological Association.

Kilburg, R.R. (2001) Facilitating intervention adherence in executive coaching: A model and methods. *Consulting Psychology Journal: Practice and Research,* 53, 251–67.

Kraus, R., Zack, J., and Stricker, G. (eds) (2004). *Online Counseling: A Handbook For Mental Health Professionals.* Boston, MA: Academic Press.

Kruger, J., Epley, N., Parker, J., and Ng, Z.-W. (2005) Egocentrism over e-mail: Can we communicate as well as we think? *Journal of Personality and Social Psychology,* 89, 925–36.

Lojeski, K.S. (2006) When distance matters: An overview of virtual distance. Virtual distance learning (TM): A proposed model for the study of virtual work. Unpublished doctoral dissertation. Stevens Institute of Technology, NJ.

Lowman, R. (2005) Executive coaching: The road to Dodo Ville needs paving with more than good assumptions. *Consulting Psychology Journal: Practice and Research,* 57, 90–6.

Luebbe, D.M. (2005) The three-way mirror of executive coaching. Unpublished doctoral dissertation, University of Cincinnati, OH.

McLaren, P., Ahlbom, J., Riley, A., Mohammedali, A., and Denis, M. (2002) The North Lewisham telepsychiatry project: Beyond the pilot phase. *Journal of Telemedicine and Telecare,* 8, 98–100.

Maheu, M.M., Pulier, M.L., Wilhelm, F.H., McMenamin, J.P., and Brown-Connolly, N.E. (2005) *The Mental Health Professional and the New Technologies: A Handbook For Practice Today.* Mahwah, NJ: Lawrence Erlbaum.

Mallen, M.J., Vogel, D.L., and Rochlen, A.B. (2005a) The practical aspects of online counseling: Ethics, training, technology, and competency. *The Counseling Psychologist,* 33, 776–818.

Mallen, M.J., Vogel, D.L., Rochlen, A.B., and Day, S.X. (2005b) Online counseling: Reviewing the literature from a counseling psychology framework. *The Counseling Psychologist,* 33, 819–71.

Miller, L.C., Devaney, S.W., Kelly, G.L., and Kuehn, A.F. (2008) E-mentoring in public health nursing practice. *Journal of Continuing Education in Nursing,* 39, 394–9. Retrieved from: http://www.ncbi.nlm.nih.gov/pubmed/18792604 (accessed July 23, 2012).

Monnier, J., Knapp, R.G., and Frueh, B.C. (2003) Recent advances in telepsychiatry: An updated review. *Psychiatric Services,* 54, 1604–9.

Morris, M., Nadler, J., Kurtzberg, T., and Thompson, L (2002) Schmooze or lose: Social friction and lubrication in e-mail negotiations. *Group Dynamics: Theory, Research, and Practice,* 6, 89–100.

Murphy, S.A. (2005) Recourse to executive coaching: The mediating role of human resources. *International Journal of Police Science and Management,* 7, 175–86.

Naquin, C.E., Kurtzberg, T.R., and Belkin, L.Y. (2010) The finer points of lying online: E-mail versus pen and paper. *Journal of Applied Psychology,* 95, 387–94.

Paul, D.L. (2006) Collaborative activities in virtual settings: A knowledge management perspective of telemedicine. *Journal of Management Information Systems,* 22, 143–76.

Penny, C. and Bolton, D. (2010) Evaluating the outcomes of an e-mentoring program. *Journal of Educational Technology Systems,* 39, 17–30.

Perren, L. (2003) The role of e-mentoring in entrepreneurial education and support: A meta-review of academic literature. *Education + Training*, 45, 517–25.

Peterson, D.B. (1996) Executive coaching at work: The art of one-on-one change. *Consulting Psychology Journal: Practice and Research*, 48, 78–86.

Plummer, C.A. and Omwenga Nyang'au, T. (2009) Reciprocal e-mentoring: Accessible international exchanges. *International Social Work*, 52, 811–22.

Podsakoff, P. and Organ, D. (1986) Self-reports in organizational research: Problems and prospects. *Journal of Management*, 12, 86–94.

Rickard, K. (2007) E-mentoring and information systems effectiveness models: A useful nexus for evaluation in the small business context (Doctoral dissertation). Retrieved from: http://wallaby.vu.edu.au/adt-VVUT/public/adt-VVUT20080407.165406/index.html.

Rickard, K. and Rickard, A. (2009) E-mentoring for small business: an examination of effectiveness. *Education + Training*, 51, 747–68.

Rizzo, A.A, Graap, K., Mclay, R.N., Perlman, K., Rothbaum, B.O., Reger, G. *et al.* (2007) Virtual Iraq: Initial case reports from a VR exposure therapy application for combat-related post-traumatic stress disorder. *Virtual Rehabilitation*, 124–30. Ieee.

Rohland, B.M., Saleh, S.S., Rohrer, J.E., and Romitti, P.A. (2000) Acceptability of telepsychiatry to a rural population. *Psychiatric Services*, 51, 672–4.

Rossett, A. and Marino, G. (2005) If coaching is good, then e-coaching is… *Training Development*, 59, 46–9.

Scott, C.R. and Timmerman, C.E. (1999) Communication technology use and multiple workplace identifications among organizational teleworkers with varied degrees of virtuality. *IEEE Transactions on ProfessionalCommunication*, 42, 240–60.

Sherpa Coaching (2011) Six annual executive coaching survey. Retrieved from: http://www.sherpacoaching.com/pdfpercent20files/SherpaExecutiveCoachingSurvey2011.pdf (accessed March 16, 2011).

Shpigelman, C.-N., Reiter, S., and Weiss, P.L.T. (2008) E-mentoring for youth with special needs: Preliminary results. *CyberPsychology and Behavior*, 11, 196–200.

Shrestha, C.H., May, S., Edirisingha, P., Burke, L., and Linsey, T. (2009) From face-to-face to e-mentoring: Does the "e" add any value for mentors? *Journal of Education*, 20, 116–24.

Single, P.B. and Single, R. (2005) E-mentoring for social equity: Review of research to inform program development. *Mentoring and Tutoring: Partnership in Learning*, 13, 301–20.

Smith, S.J. and Israel, M. (2010) E-mentoring: Enhancing special education teacher induction. *Journal of Special Education Leadership*, 23, 30–41.

Spagnolli, A. and Gamberini, L. (2007) Interacting via SMS: Practices of social closeness and reciprocation. *British Journal of Social Psychology*, 46, 343–64.

Stewart, S. (2008) CMC and e-mentoring in midwifery. In: S. Kelsey and K. St Amant (eds) *Handbook of Research on Computer Mediated Communication*. Hershey, PA: Information Science Reference. pp. 103–13.

Stewart, S. and Carpenter, C. (2009) Electronic mentoring: An innovative approach to providing clinical support. *International Journal of Therapy and Rehabilitation*, 16, 199–206.

Thompson, L., Jeffries, M., and Topping, K. (2010) E-mentoring for e-learning development. *Innovations in Education and Teaching International*, 47, 305–15.

Thoresen, C. (1997) Early career support program: Telecommunication mentoring for rural teachers. *Journal of Science Teacher Education*, 8, 283–93.

Torres, C., Brodnick, R., and Powell, D. (2009) Leader development gets a second life. *Focus/ Virtual Learning*, 29, 17–19.

Van Velsor, E., Taylor, S., and Leslie, J.B. (1993) An examination of the relationships among self-perception accuracy, self-awareness, gender, and leader effectiveness. *Human Resource Management*, 32, 249–63.

Wadia-Fascetti, S. and Leventman, P.G. (2000) E-mentoring: A longitudinal approach to mentoring relationships for women pursuing technical careers. *Journal of Engineering Education* (July), 295–300.

Wang, L. (2000) The relationship between distance coaching and the transfer of training. Unpublished doctoral dissertation, University of Illinois at Urbana-Champaign.

Wasylyshyn, K.M. (2003) Executive coaching: An outcome study. *Consulting Psychology Journal: Practice and Research*, 55, 94–106.

Wilson, M., Hannum, K. and Center for Creative Leadership (2006a) *Center for Creative Leadership Impact Study: Sonoco*. Retrieved from: http://www.ccl.org/leadership/pdf/aboutCCL/SONOCOimpactstudy.pdf (accessed June 21, 2007).

Wilson, J., Straus, S., and Mcevily, B. (2006b) All in due time: The development of trust in computer-mediated and face-to-face teams. *Organizational Behavior and Human Decision Processes*, 99, 16–33.

Workman, M. (2007) The proximal-virtual team continuum: A study of performance. *Journal of the American Society for Information Science*, 58, 794–801.

Young, D.P. and Dixon, N.M. (1996) *Helping Leaders Take Effective Action: A Program Evaluation*. Greensboro, NC: CCL Press.

# Index

Note: Page references in *italics* refer to Figures; those in **bold** refer to Tables and Boxes

*The Wiley Blackwell Handbook of the Psychology of Coaching and Mentoring*, First Edition.
Edited by Jonathan Passmore, David B. Peterson, and Teresa Freire.
© 2013 John Wiley & Sons, Ltd. Published 2016 by John Wiley & Sons, Ltd.

Printed and bound by CPI Group (UK) Ltd, Croydon, CR0 4YY

10/12/2023

08204660-0004